D1521924

A History *of the* Book *in* America

VOLUME 3

The Industrial Book
1840–1880

A History of the Book in America
David D. Hall, General Editor

· · ·

· · ·

A History

of the Book

in America

VOLUME 3

The Industrial Book
1840–1880

EDITED BY

Scott E. Casper, Jeffrey D. Groves,
Stephen W. Nissenbaum,
& Michael Winship

. . .

Published in Association with
the American Antiquarian Society
by The University of North Carolina Press
Chapel Hill

© 2007

The University of North Carolina Press

All rights reserved

Designed by Eric M. Brooks

Set in Bulmer by Tseng Information Systems, Inc.

Manufactured in the United States of America

PUBLICATION OF THIS BOOK
WAS ASSISTED BY A GRANT FROM THE
WILLIAM R. KENAN JR. CHARITABLE TRUST.

The paper in this book meets the guidelines
for permanence and durability of the Committee on
Production Guidelines for Book Longevity of the
Council on Library Resources.

Library of Congress Cataloging-in-Publication Data

The industrial book, 1840–1880 / edited by Scott E. Casper . . . [et. al.].

p. cm. — (A history of the book in America; v. 3)

Includes bibliographical references and index.

ISBN 978-0-8078-3085-7 (cloth: alk. paper)

1. Book industries and trade — United States — History — 19th century.

2. Publishers and publishing — United States — History — 19th century.

3. Books and reading — United States — History — 19th century.

I. Casper, Scott E.

Z473.I53   2007

381'.45002097309034 — dc22   2006038982

11 10 09 08 07   5 4 3 2 1

CONTENTS

FIGURES, TABLES, & GRAPHS

Figures

Tables

Graphs

CONTRIBUTORS

SUSAN BELASCO is professor of English and women's studies at the University of Nebraska, Lincoln. She is the editor of Whitman's periodical poetry for The Walt Whitman Archive (http://www.whitmanarchive.org), the coeditor (with Kenneth M. Price) of *Periodicals in Nineteenth-Century America* (1995), and the author of numerous articles on periodical literature.

CANDY GUNTHER BROWN is associate professor of religious studies at Indiana University and the author of *The Word in the World: Evangelical Writing, Publishing, and Reading in America, 1789–1880* (2004).

KENNETH E. CARPENTER is retired from the Harvard University Library, where editing the *Harvard Library Bulletin* was among his responsibilities. He is the author of *The Dissemination of the Wealth of Nations in French and in France, 1776–1843* (2002), *Readers and Libraries: Toward a History of Libraries and Culture in America* (1996), and *The First 350 Years of the Harvard University Library* (1986), as well as editor of *Books and Society in History* (1983) and the microfiche collection *The Harvard University Library: A Documentary History* (1989).

SCOTT E. CASPER is professor of history at the University of Nevada, Reno. He is the author of *Constructing American Lives: Biography and Culture in Nineteenth-Century America* (1999) and coeditor (with Joanne D. Chaison and Jeffrey D. Groves) of *Perspectives on American Book History: Artifacts and Commentary* (2002).

JEANNINE MARIE DELOMBARD is associate professor of English at the University of Toronto. She is the author of *Slavery on Trial: Law, Abolitionism, and Print Culture* (2007), which examines the centrality of juridical rhetoric to the antebellum slavery debate.

ANN FABIAN is professor of American studies and history at Rutgers, the State University of New Jersey. She is the author of *Card Sharps, Dream Books, and Bucket Shops: Gambling in Nineteenth-Century America* (1990) and *The Unvarnished Truth: Personal Narratives in Nineteenth-Century America* (2000).

JEFFREY D. GROVES is professor of literature at Harvey Mudd College and coeditor (with Scott E. Casper and Joanne D. Chaison) of *Perspectives on American Book History: Artifacts and Commentary* (2002).

PAUL C. GUTJAHR is associate professor of English, American studies, and religious studies at Indiana University. He is the author of *An American Bible: A History of the Good Book in the United States, 1777–1880* (1999), coeditor (with Megan L. Benton) of *Illuminating Letters: Essays on Typography and Literary Interpretation* (2001), and editor of *Popular American Literature of the 19th Century* (2001).

DAVID D. HALL, a historian of American culture and religion, is the general editor of the five-volume *A History of the Book in America*. With Hugh Amory he coedited volume 1 in the series, *The Colonial Book in the Atlantic World* (2000). His publications include *Worlds of Wonder, Days of Judgment: Popular Religious Belief in Early New England* (1989) and *Lived Religion in America: Toward a History of Practice* (1997). He teaches at Harvard University.

DAVID M. HENKIN is associate professor of history at the University of California, Berkeley. He is the author of *City Reading: Written Words and Public Spaces in Antebellum New York* (1998) and *The Postal Age: The Emergence of Modern Communications in Nineteenth-Century America* (2006).

BRUCE LAURIE teaches at the University of Massachusetts, Amherst, and has taught at Mount Holyoke College and the University of Warwick in Coventry, England. He is the author most recently of *Beyond Garrison: Antislavery and Social Reform* (2005).

ERIC LUPFER earned a doctorate in English and a master's degree in information studies from the University of Texas at Austin. He is director of grants and education at Humanities Texas, the Texas state affiliate of the National Endowment for the Humanities.

MEREDITH L. MCGILL teaches English and American literature at Rutgers, the State University of New Jersey. She explores the relation between copyright law and antebellum literature in *American Literature and the Culture of Reprinting, 1834–1853* (2003).

JOHN NERONE is professor and College of Communications Scholar at the Institute of Communications Research at the University of Illinois at Urbana-Champaign. He writes on the history of the media and is the author of *Violence against the Press: Policing the Public Sphere in U.S. History* (1994) and the coauthor, with Kevin Barnhurst, of *The Form of News: A History* (2001).

STEPHEN W. NISSENBAUM is professor of history, emeritus, at the University of Massachusetts, Amherst, and adjunct professor of history at the University of Vermont. His books include *The Battle for Christmas* (1996), a finalist for the Pulitzer prize; *Sex, Diet, and Debility in Jacksonian America: Sylvester Graham and Health Reform* (1980); and, with Paul Boyer, *Salem*

Possessed (1974), which won the John H. Dunning Prize of the American Historical Association.

LLOYD PRATT is assistant professor of English at Michigan State University. He is completing a manuscript on the relationship between time and nationalism in nineteenth-century Anglo- and African American writing.

BARBARA SICHERMAN is William R. Kenan, Jr., Professor of American Institutions and Values, emerita, Trinity College, Hartford. Her publications include *Alice Hamilton: A Life in Letters* (2003; first published 1984) and "Reading *Little Women*: The Many Lives of a Text," in *U.S. History as Women's History* (1995). She coedited *Notable American Women: The Modern Period* (1980) and is completing a book tentatively titled "Reading Lives: Women and Literary Culture, 1860–1920."

LOUISE STEVENSON is professor of history and American studies at Franklin & Marshall College. Her books include *Scholarly Means to Evangelical Ends: The New Haven Scholars and the Transformation of Higher Learning in America, 1830–1890* (1986), *The Victorian Homefront: American Cultural and Intellectual Life, 1860–1880* (2001; first published 1991), and an almost-completed history of everyday American intellectual life from 1730 to 1940.

AMY M. THOMAS is associate professor of English at Montana State University. She is the coeditor (with Barbara Ryan) of *Reading Acts: U.S. Readers' Interactions with Literature, 1800–1950* (2002).

TAMARA PLAKINS THORNTON is professor of history at the State University of New York, Buffalo. She is the author of *Cultivating Gentlemen: The Meaning of Country Life among the Boston Elite, 1785–1860* (1989) and *Handwriting in America: A Cultural History* (1996).

SUSAN S. WILLIAMS is professor of English at Ohio State University. She is the author of *Confounding Images: Photography and Portraiture in Antebellum American Fiction* (1997) and of *Reclaiming Authorship: Literary Women in America, 1850–1900* (2006). She has also edited an edition of Hawthorne's *The Scarlet Letter* (2007) and is the coeditor (with Steven Fink) of *Reciprocal Influences: Literary Production, Distribution, and Consumption in America* (1999) and (with Steven Fink and Jared Gardner) of the journal *American Periodicals*.

MICHAEL WINSHIP is the Iris Howard Regents Professor of English II at the University of Texas at Austin. He edited and completed the final three volumes of *Bibliography of American Literature* (1955–91) and is the author of *American Literary Publishing in the Mid-Nineteenth Century: The Business of Ticknor and Fields* (1995).

EDITORS' & AUTHORS' ACKNOWLEDGMENTS

Like the other volumes of *A History of the Book in America*, *The Industrial Book* is a collaborative work constructed on the insights, expertise, and questions of many scholars. While as volume editors we are indebted to all whose labor and goodwill, directly or indirectly, contributed to the completion of this volume, our chief debt, and hence our first acknowledgment, is to our authors. Their intellectual generosity and commitment to this project over many years, their cooperation with us and with each other, and their willingness to undertake many rounds of revision as the overall narrative took shape are ultimately responsible for the volume's completion. We would like to thank the Editorial Board that oversees *A History of the Book in America* for its invaluable engagement on this, the third volume in the series. And we are grateful for the counsel given and questions posed by many interested scholars whose names do not appear in the table of contents, especially those who contributed to the early discussions that shaped the volume: Georgia B. Barnhill, John Bidwell, Burton J. Bledstein, Stuart M. Blumin, Richard D. Brown, Janet Duitsman Cornelius, William J. Gilmore-Lehne, Michael H. Harris, Marcus A. McCorison, David McKitterick, Roger E. Stoddard, and Ronald J. Zboray.

The editors wish to acknowledge the support of the American Antiquarian Society (AAS), which began its sponsorship of *A History of the Book in America* during the presidency of Marcus A. McCorison and continues to encourage the project during the presidency of Ellen S. Dunlap. John B. Hench, vice president for collections and programs at the society, and Caroline F. Sloat, administrative assistant for *A History of the Book in America* and the society's director of scholarly programs, have both played major roles in enabling the preparation of *The Industrial Book*. Without the expertise of archivists, bibliographers, curators, and librarians, the scholarly materials that underlie and support this volume would not have been available: we thank all those at AAS and elsewhere whose patient and painstaking work with rare books, graphic materials, and manuscripts has contributed to this book.

Generous funding from the National Endowment for the Humanities made it possible for the editors and many of the contributors to meet for crucial face-to-face discussions and supported the work of the project's Editorial Board. Further financial support has been provided by The Elisabeth Woodburn

Fund of the Antiquarian Booksellers' Association of America, Inc., American Booksellers' Association, Inc., the Richard A. Heald Fund, the James J. Colt Foundation, the John Ben Snow Memorial Trust, and the Center for the Book in the Library of Congress. We are most grateful for these contributions.

. . .

Individual contributors wish to add the following
particular acknowledgments:

SUSAN BELASCO: I am grateful to Linck C. Johnson for pointing out an important primary source for my essay.

SCOTT E. CASPER: I am grateful to Robert A. Gross for his suggestions on the Introduction; to Richard R. John for his advice on Chapter 5, Part 2; and to Donald W. Krummel, Leon Jackson, Robert Blesse, and Millie Syring for their assistance on Chapter 6, Part 2.

JEANNINE MARIE DELOMBARD: I am indebted to Andrea Stone (University of Toronto) for her excellent research assistance on this project.

JEFFREY D. GROVES: I would like to thank Lisa M. Sullivan, who read and commented on drafts of Chapter 4, Parts 2 and 3.

DAVID M. HENKIN: I wish to acknowledge the research assistance of Ana Vohryzek-Griest.

BRUCE LAURIE: Research for Chapter 2 was funded in part by a National Endowment for the Humanities fellowship at the American Antiquarian Society. Thanks to David Montgomery for lending me photocopies of the records of Typographical Union No. 2, which form the foundation of Chapter 2, and to Ava Baron and William Pretzer for sharing rare materials on the labor process in printing.

JOHN NERONE: Research for Chapter 7, Part 1, was conducted during a National Endowment for the Humanities fellowship at the American Antiquarian Society in 1996. I thank the staff and office of AAS for their support.

LLOYD PRATT: The Bay State Historical League and Massachusetts Foundation for the Humanities Scholar-in-Residence program funded my time at the Nantucket Atheneum, and the Nantucket Historical Association's E. Geoffrey and Elizabeth Thayer Verney Fellowship generously supported my research there.

BARBARA SICHERMAN: Many individuals contributed to my thinking about this essay. Special thanks go to David D. Hall, Joan Jacobs Brumberg, Robert Gross, Joan Hedrick, Carl Kaestle, Mary Kelley, Bruce Laurie, James A. Miller, David Nord, Janice Radway, Dorothy Ross, Joan Shelley Rubin, and Louise Stevenson. Work on this chapter was aided by a fellowship from the National Endowment for the Humanities, a leave from Trinity College, and research funds from the William R. Kenan, Jr., Professorship of American Institutions and Values.

SUSAN S. WILLIAMS: Some of the initial research for this essay was supported by a Stephen Botein Fellowship at the American Antiquarian Society, and I thank John B. Hench and Joanne D. Chaison of AAS for their assistance and support. At Ohio State, I would like to thank James Phelan and Steven Fink for encouraging me to undertake the essay, and Jared Gardner for his helpful reading of an early draft.

MICHAEL WINSHIP: I would like to acknowledge the help of John Bidwell, James N. Green, and Georgia B. Barnhill with Chapter 1; and Jim Green for Chapter 4, Parts 1 and 4.

Introduction

Scott E. Casper

. . .

The American Book Trade Association (ABTA) opened its third annual conference on the sweltering Tuesday afternoon of 11 July 1876. It was a week to the day after the hundredth anniversary of the creation of the United States of America, and the conference was being held in Philadelphia, on the grounds of the Centennial Exhibition. On behalf of the Local Committee on Reception, J. B. Mitchell of J. B. Lippincott & Co. welcomed the participants by saluting the century of progress embodied in the exposition's displays. He pointed especially to the vivid contrasts his colleagues in the book trades might observe:

> you may see in the Pennsylvania Educational Building a representative school-room of 1776, with the meagre and crude appointments of its day, contrasted with the highly-advanced and almost luxurious appliances and aids to education of the present time. You may observe in Machinery Hall the old printing-press of Franklin, upon which, by hard labor, he could produce perhaps 150 impressions per hour, side by side with the Messrs. Hoe & Co.'s latest invention, the Web perfecting-press, printing 32,000 copies of a newspaper, on both sides, in the same time. . . . Steam, the telegraph, and the power printing-press, what have they not accomplished, and how have they changed the condition of the civilized world![1]

At this point ABTA president Anson D. F. Randolph introduced Rev. Mr. William J. Shuey of the United Brethren Publishing House in Dayton, Ohio. Shuey invoked God's providence in "the interests of the book trade—that great work of diffusing knowledge and wisdom among our fellow-men." As for President Randolph, in his opening address he described the "silent and majestic company" that the ABTA had gathered in its own display in the exposition's Main Building: the historians, poets, storytellers, travelers, economists, philosophers, inventors, and teachers whose works existed for the multitudes only through the efforts of the book trades. "Congratulate yourselves that you are American bookmakers and booksellers in this memorable year of the republic!" Randolph exhorted his listeners. But he went on to acknowledge what everyone in the room must have known: that not all was well in the trade. Indeed, Randolph devoted the remainder of his address to the hard times that plagued the nation's publishers and booksellers. Founded in the wake of a nationwide depression, "overstocked markets," and cutthroat competition to provide discounts to retail booksellers and libraries, the ABTA sought to regulate the book trade with a consistent maximum discount rate. It also aimed to unite publishers and wholesale dealers around a shared sense of their calling as "brethren."[2] Within two years the ABTA would be dead, and so would its attempts to "reform" the trade.

But on that July day in 1876, more than 150 men assembled in Judges' Hall on the Centennial grounds and applauded repeatedly as Randolph described their common objectives. The next morning they heard a report from the ABTA's executive committee, read by William Lee of the Boston publishing firm Lee & Shepard. After rehearsing the organization's brief history, Lee emphasized the role that retail booksellers needed to play if the ABTA were to survive and succeed. Its members needed to include "every bookseller in the United States, from the rising sun in the East to the Golden Gate of the West—from the deep caverns of Lake Superior in the North to the magnificent domains of the Lone Star in the South." In fact, Lee's audience included nobody from west of Denver and only one listener from the former Confederacy, a bookseller from Knoxville, Tennessee. More than half came from New York, Philadelphia, or Boston. But, as Lee pointed out, the local bookseller knew the tastes of "his townsmen," and he needed to educate them about the small profit margins in every part of the book trade. Only then would his customers cease to clamor for ever-lower prices. Later that day, booksellers' associations from New England, New York, Cincinnati, Baltimore, and cities along the Hudson River reported on the mixed results of the ABTA's recommended discount in their vicinities, and René Fouret, representing Hachette & Co. of Paris, thanked the ABTA for its warm welcome and for the opportunity to meet "my brothers here." On Thursday morning, J. A. Roys, a newsdealer from Detroit who did not belong to the ABTA, attempted to speak about the relationship between the book trade and his own profession. Roys, who only a few months earlier had "declared war" upon leading periodical publishers Robert Bonner and Frank Leslie for "promoting a system of exclusive agencies" to control the sale of their magazines, was quickly stopped when he began to ramble. The convention adjourned that afternoon after selecting the next year's officers and committee members and after hearing from General Joseph Hawley, president of the Centennial Commission and a Philadelphia newspaperman himself.[3]

On Friday the members and their wives, 250 or 300 in all, boarded a train for Atlantic City. The locomotive was festooned with American flags and a blue banner with white lettering that read "American Book Trade, 1876." Once they arrived, the banner was fastened over the entrance to the United States Hotel, where the entire group assembled for lunch after a few hours on the beach. J. B. Mitchell, the Lippincott executive who had opened the convention's proceedings on Tuesday, began the toasts by celebrating the publishers' and booksellers' "close relations to the authors, that class who, in connection with the newspapers, have so much to do with forming the moral tone and sentiment of the time, and the necessity of such relations to them in creating a circulation for their works and a market for their thoughts." The penultimate remarks came from W. W. Harding of Philadelphia, who held the distinction of being the only American publisher who also manufactured his own paper. Harding described the "inseparable relations between the press and pure book literature as an agency in educating the people and conserving public morality."[4] After a toast to "The Railroad Interests" and the Camden and Atlantic Railroad Company president's response, Wesley Jones, the ABTA's second vice president and a retail bookseller from Burlington, Iowa, thanked his Philadelphia brethren for organizing the convention. With that, the American Book Trade Association closed its proceedings for 1876.

The men assembled in Philadelphia worked for more than 110 firms and organizations in an array of the nation's book trades. Most of the largest trade publishers were represented: D. Appleton & Co. and G. P. Putnam's Sons of New York, James R. Osgood & Co. of Boston, and Philadelphia's own Porter & Coates and J. B. Lippincott & Co. A representative from one of the nation's major publishing houses was missing, however, although President Randolph reported a recent visit to the last surviving Harper brother, the semiretired, seventy-five-year-old Fletcher, "a veteran taking his repose after years of manly, honest toil."[5] The leading religious publishing societies were there, among them the American Tract Society, the American Sunday-School Union, and the American Baptist Publication Society, as were school-book houses such as Cincinnati's Wilson, Hinkle & Co., which published the popular McGuffey's readers. Not all the delegates represented large publishers or distributed their works to a diverse, nationwide audience. The westernmost of them, Denver's E. C. Narris, represented Richards & Co., which produced books about Colorado for potential tourists or mining investors. Other firms specialized in a particular genre or catered to a specific audience. Chicago's Keen, Cooke & Co. was best known for publishing Allan Pinkerton's detective stories, while Philadelphia's Lindsay & Blakiston produced medical books, mostly for physicians. S. K. Brobst of Allentown, Pennsylvania, published a few works in German. Many of the small firms represented were retail booksellers, hailing from places as far-flung as Dubuque and Peoria. The Esterbrook Steel Pen Co. of Camden, New Jersey, the American Lead Pencil Co. of New York, and the Southworth paper company of Mittineaque, Massachusetts, each sent a delegate. So did leading firms from Leipzig and Paris. Two stenographers recorded the convention's proceedings, which appeared two weeks later in one of the ABTA's official journals, *Publishers' Weekly*.[6]

The ABTA's 1876 conference, and the Centennial Exhibition on the grounds of which it took place, offer a striking window into the five major themes of *The Industrial Book*, a collaborative history of the creation, distribution, and uses of print and books in the United States from 1840 to 1880. First, these decades witnessed the ascendancy of what we call the "industrial book": the manufactured, bound product of a publisher, and the quintessential product of the industrialization of both the printing and papermaking trades. In terms of capital, workforce, and production, the manufacturing of books constituted a modest segment of America's industrial revolution. However, it represented a striking change in the production of printed matter, and the books themselves played a disproportionately significant role in justifying and embedding a market culture in the lives, homes, and ideas of Americans.

Second, during these years a national book trade system emerged in the United States. Book publishers created and became aware of themselves as participants in a trade: a system of communication, competition, cooperation, and distribution. The fundamental element of this system, discounted sales to dedicated retailers, linked publishers to booksellers across the nation, often through wholesale dealers ("jobbers"). Improved mechanisms of transportation, credit, and marketing underlay and facilitated the system, which established New York especially, and Philadelphia and Boston secondarily, as the center of America's book trades, with Chicago emerging as an important distribution center in the postbellum years.

Third, publishers, editors, and authors worked to define a sense of the "American book." This occurred narrowly in the development within belles lettres that much later came to be known as the American Renaissance, and more broadly in domains that spanned both learned and popular cultures. The notion of the American book developed certainly in conceptions of what constituted "American" themes or topics but also in the material efforts of publishers who packaged the texts in bindings and in advertisements.

Fourth, the ascendant book culture disseminated in the products of the national book trade system came to embody a set of values that was centered on, though by no means limited to, the middling classes, at once explaining and manifesting what it meant to live in a bourgeois world. Reading and writing, first enumerated in the United States census in 1840, were conceived of as essential to American citizenship, economic success, and cultural achievement. Public schooling, initiated in a few states before 1840, penetrated the entire Northeast and Midwest before the Civil War, and the former Confederate states, including their formerly enslaved populations, after it.

The fifth theme cuts across each of the other four: in each case, other factors complicated, stood against, and existed outside the consolidation and nationalization of the industrial book. The publisher's case-bound, manufactured book, the most striking material development of the period, was only one among many forms of print. Even as metropolitan publishers and printers of books and daily newspapers oversaw factories that employed hundreds of workers and large-scale presses, small shops continued to exist across the United States, printing the ephemera of everyday life (broadsides and pamphlets, railroad schedules and printed forms) and the weekly newspapers that served millions of Americans. The system of distribution that publishers such as G. P. Putnam & Co., Ticknor and Fields, and Harper & Brothers sought to create never worked entirely smoothly, and it never included all of the nation's book publishers. The ABTA itself came into existence to address publishers' imperfect sway over local retail prices, while publishers inside and outside the "legitimate" trade sparred over noncopyrighted foreign works. Those who employed nationalistic terms like "American literature" borrowed from English models in such matters as styles of magazines and modes of literary celebrity, even as Americans in parlors, Sunday schools, and learned societies read the productions of foreign pens that were also the products of American publishers. And middle-class culture existed alongside numerous communities of interest, defined by race, gender, class, ethnicity, ideology, religion, occupation, avocation, or region. As the United States became a continental nation, the printed word became the vehicle that helped define these communities' distinctive identities across geographical distance. Non-industrial printing, an imperfect and partial system of publishers' control, continued literary and economic relationships with Europe, and the efflorescence of localized and specialized identities: all of these indicate the limits of the major developments. Together they, too, form a significant part of this narrative.

· · ·

For members of the ABTA, their convention was probably a convenient excuse to visit the Centennial Exhibition, the international demonstration of the world's and especially America's progress in manufacturing, agriculture, and the arts. Bookmen on holiday may have wanted escape from the trade's exhibits, as did William Dean Howells. The July issue of the *Atlantic Monthly* featured "A Sennight of the Centennial," a travelogue in which the former Ohio newspaperman and current editor of that esteemed journal reported skipping "the display of the publishing houses: books were the last things I cared to see at the Centennial. But I heard from persons less disdainful of literature that the show of bookmaking did us great honor."[7] But if the publishers and booksellers wished, they could find evidence of all of the period's major developments throughout the fair.

Two weeks earlier, the three biggest presses in Machinery Hall had competed to determine which could print the most impressions in an hour. The press of Philadelphia's Bullock Printing Press Co. produced 14,856 copies of the *New York Herald*; New York's R. Hoe & Co. press, 21,810 copies of the *Philadelphia Times*; and that of London's John Walter, 10,455 copies of the *New York Times*.[8] These rotary web perfecting presses were the largest spectacle, especially when in operation, but almost sixty other companies, including a few from France and Germany, displayed presses designed for lighter work than the urban daily newspaper. Large presses for fine illustration and cylinder presses for producing newspapers from already-cut sheets testified similarly to industrialization. Presses for "small newspapers, book-work, pamphlet- and jobbing-work" might remind visitors that not all printed matter came from large factories. And "small job and amateur presses" indicated "the growing interest taken in the details of the art of printing by a constantly increasing number of persons not engaged in the printing business," as well as the sort of machine in use in "general printing-offices . . . enabling master-printers to employ their boys and apprentices with great advantage and saving in cost of labor."[9] Affordable at low prices, the small presses also exhibited the mass production of printing presses themselves. Myriad other machines were on display. Perhaps most striking, W. F. Murphy of Philadelphia demonstrated "a bindery and printing establishment in complete running order, with all the machinery of the most recent date and improved design," complete with "Ruling-machine, stand-press, and board-cutter, made by W. O. Hickok, Harrisburg, Pa.; a paging and numbering machine and stabbing machine, made by J. R. Hoole, New-York; Wm. Bradwood's book-folding machine; Carver & Brown's cutting and paper-perforating machines; and two Gordon presses."[10]

The machinery and productions of industrial printing could be seen outside Machinery Hall as well. The Campbell Printing Press and Manufacturing Co. of New York erected its own building, complete with a statue of Gutenberg over its entry. In the Main Building, stationery exhibits dwarfed the ABTA's display of publishers' wares. There were papers of every sort from a dozen nations: writing paper, printing paper, photographic paper, and card stock, not to mention wallpaper and cigarette wrappers and an exhibit of wood pulp from the Androscoggin Pulp Company of Portland, Maine.[11] Thaddeus Davids & Co. of New York displayed hundreds of its inks in a showcase made of walnut, cherry, and maple, topped with griffins holding gold quill pens in their mouths and containing quotations from Byron and a book titled *The History of Ink* by the firm's proprietor (Fig. I.1). No less modest, the American Lead Pencil Company's exhibit featured "a series of four octagons, one rising above the other, crowned by a little dome, on which the statue of America holds Amazonian guard." The Centennial judges responsible for Group 13, which included "Paper Industry, Stationery, Printing, and Book Making" as well as "Machines and Apparatus for Type-Setting, Printing, Stamping, Embossing, and for Making Books and Paper Working," awarded prizes to many of these companies and to a number of publishers for the material elegance of their books.[12]

The industrial book belonged to this broader industrialization within the book trades and related industries, which was itself part of the American and transatlantic Industrial Revolution of the mid-nineteenth century. From 1850 (the earliest date for which manufacturing census data are reliable) to 1880, the number of manufacturing establishments in the United States with annual product of at least $500 rose from 153,025 to 253,852, a 66 percent increase, while the number of workers in those establishments nearly tripled, from 957,059 to 2,732,595. Printing and publishing accounted for a rising share of the manufacturing economy (Tables 4.1–4). The number of those establishments multiplied more than fivefold, from 673 in 1850 (0.55 percent of the total) to 3,467 in 1880 (1.37 percent), and their employees more than sevenfold, from 8,268 (0.86 percent of all manufacturing workers) to 58,478 (2.14 percent). The value they added to the economy (value of total products less cost of raw materials) rose from 1.43 percent to 2.96 percent of the entire manufacturing economy over those thirty years. When one considers the constellation of industries involved in the production of print—largest among them bookbinding and papermaking, but also including engraving and lithography, the production of ink, type, and printing equipment, and the stationery trades—the book trades and related industries by 1880 accounted for more than 4 percent of America's manufacturing laborers and more than 3.5 percent of its total manufactured products. Although buffeted by the economic cycles of boom and bust that sank many businesses in the depressions of 1857 and 1873, the printing and bookmaking trades appear to have been relatively resilient, their establishments increasing significantly in

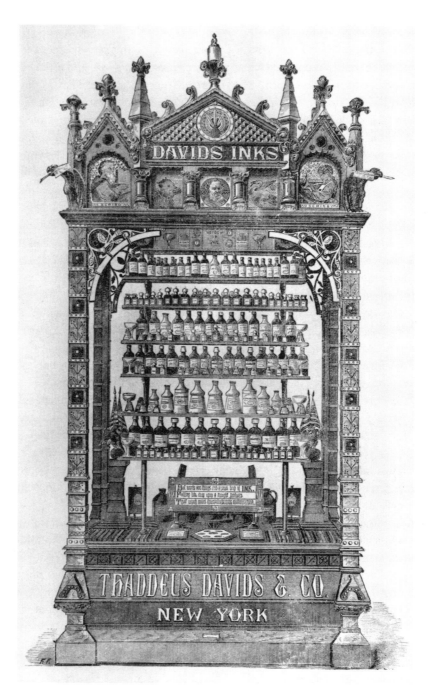

FIGURE I.1. Thaddeus Davids & Co. ink display, Centennial Exhibition, Philadelphia, 1876. From *Publishers' Weekly* 10 (1 July 1876). American Antiquarian Society.

number every decade even as the number of manufacturing establishments nationwide decreased from 1850 to 1860 and remained constant from 1870 to 1880.

Much of this increase, particularly in workforce, capitalization, and overall production, was tied to industrial mechanization. Printing presses had existed for nearly four hundred years by 1840. One difference was the use of steam to power machines that multiplied the speed and number of impressions that could be produced. Waterpower was essential to the growth of the paper industry, which by 1880 used more than 7 percent of the nation's water-generated energy. Beneath these enormous transformations lay the introduction of machines to perform tasks formerly done exclusively by hand, notably in binderies and typefoundries. As a whole, the average labor force of a printing or publishing establishment rose from 12.3 workers in 1850 to 16.9 in 1880, in a period when the average American manufacturing workplace grew from 6.3 to 10.8 employees. These aggregate numbers mask important differences: book publishers in 1870 employed three times as many workers per shop (34.75 employees) as did newspaper publishers (10.95), and nearly four times as many as job printers (9.12). Even those figures give undue weight to the scale of metropolitan newspaper and job printers, mostly in the Northeast. Elsewhere, shops employed far fewer workers than the national averages.

Printers sometimes called themselves labor's aristocracy, not only because they were highly literate but also because their wages outpaced those of other manufacturing workers: in printing and publishing, wages exceeded the national manufacturing averages by a third before the Civil War and by more than half in 1870 and 1880. Average wages across all the printing and related trades were lower, especially in bookbinding and papermaking, with their significant use of female and child labor, but still ran ahead of national averages. Industrial production swelled the number of women and children in printing and publishing, from 17 percent of their workforce in 1870 to 21 percent just a decade later. In the largest shops — the major book publishers, metropolitan daily newspapers, and job-printing establishments — industrialization brought about new roles for operatives, many of whom now tended rather than powered machines. It also brought about increasingly minute divisions of labor, with concomitant differences in skill levels and pay. But it eliminated neither high-skilled nor handcrafted work; for example, typesetting would not become heavily mechanized until after 1880, with the development of the linotype and monotype machines.

The few operatives on display at the Centennial appeared as their employers wished them to be seen, so unobtrusive as not to receive mention

TABLE I.1. Printing, book, and stationery trades in the United States, 1850

Industry	Number of states	Number of firms	Number of employees	
			Male	Female
Bookbinding and blank books	23	235	1,778	1,690
Engraving	10	112	433	47
Envelopes	1	2	6	36
Ink	3	14	49	4
Lamps	3	26	918	20
Lithography	1	11	104	58
Maps	1	3	26	63
Paper	23	443	3,835	2,950
Pens and pencils	1	4	58	0
Printing, lithographic and copperplate	7	26	241	134
Printing and publishing	25	673	6,989	1,279
Slates	1	6	109	0
Stationery	—	8	99	126
Type and stereotype	10	42	775	224
Total		1,605	15,420	6,631

Source: *Abstract of the Statistics of Manufactures, according to the Returns of the Seventh Census* (Washington, D.C.: Bureau of the Census, 1858).
Note: The thirty-six "states" reported included the District of Columbia and the territories of Minnesota, New Mexico, Oregon, and Utah.

when *Publishers' Weekly* described the machines in operation. The one exception was the "girl" who counted, banded, and boxed envelopes at Samuel Raynor & Co.'s "gumming and folding machine."[13] Beyond most Centennial visitors' view, Philadelphia's journeymen printers, organized as a local of the International Typographical Union, were seeking higher wages that June from the Employing Printers of Philadelphia in negotiations far less rancorous than the strikes that would bedevil America's larger industrial employers the following year. The Centennial judges took the occasion to praise "two journeymen" from Cambridge, Massachusetts, Joseph R. Beckett and Romeo Cervi, who had practiced hand-tooled bookbinding "out of working hours," as "an example worthy of imitation by workmen" and "of encouragement by employers." The citation commended Beckett, the Massachusetts-born son of Irish immigrants, and Cervi, born in Italy, for "not only a desire to improve on the part of the exhibitors, but an ability to originate and complete designs without outside aid." Such recognition seems out of place next to the citation to Philadelphia's Oldach & Mergenthaler for "book-binding of general uniform excellence, at a moderate price."[14]

Capital invested	Raw materials	Cost of labor	Value of products
$1,063,700	$1,560,330	$901,404	$3,255,678
$172,065	$130,714	$227,776	$566,005
$10,500	$17,180	$7,020	$45,000
$116,650	$72,673	$21,588	$213,648
$486,300	$490,862	$290,424	$1,060,022
$76,600	$49,650	$51,288	$136,000
$8,200	$6,275	$21,024	$42,100
$7,260,864	$5,553,929	$1,497,792	$10,187,177
$43,000	$59,014	$14,028	$85,300
$148,500	$59,558	$115,836	$247,200
$5,862,715	$4,964,225	$2,737,308	$11,586,549
$50,000	$13,174	$23,100	$46,700
$113,000	$207,775	$45,708	$332,900
$513,700	$298,922	$275,220	$913,200
$15,925,794	$13,484,281	$6,229,516	$28,717,479

It would be easy to misrepresent the importance of book publishing in the advent of an industrial print culture. The industrial book represented the culmination of the industrialization of printing: its paper produced in factories, pages printed from stereotype or electrotype plates and mechanically folded and cut, housed in decorated case bindings stamped in gold by machine. But in 1870 the book printing and publishing establishments that the census enumerated paled in number beside those identified with newspaper (1,199) or job printing (609). Even if the category "printing and publishing, not specified" (311 establishments) included some book publishers along with producers of photograph albums and miscellaneous objects, other sorts of printing firms employed more workers, held more capital, and produced printed matter in greater quantities and of greater economic value. The preeminence of book publishing sprang from the cultural capital of its products, derived not only from the apparent permanence of their ideas but also from their physical appearance, beginning with the binding style that the publisher selected.

. . .

Earlier in 1876, the organizers of the Centennial Exhibition had raised a furor among American publishers by decreeing that judges would award prizes only to publishers who physically produced their own books. If the organiz-

TABLE I.2. Printing, book, and stationery trades in the United States, 1860

Industry	Number of states	Number of firms	Number of employees Male	Female
Bookbinder's machinery	2	4	46	1
Bookbinder's tools	1	1	5	0
Bookbinding and blank books	27	269	2,045	2,732
Engraver's blocks and wood	2	2	12	0
Engraving and die-sinking	10	191	706	18
Envelopes	5	16	150	282
Ink—printing	5	16	79	0
Ink—writing	4	13	58	8
Lithography	7	53	760	26
Machinery—paper	1	3	33	0
Map mounting and coloring	1	1	2	0
Maps	6	15	90	110
Metal type	1	1	6	0
Music printing	1	2	11	0
Newspaper directing machines	1	1	2	0
Paper	24	555	6,519	4,392
Printers' chases, furniture, and rollers	2	8	27	0
Printing and publishing	37	1,666	17,826	2,333
Printing and lithographic presses	5	14	707	0
School apparatus	3	3	23	7
Stationery (including pencils)	7	32	365	27
Stereotyping and electrotyping	3	41	305	0
Type, type and stereotype founding	6	32	795	312
Type, wooden	1	2	32	7
Total		2,941	30,604	10,255

Source: *Manufactures of the United States in 1860; Compiled from the Original Returns of the Eighth Census* (Washington, D.C.: GPO, 1865).
Note: The thirty-nine "states" reported included the District of Columbia and the territories of Nebraska, Utah, New Mexico, and Washington.

ers' decision stood, only a handful of firms such as Harper & Brothers, which housed most of its operations within its own seven-story New York factory, would be eligible for awards. Taken to its extreme, the decision would mean that only W. W. Harding, the Philadelphia printer with his own paper factory, could win a Centennial prize. Eventually the organizers relented, and dozens of publishers won citations.[15] But the uproar illuminated two larger points. First, by 1876 most American publishers only coordinated the processes of book manufacturing: they contracted with printing firms, binderies, and other establishments to produce their wares, and they worked with job-

Capital invested	Raw materials	Cost of labor	Value of products
$26,000	$6,390	$19,068	$39,100
$3,000	$660	$1,800	$2,625
$1,654,830	$1,554,082	$1,048,930	$3,729,080
$25,600	$4,750	$4,104	$12,700
$431,650	$157,171	$330,524	$829,140
$309,600	$433,637	$117,180	$763,700
$245,700	$498,505	$33,264	$802,900
$33,050	$45,344	$18,432	$119,578
$445,250	$229,206	$338,868	$848,230
$45,000	$13,675	$14,232	$41,400
$200	$200	$816	$2,000
$218,500	$115,555	$69,108	$301,500
$50,000	$50,640	$2,304	$68,000
$18,000	$5,800	$5,280	$22,500
$2,000	$340	$240	$600
$14,052,683	$11,602,266	$2,767,212	$21,216,802
$13,900	$11,699	$10,656	$31,500
$19,622,318	$12,844,288	$7,588,096	$31,063,898
$1,015,000	$145,520	$289,684	$943,450
$8,200	$5,560	$9,936	$27,000
$144,400	$81,167	$106,380	$325,338
$126,500	$60,507	$120,840	$286,300
$1,113,600	$357,600	$416,404	$1,276,570
$26,500	$5,000	$11,520	$25,000
$39,631,481	$28,229,562	$13,324,878	$62,778,911

bers to distribute their books to retailers across the United States. Second, at moments such as this, publishers could unite to express their views, in the pages of *Publishers' Weekly* and (in this case) in the ABTA's correspondence with the Centennial organizers. Together, these elements exemplified the national trade publishing system that emerged fitfully between 1840 and 1880.

If the industrial book exemplified the influence of the Industrial Revolution upon the material appearance of the printed word, then the centrality of the publisher represented the contemporaneous organizational revolution in American business that emerging national markets at once encouraged and demanded. By the 1850s the publisher was "the entrepreneur of the book trade," as Michael Winship has explained. That trade "included a number of specialized firms, many of considerable size, dedicated to a particu-

TABLE 1.3. Printing, book, and stationery trades in the United States, 1870

Industry	Number of states	Number of firms	Steam engines HP	Steam engines Number	Water wheels HP	Water wheels Number
Bookbinding	36	500	773	77	0	0
Chromos and lithographs	13	91	186	20	0	0
Engraving	18	157	151	13	0	0
Engraving and stencil-cutting	20	136	13	4	10	1
Envelopes	4	21	129	14	30	1
Ink, printing	7	16	248	13	55	2
Ink, writing	7	25	8	1	0	0
Maps and atlases	5	18	0	0	20	1
Paper, printing	25	235	5,269	144	17,354	454
Paper, writing	6	46	731	10	6,144	146
Pencils, indelible	1	1	8	1	0	0
Pencils, lead	2	7	265	6	0	0
Pens and pencils, gold	10	21	56	3	5	1
Pens, steel	2	3	38	2	0	0
Printers' fixtures	7	21	15	3	28	3
Printing and publishing, not specified	20	311	2,698	187	20	1
Printing and publishing, book	10	40	458	28	0	0
Printing and publishing, newspaper	38	1,199	3,135	302	74	9
Printing, job	30	609	1,440	174	15	4
School slates and slate-pencils	3	21	28	2	234	17
Stereotyping and electrotyping	8	36	91	8	0	0
Type founding	10	31	166	11	0	0
Wood pulp	4	8	0	0	1,069	14
Total		3,553	15,906	1,023	25,058	654

Source: Ninth Census, Volume III: The Statistics of the Wealth and Industry of the United States (Washington, D.C.: GPO, 1872).
Note: The forty-five "states" reported included the District of Columbia and the territories of Colorado, Idaho, Montana, New Mexico, Utah, Washington, and Wyoming. Under "Steam engines" and "Water wheels," "HP" indicates horsepower.

lar branch of book manufacture and distribution: papermaking, typefounding, stereotyping, printing, binding, jobbing, or retail bookselling."[16] Unlike printers of the colonial era and the early republic, the primary role of mid-nineteenth-century book publishers — some of whom had begun their careers as printers — was to coordinate these functions. Located predominantly in New York, Boston, and Philadelphia, these publishers developed solutions to the problems that had made their business primarily local or regional a gen-

Number of employees			Capital invested	Raw materials	Wages	Value of products
M > 16	F > 15	Youth				
3,972	3,175	550	$5,319,410	$8,026,870	$3,095,821	$14,077,309
1,244	56	99	$1,533,725	$735,810	$837,732	$2,515,684
1,047	269	91	$1,744,795	$452,072	$1,022,090	$2,093,482
381	5	45	$244,000	$103,035	$155,968	$509,644
240	624	38	$874,000	$1,282,139	$314,458	$2,267,541
152	0	3	$343,300	$353,711	$100,187	$600,329
101	32	27	$276,230	$176,399	$45,962	$366,473
101	65	15	$380,500	$129,162	$87,562	$393,447
5,107	2,553	507	$16,771,920	$16,120,363	$3,400,038	$25,200,417
1,450	2,384	28	$6,314,674	$6,009,751	$1,470,446	$9,363,384
4	0	0	$20,000	$13,000	$3,000	$20,000
61	95	0	$241,150	$44,510	$48,150	$160,800
199	30	13	$268,250	$181,740	$133,556	$467,380
47	195	15	$175,000	$49,943	$60,000	$180,000
80	0	6	$55,200	$32,640	$33,931	$118,119
8,718	1,231	719	$16,839,993	$11,398,131	$7,156,332	$28,995,214
920	352	118	$2,128,993	$1,525,773	$760,275	$3,568,823
11,343	718	1,069	$14,947,887	$8,709,632	$8,168,515	$25,393,029
4,458	499	598	$6,007,354	$2,966,709	$2,710,234	$8,511,934
221	0	53	$159,620	$76,385	$88,236	$217,103
659	15	92	$1,033,200	$220,774	$446,532	$1,075,080
729	413	189	$1,704,785	$819,938	$720,105	$2,180,001
111	0	0	$191,000	$29,500	$60,178	$172,350
41,345	12,711	4,275	$77,574,986	$59,457,987	$30,919,308	$128,447,543

eration earlier: the risks of transportation, credit, and communication with others in the trade.

When publishers spoke of the "trade," they referred also to their relationships with one another. Twenty-one years before the ABTA convened at the Centennial Exhibition, the New York Book Publishers' Association had honored 153 American authors at a similarly self-congratulatory event at New York's Crystal Palace. That dinner was the highlight of a familiar occasion: a semiannual trade sale, "controlled by and strictly limited to members of the book trade," at which publishers introduced new works and attempted to dispose of slow sellers.[17] Publishers assembled for festivity and business and attempted to act in concert throughout these decades for several rea-

TABLE 1.4. Printing, book, and stationery trades in the United States, 1880

Industry	Number of states	Number of firms	Steam engines		Water wheels	
			HP	Number	HP	Number
Bookbinding and blank books	36	588	—	—	—	—
Electric lights	3	3	—	—	—	—
Engravers' materials	3	11	—	—	—	—
Engraving and die-sinking	17	246	—	—	—	—
Engraving, steel	9	55	—	—	—	—
Engraving, wood	18	167	—	—	—	—
Envelopes	5	12	—	—	—	—
Ink	14	63	—	—	—	—
Lithographing	21	167	—	—	—	—
Paper	30	692	36,301	673	87,611	1,856
Pencils, lead	3	4	—	—	—	—
Pens, gold	4	16	—	—	—	—
Pens, steel	3	3	—	—	—	—
Printing and publishing	42	3,467	15,990	1,179	335	59
Printing materials	9	27	—	—	—	—
Stationery goods	18	159	—	—	—	—
Stereotyping and electrotyping	16	45	—	—	—	—
Telegraph and telephone	9	40	—	—	—	—
Type founding	13	48	—	—	—	—
Wood pulp	12	50	—	—	—	—
Total		5,863	52,291	1,852	87,946	1,915

Source: *Report on the Manufactures of the United States at the Tenth Census (June 1, 1880)* (Washington, D.C.: GPO, 1883).

Note: The forty-seven "states" reported included the District of Columbia and the territories of Dakota, Idaho, Montana, New Mexico, Utah, Washington, and Wyoming. Under "Steam engines" and "Water wheels," "HP" indicates horsepower.

sons. One was the volatility of the American economy, combined with the low profit margins in publishing. The "Fruit Festival" banquet of 27 September 1855 was soon followed by the nationwide depression of 1857, in which several American publishers — notably John P. Jewett, the original publisher of Harriet Beecher Stowe's *Uncle Tom's Cabin* (1852), as well as Stowe's current publisher Phillips, Sampson & Co. — suspended payment and eventually went out of business. Another was the lack of international copyright protection, a situation that had existed before 1840 and would not be resolved until passage of the Chace Act in 1891. From the mid-1820s through the 1880s, many publishers subscribed to an informal system known as "courtesy of the trade" to sort out which of them had the right to publish a particu-

Number of employees			Capital invested	Raw materials	Wages	Value of products
M > 16	F > 15	Youth				
5,127	4,831	654	$5,798,671	$5,195,771	$3,927,349	$11,976,764
214	0	15	$425,000	$150,650	$117,500	$458,400
66	3	1	$54,500	$26,464	$39,840	$85,764
698	62	92	$416,840	$262,828	$419,646	$1,180,165
1,118	661	137	$2,387,050	$648,994	$1,951,745	$2,998,616
468	20	21	$183,733	$68,605	$333,590	$734,728
233	948	23	$923,800	$2,346,500	$344,143	$3,000,617
339	79	62	$1,251,050	$864,765	$230,284	$1,629,413
3,641	308	373	$4,501,825	$2,755,264	$2,307,302	$6,912,338
16,133	7,640	649	$46,241,202	$33,951,297	$8,525,355	$55,109,914
116	144	139	$341,597	$97,344	$102,233	$279,427
226	19	19	$370,150	$190,906	$172,207	$533,061
34	230	16	$182,500	$38,950	$88,500	$164,000
45,880	6,759	5,839	$62,983,704	$32,460,395	$30,531,657	$90,780,341
164	7	20	$199,900	$190,353	$98,878	$421,316
1,871	1,028	218	$3,286,325	$3,501,426	$1,159,893	$5,898,322
562	44	36	$536,000	$200,491	$312,208	$724,689
797	37	59	$636,458	$755,891	$458,406	$1,580,648
1,327	406	253	$2,772,690	$660,748	$958,693	$2,330,298
1,184	8	17	$1,898,450	$910,835	$444,778	$2,256,946
80,198	23,234	8,643	$135,391,445	$85,278,477	$52,524,207	$189,055,767

lar foreign work or author. Because American copyright law did not provide a legal protection of this right, however, the writings of the most popular British authors, such as Sir Walter Scott and Charles Dickens, became fodder for American publishers' competition. During the depression that began in 1873, publishers formed the ABTA in order to safeguard themselves against another sort of competition, "underselling" and ruinous discounting. Publishers came to know themselves as a trade through the pages of their own periodicals, beginning notably when the just-founded New York Book Publishers' Association absorbed *Norton's Literary Gazette* in 1855 and renamed it the *American Publishers' Circular and Literary Gazette*, the forerunner of *Publishers' Weekly* (1873).

The ABTA's Centennial Exhibition display, a two-story iron pavilion within the Main Building, revealed how harmoniously the trade appeared to work (Figs. I.2–4). More than ninety firms or organizations exhibited their wares, many of them specimens of fine binding and typography: schoolbooks, religious tracts and Bibles, American and English literature, legal and medical

FIGURE I.2. The American Book Trade Association exhibit, Centennial Exhibition. The A. J. Holman & Co. display is in the right foreground, lower floor. Photograph courtesy of the Free Library of Philadelphia.

works, and assorted specialized volumes. At ground level, visitors could enter between Altemus & Co.'s showcase of photograph albums and scrapbooks and J. W. Lauterbach's single publication, the Centennial book *A Century After: Picturesque Glimpses of Philadelphia and Pennsylvania* (1875), then see before them small displays of *Publishers' Weekly* and the American News Company's *American Bookseller's Guide* and the large case of the American Bible Society and the British and Foreign Bible Society. Turn left, and there were exhibits from Harper & Brothers, the medical publisher William Wood & Co., and T. B. Peterson & Bros., publisher of the popular novels of Mrs. E. D. E. N. Southworth and Caroline Lee Hentz. To the right were Kay & Bro.'s law books; E. Steiger's maps, globes, and textbooks for German schools in the United States; and the American Sunday-School Union's "wonderful variety of publications." Along the back could be found the myriad small displays of specialty publishers: John W. Griffiths's three books on shipbuilding, A. J. Bicknell & Co.'s architectural books, George R. Lockwood's "glorious" edition of Audubon's *Birds of America*, and the Seventh-Day Adventists' "health publications, together with some mysterious allegorical and prophetical literature." Upstairs, fourteen firms presented larger

FIGURE 1.3. The American Book Trade Association exhibit, Centennial Exhibition. The extensive A. S. Barnes & Co. display is visible on the upper floor. Photograph courtesy of the Free Library of Philadelphia.

displays: several major schoolbook companies' wares, D. Appleton & Co.'s *Picturesque America* and Webster's spellers, Lee & Shepard's eleven-volume *Works of Charles Sumner* with a bust of the recently deceased Massachusetts senator. Architecturally and spatially, it all might seem like the book district of an American metropolis of the day.[18]

But the stylistic cacophony of the exhibits would quickly belie any notion that the publishers had planned their pavilion together. The ABTA's three-man committee to oversee its creation had asked potential exhibitors to provide scale drawings of their "show-cases, counters, or partitions, showing clearly the elevation and ground-plan," but apparently many did not comply.[19] When the Centennial Exhibition opened on 10 May, *Publishers' Weekly* lamented that the structure lacked any sign indicating the ABTA's proprietorship and that "the style of exhibits is as various as their character," stating that the display "of the American Bible Society is perhaps the most beautiful, and from this they range down to one or two in cheap, stained wood, with tawdry ornamentation. . . . some excrescences such as Mr. Harding's large sign, which

PLAN OF THE AMERICAN BOOK TRADE ASSOC. EXHIBIT.

PHILADELPHIA, 1876.

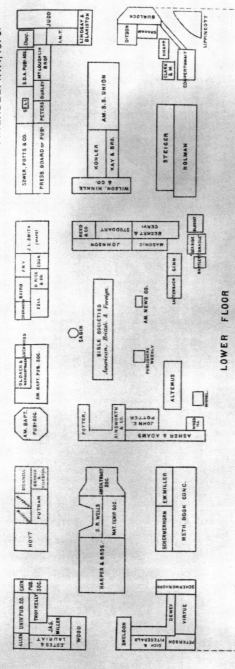

LOWER FLOOR

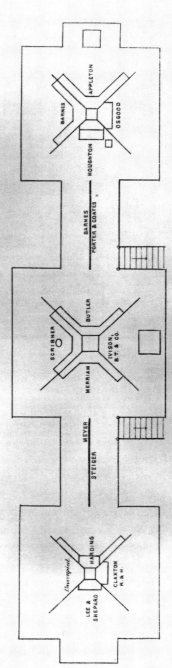

UPPER FLOOR

The Publishers' Weekly, July 1st 1876.

J. Bien Photo-Lith.

FIGURE 1.4. "Plan of the American Book Trade Assoc. Exhibit" at the Centennial Exhibition, showing both lower and upper floors. From *Publishers' Weekly* 10 (1 July 1876). American Antiquarian Society.

The firms and organizations represented in the exhibit and their specialties were as follows, beginning in the upper-left corner of the lower floor:

1. H. S. Allen (New York): *People's History of America*
2. University Publishing Company (New York): schoolbooks and maps
3. Catholic Publication Society (New York): Bibles, prayer books, *Catholic World*
4. Thomas Kelly (New York): Catholic Bibles and devotional books
5. James Miller (New York): English and American works in fine bindings
6. Estes & Lauriat (Boston): Guizot's *History of France* and other works
7. William Wood & Co. (New York): medical works
8. Henry Hoyt (Boston): juvenile books
9. J. W. Griffiths (New York): three works on shipbuilding
10. James Anglim (Washington): Lanman's *Biographical Annals of the Civil Government of the United States*
11. A. J. Bicknell & Co. (New York): architectural publications
12. Brewer & Tileston (Boston): Worcester's dictionary
13. G. P. Putnam's Sons (New York): American literature, *Putnam's Magazine*
14 and 15. American Baptist Publication Society (Philadelphia): hymn and tune books, standard religious works
16. Oldach & Mergenthaler (Philadelphia): bookbinders
17. George R. Lockwood (New York): Audubon's *Birds of America*
18. George Sherwood & Co. (Chicago): schoolbooks
19. Henry Carey Baird & Co. (Philadelphia): maps and atlases
20. H. C. Fry (Philadelphia): binders' tools and dies
21. J. L. Smith (Philadelphia): maps
22. Ezra A. Cook & Co. (Chicago): *Christian Cynosure* (reform newspaper)
23. D. Rice & Co. (Philadelphia): McKenney's Indian Tribes, *North American Sylva, National Portrait Gallery of Distinguished Americans*
24. Charles H. Davis & Co. (Philadelphia): Zell's atlas, encyclopedias, and U.S. business directory; Duyckinck's *Cyclopedia of American Literature*
25. Sower, Potts & Co. (Philadelphia): historical display of German-language publications
26. William F. Gill & Co. (Boston): miscellaneous publications and model of Bunker Hill Monument
27. Seventh-Day Adventists' Publication Society (Battle Creek, Mich.): health publications
28. McLoughlin Bros. (New York): toy books and games
29. S. D. Burley (Philadelphia): Kidder's *United States Centennial Gazetteer and Guide*
30. J. L. Peters (New York): bound and sheet music

(continued)

31. Presbyterian Board of Publication (Philadelphia): hymnals, catechisms, periodicals, other religious works
32. Rev. H. Floy Roberts: manuscript of "Interlinear New Testament" with Greek text and English translation
33. Orange Judd Co. (New York): agricultural and horticultural works
34. Lindsay & Blakiston (Philadelphia): medical publications
35. Harper & Brothers (New York): periodicals, English classics, American books
36. S. R. Wells & Co. (New York): phrenological works
37. American Tract Society (New York): tracts, Bibles, periodicals
38. National Temperance Society (New York): books, pamphlets, periodicals
39. Sheldon & Co. (New York): textbooks
40. D. M. Dewey (Rochester): color plates of fruit for fruit-growers' catalogs
41 and 45. J. W. Schermerhorn & Co. (New York): textbooks, globes, and other materials for schools
42. Virtue & Yorston (New York): quarto Bible, works on American Revolution and Civil War
43. T. B. Peterson & Bros. (Philadelphia): novels of E. D. E. N. Southworth, Caroline Lee Hentz, Charles Dickens, and others
44. Dick & Fitzgerald (New York): encyclopedias, "handy books"
45. *See* 41
46. E. W. Miller (Philadelphia): Bibles
47. Methodist Book Concern (New York): Bibles, standard religious and Sunday school books
48. Potter, Ainsworth & Co. (New York): penmanship and educational books
49. John E. Potter (Philadelphia): Bibles and Testaments in German and English
50. H. M. Hinsdale: "Office Scratch-books" (stationery)
51. Asher & Adams (New York): maps, atlases
52. J. Sabin & Sons (New York): Sabin's *Bibliotheca Americana*
53. Bible Societies: publications of American Bible Society (New York) and British and Foreign Bible Society (London)
54. *Publishers' Weekly* (New York): bound volumes of the journal and other publications
55. American News Company (New York): *American Booksellers' Guide*
56. Altemus & Co. (Philadelphia): photograph albums, scrapbooks
57. Ivan C. Michel: self-published volume of the Lord's Prayer in 500 languages
58. J. W. Lauterbach and Allen, Lane & Scott (Philadelphia): *A Century After* (Centennial volume)
59. Ginn Bros. (Boston): educational books
60. T. & J. W. Johnson & Co. (Philadelphia): law books
61. A. Reed & Co. (Philadelphia): bookbinders
62. J. M. Stoddart & Co. (Philadelphia): William Brotherhead's *Centennial Book of the Signers*
63. J. R. Beckett and Romeo Cervi (Cambridge, Mass.): bookbinders

64. Masonic Publishing Company (New York): Masonic publications

65. John Russell Bartlett (Providence): catalog of the library of John Carter Brown

66. *Seaside Oracle* (Wiscasset, Maine): American village newspaper

67. Lorin Blodget (Philadelphia): Blodget's *Climatology of the United States*

68. Wilson, Hinkle & Co. (Cincinnati): McGuffey's readers and other schoolbooks

69. Ig. Kohler (Philadelphia): German publications

70. American Sunday-School Union (Philadelphia): religious books

71. Kay & Bro. (Philadelphia): law books

72 and 84. E. Steiger (New York): globes, maps, German schoolbooks, kindergarten supplies

73. A. J. Holman & Co. (Philadelphia): historical display of American Bibles

74. J. E. Ditson & Co. (Philadelphia): Centennial sheet music

75. Samuel D. Burlock & Co. (Philadelphia): Presbyterian works

76. Andrew J. Graham (New York): phonographic (stenography) works

77. Allen E. Knapp: "Continuous Genealogical Family Record"

78. Clark & Maynard (New York): educational, juvenile, and Masonic books

79. Cowperthwait & Co. (Philadelphia): educational publications

80. J. B. Lippincott & Co. (Philadelphia): Bibles, standard works in all fields

81. Lee & Shepard (Boston): *Works of Charles Sumner*, juvenile and miscellaneous publications

82. W. W. Harding (Philadelphia): self-manufactured albums

83. Claxton, Remsen & Haffelfinger (Philadelphia): works of James Madison, standard English authors

84. *See* 72

85. Louis Meyer (Philadelphia): sheet music

86. G. & C. Merriam (Springfield, Mass.): works of Noah Webster

87. Scribner, Armstrong & Co. (New York): schoolbooks, *St. Nicholas*, *Scribner's Monthly*

88. J. H. Butler & Co. (Philadelphia): wall maps and schoolbooks

89. Ivison, Blakeman, Taylor & Co. (New York): schoolbooks, Spencerian penmanship series

90. Porter & Coates (Philadelphia): editions of Shakespeare and varied other works

91 and 93. A. S. Barnes & Co. (New York): schoolbooks

92. Hurd & Houghton (New York) and H. O. Houghton & Co. (Cambridge, Mass.): Riverside Press publications

93. *See* 91

94. D. Appleton & Co. (New York): Ripley's *American Cyclopaedia*, Bryant's *Picturesque America*, Webster's spelling books, miscellaneous publications

95. James R. Osgood & Co. (Boston): English and American literature

crosses awkwardly over to Steiger's place, interfering with all the upper lines of the edifice, and the staring advertisement of authors on the side of the Petersons' case, the Committee should request to have removed."[20] Harper & Brothers was a chief offender: after waiting too long to submit its plans and then asking for space to display its "entire catalogue, amounting to over three thousand volumes," it got just an eight-by-ten-foot space on the ground floor. There it installed a twelve-foot-high case, "in oak" and "out of tone with the other cases in the Exhibition."[21]

The national book trade "system" was similarly imperfect. Resisting the 1855 attempt by the New York Book Publishers' Association to establish control over that city's trade sales, Harper & Brothers and other firms continued to contribute to the auctions held by Bangs, Merwin & Co., and trade sales also continued in Boston, Philadelphia, and Cincinnati. Courtesy of the trade often proved difficult to enforce, especially against publishers of self-described "cheap libraries" in the 1870s that defended their reprinting as a populist revolt against a monopolistic publishing trade. The two definitions of the trade—the various industries whose efforts publishers coordinated, and the "brotherhood" of publishers themselves—were not always reconciled. Publishers of the ABTA might seek to enforce set prices and standard discounts, but the jobbers and especially the retail booksellers down the distribution chain might not comply if they could purchase stock cheaply at the trade sales or from traveling salesmen. Similar attempts at organization occurred in other industries, with varying degrees of success. By the mid-1870s, railroad executives and managers convened in trade associations, published trade periodicals, and developed successful mechanisms to control internecine competition. Boards of trade had been created to facilitate the distribution of farm products by reducing the risks of coordinating credit and information among producers, jobbers, and storekeepers. But, as in publishing, trade associations in many other industries found it impossible to enforce agreements about pricing—a difficulty that would lead after 1880 to the formation of trusts.[22] Editorially, the *American Publishers' Circular* and *Publishers' Weekly* expressed the publishers' impulse toward concerted action. For example, the latter's stenographic transcript of the proceedings of the 1876 ABTA convention was intended surely for the publishers and booksellers across the country who did not come to Philadelphia that July, as well as for those who did. Concert did not always occur, however: whether noting the ABTA exhibit's stylistic disunity or, the very next year, the demise of a schoolbook publishers' trade association, the trade journal spoke for and to a community that often failed to act as one.

Outside the book trade and the allied stationery trades represented at the

ABTA convention lay the larger, less centralized world of newspaper publishers and printers. Writing for the Bureau of the Census in 1880, special agent S. N. D. North celebrated "the localization of the American press": because "every hamlet has its mouthpiece through the printing press, and every city is independent of every other city for its daily news supply," the American press was "the freest, the most self-reliant, the most loyal to home and vicinity interest, in the world."[23] The Newspaper Pavilion at the Centennial Exhibition suggested the same story. A two-story wooden structure "on the banks of a beautiful lake glistening between the Machinery Hall and the United States buildings," rising thirty-three feet and occupying more than three thousand square feet of Centennial ground, the pavilion housed copies of each of the nation's 8,129 newspapers. Any visitor could easily find a hometown newspaper, because all were "filed away in alcoves divided into pigeon-holes," organized alphabetically from the weekly *Henry County Register* in Abbeville, Alabama, to the daily *Sentinel* in Laramie City, Wyoming Territory. Upstairs, visitors could read their "instantly accessible" papers and write home from the desks in well-lit "writing galleries." The building became "a monster reading room and an exchange for newspaper men."[24]

At the same time, the Newspaper Pavilion told its own story of encroaching nationalization. The brainchild of Geo. P. Rowell & Co., the nation's leading advertising firm, the building cost more than $10,000; staffing it and preparing a 314-page catalog ran to nearly the same amount; postage to advertise it to newspaper publishers nationwide cost another $1,200. These expenses would pay dividends, because "the exhibition would be worth its full cost as an advertisement of their [Rowell's] own business, as conductors of the most complete newspaper advertising agency in the world." The pavilion itself was "essentially a reproduction" of Rowell's New York agency, where more than 1,750 papers a day were filed in similar cubicles and where clerks checked advertisements' placement in every newspaper. Visitors to the Newspaper Pavilion would encounter striking similarities between far-flung papers: the same poetry, identical "news of the week," and the same advertisements, all "in the same position." These were the work of newspaper syndicates, which supplied patent insides (sheets printed on one side with stock material) to hundreds of newspapers, leaving the "editorials, and local news and advertisements" to be composed and printed at the local publishing office on the other side of the sheets. By 1876, syndicates in New York, "Chicago, Milwaukee, Cincinnati, Memphis, St. Paul, and other cities" boasted that they saved "the country press over $2,000,000 annually" in typesetting, printing, paper, and ink.[25] Wire services such as the Associated Press, founded in 1848, commodified news itself, transforming the older system in which publishers exchanged newspapers free through the mails and clipped from one another's papers. Syndicates and wire services may have helped struggling local publishers to stay solvent, sustaining the "localization" that the 1880 census acclaimed. At the same time, they began a long process of regional or national centralization in the sources of news and the contents of newspapers.

. . .

Describing each exhibit within the ABTA's pavilion at the Centennial Exhibition, *Publishers' Weekly* wrote that James R. Osgood & Co. (formerly Ticknor and Fields), one of the nation's premier publishers of literary books, occupied "the northern section of the western pavilion, upstairs, but by no means show their strength in the single case of books they exhibit."

> This is to be regretted, as the strength of American literature is better shown from the catalogue of this house than from that of any other, the great majority of American poets and essayists having this imprint in their books. The most prominent set in the case is Prof. Child's edition of the 'British Poets,' occupying two and a half shelves out of the eight: this edition is of course to the credit of American scholarship, in the way of editing, but the space might better have been given to American authorship proper. The case, nevertheless, contains enough good American literature to make an American proud, even if in company with an English cousin—for here are the works of Emerson, Lowell, Longfellow, Whittier, Hawthorne, Bret Harte, Howells, Agassiz, Ticknor, Aldrich, Stedman, Mrs. Whitney, and others known wherever people read books, besides the superb series of translations, Bryant's Homer, Cranch's Virgil, Longfellow's and Norton's Dante, and Bayard Taylor's Goethe's Faust, which are one of the chief triumphs of this country's literary ability, showing in this department the same cosmopolitanism we show in our welcome of the people of other nations.[26]

This description suggested a particular definition of "American literature" and "American authorship proper." Original American poetry and essays belonged; A. D. T. Whitney, who wrote popular juvenile fiction, seems a generic anomaly, perhaps a nod toward female authorship. Translation became a literary act, in which American writers might at once display a cosmopolitan spirit and make the European classics into America's own literary heritage. Indeed, although James R. Osgood & Co. and its predecessor, Ticknor and Fields, had long advertised the most renowned catalog of American literary authors, this American publisher of Alfred Tennyson, Thomas De Quincey, and Robert Browning had always placed them within a transatlantic pantheon. The works on view in Osgood's bookcase were narrow in another sense: nearly every one of the authors of the books on display either hailed from or resided in New England, the region that claimed by the 1870s to be the source of "American literature."

The publishers' displays also suggested another, broader definition of the "American book," as did books available elsewhere in the exhibition, in the city of Philadelphia, and throughout the period. American books themselves were becoming bibliographers' quarry, as seen in J. Sabin & Sons' exhibit: the first seven volumes of its *Bibliotheca Americana: A Dictionary of Books Relating to America, from Its Discovery to the Present Time.* Publishers and readers identified particular genres and formats as uniquely American, notably dime novels, not exhibited at the Centennial but surely available from the city's news agents and in railroad stations. Then there were books on particularly American topics: American history, exemplified by H. S. Allen's display "in different styles of binding (all very patriotic), of his 'People's History of America' "; American flora and fauna, seen in Audubon's *Birds of America*; and the volumes of American geology and exploration published by the United States government and on display in the Government Building.[27] In an era when conflict with Native Americans in the Great Plains climaxed in the centennial summer's Battle of Little Bighorn, publications about Native Americans spanned from scholarly work that anticipated late-nineteenth-century anthropology to Henry Wadsworth Longfellow's literary treatment in *The Song of Hiawatha* (1855) to the very first Beadle dime novel, *Malaeska: The Indian Wife* (1860).

Like these last examples, the subjects and authors of "American literature" and "American books" ranged well beyond New England. Literary historians of American regionalism have argued that post–Civil War writing about the South, the West, and even rural northern New England, particularly in such magazines as the *Atlantic Monthly*, represented either metropolitan nostalgia for the worlds that the metropolis helped "devitalize and deplete" or a vicarious tourism to the "unmodernized picturesque," targeted to an American leisured class in the making that defined itself partly through its actual vacation practices.[28] In such interpretations, which render urbanization the central development of our period, "region" becomes the antithesis of the metropolitan. It is equally true that in these years of westward expansion and sectional division, the nation was defined literarily by its regional parts: humor from the Southwest as well as from "Down East" Maine, or the western-inflected works of Bret Harte (part of the Osgood pantheon) and Mark Twain (who joined that pantheon in 1877), as much as the New England writers whom publishers such as Ticknor and Fields cast as the nation's canon. The century's most popular novel, *Uncle Tom's Cabin*, was both a compendium of American places and characters *and* a mix of American literary styles, from the dialect humor of a Kentucky tavern to Ophelia St. Clare's characteristic New England propriety. *Uncle Tom's Cabin* spawned southern proslavery novels, but the plantation fiction of William Gilmore Simms and John Pendleton Kennedy preceded Harriet Beecher Stowe's book, and a post–Civil War vogue for the "Old South" would spawn new literary representations of the region.

Another way to identify "American" culture was to define what it was not: "European" or especially "English." Essays such as Emerson's "The American Scholar" (1837) and Margaret Fuller's "American Literature: Its Position in the Present Time, and Prospects for the Future" (1846) forecast a literary future distinct from its European forebears, much as Thomas Cole's "Essay on American Scenery" (1838) laid theoretical underpinnings for the explosion of American landscape painting over the following three decades. Declarations of nationality sometimes had specious origins. At the Centennial, the Massachusetts publisher Brewer & Tileston's exhibit of Joseph Emerson Worcester's dictionary inspired *Publishers' Weekly* to recall "the war between the dictionaries, the English and American . . . one of the most curious features of American literary history," a skirmish remembered as a moment of transatlantic cultural conflict, not unlike the 1849 rivalry between American actor Edwin Forrest and English tragedian William Macready.[29] In fact, J. E. Worcester and Noah Webster were both Americans, but in the 1840s and 1850s their publishers waged pitched battle over which would become the standard work in the United States. The most famous literary authors, including Irving and Emerson, defended Worcester's dictionary. But publishers G. & C. Merriam of Springfield, Massachusetts, successfully characterized Webster's as the more national work with the audience that counted commercially: school boards and teachers who adopted books for classrooms. In this case, defining a work as "American" required a contrast with British antecedents, as minimal or even spurious as the differences might be.

For all the rhetoric of national distinction, American authors and publishers borrowed heavily from their European predecessors and counterparts. *Uncle Tom's Cabin*, Dickensian in the sweep of its human portrayals and in its moral intensity, contained elements of the transatlantic gothic and sentimental as well. Not only did "American literature" in the mid-nineteenth century owe much to Sir Walter Scott and Charles Dickens; it *was* Scott and Dickens. In the ABTA's pavilion, J. B. Lippincott & Co. and Porter & Coates each displayed busts of Shakespeare and Scott; Lippincott also included busts of Milton and Byron. Americans feted Dickens on his 1842 and 1867 tours. Americans prodigiously read the works of English authors in American editions, the proliferation of which led to publishers' courtesy of the trade and calls for international copyright protection, as well as in imported books. Indeed, imports increased massively from the 1840s to the 1870s. These were represented at the Centennial in displays by the book trades of France, Germany, and the Netherlands, a few publishers' exhibits from the British empire, and assorted books from about fifteen other nations from Egypt to Peru, which displayed its books in a locked case with its cigars.

Even efforts to define "American literature" borrowed from English antecedents and suggested a transatlantic, more than a national, canon. Samuel Kettell's *Specimens of American Poetry* (1829) and William Cullen Bryant's *Selections from the American Poets* (1840) were early efforts to make an "American" anthology. The industrious Rufus Wilmot Griswold built on such efforts with *The Poets and Poetry of America* (1842), *The Prose Writers of America* (1846), and *The Female Poets of America* (1849); the *Cyclopaedia of American Literature* (1855), compiled by the brothers Evert A. and George L. Duyckinck, was a biographical dictionary with literary excerpts. All of these works argued for a specifically American literary history, as did books about American authors' homes that first appeared in the 1850s. Collected editions of authors' works, first popularized by the edition that Sir Walter Scott prepared to extricate himself from debt in the late 1820s, were another story. An early American example, Harper & Brothers' edition of James Kirke Paulding in the 1830s, was an "edition" only in its uniform binding and numbered spines; the title pages, retained from the separately published volumes, made no mention of a collected edition. In 1847 publisher George P. Putnam made an agreement with Washington Irving to publish a full edition of Irving's works, revised by the author. The success of that edition, and G. P. Putnam & Co.'s many editions of Irving after his death in 1859, helped make him "the first canonized American author." Just months after Nathaniel Hawthorne's death in 1864, Ticknor and Fields published a Hawthorne collected edition, but that firm had already issued its own editions of Scott and Thomas De Quincey—creating a "canon" of English-language writers both British and American. The 1860s also witnessed several American collected editions of Dickens published by other firms. American literary criticism was similarly transatlantic in focus: critics writing for such journals as the *North American Review*, the *Knickerbocker*, and the *Southern Literary Messenger* copied English styles of reviewing and reviewed British and American books. Only with the publication of Moses Coit Tyler's *A History of American Literature* (1878) would the notion of an American literary tradition, broached by Griswold and the Duyckincks a quarter-century earlier, take root. Even then, the

American Men of Letters, a series of authors' biographies that Houghton, Mifflin & Co. launched in 1880, imitated Macmillan's English Men of Letters series.[30]

In other cases, transatlantic relations and communities blurred distinctions of nationality. Learned culture offers one example. Francis Child, editor of The British Poets series displayed prominently by James R. Osgood & Co. at the Centennial, was a Göttingen-trained scholar of Middle English with ties to European and British colleagues. Institutions that sought to establish an American scholarly presence in this period, notably the Smithsonian, participated in a broader discourse. Evangelical religion also crossed the Atlantic. Many of the books and tracts published by American societies were originally published by their British counterparts, and at the Centennial Exhibition the American Bible Society displayed its books jointly with the British and Foreign Bible Society. Inspired largely by evangelical and humanitarian movements, abolitionism was a third arena of transatlantic cooperation. Frederick Douglass won some of his greatest acclaim during his 1845-47 tour of England, where he traveled in part to evade American slave catchers after the publication of the *Narrative of the Life of Frederick Douglass, an American Slave* (1845). And the popularity of *Uncle Tom's Cabin* in England definitively answered Sydney Smith's 1820 query: "In the four quarters of the globe, who reads an American book?"[31] American books, the physical objects as well as the texts and ideas, were exported around the globe by 1880. Although valued at only a third of its imports, the nation's book exports reflected the growth of American industry generally and specific developments such as the United States' hemispheric significance (exports of books to Latin America swelled more than tenfold) and the opening of Japanese markets to American producers after Commodore Matthew Perry's 1852-54 expedition.

.   .   .

Among the displays at the Centennial were a schoolroom in the Norwegian exhibit and the colonial and modern American classrooms in the Pennsylvania Educational Building, which J. B. Lippincott & Co.'s J. B. Mitchell mentioned in his welcome to the ABTA. A few yards from the Woman's Pavilion stood the one-story pine American Kindergarten, where each Monday, Tuesday, and Wednesday morning Miss Ruth R. Burritt of Boston instructed eighteen orphans from Philadelphia's Northern Home for Friendless Children, while spectators could observe the system of Friedrich Froebel, "the inventor of the Kindergarten."[32] If the exposition testified foremost to industrial progress, it also showcased the advance of "culture," exemplified by the fine arts, which had their own building, and education. Schoolbooks figured prominently among the wares in the ABTA Pavilion and in foreign publishers' exhibits, and furniture makers displayed school desks designed to be fastened to the floor.[33] Most numerous of all were exhibits from schools themselves in Spain, Sweden, and other nations, and twenty-four states, the District of Columbia, and Indian Territory. States sent statistical information about their school systems, photographs of school buildings, information about colleges and normal schools, and especially samples of students' work. Individual institutions also mounted their own exhibits. The Centennial organizers' final report noted that the educational displays revealed the "growth of general interest in popular education throughout the world": national, state, and local support, school-attendance laws, commissions to systematize public education, "the steady gain of female education in most countries," and an "increase of schools and agencies for the instruction of adults neglected in youth." Moreover, "a growing appreciation of the vital importance of better instruction for every class of schools" was evidenced by rising numbers of normal schools, increasing salaries for teachers, and the "quite general revision of methods." Universities were offering more courses of study, and "public libraries and . . . newspaper and periodical literature" afforded more "popular information" to increasing numbers of readers.[34]

The decades from 1840 to 1880 witnessed massive growth in public education and other forms of schooling in the United States. In 1840 the census enumerated 47,209 primary (public) schools, with 1,845,244 students. In the next decade, although the nation's population increased only from 17 million to 23 million, public schooling expanded massively within the Northeast and across the states of the old Northwest Territory: the 1850 census counted 80,978 public schools, 3,354,011 pupils, and 91,966 teachers. By 1880 the numbers of students (9,867,505) and teachers (286,593) in public schools had tripled again while the nation's population had only doubled (to 50 million). Much of the growth occurred in the relatively new states of the Midwest and California, but most southern states also established public school systems — separate for black and white children — for the first time after the Civil War. In 1850, 56 percent of white Americans (59 percent of males, 53 percent of females) aged five to nineteen attended school for some part of the year. Thirty years later, those figures topped 60 percent for white males and females, and school attendance among nonwhite children had increased from 1.8 percent to 34 percent. Institutions of higher education also swelled: 173 colleges and universities enrolled 16,233 students in 1840; forty years later, 811 institutions enrolled 116,000 students, much of the growth having occurred in the 1870s with the creation of land-grant state universities under the Morrill Act of 1862.[35] Meanwhile, the number of Sunday schools in the United States increased from 8,268 affiliated with the American Sunday-School Union in 1832 to an estimated 69,508 Protestant Sunday schools in 1875.[36] As the Centennial judges noted, the American "common school is universal but not national," explaining that while "In theory all schools are built after the New England model," their number, operation, funding, and quality varied widely from state to state, given the lack of any "central board of control."[37]

Underpinning this phenomenal growth, no matter how decentralized, was faith in education, not new but increasingly deployed in secular as well as religious terms, toward the constellation of values associated with middle-class self-making. Historians have proposed various definitions of the nineteenth-century "middle class," an amorphous social formation that likely understood itself through shared social and cultural characteristics that paradoxically included the confidence that it transcended what contemporaneous Marxists termed "class consciousness." At least in its urban manifestation, the middle class had clear demographic characteristics. Cities were becoming more segregated by wealth, with white-collar and professional men and their families living apart from the working classes. Nonmanual employment was booming, thanks to the commercial economy that buttressed the Industrial Revolution on the mercantile side (banking, credit) and the supply side (retail shops). The number of clerks, the archetypal occupation of this economy, increased from 101,325 in 1850 (when they comprised a single census category) to 444,064 thirty years later (when nine categories of clerks worked in establishments ranging from stores, to banks, to factories).[38] Reading, writing, and mathematical skill had become increasingly important not only for Americans in these occupations but also for middling farmers who sought, in the familiar phrase, to "improve" their holdings during the simultaneous agricultural revolution. As farm families from rural New England to Illinois and California participated in regional and national markets, they came to adopt cultural styles from the northeastern middle class, even if they pointedly distinguished themselves from presumably debauched urban "fashion."[39]

More than a demographic or occupational category, the middle class came to be associated with particular cultural patterns. Many middle-class associational proclivities depended on the spoken or printed word: lyceums, debating societies, reading clubs. Others produced millions of pages of print: annual reports, proceedings of meetings, and especially religious and reform publications that attempted to spread the values of self-culture, self-restraint, and self-improvement across America. Among the most famous were the myriad publications of the temperance movement, which included flimsy tracts as well as John B. Gough's *Autobiography* (1845) and Timothy Shay

Arthur's best-selling novel *Ten Nights in a Bar-Room and What I Saw There* (1854). In temperance as well as abolition, the printed page and the spoken word worked hand in hand: the best-known reform authors, such as Frederick Douglass, gained fame for the lectures in which their published words probably originated. As household economic production waned, middle-class families also provided the essential markets for an expanding consumer culture. "Refinement" became a marker of bourgeois respectability, not aristocratic gentility. Books and magazines, whether advice manuals or the fashion plates in *Godey's Lady's Book*, taught these Americans how to comport themselves in everything from child-rearing to penmanship. Where ornately bound books had once been the handiwork of skilled craftsmen and the province of the wealthy, industrial publishers' case bindings with various degrees of ornamentation made books themselves into increasingly affordable signs of status, along with the elegant writing papers, gold pens, and assorted inks that stationery manufacturers showed off at the Centennial Exhibition.

The evolution of professionalism also intersected with the history of this middle class.[40] "Profession" was sometimes defined as the activity that supplied one's chief source of income. This was the sense the census applied when it enumerated 82 "authors" in 1850 and 216 in 1860, 458 "authors and lecturers" in 1870, and 1,131 "authors, lecturers, and literary persons" in 1880.[41] This definition was imprecise, however: members of the industrial working class might earn their income as operatives in paper mills or printing factories but likely did not view these jobs as professions. An older definition, profession as a calling, was transformed during the mid-nineteenth century. Where "professional" had formerly denoted learned training (clergymen, lawyers, and physicians), another definition gathered force after the Civil War. In its increasingly institutional sense, "profession" described a self-regulating group of practitioners, usually formally organized, that set standards, enjoyed certain social obligations, granted its members particular freedoms, and developed a technical vocabulary to speak across place and to separate itself from the uninitiated. Librarians, schoolteachers, and college professors: all established professional associations and journals, and all asserted their professional status through these actions.

Most important for the history of the book, the middle class defined itself through what scholars have described as an "ideology of literacy" that would be, ideally, available to all Americans.[42] The notion that literacy was essential to moral self-improvement and democratic citizenship was at least as old as the Republic. Harnessed to the desire to create productive citizens in a market economy, it became a cornerstone of the public school movement that gathered force in the 1830s and swept across the North in subsequent decades. It also undergirded the middle-class reformulation of gender roles. Women were urged to become exemplars of virtue and teachers of the rising generation both at home and in public, even in the reaches of the uncivilized West, according to Catharine E. Beecher's exhortation.[43] Once the census began to enumerate illiteracy in 1840, the new category offered a measure to identify those who fell outside middle-class values: immigrants with minimal ability to read and write; southern aristocrats and legislators who denied education to enslaved African Americans; ordinary southern farmers whose illiteracy rates far exceeded those of Americans elsewhere. The celebration of literacy could also become a pretext for coercion, as in school reformers' determination to bring Irish immigrants into state-controlled public schools.

However, the ideology of literacy also served those who were outside the white, Anglo-American middling classes and those who sought to improve their lot, notably slaves who "slipped and learned to read" before the Civil War, free blacks in the North and South who established their own schools and literary societies, and emancipated African Americans who insisted on public schooling during Reconstruction. At the Centennial, the sole educational exhibit from Virginia came from Hampton Normal and Agricultural Institute, the American Missionary Association's school for African Americans and a few Native Americans. In addition to its catalogs and photographs, Hampton Institute sent samples of its students' academic work and handicrafts — including the union of the two in the school's "monthly illustrated paper," the *Southern Workman*, produced in a "well-equipped printing office of the Institute" in which three male students completed their work requirement. As described by the Centennial judges, Hampton exemplified the ideology of self-improvement, as middle-class Americans applied it to others. With the institute's combination of academic study, manual work, military discipline, and attention to morality and social graces, they asked, "what may not be accomplished for the colored people of the South, through even this one institution, every one of whose graduates is a teacher and a missionary for their enlightenment and elevation?"[44]

Literacy and the printed word had more complicated meanings for other groups outside the Anglo-American middle class. Praising the U.S. Bureau of Education's exhibit of children's papers and manual work from schools in Indian Territory, the Centennial judges wrote that Native American students compared well with white children in village schools across the nation, a sign that "civilization was making steady inroads upon savage life," at least "among the more tractable tribes."[45] This reformist analysis responded both to Anglo-American neglect and to the specter of "savagery" among tribes not yet brought within the reservation system. In 1879, according to the Board of

Indian Commissioners' annual report, there were 64 Indian boarding schools and 292 day schools, with a total of 500 teachers and 13,343 students (approximately 30 percent of school-age Native American children).[46] Many of these schools, established by Christian missionaries, mirrored the Centennial judges' assimilationist stance. Native Americans' own views were more mixed. The Cherokees established their own national public school system in 1841; in two decades it grew from 8 to 30 schools, and its enrollment from 200 to 1,500. Two seminaries—one for boys modeled on Boston Latin School and kindred classical academies, one for girls modeled on Mount Holyoke Female Seminary—survived just five years (1851–56), casualties not only of inadequate funding but especially of criticism from full-blooded Cherokees. Begun with hopes of uniting and enlightening the whole nation, the Cherokee school system instead contributed to widening internal divisions that resembled those in the United States. Most full-blooded Cherokees, who spoke little or no English and were poorer than their mixed-blood compatriots, did not send their children to school: they complained that their children encountered ridicule from mixed-blood, English-speaking children, and their farms required the children's labor. Students came predominantly from the mixed-blood minority of Cherokee society, who most welcomed the ideology of improvement and the trappings of consumer culture, even as they asserted tribal sovereignty from their position as political leaders.[47]

Newspapers, the major form of printed matter produced in Indian territories, further exemplified these conflicts and contradictions. Several papers were published in a combination of English and Native American languages. In Indian Territory, the *Vindicator* (English and Choctaw, 1872–76) and the *Indian Herald* (English and Osage, 1875–?) were published by white physicians, while the *Cherokee Advocate* (English and Cherokee, 1844–48, revived in 1876) was the product of mixed-blood Cherokee leaders. All three could be found in Rowell's Newspaper Pavilion at the Centennial. In Dakota Territory, the American Board of Commissioners for Foreign Missions and the Presbyterian Board of Foreign Missions initially published the monthly *Iapi Oaye* ("The Word Carrier," 1871–1939) mostly in the Dakota language and divided it in 1884 into two editions, one each in English and Dakota. Papers published by missionaries and American agency officers adopted a predictably assimilationist stance, but Native American–published papers had a more delicate balancing act. For example, the *Cherokee Advocate* and the *Indian Journal*, also published by Cherokees, modulated their response to the Battle of Little Bighorn in June 1876, condemning the United States government's actions while distinguishing themselves from the less "civilized" Indians who had routed Custer's troops.[48]

Most Native Americans had been separated by removal from the white United States population, only to see control of their land challenged as Anglo-American gold fever and land pressures mounted after the Civil War. Also persecuted within American society, the Church of Jesus Christ of Latter-day Saints chose to separate itself geographically and established a thriving culture based on print in Utah, testimony to both its belief in education and its determination to create a communal consciousness. Early Mormon publications included the *Book of Mormon* (first published in 1830), hymnals, and newspapers such as the *Deseret News* (1850–). Institutions of print and education proliferated after the Mormons settled in Utah in 1847: the University of Deseret in 1850 (renamed the University of Utah in 1892), a territorial library (which published a sixty-three-page catalog in 1852), scientific and literary societies, the publishing firm of George Q. Cannon in the late 1860s, and Cannon's periodical for children, the *Juvenile Instructor* (1866–1929). The most ambitious undertaking, the Deseret Alphabet (1853), transliterated English into thirty-eight phonetic characters. Brigham Young promoted the alphabet as a vehicle for uniting English-speaking Mormons with non-English-speaking Mormon immigrants, and the university published a series of primers to establish it among schoolchildren. The experiment failed quickly after Young's death in 1877, but the idea suggested the extent to which the Mormons were a people of the printed word, even as evangelical Protestants published anti-Mormon tracts, exposés, and novels from the 1850s on.[49]

Mormon printing enterprises appeared nowhere at the Centennial except the Newspaper Pavilion, a fact that begins to reveal the exposition's incomplete, largely middle-class picture of American print culture—and of America itself. The *New Century for Woman*, a weekly newspaper published in the Woman's Pavilion, reviewed advice manuals and romance novels and promoted women's advancement within both the domestic sphere and "the new departments in trades and handicrafts, in artistic work, in education, in the scientific and learned professions," but it addressed neither the issue of woman suffrage nor the plight of working-class women.[50] Male or female, members of the working class themselves were effaced at the exposition. The men and women who operated the machinery in the exhibits appeared as neatly dressed, intelligent hands, not potential labor radicals with their own publishing agendas. The fifty-cent admission fee and Sunday closing policy made it difficult for workers to visit the exposition in any event; they more likely patronized a neighboring zone of cheap entertainments featuring a 602-pound woman, the wild man of Borneo, beer gardens, and ice-cream saloons.[51]

The exhibits from Hampton and other African American schools were relegated to an obscure section of the Main Building and were overshadowed in any case by the more eye-catching displays of educational furniture and photographs of northern schools. Black presence at the exposition was similarly muted: the most prominent figure of color was the Italian sculptor Francesco Pezzicar's *The Abolition of Slavery in the United States* (or *The Freed Slave*), which depicted a mostly nude black man breaking his chains and holding aloft Lincoln's Emancipation Proclamation. But it was different when one actual, self-liberated slave tried to participate in the exposition's opening ceremony: a policeman nearly denied the gray-haired Frederick Douglass his place on the platform, and only the intervention of Senator Roscoe Conkling of New York prevented the expulsion of America's foremost black leader and writer. White visitors would more likely have noticed the African American waiters in the Southern Restaurant, "a band of old-time plantation 'darkies' who will sing their quaint melodies and strum the banjo," or the four singing African American men who plugged tobacco, part of the exhibit of the Richmond firm of Archer and Brownell. Newly emancipated, identified as "the pure and unadulterated 'Essence of Ole Virginny,'" or displayed as manual laborers, African Americans hardly appeared as strivers after education or elevation.[52]

.   .   .

Then again, the Southern Restaurant was among the Centennial's relatively few depictions of the American South, white or black. Hampton Institute's was the only educational exhibit from Virginia; eight of the eleven former Confederate states displayed no educational material at all. Neither the ABTA's conventioneers nor its book exhibitors included anyone from the former Confederacy. In large measure, this omission resulted from the wide disparity between the production and consumption of printed matter in the South and in the rest of the United States. It is impossible to state precisely what role sectional division and the Civil War played in the pivotal developments examined in this volume — the emergence of the industrial book, the coordinating role of a national trade publishing system, the concept of the "American book," the centrality of middle-class values — or the countervailing pressures that worked against the consolidation of all of these. Before the war, sectional controversy produced an enormous amount of print, as antislavery and proslavery advocates committed their views to the page in hopes of swaying fellow Americans and creating communities of sentiment. Abolitionist literature provoked the most visible antebellum attempts at censorship: Andrew Jackson's order barring incendiary material from the mails; southern state laws (rarely enforced) and community pressures (more effective) to curtail spoken and printed criticism of slavery; northern and southern mobs' destruction of antislavery printing houses; and the "gag rule" by which Congress avoided action on antislavery petitions.[53] The war itself, as an event that heightened the national imagined communities of the United States and the Confederate States, reinforced several nationalizing trends in the realm of print, especially in the Union: the appeal and circulation of timely national newspapers such as *Harper's Weekly*, as well as the proliferation of common patriotic poetry, songs, and stories in various print media.[54]

The Confederacy, which developed a strikingly national consciousness in its brief existence, despite its vaunted commitment to state sovereignty, was less able to solidify that community through print. The familiar story, of a disparity in printed material and capacity at the war's beginning that became an utter lack by its end, explains a great deal. The 1860 census counted 151 printing establishments, 9 percent of the nation's total, in the eleven states that would soon form the Confederacy, which contained 29 percent of the United States population. Those establishments employed 1,014 people (5 percent of the national total) and had $936,799 in capital investment (6 percent); their output was valued at $895,230 (4 percent). The South's only stereotype foundry was in Tennessee, which quickly fell to the Union; its fifteen paper mills could not keep up with demand, and it had no manufacturers of printing presses. Given these difficulties from the outset, it is remarkable that the war spurred southerners to create several new literary magazines, most of which folded by 1864.[55] The southern states were similarly slow to adopt public schooling, in large measure because of their widely dispersed populations and the concentration of wealth among plantation owners, who were loath to subsidize the education of the majority of southern whites, let alone the enslaved. Reconstruction revolutionized the South educationally: from 1850 to 1880, southern public schools more than tripled in number (from 13,611 to 47,710) and nearly quintupled in enrollment (from 416,597 to 1,974,033, of which 36 percent were African American). It did not do the same industrially, at least not for publishing and printing, activities that were increasingly consolidated in the Northeast: southern printing establishments in 1880 numbered 7 percent of the nation's total, less than before the war, and the value of their output was 4 percent of the nation's total printing and publishing.[56] Little wonder, then, that the world of southern print had little presence either in any Centennial displays, except the Newspaper Pavilion, or at the ABTA convention.

Eleven years after the end of the Civil War, the Centennial Exhibition sought to present a reunited nation to itself and to the world. But the exposition as a whole resembled the "American literature" in James R. Osgood

& Co.'s book display and the genteel-reformist ideology of the *Nation*, the
weekly magazine launched within three months of the Confederate surrender. All promoted a United States guided by the capitalist, industrial, middle-
class, consumerist values that northeasterners sought to export south in the
1870s and 1880s. Even as a Lost Cause vision of benevolent masters and happy
slaves came to dominate imaginative literature and historical writing about the
"Old South," some southerners advocated a "New South" where industrialists — including paper manufacturers — would find cheap labor and nearby
raw materials in the 1880s and beyond. But the centralization of the book
trades in the North that was accomplished by 1880 would remain a defining
characteristic of the American book throughout the following century.

CHAPTER 1

Manufacturing and Book Production

Michael Winship

· · ·

> Of contributions by inventors and artizans to the great work of
> mental development, there are three that have been conspicuous
> in bringing out the modern outburst of thought. . . . Successfully
> employed in hastening a present, they are securing the future ele-
> vation of our race. Preventing retrogation in intelligence, they add
> daily to the general stock, and are posting it up for the use of our
> successors. . . . They are metallic types, paper and the printing
> press; — a triad of achievements in mechanical science unrivalled
> in importance and value. While water, wind, steam, electricity and
> the gases, serve to animate material mechanisms, these are the
> elements of a higher and mightier prime mover; one destined to
> agitate and expand the intellect of the world; to extend and per-
> petuate the peaceful reign of science and arts over the earth.
>
> *Report of the Commissioner of Patents, for the Year 1850* [1]

In the United States, the nineteenth century was the great period of industrialization, and the benefits of industrial ways were an article of faith. As
the epigraph to this chapter makes clear, this belief was especially true for
the manufacture of and trade in books and other printed materials: between
1840 and 1880 these objects changed substantially in their manufacture, appearance, and cost, as did the lives of those who produced and consumed
them. When examining these changes and their implications, it is important
to distinguish the invention of a new technology — the most common focus of
historical accounts or studies — from its introduction into practical use and
its widespread acceptance by industry. These two steps usually involved different people and new combinations of capital and ingenuity, and they likely
occurred at different times. By 1840 many of the manufacturing technologies
and changes described in this chapter had not only been invented, but some
had also been introduced into practice. Only during the middle decades of
the nineteenth century, however, did their use become general. Furthermore,
even as the methods of book manufacture in 1880 varied substantially from

those in 1840, the methods of 1880 would by and large continue to be in general use well into the twentieth century.

Printing from plates, one of the most important and characteristic new processes adopted in the United States during the nineteenth century, is a useful illustration of these points. Scattered experiments with various processes of producing printing plates had taken place for several centuries in Europe and Great Britain, and they had met with some success, but the method of casting stereotype plates from plaster molds was finally perfected in England in the first decade of the nineteenth century. It was first successfully used in the United States in 1813. Over the course of the following decades, this process for producing plates was supplemented by other techniques, most importantly by electrotyping, but also by stereotyping from papier-mâché "flong" molds. By the 1830s, printing from stereotype plates was becoming the standard form of book manufacture in the United States, at least by the larger firms: of the 413 volumes published by Harper & Brothers in 1834, 192 (46 percent) were stereotyped, and by 1855 almost every work at the Harper establishment was electrotyped. The use of stereotype and especially electrotype plates for book production remained standard well into the twentieth century, and the use of stereotype plates made from flong molds, introduced in 1861 and widely adopted in the newspaper industry after the Civil War, remained common into the 1970s.[2]

The development of printing plates calls attention to several other general features of industrialization. First, new technologies usually supplement, rather than replace, older ones: even after plates became predominant, much printing continued to be done directly from type. Second, technological change does not happen in isolation. The ability to produce stereotype plates from flexible flong molds solved the problem of how to produce curved printing plates that could be attached to rotary printing presses, which in turn could efficiently print on paper in rolls, rather than in sheets. Changes in plates, presses, and paper meant that the rate of printing could be greatly increased, and they were put to good use in the production of newspapers, whose editors and owners had made the currency of news a selling point. The "discovery of news," however, was neither dependent upon nor determined by these technological developments: the daily penny press emerged in the 1830s, several decades before the introduction of curved stereotype plates or the widespread use of rotary presses.[3] Even as the fallacy of technological determinism needs to be avoided, the implications of technological change demand close attention. Industrialization and the introduction of new technologies of production inevitably affected practice, even if the effect was contingent and unpredictable.

Although this chapter examines each of the many processes of book production separately, it is important to remember that they were utilized in a wide range of establishments to produce the tremendous variety of books and printed matter that characterizes the nineteenth century. The Adams flatbed platen power press used by William Dean Howells's father in his Ohio newspaper office was, in principle, the same as the twenty-eight Adams presses installed in 1855 by Harper & Brothers in their new factory in New York. Nevertheless, the two environments could not have been more different. In the Ohio shop, the Adams press, like the hand press it had only recently replaced, was originally powered manually, and Howells's father used it to print directly from type inked by rollers that were fabricated in the shop. In contrast, the Harper establishment's steam-powered presses were part of a large, modern, fireproof book-production facility designed to organize and rationalize the production process.[4] Adams presses continued to be widely used after the Civil War: in the late 1860s they could be found at both the Riverside Press — a large book manufactory in Cambridge, Massachusetts — and in the much smaller shop of the Worcester, Massachusetts, job printer Charles Hamilton. But again, these were different establishments specializing in different kinds of work. In 1868, when the Riverside Press purchased its first cylinder press, adding it to eighteen Adams presses, four hand presses, and one jobbing press, Hamilton was already operating two cylinder presses, as well as two Adams presses, two jobbing presses, and one hand press. If anything, Hamilton's equipment was more varied and up-to-date than that in Cambridge.[5]

Type, Printing Plates, and Composition

If the use of printing plates was one of the characteristic developments in book manufacturing of the nineteenth century, the reproduction of texts from movable type, a process introduced into Europe in the mid-fifteenth century, remained at the heart of printing throughout the period. Printed matter continued to be set up in movable type, just as it had been during the preceding four centuries, and much of it was printed from type in a fashion that would have been familiar to earlier printers.

Despite this continuity, a number of nineteenth-century developments in the production of type increased its availability and the variety of its design. The earliest was the invention and perfection of the pivotal typecasting machine by David Bruce Jr. of New York during the 1830s and early 1840s. The heart of the machine, a pump turned by a hand crank, forced molten type metal made of the traditional mixture of lead, tin, and antimony into a type mold with an attached matrix, a bar of metal impressed with the negative image of the face of a particular character, or "sort." The temperature, makeup, amount of type metal, and thrust of the pump had to be adjusted to match the size and width of each letter, but each revolution of the machine's handle cast and released a single piece of type from the mold. The resulting type was far more regular than type cast in a handheld mold, having especially a sharper face, but each piece of type still had to be finished and dressed manually. The greater control of the casting process that the machine allowed, however, made it possible to produce the elaborate ornamental and display types so characteristic of the period's typography. The typecasting machine was far faster than hand casting: an average of one hundred pieces of type of the ordinary sizes could be cast in a minute, though larger sizes necessarily had to be cast at a slower rate, while traditional hand casting could only produce a maximum of roughly four thousand individual types in a day — though this rate had been doubled with the adoption of the lever hand mold early in the nineteenth century. From 1845, most of the type in the United States was produced by the Bruce pivotal typecasting machine.[6]

A second innovation of the 1840s was the use of electrotyped matrices for typefounding. Traditionally, the matrix had been produced by striking a steel punch, with the shape of a letter laboriously carved on its end, into a bar of soft copper. Electrotyping eliminated the need for both the punch and the operation of striking. In this process, the model letter was cut out of type metal, which after proper preparation was submerged into an electrolytic bath with plates of zinc and copper. The action of the electric current within the bath caused the type metal to be coated with a thick shell of copper, which was then removed and backed up to produce a matrix. Although the resulting matrix was less sharp and less durable than the traditional one, electrotype matrices were widely used and served to encourage both the production and proliferation of new type designs, as type metal was far easier to work in making model letters than the steel used for traditional punches. It was also possible to reproduce any style of type already in hand by using the types themselves as the model for the electrotype matrices, though by the 1880s attempts were being made to restrict this practice by means of the patent laws.[7]

The manufacture of type remained a specialized branch within the printing trades throughout the period, with type foundries, which regularly issued type-specimen catalogs to show off their wares in all their variety, located in the large cities across the country.[8] Table 1.1, which gives the number and location of type foundries in 1866, 1874, and 1878, shows that the overall number increased by nearly a third, but that in contrast to much of the book trade, these establishments became less centralized, presumably because of the ex-

TABLE 1.1. Number and location of type foundries, 1866, 1874, and 1878

City	1866	1874	1878
Boston	3	3	4
New York	8	7	5
Buffalo	1	1	1
Philadelphia	3	3	3
Baltimore	1	2	2
Cincinnati	2	2	2
Chicago	1	1	4
Milwaukee	1	1	1
St. Louis	1	1	2
Richmond	0	1	1
St. Paul	0	0	1
California	0	2	1
Total	21	24	27

Sources: Thomas MacKellar, *The American Printer: A Manual of Typography*, 2nd ed. (Philadelphia: L. Johnson & Co., 1866), 20; 9th ed. (Philadelphia: MacKellar, Smiths & Jordan, 1874), 18–19; and 11th ed. (Philadelphia: MacKellar, Smiths & Jordan, 1878), 29.

pense of shipping heavy type. While the number of foundries in New York City fell from eight to five, new foundries sprung up across the country, especially in Chicago, where a single foundry in 1866 had multiplied to four by 1878. Type was sold by the pound and was normally divided into three classes for pricing: book and newspaper faces in both roman and italic, regular display faces, and more elaborate ornamental faces. Price also depended upon body size, which continued to be designated by time-honored names, from diamond (roughly 4½ modern points) through pica (12 points) to canon (48 points), with even larger sizes described as multiples of pica. The introduction of typecasting machinery does not seem to have reduced the cost of book and newspaper type significantly, though there seems to have been a slight reduction in cost over time, especially in the smaller sizes.[9] Body size and, to a lesser extent, height to paper, the distance between the face and the foot of the type, continued to vary slightly from foundry to foundry, which made it impossible to mix type from different sources in a single form, though an important step toward standardization occurred in 1886 when the investigation of a committee formed by the Type Founders' Association of the United States led to the widespread adoption of the American point system.[10]

In addition to regular type, foundries advertised other material in their specimen catalogs, including exotic alphabets for foreign languages such as

Greek and Hebrew, fractions and special figures, and music, as well as leading, decorative rules, borders, type ornaments, and a wide variety of stock cuts. This was also the period when American wood type emerged as an important supplement to traditional metal type, particularly for large and ornamental letter forms. The production of wood type — cut by hand or, later, by machine router from the end grain of a tight-grained wood such as cherry, apple, or boxwood — was a specialized trade and by the 1870s had come to be dominated by two firms, W. H. Page & Co. of Greenville, Connecticut, and Vanderburgh, Wells & Co. of New York City. Sorts of wood type were produced as large as 15-line pica (180 points), were priced by the character, and were particularly used for advertising and poster work.[11]

The wide variety of type styles and sizes allowed for the extravagant and eclectic appearance of much printed matter from the period. This free combination of type styles was particularly characteristic of job printing — posters, advertising flyers, and other ephemera — but it was also a feature of title pages and advertisements in books, magazines, and newspapers. The text types used for bookwork were available and used in a great, if less obviously extravagant, variety of designs. In a major shift during the 1850s, the old-style type design (with slanted stress, bracketed serifs, and less contrast between thick and thin strokes characteristic of calligraphic letterforms written with a broad-nib pen) was reintroduced to supplement the predominant modern face (with vertical stress, hairline serifs, and exaggerated contrast between thick and thin strokes characteristic of copperplate lettering but also influenced by an almost mechanical devotion to symmetry). This shift in typographic taste, in its most extreme cases, led to the peculiarly surprising use of such outdated letter forms as the long *s* in some texts printed in the 1850s and 1860s.

The widespread use of stereotype and electrotype plates contributed to the eclectic appearance of typography from the period. On the one hand, plates increased the useful life of type, especially the expensive and often delicate ornamental faces, by providing a substitute printing surface for use on the press, where most wear took place. On the other hand, since plates were cast a page at a time, a printer could make do with a smaller amount of type of any particular size or design: instead of needing sufficient type to set up an entire form before it could be proofed and sent to press, plates allowed type to be distributed and reused page by page. Inevitably, the use of plates encouraged printers to stock a greater variety, if smaller quantity, of different types, but it also meant that in large bookshops type used for stereotyped or electrotyped matter was kept separate from type used on the press. Fresh type that was free from wear was necessary for producing a sharp cast in the plate that could be used for high-quality printing—indeed, larger firms often sold type that had been used only for plates to country printers.

Plates were made by several processes. Stereotype plates produced with plaster molds predominated before 1860, but after the Civil War, electrotype plates became increasingly common in bookwork. Electrotyping, which initially was intended for reproducing woodcuts and wood engravings, was introduced in the early 1840s, most notably by the engraver Joseph A. Adams for his work on the *Illuminated Bible* (1843-46) published by Harper & Brothers. The process involved the use of a wax mold into which a page of type had been impressed. The mold was next coated with a thin layer of powdered graphite and then submerged in an electrolytic bath, where a thin layer of copper would be deposited on its surface. The copper shell, once removed from the mold, was backed up with type metal and finished in much the same way as stereotype plates. Electrotype plates reproduced finer detail than stereotype plates, and their copper surface was more resistant to wear.

Printing from stereotype or electrotype plates had many advantages, chief among them that they allowed printers to preserve or duplicate the act of composition. By the 1850s, most books for which any continued demand could be expected were being printed from plates, and it is a marked feature of publishing during this period that books, once published, remained in print. The economics of printing from plates meant that it was not unreasonable to print small runs of several hundred or fewer copies of a work to meet even a modest demand. The possession of a set of plates gave any publisher an economic advantage over a competitor who might wish to reprint the same text, a fact that certainly helped support "courtesy of the trade" conventions (see Chapter 4, Part 3). Indeed, publishers usually reckoned their capital worth as the inventory value of the plates that the firm owned, valued not as metal but as the right to publish. When plates were sold or auctioned, the sale regularly included both the physical plates and the rights to publish the text, if it was covered by copyright.

The extent to which plates served to freeze a text, discouraging its correction or revision, is not clear. Certainly there was expense involved in correcting or revising a text that had been cast in plates, a process that involved chiseling away the original text and replacing it with the new text set in type, which was then soldered in place. If the revisions were extensive, the new text might be cast separately as plates, which were then, with the originals, cut up and soldered together. Surviving evidence suggests that workmen became very skilled at working with plates, and there are many examples of texts cast in plates that were corrected or revised extensively. The longevity of plates and the skill with which old and battered plates could be renewed were also remarkable: the original 1852 plates of Harriet Beecher Stowe's *Uncle Tom's Cabin* were still in use in the late 1870s after having been used to produce several hundred thousand copies.[12]

The ability to duplicate a text by producing several sets of plates was chiefly useful in the newspaper trade, where it allowed a firm to print a late edition from multiple plates on multiple printing presses—all in the interest of getting the news into print as quickly as possible. Such a rate of production, of course, was necessary only at the largest urban newspapers that could afford the heavy investment in presses, and printing from multiple plates probably became even more exceptional once the process of using curved plates on high-speed rotary presses was perfected. In bookwork the production of duplicate plates was uncommon, though it was used occasionally for running off copies simultaneously in two locations: for instance, sometimes the British edition of an American work was printed in London from a duplicate set of the American plates. It was more common, however, for duplicate plates of illustrations, especially of stock images, to be made for distribution or sale.

Whether a text was printed from plates or directly from type, it was initially composed by hand in the traditional manner. For their work, compositors were usually paid, and customers charged accordingly, a piece rate that was based on the area of type that had been set, reckoned in ems or the square of the body size of the type used, rather than on the actual number of individual pieces that made up the composed text. The rate per thousand ems varied, depending on the nature of the text: composition set from printed copy cost less than that set from manuscript. Similarly, leaded text, which had "leads," or thin strips of metal inserted between the lines of type, was charged by area, as if it had been set solid, but usually at a lower rate. Tables and extra work involved in composing foreign-language or other unusual text were charged at an hourly rate, and the work was often done by a foreman or another specialist. If a text was to be cast as plates, the cost was roughly double that for composition alone, but the charges were reckoned on the same basis, with a small additional sum for the wooden boxes in which the plates were stored in the printer's vaults when not in use.[13]

The mid-nineteenth century was an important period of experimentation with mechanical typesetting. By 1856 the large printing establishment of John F. Trow in New York City had installed five composing machines and a distributing machine, apparently the first such machines successfully employed commercially. Designed by William H. Mitchel, they were relatively primitive: the composing machine had a keyboard with thirty-four keys—

one for each of the lowercase letters, as well as points and spaces — and when a key was pressed, the appropriate piece of type would be released from a reservoir and carried by tape to an assembly point. Uppercase and other characters were set by hand, and a second worker was required to break up the assembled type into lines for justification. The distribution machine relied upon the fact that each sort had a distinctive set of nicks on its body that allowed it to be dropped from a revolving cylinder, piece by piece, into the appropriate channel in the reservoir.[14]

A more successful typesetting and distributing machine, first produced by Timothy Alden in New York City in 1857, worked on similar principles but had 154 keys, and after improvements made during the 1860s, was used for bookwork by D. Appleton & Co. and experimentally for newspaper work at the *New York World*. During the 1870s and later, composing and distributing machines produced by Henry A. Burr were even more widely adopted. No matter how refined, all of these machines depended upon hand justification of the type by a second worker who assisted the keyboard operator, but many of their features influenced and were incorporated in the ultimately successful linotype and monotype typesetting machines that were perfected and introduced at the end of the century. From the 1850s on, women were frequently employed as the operators of these machines — most notably Augusta Lewis (Troup), who was not only one of the founders of Women's Typographical Union No. 1 but also the most accomplished operator of the Alden Type-Setting and Distributing Machine. The employment of female operators serves as a reminder that one of the major incentives for developing this technology was to reduce, especially in newspaper shops, the bargaining power of the International Typographical Union and its male membership.[15]

Paper and Papermaking

Of all the trades associated with printing and publishing, the relationship with the papermaking trade was the most complex. The paper used in printing made up a small part of the total output of the trade, which also produced paper ranging from stationery and ledger paper of very high quality and strength to the much cheaper products used for wallpaper, wrapping, and packaging. As a business, papermaking was capital intensive and international in scope, depending on the import and export of technology, raw materials, and finished product. Not surprisingly, the paper trade developed its own business systems — not only special retail and wholesale networks for printing papers, stationery, and other paper products but also separate sources of capital, specialized manufacturers of machinery, and conventions of labor relations.

The introduction and adoption of machine-made paper in the printing and book trades in the United States parallels in many ways those of printing plates, though, if anything, the substitution of machine-made for handmade paper had become even more universal by midcentury. The mechanization of papermaking involved many discrete and interdependent developments over many years, beginning with the introduction of the Hollander beater in Europe at the end of the seventeenth century for the preparation of "stuff," the slurry of fibers and other materials from which paper was made. Experimentation with and adoption of alternative sources of fibers, as well as the development of effective chemical treatments to prepare them, continued over many centuries, though major developments occurred during the mid-nineteenth century. Sizing and finishing, processes necessary to make paper usable for printing, were also continually being perfected. The signal innovation, however, was the mechanization of molding and couching, the process by which paper is formed. As with printing plates, the initial experimentation and successful development occurred in England and was adopted in the United States before 1840.

Two distinct, if related, methods of forming paper mechanically were successfully developed at what came to be known as the "wet end" of the paper-making machine. Both involved the use of a finely woven wire "web," or screen, upon which the stuff was molded to form a felt of fibers that became paper. The cylinder machine, first designed in England by John Dickinson, had the web stretched around a rotating drum submerged in the vat of stuff. A slight vacuum maintained inside the rotating drum drew the water out of the stuff so that a web of paper formed on the drum's surface. In the Fourdrinier machine, first conceived at the Didot Mill outside Paris by Nicholas-Louis Robert, but perfected and produced in London in the first two decades of the nineteenth century, the stuff was dribbled onto the surface of a moving "endless" web, and the paper was molded as the web moved away from the vat and water drained off. In both machines, the newly formed paper was then passed along to the "dry end" of the machine, where it was lifted off the wire web onto a second web, made of wool felt, and pressed between rollers to remove more water. It was then sized, polished, and cut into sheets as required. The cylinder machine was simpler and less expensive, but it produced paper of lesser quality. The Fourdrinier machine reduced the inherent characteristic of both to impart a distinct "grain" to the paper by shaking the wire web sideways as the paper was forming in order to interlock the fibers, and it eventually came to predominate, though during most of the nineteenth century both were in common use.[16]

New Jersey papermaker Charles Kinsey succeeded in making printing stock on a rudimentary cylinder machine patented in 1807, but the earliest known, commercially produced, machine-made paper in the United States came from the cylinder machine developed by Thomas and Joshua Gilpin of Wilmington, Delaware — on 15 April 1818, this paper was used to print an issue of *Poulson's American Daily Advertiser*. The earliest Fourdrinier machine, valued at $30,000, was imported to the United States in 1827. By the following year, George Spafford and James Phelps in South Windham, Connecticut, had inaugurated the production of an American-built Fourdrinier machine, which in 1829 sold without accessories for $2,000. By the early 1830s, Fourdrinier machines were being made in Morristown, New Jersey, by Stephen Vail, and others, probably imported, were available from C. M. Pickering of New York. During these early years, cylinder papermaking machines predominated in American mills; however, by 1837 a fully equipped Spafford & Phelps Fourdrinier cost just $3,750. By then, machine-made paper was well on the way to replacing handmade paper: by 1845 only two mills making paper by hand remained in operation in the United States, and by 1880 handmade paper produced in America had all but disappeared. Between 1840 and 1880, virtually all of the paper used for printing was machine-made.[17]

Another fundamental innovation of nineteenth-century papermaking was the widespread introduction of new sources of fiber, the raw material from which all paper was made. The traditional source was linen rags from used clothing, and the collection and sale of rags for papermaking remained important throughout the nineteenth century: the cost of rags in various European and Near Eastern ports remained a regular feature of lists of prices current in commercial periodicals throughout the century. However, the cotton gin, invented and adopted in the 1790s, meant that cotton, chiefly grown in the southern states, rather than linen, became the major vegetable fiber used for clothing in the Western world. More and more, the rags that were collected and traded were made of cotton instead of linen. The worn fiber from cotton rags was considerably weaker than that from linen, and increasingly rags were supplemented or even replaced for better quality paper by the stronger raw cotton waste bought directly from spinning and weaving mills. By the 1840s, cotton had become more common as a source for fiber than linen in the paper used for books, making up 65 percent of the fiber content (as opposed to 30 percent for the preceding four decades) according to one study.[18]

The long-standing search for an alternative to linen and cotton rags led to continuing experiments with almost all types of fibrous materials, including especially straw, but also wood and even wasp nests. While the cellulose strands in vegetable matter were ideally suited for making paper, the raw material contained other substances, such as lignin and resins, that quickly weakened and discolored the resulting paper. Paper made from ground wood pulp was used on an experimental basis; the first commercial paper mill to produce "mechanical wood" newsprint went into operation in Curtisville, Massachusetts, in 1867. The 7 January 1868 issue of the *New Yorker Staats-Zeitung* was printed on wood-pulp paper, and during the 1870s many city newspapers followed this lead. During these same decades, experiments were underway in developing chemical processes that would purify the cellulose fibers in wood pulp. The earliest successful method for producing "chemical wood" paper involved boiling ground wood chips in an alkaline solution of caustic soda, but the resulting pulp was inferior and was usually mixed with rag pulp. Experiments with a better method, the sulfite process, were first conducted in Paris in 1857 by two American brothers, Benjamin C. and Richard Tilghman, and then successfully developed in Sweden and England. In 1882, C. S. Wheelwright of Providence operated the first American paper mill to use sulfite pulp commercially. In succeeding decades, the sulfite and, later, the sulfate processes ensured that wood pulp would increasingly replace rags as the primary raw material used to produce the paper needed to meet an ever-increasing demand and market. Although wood fibers began to be mixed with rags in very small amounts in the 1850s to produce the paper used in books, not until the 1870s did wood fiber predominate. Even then, most paper remained mixed—in one sample of fifty books from the 1870s, only 20 percent of the paper was made from pure rags and just 10 percent from pure chemical wood.[19]

Printing papers varied considerably in weight, opacity, color, and strength, depending on the quality of the raw materials, the manufacturing method, and especially the chemicals and other materials added to the stuff in the vat or used in sizing and finishing the sheets. Machine-made paper used for printing was originally "wove" in finish, displaying the smooth surface that came from being molded on a web, but early on it was discovered that the addition of a "dandy roll," a small, cylindrical, patterned roll placed at the wet end of the machine, could impress the traditional "laid" pattern, and even watermarks, typical of sheets of handmade paper. When first introduced, the smoother and more uniform appearance of the wove, machine-made paper was prized, especially for bookwork, and suited the new typographic styles of the modern-style typefaces that were popular, but with the reintroduction of the old-style type designs in the 1850s, machine-made "laid" paper also began to be used.[20] Another major change in printing papers over the period was the increasing use of a chemical alum-rosin size in place of the traditional animal gelatin size to set the ink and keep it from spreading or offsetting, something that became increasingly important as presses became faster. Almost unknown before the 1840s, alum-rosin size was almost universal in book papers by the 1870s. As it was acidic and tended to break down the cellulose fibers, its use was one factor in the subsequent rapid deterioration of much of the paper used during the period.[21] Despite these many changes, throughout the nineteenth century papermaking remained as much an art as a science, and the quality and appearance of paper varied considerably from mill to mill and lot to lot. In placing an order for paper, printers and publishers would typically include a sample piece of paper, which they requested be matched in weight, color, and finish.[22]

The use of the papermaking machine meant that for the first time the dimensions of the final sheet were freed from the human limits imposed by the hand mold: in theory, the only limit to the dimensions of a machine-made sheet was the width of the web on which the paper was molded. Indeed, it was feasible to make a continuous roll of paper. In practice, however, the size of existing printing presses and the market's demand that products appeal to consumers' usually conservative expectations meant that paper continued to be produced in sheets in traditional dimensions and proportions. New and larger printing presses could handle larger sheets, and the size of the sheet did increase, but the larger sheets typically preserved the dimensional proportions of the handmade sheet: a table of the sizes of American book papers from 1871 shows the traditional sizes, from medium (19" x 24") to imperial (22" x 32"), as well as larger sizes from medium-and-half (24" x 30") and double medium (24" x 38") to double imperial (32" x 46"). Printers' and publishers' records bear this out, but they also indicate that, if traditional paper sizes continued to be used, the traditional names for paper sizes were soon replaced by the practice of recording the dimensions of a sheet of paper in inches, and concomitantly, by an increasing variety of sizes available for order. Not until the successful adoption of the rotary press and curved stereotype plates did the use of rolls of paper become practical in the printing trades.[23]

Throughout the period, the cost of paper was relatively high in comparison to the other costs of printing, though the general trend seems to have been toward lower prices as the production and market for paper expanded with the introduction of new raw materials and manufacturing methods. Prices were reckoned at cents per pound of a ream of paper and fluctuated considerably — the range typically varied from fourteen to twenty cents — depending not only on the specifics of a paper's material content and finish but also on the general state of the economy, reflected in the cost of raw materials and credit. Because of its expense, printers and publishers usually ordered paper only for specific jobs and from wholesale paper merchants, rather than directly from the mills. These wholesalers typically arranged for the manufacture and speedy delivery of printing paper and offered their customers extended credit — often of three, six, or even twelve months — on their orders, thus helping to finance the book trade by relieving their customers of the expense of warehousing paper and the obligation to pay immediately for a raw material that, for publishers at least, would not return a profit until a book was manufactured, distributed, purchased, and paid for. The wholesale paper trade was closely allied not only to the mills but also to the retail stationery trade, which dealt in a wide range of products beyond paper.[24]

Printing Presses and Presswork

No innovation served as a greater public symbol of industrial progress in book manufacturing than the power-driven, iron and steel printing machine. At the Centennial Exhibition in Philadelphia, the newest and largest models — Hoe's perfecting press and Bullock's rotary perfecting press, each with a mechanical folder attached — were prominently displayed in Machinery Hall, side by side with the traditional common hand press that Benjamin Franklin had used when he visited London. In the Campbell Press Building, just west of Machinery Hall, a daily newspaper was printed on a Campbell's rotary perfecting press, which stood next to another common press, borrowed from the American Antiquarian Society in Worcester, Massachusetts, that was used to print a facsimile of a 1776 newspaper printing of the Declaration of Independence. Centennial publications and guides gave extensive accounts of these exhibits that fully illustrated and described these modern newspaper presses, stressing their intricacy, size, and speed.[25]

Like many other bookmaking technologies, the printing press changed only in minor ways before the end of the eighteenth century, though the exact details of the earliest printing presses are a matter of speculation. The eighteenth-century common press, made of wood and metal, was in itself a complex machine that managed the variety of actions required to produce printed sheets: text composed in type was imposed and locked into a chase, a cast-iron frame, with wedge-shaped quoins; the chase in turn was attached to the bed of the press, where the type was inked; a blank sheet of paper, properly prepared by wetting, was held in place precisely on the tympan and masked by the frisket so that the text, once printed, would appear as a clean image in the correct position on both sides of the sheet; the bed was cranked under the platen; and the platen, lowered by means of a screw turned by a bar, applied pressure against the paper and inked type on the bed of the press to transfer the ink from type to paper. Typically, two pressmen operated the press, one of them responsible for handling the sheets of paper and making the impression, and the other for inking the type. Often, however, a single pressman worked at "half press" to perform both operations. Careful adjustment of the press and type, as well as coordination between pressmen, was required to produce printed sheets of acceptable quality.

All these processes were mechanized in one way or another during the industrial era. The screw-driven platen of the wooden common press could make an impression only on half of the form of type held in the bed, which meant that two pulls of the bar were required to print even one side of a sheet. In England at the turn of the nineteenth century, Charles Mahon, Third Earl of Stanhope, who had been instrumental in perfecting the plaster-mold method of stereotyping, also designed and built a metal hand press with a full-size platen that could print the entire form of type with a single pull. Because the traditional screw mechanism to lower the platen proved no longer adequate to apply sufficient pressure over the greater area of impression, the Stanhope press depended on a lever-powered system. These two innovations — replacing wood with metal, chiefly cast iron reinforced with forged steel, and replacing the screw with a lever-powered and later a toggle-joint system — became standard for all hand presses that were designed and produced during the nineteenth century and beyond. Copies of the original Stanhope press were in use in New York City by 1811, but over the century many different American designs for iron hand presses were patented and produced. Two, in particular, predominated. The Columbian press, designed and first produced in Philadelphia by the American George Clymer about 1814, went on to become one of the standard hand presses used in nineteenth-century British printing shops after Clymer moved his manufacturing operations to London in 1817. The Washington press, first patented in 1821 by the New York printer Samuel Rust, was a simpler and lighter machine. After the New York firm R. Hoe & Co. purchased Rust's entire establishment and patent rights in 1835, the Washington press became one of that firm's signature products and the predominant hand press used in the United States into the twentieth century, its design widely copied by other firms after the original patents expired. An 1894 article in a dictionary of printing praised the Washington press: "For simplicity and accuracy it is difficult to see how any machine can surpass it." [26]

Further developments in press design came from progress in discovering alternatives to the hand-pulled lever for applying pressure on the platen to transfer the printed image from inked type to paper. Again, experiments were underway by the turn of the century, chiefly in Europe and England, but American inventors and press makers soon joined them. Isaac Adams of Boston—drawing on innovations made by Daniel Treadwell, another Bostonian, but one who had spent time in England—developed a successful power press by about 1830. The Adams press, with continuing further improvements designed by Isaac's brother, Seth Adams, became the standard press used for book manufacturing in the United States throughout the nineteenth century. In 1859 R. Hoe & Co. purchased the patents and became the primary manufacturer and supplier. A description of the press from 1871 reported that "Hoe's Catalogue says that for letter-press and cut work of the finest quality, these presses cannot be equaled; and, in spite of the numerous improvements in cylinder presses, this assertion is believed by many experienced book-printers."[27] By century's end, however, the larger and faster cylinder press had become the choice of most book printers, though many Adams presses continued in use into the new century.[28] Although quite different in appearance, the Adams press shared a basic principle with the traditional common press, for it consisted of a flat bed—which held the form of type, and later plates, in place—and a flat platen, although on the Adams press the bed rather than the platen was lowered and raised by means of a toggle joint in order to transfer the image from type to paper, while the flat platen remained stationary.

On cylinder presses, a cylindrical platen was used in place of a flat one to make the impression, progressively applying pressure as it was rolled across the inked type. This method had the advantage of allowing an increase in the size of the sheet that could be printed from a single form, as it was no longer necessary, as with a flat platen, to apply the entire pressure required to transfer the printed image in a single instant. As early as November 1814, the *Times* of London had successfully installed the first two cylinder machines, which had been designed and perfected there by a German, Friedrich Koenig. The earliest cylinder presses used in the United States were those designed and manufactured in England by David Napier and imported during the second half of the 1820s, but around 1830 R. Hoe & Co. had begun manufacturing them in New York.[29] Cylinder machines were the primary presses for newspaper work (especially after the introduction of the penny press in the 1830s) until the end of the century and were also increasingly used in magazine offices. Their reputation for producing work of inferior quality and for causing wear or damage to type, plates, and illustrations in the process of printing, however, meant that book printers preferred the Adams press through 1880.

Further experiments during the mid-nineteenth century led to the successful development of rotary printing machines — in which the printing surface, whether composed type or printing plates, was itself attached to a cylindrical surface and rotated against the cylindrical platen to make the impression — though again, experiments with this method of printing had been longstanding. The earliest commercial successes were made with type-revolving presses, which depended on several techniques to hold rectangular type to the curved surface of the platen: making the cylindrical platen of such large diameter that the arc of the surface was only slightly curved; casting type on a tapered body or with notches and projections; and using specially prepared wedge-shaped rules and quoins to hold them in place in a curved chase called a "turtle." The *Philadelphia Public Ledger* of 22 March 1847 was issued on a type-revolving press supplied by R. Hoe & Co., though it was a primitive machine that used a flat platen to print paper supplied in sheets. Over the next decades, Hoe produced and successfully marketed an improved version of its type-revolving Lightning press: by 1855, the first twenty-three had been sold to big-city newspapers, including, incredibly, one to *La Patrie* in Paris. During the 1860s, however, William H. Bullock's Printing Press Co. of Philadelphia designed and perfected a rotary web press using curved stereotype plates that could also print both sides of a web of paper, which was then cut into sheets, all in a continuous motion able to produce over twenty thousand perfected (i.e., printed on both sides) sheets an hour. Hoe and other press manufacturers soon entered the field with web presses of their own, though the market for these fast but large, heavy, and expensive printing machines was for many years limited to urban newspapers with the largest circulations.[30]

At the same time, the industrial era brought about the development of the jobbing-platen press, a versatile and inexpensive machine that was popular in many shops and that allowed for the proliferation of printed ephemera. The "platen jobber" was a strictly American development, based on early experiments by Bostonians Daniel Treadwell, who also worked on the early development of the platen power press, and Stephen Ruggles; it was perfected at midcentury successively by George Phineas Gordon and his draughtsman, Frederick Degener. Characteristic of the platen jobber was that bed and platen, both flat, were joined by a hinge and brought together by a horizontal, rather than a vertical, movement; that the ink was distributed automatically by rollers revolving over a rotating ink disc; and that the frisket was dispensed with. These features meant that the press could be operated effectively by a single pressman, and over the century the platen jobber developed in two directions: with a treadle or lever, it became a small, hand-operated press chiefly used for small jobs or by amateurs, whereas the power-driven version was used by professional printers efficiently and rapidly for a variety of jobs and eventually would work side by side with large cylinder presses.[31]

These new printing presses depended for their success on many ancillary inventions and improvements: the replacement of traditional ink balls by composition rollers for distributing the ink; an increasing variety of faster-drying or colored printing inks suitable for use on the larger and faster printing machines; metal grippers to feed and position the sheet of paper precisely over the printing surface; fly mechanisms to remove the printed sheet from the press; and mechanical folders to cut and fold the printed sheet. For book printing, the development of patented stereotype blocks — platforms that were locked in the bed of the press, that fastened the printing plates in place by means of small hooks, and that brought the plates up to type height — simplified the processes of imposition and makeready (the preparation of the type or plates for the press run), especially with the larger sheets made possible by machine-made paper and the larger beds of power-driven printing machines. Industrial presses were powered by various means: hand levers and foot treadles persisted throughout the nineteenth century on smaller presses, especially jobbing presses, whereas horse- and water-power, transferred to the shop floor by means of belts and overhead shafts, were widely replaced by steam engines, a substitution that helps explain the frequent fires that bedeviled larger printing and bookmaking establishments. Electric power, introduced toward the end of the century, would eventually predominate in industrial printing plants.[32]

While more efficient, the new printing presses were generally less versatile. This fact explains the different arrays of equipment, mentioned earlier in this chapter, that were found in the printing establishments of Charles Hamilton and the Riverside Press: Hamilton, an industrial job printer, owned a variety of presses in order to meet many kinds of printing requirements, whereas the Riverside Press was chiefly a book-printing plant that depended on Adams flatbed presses.[33] The cost of presses was also a factor: in 1856 small jobbing platen presses and Washington hand presses cost only a few hundred dollars, depending on the size of the bed, whereas Adams presses and cylinder machines, which began at less than $1,000 for the smallest sizes, could cost as much as $4,500 for the largest double-cylinder machine.[34] In 1867 R. Hoe & Co. advertised its largest ten-cylinder type-revolving machine at $41,250, with "boxing and carting" an additional $780 and other extras, $647.[35] The large rotary presses that were being installed in big-city newspaper offices during the 1870s and that were exhibited at the Centennial Exhibition must have cost many thousands more: in 1882 the *St. Louis Globe-Democrat* paid $80,000 for a Hoe web rotary press with an attached folding machine.[36]

TABLE 1.2. Impression rates for presses, 1870

Type of press	Makeready (hours)	Presswork (hours)	Impressions per hour	Impressions per 10-hour day
Hand press:				
1 form of 7,500 impressions	1	9	167	1,500
4 forms of 250 impressions	4	6	167	1,000
Machine-powered jobbing press:				
1 form of 6,000 impressions	1	9	667	6,000
8 forms of 100 impressions	8	2	400	800
Medium cylinder press:				
1 form of 7,500 impressions	1	9	833	7,500
8 forms of 250 impressions	7	3	667	2,000
Mammoth cylinder press:				
1 form of 4,000 impressions	3	7	571	4,000
4 forms of 250 impressions	7	3	333	1,000

Source: Theodore L. De Vinne, *The Printers' Price List: A Manual* (New York: Francis Hart & Co., 1871), 75.

This great variety of presses, many of which were necessarily dedicated to particular types of work, makes it impossible to generalize about the rate and cost of production during this period. Any press's performance largely depended on the nature of the work and the number of copies to be produced: the time required for makeready could be considerable, especially on the large new printing machines or for high-quality or complicated work. Table 1.2 estimates impression rates for several kinds of presses in 1870, although these rates fall far below those that were often advertised for large cylinder and rotary presses. Theodore L. De Vinne, who made these estimates based on his practical experience, nonetheless reported that based on "the abstract of an entire year's business," the "average daily performance of a large press room" in New York—containing twelve cylinder presses, two large Gordon platen jobbers, two smaller "card" platen jobbers, and two hand presses— came to only 2,750 impressions per press.[37]

Industrial printing presses also profoundly altered the labor of printing. During the nineteenth century, the division of labor in printing establishments became more complex than the traditional, simple division between compositors and pressmen of the preindustrial era. The production of printing plates required a separate establishment and special skills, but within the pressroom itself, especially in large industrial printing plants, the introduction of new printing machines caused a further division of labor. The Harper & Brothers printing establishment of 1855 contained a pressroom

MANUFACTURING AND BOOK PRODUCTION

with twenty-eight flatbed printing machines, each serviced by a "girl" who was responsible only for feeding sheets of paper into the press, all under the supervision of one male foreman. Other men were responsible for preparing the form for the press.[38] But the diverse labor involved in printing with these new machines could be much greater, as De Vinne makes clear:

> A large press of any kind requires many servitors. The Feeder, who lays the sheets, receives from $6 to $9 per week, according to ability. For fine Book work or Color work, requiring accurate register, two Feeders or Pointers are needed on the reiteration, who double the expense of feeding. On some presses, a Fly-boy at $3 or $4 per week is needed. For the finest Wood-cut and Color work on Cylinders, it is necessary to employ a boy to interleave the sheets as they are delivered from the fly, to prevent set-off. Such work requires the undivided care of the pressman. He can run and oversee but one press. The cost of labor alone for a press employed on such work is often more than $8 per day.
>
> The Feeders, Pointers, Fly-boys, and Interleavers are attached to one press. But in every large job and book office many workmen are employed who are attached to no particular press, but who work for all, in cutting, wetting, packing, and dry-pressing the sheets, in making rollers, in caring for plates, or in general supervision.[39]

Binding

A major development of the mid-nineteenth century was the widespread adoption by publishers of cloth-cased bindings and gold stamping for the vast majority of trade books. The implications of this development are difficult to overstate: for the first time, the publisher was responsible not only for the typography and appearance of the printed sheets but also for the design and production of the binding in which they were sold to the public, bindings that in most cases were treated as permanent. Publisher and reader were connected in a new way, not just through the text of the works that the former published but also through the package in which that text appeared. In some instances, a particular style of binding became associated with a publisher: this was certainly the case with the brown "ribbed T-cloth" binding, soberly decorated on the sides with a blind-stamped arabesque ornament, that Ticknor and Fields used on most of its general trade books—including the classic works by New England's literary authors, such as Emerson, Hawthorne, Longfellow, Thoreau, and Whittier—from the late 1840s.[40]

Publishers' sale of books with cloth bindings replaced the earlier practice of retailing books in plain leather bindings or in temporary pasteboard bindings covered with paper, the production of which was usually the responsibility of publishers or wholesalers. This industrial development depended on several new binding technologies that began to be introduced during the 1820s but became predominant in the 1830s. One was the adoption of the cased binding, where what has come to be known as the "book block" (the printed sheets with binder's leaves attached) was prepared for binding independently from the decorated case or cover: the two were attached to each other only as a final step in the binding process. Unlike traditional binding structures, where boards were attached to the book block before the covering was applied, cased bindings allowed for the streamlining of work flow in the bindery and encouraged the preparation and binding of multiple copies of a single work in batches. This streamlining was particularly important in the preparation and decoration of the cases, as were additional important innovations, such as the manufacture of a suitable linen or cotton cloth that could be used as the primary covering material for publishers' trade bindings. This cloth was sized, dyed, and grained with an overall texture or pattern, processes that resulted in a material that was attractive, stable, resistant to bleed-through of adhesives and to wear, and able to support lettering and other decoration. The 1830s also saw the introduction of a new method of finishing, the application of lettering and decoration to the binding that replaced the traditional method of hand tooling in which skilled craftsmen used individual brass tools, fillets, and rolls to build up a title or design letter-by-letter or element-by-element. With the development of large, cast-iron binder's stamping and embossing presses, intricately carved brass dies could, when heated, be used to stamp a pattern in gold, blind, or—after the late 1860s—black in a single stroke to a board or the spine of a case before it was attached to the sheets.

The use of binders' cloth and die-stamped decoration accounts for the characteristic appearance of trade books of the nineteenth century, which is in marked contrast to earlier books. Publishers and booksellers quickly discovered that a publisher's binding could not only reflect a book's content or genre but in itself influence a customer's decision whether or not to purchase it. As a result, publishers devoted considerable attention and expense to the design and appearance of the binding. Binder's cloth, which was chiefly imported from England (Interlaken Mills, the first important American manufacturer, was established only in 1883), was produced and used in many colors and grains that, together with the die-stamping, could reflect the latest fashion in decorative design. Before the 1860s, it was typical for a single work to be offered for sale in a multitude of colors and grains of cloth and often in several binding designs or styles — "gilt" or "extra gilt," depending on the amount of gold applied, or even in traditional paper-covered boards or wrappers — any of which might appeal to a particular customer and his or her pocket-book. This exuberance became muted during the 1860s, though it remained common for a single work to be offered in several, if fewer, colors, even as the gold-stamped design tended to become specific to that work. Throughout the period, publishers usually offered a few copies for sale bound in a more expensive leather binding, which remained the standard binding for genres such as Bibles and prayer books.[41]

Beginning in the 1830s, the streamlining and regularization of the binding process that resulted from the adoption of cased binding led to the develop-ment of many further binding machines beyond the stamping and embossing presses used in finishing. The use of rolling machines, hydraulic-powered standing presses, and smashing machines replaced the traditional process of hammering printed sheets to prepare them for binding. In 1856 Cyrus Chambers Jr. of Philadelphia took out his earliest patent for a folding ma-chine for printed sheets, and with subsequent improvements it soon supple-mented hand folding. Once sheets were folded and gathered, grooves were cut along their spine by a sawing machine to prepare the book for sewing; pamphlets were prepared for stitching by a stabbing machine that punched holes through the sides of the gatherings. Sewing machines were also intro-duced during these decades, though the crucial breakthrough — the replace-ment of straight needles with curved ones that could carry a continuous thread through the fold of a gathering and then back out again — was first patented by David Smyth only in 1879. Guillotines and table shears, instead of the traditional plough, were used to trim the sheets and gatherings, and rounding and backing machines shaped the book block during the forward-ing process. The preparation of cases was done by hand, though millboard-cutting, gluing, and case-smoothing machines were introduced toward the end of the century. Many of these machines were power-driven, connected by leather belts to an overhead shaft driven by a steam engine, usually placed in the basement.[42]

The proliferation of bindery machinery did not mean that machine work replaced handwork. In most binderies, many operations continued to be done by hand, at least on occasion, even after the new machinery had been installed, and even power-driven machines were fed by hand. Machinery, however, sped up the binding process and allowed for the substitution of unskilled workers, especially women, for more expensive craft labor, both considerable financial advantages. Nevertheless, binding remained a labor-intensive and time-consuming process, which in some cases was a bottleneck in the process of production: in 1852 the *Literary World* reported that "from 125 to 200 book-binders have been constantly at work in binding" *Uncle Tom's Cabin* during the height of its success, and surviving copies provide evidence that several different binderies worked simultaneously to keep up with demand.[43]

This situation was, of course, exceptional. More typically, once a bindery received the printed sheets of a new edition from the printer, it would bind up and return to the publisher several hundred copies and warehouse the remainder in sheets. These were then bound up only as demand required, and publishers' records indicate that it was not uncommon for a batch of a dozen or even fewer copies, made up from the original sheets, to be bound and returned to the publisher many years, even decades, after a work's original publication.[44] This system of warehousing and binding in batches made financial sense, for although there may have been some economy of scale in binding the entire edition at once, the publisher would then have been responsible for the cost of binding the entire edition, which might remain in print for many years during which the stored copies ran the risk of being soiled or damaged. Survivals, though uncommon, give clear evidence that from the 1830s at least some bound books were warehoused in printed dust wrappers, intended to protect the binding from wear or fading but to be discarded before the binding was displayed for retail sale.[45]

The cost of binding was usually charged at a set rate per copy, which was often considerable and could, for trade books, be the largest cost of production. The rate charged for binding varied considerably, depending on the size of the book, the amount of decoration, especially if gold-stamped, and the number of copies being bound. The cost books of Ticknor and Fields indicate that in the mid-1850s the standard charge for the firm's signature brown cloth binding was 10¢ per volume. In his 1871 account, De Vinne stated that the cost for trade cloth bindings in "ordinary library style" ranged from 10½¢ to 57½¢ per volume for orders of 500 or more, with an extra charge of up to 30¢ for gilt edges. The publisher was also responsible for the cost of the brass dies used for stamping the decoration on the cloth cases: in late 1876, for example, James R. Osgood & Co., a successor firm to Ticknor and Fields, paid as much as $26.46 for the dies used on the binding of Charles Dudley Warner's *In the Levant* (1877; Fig. 1.1), which was then bound at the rate of 21¢ per copy.[46] Any binding expenses were, of course, justified if they resulted in helping to convince a customer to purchase a copy of the work because of its attractive appearance.

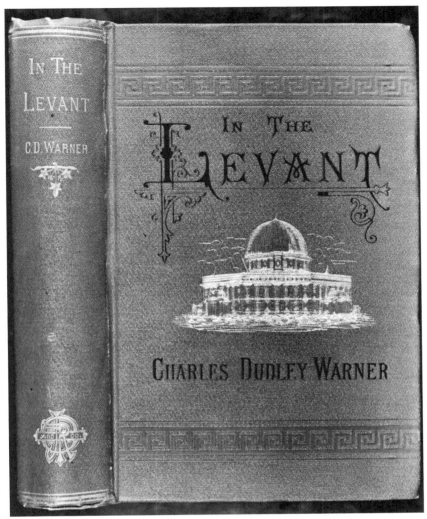

FIGURE 1.1. Charles Dudley Warner's *In the Levant* (Boston: James R. Osgood & Co., 1877) in a binding style typical of the 1870s. This copy was bound in green cloth, but the book was also available in mauve, blue, or terra cotta. American Antiquarian Society.

Illustration and Ornamentation

Before the development and introduction of successful photomechanical and photochemical techniques for the reproduction of images at the end of the nineteenth century, books remained more typographic than graphic in their appearance. Nevertheless, many books produced during the mid-nineteenth century were illustrated, and the publication of separately printed images also proliferated. The long-established graphic processes of relief and intaglio printing continued to predominate during the period, but the new processes of lithography and photography were then first introduced and adopted. Like bindings, illustrations could play an important role in affecting the ways that books were merchandised, received, and read.

Relief printing remained the most common method for the reproduction of images throughout the period, as it had been since at least the fifteenth century. Its chief advantage was that a design (which was left in relief on the surface of a woodblock after the background was cut away so that the image, once inked, might be transferred to paper) could be made of type height and thus printed as part of the same form and at the same time as text set in type. This made relief print the least expensive form of graphic reproduction, and it was used almost universally for ornamentation—borders, rules, decorated initials, headpieces, and tailpieces—as well as for most images that appeared on printed text pages. With the adoption of printing plates, relief images were locked up and cast together with type as part of a single plate, which had the added advantage of saving the original relief block from unnecessary wear on the press during printing. This practice was particularly beneficial given the new style of relief illustration, wood engraving, that was introduced at the end of the eighteenth century and that became popular and widely used during the nineteenth.

In wood engraving, the relief process drew on methods for indicating shading that were characteristic of the intaglio engraving process: the relief parts of the block, which would appear in black on the final print, often served as background, whereas the design was cut away and would typically appear as a pattern of fine white lines, cross-hatching, or dots to make up the printed image. To achieve this effect, designs had to be cut on the end grain of a closely grained wooden block, typically made from boxwood or fruit trees. For larger illustrations, cuts had to be made up of several smaller blocks bolted together: this unit might be carved as a whole, but the smaller blocks could also be carved separately by a team of engravers to speed up the process. Wood-engraving blocks were fragile, as well as time-consuming and expensive to produce, so the capability of reproducing or even duplicating them in metal for use on the press was a decided advantage. Indeed, electrotyping was originally developed as a means of reproducing woodcuts and engravings.

Relief wood engravings could be, and frequently were, printed together with text set in type on a single sheet, and in the postbellum years some of the most lavish gift books, often reprint editions of favorite or classic poems, were produced in this way. However, in order to produce the very best images, wood engravings had to be printed separately from type on different paper

and with different ink. Thus, wood engravings were usually produced independently from the printed text sheets—even at a separate shop—and then
inserted into the text during the binding process. This was the normal practice for all but the cheapest trade books in the antebellum years and continued
to be common throughout the century.

Like relief printing, the reproduction of images by the intaglio process
dated back to the earliest years of printing. In an intaglio print, an image or design was engraved, etched, or otherwise cut into the surface of a metal plate,
which was then coated with ink. After the surface of the plate was wiped clean,
ink remained in the cut lines of the image and could be transferred to damp
or absorbent paper when the plate and paper were passed through a special
"rolling press" with two rollers to apply substantial pressure. The nature of
the process meant that intaglio images were necessarily printed in a separate
operation from text set in type. During the nineteenth century, the intaglio
process continued to be used for both separate prints and illustrations inserted in books, though the need to produce increased numbers of images
meant that traditional copper plates were widely replaced with either steel
or copper plates treated by steel-facing, a process that deposited a thin layer
of steel on the surface of a copper plate by means of electroplating. Intaglio
images were more expensive to produce than relief ones and, with their distinctive look, were widely used for portrait frontispieces, as well as technical,
scientific, topographic, cartographic, and fashion illustrations.

Based on principles discovered in Germany in 1798 by Alois Senefelder,
the lithographic or, more generally, planographic process was developed and
widely adopted during the nineteenth century. The image or design was
drawn or placed on a specially treated surface—traditionally a highly polished, fine-grained, but porous limestone—in a greasy or oil-based medium,
such as a crayon. The surface was then coated with a film of water, which
was repelled by the design, and next with a layer of greasy or oil-based ink,
which was in turn repelled by the water but adhered to the design; the inked
image could then be transferred to a sheet of paper laid over the surface and
run through a suitable press. This process, like the intaglio one, required
that lithographic illustrations be produced independently from text printed
from type, and where the two were used together, the illustrations, printed
on separate leaves, were inserted at the bindery. Nevertheless, lithography
proved a versatile process for the reproduction of images. It was discovered
early on that an illustration or image drawn or prepared on specially treated
paper could be transferred to the lithographic surface for further reproduction, a process that in the early 1840s gave rise to anastatic printing, a method
of reproducing, in facsimile, printed or handwritten material. Similarly, an

intaglio image printed on transfer paper could be reproduced lithographically in large numbers with no wear to the original intaglio plate, and this process became widely used for the production of sheet music after the 1830s. Many inserted intaglio frontispieces and other illustrations must also have been reproduced in this fashion, especially in popular works, as the development of the steam-powered lithographic press during the 1850s increased the rate of production of lithographic over intaglio prints remarkably, from twelve prints an hour to nearer one thousand, though some printers claimed even more.[47]

Another lithographic process, chromolithography, was only the most spectacular of the various methods employed for producing colored illustrations before 1880. Colored illustrations could only be made in one of two ways: either an image printed in black was colored by hand, typically by a team of colorers, each of whom applied a single color with the aid of a stencil; or by printing impressions of an image from multiple, separately prepared relief blocks or lithographic stones, each inked in a different color. Both techniques were used during the mid-nineteenth century. Many lithographic prints, known as "lithotints," employed a tint stone to provide a contrasting background to the main image, much like a painter's wash, and multicolored lithographic prints were developed to a particularly sophisticated level by specialist chromolithographic firms, such as P. S. Duval of Philadelphia and Louis Prang & Co. of Boston, who produced separately published prints commonly referred to as "chromos." These firms became famous for the high quality of their prints, which could be made up from impressions from as many as several dozen separate stones: for example, in 1869 James Parton described the printing process for Prang's reproduction of Eastman Johnson's painting *The Barefoot Boy*, based on John Greenleaf Whittier's poem, as employing twenty-six stones (Fig. 1.2).[48] Less elaborately produced chromos were sometimes used as inserted book illustrations and for trade cards and advertising.

A final method for graphic reproduction during the period was photography, though its major impact occurred during the late nineteenth and early twentieth centuries. Long before 1880, however, the fad for collecting daguerreotypes and separately published photographic prints, especially carte de visite portraits, was well established. The use of photographic processes for illustrative purposes in books was more limited: the first photographic illustration in an American book was the frontispiece in *Homes of American Statesmen*—published by G. P. Putnam & Co. in late 1853, although the title page is dated 1854—but the same book also employs the more common "engravings on wood, from drawings . . . and daguerreo-

THE BAREFOOT BOY.

BLESSINGS on thee, little man,
Barefoot boy with cheek of tan!
With thy turned-up pantaloons,
And thy merry whistled tunes;
With thy red lip, redder still
Kissed by strawberries on the hill;
With the sunshine on thy face,
Through thy torn brim's jaunty grace;
From my heart I give thee joy,—

I was once a barefoot boy!
Prince thou art,—the grown-up man
Only is republican.
Let the million-dollared ride!
Barefoot, trudging at his side,
Thou hast more than he can buy
In the reach of ear and eye,—
Outward sunshine, inward joy;
Blessings on thee, barefoot boy!

Cheerily, then, my little man,
Live and laugh, as boyhood can!
Though the flinty slopes be hard,
Stubble-speared the new-mown sward,
Every morn shall lead thee through
Fresh baptisms of the dew;
Every evening from thy feet
Shall the cool wind kiss the heat;
All too soon these feet must hide
In the prison cells of pride,

Lose the freedom of the sod,
Like a colt's for work be shod,
Made to tread the mills of toil,
Up and down in ceaseless moil,
Happy if their track be found
Never on forbidden ground;
Happy if they sink not in
Quick and treacherous sands of sin.
Ah! that thou couldst know thy joy,
Ere it passes, barefoot boy!

FIGURE 1.2. Chromolithographic reproduction of Eastman Johnson's painting *The Barefoot Boy* (34 x 26 cm; Boston: L. Prang & Co., c. 1868), based on a poem by John Greenleaf Whittier. An owner of this "chromo" pasted a clipping of the poem to the foot of the print. American Antiquarian Society.

types." The frontispiece itself was a photographically reproduced "crystalotype" (a salt print made from an albumen glass-plate negative) mounted on a blank leaf. From the mid-1850s, similar techniques were occasionally used in other books, especially privately printed memorial volumes produced in limited numbers for friends and family.[49]

Given the variety of methods for reproducing images and their variety of uses, it is difficult to generalize about the costs of illustration, but the inclusion of images added expense, sometimes substantial, to the production costs of books and other printed materials. The least expensive method, wood engraving, was the most widespread and certainly became more widely used, not only in books but especially in periodicals and newspapers, as the century progressed. The presence of illustration was an important element in the publication and sales appeal of much printed matter, and different reproductive techniques became associated with specific genres or types: intaglio was widely used for frontispiece portraits and for scientific and technical works, as well as for sheet music, even when the latter was subsequently reproduced lithographically; lithography for sheet music covers or scenes of travel and exploration, the latter either to be inserted in books or issued separately as chromos; and photographs for inserted portraits in memorial volumes. In many trade books, illustrations helped define genre and appeal to customers. Increasingly during the century, individual book illustrators and artists became well known and sought after, identified by name on the title page along with the author, and in a few instances — Bartlett's *American Scenery* (1840) is an early example — the illustrator (W. H. Bartlett) rather than the author of the text (N. P. Willis) has come to be recognized as chiefly responsible for the work.

Conclusion: Impact of Industrialization

By 1880 the era of the industrial book was firmly established: new manufacturing methods had profoundly changed the way books and other printed materials were produced and what they looked like. If traditional craft methods persisted, in most places people and machines produced print in ways that would have been unimaginable during the early decades of the century. Type had proliferated in both quantity and variety of design, even as much printing was done from plates rather than type. Machine-made paper had completely replaced handmade paper for printing. The wooden common press was a thing of the past, something to be displayed as a curiosity at the Philadelphia Centennial Exhibition: books and newspapers were now printed on large, heavy, power-driven printing machines made of metal. Books were now offered for retail sale in an attractive, often stunning, new package: a decorated cloth binding, designed and paid for by the publisher, often specific to the work. Illustrations and separately published images were to be found in proliferation.

Because of the fundamental and far-reaching nature of these changes, it is impossible to make useful generalizations about their impact. If new technologies enabled the production of cheap print in quantities and at speeds previously impossible, many publications from the nineteenth century were elegant and expensive, produced slowly, with individual care and attention from highly skilled workers. If the investment in machines and equipment at H. O. Houghton & Co.'s Riverside Press in 1860 was valued at over $35,000 and the new, fast, rotary presses developed for big-city newspapers in the 1870s at over twice that figure, in 1856 the New York typefounder George Bruce (brother of David Bruce Jr.) had estimated the complete cost of new and modern equipment, including type and ornaments, for a small country weekly newspaper to be just under $810.[50] Certainly, working conditions in the printing and book trades had changed: although many highly skilled and trained laborers were still employed, these were increasingly supplemented, even outnumbered, by those less skilled who worked at the service of machines. Craft traditions were increasingly a vestigial survival in the new industrial setting. The distinction between workers and employers, always a nominal one during the earlier period, became insurmountable and institutionalized by the formation of separate organizations to represent their interests, even as a new class of foremen and engineers emerged. Nevertheless, in many small jobbing and newspaper shops that also adopted new industrial manufacturing methods, such distinctions must have seemed unnecessary or impossible — and new machines such as the tabletop platen jobber were widely available to the hobby printer and led to an explosion in the publication of amateur newspapers in the 1870s.

Nor was the process of industrialization complete by 1880. In succeeding decades there would be major new developments, especially the perfection and adoption of the linotype and monotype machines for composition and the Smyth book-sewing machine. In the twentieth century, the application of photographic techniques to the reproduction of printed images would profoundly revolutionize the production and reception of print. But between 1840 and 1880, major steps in the industrialization of the book and printing trades were taken: printing and publishing would never be the same again.

CHAPTER 2

Labor and Labor Organization

Bruce Laurie

. . .

Philadelphia's journeymen printers did not share the excitement of the thousands of visitors pouring into Fairmount Park on 10 May 1876 for the grand opening of the Centennial Exhibition. Following three years of economic depression, workers in the printing trades faced a protracted crisis marked by widespread joblessness and falling wages. In one important respect, however, printers were better off than most wage earners. Their union, Local No. 2 of the International Typographical Union (ITU), had survived the worst of the depression and its class strife. Though weakened, the local enjoyed enough influence to convince another city trade association, the Employing Printers of Philadelphia, to talk about wage concessions. The ensuing discussion, in the opinion of the union men, was blunt and direct but also cordial and respectful, and it ended "amid mutual expressions of regard."[1]

During the talks, the journeymen maintained that they were entitled to better treatment than casual laborers or factory drudges. John Funnell, for instance, vigorously chided the employers for assuming that printers were no different from ordinary workers. He cited government figures showing that carpet weavers' annual income of $380 was "barely sufficient to obtain the merest necessities of life." Surely, he said, employers would not reduce printers to the same level of penury and want. Surely employers understood that printers were intelligent men who needed more than muscles to do their work, that they had a "corresponding necessity to appear more respectable in their dress, and to keep their families in better condition than those who were engaged in menial service." Surely, he argued, printers "should be entitled to a little more consideration."[2]

It is instructive to compare Funnell's depiction of his fellow workers with the images of printers projected by historians. Some closely follow Funnell, describing privileged tradesmen jealously protective of craft skills and personal autonomy on the shop floor through quietly strong trade unions that yielded the enviable standard of living associated with a labor aristocracy.[3] A very different picture emerges from an influential study of apprenticeship that offers a familiar model of the declension of artisanship. In it, printers were craftsmen in name only, condemned to "long hours, hard work, and earnings sufficient for a modest standard of living without savings or luxuries." They were forced into "tramping around the country" in search of a "pot of gold," only to "drift into a pattern of frenzied work alternating with equally frenzied drinking binges." Tramp printers, this study holds, were "the first casualties of the new machine age." [4]

Funnell had a better understanding of his fellow tradesmen than the pessimistic school of historians. Printers did not follow the familiar script of craft declension. Of course, their livelihoods varied widely between periods of prosperity and the lean times that accompanied the disastrous inflation of the Civil War era and the depressions of 1837, 1857, and 1873. Those depressions wiped out many unions and left journeymen at the mercy of cost-conscious employers. It would be a mistake, however, to read such variation as a downward spiral. If anything, the fluctuating incomes of printers occurred in the larger context of income improvement — the fluctuation tended upward.

Members of the typographical union in antebellum America were relatively well off. In 1850, Philadelphia printers of all ages and grades of skill earned about $370 per year — over $100 more than the average for male workers as a whole.[5] This income bought the correspondingly better standard of living for which John Funnell argued, for it elevated printers to the highest income bracket of wage earners.[6] Over the ensuing thirty years, printers' incomes remained high enough to sustain middling comfort. In Philadelphia in 1880, printers averaged $520 per year, exceeding the fourteen-industry average of $465 and maintaining their distinction as the best paid of all tradesmen in the traditional crafts. Only skilled workers in the new metal trades earned more.[7]

These income figures — and those from 1880 in particular — should be used with caution, as they include both skilled and unskilled workers. Taking the average income distorts the picture because of the printing industry's notoriously wide wage disparity based on experience. Veteran printers in 1880 exceeded the $520 average in Philadelphia by as little as $100 or as much as $400. An 1883 Illinois study reveals an average yearly income for printers of $655, nearly $100 more than workers in nineteen other occupations, and the highest of all tradesmen except metal workers. The income of individual printers in this study ranged from a low of $580 to a high of about $1,000, at a time when $600 bought plebeian respectability.[8] Such workers had smaller families of two or three children, indicating some form of fertility control, and they kept their children in school as long as possible. Their wives tended households that boasted proper kitchens, sometimes equipped with washing machines, sewing machines, or both. The jewel of such households was the parlor, often redolent with the trappings of respectability: a carpeted floor, a piano or organ, and even bookcases, for Illinois printers spent up to $25 per year on reading material. The purchase of such comforts left enough money for necessities, life insurance, and, of course, union dues.[9]

To what do we attribute this popular version of the printer's good life? Several printers in the Illinois survey had no doubt that it was the ITU that secured their wages and working conditions.[10] While there is no reason to doubt such a predictable claim, there is good reason to believe that it is incomplete. It was not simply the union but the larger context in which employee and employer found themselves that explains the conditions enjoyed by printers in the industrial age. Ely Moore, one of Jacksonian America's more celebrated printers, captured this context quite well in an 1833 speech about the troubles of working men. He blamed the "evils that ever flow from inordinate desire and unrestricted selfishness" on competition and exhorted his colleagues to "establish an equilibrium of power." A Locofoco Democrat partial to small government, Moore abjured recourse to state power in favor of "unity of purpose and concert of action on the part of the producing classes." He scoffed at those who shrieked "illegal combination" at trade unionists. "Have not journeymen the same right to ask their own price for their own property, or services, that employers have. . . ? Is that equal justice that makes it an offense for journeymen to combine for the purpose of maintaining their present prices, or raising their wages, while employers may combine with impunity for the purpose of lowering them?"[11] Moore did not attack employers for organizing. In fact, he favored collective action on both sides of the class divide to reduce the competition that he and fellow workmen found so destructive. He proposed a model of corporatism in which each side established its own rules and regulations for the conduct of the trade, but in which they also came together to work out differences over matters of mutual concern.

Moore's vision, in which laborers and owners work toward "an equilibrium of power," provides the modern historian with a frame of reference for labor relations in the printing trades during the industrial age. As we consider employer organizations, trade unions, and the relationship between them, we need to keep several points in mind. The equilibrium Moore sought was never fully achieved in the nineteenth century. A persistent imbalance in power inhered in the very nature of class relations owing to the fact that union printers represented only a small fraction of employees in their industry. Unionized printers were largely white males and craft unionists, which is to say that their organizations not only excluded women most of the time but also all other workmen, regardless of skills. In addition, membership in the "typographical union" was restricted to compositors. Other workers in the printing trades either remained unorganized or formed their own organizations. Such exclusiveness restricted the compass of unionism and enhanced management's natural advantage. Moore's corporatism, moreover, proved terribly elusive because its institutional mainstays often came undone in the economic cycles of the nineteenth century. Depressions and downturns made unions easy prey for aggressive employers and left printers' associations vulnerable to loosely affiliated renegades who broke ranks at the earliest opportunity. Relations between the classes inevitably worsened in such moments, as they did in the aftermath of the panic of 1873.

The ensuing depression taught union printers two related lessons. It showed that even the more fraternal employers with much to gain from trade unions — such as standardized wages and subsidized job training — preferred union-free shops or at least compliant unions. Their corporatistic outlook did not compel class peace; it simply encouraged a sympathetic disposition, a conditional tendency to work with unionists. For their part, union men had to make themselves impossible to ignore and too strong to break. They found in the early 1880s that this could not be done without the help of workers in other trades who enjoyed some leverage over publishers, not only because of their labor power but also because they were consumers. Printers learned that there was no future in acting as a group apart from the greater body of labor.

Entrepreneurs and Employer Organizations

In the middle half of the nineteenth century, printing and publishing firms were usually structured as proprietorships or partnerships, though joint stock arrangements became more common after the Civil War. This point held true even for the largest and most prestigious firms, such as Harper & Brothers in New York. Very few firms, however, reached the scale or technological sophistication of the Harper establishment. Table 2.1, comparing the number of employees in printing firms of various sizes in Philadelphia, shows why.[12] In 1850, medium-sized firms with six to fifty employees were the most numerous, followed by the smallest firms and then by the largest. Thirty years later, the number of firms had increased nearly threefold, from 106 to 289, or just about the rate for the industry as a whole, and the distribution of firms had not changed much. As for employees, a slight majority in 1850 worked in medium-sized shops; thirty years later, they concentrated in the largest ones. This shift is just what we should expect, given the conventional wisdom on the acceleration of industrialization in the second half of the century. The fact remains, however, that this pattern represents a change in magni-

TABLE 2.1. Percentage of the workforce employed in small, medium, and large Philadelphia printing firms, 1850 and 1880

	1850			1880		
Number of employees	0–5	6–50	50+	0–5	6–50	50+
Number of firms	36	60	10	105	148	36
Percentage of workforce	5	51	44	4	37	59

Source: Adapted from Bruce Laurie et al., "Immigrants and Industry: The Philadelphia Experience, 1850–1880," *Journal of Social History* 9 (1975): 223, table 5, which is based on U.S. Census Office, *Census of the United States, Manufacturing Schedule, County of Philadelphia, 1850 and 1880* (microfilm mss., National Archives).

tude rather than kind, for the figures also tell us that in the city small shops had already been marginalized well before 1850. Later industrial development simply deepened this pattern; it did not create a new one.[13]

Printing was a competitive swirl by the 1830s. Myriad firms came into existence to produce "cheap books" and other printed matter. A printer who had earlier brought out a full range of printed products had to relinquish book publishing. "Steam and competition," he lamented, "have made sad work upon high prices."[14] So had innovative bidding systems that replaced political patronage in awarding government contracts.[15] Competitive bidding also spread more widely through the private sector. A jittery bookseller in Boston spoke of a "crisis" in the early 1850s brought on by publishers whose wholesale discounts threatened to make "losers" of everyone.[16]

Employers economized by hiring cheaper labor in the form of partially trained apprentices ("two-thirders") and women. The depression of 1837 interrupted this trend, but it soon resumed. In 1846 a revealing, if apocryphal, story circulated out of Detroit, that when apprentices went on strike there, not enough journeymen could be found to replace them.[17] By the turn of the new decade, workers in New York's 150 printing shops consisted of 1,200 pressmen and compositors and some 800 apprentices.[18] In Philadelphia's book and job houses, apprentices constituted a quarter to a third of all employees.[19] Such conditions, decided a meeting of New Yorkers in 1850, indicated that "the surrender of our business to the unregulated, unlimited operation of the vaunted 'law of supply and demand'—that is, to the law that 'might makes right'—is in effect to empower the least honorable and most avaricious employers."[20] This complaint against unbridled competition became a commonplace among printers. For them, the market revolution was not the harbinger of opportunity so much as a threat to their laboring traditions and livelihoods. They recognized, of course, that some employers were more honorable than others. New York firms, for instance, were owned by both such rugged individualists as Theodore De Vinne and the more corporatistic Russell Brothers. The Russells, when confronted with a strike of Local No. 6 of the ITU, quickly agreed to "pay with pleasure" because they were successful "only with the help of our workers."[21]

Who better typified employers, De Vinne or the Russells? The preponderance of scholarly opinion views De Vinne as representative of the industry as a whole in his reluctance to join together with fellow employers in the name of self-regulation.[22] Charlotte Morgan argues, for instance, that master printers were resistant to collusion precisely because so many of them came up through the ranks and were too individualistic to "submit to union regulations or . . . be bound by employer agreement."[23] Morgan's claim, however, can be reversed. The printer who rose from within also got exposed to the corporatistic tradition that Ely Moore so respected and that imparted an appreciation for the uses of collusion. No Gothamite represented this corporatistic ethos more ably than Horace Greeley, publisher and editor of the *New York Tribune* (1841–1924). Though an employer at the end of the 1840s, Greeley joined the New York Printers' Association, which made him its first president in 1851, because at the time he supported unionism in principle. But Greeley also used his new pulpit to call for an organization of employers. Critics ridiculed him as naive and "impracticable," none more vociferously than the editors of the *Journal of Commerce* (1827–93), the city's leading voice of acquisitive individualism. "Large and strong establishments," they argued in a cold-blooded encomium to free competition, "may think it an object to pay prices sufficiently high to break down the weak ones so they [the large ones] may have the whole ground. Small and weak establishments, on the contrary, are obliged to economize or die." This same imperative applied to prices. "Free competition on both sides," they concluded, "brings justice to all."[24]

Many employers in the 1850s, however, shared Greeley's disposition toward cooperation. Book publishers in New York, followed soon by counterparts in other urban centers, formed publishers' groups and associations.[25] Small towns and provincial cities went along as well. In early 1854, Bay State journalists organized the Association of Editors and Printers of Western Massachusetts to control a chaotic industry floundering for lack of uniform standards. Standing committees on advertising, job printing, labor, and prices drafted policies and proposed rules and regulations that went into effect when approved by the membership as a whole. The committee on advertising, for instance, developed a common scale of prices as well as uniform standards of measurement for particular categories of copy. As if to remind us that it is just as possible to invent markets as it is to control existing ones, the committee also removed meeting notices for civic, social, and religious groups from the category of pro bono work. The labor committee prohibited employment of apprentices who could not certify proper training, a longtime goal of union printers, and proscribed raiding by banning member firms from taking on apprentices already indentured to another firm.[26]

Employer cooperation reached its highest expression in the New York Typothetæ. Formed in 1865 after years of discussion and planning, the Typothetæ was inspired by such luminaries as the Harper brothers, Peter C. Baker, and John F. Trow, all of whom had strenuously resisted the trend toward collusion. They were turned around by a deluge of new entrants into the trade that drove down prices of standard works, and not primarily by an antiunion animus, although that attitude was certainly present. The organization held dinner meetings, published the *American Bookmaker* (1885-97), and encouraged proprietors in other cities to follow its example. The Typothetæ persisted in New York through the 1860s, fell apart in the early 1870s, and then reemerged in the 1880s as a mildly antiunion force that gradually made peace with unionists.[27]

For most of its early incarnation, the Typothetæ in New York focused on "unhealthy competition."[28] Its members counseled better cost accounting and other business practices that improved efficiency in order to divert competitors from the simpler and more harmful solution of underselling. Price-fixing was formally eschewed until the turn of the century, though it would be surprising indeed if it were not tried earlier. The group preferred to have each house serve its own customers, solicit new ones through trade journals and other organs, and sink or swim not in the uncertain sea of price competition but in the calmer waters of high-quality work and niche markets.[29] It is difficult to gauge the impact of Typothetæ policies on publishing practices and price policies. What is clear is that its appearance marked a triumph for corporate voices such as Greeley and Moore who had advocated market regulation to improve labor relations.

Unions

Printers boasted the earliest and most durable trade unions in nineteenth-century America.[30] In 1852, independent locals of journeymen came together as the National Typographical Union (rechristened the International Typographical Union in 1865), the country's first successful national union.[31] The debut of the NTU ended a half century of fitful organization and began thirty years of sustained, if bumpy, development. Its 16 founding locals slipped to a puny 10 by 1855 but rebounded to 34 by 1860. Ten years later, the number of ITU locals had nearly tripled, to just over 90, in part because the civilian labor shortage of the Civil War era gave organized labor increased leverage with employers, but the long and deadly depression of the 1870s collapsed about 20 locals and depleted the ranks of the survivors. The resilient ones, however, launched a massive organizing drive at the turn of the 1880s that left the ITU larger and stronger than ever. By 1885, it had more than eighteen thousand members in 174 locals.[32]

Historians usually attribute this rich tradition of self-organization to the unique psychology of printing. A strong feeling of trade consciousness flowed from a common feeling that there was something special about producing printed work. Few groups of skilled workers evinced deeper or more abiding loyalty to fellow tradesmen.[33] Printers spun a dense network of organizations steeped in reverence for what they called "the craft," from unions to fraternities. Union men suffered no greater insult than being shunned or run out of the trade—declared a "rat" for falling behind in dues payments, scabbing, or violating union rules or craft customs. Philadelphian John F. Keyser was one of many members of Local No. 2 who could not bear the stigma of being blackballed. In 1863 he petitioned for reconsideration of his expulsion for dues arrears, pleading that he would have preferred the humiliation of exposing his "shortcomings if any—but rat, NEVER," adding, "if I have one aspiration above another, it is the good will of my fellow workmen."[34]

To be a printer was to be literate in the English language, to be trained as an apprentice for four to six years, long after apprentice training vanished in other trades, and to count oneself among the "intellectuals of the working class."[35] Printers who enjoyed books or keeping up with the news did not want for reading material. Their household budgets, as we have seen, included impressive expenditures for printed work, and their unions established libraries and reading rooms. Being a printer also meant wearing the trade's signature ink-stained apron, donning a whimsical hat formed of folded newspaper, and speaking a language that derived from the craft and its union tradition ("chapels" were union locals; "fat" was the best and most remunerative work). Community life reinforced the trade consciousness of the workplace, for printers lived cheek by jowl in newer and more respectable neighborhoods.[36] This togetherness extended to life's end, as shopmen and unionists attended funerals of deceased brothers laid to rest in union or fraternal burial plots.[37]

Printers also shared a common ethnic heritage. Most of them in the middle of the nineteenth century were Anglo-Americans of Protestant stock. Even in New York, the greatest immigrant city in the nation in 1850, printing was one of the most ethnically homogeneous industries.[38] It was even more uniformly so in Philadelphia: as much as 80 percent of the city's printers in 1850 were native-born Americans; by 1880 the rate was nearly 90 percent, in spite of the huge influx of Irish and growing numbers of Germans. It was the sons of such immigrants, and not the immigrants themselves, who elbowed their way into the trade in this thirty-year span, and even then only in modest numbers.[39]

Membership was uniformly male. Women entered the printing trade (but not the unions) in appreciable numbers coincident with the steam press in the 1830s, establishing a foothold in aspects of book production over the next two decades. Their appearance aroused the opposition of unionized men, who vowed to resist the feminization of their craft.[40] Such unionists policed the gates of the trade as a whole but proved remarkably effective at keeping women out of composing, the best paid and most unionized segment of the industry.[41]

Much like its predecessors, the ITU was not circumscribed simply by ethnicity and gender. In two important respects, it also encompassed a relatively small swath of the printing industry. It was far more influential in newspaper and journal shops than in book or job houses, and it was restricted to compositors within the larger occupational mix. Compositors far outnumbered pressmen, who typically organized separately out of frustration with their minority status. For their part, the men of the composing room stood out as skilled hands, workers in a crowd of machine tenders, which is to say that they were not simply highly paid but also strategically located in the production process. Everyone knew that everything began with the compositors.

Printers also knew that they worked long and hard for their money. The typical compositor at work on a morning paper following the Civil War got to his station between 10:00 and 11:00 A.M. to prepare his case for the upcoming edition by distributing the type used for the previous edition. This somewhat mundane task, carried out at a casual pace, took about two hours. (Its easy rhythms would be recalled with nostalgia by tradesmen who, late in the century, made the transition to the more feverish work routine attendant upon the linotype machine.) The printer then took a short break to prepare for his first stint of four to five hours of setting type; he broke for dinner for an hour or so and returned to his case about 7:30 P.M., working until all matter was set. He could expect to finish this second stint at midnight but had to remain on the job until 3:00 A.M. or so, working intermittently to set last-minute items and correct copy. In unionized shops or offices with sympathetic employers, printers eased this long regime somewhat by breaking into "phalanxes," teams that alternated between late and early work after midnight, with one team staying late one night, another the next. Phalanxes allowed workers to cut fourteen- to sixteen-hour workdays by two or three hours and to return home before 3:00 A.M. at least three nights per week.[42]

Printing taxed the workman's health as well as his stamina. The question of occupational health was very much on the mind of Frank Foster, the Boston printer and prominent trade unionist who in 1883 testified before a committee of the United States Senate. Foster explained that poorly ventilated composing rooms were not simply uncomfortable; they could be hazardous to the health of workmen who had to inhale the "antimony or black lead that collects in the type especially where the electrotyping process is used, as in book-making." Night work was particularly dangerous, he added, because compositors breathed air "from which the oxygen has been exhausted" by gaslights. Such conditions explained the "unhealthiness of the occupation, and its tendency to shorten life."[43] Small wonder that such workmen, well paid though they were, took to trade unionism.

Union printers combined several tactics to achieve their objectives on the job, beginning with fortifying their ranks in individual shops. Shop committees elected chairmen, or "fathers," who doubled as delegates to the local union's governing body. The New York Typographical Association's 1833 constitution stipulated that chapel heads were to be "experienced journeymen," and for good reason. They were early versions of shop stewards: mediators and negotiators who could not work effectively without the prestige, status, and all-around knowledge of seasoned workers. Fathers were expected to dun members for dues, report rats, and enlist tradesmen on the tramp. They settled disputes between members and resolved differences with employers. They also helped draft rat lists and other communications on trade conditions that circulated freely among locals.[44]

As early as the first decade of the century, the Philadelphia Typographical Society developed the "working card" system, which gradually became a tradewide custom. Once a month, the union distributed working cards to members current in dues payments; those in arrears were given the choice of paying up or being declared rats and ineligible for "berths" in union shops at the highest scales.[45] Working cards evolved into union cards, which carried special significance for printers because of the tramping tradition. Reciprocal agreements between locals in the antebellum years assured a tramp that a bona fide union card issued in one place would be recognized in another.[46] Tramp printers and settled journeymen probably got work through word of mouth or contacts with friends and family. Such informal means, however, caused friction when there were too many applicants for too few jobs. This is why the earliest unions in the trade organized employment bureaus for the jobless, who signed a roll and took berths on the basis of seniority or their place in the queue.[47] We do not know which standard prevailed early on, only that disputes over job rights were usually settled by chapel fathers at the shop level and by union committees higher up.[48]

These basic features developed in the NTU, but they gained wider expression in the ITU after the Civil War.[49] Unions began to pay officers, offer more generous welfare packages (including benefits for the families of Civil War soldiers), and expand their committee structures. In addition to ad hoc committees appointed to deal with emergencies or negotiate with employers, locals empowered standing committees to handle day-to-day affairs. Investigating committees reviewed the background and credentials of applicants for admission and then passed recommendations on to the local for further action. Business committees handed down rulings that could be reversed only by a majority vote of the membership.[50] Union work took hours of voluntary labor.

Unlike other trade unions, printers' organizations included foremen, many of whom were leaders.[51] The president of the ITU paid tribute to such men when he observed that "most of our foremen are, and have always been, the master spirits and hardest workers of our organization."[52] The unionism that represented foremen and journeymen printers, moreover, was tactically precocious in dealing with management. It developed and perhaps pioneered collective bargaining with employers, discarding the take-it-or-leave-it system unions typically practiced before the Civil War.[53] Citywide locals negotiated with publishers as early as the opening decade of the nineteenth century. Philadelphia's printers sometimes appointed committees in between formal talks to discuss differences with employers over wages and work rules.[54] New Yorkers may have established standing grievance committees by the early 1850s, as Local No. 2 in Philadelphia certainly did by 1852.[55]

The business committee, easily Local No. 2's busiest and most important body, could quash grievances, order settlements of disputes, overrule shops poised to strike, and discipline members who violated its rulings. In its work, this committee demonstrated the same mix of pragmatism and principle that had long been the signature of labor relations in the industry. The committee flatly refused to abide violations of what it considered to be matters of craft convention. It routinely ordered strikes against employers who hired nonunion men, violated price lists, or accepted work as subcontractors.[56] But it could be equally hard on employees whose work suffered from flagging competence or alcohol abuse.[57] The committee took a more flexible position on issues that involved gray areas or matters of contract or rule interpretation. It consistently refused to entertain claims from journeymen who sought compensation in excess of union scales or tried to extract extra payment for work not specifically covered in the scales but regulated by custom.[58] The committee took its investigative mission so seriously that at times it embarrassed grievants by uncovering personal animosity masquerading as violations of principle. In April 1860, for example, the Philadelphia business committee heard a complaint against a foreman for culling, that is, diverting the best work to friends and favorites. Following a hearing, the committee ruled that "there has not been one fact sustaining the charge" and went on to apologize to the employer for wasting his time, adding that it "regretted very much that among our membership in your office so much personal feeling should exist, and to which we attribute this trouble and misapprehension."[59] Nor was this unusual. In resolving a complicated dispute among an employer and two foremen in a newspaper shop, the committee observed that "any other decision would most seriously impair that faith which . . . is the intent and purpose of our organization to foster and cultivate."[60] Union officials often found themselves cast in the position of judge or referee in a dynamic but delicately balanced system that required scrupulous attention to the facts in order to retain the trust of fellow unionists and employers alike.

Pragmatism and principle also guided Local No. 2's handling of rats within its ranks. Its investigating committee gradually lengthened the local rat list by naming miscreants. But when the list grew too long and thereby compromised the union, the membership simply declared a general amnesty, readmitted the rats, and started the list anew.[61] Such forgiveness normally occurred after strikes or economic crises in which even the most loyal union men were tempted into taking nonunion work for want of anything else. Hard times tested pragmatism in another way. The union typically responded to economic downturns by incrementally reducing wage scales, partly to spread the work but also to preempt employers from taking the more drastic action of tearing those scales up. Such flexibility did not always work. Having extracted several rounds of wage concessions in the depths of the depression, employers demanded more cuts with the return of prosperity in 1878.[62] Some broke with the union, which had the effect of forcing great numbers of workers to absorb the reductions or quit work in observance of the hoary union rule that prevented union men from working in ratted shops. Local No. 2 (and possibly others as well) resolved this dilemma by allowing workers to apply for permits that waived the rule. The union tried to limit permits to historically cooperative employers forced in the depression to compromise union standards and who, it was assumed, would resume conventional union relations when the crisis passed.[63] Not a few shops, however, got used to their nonunion status; by the early 1880s the membership of Local No. 2 demanded an end to the system. What had been envisioned as a temporary expedient designed to patch up differences among friendly foes had plunged the local into crisis.

Labor Relations

No single model of labor relations dominated the printing industry between 1830 and 1880. Instead, three distinct but somewhat overlapping tendencies coexisted before the period of mature job control in which something approaching the "equilibrium of power" that printer Ely Moore had described in 1833 was achieved. For the sake of convenience, we might call these tendencies entrepreneurial, fraternal, and corporatist, with the caveat that some features were shared, sometimes in one individual, and that individuals who hewed to a tendency at one point could later embrace another one.

Entrepreneurialism, simply put, valued rapid capital accumulation and unilateral control of the workplace above all else—above the fraternal traditions of the trade, above traditional obligations to fellow employers and employees, and above the demands of unionized workers. It was an emergent tendency that motivated the innovators who transformed printing from a craft to a modern industry. Hard-driving employers in the newspaper end of the business were its exemplars, even though entrepreneurs predominated in book and job publishing. The Boston book printer James L. Homer was an early practitioner. In an 1836 speech about the ten-hour workday to the members of the Massachusetts Charitable Mechanic Association (MCMA), he cursed the short-hours movement as an insidious import of European origins that had to be fought at all costs. He invited the membership of the MCMA to join him in a scheme to "bring master, journeymen, and apprentices together . . . upon a footing of courtesy, kindness and respect," by funding a building for an institute with social and educational programs designed to heal the social wounds opened by the recent labor unrest.[64] This feeble reform impressed no one. It fell on an audience of triumphant proprietors who had just defeated workmen on strike for a ten-hour workday for the third time in ten years.

One MCMA member who did not fully appreciate Homer's acquisitiveness was Joseph Tinker Buckingham, a leading newspaper editor and publisher and recent past president of the MCMA. Though personally crusty, treacherously outspoken, and fiercely independent-minded, Buckingham represented printing's more fraternal tradition, at least at this point in a career that took him from qualified support for a shorter workday prescribed by law to active opposition. He benefited from the trade's reciprocal ethic. Having founded a journal shortly after the War of 1812, he turned for help to fellow printers in nearby shops who lent him equipment and allowed him to set portions of text requiring exotic typefaces in their offices.[65] In the early 1830s, craft fraternalism extended to his own workers, who so admired their employer that they helped him get through personal hardship and elude debtor's prison by volunteering to defer wage payments until he balanced the books.[66] He returned their favor by openly scolding fellow employers for resisting the ten-hour movement and possibly by reducing his workers' hours.[67] Men like Buckingham valued moderation and restraint in pursuit of self-interest, even as they came to terms with the market revolution. The "chief good," he once said, derived from "subdued appetites, disciplined passions, temperate habits, moderate desires, and well-informed minds."[68]

Restraint was also a central feature of the corporatist ethos. The difference was that in the corporatist context restraint was accomplished by organization — that is, by unions of workers and trade associations of employers. The union enforced work rules, developed by the tradesmen, that subordinated the interests of the individual worker to the trade as a whole. The union also enforced contracts with individual printing houses, or preferably with printers' associations. The key to such arrangements, and to corporatism itself, was the self-organization of workers and employers alike. Without unions, rule enforcement was weak and contracts an impossibility; without trade associations, contracts were limited in scope as well as difficult to negotiate and enforce.

Such tendencies persisted beyond the Civil War. Horace Greeley, for instance, was something of a latter-day Buckingham, a man of "the craft" suspicious of excessive acquisitiveness and quite prepared to meet his journeymen halfway. Homer had a successor in Theodore De Vinne, the tough-minded New Yorker who spoke the idiom of entrepreneurial individualism and brooked no interference in running his shop, but who, at the same time, was a founding member of the Typothetæ, the employers' organization formed to discipline the market. For such men, there was no direct correspondence between one's positions on market regulation and on trade unionism. Some of the same proprietors who eagerly promoted collective control of product markets by the 1860s were not necessarily tolerant of unionism. At the same time, their acceptance of self-organization indicates just how far they had moved from the uncompromising individualism of James Homer. They moved far enough, it turned out, to accept a form of unionism that promised to standardize wages and conditions.

Print unionism after midcentury developed within this institutional context of evolving trade associationism. In the quarter century before the formation of the NTU in 1852, journeymen had struggled to maintain pay scales by constraining competition in wage and labor markets. They had more, if uneven and often fleeting, success over the next thirty years. "Every addition to the number of laborers in the market reduces their power; while the power of capital grows in a ratio commensurate with the increase of . . . capital itself," read the preamble to the *Constitution of Journeymen Printers* in 1850.[69] Unions redoubled efforts to establish citywide wage scales and restrict the number of apprentices in newspaper and book offices.[70] More and more employers began to see the advantage afforded by common labor costs in negotiated settlements with union locals.[71]

Organized printers simultaneously enjoyed a qualified breakthrough on enforcement of apprentice training. Apart from wage scales, no issue loomed larger in journeymen's circles than apprenticeship. Poorly or partially trained labor was cheap labor that necessarily flattened skills and eroded livelihoods of properly trained workmen. Such workers had clashed repeatedly with rat employers who violated training norms.[72] The delegate convention of the NTU in 1853 urged recognition of the five-year training period and called on locals to do away with apprentices in newspaper shops, but it left enforcement to subordinate unions. Locals adopted rules setting journeyman-to-apprentice ratios (usually 5:1) and capping the number of apprentices per shop. Stronger and bolder locals sought to enforce the recommended ban on apprentices in newspaper offices, limiting trainees to book and job shops. While such action made for uneven conditions between the major branches of the trade, local unions in this way resurrected a training system long since dead in most handicrafts and badly wounded in their own. Even the freewheeling book publishers in New York, who were represented by the Typothetæ in the late 1860s, eventually came around. Having fought off a training clause in the 1869 agreement signed with Local No. 6, they were brought to heel by a strike that established the union's preferred ratio of one apprentice per five workers, along with a cap of five apprentices per office.[73] The duration of this arrangement remains unclear. A committee that looked into the New York situation in the mid-1880s found apprentice training weak or nonexistent. It seems to have persisted elsewhere, however, and may have been revived in New York as well in the 1890s, when the age of the linotype arrived.[74]

Foremen were not nearly so controversial as apprentices. No one doubted that they were the most important figures in major shops by midcentury, least of all the NTU itself, which early on recognized their authority.[75] One of its first rules stated that "the foreman of an office is the proper person to whom application should be made for employment; and it is enjoined upon subordinates that they disapprove of any other mode of application."[76] Though this law helped legitimate the authority of the foreman, it hardly guaranteed his prosaic acceptance on shop floors. Critical voices heard from time to time in the 1860s built into a movement in the 1870s to expel foremen from the union for playing favorites in hiring and firing, distributing work, and designating "substitutes" to spell regular printers.[77] The movement sputtered but still reinforced the trend evident from the union's first days of circumscribing foremen's power. Rules and regulations for hiring and firing, bringing on substitutes, assigning work, and distributing fat came in gradual succession, first as work rules in local union books and then as general laws approved by the annual convention or as contract provisions.[78]

Progress, however, was patchy. Even though ITU locals weathered the depression of the 1870s, printers came perilously close to losing their union during the decade. Several convergent forces severely weakened and nearly destroyed what had become one of the most powerful craft unions in the nation. The experience of Philadelphia's Local No. 2 offers a close-up view of this brush with disaster.

The first sign of trouble predated the depression but prefigured the combative labor relations it would bring. In December 1871, the *Evening Bulletin* (1847–1982), one of the largest unionized newspapers in Philadelphia, unilaterally imposed a wage cut instead of reaching agreement with the union. The company rescinded the cut in the face of a strike but later reimposed it and broke with the local in January 1872. The *Bulletin*'s toughness began an antiunion drive that cost the local several shops and loosened its hold on many more.[79] This unmistakable trend strengthened significantly in cases where investors with no experience in publishing bought out traditional owners and installed their own managers. Several Philadelphia firms went through this cycle, most notably the *Press* (1857–1920), one of the largest papers in the city and for years a loyal union shop. Before it was sold in 1877, the *Press* broke relations with Local No. 2; the new owner, a wealthy iron founder from Pittsburgh, made reconciliation appear much more unlikely.[80] From the union's perspective, it did not matter whether proprietors came from within the trade. The resistant owners were supported by their membership in the Employing Printers of Philadelphia and aided by the long depression. Wage rates reflected the new vulnerability. Local No. 2 made incremental concessions on wage scales that gradually reduced the standard rate at the end of the decade to between 35¢ and 40¢ per thousand ems, from nearly 50¢ at its start.[81]

It was not a simple matter, however, of employers bludgeoning union men into submission. Both printers and publishers used the carrot as deftly as the stick. Some offered the most accomplished workers guaranteed lifetime employment in return for trashing their union cards; others paid union scales for a freer hand on work rules; still others recognized union work rules but not the pay scale. The result was an economic free-for-all that shredded the uniform conditions printers had long identified as the primary goal of unionism. For its part, Local No. 2 unwittingly abetted antiunionism in 1878 with the permits that allowed members to work in union shops that suspended union rules. What had been conceived as a temporary policy to help traditionally friendly employers through hard times backfired by the end of the decade. Grievants among the rank and file in the early 1880s first complained that union and nonunion men were "working indiscriminately together," in violation of the local's announced policy.[82] Then, in what became a rebellion from within, they assailed the leadership as weak, vacillating, and much too inclined to compromise.[83] Reports surfaced that "roving bands of rats" drove union men from the shops, that a rival union operated secretly, and that one-time union stalwarts were behind the mischief.[84]

This commotion exposed the weakness of Local No. 2. Several times at the turn of the 1870s the membership set up committees on the "state of the trade," only to hear reports that grew more gloomy and despairing. An 1878 assessment found the union in "sad condition," with half the membership in arrears, pervasively apathetic, and feeling that the union was of "no benefit."[85] Another report in 1880 found wildly uneven standards across the city and an enfeebled union represented in only half of the city's newspapers — and even then in a compromised way. The committee urged its readers to consider the national crisis in labor relations, a crisis abetted by an unsympathetic press and antagonistic owners. It was a great achievement, the report concluded, to have survived such a hostile climate at all and further proof that Local No. 2 was "the strongest local trade organization on the continent of North America." While the local's survival was not in dispute, there was plenty of doubt about its strength and capacity. Try as it might to gild the lily of the local, the report could not help but regret the "lukewarmness of the membership" and "defections from our ranks."[86]

This combination of internal weakness and external hostility explains why revitalization plans launched between 1878 and 1882 fell flat. Demoralized, stymied by their own lassitude, and responsive to employers who traded benefits for loyalty, most members simply yawned at a group of militants clamoring for job actions. Morale picked up in late 1882 following a failed but spirited strike the previous winter. Another state-of-the-trade report discarded the defeatism of its predecessors in favor of a proposal for a five-day workweek and abolition of the permit system. Over the next few years, this committee and its successors pursued strategic objectives through a tactical plan that had three aspects. The union appealed to the residual corporatistic instincts of the city's proprietors by promising to funnel work to union shops and away from ratted offices and by vowing to standardize wages and conditions, which punished "unfair" offices and benefited fair ones.[87] This gesture of ingratiation went in tandem with an overhaul of the union that featured a limited amnesty for those delinquent with their dues as well as a vigorous organizing drive that turned a celebration of Pennsylvania's bicentennial into a labor demonstration replete with parade and speeches.[88] Finally, and perhaps most important, Local No. 2 reached out to fellow workers in several reviving craft unions, joined the craft unionists' Central Labor Union, and cultivated cordial relations with the Knights of Labor as well as labor reform groups that emerged in the course of the decade.[89] Leaders pressed such allies for support of a massive consumer boycott of the city's press, drawing on labor's most effective weapon before the great upheaval of 1886.[90]

The turning point for Local No. 2 came two years later, in 1884, in the midst of a struggle with the *Evening News* (1879–1925). A Republican daily founded five years earlier at Local No. 2's low point, the *News* in early 1884 had second thoughts about its initial decision to recognize the union. Planning to sack the staff and rehire only those who agreed to renounce the union, the *News* inadvertently tipped its hand by inserting advertisements for replacement workers in the local press. When management refused to confirm rumors of the impending shake-up, the union authorized a walkout. Its tactics show why the mid-1880s marked a divide between the old fraternalism and the new militancy. The night the strike (or lockout, as the local called it) broke out, a delegation representing the shop committee called on the *News* management in their West Philadelphia homes. The president was evasive; his assistant refused to talk; another manager went on sleeping because his wife declined to wake him. The men then went beyond the familiar actions of the past by asking their business committee to declare a boycott, enlisting the support of local newsboys as well as fellow unionists in the region. This stronger measure turned the tide, for at an emergency meeting the *News* management suddenly called off the lockout, rehired the workers, and recognized the union.[91]

The *News* lockout and boycott proved the catalyst of an organizing campaign in which the union worked energetically and effectively with its own resources, fellow unionists, and newly found friends and allies. The local next called a boycott of the *Press*, the hostile daily that had humiliated the local some years earlier, and it went to unprecedented lengths to enforce the action: forming a boycott committee that worked with local and distant unions, distributing tens of thousands of leaflets to more than two hundred unions, and securing the endorsement of the Short-Hours League, a coalition of clerics and reformers.[92] Throughout the next year, the boycott committee coordinated its efforts with an expanding front of middle-class groups, and in October 1885 the Central Labor Union and the Knights of Labor joined forces to support the general boycott of "rat papers." Only a month later, the *Evening Bulletin* and the *North American* caved in.[93]

The victory over the *Bulletin* had the same impact as the *Evening News* job action a year before. It reinvigorated the ranks and built new momentum, so much so that the local hired an organizer, its first ever, to take full advantage of the stunning reversal. Organizer James Harper registered record numbers of members, and union negotiators gradually signed up more newspapers and journals over the next few months, bringing the rest of the city's mainstream press back into the fold.[94] The addition of printing offices that had cut the union adrift and operated with nonunion labor hit a snag over the admission of former scabs who had earned the affection of their employers and the hatred of a vocal faction of the union. Discussions nearly broke down completely when the employers insisted on blanket readmission of the men — their version of a general amnesty — as the condition for union recognition. The most controversial of these cases understandably involved the hated *Press*, the first paper that broke with the local and the one targeted by the boycott of the early 1880s. Emotions still ran high in talks with the *Press* over admission of its staff. When the union team brought a peace offering to the regular meeting, an angry member moved to demand "unconditional surrender." The motion lost, 159 to 33, and the *Press* rejoined the expanding bloc of union houses.[95]

This rebirth of trade unionism came on the heels of the revitalization and reformation of trade associationism. Members of the Employing Printers of Philadelphia shed their antiunion animus in the upsurge of union militancy during the mid-1880s. Although this friendlier version of their persistent corporatist ethos helped improve labor relations, it was not the only source of class harmony. Even the most friendly employers, after all, turned against the union in the depression of the 1870s. Perhaps it took the ensuing burst of competition — the inconsistent wage standards and uneven conditions — to convince renegade employers that they had more to gain than to lose in some form of corporatism. For an observer such as Charles A. Francis, the journeyman-turned-foreman who later became a publisher and an authority on the industry, it was clear that the force of the union had brought employers around. Given his dual perspective from the shop floor and the front office, Francis probably understood labor relations in printing better than any other commentator of his generation. Its unions, he concluded, "have been the real upbuilders of the printing industry . . . and the employers have simply followed."[96]

LABOR AND LABOR ORGANIZATION

If the corporatistic regime that Francis knew so well was never particularly secure in the nineteenth century, neither was it the product of one union. Granted, the organizational achievements of the 1880s owed partly to the agency of the ITU, but they also stemmed from the work of fellow unionists in other crafts and industrial unions in the Knights of Labor, the American Federation of Labor, and even lowly newsboys who rallied to the printers' cause at a critical moment. Put another way, a beleaguered class had come to the aid of a besieged craft that managed to elude the declension that has been the fate of tradesmen since the earliest days of the Industrial Revolution. One can only wonder if John Funnell, the printer whose demeaning remarks about lesser workers opened this chapter, quite understood.

CHAPTER 3

Authors and Literary Authorship

Susan S. Williams

· · ·

In 1821 sixteen-year-old Nathaniel Hawthorne wrote to his mother about what career he might choose. Having ruled out the traditional genteel professions — the ministry, law, and medicine — he proposed a riskier plan. "What do you think of my becoming an Author, and relying for support upon my pen," he asked. "Indeed I think the illegibility of my handwriting is very authorlike. How proud you would feel to see my works praised by the reviewers, as equal to proudest productions of the scribbling sons of John Bull."[1] Hawthorne did eventually support himself by his pen (though not as well as he would have liked) and saw his works praised by reviewers and endorsed by a prominent publisher. What is striking about his letter, however, is not only how well he anticipated his own career but also how clearly he identified the most salient problems of authorship in the mid-nineteenth century. To what extent was authorship a profession? Did earning money for one's writing cheapen or increase its artistic value? What was the relationship among authors, reviewers, and readers? And for an American author, what did the desire to be judged equal to the British "sons of John Bull" suggest about the transatlantic dimensions of authorship?

Literary historians often contrast two discrete types of nineteenth-century American authors: the "romantic genius" (male, white, antipopular, original, and in frequent conflict with the growing market for print) and the "popular writer" (often female, derivative, and catering to a commercial market). An exacting history of authorial self-conception demands that we scrutinize such contrasts. Herman Melville, for example, began his career by writing South Seas adventure stories that he hoped would sell and then moved to write works that he felt sure would alienate readers and reviewers alike. Louisa May Alcott reversed this pattern, moving from the self-consciously philosophical novel *Moods* (1864) to works commissioned for a particular popular audience, such as the "girls' book" *Little Women* (1868–69). Such examples suggest that female authors often aimed to achieve "high art" just as their male counterparts did and that male authors were often just as eager for an audience as their female contemporaries. Other authors challenged the very binaries of "literary" and "popular," or "high" and "low" art. Ralph Waldo Emerson's famous call for a poet who would know "the value of our incomparable materials" articulated a fundamental challenge for the American author: how to be representative of the country while also following one's individual artistic vision.[2]

Richard Brodhead has usefully called for a history of authorship that is a history of "acts — successful, failed, and partially achieved — by which potential authors have made themselves into authors within the opportunities and obstructions of particular social situations."[3] Applying such a historical framework to our period, several trends emerge. Between 1840 and 1880, many authors demonstrated a growing understanding of, and complex relation to, the literary market, seeking more protective copyright laws, more generous contracts, and greater earnings. They understood that relating to that market was not always a simple choice between resistance and collusion. Instead, they increasingly adopted authorial strategies that enabled them to succeed in the literary market on their own terms. Those strategies reflected the growing tensions between conceptions of the author as genius and as chronicler of everyday reality. As authors became more adept at marketing their writings, they realized the value of celebrity. Publishers too embraced this new social being — the author who stood apart from his or her own writing and commanded an audience based on personal as well as literary interest. By the 1880s, authorship was for many writers a rewarding occupation — one that could, as Hawthorne had suggested in the letter to his mother, both provide an income and stand on the same cultural plane as the ministry, law, or medicine.

The Author and the Market

The decades between 1840 and 1880 witnessed an unprecedented growth not only in the production of print but also in the payments that authors received for their work. Prior to the emergence of a trade-publishing system in the United States, the costs, risks, and profits of a publication could involve a variety of parties: printers, publishers, subscribers, and authors. By mid-century, however, trade publishers had become the entrepreneurs of literary production. While they sometimes purchased a manuscript outright or asked authors to share in production costs, these publishers usually financed the books they agreed to publish and coordinated their manufacture and production. Authors typically received a royalty, usually a percentage of the retail price, on each book sold. Terms varied, but 10 percent was common.[4] In 1848 Edgar Allan Poe signed a contract with G. P. Putnam that stipulated receiving

10 percent royalties for the prose poem *Eureka*, while in 1856 Ticknor and Fields paid Henry Wadsworth Longfellow a royalty of 20 percent of the retail price for copies of *Evangeline* bound in boards, a number that reflects not only his popularity but also the fact that he had the capital to invest in his own stereotype plates.[5] The manufacture of such plates, however, was only a small percentage of the total production cost. In 1872 Roberts Brothers claimed that each copy of its edition of Theophilus Parsons's *The Infinite and the Finite* — a spiritualist work by a noted jurist that sold for $1 per copy — netted publisher and author each only 10¢, with 15¢ going to the papermaker, 15¢ to the bookbinder, 10¢ divided between the printer and stereotyper, and 40¢ to the retail bookseller.[6]

Out of nineteen extant contracts that New York publisher Moses Dodd signed in the 1850s, five were for the outright purchase of manuscripts, and five others shared costs with authors; nine provided royalties for authors.[7] Boston's Ticknor and Fields, a firm that specialized in belles lettres, was probably more representative of trade publishers generally: in 1856 it published only two books that did not pay royalties. Throughout the 1840s and 1850s, according to Michael Winship, the "great majority of Ticknor and Fields publications by American authors were published under a royalty agreement."[8] Some publishers utilized half-profits agreements with their authors, where both risks and profits of publication were shared, although this arrangement was more common in England than in the United States.[9] During his early career, Herman Melville entered into such agreements with Harper & Brothers: he and the Harpers split the profits after the costs of manufacturing the book had been paid. With the publication of *Pierre* in 1852, however, the Harpers converted to a royalty agreement under which Melville received one-fifth of the retail price after the first 1,190 copies had been sold.[10] Under both the royalty and half-profits systems, the publisher had the upper hand in record keeping, and authors frequently complained that they received vague or padded account statements. Yet as publishers became increasingly sophisticated in managing advertising and retail sales, authors grew more dependent on them for editorial advice and royalties.

Throughout this period, the burgeoning number of magazines became an important source of income for many writers. While authors and critics often assumed that book publication constituted the artistic height of success, magazine publication often proved more economically beneficial. Even beginners could be compensated well for their contributions. Susan Warner, who later wrote a best seller, received $50 for an 1850 essay titled "Female Patriotism" that kept her father, sister, and herself clothed through the winter. A decade later, Rebecca Harding Davis, writing from West Virginia, was grati-

fied when she received the same amount from the *Atlantic Monthly* (1857–)
for her first story, "Life in the Iron Mills" (1861); by 1862 she was receiving
$8 a page from the *Atlantic Monthly* and $300 for a single story in *Peterson's
Magazine* (1842–92).[11] An 1867 article titled "The Pay of Authors" reported
that the *Atlantic Monthly* paid $10 per page, the *Galaxy* (1866–78) $5 per
page of five hundred words, and *Harper's New Monthly Magazine* (1850–) $5
per page of one thousand words. Periodical poetry received less: the *Atlantic
Monthly* paid Julia Ward Howe $5 for "The Battle Hymn of the Republic" in
1851, although a year earlier it had paid Longfellow $50 for "The Children's
Hour."[12] Publishers of story papers and cheap fiction paid even higher sums:
Joseph Holt Ingraham claimed to Longfellow in 1846 that he had earned more
than $3,000 the previous year writing twenty novels "published in the news-
papers."[13]

Henry James's career provides a case study of the way in which authors
could move from periodical publishing to royalty contracts during this period. When he published his first magazine article in 1864, James received
only $12. Following the success of *The Portrait of a Lady* (1881), the *Atlan-
tic Monthly* raised his rate of pay from $10 to $15 per page. James serialized
most of his longer works (receiving $250 for each of fourteen installments of
Portrait in the *Atlantic Monthly*), and then brought them out as books, from
which he received royalties. He actively sought out the publishers who would
pay him the most, thereby challenging the practices of trade courtesy (see
Chapter 4, Part 3). James's strategies contrasted notably with his father's long
experience with publishers. Henry James Sr. published twelve books in his
lifetime but always paid for the printing plates and paper himself. He advised
his son to do the same. When the younger James published his first two books
in 1875, he published one using his father's method, paying for the plates and
receiving a 15 percent royalty, and one using the standard trade publishing
method, assuming no expenses himself and receiving a 10 percent royalty.
He did not recover the cost of the printing plates until more than thirty years
later, and after that initial trial he always negotiated for his publishers to pay
for the plates.[14]

James's case seems to sketch an upward trajectory in which American publishers assumed more risk, including growing expenses for advertising and
promotion, on behalf of increasingly well-paid authors. In fact, the situation
was not so straightforward, particularly in the wake of rising costs following
the Civil War. Seeking to control their costs, some publishers began paying a
set price rather than a percentage royalty. This method brought a decrease in
real income for some authors as retail prices increased. Mary Abigail Dodge
followed the advice of her publisher, Ticknor and Fields, and moved in the

1860s from the 10 percent royalty she had received for her first book to 15¢ per copy on subsequent ones. When she realized that such an arrangement gave her less than 10 percent (her books were retailing for $2), she challenged her publisher, taking the firm through arbitration, for which she received a $1,250 cash settlement and the promise of 10 percent royalties thereafter.[15] Maria Cummins similarly went from receiving a 10 percent royalty on her first two novels to 15 percent on her third and then 30¢ per copy for her 1864 novel *Haunted Hearts*. This flat payment did not keep pace with the rising retail price of the novel, as a percentage royalty would have. *Haunted Hearts* retailed at $1.50 in 1865 and $2.50 in 1866, which made the payment of 30¢ the equivalent of 20 percent and 12 percent royalties, respectively. Given the instability of the American market, Cummins also worked to protect her rights to English editions of her works. Because the House of Lords had decided in *Jefferys v. Boosey* (1854) that foreign authors could gain British copyright only if they were in Britain at the time of publication, in the spring of 1860 Cummins traveled to London in anticipation of the publication of the English edition of *El Fureidîs*. Four years later, she went to Canada for the British publication of *Haunted Hearts*, a step that led to a legal dispute about whether a temporary stay in a British colony could fulfill the residency requirement.[16]

Authors did not always prove adept at business. Cummins's letters from England in 1860 suggest one reason why: the intimate relations between authors and publishers made it difficult to discuss business. "I came here on business, to be sure," Cummins wrote to her mother, "but that relation is not wholly lost in one of friendship & hospitality." She then proceeded to describe the dinners, shopping, and other entertainments she had enjoyed with her publisher and his family. After this intimacy, "I really had no discretion in the advertising & have scarcely any in the matter of the title page," Cummins concluded.[17] Women writers felt this lack of "discretion" particularly keenly, given social constructions of female propriety. Yet men also sometimes felt this constraint. According to his widow, Sophia, Hawthorne never demanded from Ticknor and Fields any written contracts or statements. Some authors avoided the business aspects of publishing altogether by letting others negotiate for them. Harriet Beecher Stowe consulted her sister, who advised her to arrange for a half-profits contract for *Uncle Tom's Cabin* (1852), but left the final details of the contract to her husband, who eventually agreed to the publisher's demand for a 10 percent royalty. Stowe subsequently received royalty payments of $20,300 in 1852, but always suspected that she could have earned more. After 1854, Stowe's works were published by a different firm.[18] Susan Warner's father circulated *The Wide, Wide World* (1850) among publishers, and he probably also negotiated the contract with George Palmer Putnam for the book's publication. Warner herself stayed with Putnam and his family while she was going over proofs, but she did not know, because she was hesitant to ask, whether her book would be stereotyped. A full week passed before Putnam's wife asked the question for her.[19] In *A Battle of the Books* (1870), a thinly veiled critique of Ticknor and Fields, Dodge countered such authorial avoidance by advising writers to "deal with publishers, not like women and idiots, but as business men with business men. If an author chooses to . . . make an outright gift of the profits to his publishers, he may leave the whole matter in their hands; but if he condescends to take any part in the spoils, he thereby becomes a business partner."[20]

Author-centered market studies frequently portray such "business" as an adversarial force that distracted writers from their real work and constrained their choice of subject matter or form. Yet some of the authors most often described as having been in conflict with the business of the market were also those who exploited connections to gain access to that market. Herman Melville wrote *Moby-Dick* (1851) as a book that would challenge the literary market through its bold style and its disregard for a popular audience. But in doing so, he was inspired by a prominent literary mentor, Nathaniel Hawthorne, and he had the support of an influential editor, Evert A. Duyckinck. Moreover, despite the challenges of reading the book, *Moby-Dick* was brought out by prestigious English and American publishers, gained some positive reviews, and by 1854 had sold 2,390 of the 2,915 copies of its first American printing. Its combined British and American sales earned Melville $1,259.45 — a substantial amount of money, but still only a twentieth of what Stowe had earned in one year for *Uncle Tom's Cabin*.[21] After the Civil War, Melville turned to writing poetry, but sales of his books were declining. The production costs of *Clarel: A Poem and Pilgrimage in the Holy Land* (1876), an epic poem published by G. P. Putnam's Sons, were covered with $1,200 he received in a bequest from an uncle. This money "covered the printing expenses," Melville wrote to his cousin, but "the supplementary charges . . . advertising, &c, and customary copies distributed for advertising purposes" would cost an additional $100 (which his cousin paid).[22]

If the story of Melville's career is one of a fall from popularity to obscurity, it is also significant that he had family resources from which he could draw. In this respect, Melville's celebrated unpopularity as an author is categorically different from that of those who had virtually no support. The late 1850s is often seen as a particularly bleak period in Melville's career, when he conducted a lecture tour without much profit, searched in vain for a publisher for a book of poetry, and attempted to procure a foreign diplomatic appointment. The late 1850s is also the time when the African American writer Harriet

Wilson was trying in vain to find an audience for her fictionalized autobiography, *Our Nig* (1859). The book was printed anonymously and inexpensively by George C. Rand in Boston, but its sale was left to Wilson herself. Rand, whose printing office was two blocks away from the headquarters of the Massachusetts Anti-Slavery Society and the American Anti-Slavery Society, was an abolitionist who had printed Stowe's *Uncle Tom's Cabin* for its publisher, John P. Jewett. But he did not publicize Wilson's book (despite advertising his printing services in local business directories and newspapers), and she found buyers not among the abolitionist community in Boston but rather among young white readers in her town of Milford, New Hampshire.[23] Indeed, *Our Nig* registered the paucity of publishing opportunities for black writers by placing literary labor in a kind of artisanal exchange economy. The main character, Frado, peddles her story to individuals in much the same way that she peddles the hats she makes working for a seamstress. Wilson imagined the market as a site of reciprocal economic relations, rather than of sales to anonymous masses. The same year *Our Nig* appeared, Thomas Hamilton started the *Anglo-African Magazine* (1859–60), the first African American monthly magazine. This magazine published the work of Martin Delany and Frances Watkins Harper, albeit without compensation ("the publisher has not yet been able to pay" the contributors, an editorial note explained at the end of the first volume, "for which we present our loving thanks").[24]

The comparison between Melville and Wilson makes clear that the modern notion of the romantic struggling artist needs to be understood within a historically specific continuum of economic hardship. When Hawthorne wrote to his mother that he wanted to support himself by the pen, he did not yet fully understand what the work would entail and the kinds of business deals that it would require. In the 1830s and 1840s, he wrote short stories and sketches that were published, often anonymously, in magazines and literary annuals, and eventually these pieces were collected and published as books. Since this writing did not pay him well enough to support his family, he supplemented his writing income by working in the Boston Custom House and as the surveyor of the Port of Salem, and in the 1850s as the American consul in Liverpool. In 1837 he earned $108, or just over $1 per page, for eight tales published in Samuel Goodrich's literary annual *The Token* (1828–42). In the same year, Eliza Leslie, a writer and editor affiliated with another annual, *The Gift* (1836–45), earned $350 for her literary work.[25] Such a comparison may seem at first to point to "a gendered tradition of entrepreneurship" that associated "women's writing more with moneymaking than with art-for-art's sake."[26] In this view, Leslie would have been more willing to negotiate for a competitive salary — especially given the fact that she, unlike Hawthorne, could not at the same time be working in the Custom House. But male writers were just as concerned with money as women. Hawthorne, for one, regretted the fact that Goodrich did not pay him better for his work. As he put it twenty years later, Goodrich was "a not unkindly man, in spite of his propensity to feed and fatten himself on better brains than his own. . . . His quarrel with me was, that I broke away from him before he had quite finished his meal."[27]

It is important to repeat that authors were not faced with a simple choice of making money or pursuing art. As the description above suggests, Hawthorne accepted the idea that he should enter the marketplace and be paid competitively for his work. Like many of the Transcendentalists with whom he associated, he thought that being paid was a necessary condition for making his work available to the public. As Emerson wrote in his journal in 1836, "The philosopher, the priest, hesitates to receive money for his instructions, — the author for his works. Instead of this scruple let them make filthy lucre beautiful by its just expenditure."[28] Hawthorne's primary concern seems to have been the extent to which he could control his writing in the marketplace. His stories and sketches were frequently reprinted without his consent or payment. A benefit of his close association with Ticknor and Fields, which began with the publication of *The Scarlet Letter* (1850), was that the firm orchestrated the publication and circulation of his work in a more controlled and deliberate way, and this orchestration helped position Hawthorne as a prominent American author (Fig. 3.1). The publisher also paid Hawthorne a 15 percent royalty for *The Scarlet Letter*. Under this arrangement, he received $663.75 in 1850 — considerably more than the $1 per page *The Token* had paid him, but less than many other authors were earning.[29]

As the examples of Melville, Wilson, and Hawthorne suggest, most mid-nineteenth-century literary authors were neither wholly divorced from the market nor wholly shaped by it. Instead, they balanced their authorial rights against the advantages afforded by an increasingly large and variegated literary market. Case studies of particular authors, then, need to attend to the author's own self-understanding of his or her profession and the host of external factors — grouped together under the rubric of the "literary market" — that influenced those self-understandings. The authors' letters, diaries, and published works give one body of evidence; publishing contracts, advertisements, reviews, sales records, and correspondence with readers, editors, and publishers constitute another.

Over the past fifty years, book historians and literary critics have mined this evidence to create descriptive bibliographies and case studies of authorial careers. Scholarly attention to the material aspects of authorship — quite often framed as the conditions of the literary market — has also often led lit-

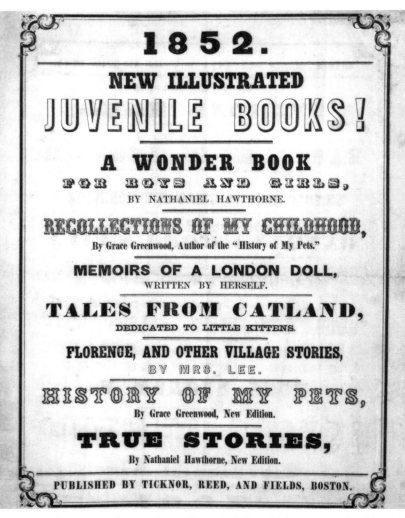

FIGURE 3.1. "1852. New Illustrated Juvenile Books!" (broadside, 39 x 33 cm). This advertisement constitutes one strategy by which Ticknor, Reed, and Fields promoted Nathaniel Hawthorne's reputation and actively marketed his books. American Antiquarian Society.

erary critics to describe the market and authorial agency as inherently opposed rather than as mutually constitutive. This group of scholars, which practices the "subversion model of criticism,"[30] focuses on the ways in which original authors attempted both to court and to distinguish themselves from an increasingly mass public, becoming simultaneously professionals with a particular expertise and cultural apostles or ambassadors who emphasized public good over personal material gain. More recently, scholars have begun recasting this notion of subversion, seeing authors less as embattled "prophets in the marketplace" than as part of a larger communications circuit that blurred the boundary between literary and sociopolitical activity. In this light, authors' editorial work or translations become as interesting as their "original" work, and previously devalued genres — sketches, occasional verse, magazine writing — become newly legible under the rubric of "authorship." This expanding notion of authorship — now more typically viewed as "writing" more generally — makes tracing the history of authorship all the more challenging. Given the shifting nature of the critical lenses through which we read the history of authorship, it becomes particularly important to see the ways in which nineteenth-century authors and critics defined literary labor.

Characterizing Authors

Since the posthumous publication of William Charvat's *The Profession of Authorship in America* (1968), the keyword associated with nineteenth-century authorship has been "profession." Charvat argued that James Fenimore Cooper was the United States' first professional author, and it has become a mainstay of book history to think about the wages of professionalism in both economic and social terms. The emphasis on the economic side of professionalism has motivated the many marketplace studies, although scholars have also attended to the public role of the professional author and how authors labored to justify their writing as socially important work. The latter studies have typically focused on the postbellum period, which is often associated with the rise of literary realism. Yet one of the first things to notice about nineteenth-century definitions of authorship is that a concern with the profession of authorship runs throughout the period. As early as 1821, Hawthorne was considering what profession he should join, with authorship being one of them. By 1870, a book reviewer in a popular periodical could conclude even more specifically that "the writing of novels has become one of the regular professions."[31] And by 1891, Rebecca Harding Davis could look back at the changing status of women writers during the period and conclude that authorship was "a profession with many castes, but fewer Pariahs in it than any other."[32] These evolving views suggest that, although writers and critics described authorship as a profession throughout the period, the definition of what constituted professional work continued to shift. In 1821 Hawthorne worried that writing was a form of devil's work of which his mother would not approve; by 1870, novel writing — previously the least valued kind of authorship — had become its own profession. Authorship itself had many subgroups, or castes, in Davis's phrase, but it was also a profession that offered relative ease of access.

The question of such access was also a recurrent theme throughout the period. How should the castes organize themselves? Who possessed the highest social cachet, and who received the most money? More recent literary history has tended to organize these castes in hierarchical terms, with the authors who were the most original and the most "distinctively American" being at the top; the writers of ephemera at the bottom; and the various kinds of popular writing (including travel narratives, poetry, sketches, slave narratives, and sentimental novels) somewhere in between. In creating such an organization, historians could take their cue from a number of nineteenth-century sources. In 1825, for example, an essay in the *United States Literary Gazette* (1824–26) argued that authors were "producers" who created something new, while writers were passive consumers who merely repeated the ideas of others. A writer's thoughts "come out as they went in," while an author's "mind has not been the highway of other men's thoughts, but a soil into which they have been cast, like seed into the good ground, and where they have died in the upswingings and full harvest of higher and brighter thoughts."[33] The essay went on to identify a "prophetic class" of authors as distinctively American, and this notion was echoed strongly by the Transcendentalists and by the Young America group in New York. When the latter group sponsored a dinner for Charles Dickens in 1842, one of its leaders, Cornelius Mathews, used the occasion to imagine an original American literature that would allow "the whole wide land [to] echo from side to side with the accents of a Majestic Literature — self-reared, self-sustained, self-vindicating."[34]

Such proclamations give a great deal of ballast to the notion that the goal of the best authors in nineteenth-century America was to be representative of a nation that was, like them, striving to be independent and original. But this notion would also necessarily be a partial reading of the historical archive. Mathews, one of the most ardent voices of American literary nationalism, chose to express his views at a dinner for Dickens, a British writer. The "self-sustained" literature he advocated was, he realized, supported by a transatlantic literary community, which was debating the importance of an international copyright agreement. And the "Majestic Literature" he envisioned was predicated on the fact of American expansionism that would later lead to the Mexican War of 1848 and continued attempts — endorsed by the political wing of Young America, among others — to annex Cuba. The rhetoric of national literary autonomy was also inherently gendered and racialized. An August 1853 article in the *United States Review* (1837–59), for example, made a direct appeal to men to create a national literature. "American authors, be men and heroes! Make sacrifices, . . . but *publish* books . . . for the hope of the future and the honor of America. Do not leave its literature in the hands of a few industrious females." This gendered rhetoric was, like Mathews's speech, in the service of advocating an international copyright, and it was motivated by the success of Stowe's *Uncle Tom's Cabin* abroad and fears of an alliance between British aristocrats and female American abolitionists.[35]

A full history of literary authorship in the nineteenth century, however, would require not only a deeper exploration of the ideology of literary nationalism but also the recognition that the representative American author was only one of many models that a writing career could take. Nineteenth-century authors, surveying their own situation, acknowledged something like Davis's caste system, but many of their comments suggest that they saw these castes as more permeable than subsequent literary history has rendered them. These authors, in the words of Kristie Hamilton, present a record "of the alternatives to literary and social categories that have been retroactively hardened."[36]

Hawthorne's case is again instructive here. He has been canonized as a high-art author of distinctively American prose—a canonization process that Ticknor and Fields began as early as the 1850s. As an author, he also gained a certain notoriety among twentieth-century literary critics because of his letter to publisher William D. Ticknor complaining about the "damned mob of scribbling women" that was outpacing him in sales.[37] Although he quickly retracted this comment (in his next letter, he claimed to like the work of Fanny Fern, among others), it has become closely associated with Hawthorne's authorship and the way in which he followed long-standing traditions allying originality with male genius and mere writing with "scribbling women." What is curious is that this mob of scribblers has received so much more notoriety than Hawthorne's earlier allusion (in the letter to his mother quoted at the beginning of this chapter) to the "proudest productions of the scribbling sons of John Bull." British writers were "scribbling sons" just as female novelists were "scribbling women." These are discrete comments made thirty years apart, and Hawthorne probably did not remember the first when he wrote the second. Historical hindsight, however, lets us see that the important thing for Hawthorne was to distinguish his authorship from "mere" scribbling and not necessarily to suggest that scribbling was an inherently gendered activity.

Hawthorne also used "scribbler" as a term in his own work. Even in *The Scarlet Letter*, he concluded his introductory "Custom-House" essay by calling on future generations to have renewed respect for "the scribbler of bygone days." This scribbler could refer to Surveyor Pue, whose manuscript he pretended to use as a source, or to himself, as the pretended reviser of that manuscript for posterity. Elsewhere in "The Custom-House," Hawthorne used a variety of terms—author, writer, editor—to describe his own work. And indeed, his career encompassed these various roles as he moved among the "castes" of children's books, sketches, periodical writing, campaign biography, and editorial work, as well as the romances for which he is now well known. "The Custom-House" also alluded to a form of authorship that he could not achieve: a kind of realism based on observation of "the page of life," as "something new in literature" that would capture the humorous and picturesque details of the quotidian here and now.[38] In this allusion, Hawthorne gestured toward another keyword of nineteenth-century authorship: observation.

"Observation" often stands in this history in direct relation to "profession" and "access." On the one hand, powers of observation were seen as the key to literary access: the prerequisite to authorship was not a certain level of education or membership in a specific trade organization but rather keen attention to the world. Everyone could observe, amateur and professional alike, and observations could also be made in unpublished writing, such as diaries and letters, that did not necessarily circulate within a culture of print. The apparent ease of observation as a direct, unmediated activity made it less threatening than more imaginative forms of writing. On the other hand, as Hawthorne's case suggests, not every published author viewed observation as easy work, and one of the hallmarks of literary professionalism was the establishment of observation as the foundation of a particular genre of writing. The emergence of high realism in the 1870s and 1880s promoted the difficulty of observation (acute observations were art precisely because they revealed more than life) and made it a viable practice for authors steeped in the tradition of romance (notably William Dean Howells and Henry James). Yet high realism also brought observation and professionalism into closer alliance with each other: the most critically successful professional writers needed not be those who wrote history, romance, or epic.

Before professionalism and observation became more fully allied, a number of writers used observation to demarcate a certain caste of author. Observation could be employed in a variety of critical contexts, but male reviewers frequently described a particular relationship between women and enhanced powers of observation. In 1853, for example, the minister and professor Austin Phelps praised his wife, the author Elizabeth Stuart Phelps who wrote under the name H. Trusta, for describing real people rather than fictional characters. In the closing years of her life, according to Phelps, Elizabeth "attached less value than she had previously done, to *fiction* as a medium of conveying truth. In her maturest efforts, she drew but little upon the resources of her own invention. Real life became more exclusively her chosen source of invention."[39] He characterized this shift as a sign of maturity and development, but in classifying his wife as an observer rather than an inventor, he reinforced a gender division between romantic invention and domestic observation. In 1865, the young Henry James echoed this division when he predicted that the best realist writers would be women, "for if women are unable to draw, they notoriously can at all events paint, and this is what realism requires."[40]

Throughout the period, however, some authors challenged the terms by which female writing in particular was allied with unmediated observation. Catharine Maria Sedgwick's story "Cacoethes Scribendi" (1830), for instance, satirized the notion that every detail of village life should be recorded in print. The village women contract a "writing itch" in which they transcribe all of their observations into stories for a literary annual. Only the heroine of the tale, Alice, objects to the notion of putting her life in print. The narrator sides with Alice's sensible restraint, which signals Sedgwick's own turn away from local-color observation.[41]

Sedgwick's story also critiqued the notion that writing is easy. The village women in Sedgwick's tale write and publish as easily as they cook and sew: they simply record observations and print. But as the demands of writing increased, professional women stressed the labor inherent in being an author. Even if observation were the goal, it took talent to pull it off. Sometimes such comments were delivered privately, as when Louisa May Alcott wrote to a fan that there is no "easy road to successful authorship."[42] But some women were willing to put demanding literary advice into print. In 1854, Elizabeth Stoddard complained that most published women writers followed their whims, rather than striving for intellectual and artistic excellence. "The eight books in ten are written without genius; all show industry, and a few talent. Their authors are Bedouins: Hagar should be the name of some, and some should be nameless."[43] Stoddard's allusion to Hagar, Sarah's handmaiden who bore Abraham's illegitimate child, suggests that not all writers were legitimately entitled to the status of author — although like Sedgwick, Stoddard conveyed legitimacy upon herself. Fifteen years later, Stowe made a similar point about artistic excellence. Addressing those with literary aspirations, especially women, she argued that the title of "author" should be reserved for "those who have confessedly some natural gift — or what is called, for want of a better word, genius — for writing," and who then succeed because of "laborious and careful study and culture." Such writers might use their powers of observation to depict "simple and homely scenes of everyday life," but those observations needed to be accompanied by genius.[44] This argument, of course, was also made about male authors (Stowe took Hawthorne to be a model of genius), but for successful female writers such as Sedgwick, Alcott, Stoddard, and Stowe, more was at stake when they tried to claim genius and originality for women.

African Americans faced a similar difficulty. In the extensive diary that she began in 1854, Charlotte Forten—an upper-middle-class freewoman born in Philadelphia—expressed her desire to become "suddenly inspired and write as only great poets can write" and to "write a beautiful poem of two hundred lines in my sleep as Coleridge did." Although Forten did publish her poetry and sketches in prestigious magazines, such as the *Liberator* (1831–65) and the *Atlantic Monthly*, she did not define herself as an inspired author; in her journal detailing a visit to South Carolina's Sea Islands, she mentioned taking travel notes and then waiting "until something further occurs which is *writable*."[45] Many African American women complicated the hierarchical discussion about literary genius by positioning themselves as amateurs in relation to white mentors. In *Incidents in the Life of a Slave Girl*, for instance, Harriet Jacobs deferred to the authority of Emily Post and Lydia Maria Child, whose letters of endorsement prefaced her narrative. By positioning her narrative as "written by herself" and using the pseudonym of Linda Brent, Jacobs established the authenticity of her text. She tempered this authenticity, however, by representing herself as a "girl": a young person who had been denied the innocence of childhood, but who also did not yet have the authority of experience. At the same time, writing was politically expedient during the abolitionist movement and Reconstruction. The history of slavery and the experiences of African American people needed to be told as realistically as possible. A review of Frank J. Webb's novel *The Garies and Their Friends* (1857) applauded Webb's ability to "take up the pen and paint their [northern blacks'] manners in vivid and pleasing colors. . . . If he has turned author in order to give us some idea of the inner life of his race, he has done good service to the cause of humanity and progress."[46] Mimetic painting here became a primary virtue rather than a secondary art. Webb moved beyond the surface observations that Forten called "writable," but as an African American writer, he made sure that his authorship was in the service of social uplift and community building.

By the time Henry James wrote "The Art of Fiction" (1884), he had expanded the notion of "painting manners" into a general theory of fiction, making it a general tenet that fiction writers should be those "on whom nothing is lost," those who are hyperobservant and translate that observation into their work. Although James himself practiced a highly aestheticized version of this theory, its general idea was applicable to southwestern humor as well as to New England regionalist writing, and to international travel writing as much as to realist poetry. The consolidation of realism as a "literary institution" was accompanied by an increased public interest in—and access to—details about authors' lives.[47] Authors' portraits were circulated in periodicals, books, and photographic cartes de visite, and fans began to picture the daily lives of authors by reading excerpts from their letters and seeing reproductions of their homes. The authors who endorsed the value of observation in aesthetic terms also became public celebrities who were themselves the object of observation.

The Author as Icon and Celebrity

If the history of authorship is to be understood on the one hand as a history of artistic self-conception, and in particular, of the relationship among the key concepts of professionalism, access, and observation, it must on the other hand also be considered as a set of external projections about what authorship entails. During the nineteenth century, authors came to define themselves in relation to a market in which public perception had great value. Professional recognition was also important, and aspiring writers wanted to hear advice from established authors in part because they knew them to be celebrities in the literary world, familiar not only through their works but also through a complex network of advertisements, portraits and photographs, and biographies.

In broad terms, the period between 1840 and 1880 witnessed a shift in literary publicity from an emphasis on the author's relation to his or her work to emphasis on what we might term a "cult of personality": an interest in the private as well as the literary lives of authors. At the beginning of this period, biographical sketches of authors frequently referred back to their works: to know the work was to know its creator. By its end, readers clamored for details about the author's life that were not revealed in his or her writings. As consumers, readers also increasingly participated in the commodification of authors—a shift revealed by the large number of portraits of authors circulated by magazines, photographic studios, and even card games. (On the commodification of literature more generally, see Chapter 9, Part 2.) The challenge for authors and their publishers was to control the terms of that circulation within an increasingly diverse market—a difficult task that sometimes proved impossible.

Letters from readers to authors they admired provide one index of the shifting terms of literary celebrity. Before the Civil War, these letters often made no distinction between the narrator or character in a book and the author beyond it. In the 1850s, for example, the novelists Susan Warner and Maria Cummins received mail from readers that spoke to them as if they were the characters they had created and that claimed emotional, private ties to the authors through their characters. "I feel as if I knew you and you were my personal friend," wrote Ella Blake to Warner. "I have smiled and wept, over our story," Paul Swanwick wrote to Cummins.[48] A generation later, another young reader used similar language to conflate Louisa May Alcott and her character Jo March. "We have all been reading 'Little Women,' and we liked it so much I could not help wanting to write to you. We think *you* are perfectly splendid; I like you better every time I read it. We were all so disappointed over your not marrying Laurie."[49]

Given the passion of readerly identification represented in such letters, it is not surprising that some midcentury writers parodied their fan mail, a sign both of its pervasiveness and of the growing sense that celebrity authors needed to distance themselves from their readers. Fanny Fern (Sara Willis Parton) devoted several chapters to fictionalized fan mail in her autobiographical novel *Ruth Hall* (1855), showing how many liberties readers took with authors as they demanded everything from literary advice to money to marriage. In *Jo's Boys* (1886), Alcott took this satire one step further when she described a fan who comes to Jo's house in order to glimpse the now-famous author, peeps into her study, and grabs a few mementos from her desk. This scene is reminiscent of an entry in Alcott's journal: "Reporters sit on the wall and take notes; artists sketch me as I pick pears in the garden; and strange women interview Johnny [her nephew] as he plays in the orchard. It looks like impertinent curiosity to me; but it is called 'fame,' and considered a blessing to be grateful for, I find. Let 'em try it."[50]

Attempting to commercialize the intimacy of a private letter while avoiding overzealous fans, some authors permitted their portraits to circulate with their autographs. The author and editor Sarah Josepha Hale included a portrait of herself in the December 1850 issue of her magazine *Godey's Lady's Book* (1830–98) that included her signature with the phrase, "Truly yr. Friend." Since she could not send an individual autograph to every reader who might want one, she did the next best thing by providing a facsimile. Such a practice echoed the narrative style in sentimental writing of the time, which featured direct addresses to readers by engaging narrators.

Another contributor to *Godey's*, Edgar Allan Poe, also understood the advantages of seeking publicity through the circulation of his portrait. Poe, however, was unable to control the terms of that circulation as carefully as Hale, since the image he tried to formulate during his life shifted after his death in 1849. An experienced editor as well as poet and fiction writer, Poe worked throughout his career to create interest in himself and his writings. In 1843 his woodblock portrait in the *Philadelphia Saturday Museum* (1842–44) was accompanied by a biographical essay that Poe probably helped to write, or at least provided much of the information for. His pose in the portrait, with his arm resting on books, was a standard occupational pose used by daguerreotypists of the time, and it established Poe as the leisured and gentlemanly author of books, while obscuring the work involved in producing them. In fact, Poe was struggling to make a living at this time, having left his editorship of *Graham's Magazine* (1840–58) the year before.[51]

Despite Poe's efforts, his success in crafting his authorial image did not last long. After his death, a counterimage of Poe as a tortured, tragic genius with a diseased mind and drug addiction quickly surfaced. Rufus Griswold's verbal description of Poe as "thin, and pale even to ghastliness, his whole appearance indicat[ing] sickness and the utmost destitution" was solidified by the circulation of similarly revisionist portraits.[52] They pictured Poe with a furrowed brow, wide forehead, and exhausted eyes: the prototype of the author as romantic genius, as in the portrait of the tortured, brooding Poe featured in William Fearing Gill's literary anthology *Laurel Leaves* (1875), in which he is surrounded by shadowy scenes from his poems. Poe was identified with his works, and the selective identification perpetuated the popular legend of him as tragic visionary. Despite the fact that the romantic model of authorship was under constant negotiation throughout the second half of the nineteenth century, and despite the fact that Poe himself was a savvy participant in the literary market, this image — rather than that in the *Saturday Museum* — proved to be the lasting one.

Walt Whitman was more successful than Poe in controlling which of his many personas would appear before the public. He first used a portrait as a form of authorial self-fashioning when he substituted an engraved, uncaptioned image of himself for the usual authorial attribution in the frontispiece to *Leaves of Grass* (1855). In this well-known engraving, Whitman's pose suggests a natural "rough" more than a literary author: he slouches slightly and looks directly at the reader. Whitman created this "natural" portrait by thinking carefully about its construction, and he continued this pattern of self-conscious portraiture throughout the rest of his life. There are at least 130 known photographs of Whitman, many of which stress his role as cultural prophet (his long white beard evoking Moses for some viewers) and lover of nature.

Biographical sketches of Whitman echoed this self-fashioned image of a natural rather than literary man; he was rarely pictured with a book or pen. In *Authors at Home* (1889), an anthology of "personal and biographical sketches

FIGURE 3.2.
Frontispiece to the 1860
edition of Walt Whitman's
Leaves of Grass (Boston:
Thayer and Eldridge). Unlike
the famous frontispiece to
the 1855 edition that showed
Whitman as a "rough," this
portrait employed more
standard conventions of how
a poet should look. American
Antiquarian Society.

of well-known American writers," George Selwyn described Whitman as living on a "quiet, democratic street" that "has all the rudeness, simplicity, and free-and-easy character of the quarters of some old sailor."[53] As a poet who imagined himself to represent the American nation, it was fitting that Whitman should live on a "democratic street" and that his house would be adequate but not elegant, more akin to a sailor's retreat than the genteel study of a literary man. It was also an appropriate house for the image of the "rough" pictured in the first edition of *Leaves of Grass*. Later editions of that work experimented with Whitman's image. The Thayer and Eldridge 1860 edition, for example, was advertised (with Whitman's endorsement and assistance) as "An Elegant Book" and included a frontispiece that featured a more refined, "authorlike" Whitman in a studio pose, wearing a jacket and cravat, rather than a work shirt open at the neck (Fig. 3.2).

Like Hawthorne, Whitman worked at various times in his career to foster a myth of readerly neglect and critical underappreciation, but by the 1880s he had succeeded in making himself into a celebrity—a fact that derived in part from his own efforts at self-representation through portraiture. In addition to circulating his image, he gave well-attended public lectures in New Jersey and Manhattan, received visits from prominent artists and intellectuals, was the subject of a successful lecture given in New York by the British publisher Ernest Rhys, became the unofficial poet laureate of the *New York Herald*, and received numerous letters from readers. He even witnessed the increasing commercialization of his name with the appearance of a Walt Whitman cigar. From the 1870s, Whitman began the practice of including his signature, either in autograph or in facsimile, on the title page of special editions of *Leaves of Grass*. At that time, he claimed that 60 percent of the letters he received were requests for his autograph; he put the letters into the fire but marketed his autograph through his books.[54]

Perhaps intuiting the difficulties of controlling one's own image, many authors tried to limit their publicity. For every Poe, Whitman, and Twain who courted his public image, there was a Melville or Hawthorne who resisted it. Hawthorne was less extreme in this regard than Melville; although he felt uncomfortable sitting for a portrait or photograph, he frequently did so, and his image regularly appeared in print. American periodicals, such as the *International Magazine of Literature, Art, and Science* (1850–52), the *National Magazine* (1852–58), and the *Boston Museum* (1848–54?), included engravings of his image beginning in the early 1850s. Ticknor and Fields commissioned an engraving of Hawthorne for the first edition of *Twice-Told Tales* (1851), and he often asked the firm to put a copy of his portrait into the books it sent as complimentary copies. In England, Hawthorne had the uncanny experience of seeing his image reprinted in pirated editions of his works for sale in railroad stations and bookstalls, in one case noting that the portrait was "so very queer that we could not buy it."[55] The author who had early aimed to write works praised as equal to that of the "scribbling sons of John Bull" now was faced with the underside of that ambition: his portrait could be at once internationally available and unrecognizable. Melville resisted portraiture more categorically. Over the course of his career, he is known to have sat for only two painted portraits and ten photographs, only a fraction of the fifty-eight known original portraits and photographs of Hawthorne. Melville, like his character Pierre Glendinning, resisted being "oblivionated" by daguerreotypy, believing that it was easier to stand out by remaining invisible than to join all of the "nobodies" pictured in magazines.[56] He wanted his name and works to be famous, even as he protected his privacy by withholding his image.

Melville, to some extent, participated in the logic of separate spheres, which distinguished between the public world of the marketplace and the private world of the home and the literary study. This logic was especially pervasive for women, leaving female authors in the difficult position of maintaining their domestic privacy while also working in an increasingly public literary world. Yet they did succeed as celebrities within that world, for at least three reasons. First, the early publicity of women writers tended to present them as idealized types, rather than as distinct individuals, focusing successively on their piety, their nationalism, and the domestic space in which they wrote. Second, after the Civil War, as publicity became more individualized, it largely took the form of depicting women writers properly at home or in their studies, rather than as involved in the business of publishing. And third, women writers, such as Harriet Beecher Stowe, who went on public lecture tours spoke largely on topics deemed appropriate to their sex.

To a greater extent than those of their male counterparts, biographical sketches of female writers in the mid-nineteenth century presented idealized types more than individual personalities, doing little more than extrapolating from their writings what one might know about their private lives. But throughout the 1850s, interest in the home lives of prominent authors grew, and such publications as *Homes of American Authors* (1853) were intended to serve it. As John Hart explained in *The Female Prose Writers of America* (1852), "It seems to be an instinctive desire of the human heart, on becoming acquainted with any work of genius, to know something of its author." This was particularly true in the case of women writers, he wrote, because "women, far more than men, write from the heart. Their own likes and dislikes, their feelings, opinions, tastes, and sympathies are so mixed up with those of their subject, that the interest of the reader is often enlisted quite as much for the writer, as for the hero, of a tale."[57] Even as Hart emphasized the emotional appeal of women writers, he also suggested that such appeal built a national community, as the frontispiece to his book vividly illustrates (Fig. 3.3). This chromolithograph creates an icon of the woman writer, subsuming individual differences into an idealized female image that symbolizes patriotism and national service. She leans on the flag, holding a bouquet of flowers rather than a pen. At the same time, the natural background, a tranquil and almost sublime landscape of mountains and streams, suggests that women writers are natural as well as inherently American. This iconography makes all women writers into a generic whole that emphasizes nature, friendship, fidelity, and patriotism, rather than possessive individualism.

This nationalistic iconography was supported by a sense that women writers had a particular contribution to make to American literary nationalism. As Mrs. A. J. Graves put it in 1847, "in our national female character there is a rich mine for our writers as yet unexplored, which will amply reward all who seek for its virgin ore," and it will produce "beautiful revelations of character, more full of originality and deep interest than are to be found in the creations of the most gifted genius."[58] Graves applied the key terms of literary nationalism — genius, originality, national character — to women's sphere. The domestic, for her, became equivalent to the national.

FIGURE 3.3. Frontispiece and title page of John S. Hart's *The Female Prose Writers of America* (Philadelphia: E. H. Butler & Co., 1852). American Antiquarian Society.

Such depictions of women authors in biographies and portraits were part of a larger national project of defining and civilizing the new nation, especially through normative depictions of white womanhood. It became less important what a writer was really like than that she fulfill certain ideals about what she should be like. For example, a January 1843 *Graham's Magazine* engraving entitled "Our Lady Contributors" contains framed portraits of Lydia Sigourney, Catharine Maria Sedgwick, Frances Osgood, Elizabeth Oakes Smith, and Emma C. Embury but subsumes their individual traits into the nationalistic iconography of the whole, with an eagle at the top sitting on an emblem of the Stars and Stripes. Like the Hart frontispiece, this engraving also contains allusions to Greek poetry, with the muses in the center and the lyre at the bottom. It is thus an image both of national solidarity and of particular cultural origins. Although each woman pictured in *Graham's* holds an individual place in the engraving, a curtain framing the portraits suggests the theatricality of the scene: the curtain could be drawn to give public exposure or closed to maintain privacy.

FIGURE 3.4.

Frontispiece of Jarena Lee's
*Religious Experience and
Journal of Mrs. Jarena Lee:
Giving an Account of Her
Call to Preach the Gospel*
(Philadelphia: Privately
published, 1849). American
Antiquarian Society.

The tradition of publicizing female writers in stylized and idealized images continued throughout the nineteenth century. Portrayals of the black female body were especially carefully orchestrated. Following the tradition begun in Phillis Wheatley's *Poems on Various Subjects* (1773), the evangelist Jarena Lee included her portrait as the frontispiece to her spiritual autobiography, *Religious Experience and Journal of Mrs. Jarena Lee* (1849; Fig. 3.4). Lee's white hat and garment associate her with simple Quaker clothing and lead the viewer to the light on her eyes and on the books at her right arm. As in most portraits of women writers during this period, she does not look directly at the viewer but rather at a distant place.

Although such idealized images persisted after the Civil War, they were countered by more realistic portraits of women at home or at work in their studies. This was part of the larger move to depict authors in private spaces, indicating a shift from focusing on them exclusively through their texts to seeing them as people whose lives were interesting in their own right. One of the best-known authorial portraits of this period was Christian Schussele's

Washington Irving and His Literary Friends at Sunnyside (1863), a composite painting of Irving in his study with fourteen fellow writers that was widely circulated as a print (1864). But such depictions were still gendered in particular ways. Richard Stoddard's *Poets' Homes* (1879), for example, included a detailed engraving of the novelist Elizabeth Stuart Phelps (Ward) at work in her study.[59] Unlike Schussele's portrait, which filled the study with writers and put Irving front and center, this engraving barely pictures Phelps. Sitting at the far left of the image, she is visible only through her back and part of her silhouette, her body almost lost in an overstuffed chair and large, solid writing desk. The accompanying biographical sketch similarly draws attention to all of the objects in the room, rather than to the author herself: "All the day the sun shines in as cheerfully as it can, struggling through those little windows and those little panes. There are subdued green curtains at these windows; and about the room are books, pictures, a few easy chairs, tables, and many of the nothings which make a study pleasant."[60] Rather than calling attention to Phelps herself, this sketch emphasizes the "nothings" that make up her domestic surroundings, suggesting both a woman of taste and one who shares the sensibilities of her readers. If the sun could only partially penetrate this private space, so too did readers receive only a carefully constructed glimpse of the private life of the woman whose writings, at least in *The Gates Ajar* (1869), had not only had tremendous sales but also set off a highly successful marketing campaign for items associated with the book.

Phelps's case was typical of other nineteenth-century women authors whose books garnered large sales. The more successful the author, the more the surrounding publicity worked to show her to be a "normal" woman working quietly at home. Alcott's success with *Little Women* and its sequels helped her become one of the most famous novelists in the nineteenth century, with readers making pilgrimages to Concord to catch glimpses of her. Her association with other prominent authors was clear in a full-page illustration in an 1880 issue of *Frank Leslie's Illustrated Newspaper* (1855–1922) titled "Four Luminaries of American Letters" (Fig. 3.5). The top of this engraving groups Alcott with Emerson, John Greenleaf Whittier, and her father, Bronson Alcott. The fact that she is on the same level with these authors (her portrait being merged with theirs and printed the same size) suggests that women were not necessarily seen as inhabiting a separate literary sphere, especially in the second half of the century. Yet of the four authors, only the home of "Miss Alcott" is pictured, as if it were especially important to picture the domestic space in which she lived. At the bottom, her father is pictured lecturing in the public hall of the Concord School of Philosophy (ironically, a school that began in Bronson's study at Orchard House) with a few women

RALPH WALDO EMERSON   A. BRONSON ALCOTT   LOUISE ALCOTT   JOHN G. WHITTIER

THE SUMMER SCHOOL

THE HOME OF MISS ALCOTT.

SCENE IN THE INTERIOR OF THE CHAPEL DURING A LECTURE BY A. BRONSON ALCOTT.

MASSACHUSETTS.—SECOND TERM OF THE SCHOOL OF PHILOSOPHY, IN THE CHAPEL ON THE ORCHARD GROUNDS, CONCORD. FROM SKETCHES BY W. PARKER BODFISH.—SEE PAGE 398.

FIGURE 3.5. "Four Luminaries of American Letters," from *Frank Leslie's Illustrated Newspaper*, 14 August 1880. General Research Division, the New York Public Library, Astor, Lenox, and Tilden Foundations.

in the audience, but none on the stage. Women writers could be luminaries, the illustration seems to suggest, but that celebrity status needed to be balanced by a close tie to the home, rather than the lecture hall. When Louisa May Alcott was pictured addressing a crowd, in the frontispiece to Ednah D. Cheney's *Louisa May Alcott: The Children's Friend* (1888), she sat in a chair reading to a throng of rather etherealized children, as if Jo March herself were reading to her boys.[61]

A year after publishing *Louisa May Alcott*, Cheney released a compilation of Alcott's private journals and letters. This release was typical of a larger trend toward publishing such "life and letters" volumes. The 1880s also marked the publication of Julian Hawthorne's account of his father and the beginning of Horace Traubel's daily visits to Whitman that would result in the nine-volume biography *With Walt Whitman in Camden* (1906–96). All of these volumes were biased toward celebrating the author and were edited with a heavy hand, but they also indicated the extent to which the lives of American authors had now become subjects in and of themselves. But Cheney justified publishing her volume by returning to the long-standing and familiar notion that works revealed what readers needed to know about their authors. "Of no author can it be more truly said than of Louisa Alcott that her works are a revelation of herself," Cheney wrote. "It is therefore impossible to understand Miss Alcott's works fully without a knowledge of her own life and experiences."[62] The logic here was tautological; the works reveal the author, but it is important to know something about the personal life of the author in order to fully understand the works. Such thinking resulted from shifting ideas of authorship in the late nineteenth century. Vestigial notions of the private sanctity of the author merged with public demands to know more about authors' lives, with the compromise being that biography would enhance understanding of the work itself. Alcott herself probably would not have supported publication of such a volume. Cheney acknowledged that Alcott wished to have most of her letters destroyed, and she quoted an 1885 letter to publisher Thomas Niles in which Alcott declined to give information for another biographical sketch: "I don't like these everlasting notices; one is enough, else we poor people feel like squeezed oranges, and nothing is left sacred."[63] In her earlier writing, particularly sensational and gothic fiction, Alcott had avoided such scrutiny by publishing anonymously; even as late as 1877, she published *A Modern Mephistopheles* in the Roberts Brothers' No Name series.

Alcott's letter was a far cry from Hawthorne's youthful conviction that his mother would take pride in his aspiring authorship. In some respects, this shift was simply that from a young artist to a seasoned professional; as a teenager, Alcott herself had sounded equally enthusiastic about the possibilities of authorship. Yet it also registered the overall shift in the terms of authorship between 1840 and 1880. In the 1840s, Emerson and his followers had embraced a cultural patriotism that encouraged Americans to become authors, but by the 1860s, writers such as Thomas Wentworth Higginson and Harriet Beecher Stowe worried that too many citizens had heard the call and that the flood of writers would drown out the voices of true talent.[64] In the 1840s, authors such as Poe had begun nascent publicity campaigns for emergent authors, but by the 1880s, authors such as Melville and Alcott had declared themselves exhausted by publicity requests. The vision in Sedgwick's "Cacoethes Scribendi," in which amateur village women can easily put their works into print, was succeeded by that in Elizabeth Stoddard's "Collected by a Valetudinarian" (1870) and Constance Fenimore Woolson's "Miss Grief" (1880). In Stoddard's story, a talented author chooses not to publish her work; in Woolson's, another talented author wants to publish her work but lacks the requisite professional connections.

The market that enabled authors to create a viable profession writing American literature eventually became a subject of that literature. At the same time, critical conventions moved from encouraging readers to find authors in their works to imagining the conditions of those works' production. "In reading the following pages one gets a closer and more intimate view of the authors sketched than their writings could possibly afford," editors J. L. Gilder and J. B. Gilder noted at the beginning of *Authors at Home*. Yet one is "relieved of any sense of intruding upon their privacy by the fact that the papers here gathered together . . . were all written with the approval of the authors whom they portray."[65] That privacy would become increasingly difficult to preserve in the following decades, leading to a modernist aesthetic that valued reclusivity, alienating style, and expatriation. But by the 1880s, American authors were indeed at home, firmly ensconced within American culture and recasting literary nationalism within the terms of an increasingly complex profession of authorship.

The National Book Trade System

Distribution and the Trade

Michael Winship

· · ·

On 17 September 1850, New York publisher A. S. Barnes & Co. wrote to Lea & Blanchard, a Philadelphia publisher chiefly of medical books, introducing Joseph S. Taft of Houston, Texas, who "is in Book business at that place, and sells many of your Books" and whom Barnes had found to be "true & faithful." Three days later, Taft visited Lea & Blanchard in Philadelphia and placed an order for that firm's books, received on credit, in the amount of $180.48. On 2 October, back in Houston, Taft wrote to the firm:

> I find more ready sale for your medical works than I anticipated. The small invoice I purchased from you are nearly all sold. It is but a week since I received them. Enclosed I send a list of such as are enquired for and a few others I think will sell. Also of a few other works I want. Please forward early as convenient. Shipped as before unless you have an opportunity to send direct from your port.

This second order amounted to $121.50, also sent on credit, and during the 1850s Taft was to place thirteen further orders of Lea & Blanchard's books for stock, a total of $1,317.68.[1]

Lea & Blanchard had other dealings with Texas in 1850. On 11 February, George C. Read of Washington-on-the-Brazos placed an order for subscriptions to the firm's two medical journals, the *American Journal of Medical Sciences* and the *Medical News and Library*, enclosing a draft for $5 on the Canal Bank of New Orleans. On 6 March, A. M. Alexander & Bros. of Dallas placed an order for the same journals on behalf of Perry Dakan, M.D., as did Pratt, Woodford & Co. of New York, acting as agents for E. Stephens of Brazoria, on 27 May. Finally, on 29 October, Daniel Baker of Huntsville wrote to Lea & Blanchard, referring to one of its nonmedical publications: "The beautiful copy of the Encyclopedia Americana, which you have so kindly donated to the Library of Austin College, Texas, has been received. Accept, Gentlemen, my very sincere thanks for this substantial expression of the interest which you take in the cause of Education, in that distant frontier state."[2]

As these dealings indicate, by the mid-nineteenth century a national book distribution system was at work in the United States, one that made books and periodicals that were published in Philadelphia, one of the publishing centers in what was becoming an increasingly centralized industry based in a few East Coast cities, readily available to booksellers and customers even in Texas. It is difficult to know the precise contours of book culture in that "distant frontier state," which had joined the Union only five years earlier. However, for those who wished to acquire books published on the East Coast and who had the means—and surely there were many who did not—these books were readily accessible.

As publishers assumed the central entrepreneurial position of the American book trade in the first half of the nineteenth century, they relied on the development of efficient systems for distributing their publications from the increasingly concentrated sites of production to a dispersed and diverse audience of readers and consumers. Paradoxically, whereas the economics of industrialization encouraged the production of multiple copies of a single work in a single location, the economics of consumption required that each work be marketed singly, copy by copy, in multiple locations, whether local, national, or international. Conditions within the industrializing United States—a diffuse and expanding territory with a population still largely rural or living in widely scattered small towns—exacerbated the problem. In many ways, the problem of distribution has always defined and characterized the American book trade. Distribution is also one of the most understudied and least understood aspects of the nineteenth-century book trade, in part because of the paucity of surviving evidence that documents earlier practices.

Books are, of course, not unique: the production and consumption of many products faced the very same difficulties during the industrial era. In the American economy, the success of the industrialization of consumer goods depended on the development of systems, or "technologies," of distribution. The development of three separate, interrelated distribution networks enabled the exchange of information, goods, and credit. The network for the distribution of information allowed producers and consumers to learn, on the one hand, what products were desired and, on the other, what products were available; knowledge that was essential for the working of a viable market system. The network for the distribution of goods enabled the transfer of goods, in this case books and other printed matter, from the site of production to that of consumption, from factory to customer. The network for the distribution of credit worked in reverse, requiring consumers to provide, one by one, the money that fueled industrial production. In examining each of these networks, it is useful to recognize that the particular developments that relate to the book trade were often, even usually, shared by the distribution of consumer goods more generally.

Information about the availability of books and the demand for them was essential, and during the middle decades of the nineteenth century, the trade developed regular means for communicating such information (as Part 2 of this chapter explains in greater detail). By 1880, *Publishers' Weekly*, under the direction of Frederick Leypoldt and R. R. Bowker, was well on its way toward establishing its present role as a semiofficial organ for the book trades, providing a systematic record of new publications and a forum for exchange of information and opinion. The Publication Office of *Publishers' Weekly* supplemented the periodical with a range of further publications: the *American Catalogue of Books*, first issued in 1870; the annual August education number of *Publishers' Weekly*, from 1872 also issued separately as the *American Educational Catalog*; and the *Publishers' Trade List Annual*, begun in 1873. In addition, the firm published the *Library Journal*, the "Official Organ of the American Library Association," from 1876.[3] In subsequent decades, under the proprietorship of R. R. Bowker, the firm would issue further periodicals and reference works to serve the book trades, especially those concerned with trade publishing, while related trades, such as those of music and stationery, developed their own specialized publications by 1880.

Publishers' and bookshops' communication with their customers, as opposed to communication with other members of the trade, continued to be chiefly managed in traditional ways. Publishers regularly advertised their new books in newspapers and periodicals, and they encouraged, sometimes with financial incentives, booksellers to do the same in local publications. The publishers often supplemented these advertisements with squibs and longer reviews. They sometimes put aside as many as two hundred copies of the first printing of a new book for reviewers, who might be supplied with promotional text to use in their notices. Publishers regularly produced trade lists and more comprehensive catalogs for distribution and consultation and provided booksellers with printed shewbills (large posters for mounting) and flyers for their new books. With the founding of *Harper's New Monthly Magazine*, *Putnam's Monthly*, and the *Atlantic Monthly* in the 1850s, a number of the major trade publishers began to issue general-interest monthly magazines that, while not specifically house organs, could be counted on to preview, puff, or advertise that firm's new publications. From the 1870s, *Publishers' Weekly* and some of the larger book distribution firms published regular monthly circulars, which book dealers could have individually imprinted with their own name for further distribution to customers.[4] However, publishers and booksellers carried on much of their direct communication with customers through the mails or in person.

Between 1840 and 1880, the United States grew from an area of 1,788,006 square miles to 3,022,387, and its population grew from 17,069,453 to 50,155,783. However, most Americans continued to live in rural areas (15,224,398 in 1840; 36,026,048 in 1880), and population density increased only from 9.8 per square mile to 16.9. As the nation expanded, traditional means of transportation—those using roads, coastal waterways, rivers, and canals—continued to be important, but the chief new development of the period was the introduction of the rail network: railroad mileage increased more than fortyfold, from just 2,818 miles in 1840 to 115,647 in 1880.[5] Nevertheless, the transportation of goods from manufacturer to consumer remained a central problem of distribution, especially as book publishing and production became concentrated in only a few, mostly eastern, urban centers. The key development was the emergence of express companies, which served as middlemen and managed the movement of shipments of small packages from place to place. Agents for express companies arranged for shipment of book packages, their receipt, and if necessary, their transfer from one form of transportation to another. From the 1840s, publishers depended on express companies to ship orders of books to their distributors, who paid extra for the service, though large orders continued to be sent by freight. Small packages of books, especially to individual customers, could also be sent by U.S. mail, also an important vehicle for the distribution of magazines and newspapers that were subsidized by favorable low rates. Publishers found ways to take advantage of this postal subsidy: in the 1830s and early 1840s, by issuing the mammoth weeklies, large weekly newspapers that printed an entire novel in a single issue; and in the 1870s, by producing a number of inexpensive "libraries" and "series" that at least nominally appeared regularly as periodicals and could be registered as second-class postal matter.[6]

The transfer of credit was also a problem for the distribution of books, especially between 1836, when the charter of the Second Bank of the United States expired, and 1862, when the federal government first issued greenbacks, paper notes that it backed as legal tender. Throughout the period, the transfer of credit—within the book and printing trades, as well as between publishers, booksellers, and private customers—was difficult: hard money and specie remained scarce; paper bills and notes were unreliable. Banknotes often traded below par and might well prove to be counterfeit or to have been issued by distant, failed banks. The situation improved after 1863, when the federal government first authorized the charter of national banks that could issue paper money backed by federal bonds. Still, much of the business in the book trades continued to be managed on account and relied on extending credit to both trade firms and retail customers, often for long periods.

A chief characteristic of the mid-nineteenth century was the emergence of a variety of middlemen and businesses — advertising agents, express companies, credit reporting firms — that served generally to foster American commerce. Individual agents, such as Charles B. Norton in the 1850s and Frederick Leypoldt after the Civil War, fostered trade communication by editing and producing periodicals and publications for the book trades. The international trade in both books and texts depended on the services of specialist London firms directed by agents such as Sampson Low and Nicolas Trübner. More important for the efficient distribution of books was the development of jobbing by firms that acted as middlemen between publishers and retail booksellers. Much remains to be uncovered about the history and working of jobbing in the book trades, but during the 1850s many firms that are better remembered as publishers — for example, Phillips, Sampson & Co. in Boston, D. Appleton & Co. in New York, and J. B. Lippincott & Co. in Philadelphia — supplemented their publishing business, often substantially, by acting as jobbers. In 1854 the Lippincott firm was described as possibly the "largest book distributing house in the world"[7] (Figs. 4.1 and 4.2). During the 1850s, jobbers might act chiefly as agents, gathering orders from a number of publishers and sending them on as a single shipment to retail establishments, which maintained accounts directly with those publishers. Jobbers might also purchase books in large lots directly from publishers to be divided up and sold on their own account to retailers, who were thus saved the difficulty of establishing credit and maintaining separate accounts with multiple publishing firms.[8]

After the Civil War, a number of specialized jobbing firms made wholesaling rather than publishing their main business, though these firms supplemented their business in trade books with other merchandise, including periodicals, schoolbooks, stationery, sheet music, and even musical instruments. The most important of these, the American News Company of New York, was established in 1864 with the merger of Sinclair Tousey & Co. with the rival firm of Dexter, Hamilton & Co.[9] Both firms were already well-established as distributors of periodicals and newspapers, but the American News Company signaled its interest in the distribution of trade books when it started publishing the *American Booksellers' Guide* (1868–93), a periodical initially sent free to every "bookseller, newsdealer, music-dealer, and stationer in the United States" (Fig. 4.3). During the 1870s, this periodical, which became the *American Bookseller* in January 1876 and which from 15 July 1876 to 15 Sep-

FIGURE 4.1. "View of One of the Salesrooms of Lippincott, Grambo, & Co." (Philadelphia), from *Godey's Lady's Book* 45 (November 1852). American Antiquarian Society.

tember 1877 styled itself as an "official organ of the American Book Trade Association," came to rival *Publishers' Weekly* as an important source of information to the trade.

During the 1870s, several other jobbing firms emerged in New York. In 1874 Baker, Pratt & Co. — which traced its ancestry back to the bookstore, bindery, and subscription book publishing business formed by David F. Robinson and B. B. Barber in Hartford in the late 1820s — was formed to dedicate itself to the jobbing of books and stationery. The firm specialized in schoolbooks but also dealt in trade and imported books.[10] The following year, Charles T. Dillingham, who had worked as a clerk and agent for various New York and Boston firms since he entered the trade as a fifteen-year-old in 1857, went into jobbing on his own account and remained an important wholesaler of books until his firm merged in 1896 with what had then become the Baker & Taylor Company.[11] Elsewhere, the traditional pattern of combining jobbing with publishing persisted. In Philadelphia, J. B. Lippincott & Co. was both one of the country's largest jobbers, specializing in supplying retail outlets in the southern states, and an established trade publisher. In 1872 the Chicago firm

FIGURE 4.2. "Packing Room and Counting House of Lippincott, Grambo, & Co.," from *Godey's Lady's Book* 45 (November 1852). American Antiquarian Society.

Jansen, McClurg & Co. was formed as a separate enterprise from S. C. Griggs & Co. (both of which traced their origins back to the Chicago bookshop of William W. Barlow & Co., established in 1844) so that the Griggs firm could concentrate on its publishing activities. The former firm, especially after it became A. C. McClurg & Co. in 1886, would go on to become the Midwest's largest wholesaler of books and related merchandise but would continue to maintain substantial retail and publishing operations for many years.[12] Even the American News Company—primarily a jobber of periodicals, books, and music—also published a number of standard out-of-copyright works for supply to its retail customers.[13]

The rise of jobbing went hand in hand with the emerging dominance of the discount system as the chief means for the distribution of books, increasingly making exchange (where two publishing firms traded stock) and commission (where retail establishments acted as agents of the publisher, taking a commission of, say, 10 percent on the sale price of any copy of that publisher's books that they handled) vestigial and irrelevant. At its most basic, the discount system of book distribution meant that a dedicated bookshop ordered

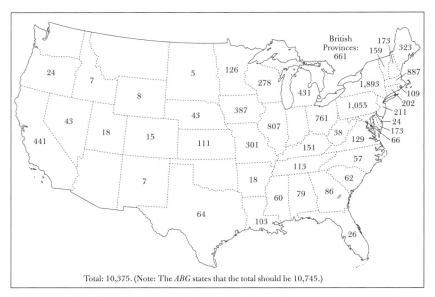

Total: 10,375. (Note: The *ABG* states that the total should be 10,745.)

FIGURE 4.3. Map showing the agents in each state or territory who received the American News Company's *American Booksellers' Guide*, which was sent free of charge to every "bookseller, newsdealer, music-dealer, and stationer in the United States" (2 [1870]: 19). This map suggests the extent of the national retail distribution network for printed materials in 1870. Although no numbers are given for Arizona, Indiana, Montana, Washington, and the Indian Territory (i.e., Oklahoma), this is clearly an oversight for Indiana and perhaps for some of the others as well.

books directly from a publisher or jobber, receiving a discount off the nominal retail price large enough to cover the expense of shipping and overhead costs and to allow for profit once the book was sold. Typical terms, which were open to negotiation and varied depending on the size of an order, were a discount of one-quarter to one-third off the retail price, with payment due in three months. As the system developed, it was further refined: publishers arranged to ship a number of copies of their new publications directly to retail firms on account, that is, without a specific order, with the understanding that such copies, if fresh and undamaged, could be returned within a set time period for credit. The practice of allowing returns benefited publishers, and book distribution generally, by ensuring that new works were widely available to customers. But it also complicated the accounting of sales, royalties, and profits and often caused misunderstandings and disputes.

The discount system ultimately depended upon the establishment of a fixed retail price from which the discount could be reckoned, a practice that became feasible only after the standard was established of offering books for sale in a publisher's cloth- or paper-covered binding. During the 1850s, the Boston publisher Ticknor and Fields offered its distributors a regular discount of 25 or 30 percent, with larger discounts available to firms that placed substantial orders or that could pay with cash instead of credit.[14] The inflation during the Civil War brought about a rise in retail prices of books: new publications that in the 1850s typically retailed for 75¢ might be priced at $2.00 in the 1870s. Simultaneously, discounts to the trade edged up — reaching 40 percent, or even higher — though many booksellers also regularly offered a discount from the nominal retail price to many of their retail customers. One of the chief goals of the trade organizations formed after 1873 was to insist on a standard trade discount of 20 percent, accompanied by a reduction of the retail price that would be charged all retail customers. These attempts at "reform," in turn, led to the formation of a national American Book Trade Association (ABTA) the following year, but the attempt to regulate prices and discounts proved unsuccessful, and the ABTA ceased to be a force by the end of 1877.[15]

Many in the trade associated this failure in self-regulation with the persistence of trade sales, regularly scheduled auctions of books that were strictly limited to members of the trade and that provided an alternative, and generally effective, means of book distribution from August 1824, when the first regular trade sale was held, into the early twentieth century. Trade sales occurred semiannually, spring and fall, in New York, Philadelphia, and Cincinnati, and annually every August in Boston, and lasted several days (Fig. 4.4). Participating publishers offered an announced number of both new titles and old stock, and jobbers and retail booksellers purchased the books in lots at prices established by a Dutch auction system. The first or final days were usually devoted to the sale of stationery and sets of printing plates. Trade sales served several important functions in the distribution of books: they brought the trade together and thus fostered communication and cooperation; they allowed publishers to introduce new works and gauge the demand for books on their backlist; they provided a clearinghouse for credit, as the auctioneer or other sponsor made arrangements to collect payment from purchasers and transfer it to participating publishers; and the printed trade-sale catalogs served as a record of books available.

Because of trade sales' importance for book distribution, their management was a constant source of conflict. In 1855 the New York Book Publishers' Association was formed to oversee the trade sales, which the auction house of Leavitt, Delisser & Co. managed from 1856. For several years, until 1858, competing trade sales were held in New York, and several important publishers, including Harper & Brothers, chose to participate only in the

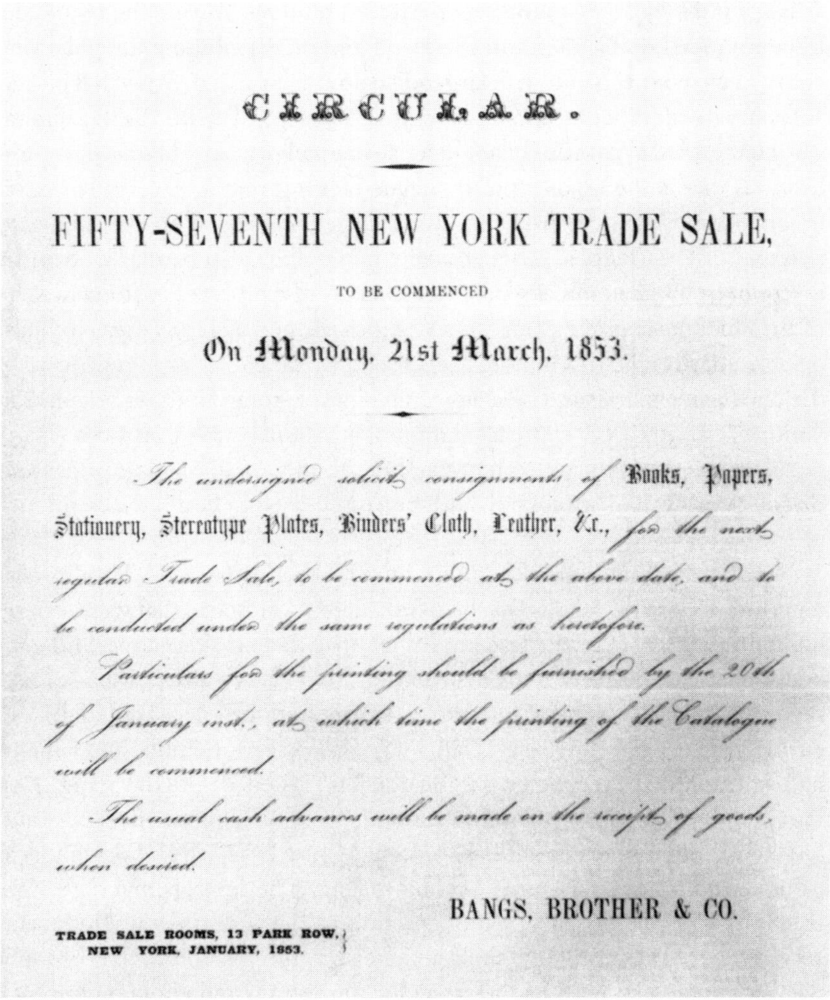

CIRCULAR.

FIFTY-SEVENTH NEW YORK TRADE SALE,

TO BE COMMENCED

On Monday, 21st March, 1853.

The undersigned solicit consignments of **Books, Papers, Stationery, Stereotype Plates, Binders' Cloth, Leather, &c.,** *for the next regular Trade Sale, to be commenced at the above date, and to be conducted under the same regulations as heretofore.*

Particulars for the printing should be furnished by the 20th of January inst., at which time the printing of the Catalogue will be commenced.

The usual cash advances will be made on the receipt of goods, when desired.

BANGS, BROTHER & CO.

TRADE SALE ROOMS, 13 PARK ROW,
NEW YORK, JANUARY, 1853.

FIGURE 4.4. "Circular — Fifty-Seventh New York Trade Sale," from Bangs, Brother & Co. (New York), soliciting consignments of books, papers, and printing and binding materials for its spring trade sale, March 1853. G. & C. Merriam Collection, American Antiquarian Society.

long-established trade sales managed by Bangs & Co. In July 1875 the regular trade sales were suspended and replaced by a series of book fairs organized by the ABTA, but by the spring of 1877, regular trade sales had returned and would continue in one form or another until 1903. Nevertheless, the Civil War marked a decline in the trade-sale system: the final trade sales in Philadelphia and Boston were held in March 1865, and those in Cincinnati, suspended during the war years but revived in 1865, were opened to the public in 1879. More and more, the surviving New York trade sales were reputed to be a place where publishers dumped dead stock and remainders.[16]

As trade sales declined in importance, a new distribution system emerged. Increasingly, retail booksellers placed their orders with traveling sales agents. Known as commercial travelers, these agents, each employed by a publisher to visit retailers and push the publisher's list of new and backlist books, spared retailers the expense of traveling once or twice a year to the urban centers where publishing was becoming concentrated and where the trade sales were held. This shift to the use of commercial travelers occurred throughout American commerce during this period, and book travelers, representing both the larger publishers and jobbers, were important within American book distribution for more than a century. Commenting on this change and its initial consequences, Charles T. Dillingham spoke to the Booksellers' League at that association's first annual dinner in April 1895:

The retail bookseller was prosperous until late in the 70's. The facilities of transportation, fast freight, express and mail became such that the bookseller came less often to market, and in very many cases not at all, sending forward his order by mail and buying his large bills from travellers. The publishers having generally retired from dealing in outside books, confining themselves to their own publications, organized a system of sending travellers to, first, the larger cities, and later, to the small towns and hamlets. This appeared at first to be an advantage to the bookseller, as it saved him the time and expense of visits to market, although it allowed him to see *only* such goods as it was especially desired he should buy. The serious disadvantage was that naturally the enterprising travelling salesman in his eagerness to swell his sales and secure for his employer as large a return as possible for his outlay, diligently sought new outlets for his wares outside the bookseller, and we so well know he found them, and the hard times for booksellers then commenced. The salesman found he could sell large bills of prominent popular books to a class that look for sensations in way of advertising, and owing to the wide margin between the advertised retail price and the net price of books they were a shining mark for such a purpose. These dealers would sell books only during the holidays, never buying a regular line through a publisher's list, and by advertising and selling at no profit, or less than cost, the well-known books of the day, they could derive great benefit by attracting people to their emporium, and by piling up cheap 12mos in great confusion with the advertised books enough would be bought at a large profit to make up for loss on the advertised books.[17]

As Dillingham's tirade indicates, trade books were not only distributed through dedicated retail bookshops. Even the professional book travelers employed by trade publishers often sought to expand the market for their wares beyond the traditional bookshop by approaching alternative retail outlets, which purchased large orders of the most popular works at large discounts that allowed them to compete successfully by underselling traditional dedicated bookshops. Furthermore, like periodicals, some classes of books depended on alternative distribution systems or specialized retail outlets to reach their customers. Sheet music and songbooks were chiefly sold in music shops that also carried musical instruments; schoolbooks and textbooks were purchased and made available by agents employed by public or private educational organizations; religious works were made available at churches and Sunday schools. Colporteurs sold religious tracts door to door, and the years after the Civil War saw the rise of a form of subscription publishing that depended upon amateur agents who canvassed a single work or limited list directly to customers, both urban and rural, by means of a sample or prospectus.

Nevertheless, the dedicated bookshop remained the most important site for the distribution of the full range of American trade books throughout the nineteenth century. Available evidence, though scarce, suggests that the bookshop was quite different from those that modern readers know. Although the most recently published titles were advertised by means of shewbills or displayed in store windows, and other new books were laid out on open tables in the shop, the general stock was chiefly shelved behind counters and not accessible for browsing. Customers depended on sales clerks for advice and service. The books themselves were shelved by publisher rather than by subject, a system that made maintaining inventory more straightforward but depended on the clerks' knowledge of the stock when serving customers (Fig. 4.5). Most retail bookshops supplemented their business in trade books by offering periodicals, stationery, fancy goods, and even patent medicines.[18]

Dedicated retail bookshops were viable only in towns and cities, where the customer base was large enough to allow for a reasonable profit. Most Americans, who even in 1880 lived predominantly in rural settings, also depended on other sources for their reading material, although there is little evidence that access to printed material was impossible for those who desired it. Locally produced printed matter—newspapers especially—was readily available, and the postal system provided a means of direct communication

FIGURE 4.5. "D. Lothrop & Co.'s New Bookstore — Interior View" (Boston), from *American Bookseller* 1 (1 June 1876), showing the role of clerks in providing customers with access to books and material in display cases. American Antiquarian Society.

and distribution between customers and book firms in the main publishing centers. General stores stocked some books, but a number of institutions made many more available: libraries of various sorts, schools, and churches. Many avid readers formed clubs to share the expense of periodical subscriptions or book purchases. Even more informally, individual readers relied on family, friends, and neighbors to share and pass around reading material.

If distribution remained a concern for the book trade throughout the industrial era, there is no doubt that between 1840 and 1880 systems were put into place that allowed a national market for books and print to function successfully and efficiently. As indicated by title-page imprints, an earlier practice of building ad hoc or formal alliances for the regional distribution of some publications died out among trade publishers during the 1840s and 1850s, though it continued among subscription publishers. The establishment of a national market for books, even as the centers of publication became concentrated, was the major development of this period. During the 1850s, many books published in New York were purchased and accessed within several weeks by the St. Louis Mercantile Library, a subscription library founded in 1846. St. Louis was a major transportation center, but books were also reaching the frontier. A copy of W. L. G. Smith's *Life at the South; or, "Uncle Tom's Cabin" as It Is*, published in early August 1852 by Geo. H. Derby & Co. of Buffalo, survives with the inscription "Aug 21st 52 in trade for 3 Mudie Books to a pedlar" and a printed slip identifying the purchaser as John Deichman, dealer of drugs and medicines, Whitewater, Wisconsin. By the 1860s, the system for the distribution of books was even more efficient: the St. Louis Mercantile Library acquired books published in Boston immediately on publication, in some cases on the very same day that the library of Harvard College accessed them.[19] The market for trade books was a national one by 1880.

<hr />

PART 2

Trade Communication

Jeffrey D. Groves

. . .

Late in 1833, George Palmer Putnam, a nineteen-year-old clerk in a New York publishing and bookselling shop, set out to fill what he deemed "a *desideratum* in the trade" by editing and arranging for the publication of the *Booksellers' Advertiser, and Monthly Register of New Publications, American and Foreign*.[20] The inaugural issue appeared in January 1834, and Putnam believed it to be "the first attempt in this country to furnish a booksellers' journal with a statistical record of American publications."[21] In spite of what its young editor described as the journal's favorable reception, the *Booksellers' Advertiser* ceased publication after twelve issues. It was revived in 1836 as a quarterly, but only one number was printed. Putnam had too few hours to devote to the project, and the journal, which " 'promised to pay' in time," did not attract enough advertisements from other members of the trade to make it profitable.[22] Publishers and booksellers of the day, it seems, were not convinced of the necessity of such a journal.

Two decades later the situation had changed. With the market for books becoming both more extensive and more competitive, publishers, jobbers, and booksellers more fully understood the desirability of staying informed about recent publications, trade practices, and the business conditions for bookselling. In September 1855 Putnam saw his earlier vision materialize when the fledgling New York Book Publishers' Association, of which he was a founding member, brought out the first issue of the *American Publishers' Circular and Literary Gazette*, a trade journal meant "to promote the acquisition and circulation of early and authentic intelligence on all subjects connected with Publishing and the Trade in Books."[23] Unlike the *Booksellers' Advertiser* and several other more recent attempts to maintain a trade journal, the *American Publishers' Circular* had a substantial life: after changes in title, ownership, and place of publication, it merged in 1872 with another periodical to become the *Publishers' and Stationers' Weekly Trade Circular*, a journal that recorded Putnam's death that same year.[24] In 1873 the *Trade Circular* was renamed the *Publishers' Weekly*, and that journal is still with us.

The realization of Putnam's "*desideratum*" points to an important development: between 1840 and 1880, the American book trade established a dependable, easily accessible communication system that relied on a variety of printed works to coordinate the efforts of publishers, jobbers, and booksellers throughout the nation. All three segments of the trade needed ways of disseminating and gathering information about both the centralized production of books and the local markets for them, and time-honored methods for doing so were increasingly inadequate as the trade expanded. The need for efficient trade communication predated 1840, of course, and earlier practices persisted through the nineteenth century. In many cities, the proximity of publishers, printers, and booksellers made word of mouth an important means of sharing information. Trade sales gathered trade members for conversation as well as for buying and selling. Letter writing remained an important part of the daily routine and an essential means of doing business, and publishers in particular were prolific correspondents. Supplementing such traditional practices, certain kinds of printed works produced primarily outside the book trade helped to distribute needed information. Newspapers were important venues for trade advertisements and publishers' announcements that coordinated the reprinting of foreign works. In the middle of the century, magazines became increasingly useful periodicals for publishers' advertisements, reviews, notices, and extracts. Beginning in the 1850s, printed credit reports from agencies such as the John M. Bradstreet Company and R. G. Dun & Co. allowed publishers and jobbers to assess risk more accurately when extending credit to booksellers.[25]

Although these ways of allowing access to "early and authentic intelligence" were routinely used within the nineteenth-century book trade, the signal development in trade communication was the emergence of trade periodicals. Early attempts to distribute such publications displayed a top-down approach, serving primarily to inform booksellers and book buyers about publishers' new and recent books. Over time, trade periodicals became more multidirectional and participatory, allowing booksellers to communicate by letter through their pages, jobbers to advertise their ability to fill orders for booksellers and country merchants, and publishers in different cities to debate topics such as discounting and underselling. By 1880, *Publishers' Weekly* had become the trade's semiofficial periodical, and its pages displayed not only a means of circulating business information and trade correspondence but also a strong advocacy for trade reform that—together with the journal's numerous associated trade publications—became a key element in its rise to prominence.

The success and durability of *Publishers' Weekly* stands in marked contrast to the relative transience of earlier efforts in trade journalism. After Putnam's *Booksellers' Advertiser* ceased publication in 1836, the most robust trade periodicals to follow immediately in its wake were produced by publishing houses that also specialized in jobbing both domestic and imported books. *Wiley & Putnam's Literary News-Letter and Monthly Register of New Books, Foreign and American* (1841–47) demonstrated Putnam's continuing commitment to trade periodicals, while *Appleton's Literary Bulletin: A Monthly Record of New Books, English and American* (1843–47) expanded the coverage of Appleton & Co.'s earlier *Home Book-Circular* (1840–43). Essentially catalogs of recently published books, these monthlies were distributed free of charge to a large number of booksellers, lawyers, doctors, and other professionals, as well as to many colleges, schools, and libraries.[26] As their titles suggest, they promoted the publications and importations of their respective houses. "It is proper to observe," noted the first number of *Appleton's Literary Bulletin*, "that one of the features of this list will be the communicating intelligence regarding Messrs. Appleton & Co.'s own Publications at greater length than they have an opportunity of doing elsewhere."[27] Indeed, this first number mentioned only a handful of books from the lists of other publishers. Although by 1847 *Appleton's Literary Bulletin* did announce a larger range of American books from other houses, the overwhelming majority of titles publicized in its pages were Appleton's own or European books that the firm could supply. If the leading trade periodicals of the 1840s were openly self-promotional, they were nonetheless of substantial value to the American book trade. A bookseller in Cincinnati, for instance, who had access to both *Wiley & Putnam's Literary News-Letter* and *Appleton's Literary Bulletin* would have been able to stay informed about the new and recent publications of the periodicals' owners and numerous other American houses. The bookseller could also have purchased books that Wiley & Putnam or Appleton &

Co. had already imported or could have utilized the services of their London branches to order works that had been announced in their journals.

Like the recipients of *Wiley & Putnam's Literary News-Letter* and *Appleton's Literary Bulletin* who used them side by side, the publishers of these monthlies began to conceive of their periodicals as together serving a growing need in the trade for the circulation of information. In 1847 Wiley & Putnam and Appleton & Co. articulated this need jointly in a somewhat surprising way—by announcing the cessation of their respective periodicals.

> The objects for which these journals were commenced, have become extended with the advance and growth of the trade, and the establishment of an enlarged journal, *in which all Publishers and Booksellers could unite*, and a full statement of the merits of the books of the day be presented to the public, has become an affair of importance. We have, therefore, discontinued the News-Letter and Bulletin, the usual contents of which will hereafter appear in the *Literary World*. We warmly commend this undertaking to the support, by advertising and subscription, of all who have received the former journals.[28]

The weekly *Literary World: A Gazette for Authors, Readers, and Publishers*, published jointly by John Wiley and Daniel Appleton, began with great promise, but within three months disagreements between the publishers and their editor, Evert A. Duyckinck, resulted in Duyckinck's replacement by Charles Fenno Hoffman.[29] By 1848 Wiley's and Appleton's warm commendations of the journal had cooled considerably, and in October they sold the *Literary World* to Duyckinck and his brother George.[30] The new owner-editors worked hard to reach Hoffman's announced goal of offering "a medium where the *Author* and the *Publisher, the Bookseller* and *the Bookbuyer*, the *Reader* and the *Critic*, may all communicate with each other, as in a *Literary Exchange*."[31] They noted American and foreign publications, printed "literary intelligence" from both sides of the Atlantic, included literary criticism and opinion, and provided a widely circulated advertising medium used by numerous publishers, jobbers, booksellers, and others associated with the trade. The *Literary World* was clearly intended to serve as a national organ: its printed lists of agents show that subscriptions could be purchased from publishers and booksellers from Portland to Savannah, from Washington to St. Louis, from Cincinnati to New Orleans.

Despite its ambitions, the *Literary World* failed in 1853. In the end, the journal proved too true to its title: the Duyckincks envisioned it primarily as a literary periodical and struggled to attract a general readership. What the trade really needed was a periodical dedicated solely to its interests. Briefly surveying the history of "the newspapers of the trade" in 1852, Charles B. Norton argued that "those publications of this class which will prove most successful, will *most thoroughly identify themselves with the interests of the Trade.*"[32] By the time he wrote these words, Norton had already put his argument into practice. In 1851 he founded *Norton's Literary Advertiser* to bolster his jobbing business as book agent and purchaser for libraries. The following year, he expanded the periodical's scope, capturing the larger purpose for the trade in a new title, *Norton's Literary Gazette and Publishers' Circular*, and competing head-to-head for trade advertisements with the *Literary World*. He attempted to boost the authority of his journal by summarizing the publishing activities of the previous year in an annual supplement between 1852 and 1856.[33]

In 1855 the newly founded New York Publishers' Association, which had been organized in part to regulate trade sales, took over the publication of Norton's journal and renamed it the *American Publishers' Circular and Literary Gazette*. The first issue, edited by Norton, outlined the difficulties that an authoritative trade periodical might overcome:

> That the Book Trade requires a better method of communication between its members than any other branch of business is self-evident. The Publisher, anxious to draw the attention of the Bookseller to his newly published, or forthcoming books, must necessarily, especially if his business is extensive, either advertise largely, or send circulars to his customers through the post-office. The latter expedient is both expensive and uncertain. The difficulty of ascertaining the precise location of all Booksellers seems insurmountable; and many of the circulars frequently never reach their destination. To advertise largely in either a daily or weekly newspaper (except in one exclusively devoted to the trade) is, when the object of the Publisher is to reach the eye of the Bookseller, almost as uncertain.

The *American Publishers' Circular* earnestly, and to a large extent successfully, attempted to construct "a better method of communication" for the trade. It did not, however, occupy the field exclusively. From 1858 until 1861, for instance, O. A. Roorbach competed with the *American Publishers' Circular* by bringing out the *Bookseller's Medium and Publisher's Advertiser*. Nonetheless, the *American Publishers' Circular* became, almost from the beginning, the most obvious avenue through which individual publishers and booksellers could communicate with the larger trade.[34]

Published in New York until 1863, the *American Publishers' Circular* represented the eastern trade most fully, but its early editors — Norton until 1856, and then Charles R. Rode until 1863 — envisioned it as serving the entire trade. In 1856 Norton announced that he would travel extensively in the South and West, soliciting subscriptions and advertisements for the journal.[35] Its pages demonstrate that booksellers and jobbers far distant from New York understood themselves to be participating through its pages in a national communication system. During the financial panic of 1857, Rode reported that a group of New York publishers was considering offering credit at four months, rather than six, and then followed up on that report by printing a large number of letters from subscribers in the next seven issues. Introducing the first set of letters, Rode wrote that "Correspondents may rest assured that this journal desires only to further the best and broadest interests of the Trade, and that it is committed to no special or narrow policy," and the reprinted letters attested to the journal's efforts to serve the entire trade.[36] Many geographically distant members of the trade — booksellers from western New York and Charleston, South Carolina, jobbers and retailers from Wisconsin and Illinois — wrote to support or criticize the proposed change. Some of the correspondents chastised the *American Publishers' Circular*, suggesting that it was merely a slave to the "cliqueism" of New York publishers, yet Rode published their letters to demonstrate the impartiality of the journal's editorial policies.[37]

In 1863 the new owner of the *American Publishers' Circular*, George W. Childs, moved the periodical to Philadelphia. Childs renamed it the *American Literary Gazette and Publishers' Circular* and remained its publisher until 1872. That year Frederick Leypoldt purchased the periodical and merged it with his own journal, the *Trade Circular and Literary Bulletin*, which he had founded in 1869. The resulting periodical, the *Publishers' and Stationers' Weekly Trade Circular*, was again renamed in 1873, becoming *Publishers' Weekly*. From the beginning, *Publishers' Weekly* trumpeted its pedigree, noting in its masthead and in advertisements that it was descended from periodicals that dated back, through *Norton's Literary Gazette*, to 1852. Facing an initial challenge from a rival publication, the American News Company's *American Booksellers' Guide*, the first issue of *Publishers' Weekly* boosted its authority by advertising itself as an "Official Organ of the Publishers' Board of Trade," a body that had been founded in 1870 to regulate the textbook market. By 1874 Leypoldt could also proclaim that his journal had been recognized as the "established organ of the entire trade" by the newly founded American Book Trade Association.[38] Even though the ABTA proved to be short-lived, this designation must have particularly pleased Leypoldt, who from the beginning had claimed that *Publishers' Weekly* was a journal with a national readership. An advertisement from 1873, for instance, was made up of testimonials excerpted from twenty-nine letters to the *Publishers'* *Weekly* offices. Four of these were from the state of New York, and one from Philadelphia, but the others were chosen to suggest a widely diffused distribution, coming as they did from Georgia, Alabama, Kansas, Illinois, Minnesota, Michigan, Maine, and California. A testimonial from a Wisconsin bookseller concisely embodied the spirit of the advertisement: "We, who are so far from the market, need such a paper."[39]

Leypoldt's commitment to trade bibliography addressed a different need: jobbers and booksellers required full and reliable information not only about new publications but also about all books that were currently available for sale. A full record of books in print, distributed in easily referenced lists or catalogs, would allow the bookseller to "save time and trouble, and will generally induce him to send fuller orders, on detecting at a glance the deficiencies of his stock."[40] Trade-sale catalogs, which listed books from numerous firms, had served as useful references in addition to publishers' trade lists, advertisements, and in-press announcements. In 1847 Alexander V. Blake compiled *The American Bookseller's Complete Reference Trade List*, which reprinted the trade lists from a number of publishers in a single volume for sale to booksellers. Similarly, in the late 1850s, the *American Publishers' Circular* regularly printed publishers' trade lists in its pages and even called for a standard size for such lists so that they would be easier to use and preserve.[41] Howard Challen took up the practice in his *Uniform Trade-List Circular* (1866–68), continued as *Publishers' and Stationers' Trade-List Directory* (1869). During this same period, booksellers and other members of the trade could also refer to O. A. Roorbach's *Bibliotheca Americana* (1849), a catalog that through a series of supplements (1850, 1852, 1855, 1858, and 1861) attempted to compile a cumulative list of American and foreign books published in the United States between 1820 and 1861. As Roorbach noted in the initial volume, the catalog's purpose was "to supply Booksellers with a practical Manual of information respecting all books printed in this country during the last thirty years; in other words, all American editions now in the market."[42] James Kelly's *American Catalogue of Books* (1866, 1871) continued Roorbach's work, covering in two volumes American books published between 1861 and 1871. In addition to fuller guides to books in print, the book trade also needed reliable information about its own membership, and John H. Dingman addressed this need with *A Complete List of Booksellers, Stationers, and News Dealers in the United States and Canada* (1867) and the *Directory of Booksellers, Stationers, Newsdealers, and Music Dealers and List of Libraries in the United States and Canada* (1870).

Leypoldt, taking inspiration from such earlier publications and from the

German book trade, which was much more systematically organized than its American counterpart, began to create a mechanism for the regular circulation of information about American books through "a general plan of trade helps."[43] *Publishers' Weekly* was at the heart of this project. In every issue, Leypoldt included announcements of forthcoming works and a record of recently published works. Although he could not claim completeness in this effort—he deliberately excluded some classes of books, such as cheap reprints, and a substantial number of publishers neglected to send him the imprint information he regularly requested from them—the relative fullness and regularity of these order lists were of great use to the trade.[44] In 1879 *Publishers' Weekly* followed Dingman's lead and began in its pages to publish installments of a geographically organized "Book and Stationery Trade Directory," the parts of which were ultimately to be collected in a volume.[45] Although this project was never completed, the effort seems to have influenced C. N. Caspar, who in his *Directory of the American Book, News and Stationery Trade* (1889) recognized the rationale for Leypoldt's plan: "in no trade or profession are so many letters, circulars, prospectuses, price-lists and catalogues sent out to dealers as is done daily among the booksellers' and stationers' fraternity."[46]

Beyond these attempts to record the products and map the contours of the American book trade, Leypoldt and his associates at *Publishers' Weekly*, including R. R. Bowker by 1872 and Adolf Growoll by 1877,[47] inaugurated during the 1870s two major "trade helps," the influence of which would last long beyond the decade. In 1870 Leypoldt published the *American Catalogue of Books for 1869*, a compilation of the monthly lists from his journal, the *Trade Circular and Library Bulletin*, to which were added indexes and a supplementary list. Two similar volumes appeared in 1871 and 1872, the latter one containing trade lists from twenty-six publishers.[48] But the annuals were not remunerative, and uncooperative publishers made the collection of information difficult, so Leypoldt, in spite of his dedication to the project, ceased publication after those three volumes. He revived the idea in the mid-1870s, and in 1878 the first part of the *American Catalogue* appeared, which included author and title listings for "books in print and for sale (including reprints and importations) July 1, 1876."[49] The complete work was published in volume form in 1880, and thereafter the *American Catalogue* continued on, a standard tool for jobbers and booksellers, in the form of supplements and multiyear volumes, until 1910.[50]

The *American Catalogue* came to fruition in the decades after 1880, but the *Publishers' Trade List Annual* quickly matured in the 1870s. This collection of publisher trade lists, first issued in 1873, was bound in New York and distributed throughout the country. Like the *American Catalogue*, the *Publishers' Trade List Annual* included the trade lists of a large portion of the trade and thus was of use especially to jobbers, booksellers, and book buyers. The volume's utility was quickly recognized by the trade and its customers, as L. Thorvel Solberg, a bookseller in Omaha, noted in an 1874 letter to *Publishers' Weekly*: "I find occasion to refer to it so often, that a facetious customer, noticing my hesitancy in answering a question relating to some book, said, 'Go get your *Booksellers' Bible.*'"[51] The first volume contained lists from 59 publishers; by 1880 that number had almost doubled, to 104. Not surprisingly, lists from New York, Boston, and Philadelphia houses predominated, but a substantial number of lists and advertisements came from firms in cities such as Baltimore, Cincinnati, Louisville, Chicago, and San Francisco.

Improved trade bibliography was not the only important development to be featured in the pages of *Publishers' Weekly*. Leypoldt's journal also made itself indispensable by becoming both a site for trade communication and an editorial advocate for trade reform. In 1872 it began to editorialize about the need for a national trade organization to combat "the great difficulty of underselling," by which Leypoldt meant the erosion of booksellers' profit margins by publishers who offered large discounts from the retail price to purchasers outside the trade.[52] These discounts were often given to libraries, to school districts, and to professionals such as doctors, lawyers, and teachers, but many booksellers claimed that books could be purchased below their retail prices by virtually any individual who troubled to contact a publisher. This practice had an impact on jobbers, whose own profit margins were affected, and *Publishers' Weekly* for the most part sided with booksellers and jobbers when it criticized "underselling" by publishers directly to retail customers. Letters from all segments of the trade quickly began to debate various avenues for reform, including altering the management of the trade sales, which were widely believed to encourage underselling. Inspired by the rallying calls for reform in *Publishers' Weekly*, a group of "booksellers of the West," primarily from Ohio and Illinois, met in 1873 to discuss reform, and this meeting resulted in the formation of the Booksellers' Protective Union and the gathering of a larger group (including R. R. Bowker as representative of *Publishers' Weekly*) in Cincinnati the following February.[53] *Publishers' Weekly*'s reporting on and editorializing about this movement spurred the trade to hold a yet larger convention in July 1874 at Put-in-Bay, Ohio, and at this convention, the American Book Trade Association was founded. *Publishers' Weekly* reported extensively on the convention to its large readership, focusing attention particularly on the debate about a standard trade discount of 20 percent.

At the 1874 convention, *Publishers' Weekly* was declared the "established organ of the entire trade," and Leypoldt took this election very seriously. The journal publicized trade meetings, both large ones, such as the ABTA conventions in Niagara Falls (1875) and Philadelphia (1876), and smaller ones sponsored by regional trade associations. Between 1874 and 1876, trade reform was the constant refrain in the pages of *Publishers' Weekly*. By the end of 1877, however, the ABTA had become moribund, and the standard 20 percent discount, at first embraced by a large and influential portion of the trade, had disappeared in the face of emergent department stores and book discounters who sold directly to the public at steeply reduced prices.

Although this attempt at discount reform and price maintenance failed in the 1870s, *Publishers' Weekly*'s position as an advocate for the trade was strengthened in the process. The journal had, after all, marshaled a trade-wide conversation about reform that was national in scope, and in doing so it had decisively shown the trade's need for such a stable means of communication. In combination with its continuing production of trade helps, this advocacy role made *Publishers' Weekly* by 1880 the trade's leading voice. And as *Publishers' Weekly*'s growing authority in the trade suggests, print allowed publishers, jobbers, and booksellers to organize themselves most effectively. As these merchants of the word sought "authentic intelligence" about the growing American taste for books, they utilized the qualities and forms of the very medium they marketed. Along with the economic and technological developments that characterize publishing during the middle of the nineteenth century, this use of print was one of the main contributors to the maturation and nationalization of the book trade.

PART 3

Courtesy of the Trade

Jeffrey D. Groves

. . .

Until the United States recognized international copyright in 1891, American publishers could legally reprint books and articles by foreign authors without the author's or original publisher's permission and were not legally obligated to pay either of them anything, although by midcentury many prominent American trade publishers did offer such remuneration. The established or growing reputations of many foreign authors, especially English ones, guaranteed a strong American market for their works, while their names added distinction to publishers' book lists. These incentives were powerfully conditioned, however, by the absence of copyright's limited-term monopoly, without which a publisher could neither effectively predict nor control the market for a foreign work, because any other American house might also legally reprint it.

As a result, many American publishers worked together to manage these incentives through so-called courtesy of the trade, a set of extralegal trade conventions that governed competition and shored up profits on reprints. The trade publishers who upheld these conventions generally described trade courtesy as a mutually beneficial agreement between respectable houses that recognized the rights of foreign authors, while those firms that did not — firms that trade publishers often referred to as pirates — characterized courtesy of the trade as a trust that benefited only "the clique of publishers who framed it."[54] Although the rules of courtesy of the trade were never overtly and systematically articulated, they were frequently referred to in the business correspondence of trade publishers and reinforced by articles supporting the conventions in influential trade journals, such as the *American Publishers' Circular and Literary Gazette* and *Publishers' Weekly*. Overall, courtesy of the trade proved generally successful throughout most of the nineteenth century, functioning, in Henry Holt's memorable formulation, as a "realization of the ideals of philosophical anarchism — self-regulation without law."[55]

As it had evolved by midcentury, trade courtesy consisted of two major principles based on priority and association. One held that the publisher to first announce publicly that it had a foreign work "in press" had the right to control the publication of that book in the United States without competition from others. In the case of a conflict, any firm that was not first to announce the book was expected to relinquish its plans to publish it or to risk having its own noncopyrighted books "printed on" or "interfered with" by the "wronged" house. Initially, the claim that a work was in press was probably literal, indicating that production had actually begun, but very quickly the phrase came to mean simply that a publisher *intended* to publish the work.[56] "In press" could also indicate that a publisher had made payments to a foreign publisher or author for advance sheets to be sent to America prior to the book's foreign publication, which would allow the American publisher to produce and distribute its edition before any foreign copy could cross the Atlantic, thus giving the publisher actual priority in the market.

The second principle of trade courtesy, the rule of association, was built on the first. The publisher who initially reprinted the work of a foreign author could exercise a claim on all of that author's subsequent works, thus associating that author with the house. For instance, after William D. Ticknor successfully built a claim to Tennyson's *Poems* in 1842, other trade publishers respected the Boston firm's "right" to publish Tennyson's subsequent works. As late as 1868, Fields, Osgood & Co., a successor firm of William D. Ticknor, could write to an English publisher, "In America we have always published Mr. Tennyson's Poems by arrangement with him, and our communication with him has been generally recognized and respected by the trade."[57] The association of a popular foreign author with an American house demanded that the publisher invest substantially in that relationship in the form of printing plates, advertising, and usually payments to the author or, more often, his or her foreign publisher. Members of the trade who did not want their own investments in reprinted works interfered with were likely to respect the investments of others. The rule of association was also carried over to cover American authors: it was considered a violation of trade courtesy for a publisher to approach American authors in order to recruit them away from the firm with which they were already associated, though a firm was free to publish an author's later work if the author approached it on his or her own.[58]

An early form of trade cooperation in the United States dated back to the eighteenth century, when booksellers and printers often joined together to share the risks of publication and to limit competition.[59] The origin of trade courtesy itself was likely Irish: before English copyright law was extended to Ireland in 1801, the Irish trade was free to reprint English works, and thus Irish publishers developed a system for regulating reprinting that anticipated the American one.[60] The American trade in foreign reprints—and with it, courtesy of the trade—emerged during the opening decades of the nineteenth century, especially after the Tariff Act of 1816 raised the duty on foreign books and thereby encouraged their American manufacture. By the early 1820s, some American publishers had begun to purchase advance sheets of popular British authors in the hope of bringing out a work before other American firms could reprint from an imported copy of the published English edition. Carey & Lea, for instance, made payments to Sir Walter Scott or his publisher throughout much of the 1820s and early 1830s, and Harper & Brothers made similar payments to Edward Bulwer, even forming a contract with him in 1835.[61]

During the 1830s, the conventions of trade courtesy were defined even as its evolving rules were tested. Houses such as Carey & Lea, Carey & Hart, and Harper & Brothers had come to dominate the reprint business, and finding themselves in constant competition to secure foreign titles for the American market, they were primarily responsible for articulating the rules of courtesy.[62] The economic depression that began in the late 1830s had an important effect on the reprint business and thus on the development of trade courtesy. At the beginning of the depression, overall book production seems to have contracted: Carey & Lea, for instance, which had brought out 112 new titles in 1835, printed only 52 in 1837. A new form of competition developed with the rise of the mammoth weeklies. By the middle of the 1840s, however, the weeklies were no longer a threat to trade publishers, having been largely extinguished by postal reforms, competition from scrappy publishers, and their own undercapitalization. Courtesy of the trade, which had continued to operate between most publishers, enjoyed a resurgence after the demise of the weeklies. Perhaps in response to the aggressive competition of the early 1840s, it very quickly became a practice that helped publishers to expand and shape their lists as the economy, in fits and starts, began to improve.[63]

Dependent on rapid and widely circulated modes of communication, courtesy of the trade matured alongside the newspapers and magazines that proliferated by midcentury. To secure a title in the 1850s, publishers would place in-press announcements in a leading newspaper. Particular publishers might favor a particular paper, as Harper & Brothers favored the *New York Commercial Advertiser*, but at this time there was no single, agreed-upon organ for such announcements. Publishers routinely placed their announcements in daily papers, rather than less frequently published editions, because dailies provided a prompter record. For their own protection, publishers kept files of their printed announcements so that they could prove their claims against others. Harper & Brothers methodically clipped its in-press announcements, pasted them into memorandum books, and saved other publishers' announcements when there was competition for a particular book.[64]

Ticknor and Fields's relationship with Robert Browning illuminates the details of trade courtesy as it was practiced by midcentury. In 1849 the firm published Browning's *Poems*. Subsequently, the poet became associated with Ticknor and Fields, the American editions of his works often containing an authorization statement from Browning recognizing the firm as his preferred American publisher. Ticknor and Fields took care to safeguard its prize: in September 1855, having heard that Browning would soon publish a new work, the firm sent a letter to the poet's London publisher, Chapman & Hall, asking it to "do us the favor to name the title & when it is coming that we may announce it as in Press according to an understanding with Mr. Browning himself."[65] Several days later, Ticknor and Fields wrote a letter to Browning outlining its terms of payment and its desire for priority in the market:

Dot us down your debtor £60 for the two vols & send them just as early as it is possible to do so that we may have a full months start before our brethren of the trade smell the English copies across the sea. They are keen-scented rascals, our friends in the *Craft*. Dont let Chapman bring out the English copy till we are in full possession of the sheets, and have them printed. He might delay till Dec[r] 1st perhaps. However, you will do what is best I am sure, that we may not be interfered with. . . .

. . . We wish to be your publishers, whatever you may prepare for the press. Please remember this. There are certain names we should feel a deep mortification to see any where else than among our list of worthies, & we mean to be just.[66]

While Ticknor and Fields had established a claim to Browning with the publication of *Poems*, it wanted to bolster that connection by offering the poet handsome terms for his works and to guard against interference in its market by getting the new book through the press before any other American publisher could possibly print it. Doing so would allow the firm to control the early sales of the book, with no competing editions to meet the immediate demand. That Ticknor and Fields worried about being interfered with indicates that trade courtesy did not always protect publishers, but the firm's clear understanding of how best to defeat interference nonetheless depended on the widely accepted courtesy system.

As Ticknor and Fields made clear in the same letter, the firm also hoped to publish Browning's wife, Elizabeth Barrett Browning. Since 1850, however, she had been associated with a New York publisher, C. S. Francis & Co., which had informed Ticknor and Fields that it would not surrender the association even if Barrett Browning wished her books to be published by the Boston firm. Ticknor and Fields communicated this information to Robert Browning:

Willingly would we (Ticknor & F) pay Mrs. Browning for her poems; but, as I once told you, Francis would print at any rate, and at a cheaper rate, and perhaps set on our other books full chase, & to try to injure us in every way. We are a funny set of christians over the waves. . . .

. . . I regret, and always have done so, that Mrs. Browning does not belong to us, but when her writings first saw America, I was guiltless of book-publishing and innocent of ink. And now that I am reckoned among Publishers and sinners, it is too late to claim her. This is, and always will be annoying to us.

I shall meet Francis in New York next week. . . . I once tried to buy the plates & the right of him to issue Mrs. B's works, but he groaned and held on.[67]

In 1856 Ticknor and Fields again tried in vain to purchase Francis's "right." As much as the Boston firm would have liked to publish Barrett Browning, and as much as she would have provided prestige for the house, the firm did not challenge its New York rival by printing on it: Francis brought out Barrett Browning's next work, *Aurora Leigh*, in an "author's edition" in 1857. Such willingness on the part of Ticknor and Fields to surrender its immediate interests to the larger goal of protecting its list from poaching was common under courtesy. The extensive correspondence of this firm shows repeatedly that it either succeeded in getting other houses to cease publication of a book, or itself ceased publication when pushed by another firm.

If these principles were widely observed by midcentury, they were also often strained or broken. Sometimes different understandings of literary property and trade courtesy clashed. Most English publishers assumed that when they published a domestic work, they also acquired the foreign rights to it. American publishers, to the contrary, generally acted as agents for authors in placing their books with foreign publishers, not as holders of the foreign rights. Where payments in advance of publication were involved, misunderstandings might occur because of the nebulous right that was being purchased: one American publisher might pay a foreign author for the reprint rights to his or her work, while another American publisher might conclude negotiations with the foreign house that would first print the book. In such cases, the two American publishers typically came to an amicable agreement, with one firm surrendering its claim on the book in return for reimbursement of expenses from the other.[68] Regardless of such misunderstandings, it is clear that courtesy of the trade favored those publishers that could obtain and afford advance intelligence about forthcoming foreign books (intelligence that might be carried in a foreign journal or, more effectively, provided by a foreign agent) and deal expeditiously with foreign authors and publishers.

The claim of right by association was also often difficult to maintain when the author was a popular novelist. Courtesy of the trade could not effectively govern the reprinting of Scott's romances or Dickens's novels: for many publishers, the temptation to profit by reprinting works by these extraordinarily popular authors was stronger than the urge to cooperate. Nor could courtesy be used to associate a "classic" author to a house, and collected editions of standard foreign writers were generally held to be fair game.[69] Printing on another publisher in retaliation for a breach in courtesy could erode the value of an association. In 1870, after failing to resolve a courtesy dispute with Fields, Osgood & Co., Harper & Brothers published an illustrated edition of Tennyson's works that substantially weakened the thirty-year association between the Boston house and the poet laureate. Adding insult to injury, this punitive measure encouraged other publishers to bring out rival editions.[70] Once a publisher lost control of an association, it could not be reclaimed — almost as if a copyright had expired and a book had slipped into the public domain.

This point was made a matter of public record in 1865 when Sheldon & Co. took H. O. Houghton & Co. to court over an alleged breach of trade courtesy. In 1861 these two firms had contracted to publish a uniform edition of Dickens's works. Houghton owned the plates and printed the books, while Sheldon marketed and distributed them for a limited term of years. In 1864 Houghton notified Sheldon that this term would not be extended. Subsequently, Sheldon filed a bill of complaint in New York, claiming that the two firms had in effect formed a partnership in the Dickens edition and that the association of Dickens with both firms constituted a goodwill, a partnership commodity that had significant monetary and prestige value for both firms. The trade watched this lawsuit with interest. Attorneys for both the plaintiff and the defendant deposed numerous prominent publishers about their understanding of the workings of courtesy of the trade. After hearing the arguments, the judge ruled for Houghton. No partnership had existed, he said, but even if it had, the "incorporeal property called good-will" had no legal force because the courtesy of the trade was constituted by extralegal agreements among firms that volunteered their cooperation.[71] This ruling could not have surprised many publishers, most of whom probably concurred with a writer in *American Literary Gazette and Publishers' Circular*: "It is not easy to see from what is stated by the court . . . how a different conclusion could have been reached."[72]

Some twentieth-century scholars have suggested that *Sheldon et al. v. Houghton* weakened courtesy of the trade, but in fact the decision left the system precisely where it had been prior to the controversy, a point made evident in the testimony for a later lawsuit.[73] In February 1893, Isaac K. Funk, of Funk & Wagnalls, lost a libel suit against the *New York Evening Post*. In an editorial two years before, the *Evening Post* had charged the publisher with piracy and theft for having reprinted the *Encyclopedia Britannica*. Funk had sued for $100,000 in damages. During the trial, several publishers testified about the role courtesy had played in American reprinting prior to the establishment of international copyright in 1891. While those who testified had an interest in reinforcing the courtesy of the trade, their testimony demonstrates that in the second half of the nineteenth century, courtesy was the dominant regulatory practice in reprint publishing.[74]

By the 1870s, the practice of purchasing advance sheets was largely replaced, at least in relation to popular works by well-known authors, by a voluntary royalty system.[75] Beginning early in the decade, the American News Company circulated in-press announcements through its nationally distributed *American Booksellers' Guide*, while *Publishers' Weekly* attempted to standardize the practice of trade courtesy by reporting in-press announcements from the previous week's *New York Commercial Advertiser*, which effectively made the *Commercial Advertiser* the paper of record for the reprint trade.[76] Such movements toward standardization, however, do not indicate the general health of trade publishing. During the late 1870s, a new breed of publishers that specialized in reprinting attacked courtesy of the trade. The most aggressive challenges came from John W. Lovell, Isaac K. Funk, and George P. Munro: like the publishers of the mammoth weeklies nearly forty years earlier, these entrepreneurs printed inexpensive versions of foreign works, often as part of a cheap series or library that was designed to take advantage of postal regulations that subsidized second-class mail and to cut into the market of the established trade publishers. Relying on noncopyrighted works and large sales to make a profit, not only did these publishers disregard courtesy but, appealing to a growing anticorporate, populist sentiment, they attacked it as bad for the book-buying public and described it as monopolistic in intent. In 1879 Lovell, one of the most ambitious of these new publishers, denounced trade courtesy in the pages of *Publishers' Weekly*:

> I can say to the younger and smaller houses from my own experience, Go in heartily for the "courtesy of the trade" and — starve. You will find everything is expected of you and very little given you. As for my part, I prefer to follow the examples that led to success in the past rather than the precepts now advocated to prevent others from attaining it.[77]

In the same journal a year later, Funk complained that "No one pretends to claim that the law of courtesy was framed in the interest of authors or of the public. It is a 'right of possession' based primarily on the principle, or lack of principle, of *first grab*."[78] In 1884 Munro, the creator of the famous Seaside Library of cheap reprints, argued in the *New York Tribune* that he was not a pirate but "a reformer" breaking down "the Chinese or rather American wall of trade courtesy and privilege" that had been erected solely for the benefit of "a monopoly of publishers in this country."[79]

This "new competition," as *Publishers' Weekly* called it, developed in the midst of a difficult period for the book trade in general.[80] The depression of the 1870s caused established trade practices to erode: publishers offered ever-deeper discounts on their works to the trade and quite often to the public. Steep discounts and floating prices reduced the profitability of both jobbing and retailing, and booksellers especially began to complain about their treatment at the hands of publishers. An 1880 correspondent to *Publishers' Weekly* summed up the situation: "the trade has been going down hill in so far as harmony of action is involved."[81] Publishers such as Lovell, Funk, and Munro took advantage of this disarray to challenge the established reprinters. Unlike the proprietors of the mammoth weeklies, these cheap publishers had staying power. Established trade publishers screamed about raids on their lists. When Lovell brought out an edition of Jean Ingelow's *Poems* in 1880, Roberts Brothers, the Boston firm with which the English poet had been associated for more than fifteen years, took out advertisements "To Booksellers throughout the United States" encouraging them not to "sanction a moral wrong by vending this unauthorized version," but rather to "show their admiration for this beloved authoress by favoring only the Author's Editions, issued by her own publishers."[82] In the same year, *Publishers' Weekly* spoke for trade publishers when it argued that Lovell and the other pirates benefited from a form of "getting something for nothing, by reprinting books without recognition of the cost of writing them" and by "interfering with the vested rights of American publishers who publish under arrangement with foreign authors or their representatives, or who have taken the risk of making a market for these authors."[83] Unless a trade firm was willing to bring out a cheap edition to compete head on with a reprinter, however, such moral arguments were the best that could be mustered, for there was no legal recourse against "interfering" publishers such as Lovell. The traditional punitive measure of printing on a publisher who infringed a courtesy association had little effect because the new publishers were attempting not to control the market for a particular book but merely to cut into an existing market.

Between 1840 and 1880, courtesy of the trade proved a generally effective system for managing competition among a large number of publishing firms. The "new competition" provided by reprinters of the late 1870s certainly challenged its basis, but courtesy nonetheless continued to organize reprinting until international copyright replaced its economic function in 1891. Even after that, many trade publishers respected the rule of association, and courtesy conventions served as guidelines for the reprinting of American works that had entered the public domain.[84] The cooperation between publishers that this system had helped to shape allowed the ghost of courtesy to persist among some of the older firms well into the twentieth century — not as the means to create a "vested right" in a noncopyrighted text but as an extralegal means of maintaining trade cooperation.

PART 4

The International Trade in Books
Michael Winship

．　．　．

Throughout the middle half of the nineteenth century, the United States was fully and actively involved in the international trade in books.[85] The broad outlines of this involvement are preserved in the annual Commerce and Navigation reports submitted to the House of Representatives by the Treasury Department. The statistics reported there reveal the tremendous, even exponential, growth in international trade over the period. Between 1846 and 1876, American book imports grew almost tenfold, exports by a factor of just over thirteen, though imports always exceeded exports by several times. The trade was chiefly transatlantic—the trade with Great Britain strongly predominated—but over the period, exports to Canada and various South American countries increased substantially. Imports of books entered the United States overwhelmingly through New York, which was increasingly becoming the major center of the publishing industry, but the growing trade with Canada meant that by 1876 the greatest value of exported books passed through Niagara and other centers of trade along the Canadian border. (For an overview of U.S. book import and export statistics, see Graph 4.1 and Tables 4.1–4.)

Such statistics provide an overview of the international trade in books. If similar records for the domestic book trade were available for these years, historians could determine the relative importance of the international and domestic trade in books. It is, however, important to remember exactly why one set of statistics survives and the other does not: customs statistics are a direct result of governmental regulation of international trade, a form of control that many Americans feel would be an inappropriate abridgment of First Amendment rights if applied to the domestic book trade.[86] In contrast, governmental regulation of the foreign trade in books through the collection of tariffs, a duty on foreign books as merchandise, was widely accepted not only as a source of revenue but as a means of protecting the domestic manufacture of and trade in books.

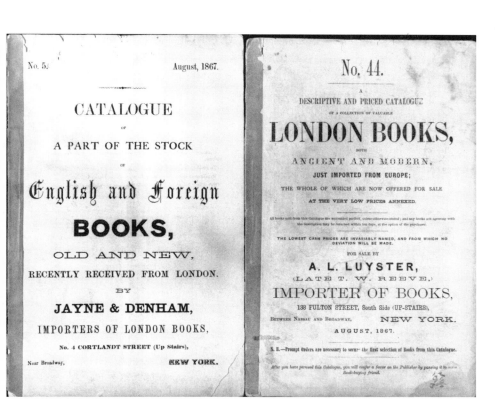

FIGURE 4.6. Two catalogs listing books imported from London for retail sale in New York, both dated August 1867. Courtesy of Michael Winship.

Tariff rates on books in both the United States and Great Britain indicate that the second of these functions was the more important during the nineteenth century. In both countries, the use of tariffs to restrict the international trade in books must have been made acceptable in part by the support it provided the domestic book trade. In the United States between 1824 and 1846, duties on imported books were charged according to a complicated schedule, depending upon the language in which they were printed, the number of years since original publication, and the binding. The Walker tariff of 1846 simplified the duty on books, which was set at a flat rate of 10 percent ad valorem and 20 percent on any book "in the course of printing and republication in the United States." These rates were lowered in 1857 to 8 and 15 percent respectively, but with the Civil War, rates were raised in 1861 to a flat 15 percent, in 1862 to 20 percent, and in 1864 to 25 percent.[87] At midcentury, the British government charged a duty on imported books at a basic rate of five guineas per hundredweight, reduced by half for books printed in a "living" foreign language or printed in English in a British colony or possession, and

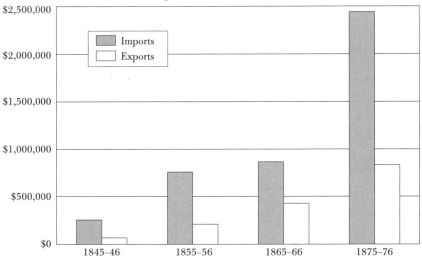

GRAPH 4.1. U.S. import and export figures for books and other printed matter, 1845–1876

Sources: United States Congress, *Commerce and Navigation*, 29th Cong., 2nd sess., House Executive Document 2, no. 11 (Washington, D.C., 1846; serial set 498), *Commerce and Navigation of the United States for the Year Ending June 30, 1856*, 34th Cong., 3rd sess., House Executive Document 13 (Washington, D.C., 1856; serial set 910), *Commerce and Navigation of the United States for the Year Ending June 30, 1866*, 39th Cong., 2nd sess., House Executive Document 17 (Washington, D.C., 1867; serial set 1301), *Commerce and Navigation of the United States for the Fiscal Year Ended June 30, 1868*, 40th Cong., 3rd sess., House Executive Document [16] (Washington, D.C., 1869; serial set 1384), and *Commerce and Navigation of the United States for the Fiscal Year Ended June 30, 1876*, 44th Cong., 2nd sess., House Executive Document 13, no. 46 (Washington, D.C., 1877; serial set 1760).

Note: This graph and Tables 4.1–4 indicate general trends for book imports and exports between 1840 and 1880 but do not include information about reexports (books imported to the United States and then immediately exported) and indirect trade (books that were reexported to the United States from another country). Each decade is represented by its midpoint fiscal year (1845–46, 1855–56, etc.), and all figures are in unadjusted dollars. The data from the Commerce and Navigation volumes of the American serial set are statistical representations that simplify and standardize the congressional reports on which they are based, which do not all use the same set of categories or collect exactly the same set of information. Moreover, the Commerce and Navigation reports do not systematically discriminate between books, maps, periodicals, pamphlets, and other forms of printed matter. For ease of reference, country names have been standardized across the period.

further reduced to one guinea per hundredweight for all books printed prior to 1801.[88]

Examining the international book trade in terms only of tariffs fails to give any sense of just what books and texts were being traded and how the business was managed. Several examples of the transatlantic trade between London and the Boston literary publishers and booksellers Ticknor and Fields help

TABLE 4.1. Books and other printed matter: U.S. imports
by place of origin, 1845–1876

Place of origin	Value of U.S. imports in dollars			
	1845–46	1855–56	1865–66	1875–76
Belgium	5,261	3,045	296	8,525
Brazil	0	0	116	125
China	73	164	904	8,749
Colombia	0	2,073	2	1,040
Denmark	192	0	0	0
France	53,126	90,610	39,559	208,044
Germany	16,179	81,745	139,985	614,775
Hawaiian Islands	0	0	0	1,674
Italy	399	772	1,002	6,963
Japan	0	0	64	5,294
Mexico	37	45	135	831
Netherlands	2,161	5,551	1,601	19,110
Russia	12	103	10	20
Spain	120	313	4,105	458
Sweden and Norway	97	10	0	2,261
United Kingdom	176,960	580,392	668,519	1,536,559
Canada	513	1,915	9,023	23,812
Other British Possessions	130	562	1,231	393
Venezuela	4	8	7	122
Other Central and South America	56	0	0	83
All other	84	0	0	0
Total	255,404	767,308	866,559	2,438,838

Sources: See source note for Graph 4.1.

to fill out the picture. In order to participate successfully in the transatlantic trade in books and texts, any firm needed to be able to transfer information, merchandise, and credit. An information network enabled the partners of Ticknor and Fields in Boston to learn what books were available in London. They relied primarily on advertisements, notices, and reviews in periodicals — especially trade journals, such as Sampson Low's *Publishers' Circular* (1837–1959) — as well as on publishers' and booksellers' catalogs. Public sources of information did not fulfill the firm's needs, for the conventions of trade courtesy required that the partners have early knowledge of gossip, especially of forthcoming London publications. To this end, both partners made several trips to England to establish personal acquaintance with London publishers and authors. More important, the firm employed Nicolas Trübner as its agent in London, paid to keep Ticknor and Fields abreast of

TABLE 4.2. Books and other printed matter: U.S. exports by destination, 1845–1876

Destination	Value of U.S. exports in dollars			
	1845–46	1855–56	1865–66	1875–76
Argentina	759	1,667	3,447	7,525
Belgium	200	992	0	659
Brazil	496	1,659	29,443	58,845
Chile	3,214	6,600	2,210	1,563
China	1,280	1,573	3,453	4,718
Colombia	208	8,604	88,817	43,727
Denmark	873	1,134	4,317	750
Dominican Republic	0	22	85	1,947
France	2,585	8,119	14,086	13,713
Germany	1,132	4,678	5,394	38,774
Hawaiian Islands	0	5,294	6,936	7,334
Italy	200	100	1,480	10
Japan	0	0	845	18,962
Mexico	5,080	2,425	9,822	15,271
Netherlands	114	1,516	1,634	1,178
Peru	0	550	1,247	275
Russia	1,002	0	0	0
Spain	3,779	6,344	34,031	9,867
Sweden and Norway	0	30	0	60
Texas	1,876	—	—	—
Turkey	17	0	1,235	0
United Kingdom	14,954	21,640	97,296	97,499
Canada	9,869	110,366	94,072	481,148
Other British Possessions	8,053	9,101	16,596	24,252
Uruguay	200	381	200	1,552
Venezuela	1,410	3,284	4,378	6,755
Other Central and South America	275	544	5,089	999
All other	5,991	5,879	1,043	646
Total	63,567	202,502	427,156	838,029

Sources: See source note for Graph 4.1.

new and interesting publications. A letter of 7 April 1856 to Trübner indicates what was expected:

Touching the works we wish you to buy for us for reprinting, we meant to have explained to you, when you were here, and thought we did, the class of publications which we naturally choose. You see how impossible it is for us to name authors as you suggest, for new ones are springing up every day. Books like Rogers' 'Table Talk', Mrs. Gaskell's 'Life of

TABLE 4.3. Books and other printed matter:
U.S. imports by tariff collection district, 1855–1876

Tariff collection district	Value of U.S. imports in dollars		
	1855–56	1867–68	1875–76
Baltimore	2,012	6,637	44,869
Boston	106,634	101,974	177,939
Buffalo	30	217	459
Champlain, N.Y.	1,440	550	2,460
Detroit	28	1,885	4,272
New Orleans	23,227	10,198	14,549
New York City	590,306	1,043,421	2,000,437
Niagara	115	2,815	2,458
Passamaquoddy Bay, Maine	0	167	769
Philadelphia	34,602	2,169	121,023
Port Huron, Mich.	0	11,715	3,861
San Francisco	7,576	25,133	54,319
Vermont	18	11,898	7,388
Other Great Lakes districts	30	841	1,994
Other Atlantic districts	937	401	820
Other Gulf State districts	353	327	1,098
Other Pacific districts	0	78	123
Total	767,308	1,220,426	2,438,838

Sources: See source note for Graph 4.1.

Note: "Tariff collection district" indicates the route by which imported and exported books and other printed materials entered or left the United States. Tariff collection district tables were not introduced in the Commerce and Navigation reports until 1855–56. The 1865–66 report does not contain such information; the next report to do so is 1867–68, and those tables are summarized here and in Table 4.4.

Jane Eyre', Tennyson's 'Poems', &c. &c. are what we want. First rate things you know as well as we do. A new poet, for instance, we should be shy of, but another shot from Alexander Smith, for instance, would suit us exactly. Will it not be a good plan for you to enquire of publishers occasionally what is *talked* of as coming out?[89]

The nineteenth-century networks for the transfer of merchandise and credit used by Ticknor and Fields were also well-established and relatively stable. For most of the century, the packet lines (the Cunard line was the most famous) connected Liverpool to Boston and New York with regular, twice-a-month service, first sail and then steam. The packets carried the mails — thus supporting the information network — and all but the very largest shipments of books that Ticknor and Fields ordered from London. Finally, a network

Tariff collection district	Value of U.S. exports in dollars		
	1855–56	1867–68	1875–76
Baltimore	2,542	1,216	8,042
Boston	29,766	20,491	53,368
Buffalo	7,691	104	600
Champlain, N.Y.	27,377	3,095	17,670
Detroit	225	1,473	10,607
New Orleans	379	4,765	315
New York City	61,522	239,370	293,843
Niagara	7,191	305	344,222
Passamaquoddy Bay, Maine	20,893	10,153	11,576
Philadelphia	5,644	4,150	4,291
Port Huron, Mich.	0	54	0
San Francisco	1,946	21,217	35,215
Vermont	5,517	30,689	35,337
Other Great Lakes districts	31,763	8,969	21,317
Other Atlantic districts	46	1,753	777
Other Gulf State districts	0	2,054	845
Other Pacific districts	0	135	4
Total	202,502	349,993	838,029

Sources: See source note for Graph 4.1.

for the transfer of credit provided Ticknor and Fields with the means to pay for its London purchases, involving the firm with large international bankers. Typically the firm purchased a bill of exchange with cash from the Boston bankers Brown Brothers and deposited it with Baring Brothers, bankers in London. Ticknor and Fields could then pay the London trade for purchases with promissory notes drawn on Baring Brothers.

By midcentury, Ticknor and Fields was well established as publisher and bookseller, very much involved in the import book trade. The firm regularly imported some works in bulk for wholesale distribution and also imported small quantities of other London publications for retail sale. Books were not the only imports, however, for once connections were made, the firm began to import all sorts of other products related to the book trade. These included type, ink, paper, binding cloth, leather, stationery, and, on occasion, stereotype or electrotype casts of relief engravings done by British artists — at one point the firm inquired whether there might be a promising young British engraver that it could lure to Boston and set up in business.

Which books did Ticknor and Fields import from England? The range was considerable. For wholesale distribution, the firm regularly imported British Bibles and testaments, as well as illustrated children's books, including the so-called indestructible books printed on cloth for the very young. Another specialty was elegantly illustrated gift editions for the Christmas trade — including British editions of the firm's own American authors Henry Wadsworth Longfellow and Oliver Wendell Holmes. Smaller quantities of British books and magazines were regularly received for retail sale at the firm's Old Corner Bookstore. Finally, the firm sent special orders for single books to London for its retail customers, who included many of the intellectual elite of Boston and Cambridge.

A single transaction exemplifies the range of the firm's activities as an importer of books. On 12 March 1858, Ticknor and Fields received a shipment of books from its London agent, Trübner & Co., via the Cunard steamship *Niagara*, which had just arrived from Liverpool. The contents of "Case #206" were various. It contained small shipments of new books purchased directly from two London publishers, Richard Bentley and H. G. Bohn, which had been ordered on 27 January and 9 February, respectively, and had a total value of £14 13s. From Bentley, the firm received eleven copies of volume 8 of a new edition of Horace Walpole's works; from Bohn, a selection of sixty-six volumes from his famous "library" series. A third group of new books, eleven titles valued at £4 10s. 5d., had been gathered together by the London agent and included three dozen copies of *Our Favourite Picture Books* for children. Several newly published books detailing the siege at Lucknow, which had been lifted only the preceding autumn, provided current intelligence of imperial politics. Boston customers could also keep up with the latest London serials, for Trübner also sent a collection of recent issues of magazines and newspapers, valued at £5 1s. 6d., including eight copies of Dickens's *Household Words*, five each of *Chambers's Journal of Popular Literature, Science and Arts* and the *Illustrated London News*, and twelve copies of the most recent monthly part of Thackeray's *The Virginians*, then being serialized in London. The shipment also contained special orders for individual patrons: twenty-one titles in all, valued at £7 1s. 2½d., including medical books, sheet music, and back issues and bound volumes of magazines. Finally, the agent had included with the shipment fourteen parcels that had been delivered in London for transfer to Boston. This was a service that Ticknor and Fields regularly performed for its customers, and included with this shipment were parcels for Ralph Waldo Emerson, Eliza Follen, and the American Board of Commissioners for Foreign Missions.

The total cost of the books in this shipment came to just over £31. The packing case cost another 7s. 6½d.; freight came to £1 12s. 5d. (paid to Baring Brothers' branch in Liverpool); a further 3s. was charged for postage. Trübner & Co. also charged a commission of 7½ percent on the value of the books that it had gathered (a total of £1 5s. 10d.) and included a report with the shipment to keep the Boston firm up to date on its book orders and to provide the latest news of the London trade. For example, with this shipment Trübner reported that the London firm Kent & Co. was not able to supply a portrait of Alfred Tennyson that Ticknor and Fields wished to use as the frontispiece for a collected edition of that poet's works, as no copies were in stock.[90]

Just as important as the importation of merchandise—books, serials, and other items—was the transatlantic trade in texts. The conventions of trade courtesy allowed American firms to acquire the right—if not a de jure copyright, at least a trade-sanctioned de facto right—to English publications. Since British copyright law required first publication in the United Kingdom, American publishers of British works usually strove for simultaneous or nearly simultaneous publication in order to discourage competition. This frequently resulted in a payment to the British publisher or author for early sheets, proofs, or even a second copy of the manuscript, sent from London. Similarly, American publishers often held off their publication of an American work until it could be brought out in London in order to establish a claim on British copyright for the author.

The trade in texts—as opposed to their piracy—was much more important and regular than many scholars recognize. When the firm published a two-volume edition of Tennyson's *Poems* in 1842, for example, it made a payment of $150 to the poet to establish the publisher's "rights" to his work.[91] From time to time, when the firm acted as the sole "authorized" American distributor of a British edition, it could be said to be involved in the importation of both books and texts in a single transaction. These imported editions (which included works by Mary Russell Mitford, Richard Hengist Horne, and Mayne Reid, among others) were shipped in sheets or bound but usually had a specially printed title page with the Ticknor and Fields imprint. A typical example of this type of transaction involving the collected works of Charles Dickens, a vocal supporter of international copyright and critic of American publishers for their so-called piracies, is illustrative.

On 9 March 1858, Ticknor and Fields wrote to the London publisher Chapman & Hall to inquire what price and size of order would guarantee exclusive rights to the American market for an authorized edition of Dickens's collected works that the London firm had announced for serial publication. Terms were quickly agreed upon, and on 15 June the first shipment containing five hundred two-volume copies each in sheets of *The Pickwick Papers*,

The Life and Adventures of Nicholas Nickleby, and *The Life and Adventures of Martin Chuzzlewit* left London. Chapman & Hall charged 2s. per volume, a total of £300; the cost of packing cases, bills of lading, dock charges, entering, clearing, and insurance was another £12 9s. 5d., though the Boston firm received a drawback, a refund of the paper duty, of £20 10s. 10d. The total cost of the shipment thus came to £291 18s. 7d. ($1,297.46), which was posted to Chapman & Hall's account on 24 October 1858. When the sheets arrived in Boston, their cost came to 86½¢ per copy. Another 30¢ was charged for binding, but the total cost per copy ($1.16½) was less than half the retail price of $2.50. Because Ticknor and Fields was the sole American distributor, the firm was able to increase further the profit on the work by reducing the trade discount to only 20 percent, or 25 percent on orders of twenty-five copies or more. The first lot of sheets was shipped by freight directly from London and not, as was normal, via the Liverpool packets. It was not received in Boston for three months, and this delay held up publication of the subsequent volumes in the set that arrived in Boston before the first were in hand. Furthermore, freight costs on the shipment (£12 9s. 5d.) were heavy, and further charges came due upon arrival in Boston.[92] When the firm finally began to distribute the series at the end of October, a fourth volume — *The Old Curiosity Shop* — was included, though it had not been issued in London until well after the original three titles.[93]

The transactions between Ticknor and Fields and Chapman & Hall exemplify how, and especially in what quantities, both books and texts crossed the Atlantic during the nineteenth century. Of course, particular arrangements and costs varied from place to place, time to time, and transaction to transaction. Nonetheless, it is clear that during the nineteenth century, the transatlantic trade in both books and texts was an active and thriving business. Ticknor and Fields — a preeminent literary publisher — issued not only the works by William Cullen Bryant, Richard Henry Dana, Ralph Waldo Emerson, Nathaniel Hawthorne, Oliver Wendell Holmes, Henry Wadsworth Longfellow, James Russell Lowell, Harriet Beecher Stowe, Henry David Thoreau, and John Greenleaf Whittier, but also, for the same market and for the same audience, those by Robert Browning, Thomas De Quincey, Charles Dickens, Charles Kingsley, Mary Russell Mitford, Charles Reade, Sir Walter Scott, Alfred Tennyson, and William Makepeace Thackeray.

CHAPTER 5

The Role of Government

Copyright

Meredith L. McGill

. . .

The history of copyright law in the nineteenth century has been told as a story of gradual progress toward the copyright system we are familiar with today, including the broadening of a narrow definition of authors' rights to include translation and dramatization; the extension of copyright protection from the original "maps, charts, and books" to a wider range of mass-produced and fine-art objects; the centralization of the administration of copyrights; and the emergence by the 1880s of a consensus within the publishing trades as to the need for an international copyright agreement. But to identify this period with the belated settling of American copyright law on a strong authors'-rights foundation is to narrow the spectrum of nineteenth-century thinking about intellectual property and to overstate the role that copyright played in the explosive growth of the printing and publishing trades.[1] If, in retrospect, nineteenth-century law appears inadequate, inconsistent, and unsettled, it is because a variety of models of intellectual property still vied for dominance in popular opinion, in Congress, and in the courts. For example, the seeming incongruity of a law that protected citizens and residents but not foreign authors did not simply reflect the power of opportunistic publishers of foreign reprints; it was the product of a strong cultural emphasis on the free circulation of print that depended on limiting authors' and publishers' property rights in texts. Americans disagreed both about the nature of copyright and about where exactly this property resided. A narrow definition of copyright as a trade privilege — the right to the copy — made sense so long as publishers' property was tied up in printed sheets. The increased use of stereotype plates, however, raised questions as to whether copyright had a material correlative or whether it was an abstract right independent of plates, sheets, or the words of the author.

Although historians and critics have long regarded the emergence of authors' rights as a threshold condition for a mass market for books, the strengthening of the copyright laws was not a significant catalyst for growth in the book industry. Rather, nineteenth-century markets tended to flourish — at times in cutthroat fashion — precisely where the law stopped short of protecting authors' rights. "Piracy" and "legitimate publishing" cannot simply be opposed to each other. Indeed, most publishing firms included both American works and foreign reprints on their lists. Moreover, publishers found ways of regulating markets outside the reach of the copyright laws, through the courtesy of the trade and through elaborate transatlantic arrangements that provided for de facto copyright protection in both England and the United States. Changes in the copyright law were avidly sought by many authors, publishers, and playwrights; they helped to stimulate the production of genres such as printed play-texts and served as an instrument for the consolidation of authors', publishers', and theater managers' power. Yet for much of this period, copyright laws were unenforced and technically unenforceable; they played more of a shadow role than a central part in the growth and regulation of the market for printed materials.

The first fifty years of American copyright jurisprudence produced a divided legacy. While the Supreme Court maintained that copyright was a reward for, and a spur to, civic duty and insisted on strict adherence to the statutory requirements in order for copyright to be defensible at law, Congress's passage of the act of 1831 redefined copyright as something approximating a personal property right, making copyrights familial and heritable, although only for a single generation (Table 5.1).[2] Over the following decades, Congress tinkered with aspects of the law, changing deposit requirements and extending copyright to include performance rights in dramatic texts and photographic images, but it did not undertake another major revision of the copyright code until 1870.

In the period between these two copyright acts, public debate over the restriction of copyrights to citizens and residents repeatedly came before Congress. Many authors and publishers believed that the free reprinting of foreign works devalued American copyrights. Indeed, many profitable texts — staples of the publishing trades such as magazines, school texts, reference works, and popular European novels — continued to circulate, unprotected by copyright. Despite support by prominent literary figures, publishers, and statesmen, Congress turned back numerous international copyright bills, and in 1854 the Senate blocked the ratification of an Anglo-American copyright treaty.[3] Although nominally a debate over foreign authors' rights, the question of international copyright became the focal point of a domestic struggle over the nature and structure of a rapidly expanding market for print. In newspaper and magazine articles, discussion at public meetings, and petitions to

Date of U.S. act	Major provisions of U.S. act	British enactments
31 May 1790: First U.S. copyright law	· establishes fourteen-year copyright term for citizens and residents, and fourteen-year extension for living authors who reregister their titles · sets prerequisites for copyright: depositing a printed copy of the title in the district court; publishing a copy of this record in one or more newspapers for 4 weeks; delivering a copy of the work to the Secretary of State within 6 months · assures the public that copyright does not "extend to prohibit" the importation, sale, or reprinting of any map, chart, or book published by a noncitizen outside of the jurisdiction of the United States	
29 April 1802	· extends copyright to "historical and other prints" · requires notice of copyright to be inserted into books themselves, either on the title page or the page just following · requires a record of copyright to be impressed on the face of maps and charts	
3 February 1831: First general revision of the copyright code	· extends the initial term of copyright to 28 years, including copyrights in force · extends the right of renewal to widows and children of authors and proprietors · extends copyright protection to musical compositions · eliminates the requirement to publish notices in the newspaper to establish copyright, but retains this requirement in the case of copyright renewals · requires a copy of the work to be delivered to the clerk of the dis-	1833: Dramatic Property Act: provides performance rights for dramatic compositions 1838: International Copyright Act: provides protection in Great Britain for books published by foreign authors whose governments extend reciprocal rights to British citizens 1842: Literary Copyright Act: extends the term of copyright to 42 years from the date of

TABLE 5.1. *Continued*

Date of U.S. act	Major provisions of U.S. act	British enactments
	trict court, who is newly required to transmit a certified list of copyright records as well as copyright deposits to the Secretary of State	publication, or the life of the author plus 7 years
		1844: International Copyright Act: amends the 1838 law to include a wider range of objects, including dramatic works, music, drawings, prints, and engravings
10 August 1846	· requires the delivery of deposit copies to the newly established Smithsonian Institution	1846: Anglo-Prussian treaty: first of a series of bilateral copyright treaties made possible by the broader provisions of the 1844 International Copyright Act
		1851: Anglo-French copyright treaty
18 August 1856	· provides performance rights for dramatic compositions	1854: In *Jefferys v. Boosey*, the House of Lords overturns on appeal an earlier case granting foreign authors' rights, insisting on residency in Britain at the time of publication, rendering void American authors' contracts with British publishers, and stimulating the production of cheap reprints of American texts
5 February 1859	· shifts the responsibility for retaining copyright deposits from the Department of State to the Department of the Interior	
3 March 1865	· extends copyright to photographs and negatives · provides for free postage for copyright deposits sent to the Library of Congress within one month of publication · stipulates that a default of deposit requirements within one year of publication forfeits the copyright	

TABLE 5.1. *Continued*

Date of U.S. act	Major provisions of U.S. act	British enactments
	· defines "book" to include all volumes or parts thereof, all engravings, maps or prints belonging thereto, and any further edition that includes additions	
8 July 1870: Second general revision of the copyright code	· shifts authority for copyright record keeping to the Librarian of Congress	
	· extends copyright protection to paintings, drawings, chromos, statuary, and models or designs "intended to be perfected as works of the fine arts"	
	· retains the right of public performance for dramatic compositions, and grants the right of dramatization and translation to copyright authors	
	· stipulates deposit requirements: *a printed copy of the title page* for books and other printed works, or *a description* of a work of the fine arts, to be sent to the Librarian of Congress; within 10 days of publication, 2 *copies* of a copyright book (or *a photograph* of a work of the fine arts) also to be sent to the Librarian of Congress	
	· reiterates that copyright does *not* "extend to prohibit" the printing, publishing, importation, or sale of works made by noncitizens	
	· establishes a two-year horizon for legal action after cause	
	· stipulates that all copyright deposits and records that had been removed by the Department of the Interior from the Department of State shall be moved to and under the control of the Librarian of Congress	

TABLE 5.1. *Continued*

Date of U.S. act	Major provisions of U.S. act	British enactments
	· requires that the clerks of the district courts transmit to the Librarian of Congress all prior deposit copies *not* sent to the Department of the Interior, and that duplicate copies of legal, scientific, and mechanical works be sent to the library of the Patent Office	
18 June 1874	· provides for a shorter form of the copyright notice that must be inscribed upon "some visible portion" of the article in question: "Copyright, 18-, by A. B." · specifies that the words "engraving," "cut," and "print" refer only to pictorial illustrations and not to prints or labels designed for manufacture, which may be registered in the Patent Office	1878: Royal Commission on Copyright recommends the modernization and codification of British copyright law and the establishment of a bilateral copyright treaty with the United States
1 August 1882	· permits manufacturers of designs for decorative articles, tiles, plaques, and articles of pottery and metal to place copyright notices on the back or bottom of these articles	1886: The Berne Convention for the Protection of Literary and Artistic Works is signed by 7 European nations, Haiti, Liberia, and Tunisia, providing for international copyright protection without the requirement to register, and the exclusive right to import or produce translations
3 March 1891: "Chace Act"	· extends international copyright protection to foreign authors whose governments offer reciprocal rights to American authors, provided that the foreign authors' works are entirely manufactured in the United States and are published in the United States no later than the date of foreign publication	1887: The United Kingdom ratifies the Berne Convention

Congress, the question galvanized not only authors, editors, and publishers but also booksellers, printers, bookbinders, and typographers.

The most intense period of agitation for and against an international copyright law began in the spring of 1836, when the British publishing firm Saunders & Otley set up a branch office in New York, hoping to control the American reprint market for its books. Soon realizing that its claims were unenforceable at law, the firm circulated a petition to prominent British authors, gathered signatures, and submitted it to Congress, setting off a polarized reaction in the publishing world. This petition appealed to American generosity, national pride, and respect for individual rights, charging that British authors' reputations and profits were badly injured when their works were reprinted without their consent.[4] Many American authors and publishers supported the British authors' petition, expecting American literature to flourish in the absence of competition from cheap reprints.[5] However, members of the book trades — periodical editors who relied on foreign sources for much of their material, some publishers, and printers' trade organizations — successfully blocked a series of international copyright bills that were brought before Congress. Opponents of international copyright argued that it threatened the availability of cheap reading for an increasingly literate citizenry and jeopardized the jobs of thousands of men and women employed by publishers of reprints.[6]

Congressional support for international copyright tended to be Whig, northern, and avowedly protectionist, linked by association and ideology with Henry Clay's American System of developmental nationalism.[7] Clay spearheaded the first congressional campaign for international copyright, putting forward bills in 1837, 1838, 1840, and 1842, only to see them rejected or stalled by unfavorable committee reports. International copyright proponents contended that requiring payments to foreign authors would benefit the American public, describing the granting of reciprocal rights as a sign of cultural independence, as well as a matter of justice to British authors.[8] But their cause foundered on a central contradiction: those pressing for payments to foreign authors were clearly more interested in protecting the profitability of American authors and publishers than in protecting the printing and book trades as a whole or in responding to the desire of American readers for cheap books. Although an international copyright law was consonant with Clay's platform, critics attacked the measure for not being protectionist enough.[9]

Opponents of international copyright, articulating a protectionist policy that sailed under the flag of free trade, claimed that not paying foreign authors kept trade restrictions to a minimum, employed American printers, and enabled American publishing to flourish. Instead of viewing the burgeoning market for foreign reprints as a sign of provincialism, opponents claimed that national values were instantiated in the process of production. An American book could be identified by its physical appearance — its cheap paper and closely set lines of type enabling three expensive volumes to be compressed into one or two — as much as by its contents or by the nationality of its author. Opponents of international copyright contended that extending authors' rights only as far as national borders would provide adequate returns for foreign authors in their home markets and keep book prices low in the United States. Their canny analysis of the structure of the market for print spoke to Jacksonian fears about the concentration of economic and political power. Opponents argued that the uncopyrighted status of many of the most valuable texts worked to forestall the development of monopolies. They worried that, when combined with copyright, stereotyping would be used by publishers to regulate the supply of books and would augment the power of the large publishing houses. Opponents feared not only that American tradesmen would be thrown out of work but also that British publishers, who had neither market incentives nor nationalist motives to produce affordable editions, would be able to control both the price and the availability of American reading. Unlike the British market, in which powerful London publishing houses exerted control over what circulated in the provinces, American publishers could legally, at least in theory, reprint any foreign text that they thought would sell.[10]

Copyright opponents had a historical precedent in mind. American publishers employed numerous members of the Irish printing trades who had emigrated when the extension of British copyright to Ireland under the Act of Union (1800) caused the Irish reprint trade to collapse.[11] American printers were thus acutely aware of the vulnerability of provincial trade to centralized capital and all too familiar with London publishers' use of copyright to extend their power. Henry C. Carey — publisher, economist, and son of Philadelphia's most prominent emigré printer and publisher, Mathew Carey — helped defeat the 1854 Anglo-American copyright treaty by publishing *Letters on International Copyright* (1853), which argued that the unification of Great Britain and the consolidation of capital and political power in London had impoverished Scots and Irish literary culture.[12]

Advocates of international copyright attempted to satisfy opponents by adding a manufacturing clause to their bill, requiring that foreign books be produced in the United States in order to be granted copyright; they also toyed with building price-control provisions into the proposed copyright treaty, requiring British publishers to produce cheap editions for the American market. These measures could not, however, answer critics' concerns. While supporters of an international copyright law chiefly sought to bring order to the transatlantic book trade, opponents defended a system that served the publishers of newspapers, magazines, and pamphlets, as well as books. In the antebellum period, reprinting occurred in a variety of forms: poetry and tales that were first published in expensively bound gift books reappeared as filler in local newspapers; elite British magazines were reproduced in their entirety or mined for essays that were reassembled into regionally published "eclectic" magazines; and uncopyrighted evangelical tracts, works of popular science, and medical, legal, agricultural, and school texts were freely excerpted, imitated, plagiarized, and reissued. Resistance to international copyright protected a culture of print that was both provincial and cosmopolitan. While they were successful in blocking proposed laws and treaties, the printing trades' opposition to international copyright did not, however, prevent the consolidation of publishers' power.

George Palmer Putnam's early advocacy of international copyright provides one measure of the shift from a market dominated by reprinting to one in which publishers increasingly regarded copyrighted domestic texts as good investments. Putnam founded *Putnam's Monthly* in 1853 as an answer to Harper & Brothers' extraordinarily successful *Harper's New Monthly Magazine* (1850–), which was made up largely of reprinted material. Putnam sought to publish only American writing that was original to his magazine, a more risky venture than the Harpers', though he stood to profit by developing a stable of domestic authors and retaining control over their texts. *Putnam's Monthly* published now-classic works of American literature by Herman Melville, Henry David Thoreau, and Henry Wadsworth Longfellow, and yet *Harper's* eclectic mix of essays, travel narratives, and serialized novels by British authors such as Charles Dickens, William Makepeace Thackeray, and George Eliot outlived and far outsold *Putnam's*.[13] The publication of copyrighted texts did not simply or immediately displace readers' and publishers' reliance upon reprints. As the catalog of works on hand at the time of the disastrous Harper's fire in 1853 shows, most publishers invested in both these modes of publishing: if copyrighted works outnumbered reprints in the genres of "Travel and Adventure," "Theology and Religion," "Educational," and "Dictionaries and Gazetteers," reprints were twice the number of original works in the category of "General Literature."[14]

Even when Congress enacted alterations to domestic copyright law, these proved ineffective without corresponding changes in cultural and business practices. For instance, playwrights George Henry Boker and Dion Boucicault successfully lobbied Congress for a Dramatic Authors Bill in 1856. Boker, in particular, longed to publish a representative collection of his writing without, by dint of publication, effectively surrendering future payments for permission to stage his plays. While passage of the bill encouraged Boker to publish his *Plays and Poems* with Ticknor and Fields (1856), it did not bring about the kinds of changes in theatrical practice that would enable playwrights to exert control over, and profit from the performance of, their published texts. Fierce competition for audiences, the piracy of dramatic texts through oral transcription, and the quick turnover of plays in repertory theater all worked to defeat copyright registration rules that were designed for texts not tied to performances.[15] Because midcentury American theater relied on touring stars, property in dramatic works lodged not with the text or its author but with the performer. Despite the addition of performance rights to the copyright law, in practice playwrights continued to depend on individual performers for remuneration, either receiving payments directly from actors or accepting the proceeds from third-night benefit performances. Although printed plays were convenient for rehearsals and valuable stock for a theater company, playwrights and theater managers also desired to protect their property from rivals and knew that under the common law they could maintain perpetual rights in unpublished works. One solution to this dilemma was to print the text of a play as an "Acting Edition," but to claim on the title page that the work was "Printed, Not Published," marking the work as valuable because it was outside the bounds of federal copyright law (Fig. 5.1). By the 1870s, when actors' standard contracts had been renegotiated and theater companies recapitalized so that both actors' and owners' livelihoods depended on a long run of a single play, theater managers and playwrights began to seek to protect their literary property in courts of law.

As the limited effect of the copyright act of 1856 suggests, for most of the nineteenth century even legitimate property claims in printed texts were often unenforceable. The 1831 act provided for registration and deposit at district courts, but when deposit copies were sent on to Washington, they remained uncataloged in a dark, inaccessible storeroom, often still unwrapped.[16] Although publication evidence was routinely introduced in copyright cases, the ability of the federal courts systematically to verify property claims against printed evidence was not in place until the act of 1870, which began to rationalize the system by shifting authority for copyright record keeping to the librarian of Congress, funding annual reports on copyright deposits, and providing for deposit copies to be delivered free of charge through the mails.[17] That the copyright laws were technically unenforceable for much of the period, however, does not mean that they were not in force; authors, publishers, and readers continued to respond to copyright claims and to turn to the courts to uphold them. Indeed, the number of copyright cases tried

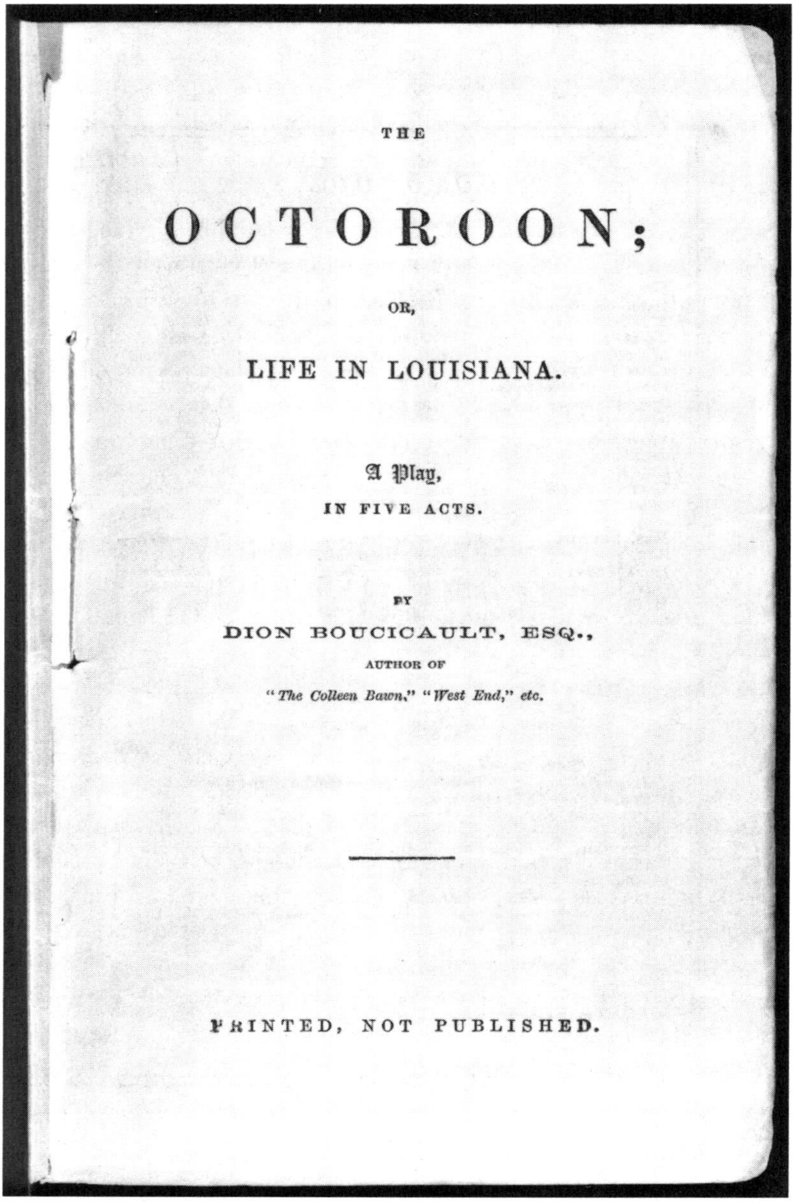
THE

OCTOROON;

OR,

LIFE IN LOUISIANA.

A Play,

IN FIVE ACTS.

BY

DION BOUCICAULT, ESQ.,

AUTHOR OF

"The Colleen Bawn," "West End," etc.

PRINTED, NOT PUBLISHED.

FIGURE 5.1. Title page of an acting edition of Dion Boucicault's *The Octoroon* (1859 or 1861). The notice at the foot of the page—"Printed, Not Published"—represents Boucicault's attempt to classify his play as unpublished and thus maintain a perpetual right to his intellectual property under common law, rather than limited-term protection through statutory copyright. Reproduced by permission of the Houghton Library, Harvard University.

in federal courts increased dramatically in the years after 1840. While fewer than twenty cases were heard in the first fifty years after the passage of the 1790 act, the courts decided more than one hundred twenty cases between 1840 and 1880. Changes in the law, such as the 1865 inclusion of photographs and the 1870 extension of copyright to encompass dramatization and translation rights, prompted publishers to test the reach of the statutes. In the 1870s, at least sixty copyright cases were reported, a sharp increase partly due to changes in the theater industry that made property rights in plays, both published and unpublished, valuable enough to defend in court.[18]

In his groundbreaking attempt to elucidate and systematize the copyright law, *A Treatise on the Law of Property in Intellectual Productions* (1879), Eaton S. Drone complained bitterly about "the condition of the law," blaming an ill-informed legislature for "meaningless, inconsistent, and inadequate statutory provisions" and inexperienced judges, who rarely heard copyright cases, for "ambiguous, erroneous, and conflicting decisions."[19] Despite the disorderly state of the law, a number of far-reaching judicial doctrines emerged as a result of mid-nineteenth-century copyright cases, including the property status of private letters, the concepts of "fair use" and "work-for-hire," and what would come to be known as the "idea-expression" dichotomy. A wide range of texts came before federal judges in this period, illustrating both the expanding reach of copyright and the new kinds of texts that were considered valuable enough to defend at law (Table 5.2). Some were books with obvious national appeal, others were practical or useful works, and yet others testified to a growing market in popular culture. While only a handful of copyright cases in this period involved works by literary authors, a large number of cases featured well-known theater managers, playwrights, and actors.

An important subset of these cases put the democratic ideal of the cheap distribution of useful texts into direct conflict with the property claims of authors. These cases involved rights in texts that of necessity differed little from their sources: abridgments, translations, compilations, dramatizations, and musical arrangements. Beginning in the late 1830s, Justice Joseph Story wrote a number of important decisions on the property status of texts that repackaged and recirculated already printed materials. In *Gray v. Russell* (1839), Story considered whether the notes and critical apparatus appended to a frequently reprinted Scottish schoolbook were subject to copyright even if they could all be found "in other works antecedently printed." Reflecting his understanding of the high value placed on compilations, Story had little difficulty deciding that a compilation could be copyrighted, provided the "plan, arrangement, and combination of the materials be new." Without such

TABLE 5.2. Copyright in the U.S. courts: selected cases, 1834–1880

Case	Text at issue	Key ruling
Wheaton v. Peters (1834)	*Wheaton's Reports*	An author's common-law property in his text ceases upon publication; strict compliance with statutory requirements is necessary for establishing title in a printed work.
Gray v. Russell (1839)	*Adam's Latin Grammar*	A compilation can be copyrighted, provided the plan, arrangement, and combination of materials are new.
Folsom v. Marsh (1841)	*The Writings of George Washington*	An abridgment that extracts the essential or most valuable parts of a work is an infringement; this case marks the first articulation of the judicial doctrine of "fair use."
Jollie v. Jacques (1850)	"The Serious Family Polka"	Copyright pertains to the contents of a work, not to the title.
Stowe v. Thomas (1853)	*Onkel Tom's Hütte*	A translation is not a copy, therefore it does not infringe copyright.
Woolsey v. Judd (1855)	Private letters	The writer possesses the exclusive right to publish letters; the receiver can publish them only for his own vindication.
Heine v. Appleton (1857)	Sketches made on Commodore Matthew Perry's expedition to Japan	Since plaintiff agreed that all sketches made on the voyage would be government property, he cannot subsequently recover copyright.
Keene v. Kimball (1860)	*Our American Cousin*	The re-presentation of a play for which the proprietor has no copyright and that he has previously exhibited is not a violation of property right.
De Witt v. Brooks (1861)	*The Life and Confession of Albert W. Hicks*	The person who writes a book, not his employer, is the author, even if the employer is the subject of the book.
Boucicault v. Fox (1862)	*The Octoroon*	The reproduction of old materials in a new form may be copyrighted; public performance of a play does not constitute abandonment of copyright.
Drury v. Ewing (1862)	Clothing patterns	A clothing "chart" falls under the definition of "book"; if a material part of a publication is used, even if

TABLE 5.2. *Continued*

Case	Text at issue	Key ruling
		improvements are made, copyright is infringed.
Sheldon et al. v. Houghton (1865)	Uniform edition of Charles Dickens's *Works*	Courtesy of the trade does not establish property rights that are defensible under the copyright law.
Rossiter v. Hall (1866)	"The Home of Washington"	Reproducing an engraving by photography is an infringement of copyright.
Wood v. Abbott (1866)	"The Golden Age" and "School Days"	A picture made from a glass negative is not a print, cut, or engraving under copyright law.
Martinetti v. Maguire (1867)	*The Black Crook* and *The Black Rook*	Copyright does not extend to "grossly immoral or indecent" productions.
Collender v. Griffith (1873)	Engraving of billiard table	A billiard table design cannot be patented, therefore an engraving of that design cannot be copyrighted.
Harte v. De Witt (1874)	Bret Harte's name and reputation	The author's interest in his name and reputation entitles him to aid from a court of equity in restraining work falsely attributed to him.
Isaacs v. Daly (1874)	*Charity*	Words that denote virtues cannot be appropriated for exclusive use as titles.
Boucicault v. Hart (1875)	*The Shaughraun*	A work must be published within a reasonable time after registering title to secure copyright.
French v. Connelly (1875)	*Around the World in Eighty Days*	Memorization and later reproduction of a play is an infringement of copyright.
Rees v. Peltzer (1875)	Maps of Chicago	Copyright in a map is lost by sale of the right to make copies without restriction.
Centennial Catalogue Co. v. Porter (1876)	Catalog of the Centennial Exhibition of Philadelphia	There can be no copyright of an inchoate intended publication; a book, not its subject, is the subject of copyright.
Kiernan v. Manhattan Quotation Telegraph Co. (1876)	Financial news	News is property; transmission to subscribers over the telegraph is not a general publication.
Richardson v. Miller (1877)	Playing cards	Cards are subject to legal protection even though they can be used to violate the law.

TABLE 5.2. *Continued*

Case	Text at issue	Key ruling
Perris v. Hexamer (1878)	Maps of Philadelphia and New York City	The style or key of a map is not a subject of copyright.
Baker v. Selden (1880)	*Selden's Condensed Ledger*	The copyright of a book does not extend to the bookkeeping system explained therein.

a ruling, he acknowledged, "it would be difficult to say that there could be any copyright in most of the scientific and professional treatises of the present day."[20] Abridgments posed more of a problem for the court, because they tracked closely the "plan, arrangement, and combination" of the work they shortened and thus confounded the sharp distinction jurists liked to draw between "independent labor," which constituted grounds for a property claim in a new work, and "servile imitation," which was the sign of infringement.[21] A successful abridgment required an extraordinary fidelity to the source text in order for its value to be retained; yet, while abridgments sought to preserve what was most valuable in the original, they did not copy but condensed and therefore transformed the text. Considered as a group, the abridgment cases brought home to American judges the limitations of the eighteenth-century understanding of copyright as a trade privilege: abridgments deserved protection as literary property because they promoted learning, although they did so at the expense of authors' rights by threatening to supersede the original text.[22] As Justice Story reminded the court in *Gray v. Russell*, law publishers had long produced valuable abridgments, and the legal profession as a whole "must depend on faithful abstracts."[23]

In *Folsom v. Marsh* (1841), provoked by Charles Upham's two-volume abridgment of Jared Sparks's twelve-volume *Writings of George Washington* (1833-39), Story elaborated a theory of copyright that also took into consideration the market, or potential market, for a particular work. Upham had transformed Sparks's exhaustive collection of Washington's letters, addresses, and public acts into a ventriloquized autobiography "in which Washington is made mainly to tell the story of his own life."[24] Even though Congress had spent $25,000 to acquire Washington's papers from his nephew, Justice Bushrod Washington, Story ruled that Washington's papers were national, not public property. In navigating the largely uncharted legal territory beyond literal copying, Story offered a fourfold test of infringement that was formally written into law in the late twentieth century as a set of guidelines for establishing the "fair use" of material under copyright (Copyright Act of 1976).

Story argued that where piracy was unclear, jurists needed to consider the "nature of the new work, the value and extent of the copies, and the degree in which the original authors may be injured thereby." Paradoxically, Upham's care in making his selections worked against him: because his excerpts so well represented Sparks's whole, Story ruled that "the value of the original is sensibly diminished."[25] In taking into consideration the value of the specific material extracted and the potential injury to the market for the original work, Story expanded copyright to embrace abstract rights that necessarily exceeded the boundaries of the text.

Despite Story's expansion of the purview of copyright in *Folsom v. Marsh*, a narrow understanding of copyright as nothing more than a printer's right to multiply copies of a text exerted a tenacious hold on American case law. This is readily apparent in *Stowe v. Thomas* (1853), which centered on an unauthorized German translation of Harriet Beecher Stowe's *Uncle Tom's Cabin* (1852). Translations, like abridgments, posed a problem for the court because they reproduced the work without duplicating the text. Justice Robert Grier remarked that "The same conceptions clothed in another language cannot constitute the same composition; nor can it be called a transcript or '*copy*' of the same '*book*,'" ruling that Stowe's copyright extended no further than the words of her text in the order they appeared:

> By the publication of her book the creations of the genius and imagination of the author have become as much public property as those of Homer or Cervantes. Uncle Tom and Topsy are as much *publici juris* as Don Quixote and Sancho Panza. All her conceptions and inventions may be used and abused by imitators, playrights [*sic*] and poetasters. They are no longer her own — those who have purchased her book, may clothe them in English doggerel, in German or Chinese prose. Her absolute dominion and property in the creations of her genius and imagination have been voluntarily relinquished; and all that now remains is the copyright of her book, the exclusive right to print, reprint, and vend it.

Grier's decision drew on a long tradition in American law of regarding publication as incommensurate with "exclusive possession," favoring readers' rights when they conflicted with tight control over authorial property.[26] While the 1870 act would expand copyright to include the right to translation, the narrowness with which the court defined the subject of copyright in this case outlived this particular decision. As late as 1908, in *White-Smith v. Apollo*, the court determined that copyright in a published song was not infringed by its material "translation" into music rolls for use in player pianos.[27]

As is clear from Story's expansive definition of authors' rights and Grier's contrary, narrow interpretation of copyright, mid-nineteenth-century case law was replete with conflicting decisions in which different rhetorics and rationales for copyright converged. Some striking patterns emerge from these cases, however. For instance, while the idea that copyright should protect original works of authorship was a common feature, defendants often argued that the texts on which they based their own either failed to meet a test of originality or were ineligible for copyright protection because they were drawn from materials in the public domain. In responding to such claims, the courts repeatedly insisted that copyright did not depend on originality. As Drone explained in his *Treatise*, copyright law's understanding of originality was more "comprehensive" than the ordinary definition of the word; it included "almost every product of independent literary labor." Drone advanced a broad, negative definition of originality as anything that is "not copied" from another, establishing a low threshold for claiming property in a new work.[28] Although jurists made frequent, and contradictory, analogies to patent law when grappling with the question of originality, nineteenth-century case law demonstrated an emerging consensus about the differences between patents and copyrights: whereas patent law required proof of originality and held accidental copying to be infringing, copyright law generally protected against copying regardless of the novelty of the text in question and found independent reorigination, though unlikely, to be perfectly acceptable. The court in *Boucicault v. Fox* (1862) represented its refusal to take literary value into account as a sign of the law's objectivity and as the cost of a democratic print culture: "the law rests upon no code of comparative criticism. It protects alike the humblest efforts at instruction or amusement, the dull productions of plodding mediocrity, and the most original and imposing displays of intellectual power."[29]

In other cases, courts also significantly limited copyright, frequently relying on the Constitution's justification for copyrights and patents to define what lay outside of copyright protection. For example, in *Martinetti v. Maguire* (1867), a case that centered on the popular musical extravaganza and burlesque *The Black Crook* (first performed in 1866), the court ruled that obscene works were uncopyrightable because, rather than promoting "the Progress of Science and the Useful Arts," their only imaginable effect was "to corrupt the morals of the people."[30] Similarly, commercial texts such as labels and advertisements were found to be ineligible for copyright because they exhausted themselves in the course of use. A copyrighted text needed to hold its value over time in order to justify federal protection. Following a line of reasoning laid out in *Clayton v. Stone* (1829), in which the court held that

THE ROLE OF GOVERNMENT

newspaper "prices current" were too ephemeral to qualify for copyright, the court determined in *Scoville v. Toland* (1848) and *Collender v. Griffith* (1873) that a medicine label and an engraving of a billiard table were too referential to qualify for copyright. In both cases, value was thought to lie in the object to which the text referred and not in the text itself. Courts frequently probed the meaning of "book," "chart," or "print" to determine whether an object could be brought within the purview of copyright, deciding in *Drury v. Ewing* (1862) that a set of diagrams for making ladies' dresses could count as a book due to interspersed instructions. However, in *Wood v. Abbott* (1866), the court ruled that photographic processes were too passive to qualify as printing or engraving, both of which required the application of force. In many cases, the use of a text proved decisive, not its form or medium. For instance, in *Richardson v. Miller* (1877), the court held that, despite the fact that playing cards could be used to break the law, their use was not restricted to gambling; therefore they could qualify as prints under the copyright law.

The difference between manuscript and print, on which the distinction between common-law copyright and statutory copyright depended, continued to serve as a structuring opposition in nineteenth-century copyright law. Common-law rights to handwritten texts were absolute and perpetual, whereas copyrights in printed texts were rights of limited duration and were contingent on the successful performance of a number of public acts, such as filing a printed copy of the title page, publishing the work within a reasonable amount of time, and submitting a deposit copy for future reference. Playwrights, theater managers, and public lecturers routinely attempted to prolong their common-law copyright by deferring the formal publication of their works, although they often printed a few copies for private use. Even though stage audiences might be as numerous as a book's readership, the fact of live performance and the limited number of viewers in each audience led courts in *Roberts v. Meyers* (1860), *Boucicault v. Fox*, and *Palmer v. DeWitt* (1870) to decide that theatrical exhibition fell short of the wholesale abandonment to the public signified by the medium of print. Similarly, in *Bartlett v. Crittenden* (1849), the court ruled that neither the private circulation of lecture notes nor the lectures themselves were addressed to "the public at large." Allowing or requiring students to copy out a textbook—a popular method of instruction in the antebellum period—was understood to be fundamentally different than printing these notes "for general use."[31] In *Kiernan v. Manhattan Quotation Telegraph Co.* (1876), the transmission of financial news to subscribers over telegraph wires was ruled to be more like letter writing than publication in print. In these cases, the court's distinction between "general and unrestricted" and "qualified or limited" publication turned on the difference between the limited reach of handwritten copying and the inescapable publicity of print.[32]

Heine v. Appleton (1857) and *Boucicault v. Fox* took up the question of the property status of work composed at the behest of an employer. *Heine v. Appleton* concerned the property status of drawings and sketches made on Commodore Matthew Perry's expedition to Japan, illustrations the artist sought to copyright after the publication of the congressional report. The court observed that when Heine signed onto the voyage, he agreed that his sketches would become the property of the United States government, but it also considered the fact that he had been paid by D. Appleton & Co. to reduce several drawings from the unwieldy government report, published in quarto size, for an octavo popular edition. The court ruled that being paid to assist in publication implied assent to publication and thus forfeited future copyright claims. However, copyright in works written for an employer was generally presumed to reside with the author unless explicitly signed away. For instance, in *Boucicault v. Fox* the court ruled that actor, stage manager, and playwright Dion Boucicault retained copyright in *The Octoroon* (1859), despite the fact that he was hired to write the play for exclusive performance at New York's Winter Garden Theatre. The court distinguished between the work Boucicault performed at the theater and the work of authorship, yoking respect for authors' rights to a respect for contracts: "The title to literary property is in the author whose intellect has given birth to the thoughts and wrought them into the composition, unless he has transferred that title, by contract, to another."[33] Although both cases asserted the author's right to the product of his labor, they entertained the possibility that employers might require that employees surrender copyright as a condition of employment, thus opening the door to the twentieth-century doctrine of "work-for-hire."

Baker v. Selden (1880) similarly acted as a pivot between nineteenth- and twentieth-century thinking about copyright. This case originally sought to limit the extension of literary property but has, paradoxically, played a crucial role in expanding the scope of copyright. Frequently cited as the origin of what modern lawyers call the idea-expression dichotomy (the doctrine that copyright protects the particularity of an author's expression, while leaving ideas open to all as inalienable public property), *Baker v. Selden* concerned the nature of the rights extended to *Selden's Condensed Ledger; or, Book-Keeping Simplified* (1860). Selden charged that Baker had unlawfully copied "certain forms or blanks, consisting of ruled lines and headings, illustrating the system and showing how it is to be used and carried out in practice." Because these forms had been "annexed" to Selden's fifty-one-page pamphlet as illustrations of his system, the decision turned on the relation of these forms (and the accounting practice that they enabled) to the book that was protected by copyright. Were the forms an indispensable part of Selden's book? Could property rights inhere in the minimally ruled spaces of an empty account-book page?[34] In distinguishing "between the book as such and the art which it is intended to illustrate," the court acknowledged that to extend copyright protection to the forms that readers needed to copy in order to employ Selden's system of accounting would be to prescribe a kind of compulsory piracy. The court ruled that Selden's "forms or blanks" must be regarded as given to the public, not "for the purpose of publication in other works explanatory of the art, but for practical application." As such, they were fundamentally unlike "ornamental designs or pictorial illustrations addressed to the taste," the purpose of which was to produce "pleasure in their contemplation." Explaining why Selden's explanation of his system could be copyrighted, but the forms readers used to apply it could not, the court contrasted the opacity of aesthetic language with the ideal transparency of commercial speech, the intransitivity of aesthetic appreciation with the iterability of scientific truth, theory with practice, and the uniqueness and physicality of the embodiment of ideas in writing with the elusive nature of disseminated habits and routines—a catalog of opposing terms that have come to underwrite the legal dichotomy between expression and idea.[35]

Throughout the postbellum period, lobbying organizations such as the American Copyright Association kept steady pressure on Congress, prompting congressmen to introduce international copyright bills in 1868, 1871, 1872, 1874, 1882, 1883, 1884, and 1885. These bills were repeatedly stalled in committee; only the 1871 and 1884 bills reached the floor of the House before being abandoned. Reciprocal copyright treaties with Great Britain were proposed in 1870 and 1878 but also failed at early levels of negotiation. Proponents of international copyright were helped in their cause by the mounting number of European copyright treaties that made the United States' refusal to enter into such arrangements seem anomalous, and by 1880 the tide was turning.[36] A British Commission on Copyright, convened in 1875, tendered a blistering report in 1878 that attacked the obscurity and inconsistency of British law and recommended that Great Britain accept American protectionist demands that copyrighted foreign texts be manufactured in America.[37] In response, Harper & Brothers—a firm that had long been an important opponent of international copyright—wrote to Secretary of State William Maxwell Evarts in November 1878, suggesting that a joint Anglo-American commission be formed to negotiate an international treaty and proposing a draft of treaty conditions. The following January, George Haven Putnam—long a supporter of international copyright—responded to the "Harper draft" in an address delivered to the New York Free Trade Club, marking a shift in the rhetoric of international copyright advocacy from protectionism to free trade. The Harper draft became the focus of ongoing discussions by American supporters of international copyright. The annual presidential messages in 1884 (Chester Arthur) and 1885 (Grover Cleveland) both recommended the passage of some kind of international copyright measure. In January 1886, Senator Jonathan Chace of Rhode Island introduced a protectionist international copyright bill into Congress that would, in heavily amended form, finally become law in March 1891. This international copyright statute acceded to the demands of the International Typographical Union and others that foreign works could be copyrighted only if they were manufactured within the United States.[38]

The granting of copyrights to foreign authors helped to standardize copyright as a tool of regulation, while the extension of copyright law to cover an ever-wider range of objects laid the groundwork for the shift from a public-good to an author-centered rationale for copyright. In a 1903 ruling concerning circus advertisements, Justice Oliver Wendell Holmes would vastly expand the purview of copyright, suggesting that the mere presence in a text of marks of personality could afford a ground of ownership.[39] This shift in thinking would be codified in the 1909 rewriting of the copyright law, in which the 1790 statute's emphasis on the protection of useful works was expanded to cover "all the works of an author."[40] Between 1840 and 1880, however, copyright was extended to some texts and not to others; competing rationales for literary property were offered in Congress, the courts, and public debate; and property rights in texts at the limits of the law were maintained by other means.

PART 2

The Census, the Post Office, and Governmental Publishing

Scott E. Casper

· · ·

From the founding of the United States, governments at all levels have been among the nation's most prolific publishers. In the mid-nineteenth century, city, county, and state publishing expanded rapidly. For example, Texas's state penitentiary, institute for the deaf and dumb, lunatic asylum, immigration bureau, and state treasurer all published annual reports through the state printer by the 1870s.[41] But while the volume of publications grew, the system remained the same: patronage dictated who received public printing contracts. In New Jersey, German-language newspaper printers received contracts to publish laws and agency reports, not only to disseminate useful information to a growing immigrant community but also to reward loyal partisan printers.[42]

At the national level, however, governmental involvement with American print culture changed dramatically. In addition to the evolution of copyright law, the role of the federal government was transformed in three critical ways. First, the Bureau of the Census began enumerating information about American illiteracy in 1840, and over the subsequent decades it collected information about education as well as periodical publication. Second, new postal regulations, culminating in the 1879 law that redefined second-class mail, encouraged the broad distribution of diverse forms of print. Third, beginning in 1860 the newly established Government Printing Office replaced patronage systems of federal publishing. By 1880 the United States had a census that sought to measure "progress" toward an enlightened citizenry, a classified mail system that worked hand in hand with a capitalist publishing industry, and a governmental printing system that disseminated scientific and agricultural intelligence as well as legislative and executive documents across the continent.

Each of these developments helped forge a more truly "United States." At the same time, each also revealed or stoked internal divisions: between rural and urban America, between North and South, between native-born and foreign-born Americans, between patronage-based and bureaucratic cultures. What seems a largely administrative history — of statistical categories, postal regulations, and a printing bureaucracy — is also a political, social, and ideological one.

The census of 1840 introduced a set of tables designed to measure the nation's progress after fifty years under the federal Constitution.[43] These tables included an enumeration of literacy. (Over the next three decades, they would also come to include the number of Americans attending school and the number of newspapers and periodicals published in every state.) The 1840 census asked household heads how many white adults in their families could not read or write. Individuals answered the question beginning in 1850, and from 1870 on, the census elicited this information from everyone older than nine. In 1870 it also divided the question into two, asking Americans, "Can you read and can you write?" and recording the results in separate columns.[44] The census report explained the rationale for this change:

great numbers of persons, rather than admit their ignorance, will claim to read, who will not pretend that they can write. . . . If a man cannot write, it is fair to assume that he cannot read well; that is, that he really comes within the illiterate class. . . . Taking the whole country together, hundreds of thousands of persons appear in the class "Cannot write" over and above those who confess that they cannot read. This is the true number of the illiterate of the country.[45]

Foreign-born Americans who could read or write in their native language were supposed to be counted as literate. However, many enumerators in 1870 apparently neglected or ignored this instruction when counting Chinese immigrants—an error acknowledged in the 1880 report.[46]

Other inconsistencies and procedural changes pose interpretive dilemmas for contemporary scholars who use census data to measure American literacy. But nineteenth-century Americans freely deployed the census for precisely that purpose. From the beginning, this new category promised to announce America's relatively high literacy rates in a period in which an ideology of literacy dominated the national culture, fueled New England's movement for statewide common-school systems, and pervaded Anglo-American schoolbooks. The Census Bureau's literacy queries similarly helped promote republican citizenship, middle-class entrepreneurship, and Protestantism.[47] An 1876 review of America's first century, published by Harper & Brothers, used the literacy data to celebrate just this progress. Answering a critic in the *London Quarterly Review* who had cited America's 5.6 million "illiterates" to attack "the American system of teaching," this American writer commented—also with census data—that 4 million of these illiterates lived "in the former slave territory, where the common schools were never suffered to come, and where a large part of the people were forbidden by law to learn even to read and write." Moreover, 665,000 of the 1.3 million illiterates from the northern states were "foreign born," leaving only 690,000 "native-born illiterates"—and most of these were *children* of immigrants.[48] In other words, the American public school was achieving its mission.

The phrasing of the census queries was usually in the negative, and the data were often used to define an American "illiterate class." To the Census Bureau, "class" may have been short for "classification." To other Americans, the enumeration identified particular places or groups as disproportionately "illiterate." When the 1840 and 1850 censuses revealed a far higher proportion of illiteracy in southern than in northern states, many commentators blamed the paucity of common schools south of the Mason-Dixon line. Virginia economist George Tucker attributed that disparity to the South's

THE ROLE OF GOVERNMENT

low population density.[49] Hinton Rowan Helper, the North Carolina sociologist whose *The Impending Crisis of the South* (1857) became an abolitionist touchstone, blamed "oligarchal politicians [who] have kept learning and civilization from the people [and] . . . have outraged their own consciences by declaring to their illiterate constituents, that the Founders of the Republic were not abolitionists."[50] At least one southern legislator used the statistics to argue for creating a public school system. W. H. Stiles, speaker of the Georgia House, described his "Empire State of the South" as "an empire of matter, and not of mind, of darkness and not of light" and urged his fellow legislators to "Enlighten this darkness, efface from her escutcheon that foul blot of illiteracy which the census discloses, or never call her again the Empire State."[51] If states would not provide school systems themselves, contended Congressman George F. Hoar of Massachusetts during Reconstruction, the federal government should do it for them.[52]

Catharine Beecher, a veteran proponent of women's education, also used census data to express her concern about the dire consequences of "the rule of ignorant majorities," but she worried most about the illiteracy of uneducated immigrants, especially women. Beecher cited the 1870 census to claim that

> there are over one million more illiterate women than men, that illiteracy increases faster among women than among men, that the increase of children is far greater among the ignorant classes than among those most educated, that it is the illiterate who care least for the proper education of their children, that vice and poverty are nearly in the same ratio as illiteracy, and that immigration, both on the Atlantic and Pacific shores, is chiefly from the more ignorant classes and is increasing every year.[53]

Immigrants needed public schools, Beecher argued. Other commentators concluded that America needed fewer immigrants. In 1856 Samuel C. Busey proclaimed that foreign-born New Englanders had a much higher illiteracy rate than "the free colored in the same States" and that "immigration is the source or cause of much the largest proportion of ignorance, blind and superstitious ignorance, which is spreading over this land, marring the beauty of its institutions and clogging the wheels of a free government."[54]

Rising illiteracy rates in New England after the Civil War contributed to a new debate, which would soon assume pernicious form. In 1872 Rhode Island's superintendent of schools, T. W. Bicknell, used census data to show rising numbers of "illiterates" among the foreign born. (By 1880 the Census Bureau itself reported "marked changes observable in Rhode Island" due to "the influx of French Canadians.")[55] Like Beecher and others, Bicknell argued for strong common schools, but he went further. He advocated the enforcement of child-labor laws, including a requirement that all children employed in manufacturing attend school five months per year, a tough truancy and vagrancy law, and evening schools for people over sixteen. He also urged "a constitutional enactment, which shall require of every person who shall possess a franchise in the State, a certificate of his ability to read and write."[56] Thomas B. Stockwell, who compiled an 1876 history of Rhode Island's public education, opposed literacy tests: "Enfranchise all, and it is for the obvious interest of every man of wealth that all should be educated. Disfranchise the ignorant, and every rich man is tempted to leave the common people in ignorance, lest they should acquire votes."[57] That, of course, is exactly what happened in the South along racial lines. In state constitutional conventions from the 1880s to the early twentieth century, Jim Crow southern governments enacted literacy tests to disfranchise African Americans. But the impulse was nationwide. Northern political reformers argued for literacy tests for suffrage as early as 1865, and by the 1890s some northerners (including the American Federation of Labor) proposed similar tests to curb immigration.[58]

When in 1840 the Census Bureau began enumerating American literacy — or illiteracy — it did not realize how its data would be manipulated for diverse political and social causes: abolition, nativism, "good government," suffrage reform. In contrast, postal regulation was political from the start. The idea that a postal system diffused enlightenment throughout the citizenry was as old as Benjamin Franklin's days as colonial postmaster. That ideology underlay the postage-free exchange of papers by newspaper publishers, customary in the colonial period but not enacted into law until 1792. High postal rates on single-sheet letters helped subsidize low rates for newspapers mailed to subscribers. Because magazine rates were also high and postmasters had the discretion to refuse them if their size or weight would hamper delivery of other mail, magazine publishers before 1840 largely did not use the postal system, and most American magazines circulated only locally or regionally.[59]

From 1845 to 1863, Congress enacted a series of postal laws that reduced the rates on every category of mail (Table 5.3). Competition from private express companies provided the initial impetus for lower rates. Although such companies could legally deliver only what and where the United States Post Office did not, new companies after 1839 covertly or overtly defied the law, augmenting earlier, informal competition (for example, letter delivery by businessmen traveling from one city to another). Reformer and businessman Lysander Spooner, who operated the American Letter Mail Company, challenged the long-standing convention that the Post Office had a monopoly on

TABLE 5.3. Letter, newspaper, and magazine postage, 1825–1863

Law	Postage in cents		
	Letters[a]	Newspapers	Magazines[b]
1825	25.0	1.5	9.0–17.5
1845	10.0[c]	1.5	7.5
1851	3.0[d]	1.15[e]	3.0[f]
1852	3.0[d]	0.5[g]	2.0[f]
1863	3.0	0.38	2.0

Source: Adapted from Richard Burket Kielbowicz, *News in the Mail: The Press, Post Office, and Public Information, 1700–1860s* (New York: Greenwood, 1989), 181. Kielbowicz based his table on several sources: U.S. Post Office Department, *United States Domestic Postage Rates, 1789–1956* (Washington, D.C.: GPO, n.d.); Jane Kennedy, "Development of Postal Rates: 1845–1955," *Land Economics* 33 (May 1957): 99; *U.S. Statutes at Large*; Frank Luther Mott, *A History of American Magazines*, vol. 1 (New York: D. Appleton & Co., 1930), 517.
Note: Prices shown are for each piece sent up to 500 miles.
[a] Postage for a single-sheet letter; rates rose in proportion to the number of pages.
[b] Postage for an average monthly, usually about 6 ounces.
[c] Beginning in 1845, a single-sheet letter was defined as one weighing one-half ounce or less.
[d] Postage if paid by sender; 5 cents if paid on delivery.
[e] Postage if paid quarterly in advance.
[f] Postage if paid quarterly in advance; postage was doubled for cash on delivery.
[g] Postage if paid quarterly in advance at either the office of mailing or delivery; postage was doubled for cash on delivery.

post roads, while other new companies maintained a lower profile and succeeded by taking advantage of the Post Office's high letter rates. Those monopoly rates subsidized six constituencies: coach contractors, rail and steam companies, local postmasters, publishers (especially of newspapers), public officials with franking privileges, and rural voters (whose post roads generated far less postal revenue than did the major roads connecting northeastern cities). To counter the new competition, Congress revised postal rates downward in 1845, 1851–52, and 1863.[60]

The intricacies of postal law reflected other pressures—usually from publishers. In every case, these publishers' legislative successes helped define the balance between locality and nationality. In 1840 a diverse group of magazine publishers lobbied to narrow the gap between newspaper and magazine rates. Challenging the decades-old principle that newspapers possessed a uniquely vital character as vehicles of political intelligence, they argued that their works were "of fully as elevating and improving a character as that of Newspapers." Whereas the 1825 law had based magazine rates on the number of sheets and the distance traveled (hence the range shown in Table 5.3), the

1845 law charged magazines by weight alone. The 1851 act reduced magazine rates by another 60 percent. As a result, readers anywhere in the nation could now receive in the mails a vast array of periodicals that catered to their particular interests. Studies of the periodicals that passed through local post offices reveal how the mail system fostered nationwide imagined communities. The census told the story from 1850 on by classifying and enumerating American periodicals: "advertising," "agricultural and horticultural," "benevolent and secret societies," "commercial and financial," "illustrated, literary, and miscellaneous," "devoted to nationality," "political," "religious," "sporting," "technical and professional."[61] Perhaps ironically, it was in southern post offices that incoming periodicals expanded horizons most. Because the vast majority of periodicals emanated from northeastern publishers, readers in the Northeast were less likely to subscribe to southern periodicals than the converse.[62]

This fact naturally caused anxiety among some southerners. More broadly, the influx of urban magazines and especially the weekly "national" editions of urban daily newspapers worried rural publishers of weekly "country" papers. If papers such as Horace Greeley's *New York Tribune* and Benjamin Day's *New York Sun* could penetrate all America at cheap postal rates, would they not drive local papers—with their lesser capital and their greater distance from "news"—out of existence? In the words of North Carolina congressman Abraham W. Venable,

> The poisoned sentiments of the cities, concentrated in their papers, with all the aggravations of such a moral and political cesspool, will invade the simple, pure, conservative atmosphere of the country, and, meeting with no antidote in a rural press, will contaminate and ultimately destroy that purity of sentiment and purpose, which is the only true conservatism. Fourrierism [*sic*], agrarianism, socialism, and every other ism, political, moral, and religious, grow in that rank and festering soil; and if such influence and such channels of communication are to be the only ones felt and employed, the press would be the greatest calamity instead of the greatest blessing. We desire our country papers for our country opinions, our provincial politics, the organs of our conservative doctrines, and to assert the truth, uninfluenced by the morbid influences of city associations.[63]

Venable was not alone in wondering what cheap newspaper postage meant for local papers. Petitions for free local mailing of newspapers deluged Congress in the 1830s and 1840s, leading to a series of legislative balances: a "30-mile postage-free zone" in the 1845 act, and free circulation of newspapers in their county of publication in the 1851 law. The influx of the "national" urban papers and the supralocal magazines thus found its counterweight in the free dissemination of country papers. New technologies would soon undercut some of the urban papers' advantage in rural America, because national news traveled faster by telegraph than New York or Chicago papers did by mail.[64]

Venable's concerns spoke not just to city papers' competitive advantage but also to their danger for "conservative institutions." Some Americans offered another solution to this "problem": postal censorship. Anxiety about one "ism" in particular—abolitionism—led to the postal censorship of incendiary material, initiated by Andrew Jackson's postmaster general in the 1830s and continued through the Civil War. The earliest state antiobscenity law appeared in Vermont (1821), followed within fifteen years by Connecticut and Massachusetts. In 1865 federal legislation "criminalized the use of the mail to transport 'obscene' material" in an attempt to stem a tide of domestic pornography that had titillated Civil War soldiers. Reformer Anthony Comstock tried to use this law to prosecute Victoria Woodhull in 1872 for publicizing several sexual scandals in *Woodhull & Claflin's Weekly* (1870–76). Thwarted by the fact that the 1865 law did not apply to newspapers, Comstock lobbied successfully for new federal legislation to keep "vice" out of the mails, the ostensible conduit between licentious public spaces and the domestic sphere.[65] The 1873 antiobscenity act stipulated

> That no obscene, lewd, or lascivious book, pamphlet, picture, paper, print, or other publication of an indecent character, or any article or thing designed or intended for the prevention of contraception or the procuring of abortion, nor any article or thing intended or adapted for any indecent or immoral use or nature, nor any . . . book, pamphlet, advertisement or notice of any kind giving information, directly or indirectly, where, or how, or of whom, or by what means either of the things before mentioned may be obtained or made . . . shall be carried in the mail.[66]

The Post Office's nationwide reach, as well as lowered postal rates and the growth of mail-order businesses, made it the logical target of a nationwide moral crusade. By 1885 twenty-four states had enacted their own versions of the federal "Comstock Law."[67]

The 1851 rates had reduced magazine postage, but magazines published less often than once a week still cost nearly six times as much to mail as did daily and weekly papers. The creation and refinement of second-class mail addressed this disparity. Intended initially to simplify the 1852 system of more than three hundred classifications based on format, distance, and frequency of publication, the 1863 law created three classes: correspondence (first-class mail), regular periodicals sent by their publishers (second-class), and everything else—occasional publications, "transient" periodicals (sent by someone other than the publisher), advertising circulars, books, seeds, cuttings, and engravings (third-class). The 1863 system maintained the discrimination against periodicals published less often than once a week, however. Over the next sixteen years, publishers and postal administrators negotiated a series of revisions. In 1874, postmasters got what they had long wanted: mandatory publisher prepayment for mailing periodicals, to alleviate the problem of uncollected postage and to eliminate the burden of keeping local lists of magazine subscribers. For publishers the 1874 law provided that periodical postage be calculated by bulk weight rather than per piece (2¢ a pound for newspapers, 3¢ for magazines). Finally, in 1879 Congress enacted a uniform rate for all periodicals (2¢ per pound), dispensing with the old problem of what distinguished a newspaper from a magazine. The culmination of thirty-five years of legislation, the 1879 act established the essential lineaments of the classification system that has existed ever since.[68]

Magazine publishers found something else to appreciate in the new classifications. Throughout the 1870s, many of their periodicals included advertisements, often in separate inserted sections. At the same time, less "respectable" publishers were producing advertising circulars and mail-order catalogs, which resembled magazines in format. Such publications, according to the 1874 act, belonged in third-class mail (1¢ per two ounces, rather than 2¢ or 3¢ per pound)—but the Post Office had to decide the postal status of every one. And if magazines included separable advertising supplements, should they not also pay the third-class rates? Arthur H. Bissell of the Post Office's legal department met with New York and Philadelphia publishers in 1878. Together they defined four criteria for second-class publications: "first, they had to be issued at regular, stated intervals; second, they had to be sent from a known office of publication; third, they had to be made of printed paper without substantial bindings such as books; and fourth, they had 'to be originated and published for the dissemination of information of a public character, or devoted to literature, the sciences, arts, or some special industry, and having a legitimate list of subscribers.' " The "legitimate" publishers pressed for registration of periodicals that carried second-class status—a version of the venerable system in which local postmasters had to judge the postal status of publications, now centralized in the urban post offices from which most periodicals issued. Rural congressmen scuttled the registration system, which seemed (as it was) a collusion between major urban publishers and the Post Office. But the 1879 act preserved the four-part definition of second-class eligibility and relegated to third-class mail "publications designed primarily for advertising purposes, or for free circulation, or for circulation at nominal rates." Magazine publishers had won a double victory: the same postal rates as newspapers, and added attractiveness to advertisers over the third-class circulars.[69]

If it seems difficult for modern scholars to distinguish firmly between magazines and newspapers, it was hardly less troublesome for postmasters and Post Office administrators between 1840 and 1879, when they discarded the distinction. Under the 1825 statute, "newspaper" implied both format and content: full sheets folded once but not stitched; appearing at least weekly; offering "an account of political or other occurrences." "Magazines" appeared less often and had more diffuse contents. If a periodical was "a large sheet, in the common form of a newspaper," it was so designated; otherwise, content dictated the determination. The indeterminacy of this definition invited publishers to experiment with various formats to mail their wares. Most famously, between 1839 and 1845 several publishers produced mammoth weeklies, which reprinted full-length British novels as gargantuan newspapers. The 1845 law, which placed postal surcharges on "newspapers" larger than 1,900 square inches, helped kill the mammoths. So did mainstream publishers such as Harper & Brothers, which used the now-lower postal rates on pamphlets to disseminate such works themselves.[70] The reach of the postal system also encouraged innovations in the material form of the printed word. In addition to the weekly country editions of newspapers such as Greeley's *Tribune*, several papers published "steamer editions" for readers on the Pacific coast. The letter sheet, a form of stationery often printed with woodblock engravings of California life, became a popular way for Gold Rush emigrants to send news back east.[71]

For the most part, publishers did not distribute books through the postal system. Bound volumes were barred from the mails until 1851. Under the 1863 classification system, books joined transient periodicals, seeds, cuttings, and other parcels as third-class mail. Other modes of distribution were more cost-effective and reliable. Publishers employed express or freight companies and developed networks of wholesalers and retailers. They used the mail to correspond with members of the trade (sending catalogs, sample copies, bills, and orders).[72] Major trade publishers also used the mails to distribute their house magazines, which served also to advertise their books—hence their interest in the development of the second-class mail system.

The story of how the postal system transmitted the printed word reveals transformations both in the relative power among America's publishers and in the American polity itself. Before 1840, newspaper publishers enjoyed the greatest sway with the postal system. Congress took an active interest in making postal policy, and most newspapers affiliated with a political party and provided a vehicle for partisan messages. As a result, local or "country" publishers enjoyed advantages in postal regulations. By 1880 Congress had relinquished the crafting of postal policy to administrators in the Post Office, who increasingly worked with the nation's major publishers of books and magazines. In an emerging bureaucratic state, the administrative arm of the federal government enhanced its own authority.

In the realm of the printed word, nowhere was this last fact more apparent than in the creation and growth of the Government Printing Office. Between 1840 and 1860, Congress alternated between two systems of public printing: a patronage system in which the majority party in each house of Congress selected the printer of that house's proceedings (1819–46 and 1852–60); and a contract system in which public printing went to the low bidder (1846–52). Executive departments commissioned Washington printers loyal to the administration's party to produce their documents and reports. The secretary of state contracted with party newspapers in each state to publish the federal laws. Each of these systems was open to criticism. The patronage system seemed corrupt, but the contract system proved worse, as the lowest bidder routinely did poor, delayed work. The costs of government publishing skyrocketed during the Pierce administration (1853–57), largely due to multiple layers of subcontracting and patronage contracts far above the prevailing Washington printing rates. From 1857 to 1860, four different congressional investigating committees found fraud, corruption, and overspending in the public printing. Finally, in 1860, Congress acted on a recommendation it had received in 1819, 1840, 1842, and 1858: to establish a government printing office. The superintendent of public printing, a position created in 1852 as little more than an auditor, was now to "execute the printing and binding authorized by the Senate and House of Representatives, the executive and judicial departments, and the Court of Claims." Congress appropriated $150,000 for "the necessary buildings, machinery, and materials." The superintendent arranged to buy an existing four-story printing plant, and Congress completed the purchase in 1861.[73]

Within two decades, the Government Printing Office bore witness to national power and industrial print. Its massive, 160,820-square-foot edifice (expanded four times from the initial 46,397-square-foot building) rose four stories and covered a full block. The monumental office-cum-factory dwarfed the surrounding structures. An 1881 engraving by H. H. Nichols showed five smokestacks at work, a team of horses emerging from a front entrance, telegraph wires running prominently across the front of the building, and an

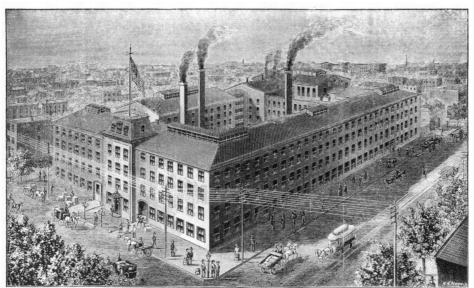

GOVERNMENT PRINTING OFFICE BUILDING, showing the new addition now (June, 1881) in course of erection.

FIGURE 5.2. H. H. Nichols's engraving of the Government Printing Office building, from R. W. Kerr, *History of the Government Printing Office (at Washington, D.C.): With a Brief Record of the Public Printing for a Century* (Lancaster, Pa.: Inquirer Printing and Pub. Co., 1881). The image suggests both the scale and the modern technologies of this agency, which was among the nation's largest printing factories. American Antiquarian Society.

enormous American flag hanging from a pole atop the ornamented Victorian facade (Fig. 5.2).[74]

This engraving served as the frontispiece to the first history of the GPO (also 1881), which author Robert Washington Kerr depicted in ideological as well as descriptive terms. Kerr, assistant foreman in the GPO's document room, initially planned to write a brief guidebook for visitors because Washington became a tourist mecca after the Civil War. But the volume swelled to 196 pages, including a history of American public printing, descriptions of the GPO's many specialized departments and labor-saving machinery, and appendices listing the entire current GPO labor force (roughly 1,800 strong, six times as many as in 1860). Kerr's whiggish narrative sketched the transformation from patronage-driven public printing to an efficient, nonpartisan governmental agency. The GPO connected the capital to the farthest-flung states and territories. The telegraph lines in Nichols's engraving linked the GPO building not only with Congress, the executive mansion, and various executive departments, but also with lines of the "Atlantic and Pacific and American Union Telegraph Companies." Telephone lines had been installed, too.[75]

The labor force, in Kerr's telling, became a microcosm of an idyllic industrial America, segmented by task and skill and working in happy harmony. In the document room, highly literate compositors and proofreaders, aided by Webster's dictionary, converted "rumpled monstrosity" of text, "kicked from pillar to post at the committee-rooms of the Capitol for days," into meticulously edited proof that placed senators and representatives "in the first ranks of modern writers." Although none of these workers "ever had the advantage of a collegiate or classical education," they corrected prose in "all the modern and dead languages"—drawing upon skills learned "in the printing business." This workforce was even integrated racially: once stereotyped and "lowered into the Press Room by steam power," every plate

> is taken in charge by one of our "colored brethren," and placed upon the bed of the press, the irregularities in the surface of the type planed down by the pressman, and it is now ready for the clean white paper. The young lady who is to manipulate these snowy sheets with her delicate taper fingers, now ascends to the raised platform at the side of the press, and by a peculiar push and pull separates a single sheet from the pile of paper at her elbow, and gently lowers it within reach of the steel fingers of the press, which clutch it viciously, and drag it into a dark abyss.

African American men and white women toil here in shared spaces without the hints of racial impurity that became a refrain in the post-Reconstruction South. (Women made up more than a third of all GPO employees in 1880.) Borrowing imagery recently used for the gargantuan Corliss Engine at the 1876 Centennial Exhibition, Kerr depicted an almost terrifying press, whose "steel fingers" counterpoint the more "delicate taper" ones of the women workers. But all sorts of hands—black and white, skilled and unskilled, human and mechanical—produced the government's imprints.[76]

Only obliquely did Kerr hint at labor problems in the GPO. The press room, he noted, had been the province of "men and boys" under the old contract system, but now "women have taken the place of boys altogether, and they are found to be much more attentive to their work, and give greater satisfaction, and endure the labor with less complaint." In the patent office specification room, which published the monthly report of new patents complete with "photolithographic illustrations," compositors were "paid for their labor by the piece." Kerr believed this "the only correct system of discharging obligations for the composition of type—and, as a result, there is less jar and dissatisfaction among these compositors than in any other branch of the establishment." This assertion belied a long-standing dispute. In 1864 federal law set GPO compositors' wage at $24 per week, a rate that held as prevailing wage scales sagged during the depression of the mid-1870s. A House committee investigating the GPO in 1876 noted that GPO weekly wages based on an eight-hour day topped those of New York printers, who received less weekly pay and worked a ten-hour day. The investigation resulted in a 20 percent cut in printers' wages the following year. GPO printers petitioned Congress unsuccessfully the next year to restore their former pay scale.[77] The vaunted labor-saving machinery, furloughs during off-peak periods (when Congress was not in session), and lower employee wages all helped the GPO hold expenses in check.

As a producer of print, the GPO was America's largest alternative to the commercial publishing system that had developed since the 1830s. But unlike commercial firms, the GPO did not need to consider the relationship between advertising and sales. It did not need to run a profit, although Congress scrutinized its accounts and criticized its expenditures. Also unlike the trade, the GPO enjoyed an existing national distribution system: the Post Office, which disseminated its products free of charge to a mostly static "readership" — legislators and their designated constituents, and the document repositories in every state (designated by federal laws of 1813 and 1857).[78] The GPO's monopoly expanded in 1873, when it took over publishing the proceedings of Congress from the private firm of Rives & Bailey (and changed the name from *Congressional Globe* [1833–73] to *Congressional Record* [1873–]), and again in 1879, when it replaced loyal local printers as the publisher and disseminator of the federal laws, ending the last bastion of the patronage system. According to an 1885 compendium of all United States government publications to mid-1881 — itself a massive GPO publication — the GPO during the Forty-sixth Congress (1879–81) produced more than twice as many publications as any pre–Civil War Congress.[79]

The GPO also sustained a role that dated back to the days of the patronage and contract systems: federal publication of learned work done under government auspices, notably in the sciences, exploration, and ethnography. Before the GPO, such work went to the authorized federal printers (or to leading commercial firms when especially voluminous or potentially profitable). Thus Washington printers produced Alfred Mordecai's reports on experiments with gunpowder, A. Guyot's meteorological tables, and the serial *Smithsonian Contributions to Knowledge* (begun 1848), while major metropolitan firms produced the federally authorized works of Alexander Hamilton (New York's C. S. Francis & Co., 1851) and Daniel Webster (Boston's Little, Brown, 1851) and, most important, Henry Rowe Schoolcraft's multivolume history of the American Indians (Philadelphia's Lippincott, Grambo & Co., 1851–57). Several works appeared from congressional printers and metropolitan firms, including Robert Greenhow's *Memoir, Historical and Political, on the Northwest Coast of North America* (1840) and John C. Frémont's *Report of the Exploring Expedition to the Rocky Mountains* (1842), both of which Wiley & Putnam published after their initial Washington appearance. Many of these publications included illustrations — some 1,600 in eighteen governmental reports on the West (1843–63) alone — making the federal government a leading patron of the emerging lithographic industry.[80]

By 1880 the GPO was taking on publication of even the largest projects. The geological and ethnographic work of John Wesley Powell extended knowledge about the American land and its peoples. The annual agricultural reports, first issued in 1849, proved especially popular: Congress authorized printing 200,000 copies in 1876 and twice that number in 1884. The GPO's most ambitious publication of the nineteenth century was *The War of the Rebellion: A Compilation of the Official Records of the Union and Confederate Armies* (70 vols., 1880–1901), intended to be the definitive documentary history of the Civil War. When complete, this work would attest to reconciliation between North and South, just as Powell's publications introduced Americans to the old and new West. As Kerr boasted, the GPO's role lay in dissemination, not just publication, for every GPO publication made its way "to every State and Territory of the Union" and even to "foreign governments."[81]

The federal government also exercised considerable power over territorial printing. In the federal territories (which included most of the West between the Sierra Nevada and Rocky Mountains), territorial secretaries had oversight of public printing but depended heavily on the federal treasury to pay for it. Federal law required that secretaries send to Washington all printing for which they wanted federal payment (to check for "fat" in the composition) and that printing had to be executed in the territory itself. The latter often proved impossible because local printers, who also published newspapers, could not tie up their type — if they had enough — for the enormous, unprofitable job of printing laws and journals. Territorial printers routinely violated federal laws, sending the manuscripts off to printers in the nearest large city (often San Francisco) but placing a local printer's name on the imprint.[82]

Between 1840 and 1880, the United States government played an expanding role in publishing and distributing the printed word and in disseminating an ideology of literacy. The Census Bureau, the Post Office, and the Government Printing Office were three of the largest federal civilian bureaucracies by the 1870s. All prided themselves on increasing "professionalism," even before the Pendleton Civil Service Act of 1883. The intersections of each with the history of books and readers tell a richer story. Thanks largely to the census, illiteracy became a category that Americans could use to argue either for

THE ROLE OF GOVERNMENT

education or for disfranchisement, depending on who was making the case and what region's or group's illiteracy was the subject. The postal system made correspondence steadily cheaper from 1845 to 1879 and became the primary distribution network for America's periodicals, while debates over postal rates revealed both the enduring clout of country newspapers and the emerging power of the largest metropolitan publishers. Government printing, most evidently a saga of bureaucratization and nationalization, is also a story of a publishing system that came to exist outside the retail trade, disseminating scholarship that might have failed in the marketplace as well as the legislative and executive documents of the expanding nation. By the Civil War years and beyond, both the Post Office and the GPO encouraged Americans' "literacy" *as* Americans, but also a range of "literacies" far beyond what the census enumerated: in the useful knowledge contained in the GPO's ethnographic, scientific, and agricultural reports; and in the booming, multifarious range of periodicals that the census counted and the postal system carried.

CHAPTER 6

Alternative Publishing Systems

Diversification in American Religious Publishing

Paul C. Gutjahr

· · ·

E pluribus unum: out of many, one. Drawn in the broadest strokes, the story of American religious publishing in the nineteenth century actually inverts that progression. It is a story dominated by Protestants, who in the opening decades of the century enjoyed an optimistic, postmillennially inspired vision of Christian unity and who established powerful interdenominational publishing societies to influence their nation for Christ. As the century wore on, American Protestants moved away from such ecumenical endeavors and began to show more faith in, and commitment to, denominational printing enterprises to bring about the conversion of their wayward fellow citizens. While the motto of the country may have been "out of many, one," the motto of religious publishing beginning in the middle decades of the century could have been easily encapsulated as *ex eodem multi*: out of one, many.

Nor were fragmentation and diversification restricted to Protestant publishing. The same decades also saw the emergence and growth of ever-stronger Catholic and Jewish presses. Taking each of these strands in turn, two things become clear in regard to religious publishing in the United States between 1840 and 1880. First, the size of production and the scope of distribution made religious publishing one of the largest and most influential components in the nineteenth-century American marketplace for print. Second, religious publishing responded to ever-multiplying theologies, which drove various bodies to establish their own printing enterprises to help propagate their views and consolidate their base of support.

By 1840 many Protestants — particularly fast-growing movements such as the Methodists, Millerites, Baptists, and Disciples of Christ — placed a messianic faith in the power of the press. Horace Bushnell commented in 1844 that American Christians operated as if "types of lead and sheets of paper may be the light of the World."[1] Whereas spreading God's word had once primarily been the realm of preachers, an unprecedented increase in the production and consumption of printed material led countless Protestants to believe that print itself would help turn the unfaithful multitudes toward Christ. In this spirit of ecumenical optimism, three important interdenominational societies sought to spread the Gospel message largely, if not entirely, through print. What their leaders came to call the "bond of union" produced the American Bible Society (ABS) in 1816, the American Sunday-School Union (ASSU) in 1824, and the American Tract Society (ATS) in 1825. By the 1830s, years ahead of most trade publishers, the interdenominational ABS, ASSU, and ATS were taking full advantage of changes in papermaking technology, stereotyping, centralized mass production, and power presses.[2] By the 1840s these societies reported publishing several million pages per year: gargantuan press runs of Bibles, tracts, Sunday school lesson books, religious biographies, sermons, and devotional classics. By 1855 the output of these three societies accounted for approximately 16 percent of all books produced in the United States.[3]

The interdenominational societies were joined by both denominational and trade publishers who produced their own editions of the Bible, religious newspapers for age-related audiences, a diverse array of sophisticated theological periodicals such as *Bibliotheca Sacra* (1844–73) and the *Princeton Review* (1825–88), catechisms, and a wide spectrum of hymnals. Religious publishers were producing not only biblical encyclopedias and devotional guides but also religious versions of such best-selling genres as gift books, schoolbooks, farmer's almanacs, and even novels.

This evangelical belief in the unifying power of the press was not lasting. To form their bond of union, the interdenominational societies had tried hard to avoid reference to doctrinal differences. Largely Congregational and Presbyterian in their founding and organization, these societies reached across denominational boundaries by producing Bibles "without note or comment" and tracts that focused less on fine theological distinctions and more on the most accepted elements of American Protestant orthodoxy. Nonetheless, fragmentation began in the 1830s and gathered momentum in the succeeding decades. Methodist and Baptist publishing exemplified this trajectory. In the years leading up to the Civil War, Methodists became increasingly convinced that the work of the ATS was too Calvinist.[4] In response, they poured more of their resources into their own publishing enterprise, the Methodist Book Concern, founded in 1789. Baptists evinced similar doctrinal issues with the ABS, which in 1834 had refused to produce Adoniram Judson's Burmese translation of the Bible because he had used the word "immerse" rather than "baptize." Because they could not come to terms with the ABS, the Baptists seceded in 1838 to form their own organization, the American and Foreign Bible Society.[5]

Not only doctrinal difference but also the rising awareness of the efficacy of printed material as a means of communication and connection within denominations fueled the growth and power of denominational publishing. A Presbyterian author captured this awareness precisely when he stated that every

> denomination should have a literature of its own. . . . [I]t should have its own constructive and defensive lines of information and operation. It has its own peculiar polity, doctrine, agency, history, life and activity, and it should keep its people as well as others informed on these phases of existence. It has its own thinkers, scholars, and institutions, and out of them should emerge those who are able to enlighten the public. . . . It has a special mission in the world, and the pen is one of the greatest and most telling agents of the day for making known what it stands for and what it is doing.[6]

Every denomination and religious tradition shared these sentiments and founded some sort of printing enterprise to help unify its adherents.

Periodicals became central to this enterprise, even among aspiring denominations and smaller religious bodies. While the first strictly religious newspaper appeared in the second decade of the nineteenth century, by 1860 there were 277 religious newspapers in circulation. Just over ten years later, that number had grown to more than 400.[7] The scope of these periodicals was on display in the mighty efforts of the Methodist Book Concern, which by 1850 employed twenty-five printers to produce five different periodicals that combined to reach more than 85,000 subscribers.[8] By 1871 the combined subscription of various Methodist periodicals numbered nearly 160,000.[9] Many denominational periodicals had only a fraction of these circulation figures, but they were no less important as indicators of how important the press had become to denominational identity. The Mennonites began publishing their first periodical, the *Herald of Truth*, from Chicago in 1864 with a circulation of just over 1,000, while in 1858 the Lutherans started their first of many papers in Knoxville, Illinois, for just over 400 subscribers.[10] All these periodicals served as vital instruments to communicate with adherents who, however few in number, were spread across a wide geographical area.

Denominational publishing enterprises also showed a growing diversity in the sites of production. While the ABS and ATS kept their operations centered in New York, and the ASSU remained in Philadelphia, other denominational publishing enterprises were located in an ever-expanding group of cities that were closer to dense concentrations of their followers. Denominations that were particularly strong on the frontier, such as the Methodists and the Baptists, were the first to move outside the traditional publishing centers. The Methodists set up shop not only in New York (1789) but also in Cincinnati (1820). The Lutherans established a center in Rock Island, Illinois, and the Baptists settled in Nashville, Tennessee. The Disciples of Christ did much of their early printing in Bethany, Virginia.

In the decades preceding the Civil War, the three largest denominations in the United States experienced schisms over the issue of slavery: the Old and New School Presbyterians separated in 1837; the Methodists formed into the Methodist Episcopal Church, North and South, in 1844; and a year later the Southern Baptist Convention was formed out of the Baptist General Convention. Among the consequences of these splits was the emergence of still more publishing enterprises that could serve the newly fractured denominations.[11] New School Presbyterians created their own publication committee in 1852, finally breaking from their Old School comrades after years of working together despite the denomination's earlier schism.[12] For a decade after the Methodists split, the two new bodies wrangled in the country's courts over the Methodist Book Concern's publishing properties in both New York City and Cincinnati. Eventually this litigation helped lead the Methodist Episcopal Church South to establish its own publishing center in Nashville, while the northern wing continued to control the New York and Cincinnati centers. The African Methodist Episcopal Church—formed in 1816 by delegates from five African American congregations—had established its own Book Concern in 1817. The American Baptist Publication Society continued to serve both wings of the Baptist Church until 1847, when the Southern Baptists started their own publishing concern in Charleston, South Carolina. Their enterprise never grew to the size of its American Baptist counterpart in these years, although it served the South until it collapsed in the financial panic of 1873.[13]

The ATS, ABS, and ASSU did not disappear as denominational publishing grew. They remained strong publishing enterprises throughout the nineteenth century. By 1877 the ATS had circulated more than 27 million copies of 1,200 volumes and 344 million copies of 755 tracts, and in the 1880s the ABS began its fourth attempt at a national general supply of Bibles to every household in the country. In 1880 alone, the ABS produced a million Bibles for this mission.[14] Like its previous attempts, this one too would fall short, signaling once again that even a publishing enterprise as large as the ABS could not serve the entire country. Equally clear by the 1880s was that the denominations no longer wished for one entity to do so. Denominational publishing had become as important and influential among Protestants as the great inter-denominational printing enterprises had been in the opening decades of the century.

Religious publishing in the United States differed from its secular counter-part in two significant ways in this period: finance and distribution. Inter-denominational and denominational societies remained nonprofit organiza-tions that solicited funds from individuals and religious bodies to support their work. They sold their materials for a price but also gave them away. Their goal in charging for material was never profit but a firm conviction that people valued more the things they had to pay for, even if they could not pay the full amount. Any profits were poured back into the publishing enterprises.[15] Like their commercial counterparts, denominational societies sometimes sold stock to raise capital for buildings, machinery, and printing supplies, but religious publishers had avenues of finance not available to the common trade house: church bodies and religious individuals who contrib-uted money to help support the mission of religious publishing.[16] This stream of charitable contribution did much to keep countless religious publishing enterprises afloat. It was also a significant source of tension with commercial publishers, who sometimes complained that they could not compete with the low price of religious publications subsidized by charitable contributions and that religious houses did not respect trade courtesy.[17] Such underwrit-ing differed from denomination to denomination. The more centralized and hierarchical bodies such as the Presbyterians were more formal in their col-lection efforts, often dedicating a single Sunday each December on which congregational offerings were earmarked for the Presbyterian Board of Pub-lication. Less centralized denominations such as the Baptists collected funds less formally because of the heavily autonomous, congregational model of their polity. Local congregations in such denominations had a larger say in how they spent the monies they received. As a result, the boards of publica-tion for the various Baptist conventions experienced financial duress when the nation's economy was poor and donations from individual congregations and congregants dwindled.[18]

To distribute their vast output, the ATS, ASSU, and ABS pioneered meth-ods of nonprofit distribution that set the standard for denominational and interdenominational publishing for the entire century.[19] What set religious publishers' distribution efforts apart from those of their secular counterparts was the vast network of churches, Sunday schools, and other auxiliary soci-eties that made up the structure of religious bodies. Churches and individuals across the nation could become repositories. Every pastor, Sunday school teacher, and benevolent worker affiliated with a church became a potential courier of printed material from denominational or interdenominational publishers. To a large extent, the early Methodist publishing enterprise had owed its great success to every circuit-riding Methodist preacher, who became a de facto salesman and distributor of Methodist literature.[20]

Whereas the Methodists had tapped their mobile ministerial corps to distribute printed material, other denominations turned instead to a system that came to be known as "colportage." In 1841 the ATS hired its first two colporteurs, itinerant agents who sold the books and tracts of the society. Work that had previously been the purview of missionaries and other volunteers increasingly fell to hired colporteurs, who combined book distribution with more spiritual activities such as preaching, counseling, and relief work.[21] Colporteurs provided publishers with a more dependable distribution network than strictly volunteer societies could. They also penetrated less settled parts of the country, which were neither serviced by established churches nor touched to any great extent by the printed material of the country's commercial publishing enterprises. Within a decade, the ATS had 569 colporteurs in the field.[22] The ABS followed suit in the 1840s by hiring special agents to oversee national Bible distribution and help coordinate the volunteer activities of countless churches and auxiliary societies.[23] By the 1850s, various denominations had begun to use colporteurs. The Baptists, who reported publishing millions of pages of printed material, fielded 109 of them in eleven different states, while the Presbyterians had more than 200 by the outbreak of the Civil War.[24] Even denominations with smaller printing enterprises, such as the Congregationalists, were hiring colporteurs by the 1860s.[25] It is possible that the effectiveness of the agency system encouraged trade publishers after the Civil War to renew their own efforts in more personalized, door-to-door sales, although the gathering of subscriptions had long been a part of commercial publishing.

Religious publishers also took advantage of established trade booksellers and depositories to distribute their works. They formed broad-based publishing alliances in their distribution networks. For example, the Southern Baptist Publication Society in Charleston, South Carolina, advertised in 1857 that its depositories sold not only Baptist works but also religious works published by the ATS and ASSU and the country's largest trade publishers.[26] By 1879, according to *Publishers' Weekly*, agents of the Methodist Book Concern recommended "the use of the more general means of selling books," noting that " 'We publish a large line of historical and other books adapted to general readers, and we have no doubt of our ability to sell them if permitted to enter the market with other houses.' "[27]

Unlike Protestant denominations, the Catholic Church had neither a central, official church publishing office in the United States nor denominations to compete with one another for adherents or readers. To respond to the prodigious growth in the American Catholic Church—from a little more than a million members in 1860 to more than seven million by 1890—there was at least one major attempt to establish a national, nonprofit publishing enterprise.[28] In 1866 Father Isaac Hecker, who had founded the Paulist Order the previous year, established the Catholic Publication Society.[29] Before the official establishment of the society, Hecker had begun to publish the widely read periodical *Catholic World* (1865-1996). By 1890 the society had produced 605 Catholic book titles and more than 70 tracts.[30]

Otherwise, Catholic publishing during the mid-nineteenth century was dominated by independent publishers that produced Catholic works and often a wide range of non-Catholic materials as well. Before the Civil War, the main centers of Catholic publishing were New York, Philadelphia, and Baltimore. After the war, important private Catholic publishing enterprises could be found in a greater number of cities as the country's population continued to spread westward. By the 1860s, D. & J. Sadlier of New York had become the largest and most important producer of Catholic material in the country. After the 1869 death of its leading light, James Sadlier, the firm fell upon hard times, and P. J. Kenedy & Sons of Baltimore (and later New York) bought its list of titles. Kenedy & Sons was typical of, if considerably larger than, the other firms that provided Catholic material during these years. Such publishers carried a wide range of goods, including scapulars, rosary beads, lithographs of famous bishops, and candles, as well as Bibles, theological works, tracts, catechisms, and schoolbooks.[31] German-language Catholic publishers appeared after the Civil War in New York, St. Louis, Chicago, Dayton, Milwaukee, and Cincinnati. By 1880 there were sixteen such publishers in seven states, selling not only Catholic books in German but a similar assortment of religious articles and vestments.[32] Unlike most Protestant publishing endeavors, the Church did not officially underwrite these independent Catholic publishers, though it did hire them to do presswork.

Jewish publishing in this period was in its formative stages. There were only two Jewish publishers of note prior to the Civil War. Rabbi Isaac Leeser of Philadelphia was the first American to translate the Hebrew Bible into English; published in 1853, it achieved great popularity among America's Jews. While Leeser's publishing interests were almost entirely religious, Edward Bloch of Cincinnati had a broader agenda.[33] In partnership with his brother-in-law, Rabbi Isaac Mayer Wise, Bloch published a series of prayer books known as the *Minhag America* (begun in 1847) and spearheaded the production of the two prominent Jewish magazines: the *Israelite* (1854-74) and *Deborah* (1855-1900). The Jewish Publication Society would be founded in

1888 to educate and unite the American Jewish community, following two failed attempts in 1845 and 1871 to create such a publishing concern.[34]

Besides the denominational, interdenominational, Catholic, and Jewish publishers, trade publishers produced a great deal of religious material. Such publishers often had strong religious ties, as did the Methodist Harpers, who refused to work or have others work for them on Sundays. Harper & Brothers published religious materials ranging from its famous illustrated Bible (Fig. 6.1) to collections of popular sermons. Other "secular" trade firms were no different. By midcentury, J. B. Lippincott & Co. was a leading supporter of the Episcopal Church in America, and Charles Scribner had close ties to the Presbyterian Church.[35] While religious publications by commercial houses went some distance in closing the gap between the worlds of religious and trade publishers, distinct differences remained in how trade publishers financed and distributed their materials.

In the 1870s, a new kind of denominationalism produced a new kind of Protestant publisher. These emerging enterprises capitalized on a wing of late nineteenth-century American Protestantism that was ever more militantly committed to biblical literalism and espoused theological stances focused on the centrality of the Bible in everyday life. Drawing from conservative elements among Methodists, Presbyterians, and Congregationalists, along with Plymouth Brethren and other independent churches, this wing would eventually be known as "Fundamentalist." New interdenominational publishers sprang up to serve its cause, seeking to work with broader constituencies that shared core theological beliefs, rather than denominational labels. In important ways, these interdenominational firms found their precedent in the earlier publishing efforts of the ABS, ATS, and ASSU. This new type of Protestant publishing first appeared when Fleming H. Revell founded Chicago-based Revell Publishing in 1870.[36] The brother-in-law of the renowned evangelist Dwight L. Moody, Revell quickly built a publishing house that eclipsed all other firms in its annual production of Christian titles. In 1875 the firm of David C. Cook of Chicago and Elgin, Illinois, emulated Revell's vision for a new kind of evangelical publishing. Other firms later followed suit, including Broadman (1891), Moody (1894), Kregel Books (1909), and Eerdmans Publishing (1910).

The interdenominational impulse that had so profoundly marked religious publishing at the beginning of the nineteenth century thus found its echo in a new (and in other ways quite different) breed of religious publishers at century's end. In the intervening decades, however, religious publishing was not only one of the most vibrant areas of American print culture but also one of the most conflicted and diverse. Protestants who had so proudly been known

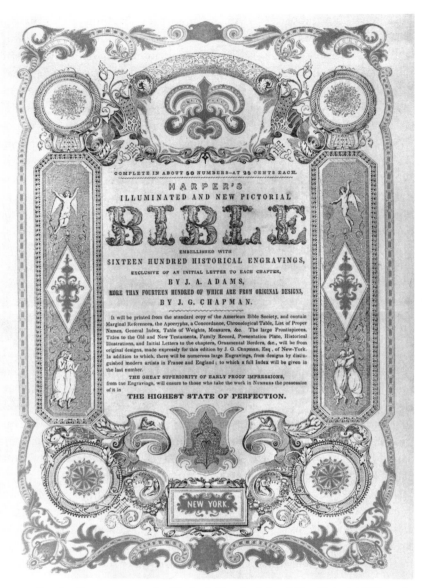

FIGURE 6.1. An 1843 prospectus for *Harper's Illuminated and New Pictorial Bible*, published by Harper & Brothers, New York, 1843–46, in fifty-four numbers, "at 25 cents each" (broadside, 34 x 23 cm). This profusely illustrated Bible, which pioneered the use of electrotype plates and included some pages printed in two colors, proved very popular and influenced the design of family Bibles for decades to come. American Antiquarian Society.

during the eighteenth century as a people of the book were now a people of books upon books upon books.

Other Variations on the Trade

Scott E. Casper

. . .

As discussed in the preceding chapters, trade publishers presented a large and general readership with publication lists that were wide ranging and topically diverse. For the most part, they made their books available through general bookstores. And their businesses, in both their economic and social aspects, were shaped by participation in the conventions of trade cooperation, including trade sales and courtesy of the trade. But as important as trade publishers were to the development of American culture, their activities were only part of a large and diverse publishing business that employed a wide variety of practices. Specialized firms collectively published far more printed matter than did Harper & Brothers, Ticknor and Fields, and the other trade publishers. The primary genres and methods of these specialized firms — such as sheet music, schoolbooks, or subscription publishing — mark these publishers as different from the "regular trade," but the distinctions between kinds of publishing should not be overstated. Trade publishers often included schoolbooks on their lists of publications, and they sometimes published books by subscription. Likewise, specialized firms occasionally behaved like trade publishers, marketing a particular book for a general audience. In both realms, many practices were similar, even if they developed independently and idiosyncratically. Music and schoolbook publishers, for instance, devised extralegal economic arrangements akin to courtesy of the trade, and they communicated through trade associations and periodicals similar to the *American Publishers' Circular* and *Publishers' Weekly*. Still, if the boundaries between trade and specialized publishing were fluid, contemporary publishers nonetheless recognized, and often insisted on, the distinctions between the two ways of doing business.

Specialized publishers typically targeted well-defined audiences, and several brief examples suggest their variety and the markets they served. Religious publishing, the largest of the specialized fields, targeted members of faith communities and those who might be converted. Other specialized publishers' focus narrowed to a single profession. Legal publishers participated in a long tradition, dating back at least as far as the eighteenth century, of depending upon the patronage system of printing state and local laws. Another important source of income was the sale of legal books and forms: as early as 1821, William Gould & Co. of Albany and its sister firm, Gould & Banks of New York, had included the phrase "law booksellers" on their title pages. Forty-seven years later, the title pages of Baker, Voorhis & Co. identified that New York firm as "law booksellers and publishers." It published the short-lived *Law Bookseller* (1868–?), a journal whose "object is to inform the profession what works are issued or on sale by the publishers."[37] Several trade firms also became leading publishers of law books, notably Boston's Hilliard, Gray & Co. and its successor, Little, Brown and Company, which published Justice Joseph Story's volumes of commentary on the law (1832–43). Beyond the law publishers and booksellers, entrepreneurs of the 1870s and 1880s devised systems of legal communication that helped create a national legal community. Brothers John and Horatio West, who operated a St. Paul bookstore specializing in law books and forms, created a publishing company in 1876 to remedy Minnesota lawyers' frustration with lack of access to recent judicial decisions and legislative actions. Their weekly pamphlet the *Syllabi* became, by 1887, the *National Reporter System*, which embraced the entire United States in seven regional reports and continues to this day. *Shepard's Citations*, still a staple of legal research, also appeared in the 1870s, when Illinois law bookseller Frank Shepard began to publish citations of his state's supreme court decisions. Finally, in 1882 New York attorneys James and William Briggs and Ernest Hitchcock devised the Lawyers' Cooperative Publishing Company, a subscription reprint system that made out-of-print law books affordable to lawyers across the United States.[38]

Like lawyers, doctors belonged to a profession that relied on books and journals, and by midcentury several publishers were serving their needs. Lea & Blanchard, successor to the Philadelphia firm founded by Mathew Carey in 1785, began in 1851 to concentrate on medical books. This firm already published the *American Journal of the Medical Sciences* (1827– , founded in 1820 as the *Philadelphia Journal of the Medical and Physical Sciences*) and had in 1843 acquired the "lighter" *Medical News and Library* (1843–1905, founded in 1837 as the *American Medical Intelligencer*). Lea & Blanchard's turn toward medical books began as a retrenchment from competition with Harper & Brothers and other emerging trade publishers. Other firms in this market niche included William Wood & Co. and P. Blakiston's Sons. Homeopathic medicine had its own publishers of books and journals, notably Philadelphia's Boericke & Tafel (publisher of *Boericke and Tafel's Bulletin of Homeopathic News*, 1871–85) and Chicago's C. S. Halsey (*United States Medical and Surgical Journal*, 1865–74).[39]

Still other firms concentrated on a particular subject, not a specific audience, and devised their own distribution networks. For example, Fowler & Wells not only published phrenological books but also sold phrenological busts, thermometers, and other self-help products, and members of the Fowler family performed phrenological examinations in the firm's New York headquarters. Its monthly, the *American Phrenological Journal* (1838–1911), advertised all these products, and a network of agents organized clubs to spread the movement's gospel, solicit customers for the firm's other merchandise, and attract readers to the *Journal* itself: whereas there were 900 subscribers at the end of 1842, the firm was printing more than 50,000 copies a month by 1853.[40]

Orange Judd began publishing agricultural books in the late 1840s, became an editor of the *American Agriculturist* (1842–1912) in 1853 and the journal's owner three years later, and bought out the leading agricultural publishing business, New York's C. M. Saxton, in 1864. The audience for agricultural books and journals was nationwide, with circulation of agricultural periodicals reaching 350,000 by 1860.[41] In the 1860s and 1870s, Chicago became a publishing hub for atlases and county histories. William H. Rand and Andrew McNally, job printers who incorporated in 1868 to specialize in railroad tickets, soon became the nation's leading producer of maps and atlases. Rand, McNally & Co. capitalized on the postwar boom in railroad travel. Their works sold at retail in railroad stations and aboard trains as well as in bookstores and newspaper offices, and railroad companies bought large numbers of their maps to publicize their routes.[42] Midwestern county atlases, pioneered by publisher A. T. Andreas in the late 1860s, soon grew to include local history and biography; after the Centennial Exhibition, this trade in "mug books" burgeoned for nearly two decades. The Chicago publishers of these books sent agents to gather biographical and historical information in the county or state in question and then sought subscriptions from among the same citizens who provided that information.[43]

If these brief examples suggest the variety of specialized publishing, a closer examination of music, schoolbook, and subscription publishing can describe the range of practices within these fields. Faced with apparent chaos in a field where copyright issues loomed large, major music publishers devised their own version of trade courtesy to regulate a competitive market. When public school systems began to enroll millions of children, schoolbook publishers accelerated their production and experimented with several ways to reach the actual market of school boards and superintendents who chose the books. Subscription publishers seem an anomalous case. The myriad firms that sold only by subscription after the Civil War did not create their own professional organization or trade journals, and their output ranged from Bibles to medical self-help books to Mark Twain's *The Innocents Abroad* (1869). However, these publishers developed distinctive methods of marketing and distinctive kinds of books.

The New Era in Indigenous Music

On 1 January 1855, the music publisher Wm. Hall & Son of New York announced that it was reducing the prices of its noncopyrighted music by one-half. The *New York Times* hailed this "great revolution in the music trade" and wondered why heretofore "so high prices should be charged for music where nothing was paid for a copyright, and the expense was only for engraving, printing and paper."[44] "War among the Music Dealers" ensued, according to a headline in *Dwight's Journal of Music* (1852–81). Fellow publishers Schuberth & Co. and Horace Waters joined Hall, and a third, S. C. Jollie, announced its own reductions. The other music publishers of America's major cities, *Dwight's* reported, planned a convention, "indignantly protesting the sacrifice of the tons upon tons of sheet music that have been accumulating on their respective shelves, and threatening in self-defence to refuse all dealings or exchanges with the obnoxious innovators." *Dwight's*, published in Boston, questioned whether this "revolution" was good for "*good* music" — "the works of Beethoven, Mozart, Mendelssohn, Schubert, Chopin, Rossini, &c., &c." On the one hand, it would make such music more affordable than America's copyrighted works, "the most superficial, trashy stuff that is in vogue: the negro melodies, the namby-pamby sentimental ballads, the flashy fantasias, polkas, waltzes, marches, &c., of native American, or tenth-rate resident German manufacture." On the other hand, when copyrighted American songs were the surest source of publishers' fortunes, publishers had little incentive to reprint European composers' work, which sold less well even at half price.[45]

In order to understand the January 1855 price war — and its resolution five months later — it is necessary to sketch the music-publishing trade of the previous fifteen years. According to one study, in 1840 approximately fifty-five music-publishing firms existed in the United States, thirty-one (56 percent) of which had been in operation for fewer than ten years. Half of those thirty-one would not remain in business ten years later. By 1850 the total had swelled to sixty-eight firms; thirty-six (53 percent) of these had not existed in 1840, and twenty-seven (40 percent) would not survive until 1860. If anything, this study underreports the reality, and music publishing was even more volatile than these figures suggest.[46] Especially in the Midwest, many of the music publishers of the 1840s started as music dealers, selling the publications of established eastern firms.[47] Music publishers generally maintained their own music stores, where they also sold musical instruments. Prosperous businesses occasionally illustrated their sheet music with engravings of their own establishments. For example, the cover sheet of Thomas Baker's "The Sparkling Polka" (1855) showed the two floors of Horace Waters's store—piano "saloon" above, music "saloon" below.[48]

Cooperation and competition existed side by side. Because music engraving required specialized punches for musical notation and specialized skills, midwestern publishers before the 1850s routinely had their engraving done in Boston, New York, or Philadelphia; engraved plates were created and sent to Cincinnati, Louisville, or Detroit for reproduction and sale in the city of publication.[49] Publishers routinely bought stock from one another because none individually produced enough of a variety to meet customers' demand. They also built distribution networks with smaller music stores (the proprietors of which published little or no music) and music teachers across the nation. The publishers supplied music at substantial discounts, as much as 40 percent to music teachers, who could then sell the music at retail prices to their students. Chaos and risk reigned: small dealers and teachers shopped around for the best prices and discounts, and publishers negotiated the best deals they could. The lack of international copyright laws meant that any firm could publish foreign music, a desideratum in a field where virtually all the "classics"—and the pieces for music study—were European. Firth, Hall & Pond in 1846 announced itself as "Sole agents for the extensive catalogue of music, published at J. A. Novello's 'London Sacred Music Ware House.'" But the same firm implied its competition with other American publishers when it noted, "Just received, a cheap edition of all the masses by Haydn and Mozart . . . and the price is only about one half of the former editions of the same works."[50]

In this volatile market, when Wm. Hall & Son and its few compatriots reduced their prices on noncopyrighted works, the other publishers' boycott forced a truce. The quasi-war ended with the establishment of the Board of Music Trade of the United States of America in June 1855. More than a dozen firms, including several of the price-cutters, joined the board. These initial members, who hailed from the eastern music-publishing centers of New York, Philadelphia, Boston, and Baltimore and from the newer cities of Louisville, Cleveland, Cincinnati, and St. Louis, agreed to sell noncopyrighted music at 20 percent below its retail price before the recent skirmish.

Following Hall's lead, they brought pricing into a new age by replacing "shillings" and "pence" with dollars and cents. They established a common discount of one-third on sales to small dealers, defined as those who held stock worth $250 or less, including music teachers. Most important, the board's members agreed, as one newspaper reported, to refrain "from republishing a non-copy-right, or foreign piece which has already been issued by a member of the Board. This is supposed to place copy-right, or American compositions, on an equal business footing with non-copy-right, or foreign compositions, inasmuch as the latter will hereafter have but *one* publisher instead of half a dozen or more, as formerly."[51]

Between 1855 and 1880, the Board of Music Trade and the large firms regulated the market in a variety of ways. To outsiders, this new form of trade courtesy seemed more like collusion. Membership was restricted to publishers that had produced at least a thousand separate pieces of music, shutting out in particular small midwestern firms. The standard discount disadvantaged music teachers, who had grown accustomed to a 40 percent discount and who, according to the New York *Musical World* (1849–60) in 1855, sold three-quarters of the nation's music. In response, groups of teachers met in 1857 in Lexington, Kentucky, and Cincinnati to form their own association against the board's "tyrannical monopoly." Anticipating the board's 1858 meeting in Cincinnati, *Dwight's Journal of Music* reminded its readers that musical publishers' trade courtesy had resulted in lower prices and more available music. It also observed that "An 'Association of Music Teachers' (of the Western and South Western States), — a sort of league for fancied mutual protection against music-publishers — is to meet in the same city at about the same time, and it is confidently hoped the difficulties between the two bodies will be amicably settled."[52] Such protests held no clout against the large firms. The board met at least four times before the Civil War and annually from 1864 to 1877 (with a hiatus in 1872). In 1871 the Board of Music Trade published its 575-page *Complete Catalogue of Sheet Music and Musical Works*. This early attempt at a union catalog of music in print included 80,000 works of foreign and domestic origin and classified all by instrument and genre. However, it included only works published by the board's twenty member firms and thus defined the field selectively for potential customers, presumably music dealers nationwide.[53]

The major firms in cities large and small nevertheless spread a transatlantic musical culture to a nation eagerly embracing music in the home and in public.[54] In 1855 *Dwight's Journal of Music* noted that "Musical Journals, of one class or another, are springing up in all parts of the country with such rapidity that one can scarcely keep the run of them."[55] *Dwight's* regularly informed its readers about the spread of musical culture, including its manifestation in print. The magazine displayed some Bostonian snobbery, however. Describing Chicago's *The Flower Queen, Dwight's* editorialized that "the vast West surely needs the humanizing influence of music, especially when sham Democracy and Slavery are so active to demoralize and drag us back to barbarism." But the periphery could talk back. In 1858 *Dwight's* published a letter from Louisville describing a flourishing scene of concerts and musical societies that were "worthy competitors to your own."[56] After the Civil War, the major firms west of the Appalachians promoted music within their cities by publishing magazines, among them *Brainard's Musical World* (Cleveland, 1864–95), *Church's Musical Visitor* (Cincinnati, 1871–97), *Hempsted's Musical Echo* (Milwaukee, 1873–75), Wm. McCarrell's *Southern Journal of Music* (Louisville, 1867–68), Root & Cady's *Song Messenger of the Northwest* (Chicago, 1864–75), and *Sherman & Hyde's Musical Review* (San Francisco, 1874–79). These magazines, many of them short-lived, sought to replicate their sturdy metropolitan cousins, such as *Dwight's* (published by Oliver Ditson & Co. beginning in 1858) and the *New York Musical Review and Choral Advocate* (1850–73). These magazines reported on musical happenings and culture elsewhere, offering readers a connection to a wider aesthetic culture.

Many of these journals also covered another musical culture: sacred music. In the early decades of the nineteenth century, a self-styled reform movement in New England had advocated the reorganization of singing in worship. Reformers emphasized ancient European tunes and American ones modeled on European harmonies as well as choral education for the edification of choir and congregation alike. The intersection between this reform and secular music appeared nowhere more than in the career of Lowell Mason, who began as a psalmodist in the 1810s. In the 1830s and 1840s, Mason became a champion of secular music education: he helped found the Boston Academy of Music (1833), advocated the introduction of singing classes in Boston public schools, and in the 1850s created programs for training music teachers — also a key constituency for his own publications. Mason never lost his passion for religious music, composing about 1,700 hymn and psalm tunes over sixty years. His published work, which included hymnbooks as well as vocal-education manuals, promoted the formal teaching of musical principles in Sunday schools and congregations.[57]

In the South and rural areas elsewhere, another sort of sacred music flourished: the shape-note tradition. The earliest American shape-note tune books, which had appeared around 1800, found popularity in rural areas and tended to be published in recently settled places such as Harrisburg, Pennsylvania, and Cincinnati. Whereas congregational hymn-singing in New England emphasized refinement, and secular sheet music boomed in popularity with the rise of middle-class parlor culture and private piano lessons, shape-note singers learned music in groups. Unlike the sacred-music reformers, compilers of shape-note books emphasized American tunes with little kinship to European hymnody. Like turn-of-the-century revivalism, shape-note publication leveled distinctions of class, in this case between the author or compiler and the buyer, even as cultivated New England psalmodists criticized shape-note publications and their singers as unschooled rubes. Two books, both published in the North where suitable type was available, did much to bring shape-note singing to the Deep South. *The Southern Harmony* (New Haven, 1835), compiled by William Walker in Spartanburg, South Carolina, sold 600,000 copies in three decades. *The Sacred Harp* (Philadelphia, 1844), the work of two singing-masters in Hamilton, Georgia, Benjamin Franklin White and Elisha J. King, remains in revised forms in print and in use to this day. Oblong and printed from type, shape-note books had press runs in the thousands, ten times the typical press run for engraved sheet music. The popularity of sacred music in its various forms would eventually fuel the publication of gospel songs.[58]

The most significant postwar development in secular music publishing was consolidation within the trade. Numbers tell part of the story. From a peak of eighty-three music publishers in 1860, the totals declined over the next two decades: seventy-three in 1870, sixty-six in 1880. Survival rates increased as the number of new entrants apparently diminished. In 1870, fifty-four (74 percent) of the seventy-three firms had existed since before the Civil War. In 1880, only fifteen firms (23 percent) had been founded since 1870, whereas thirty-eight firms (58 percent) predated the Civil War—a twenty-year persistence rate that was two-and-a-half times that of 1850.[59] Descriptions of metropolitan firms' headquarters reveal the creation of temples of music. Oliver Ditson & Co.'s five-story music store, built in 1857, contained rooms and compartments for each different sort of music; a basement full of sheet music for the wholesale trade; a safe "large enough to hold quite a dinner party" to protect 60,000 engraved plates; a pianoforte room on the second floor; a "'Book Room,' in itself a National Curiosity," on the third, containing virtually everything Ditson published; and the two upper floors for paper and sheet music presses (Fig. 6.2).[60]

Large firms also solidified their control by purchasing smaller rivals. Before the Civil War, such consolidation typically occurred within a city. For example, P. P. Werlein took over New Orleans rival W. T. Mayo in 1854; and Philadelphia's J. E. Gould & Co. acquired A. Fiot in 1855 and was itself acquired two years later by the local Beck & Lawton. Stephen T. Gordon of

FIGURE 6.2. The five-story building of Oliver Ditson & Co., Boston's leading music publisher and seller, featured on the cover of sheet music titled *Thou Hast Learned to Love Another* (originally published in 1849). *Dwight's Journal of Music* called the building, erected in 1857, "an honor not only to Boston, but to the whole Union." American Antiquarian Society.

New York acquired the catalogs (that is, the copyrights) of numerous eastern firms sometime before 1861. After the war, Oliver Ditson & Co. emerged as the trade's titan. Ditson had swallowed rival Boston firms since the late 1840s. Between 1855 and 1895, the firm took over leading publishing houses in Philadelphia, Baltimore, New York, Buffalo, Louisville, Cincinnati, Chicago, and San Francisco. Oliver Ditson & Co.'s 1890 catalog listed 100,000 titles—20,000 more than the entire 1871 Board of Music Trade's *Complete Catalogue*.[61]

By 1880 the large music publishers appeared to have conquered the chaos of four decades earlier. The Board of Music Trade languished in the early 1880s. Its meetings in 1880, 1882, and 1883 attracted only seven publishers, and coverage of those meetings in the trade journals was scant. Oliver Ditson & Co.'s consolidation may have reduced interest in tradewide gatherings. Perhaps the growth of the piano trade, which in Chicago grossed $4.6 million in comparison to $500,000 for book and sheet music sales in 1888, led music journals to reduce their coverage of the publishing business. But turmoil bubbled beneath the surface. The *Etude* (Philadelphia, 1883–1957), a new journal for music teachers, continued the old complaint against the prices on noncopyrighted music imposed by the "monopoly" of the "few leading houses." "Five-cent publishers" reprinted board members' noncopyrighted works; the leading publishers seem to have met this "piracy" mostly with ridicule, counting on the market to bankrupt flimsier operations. More troublesome was copyright infringement by Canadian publishers, a complaint that linked United States music publishers with American publishers more generally in the 1880s.[62] Even so, the music-publishing trade had achieved a stability unimaginable in 1840, as well as a staggering output that offered Americans everywhere a connection to transatlantic musical culture.

Nationalizing the Schoolbook Trade

On 16 March 1870, publishers of schoolbooks met in New York to form a Board of Trade, much as their compatriots in music publishing had done fifteen years earlier. Their motives resembled those of the music publishers: regulating their market seemed the answer to increasingly cutthroat competition. However, schoolbook publishing differed in essential ways. First, whereas music publishers constituted a world of their own, with specialized production techniques and closer connections to musical instrument sales than to the general book trade, the producers of schoolbooks included many of the nation's leading trade publishers as well as several firms that by 1870 specialized in textbooks. Second, competition arose not from the republication of foreign, noncopyrighted works but rather from producing rival text-books in the same school subjects. Third, the market was increasingly identifiable: the number of schools, and especially school systems, in America's counties, cities, and states was growing rapidly. Between 1850 and 1870, the number of schools in the United States increased 62 percent, from 87,257 to 141,629; the number of pupils doubled during the same years, from 3,642,694 to 7,209,938. Schools' total budget in 1850 was $16,162,000, less than half of which was from public funds; by 1870 their total budget grew almost six-fold, to $95,402,726, two-thirds of it from public funding. By one estimate, schools spent $18 million on textbooks in 1868. This was a lucrative market, organized into school systems with obvious access points: the individuals and boards who made adoption decisions.[63]

Before 1840, "system" was not a word often used to describe either American schooling or American schoolbooks. Early efforts to centralize public education were halting at best. Several states (New York, Maryland, Ohio) created school superintendent positions, only to abolish the office within a decade. By 1840 the state of New York had legislatively chartered academies, locally controlled high schools, and a separate public school system in New York City. Several states' and territories' early public school laws did not require localities to follow them. Michigan Territory in 1829 established only a structure for local school-district governance, and Pennsylvania counties and towns could collect the state's 1834 school tax if they wished a share of the proceeds for public schools. (This tax became mandatory fourteen years later.) Control of schooling remained predominantly local. In most parts of the nation, schools—if they existed—were not separated into grades; children of all ages attended together; and farming seasons dictated the length of the school year.[64]

The supply of schoolbooks was equally haphazard. An 1830 Connecticut pamphlet reported that "The selection of school-books, is sometimes made by the teachers, sometimes by the board of visitors; but more commonly by chance, rather than the choice of any one. The parents send such books to school as they happen to possess, and the pupils use such as are the most numerous."[65] Successful schoolbooks, such as Lindley Murray's *English Reader* and Noah Webster's spellers, readers, and grammars, were stand-alone works; in the absence of international copyright protection, Murray's was reprinted all over the United States. At this time, according to the 1870 recollection of publisher J. C. Barnes, "new books found their way into schools through merchants who purchased their semi-annual supplies from the booksellers in the large cities."[66] An 1842 broadside for G. & C. Merriam of Springfield, Massachusetts, listed sixty booksellers from Maine to Alabama as distributors of its *Village Reader*, *Easy Primer*, *Intelligent Reader*, and *Child's Guide* (Fig. 6.3).[67]

Beginning in the late 1830s and accelerating in the following two decades, systems of several sorts emerged. A cadre of reformers championed statewide governance of public schooling, notably Horace Mann, who became secretary of Massachusetts' new State Board of Education in 1837, and Henry Barnard, who assumed the same position in Connecticut the following year. Some states in the Northeast and Midwest created statewide school systems, but most states, including the entire South, did not. Nevertheless, the notion that universal public education served the common good and a developing capitalist society gathered strength. The United States census buttressed the idea when it began in 1840 to enumerate school attendance, although the federal government neither developed national educational standards, as occurred in Great Britain in the 1860s and 1870s, nor built a national, state-centered school system, as in France.[68]

The development of state and district school systems created a new, identifiable market for the bulk sale of textbooks, and publishers responded. Harper & Brothers introduced the "School District Library," which eventually comprised 187 volumes of assorted histories, biographies, travel narratives, and other nonfiction for school libraries. Other publishers targeted the classroom, not the library. Beginning with Lyman Cobb's *The Juvenile Reader Number One* (1830), authors and publishers produced graded series of readers.[69] Most successful was the Eclectic Series of School Books, published by the Cincinnati firm of Truman & Smith. The Eclectic Series, introduced in 1834 with an arithmetic book by Dr. Joseph Ray, gained national prominence with the publication in 1836 and 1837 of four readers by Professor William Holmes McGuffey of Miami University. Thanks to power presses, an expanding workforce, and Cincinnati's place at the center of the western network of rivers and canals, Truman & Smith by 1841 produced and sold more than 700,000 books in the Eclectic Series, advertised as "the STANDARD SCHOOL BOOKS of the West and South," with potential use as far away as Texas.[70] Over the next two decades, other houses also came to specialize in schoolbook publishing, notably New York's A. S. Barnes & Co. and Ivison & Phinney, as well as Cincinnati's W. B. Smith & Co., successor to Truman & Smith. Numerous general trade firms, such as D. Appleton & Co., also advertised their educational offerings. Harper & Brothers ventured into the classroom textbook market relatively late, commissioning a series of readers in 1859.[71]

Marketing schoolbooks began within the books and extended outward. Series of graded readers and arithmetics encouraged school committees and

FIGURE 6.3. G. & C. Merriam's 1842 advertisement for its Springfield Series (broadside, 54 x 43 cm), demonstrating an early method of distributing schoolbooks through firms and stores nationwide, before district and state school systems assumed responsibility for adopting textbooks. American Antiquarian Society.

principals to commit to one publisher for a curriculum that was increasingly defined by grade levels. Many schoolbooks contained advertisements for their publishers' other wares. An 1857 edition of *McGuffey's New Sixth Eclectic Reader* included advertisements and testimonials for Ray's arithmetic series (now nine books, culminating with algebra), Pinneo's series of grammars, and a "school music" series, as well as acclaim for the McGuffey's readers from state superintendents in Ohio, Indiana, Illinois, and Iowa.[72] Publishers' broadsides and catalogs also spread the word. For example, a four-page 1848 listing of "VALUABLE SCHOOL BOOKS" in geography, history, grammar, science, mathematics, Spanish, French, and Latin, from the Philadelphia firm of Thomas, Cowperthwait & Co., advertised that S. Augustus Mitchell's *Primary Geography* (1840) had been "introduced into the Public Schools of Boston, New York, Philadelphia, Baltimore, New Orleans, St. Louis, Louisville, Cincinnati, Pittsburgh, and many other cities and towns in the United States."[73] Publishers and school officials increasingly engaged in direct contact, bypassing the retail booksellers. As superintendents, local school committees, and principals came to make adoption decisions, publishers hired networks of traveling agents to promote the books.

Given the potential profit in schoolbook publishing and the growing but relatively finite market of school districts and officials, competition became fierce. In October 1838, a lawsuit threatened the two-year-old McGuffey's readers series. Samuel Worcester, a prominent author whose readers, spellers, grammar, and geography were published in Boston, filed a plagiarism suit against McGuffey and his publishers. Truman & Smith settled out of court for $2,000 and revised McGuffey's books to remove the offending passages. But Cincinnati observers saw a clear competition between East and West: the eastern booksellers were trying to drive the Ohio upstart out of the market by linking the plagiarism charge to a concerted effort to place eastern school books into Cincinnati bookstores. One Boston firm contracted with a Cincinnati firm to republish Boston books with a local imprint.[74] As more firms published rival series of readers and arithmetics, their agents fueled the fires. Agents routinely disparaged their competitors' wares, while offering school boards and principals ever-better deals to adopt their books: liberal discounts, exchanges for other firms' books, and (according to some observers) bribes. Publisher S. A. Rollo retired from the textbook trade in 1859, complaining that agents and competition had created "too much of a patent medicine business for educational publishers."[75]

A different sort of conflict developed as sectionalism divided the United States. Antebellum southern critics and politicians expressed a desire for southern textbooks to combat the ostensibly northern bias of most reading books. During the Civil War, that concern combined with the inability to procure schoolbooks published in the Union. North Carolina teachers convened in 1861 and 1862 to promote the publication of state-sponsored works. On 28 April 1863, delegates from across the South met in Columbia, South Carolina, to form the Educational Association of the Confederate States of America. The sixty-nine teachers, professors, and commercial printers in attendance appointed a Committee on General Interests of Education and Textbooks, chaired by Richard Sterling. Sterling's firm, Sterling, Campbell & Albright, of Greensboro, North Carolina, published numerous textbooks during the war; and from 1863 to 1865, Texas newspaper editor E. H. Cushing published a "New Texas" series of textbooks, mostly lifted or adapted from antebellum northern books. But while most states encouraged textbook writing, few of the works ever saw print.[76] After the war, a group of "patriotic Southern men" formed the University Publishing Company to promote a schoolbook series that would counter the offenses in northern-published books: readers that "stigmatized" southern children's fathers "as traitors," histories that presented the war from the victors' side, even "arithmetics which present to the youthful mind as problems for solution the relative losses of the 'Rebel' and Union armies in the various battles of the 'wicked Rebellion.' " No evidence survives that this company ever published a single schoolbook.[77]

In fact, the postwar years witnessed intensified competition nationwide among northeastern and midwestern firms. In February 1865 the *American Educational Monthly* (1864–76), published for schoolteachers, launched a five-year crusade against schoolbook agencies. The magazine wrote nostalgically that the earliest book agents had behaved in gentlemanly fashion, introducing school officials to the virtues of their wares and letting teachers judge for themselves. Now, however, agents conducted their publishers' book wars at the expense of the nation's teachers and children: defaming rival books in anonymous pamphlets and circulars, offering free introductions in order to supplant a system's current textbooks, and then creating virtual monopolies by persuading boards of education to pass bylaws that forbade changing textbooks at any cost to the schools. The *American Educational Monthly* had its own agenda. It perceived the centralization of adoption decisions as an invitation to collusion between superintendents and publishers, and it argued that teachers should play a greater role in choosing books.[78] Under the prevailing system, teachers became "mere cats-paws in the hands of corrupt manipulators, the paid agents of wealthy publishers."[79] The *Massachusetts Teacher* (1848–74), one of the myriad educational periodicals that appeared in most states by 1870, wrote, "The 'Battle of the Books' as described by Gail Hamilton is a misnomer, and but a pop-gun affair as compared with the school-book battle in State capitals for State supremacy, or in large cities for a commanding position. Just now, no doubt, a general disarmament will be beneficial to all concerned."[80]

Disarmament was exactly why the schoolbook publishers created their Board of Trade in March 1870—for their own sake, not the teachers'. J. C. Barnes, addressing the board that spring, explained the problem from the publishers' perspective. Now that there were more than 350 agents representing twenty competing publishers, "it is not strange that some sharp practice is resorted to," bribing everyone from teachers to superintendents to local book dealers with everything from free samples to cash. The publishers themselves, Barnes claimed, often did not know exactly what their agents were doing, until the agents' deals for free adoption meant higher expenses and lower profits.[81] At its first meeting, the School Book Publishers' Board of Trade adopted a series of bylaws. All agents were to be withdrawn as of 1 July 1870, and none employed thereafter. Introduction of schoolbooks could not occur as a free exchange of new books for old, and there would be maximum discounts for introduction copies (still liberal at half to two-thirds, but now codified): "No money, nor anything that can be converted into cash, no maps or charts or school furniture, nor any undue means whatsoever, shall be used to secure the introduction of books." Instead of agents and bribes, publishers were to use "circulars and the press," potentially guaranteeing advertising revenue to the nation's educational journals.[82]

Publishers complied at first, and their Board of Trade met quarterly for more than three years.[83] They worked with the *American Literary Gazette and Publishers' Circular*, which had modestly begun an "education issue" devoted largely to textbook advertisements in 1869. Just as the publishers created the Board of Trade, the *American Literary Gazette* announced that education issues would appear twice yearly and could be sent free, postage paid, "to any schoolmaster or teacher" who furnished an address.[84] The publishers advertised in force and pulled their agents from the field. But the regulatory system began to crack within a year. When the board met in January and April 1871, several firms complained that they had "been attacked in their interests by outside parties and compelled in self-defence to put travelling agents in the field." Publishers proposed amending the bylaws to allow agents again: rejecting A. S. Barnes's suggestion of one agent per publisher, the board voted to allow each publisher as many as ten. Over the next six years, the association increased this number to fifteen and then to twenty-five. The old abuses reappeared, and firms called on the board's arbitration committee to adjudicate conflicts caused by one another's agents. The Board of Trade formally disbanded in 1877 after the leading firm of Ivison, Blakeman, Taylor & Co. withdrew. *Publishers' Weekly* argued that public opposition to the monopolistic, price-fixing "textbook ring" had led publishers to sacrifice the board, but it was equally clear that the attempt at "reform" had failed from within.[85]

After 1877 the leading schoolbook publishers directed their efforts toward consolidation, much as Oliver Ditson & Co. was doing in the music trade. The four largest—Ivison, Blakeman, Taylor & Co., A. S. Barnes & Co., Van Antwerp, Bragg & Co. of Cincinnati, and D. Appleton & Co.—formed a syndicate by 1883 and formally merged seven years later. Their new American Book Company dominated the field; contemporaries estimated that it controlled 50 to 90 percent of the market.[86] States continued to complain about textbook rings, but to little effect. Californians passed a constitutional amendment in 1884 requiring that the state publish its own textbooks.[87] Most of the general trade publishers that had competed in the textbook market abandoned the field. Ivison bought Scribner's textbook business in 1883, and Harper & Brothers sold its textbook division to the American Book Company in the mid-1890s. A few found specialized niches in their own backlists. The Harper & Brothers literature list provided the foundation for its English Classics for School Reading series (begun in 1870), and the Riverside Literature Series (begun in 1882) helped create a literary canon of American authors from Houghton, Mifflin & Co.'s extensive copyright holdings.[88]

Like music publishing, schoolbook publishing experienced upheaval between 1840 and 1880, ending in consolidation after successive rounds of expansion, competition, and attempted self-regulation. Two controversies forty-three years apart suggest the magnitude of change. When Samuel Worcester sued William H. McGuffey and his publishers in 1838, the dispute was personal (one author against another), locally articulated (Boston vs. Cincinnati), and easily resolved—even as it augured the enormous profits to be made in textbooks. In 1881 *Publishers' Weekly* investigated schoolbook publishers' discounting and business practices and found that the "big four" firms, soon to become the American Book Company, spent $200,000 a year on agents and book introductions. By this date, "McGuffey's" was a brand name, and textbook publishing was a national industry, aimed at winning bulk contracts with city and state school systems that had not existed four decades earlier.

The Heyday of Subscription Publishing

Unlike schoolbook or music publishers, firms that published books exclusively by subscription had no clear outlets, such as school boards or music stores, for their products. They usually did not offer directly competing merchandise, such as versions of the same European music or rival series of reading books. They did not form associations to regulate their operations. They did, however, develop a distinct system of distribution, using agencies and canvassing agents to reach readers directly. Moreover, trade publishers imagined subscription houses as a discrete realm and a potential threat.

By the 1850s, the major marketing and distribution elements were taking shape for what would become the post–Civil War boom in subscription publishing. Since the eighteenth century, American authors, printers, and publishers had followed British precedent in using the subscription method to reduce the financial risk entailed in publishing a work. Such books were generally advertised in broadside sheets or newspapers. Nineteenth-century subscription publishers, then, innovated on a time-honored practice.[89] As early as 1833 a New Haven publisher experimented with a more substantial prospectus that included sample text and illustrations, terms of sale, and blank ledger pages for purchasers' names. Publishers in the 1850s created networks of sales agents by advertising in local newspapers nationwide. City directories identified book agents, some of them booksellers who sold for subscription publishers. In the Midwest, city booksellers often acted as "general agents" for eastern book publishers and hired canvassers to sell subscriptions in the city or around the region.[90]

After the war, the number of publishers who sold "by subscription only" multiplied, as did their output. Hartford, described in 1872 as "the headquarters of this business for the whole country," had at least sixteen such firms by 1870, including Elisha Bliss's American Publishing Company, publisher of Mark Twain's *The Innocents Abroad*.[91] But subscription publishing may have been less centralized than the general trade, or even music or textbook publishing, had become. Subscription publishers existed in cities of the Northeast, Midwest, and Far West. When a subscription book's title page listed multiple firms, it is likely that the first was the actual publisher who had worked with the author, created the printing plates, and prepared the canvassing book (a tantalizingly incomplete sample book that was also known as the "prospectus," or "salesman's dummy"). Firms in other cities may well have served as general agents for the book's sale, responsible for hiring canvassers and collecting subscriptions. Numerous San Francisco companies, some of them publishers in their own right, played this role on behalf of eastern publishers. At times, the San Francisco publisher Hubert Howe Bancroft also used eastern publishers as agents for his subscription books.[92] Subscription books ranged widely across genres: Civil War histories, how-to books, biographical or literary anthologies, memoirs of foreign travel, and Bibles and assorted religious works. The firms that published county atlases and histories also used the subscription method but depended on sales within the particular locality whose lands and citizens the book described. Other specialized examples of subscription publishing included expensive scientific or scholarly books, often published in parts, and books published in series to be distributed as second-class mail.

Canvassers, including women such as Annie Nelles and Mrs. J. W. Likins, responded to newspaper or magazine advertisements that promised fortunes in commissions. The sales kits that they bought from the publisher or general agent became more elaborate over time: canvassing books came to include testimonials, binding samples, and illustrations, and publishers added scripts to guide canvassers' conversations with potential customers. The canvassers' territory could range from a sector of San Francisco and a nearby county (Likins's territory for Twain's *Roughing It* [1872]) to entire western territories. After returning their subscribers' orders to the general agent or publisher, they had to traverse their territory again to deliver the books. For every patron who subscribed, the canvasser probably endured the impatience or hostility of many others who did not. Some subscribers refused to pay when their book was delivered, and given the peripatetic habits of many Americans, canvassers often had a difficult time of even finding the subscriber. By the 1870s, both the canvassers and their pitch were all too familiar to Americans, many of whom had experienced a book that failed to meet its promise or a salesperson who took the order but never returned.[93]

Subscription publishers described themselves as a boon to authors and to readers beyond the reach of bookstores. They promised authors a richer return than the trade publishers' standard 10 percent royalty. Although the well-known financial successes of Twain's subscription books and Ulysses S. Grant's *Memoirs* (1885) suggest the possibility of such fortunes, it is impossible to tell whether the typical author of a subscription volume earned more than a counterpart who published with a trade firm. However, a subscription canvasser sold one book at a time, in contrast to trade publishers who placed their seasonal lists into bookstores. Twain's publisher, Elisha Bliss, explained in 1874 why subscription books benefited ordinary readers and, by extension, publishers of all sorts:

Instead of injuring the book business I think we create a thirst for knowledge and thus increase the sale of all kinds of books. In the little towns where there are no bookstores the book agent induces the people to buy. One book thus sold is read with avidity by the whole household, and when another agent comes it is ready to buy another book. In that way a nucleus is formed for hundreds of thousands of little libraries throughout the country, which never would have existed except for the book agent.[94]

As Bliss's first phrase suggests, he was responding to complaints from retail book publishers and their trade organs, which feared subscription firms as potential competitors and denigrated subscription books as gaudy pretenders to literary merit. The *American Literary Gazette* distinguished in 1870 between, on the one hand, encyclopedias and kindred works, which could earn a return only by subscription sales, and on the other, the bulk of subscription books, which were "often absolutely worthless" in content and manufacture.[95] Two years later, the *Publishers' and Stationers' Weekly Trade Circular* (successor to the *American Literary Gazette* and soon to become *Publishers' Weekly*) called the

> great proportion of the books issued to-day from Hartford . . . either actually bad or very like humbug. A gorgeous binding, usually in very bad taste, thick but cheap paper, outrageously poor wood-cuts, the largest type with the thickest leads, add up into a very big, gaudy book which a glib tongue or persistent boring cheats folks into buying at five dollars, when the reading matter which it contains, if worth anything, would make about a dollar-and-a-half book in the regular trade.[96]

Trade publisher S. R. Crocker conceded in 1874 that authors could make more money on the "subscription plan" but hoped the best authors would not elect that direction because "Subscription books are in bad odor, and cannot possibly circulate among the best classes of readers."[97]

These laments masked the relationship and penetration between the regular trade and subscription publishing. Subscription publishers advertised for canvassers not only in local newspapers across the country but also in *Harper's Weekly*. As the *American Literary Gazette* noted, "retail booksellers often surreptitiously get hold of subscription books, and undersell, to the injury of the business"; subscription publishers threatened to retaliate by underselling retail books.[98] Beginning in the 1870s and accelerating after 1880, every major trade publisher built its own subscription department to sell particular books or sets of books, such as an author's collected works. In contrast to their descriptions of subscription firms' overpriced, gaudy wares, trade firms tended to characterize their own subscription books as elegant and to package them as "limited editions."[99]

Music, schoolbooks, and subscription offer three alternatives to the regular trade. Music-publishing firms, whose practices were distinct from those of the trade publishers, created a parallel universe. They sold through retail outlets across the United States, published trade journals, and established a version of trade courtesy in response to problems of international copyright. Textbook publishing intersected repeatedly with trade publishing from the 1840s to the 1870s, because many producers of schoolbooks were also trade houses. As schoolbook publishing diverged more fully from trade publishing in the 1880s, the nation's major firms were embracing some of the methods of the subscription publishers they disdained. In a sense, it was those subscription publishers who resisted the trend toward centralization, but even they formed distribution networks of canvassers and alliances among publishers and general agents across the country. In coming decades, Boston's music-publishing titan Oliver Ditson & Co., the textbook syndicate that became the American Book Company, and the metropolitan trade publishers that combined retail and subscription methods would all achieve increasing control of their respective markets.

CHAPTER 7

Periodicals and Serial Publication

Introduction

Jeffrey D. Groves

. . .

All producers of printed works—members of the regular trade and specialized publishers, authors, small-town printers, and workers at large urban newspapers—understood the economic and cultural importance of periodical publication. According to the Eighth Census, periodicals made up just over half of the total value of printing reported for 1859-60.[1] Readers, responding enthusiastically to this widespread production and attuned to the rhythm of daily, weekly, monthly, quarterly, and annual publication, possessed an ingrained sense of the key characteristics that generally distinguished these printed works from books. Published serially with a continuing title and maintaining topical character and timeliness in content, periodicals forged an ongoing relationship with subscribers who often formed a community by means of print.

Understanding these characteristics does not mean that the quantity and extent of periodical publication were easily measured. For the United States Census Bureau, amassing statistics for such publications was neither practically easy nor conceptually straightforward. As Superintendent of the Census Francis A. Walker reported in 1872, "In a country where literary as well as business enterprises are so ephemeral as in the United States, it will of course be impossible to secure absolute uniformity between the statistics of newspapers, magazines, and other periodicals."[2] Many short-lived publications were born and died between the decennial gathering of census information; newspapers were "constantly being started and abandoned in every section of the United States."[3] Knowing what to count was also a problem. It was an "open question," for instance, as to whether the large number of periodicals devoted primarily to advertising should be reported.[4] While there was consistency over time in a few census categories, such as the number and frequency of periodicals, the precise information gathered varied considerably from decade to decade. Perhaps more significantly, the census reports did not typically divide periodicals into familiar categories of newspapers and magazines but rather favored division by frequency of publication, a practice that made it difficult to delineate any precise boundary between these two genres.[5] The problem of knowing what to count and how to count it was serious enough that Superintendent Walker and his staff compared the reports of census agents with lists from two unnamed advertising agencies that had "thoroughly worked up" the "newspaper field" in the United States in order to present a report of the quality called for by the census legislation.[6] Such comparison almost certainly made the census statistics for 1870 and 1880 more reliable than previous reports had been: J. D. B. DeBow, an earlier superintendent of the census, had noted that the "newspaper and periodical statistics of 1850 fall short of, rather than exceed, the reality."[7] While the census records overall may not paint an absolutely accurate picture of periodical publication, they nonetheless suggest large-scale trends.

Not surprisingly, the key trend is the proliferation of newspapers, magazines, and other periodicals in the nineteenth-century United States. Table 7.1 depicts the proliferation and geographical spread of periodical publication between 1840 and 1880. The growth in the number of periodicals reported was tremendous—from 1,631 to 11,314, almost a sevenfold increase. Growth, however, was not steady over the period. During the decade of the Civil War, periodical publication slowed considerably, especially in the South. And in spite of the economic depression of the 1870s, the number of periodicals very nearly doubled in that decade. Throughout the period, New York was by far the largest center for periodical production, but there was strong growth in other states, especially those in the Midwest and West.

Individual census reports, depending on what information they collected, provide more in-depth images of the characteristics of periodical publication at particular moments. In 1880, an overwhelming majority of these publications were in English. German-language periodicals made up 6 percent of the total, and other languages, such as French, "Scandinavian," and Spanish, just over 1 percent.[8] Table 7.2 depicts frequency of issue for different periodicals by state or territory in 1880. In that census year, weeklies constituted 76 percent of the total number of periodicals reported. Monthlies trailed at 10 percent, dailies at 9 percent. Quarterlies and other periodicals made up the remaining 5 percent.

In reporting circulation, however, the 1880 census divided periodicals into just two categories, dailies and everything else. From a total average circulation per issue of almost 32 million, dailies made up 11 percent. That percentage seems to have been relatively constant over the previous decade: the 1870 census reported that dailies made up 12 percent of periodical circulation. The 1870 census also categorized frequency of issue more fully than the

TABLE 7.1. Number of newspapers and periodicals by
state or territory and decade, 1840–1880

State	1840	1850	1860	1870	1880
Alabama	28	60	96	89	125
Arizona	—	—	—	1	17
Arkansas	9	9	37	56	117
California	—	7	121	201	361
Colorado	—	—	—	14	87
Connecticut	44	46	55	71	139
Dakota	—	—	—	3	67
Delaware	8	10	14	17	26
District of Columbia	17	18	13	22	44
Florida	10	10	22	23	45
Georgia	40	51	105	110	200
Idaho	—	—	—	6	10
Illinois	52	107	286	505	1,017
Indiana	76	107	186	293	467
Indian Territory	—	—	—	—	3
Iowa	4	29	130	233	569
Kansas	—	—	27	97	347
Kentucky	46	62	77	89	205
Louisiana	37	55	81	92	112
Maine	41	49	70	65	123
Maryland	49	68	57	88	143
Massachusetts	105	209	222	259	427
Michigan	33	58	118	211	464
Minnesota	—	0	49	95	223
Mississippi	31	50	73	111	123
Missouri	35	61	173	279	530
Montana	—	—	—	10	18
Nebraska	—	—	14	42	189
Nevada	—	—	—	12	37
New Hampshire	33	38	20	51	87
New Jersey	40	51	90	122	215
New Mexico	—	2	2	5	18
New York	302	428	542	835	1,411
North Carolina	29	51	74	64	142
Ohio	143	261	340	395	774
Oregon	—	2	16	35	74
Pennsylvania	229	310	367	540	973
Rhode Island	18	19	26	32	44
South Carolina	21	46	45	55	81
Tennessee	56	50	83	91	193
Texas	—	34	89	112	280
Utah	—	0	2	10	22

TABLE 7.1. *Continued*

State	1840	1850	1860	1870	1880
Vermont	33	35	31	47	82
Virginia	56	87	139	114	194
Washington	—	—	4	14	29
West Virginia	—	—	—	59	109
Wisconsin	6	46	155	190	340
Wyoming	—	—	0	6	11
Total	1,631	2,526	4,051	5,871	11,314

Sources: *Compendium of the Enumeration of the Inhabitants and Statistics of the United States . . . from the Returns of the Sixth Census* (Washington, D.C.: Thomas Allen, 1841), 362–63; Francis A. Walker, *A Compendium of the Ninth Census* (Washington, D.C.: GPO, 1872), 510, table 39, and *Compendium of the Tenth Census (June 1, 1880)* (Washington, D.C.: GPO, 1883), 1628, table 131.

Note: The decline in the number of periodicals in Virginia between 1860 and 1870 was partly due to economic conditions during and after the Civil War, but it also stems from Virginia's loss of territory when West Virginia gained statehood in 1863.

1880 report. While weeklies accounted for 51 percent of issues circulated in 1870, there were also many more weeklies than there were dailies or monthlies. The average circulation for a weekly, then, was 2,467, but for a daily it was 4,532, and for a monthly 9,085.[9]

Dailies and weeklies were published in towns and cities across the nation, and they circulated predominantly within the region where they were produced. It is inaccurate, however, to understand these periodicals as serving only local needs. After the Civil War, dailies and weeklies were the most affected by the growth of syndication agencies, which offered nationally syndicated matter in the form of partially printed sheets, plates, or galley proofs to local newspapers, and of advertising agencies that sought regional or nationwide exposure for particular products.[10] Monthlies differed from dailies and weeklies in that their production was more centralized. In 1880 five states with leading publishing centers — Illinois, Massachusetts, New York, Ohio, and Pennsylvania — accounted for 62 percent of all monthlies reported. While these periodicals were fewer in number than dailies and weeklies, their larger average circulation suggests a wider, often even a nationwide, distribution.

The geographic spread of periodicals did not mean that local needs were being met straightforwardly by local publications. Small newspapers that featured nationally distributed advertisements, religious periodicals that created a sense of belonging among subscribers at great distances from each other, general-interest monthlies that aimed not only at a nationwide distribution but also at representing a particular concept of the nation — all such publica-

TABLE 7.2. Number of newspapers and periodicals by state or territory
and frequency of issue, 1880

State	Daily	Semi- or triweekly	Weekly	Biweekly, semi- or trimonthly
Alabama	6	1	109	2
Arizona	6	0	11	0
Arkansas	6	1	104	4
California	58	13	250	6
Colorado	19	1	63	0
Connecticut	17	2	99	3
Dakota	9	1	57	0
Delaware	5	0	20	0
District of Columbia	5	0	23	0
Florida	3	2	40	0
Georgia	16	7	163	3
Idaho	0	3	7	0
Illinois	74	23	758	22
Indiana	40	4	390	6
Indian Territory	0	0	3	0
Iowa	30	4	500	3
Kansas	20	1	310	1
Kentucky	11	9	160	2
Louisiana	13	2	94	1
Maine	12	1	90	1
Maryland	15	0	111	4
Massachusetts	39	14	279	8
Michigan	33	6	397	6
Minnesota	10	1	205	1
Mississippi	5	6	109	0
Missouri	43	10	415	9
Montana	4	0	14	0
Nebraska	15	1	165	1
Nevada	14	0	22	0
New Hampshire	10	0	66	4
New Jersey	27	7	163	2
New Mexico	3	0	15	0
New York	115	29	892	45
North Carolinia	13	5	113	4
Ohio	56	12	584	21
Oregon	7	0	59	1
Pennsylvania	98	7	674	17
Rhode Island	8	1	31	1
South Carolina	4	4	69	0
Tennessee	12	2	154	6
Texas	30	3	231	2

Monthly	Bimonthly	Quarterly	Semi-annually	State total
7	0	0	0	125
0	0	0	0	17
2	0	0	0	117
32	0	2	0	361
4	0	0	0	87
15	1	2	0	139
0	0	0	0	67
1	0	0	0	26
15	0	1	0	44
0	0	0	0	45
11	0	0	0	200
0	0	0	0	10
118	0	21	1	1,017
27	0	0	0	467
0	0	0	0	3
31	0	1	0	569
15	0	0	0	347
23	0	0	0	205
2	0	0	0	112
18	0	1	0	123
12	0	1	0	143
80	0	7	0	427
19	1	1	1	464
6	0	0	0	223
3	0	0	0	123
50	2	1	0	530
0	0	0	0	18
7	0	0	0	189
1	0	0	0	37
7	0	0	0	87
13	1	2	0	215
0	0	0	0	18
282	5	40	3	1,411
7	0	0	0	142
90	0	11	0	774
6	0	1	0	74
159	1	16	1	973
3	0	0	0	44
3	0	1	0	81
16	1	2	0	193
14	0	0	0	280

TABLE 7.2. *Continued*

State	Daily	Semi- or triweekly	Weekly	Biweekly, semi- or trimonthly
Utah	5	4	8	1
Vermont	5	0	72	1
Virginia	20	11	124	2
Washington	4	0	23	0
West Virginia	2	3	96	1
Wisconsin	21	5	283	11
Wyoming	3	0	8	0
Total	971	206	8,633	202

Source: Francis A. Walker, *Compendium of the Tenth Census (June 1, 1880)* (Washington, D.C.: GPO, 1883), 1628, table 131.

tions reached beyond their place of production to support the constitution of communities of print, both national and local, represented in commercial, political, or cultural terms.

PART 1

Newspapers and the Public Sphere

John Nerone

. . .

Newspapers did important work in enabling the development of the book industry in the nineteenth century. They reviewed, advertised, and serialized books and served as a training ground for authors. Many well-known authors were schooled in newspapers: Walt Whitman, John Greenleaf Whittier, Harriet Beecher Stowe, Mark Twain, William Dean Howells. Newspaper plants remained important regional book printers, and book publishers also produced newspapers—such as Harper & Brothers, which published the nationally distributed illustrated *Harper's Weekly* (1857–1916). But as books and newspapers both industrialized, they also differentiated their functions. Newspapers mark the horizon at which the history of the book meets the enveloping history of communication. Book culture emphasized timelessness, the authorial persona, and the cultivation of the reader's interiority. News

Monthly	Bimonthly	Quarterly	Semi-annually	State total
4	0	0	0	22
3	0	1	0	82
33	1	3	0	194
2	0	0	0	29
6	0	1	0	109
20	0	0	0	340
0	0	0	0	11
1,167	13	116	6	11,314

culture emphasized ephemerality, collective anonymous production, and the collision of the reader's mind with the exterior world.

As book culture and news culture became differentiated, their shared relationship to public life changed. In the United States, unlike in western Europe, a republican ethos had linked newspaper and book forms. European commentators worried that newspapers would supersede books and turn a culture of orderly reflection into chaotic novelty.[11] Before the Industrial Revolution, American commentators saw no such natural opposition between book and newspaper. Instead, they cited the growth of newspapers as evidence of the increasing intelligence and literacy of the population, assuming the newspaper to be the necessary vanguard of print culture. Likewise, both newspapers and books were considered key to the successful functioning of a public sphere that would produce a national culture, both political and literary. Underlying the boastful enumerations of the nation's print output was an assumption that quantitative growth was producing a stronger and more democratic community. Even pessimists who feared that the rise of popular amusements in print would eviscerate national morality never doubted that the press itself was a necessary political institution.

Industrialization changed this bland assurance. Amid transformations in technology, transportation, and political culture, the routinized flow of information through the wire services and the emerging "beat" system of reporting seemed to overwhelm the culture's capacity to make sense of it all. Commentators began to voice a sense that news culture inevitably sundered the meaningful worlds that book culture wove.[12] This development reflected fundamental changes in the newspaper system.

Newspapers work because they connect a persisting audience with predictable content in a consistent form. More than book publishers, newspapers survive by establishing a network of relationships between communities of readers and a spectrum of content producers — reporters and editors, advertisers and syndicates, and newsmaking organizations such as political parties, stock exchanges, sports leagues, and show business. The flow of content is channeled into familiar forms, constructing a meaningful representation of the social.[13] In this way, the newspaper turns the transmission of information into a ritual of social continuity.[14] Readers, bombarded daily with disjointed information, encounter in the *form* of news a representation of a coherent, common life.

Americans in the early republic imagined this common life as the public sphere. The new federal government recognized the importance of the newspaper to the public sphere by setting up postal regulations to subsidize newspaper production and the circulation of political information. The newspaper system was to exert a centripetal force, drawing a diverse and dispersed population together into a common national allegiance. To the chagrin of many, warring parties soon enlisted newspapers to turn the public sphere into a perpetual combat zone. But partisans explained that conflict was as natural to politics as competition was to the market and that their competing newspaper networks allowed the people to weigh arguments and come together in judgment. By 1840 the party press occupied the core of the newspaper system.

Centrifugal forces also acted through the newspaper system. In the years between 1840 and 1880, a growing periphery of newspapers and journals invited readers into alternative and subaltern spaces segmented from the great public. Meanwhile, an increasingly commercialized mainstream press invited segmented readerships into private spaces of consumption. Core and periphery interacted as nonmainstream publications demanded that public attention be given to their group interests or ideas; some succeeded in joining or influencing the mainstream.

By 1880 the relationship of the newspaper system to the public sphere had grown far more complex. Party loyalties continued to reside in the core but were now ghettoized in an editorial section, surrounded by more prosperous neighborhoods of news, entertainment, and advertising matter. News had become a commodity bought and sold by wire, rather than intelligence shared through the mails. Publications on the periphery produced a chorus of voices largely ignored by the parties and the mainstream press. And it was no longer clear that the point of the newspaper system was to service the public sphere. Critics complained that its commercial interests had overwhelmed its political mission.

The Party Press

The party-press system operated at full maturity in the presidential election of 1840. Remembered for its raucous and populist atmosphere, the "Log Cabin Campaign" saw both parties deploy media strategies aimed at mobilizing mass coalitions of voters. Their newspaper networks anchored this effort.

Both parties took advantage of the postal system to run national newspaper networks. The postal system allowed editors to send "exchange" papers to each other without charge, a provision meant to facilitate a national flow of information. Because these exchanges were the primary source for nonlocal news, editors eagerly sought out exchanges with nationally prominent newspapers, with editors who shared a point of view, and with other newspapers in the same state or region. To maintain a good exchange list, an editor would have to provide content that other editors would want to "clip." This meant that editors had other editors in mind as an audience when composing their original material, especially their political news. Among Whigs and Democrats, the newspaper exchange system allowed editors to run a kind of partisan news service and a virtual party convention.[15]

The center of the Whig effort in 1840 was a weekly newspaper called the *Log Cabin* (1840–41), edited by Horace Greeley, a protégé of newspaper editor and Whig eminence Thurlow Weed. Greeley's career would span all the changes in the national press system, from the world of the country print shop to the dawn of mass circulation newspapers. Editing the *Log Cabin*, the circulation of which reached 80,000, made him the first among equals in the national system of Whig editors. All exchanged with him, copying his material and giving him copy. He also carried on highly visible conversations with opposing Democratic editors.

This system provided legitimacy for the whole political process. In theory, the party-press system promised equality, multivocality, and a bottom-up process of deliberation. Any newspaper voice, just like any voter or postal address, would be equal to any other. Starting a newspaper was relatively cheap, and the system of mass politics called for (and subsidized through patronage) competing party papers in every locality. The whole system gave the appearance of grassroots democracy. Any citizen anywhere could write a letter to a newspaper that could be copied by its exchanges and come to the attention of the entire nation. So open-ended a system would produce a rich, diverse, and democratic national discourse.

The practice differed. Hezekiah Niles, the publisher of one of the nation's most important newspapers, the *Weekly Register* (1811–49), had an immense exchange list and was well positioned to observe the system in action. He complained that parties corrupted newspapers: editors acted "together as if with the soul of one man, subservient to gangs of managers, dividing the spoils of victory, of which these editors also liberally partake — more than one hundred and fifteen of them being rewarded with offices, or fat jobs of printing, &c. *This is a new state of things.*" He complained that "a falsehood manufactured or a calumny forged, runs through the whole line of hired presses."[16] Niles explained how he had detected a covert "opinion ring" in the state of New York while clipping items for his own paper: "in a period of eight or ten days, I cut out and laid aside nearly forty 'EDITORIAL' articles, which all had the same 'ear mark,' and were evidently prepared by one hand; and these articles were afterwards collected in the 'Albany Argus' and sent through the state as 'PUBLIC SENTIMENT,' and so 'public indignation' has been more than once MANUFACTURED!"[17] The phrase "manufacturing public opinion" remained common in newspaper commentary throughout the rest of the century.[18]

"Represent" describes the situation better than "manufacture." The national press system had intentionally been set up as a mechanism for representing public opinion. In initial, utopian formulations, the press and its editors would passively represent the public. But by the 1840s, observers and participants realized that representation was a far more active process. Niles and others saw editors standing in for the public, in the way that congressmen represented their constituents. When they published, they communicated not just with the public of citizens but also with the active public of fellow editors, who in turn mediated their messages both to their readers and to yet other editors. This practice confounded observers who thought newspapers should work by enabling citizens to represent themselves in public. Even party enthusiasts recognized the element of humbug here.[19] Rather than empowering individuals by giving them information that they could reason over and transform into their own voices, the party-press system allowed political professionals to contend with one another to represent public opinion.

In the process, this system policed the public sphere. The structure of American electoral politics encouraged parties to piece together coalitions that could capture a national majority. To do so meant knitting together blocs of diverse factions. Because any majority party would contain factions with conflicting interests, it could persist only by diverting attention from these conflicts. Both parties needed to repress divisive issues. They counted on their editors to play a gatekeeping role in keeping some issues out of electoral politics. In the years before the Civil War, the major repressed issue was slavery. Because southern states could effectively veto a presidential bid, both parties considered antislavery activism toxic and sought to avoid its stain, while hoping that the opposing party got labeled as lousy with abolitionists.

But the nature of the press system gave antislavery activists an opening that editors like William Lloyd Garrison were quick to exploit. Garrison (like Greeley) came from the Northeast, imbibed the fervor generated by evangelical and reform movements, and worked in printing shops and edited party newspapers before encountering a mentor (Thurlow Weed for Greeley, Benjamin Lundy for Garrison) who would promote him to national prominence. Greeley opened his paper to many of the winds of doctrine that blew through Garrison's, but party loyalty restrained him. Garrison, however, operated at the periphery of the system that Greeley moved at the center of.

Garrison's *Liberator* (1831–65) illustrates one of the key features of reform publications at the dawn of mass politics — the dialectic between core and periphery. The newspaper system had established a polarized but truly national conversation about political matters; the competition between the major parties for a majority of voters had established a boundary to that conversation. Antislavery activists tried many different strategies to influence mainstream political discourse. Many espoused the Enlightenment notion that the power of truth over a candid mind could drive public opinion. Newspapers such as James G. Birney's *Cincinnati Philanthropist* (1836–43) ran regular lawyerly debates with slaveholders over the constitutional powers of Congress and biblical support for slavery, confident that truth would prevail in a well-conducted fight against falsehood. Birney, a lawyer and 1844 candidate for president on the Liberty Party ticket, had not been socialized through the emerging popular media or he would have known better. Evangelicals, schooled in the techniques of revival and sentimental fiction, were more effective. Gamaliel Bailey's *National Era* (1847–60) produced the publishing marvel of the age by serializing *Uncle Tom's Cabin*, deploying the symbols and pathos of awakened Christianity, rather than the courtroom persuasion.

Garrison came from the party press. His experience in partisan newspapering taught him how to manipulate the system, not by making powerful arguments but by making news. His subscription list dropped as low as four hundred, and he depended on free black subscribers, especially in Philadelphia. But his national voice had little to do with his subscription list and everything to do with his exchange list, which exceeded two hundred and included many southern newspapers, which copied selectively from the *Liberator* to terrorize their readers. Frequent quotation magnified the paper's voice out of all proportion to its public support.[20]

Garrison's notoriety underscores the terms on which the periphery could direct mainstream discourse. Activists could attract mainstream attention through "deviant" action, and ironically, the mainstream eagerly helped. The

New York office of the American Anti-Slavery Society aimed propaganda at southern audiences, including mass mailings to post offices in the South. These media reached few people directly, but the hyperbolic response— public burnings, gag laws— occupied national attention. Whether such spectacular action furthered the cause remains a matter for debate. The flip side for antislavery media was the patient work of building a network of sympathetic newspapers. Abolitionists co-opted existing party newspapers, either through converting editors or by offering financing. Because the system of party newspapering was so decentralized, there were always leaks in the anti-abolitionist hegemony. By the 1850s, a national network of antislavery publications encroached on the mainstream press. In states like Ohio, where antislavery activists came to hold the balance of political power and could elect antislavery senators, local antislavery newspapers became common.[21]

Antislavery's relationship with the public sphere exemplified the careers of other movements. In an age known for reform movements, the appearance of movement newspapers should not be surprising. Some of them, like the antislavery papers, aimed to convert the great public. Anti-Masonry, the Workingmen's Party, temperance, and women's rights all produced journals that criticized and tried to intervene in mainstream press discourse. Other movements concentrated on building their own public. The Millerites, for instance, produced a vast array of publications, most famously the *Midnight Cry* (1842–44).

Other newspapers worked to give voice to ethnic or racial groups. These presses entered a complex relationship with the mainstream public, simultaneously offering a safe haven for group discourse and making a claim on the larger public to take notice. African American newspapers displayed a sort of double consciousness, intending both to build community among their readers and to demonstrate the maturity of the race to white people (see Chapter 10, Part 2). At least one antebellum black journalist, Frederick Douglass, learned from Garrison's style of newspapering. Douglass's *North Star* (1847–51) was read and clipped by editors in both the partisan and reform press; a large British readership further magnified its voice.

The double work of the foreign-language press matched that of African American newspapers. The number of foreign-language papers increased simultaneously with the rise of mass politics and the party press, and they shared the party papers' forms and intentions. Among the premier foreign-language papers before the Civil War were the German-language newspapers of the Midwest, especially in Cincinnati and St. Louis. Each city supported three or four competing German dailies of varying political and religious persuasions. A growing number of weeklies— some devoted to religion, reform, literature, or humor, and others that were the weekly editions of the daily papers—achieved broad regional circulation.[22]

The German press underscores the dialectic between separateness and assimilation in nonmainstream media. Adopting forms and rhetoric from the mainstream partisan press, German papers provided immigrants a gateway to American institutions. Success in this mission meant the papers would obsolesce, feeding their readers into the mainstream-press system. Maintaining linguistic separation could prevent this, and the press of older immigrant groups, such as Germans, often survived out of vestigial devotion to the mother tongue. Foreign-language papers also retarded assimilation by maintaining ties with the mother country, and in fact they circulated abroad and facilitated both remigration and the construction of overseas national identities.

The Transformation of the Press and the Public Sphere

As the party-press system faced challenges from the periphery, it also began to change in its structure and practices. As it labored throughout the century to repress dissident voices and integrate new populations, it also contended with sweeping changes in techniques of production and distribution, adopted new business models, and undertook new tasks. In the process, it participated in a significant transformation of the public sphere.

Liberal models of the public sphere assign the political and the economic to separate and relatively autonomous spheres. Politics and the market operate by different distributive principles—"one person, one vote" versus "one dollar, one vote"—and produce different kinds of outcomes; in theory, democracy in politics will preserve the virtues and ameliorate the inequalities of freedom in the market. Newspapers occupied a liminal position in this logic. They were supposed to service the political system, supporting citizenship and polity, but increasingly they relied on the market for support. Although eventually newspaper publishers and editors would come to think that the marketplace had freed them from the captivity of partisanship, in the 1840s this conclusion was far from obvious.

Horace Greeley's career expresses the tension between the market and politics particularly well. After his successful stint with the *Log Cabin*, Greeley's Whig backers decided to finance a penny paper in New York. The penny press had become an established subgenre in the mid-1830s partly because of its criticism of most papers' party ties. Despite proclamations of nonpartisanship, however, most penny papers were Democratic. Hence the desire to establish a Whig alternative, funded by Whigs and edited by a party loyalist. Greeley's *New York Tribune* (1841–1924) became a terrific success; its weekly edition, which circulated nationally, made Greeley one of the most widely read, influential editors in the country. The paper recruited impressive talent to provide content, including a generation of social thinkers from Margaret Fuller to Karl Marx. In its openness to movements such as antislavery and Fourierism, the *Tribune* continually drew attention to the vexed relationship between the marketplace, the political system, and the utopian expectations that democracy still conjured up.

The *Tribune* retained the voice and argumentation of the partisan press but coupled them with the arrangements of a more commercialized press. Early on, realizing his shortcomings as a businessman, Greeley partnered with Thomas McElrath, who took over all business operations. This division of labor between the sacred world of politics and the profane world of commerce, although frequently violated, would become a standard feature of newspapers' organizational structure, allowing editors and news workers to assert a manly independence from finance and advertisers.[23]

Over the next forty years, the editor's paper, composed by clipping from exchanges, would yield leadership to the industrial paper, produced in factories with ever more elaborate divisions of labor for growing markets of diverse consumers. The commercial work of the press would engulf its political voice. This transformation coincided with a tremendous expansion of the newspaper system. Growth was uneven, concentrated in certain genres and places. Metropolitan dailies expanded rapidly. The South remained underdeveloped, a fact that made southerners far more likely to see vast media conspiracies in the North.[24] New York became the news capital, replacing a more decentralized, partisan reliance on chains of influence anchored in Washington.

New York's dominance, although modest by comparison with that of London or Paris, had much to do with technological changes in production, distribution, and news transmission. Production technologies (see Chapter 1) included steam-powered cylinder presses, stereotyping, and engraving. Presses that employed steam power and curved plates turned out vastly more impressions per hour than hand-powered flatbed presses. When fully developed, the Lightning press produced by R. Hoe & Co. made eight thousand impressions per hour. The new presses cost far more than their predecessors; the Lightning press cost up to $25,000.[25] The resulting economies of scale appealed to metropolitan newspapers, which were able to expand circulation by cutting prices.

Newspapers could sell their expanded readerships more profitably to advertisers. Newspapers in the United States had always printed advertisements, but usually as short notices. In the early republic, advertising expanded with the rest of the newspaper, and advertisements from merchants came to be long and detailed. By the 1830s, advertising typically occupied three-quarters of the space of a daily newspaper. The constant pressure for space led advertising to become less, rather than more, distinctive in the 1820s and 1830s, a retrograde process that climaxed in James Gordon Bennett's famous "agate rule" in 1847: the *New York Herald* (1835–1920) would no longer carry two-column advertisements or advertisements with enlarged initial capitals or engraved illustrations. This design conservatism spread outward to the provinces, dampening but not extinguishing experimentation there.

Stereotyping made it easier to reproduce pictorial advertisements. Now a manufacturer, especially of patent medicines, could hire a woodcut firm to execute an advertisement, stereotype it, and have it inserted in newspapers around the nation. By the end of the 1860s, advertising columns pulsed with pictures, typographical variations, and white space—all the tactics of contemporary handbills and broadsides—while the rest of the newspaper became continually grayer. Newspapers came to use stereotyping for all sorts of "boilerplate" material and also to speed up production of the newspaper by casting multiple forms for multiple presses.

Newspapers took advantage of new transportation technologies to change the shape of distribution; again, metropolitan newspapers benefited most. Within cities, they used increasingly efficient transit to move their copies. They were also quick to focus on the nodes in the transportation system —streetcar stations, for instance—as sites for sales. By 1880 metropolitan dailies had to contend with monopolizing wholesalers. In New York, a wholesale firm appeared in 1854 and began to dominate distribution to retailers; in 1864 it named itself the American News Company; by 1887 it had grown to encompass some twenty thousand agencies across the continent (see Chapter 4, Part 1).[26] Regional distribution also shifted. The railroad allowed metropolitan dailies to expand into the hinterland, delivering newspapers on the same day to once-distant locales. A new division of labor appeared between metropolitan and country papers: the former carried the news of the day, leaving the latter free to concentrate on local events.[27]

The overwhelming bulk of newspaper sales still went to individual subscribers through carriers. Historians of journalism conventionally credit the penny press with moving circulation from steady subscribers to street sales. However, even in 1870 the *Philadelphia Public Ledger*, one of the most important penny papers, distributed more than 55,000 of its 70,000 daily press run to carriers and only 3,708 to newsboys for street sales.[28] The cultural significance of the newsboy hawking "extras" did not translate into a routine economic practice.

Capping the ensemble of new technologies was the telegraph. Greeley's *Tribune* greeted the telegraph as "literally material thought . . . annihilating space and running in advance of time," and anticipated that it would comprise "a net-work of nerves of iron wire, strung with lightning, [that] will ramify from the brain, New York, to the distant limbs and members — to the Atlantic seaboard town, to Pittsburgh, Cincinnati, Louisville, Nashville, St. Louis and New Orleans — and that every commercial, political or social event transpiring at either of these points will be known at the very instant it happens, in all!"[29] Presciently describing the developing urban backbone of the nation, Greeley envisioned a time when all points on the map would simultaneously know and respond to political events at Washington. But he completely misread the implications for newspapers, speculating that they would turn from novelty to deep philosophy.

First adopted regularly by newspapers in the mid- to late 1840s, the telegraph seemed to contemporaries to allow for instant communication among all parts of the nation. Counterbalancing this new transparency was a new opacity. The telegraph allowed instantaneous flow only through built channels, and these channels had bottlenecks that could be controlled. Once again, the metropolitan papers benefited. A cooperative of New York newspapers organized to capture a telegraph bottleneck for news from Europe. It then leveraged this monopoly into a national monopoly on all telegraphic news. This complicated story, worked out in marketplaces, capitals, and courts over several decades, set a pattern for the future exploitation of communication technology in the United States. Not only would technologies drive monopolistic enterprises through canny manipulation of markets, regulations, and intellectual property laws, but the outcomes would be presented as natural and necessary, dictated by the technology, and apolitical.[30]

It was hardly inevitable that the telegraph system and then the news wires would become monopolies. Any particular telegraph *line* between two points was a natural monopoly: a competing line would be prohibitively wasteful, and one of them would go out of business quickly. It does not follow that the nation's telegraph *system* should have become a monopoly. Different lines might have been operated by different companies, as occurred with the railroads despite numerous attempts to monopolize. Even more remarkable was the emergence of a *news* monopoly. Efficiencies existed in consolidating news transmission from specific places: why have competing wholesalers of market information? But that is information that is predictably produced and consensually understood. News, by its definition, is unpredictable and conflicted, its value determined not by impersonal market forces but by competing political and cultural agendas. In theory, wire services could have been partisan, as were newspapers. The monopolies that the Associated Press (1848) and Western Union (1851) built emerged only after great struggle, often through means that would be outlawed later in the century. Their hegemony never went unchallenged. In other countries, telegraphic communication was integrated into the postal system.

As monopolistic news services converged with the rising metropolitan daily paper, it became possible for the first time for the entire nation to be exposed simultaneously to the same diet of information—a monolithic "news of the day." On particularly dramatic occasions, such as John Brown's raid at Harper's Ferry or Abraham Lincoln's assassination, the impact of the news could seem unprecedented and revolutionary.

The appearance of an illustrated press magnified the emotional impact of news. Pioneered by national weeklies based in New York, illustrated papers created a storehouse of images for the entire country, providing virtual presence for people otherwise remote from the drama of the polity. P. T. Barnum's *Illustrated News* (1853, absorbed by *Gleason's Pictorial Drawing-Room Companion*), *Frank Leslie's Illustrated Newspaper* (1855–1922), *Harper's Weekly*, the *Daily Graphic* (1873–89), and many imitators used illustration to tell stories and break up a gray page. Often pictures were surrounded with florid borders, to set them off from the type. These design conventions likened news pictures to paintings in a gallery, invoking the artist's eye and hand.

Illustrated news drew on photography but resisted photorealism, partly because of a technological gap. The technology to reproduce photographs, which made possible the market for cartes de visite, existed decades before the technology to print photographs alongside text. Halftone reproduction, a version of which was demonstrated as early as 1873, was considered one of the many available techniques of photoreproduction, not the best one.[31] Engravings made from photographs claimed a fidelity and authority unavailable to simple portraiture. But in any engraving, whether or not from a photograph, an artist intervened. News artists became stock figures. The *New York Illustrated News* (1859–64), for instance, boasted of how its artists fanned out across the world in search of news and included comic illustrations of them going about their business. These artists were scavengers, not experts or authorities. Whether they drew from life or from photographs, they were supposed to be recorders, but their illustrations also always commented. News illustration required its images to tell a story, or to make a moral point, or to convey some sensation or sentiment. Photographs were too stilted and cluttered to communicate clearly. In the process of translating a photograph to an engraved plate, the artist freely excised clutter, played with foreground and background, and sometimes introduced elements.[32]

The development of illustrated news anticipated the increasing design sophistication in general newspapers. Advertising was the leading edge. The visual elements of advertising matter migrated into news columns, arranging and articulating content. Headlines appeared first in advertising matter, typically designed to draw attention to the merchandise for sale (HATS) or to the establishment offering the goods or service (WOODSTOCK ACADEMY). By midcentury, printers routinely used headlines of this nature in news content, whether generic headlines (MELANCHOLY OCCURRENCE) or references to the actors in events (MONSTER CLAY PARADE). The function of headlines in news gradually shifted. First, again imitating advertisements, they began to outline the story, with stacks of lines above important stories and especially telegraphic reports. Printers experimented typographically, varying sizes and fonts for headlines. By 1880, especially on front pages, headlines changed from labels to sentences, to tell the point of the news. In the larger printing shops, foremen began to lay out pages in a visually coherent fashion.

The development of layout clashed with some of the practical imperatives of composing a newspaper. The four-page format dictated that news be crowded into a tight space. The result was a dense page, characterized by thin columns, small type, and little white space.[33] Foremen addressed the problem of fitting news into the page in two ways. One was to keep it all gray, a continuous march of little type with no variation and minimal breaks for headlines and other devices. This was a style that signaled prestige, embodied by the *New York Times* (1851–), following the *Times* of London. The other approach, equally Victorian, was a busy, crowded, varied front page — the print equivalent of a crowded shop window. Sometimes these busy pages were organized in some way; a common practice positioned tall stacks of headlines atop alternating columns. Until well into the twentieth century, the typical daily edition did very little to map the news for the reader. Victorian news pages left hierarchy and meaning out of the arrangement of news, in much the same way that the content of news items often eschewed explanation. Foremen were not designers, just as reporters were not experts. Instead, the arrangement of news followed streams of transmission.

The Civil War: A Moment of Change?

The Civil War experience shows all these developments in dynamic play. Newspaper voices with national reach, information flowing through telegraph lines, and illustrations meant to convey a visceral, if sanitized, impression of action reached all parts of the nation. Meanwhile, political forces fought to channel news and control the representation of public opinion.

Wartime conditions called for control over military information especially. The press was a ubiquitous feature of life in the military. Correspondents accompanied armies, seeking to supply their newspaper clients with compelling information and sketches of camp life. In turn, copies of newspapers migrated through the ranks of soldiers, who read them aloud, eager for news from home and information about the state of the country.[34] Photographers accompanied the troops not only to shoot the now-famous pictures of the dead but also to make money selling portraits to soldiers, who sent them home to loved ones. Of the array of media tools, the telegraph drew special attention from military planners. The Lincoln administration early on recognized the strategic importance of the telegraph and put the lines, operated at the time by three competing companies, under the control of the War Department. The telegraph lines provided a bottleneck through which the administration could monitor and censor information.[35] But control of military information remained porous. Armies moved through a sea of civilians, accompanied by schools of correspondents, all capable of reporting movements and intentions. Military secrecy demanded the active cooperation of reporters and media outlets. The notorious outbursts of Generals Sherman and Burnside should not obscure the loyalty of the typical member of the Bohemian Brigade, as northern reporters were called; in the Confederacy, loyalty was even more pronounced.[36]

The Lincoln administration has been justifiably praised for respecting the rights of dissenting politicians—not throwing all the Democratic editors in jail and keeping them there—and the level of criticism directed at it during the war was high.[37] Instead of state repression, Lincoln and other political leaders used the techniques honed in decades of partisan struggle to manage the public sphere. A cadre of quasi-independent editors at important newspapers constituted a kind of informal propaganda agency for the administration. Horace Greeley's often testy relationship with Lincoln typified the relatively open way in which fealty and independence coexisted in the party press. This openness legitimated the representation of public opinion that the party press was devoted to crafting. Within the traditions of partisanship, Lincoln not only tolerated the opposition press, he needed it. The ritual of contest, which included heated, intemperate, and apparently treasonous rhetoric, enabled the government to claim legitimacy before a free citizenry.

Even so, the administration possessed many tools to rig the game. Some high-level imprisonments, a few newspaper closings, and the suspension of habeas corpus are well known. More interesting and less well studied is a wave of mobbings of newspapers, often involving soldiers on leave and usually coinciding with important elections. Again, the ritual aspect of these actions overrides their violence. They resemble earlier antiabolitionist actions, in which mainstream partisan leaders coordinated attacks designed less to silence abolitionists than to label them as repulsive, un-American, and weird — to make their voices not worth listening to.[38] Such partisan mobbing shared little with the more intense, popular, and violent targeting of Greeley and his *Tribune* during the 1863 New York draft riots.[39]

Both in the newspaper and in the government, Civil War newspapering shows the uneven interaction of new and old content and uses. The editor's paper worked the war in the tradition of party struggle, while the streams of content coming from correspondents and the telegraph recognized the demands of loyalty and prompted novel forms of state control. Some historians of journalism discern the emergence of modern forms of news here, arguing that the war gave rise to the modern reporter and the front page. Such intimations of innovation were premature, as the history of the front page exemplifies. Craft shops that produced four-page newspapers traditionally placed prime news and original editorial matter on inside pages and printed outside pages earlier, with less timely matter, so that the ink would not smudge in delivery. Long after changes in print technology made this practice vestigial, the front page continued to be a ghetto of advertisements, essays, and other devalued material. The exceptions to this rule were the "extra" editions of newspapers published to report immediately on unexpected events of grand importance. Although the front pages of Civil War newspapers from time to time took on the appearance of extras, filled with the latest news, this did not become prevailing industry practice until the wave of newspaper innovations of the 1870s.

The Late-Nineteenth-Century News System

The public could see a new newspaper system on display at the 1876 Centennial Exhibition in Philadelphia. Frank Leslie, the proprietor of *Frank Leslie's Illustrated Newspaper*, chaired the entire event's organizing committee. George P. Rowell, head of the nation's leading advertising agency, installed a Newspaper Pavilion, at once a press room for journalists and a reading room for the general public, featuring a copy of every one of the nation's 8,129 newspapers. Rowell succeeded in drawing journalists to the fair: more than a thousand were accredited during its seven months.[40] Some of the New York dailies sent stereotype plates by an early train to the exhibition

PERIODICALS AND SERIAL PUBLICATION

and printed their own daily editions on the spot.[41] Meanwhile, in Machinery Hall, powered by the celebrated Corliss Engine, working installations of Hoe and Bullock web presses displayed state-of-the-art printing technology. Positioned next to a hand press billed as Benjamin Franklin's own, the Hoe web press, one of only twenty-three in the world, printed on a "continuous sheet 4½ miles long, and running through the machine at the rate of 750 feet per minute."[42] Commentaries on this equipment implied that the unsurpassed output of its printing presses—1,250,024,590 copies of newspapers in 1876, Rowell figured—demonstrated industrial America's superiority to the rest of the world.[43] Other communications technologies displayed at the exhibition became points of national pride: telegraphy, photography, new systems of engraving, even typewriters, though observers took little notice of Alexander Graham Bell's telephone. Such technological and industrial marvels appeared to leave behind a world in which rugged, ink-stained individuals handcrafted little sheets with powerful voices.

In the standard histories of the United States press, the chief plotline in this period is the replacement of the party press with the commercial press. Most consider this a happy history: the marketplace freed the newspaper from a reliance on party subsidies and obliged it to serve the public by telling the truth without fear or favor.[44] Others see it as a decline: a system devoted to serving the popular deliberations of a raucous democracy was colonized by the forces of retail.[45] Either way, this narrative omits many subplots and too eagerly sees the homogenized, objective professional press of the late twentieth century emerging automatically from social forces.

After the war, a dramatic spurt of new popular newspapers recalled the appearance of the penny press in the 1830s. Cheap newspapers with a vernacular flair and a penchant for illustration appeared in cities of all sizes. The most important were innovators in second- and third-tier cities: Melville Stone's *Chicago Daily News* (1875–1978), Joseph Pulitzer's *St. Louis Post-Dispatch* (1878–), Henry W. Grady's *Atlanta Constitution* (1868–), and the *Chattanooga Times* (1869–), which Adolph Ochs, who would later turn the *New York Times* into the nation's premier newspaper, purchased for $250 in 1878. Pulitzer, who bought the *St. Louis Dispatch* and merged it with the city's *Post* in 1878, emerged from the nexus between politics and the German-language press. Carl Schurz hired him as a reporter for the *St. Louis Westliche Post* (1857–1938) in 1868; faithful to the partisan tradition of German newspapers, Pulitzer was elected to the state legislature in 1870 and worked for Horace Greeley's 1872 presidential campaign. The new papers of the 1870s, remembered because they or their proprietors achieved journalistic distinction, capitalized on a formula pioneered by less-remembered entrepreneurs, the most important of whom were the Scripps brothers, James and Edward Wyllis.[46] In addition to founding individually important newspapers in midwestern and western cities, Edward Wyllis Scripps established the first modern newspaper chain, with centralized policies and editorial direction and with national services for features and news.

The commercial press remained highly partisan. The editor's paper did not disappear; rather, it was folded into the commercial form. The editor's section of original paragraphs and clipped news stayed in the middle of the paper, moving to page 4 or 5 as metropolitan papers doubled to eight pages. The wire services, especially the Associated Press, remained partisan enough that critics during the disputed presidential election of 1876 referred to the AP as the "Hayesociated Press."[47] Barriers to entry into mainstream political discourse continued to exist, sometimes in new ways. The woman suffrage movement, which arose in the milieu of antislavery, adopted many of the same organizational and media strategies but failed to drive public discourse as abolitionists had done. As peripheral movements found it harder to break into mainstream discourse, their publications increasingly sought to build a movement culture among the already sympathetic, while accepting the indifference of the general public or at least of its media. For example, among labor publications, ambitious general-interest newspapers such as the *Workingman's Advocate* (Chicago, 1864–77) declined. Organizing papers appeared, such as the *Journal of United Labor* (Philadelphia, 1880–89, continued until 1917 as the *Journal of the Knights of Labor*), the central newspaper of the Knights of Labor, which aimed at informing members of the leaders' decisions and actions. Emancipation closed the door between African American newspapers and the mainstream press. After the Civil War, African American papers were likely to be noticed only by other African American editors, unless they were being scapegoated.[48] The wave of newspapers founded by blacks after the Civil War—especially in the South, where Republicans tried to establish a presence that would endure beyond the states' readmission to the Union—circulated for the most part in an autonomous, middle-class subculture.

As the individual newspaper became more of a factory product, the division of labor in the newsroom became departmentalized, and more by technology than by topic. Postal content, the clipped news, correspondence, and editorials that had been the entire content of the editor's paper remained the "voice" and "face" of the new paper. A second department featured telegraphic news. At first, all telegraphic news appeared in a single column under a standard heading. Later, telegraphic news split into different columns, with general news moving to the front of the paper and business news to the back. A third department featured original reporting.[49] In metropolitan newspapers, a crew of reporters who worked under a city editor scavenged the city for interesting news, often from the police courts and entertainment venues. These reporters should not be confused with correspondents. Correspondents, originally amateur letter-writers but later semiprofessional columnists, commented on the scene in faraway places, using their own voices and values. Reporters, like the court reporters for whom the term was first coined, were mere stenographers by comparison, recording what was said and done. Organizationally, editorial advocacy was becoming separate from the production of news, which news workers came only gradually to see as apolitical facts independent of positions on the editorial page.

Reporting and telegraphic news, unlike clipped news and editorials, could be bought and sold. Begun as a cooperative organization designed to cut costs for its members, the New York Associated Press (which later evolved into the Associated Press) became a news broker, retailing telegraphic news to the nation's newspapers.[50] More subtly, newspapers realized that using their own reporters to gather news would allow them to "brand" their content. Whereas earlier newspapers intended their matter to be copied, now they complained regularly that other papers were "stealing" their news.[51]

Historians often overemphasize the role of telegraphic technology in reshaping the textual qualities of modern news. By their accounts, the telegraph encouraged terseness, to save both time and money; the inverted pyramid style of writing, which places the most important point at the top and puts details in order of decreasing importance, a practice that inverts the usual pattern of telling a story from beginning to end; and neutrality, to facilitate sale to a variety of newspapers.[52] But telegraphic terseness did not influence the language of correspondents, who, following the traditions of letter writing, remained luxuriant and periphrastic. Discipline in the newsroom — the domain of the city editor and the birthplace of the professional copy editor, whose blue pen axed nickels and dimes from the wages of reporters who were paid by the line — resulted more from the foreman's insistence on space limits than from the telegraph. The inverted pyramid style seems to have emerged not from newspapers but from the internal communications of bureaucratic organizations. The first examples in newspapers were Civil War dispatches from War Secretary Edwin Stanton, but newspapers did not adopt the style in general reporting for decades after that.[53] Partisanship remained a viable commercial strategy through most of the century.[54] In a market with more than two competing newspapers, claiming to be *the* Democratic paper asserted that one controlled half the market. The directories compiled by advertising agencies continued to list newspapers' party affiliations: not only did papers remain partisan, but advertisers wanted them that way.

Some advertisers did want to reach an entire market. National manufacturers placed advertisements in newspapers of all sorts to mass-market products; medicines, including contraceptives and narcotics, provided a large share of advertising revenue. Department stores had a more direct impact, particularly on metropolitan dailies. These stores required advanced graphic capabilities and wanted ever more space, an important factor in expanding the daily newspaper beyond four pages. Unlike national manufacturers, department stores changed their advertisements frequently and wanted the newspaper to set them in type each time. To become the "one-best" medium for department store advertising, newspapers saw a significant increase in their fixed costs of production. Along with the availability of a standard menu of telegraphic news and the increasing costs of print machinery, advertising would help consolidate local newspaper markets in the twentieth century. Only then would partisanship become forbidden.

The Civil War altered the newspaper norm that the early republic had idealized. Traumatized by slavery, sobered by disunion, news culture lost its obsession with simulating public deliberation. Partisanship survived, but romance with the public sphere gave way to an emphasis on supplying facts and a practical marriage to markets. The changes in the public sphere by 1880 raised new questions about the role of the press in the republic. The media seemed to carry increasing power, and as they industrialized and as new bottlenecks and elements of monopoly appeared, it seemed to many that self-interested entities could control this power. It was in response to that impulse that journalism moved to professionalize at the beginning of the twentieth century—a complicated story for another volume.

PART 2

The Business of American Magazines

Eric Lupfer

. . .

Greeting readers from the "Editor's Easy Chair" of *Harper's New Monthly Magazine* (1850–) on the first day of January 1863, George William Curtis reviewed the history of his magazine and considered its place in the American literary scene. He boasted of *Harper's* contribution to national culture, its nurture of authors, and its efforts to provide the best of both British and American writing to its readers. Curtis recognized, however, that perhaps *Harper's* most salient characteristics as a magazine were its stability and wealth. *Putnam's Monthly Magazine* (1853–57), he wrote, "fell silent by the way about five years ago, and as if from its ashes rose the *Atlantic*, which is still our contemporary. Of yet later date is the *Continental*. The old *Knickerbocker* has been in failing health for some years."[55] Meanwhile, countless other weeklies and monthlies had come and gone. And during this period of "such mutations and sad mortality in magazines," *Harper's* had endured and even flourished.[56] Unable to resist a pun, Curtis suggested that some of these now-defunct periodicals might have lasted longer if "they had had a more solid foundation, which is the *capital* necessity."[57]

Curtis's reference to the Harper firm's wealth points to a fact of central importance in the development of American magazines. As contemporary observers frequently noted, the mid-nineteenth century was a period of "magazine mania" in the United States.[58] The sheer variety of periodicals is astonishing. Not only did magazines represent an opportunity for literary amateurs and professionals to participate in public discourse, they also became a key component of group identity. Nearly every occupation, pastime, and special interest had its own set of related periodicals. By the 1870s, a young, professionally minded schoolteacher in Ohio might have read (and even contributed articles to) the *Ohio Educational Monthly* (1852–1926), the official publication of the state's teachers' association, and national organs such as the *American Educational Monthly* (1864–76), the *American Journal of Education* (1855–82), the *Teachers' Institute* (1878–1906), the *School Journal* (1871–1916), the *Kindergarten Messenger* (1873–77), and the *Primary Teacher* (1877–83). She might also have followed several general-interest monthly magazines such as *Harper's* and *Scribner's Monthly* (1870–1930, renamed *Century* in 1881), assuming that while they constituted pleasure reading they were also relevant to her career aspirations. Whatever her choices, it is near certain that multiple magazines would have played a central role in the development of her sense of professional and personal identity.

Yet as Curtis suggests, the mania for magazines was matched by a pessimism with which many observers viewed them as business enterprises. In magazines and newspapers, literary professionals frequently noted that there were too many magazines, that subscribers rarely paid in full, and that newspapers were far more popular. As one observer wrote in 1853, "There is something awful in the contemplation of the number of periodicals, started with the most confident enterprise, and the most sanguine expectations, that never reach a third number."[59] These pessimists had a point. Only a fraction of the magazines founded during this period survived. Indeed, most were risky ventures — undercapitalized, poorly advertised, haphazardly managed, and with limited circulation. Publishing historian Frank Luther Mott estimates that between 1850 and 1865, 2,500 distinct magazines were issued in America; their average lifespan was about four years.[60]

Even those magazines that seemed relatively well established were vulnerable to the vicissitudes of an expanding but highly unstable economy. The financial panic of 1857 wiped out *Putnam's, Graham's American Monthly Magazine* (1840–58), and the *United States Magazine and Democratic Review* (1837–59). The Civil War was an even severer trial, as was the financial crisis of the early 1870s. While there is no doubt that magazines became increasingly important to American literary culture, we should recall Curtis's reflections upon the capital necessities of their publication. This period of unprecedented expansion in periodicals was marked by a high incidence of "mutations and sad mortality."

If the proliferation and vulnerability of magazines are obvious features of this period, so is their increasing integration within a culture of print. After 1840 the production of magazines became ever more bound up with the production and promotion of books, newspapers, and other printed materials. Book publishers began issuing their own house magazines, magazines printed advertisements for newspapers and books, and the text generated by editors and contributors flowed freely between them all. Even at the material level, classification could be difficult. Readers regularly had entire volumes of their favorite magazines bound in book form—a practice that publishers encouraged by selling covers for binding. The public could also purchase volumes bound by the publisher, complete with title pages, indexes, and tables of contents. Some books, such as Joseph Holt Ingraham's *The Lady Imogen; or, The Wreck and the Chase* (1861), were either comprised of sheets left over from the original periodical publication or produced from the plates thereof.[61] The cheap reprint series that emerged in the 1870s, such as George Munro's Seaside Library, consisted of books that sought to look and act like magazines. The text of the constituent novels appeared in three closely printed columns per page, and the books were issued on a regular basis in flimsy paper covers, each with its series number and date of publication featured prominently on the front.

Books and periodicals thus represented not discrete domains but mutually supporting and constitutive ones. Magazines, for example, often emphasized their connection to books, which remained the most permanent and authoritative form of print. Consider the illustration that adorned the cover of *Harper's* through the end of the century. In the illustration, the magazine's title is set within a small shrine, replete with fluted columns, decorative ribbons, and at the top, a pair of angelic children strewing flowers over the scene.

As if to anchor the enterprise both culturally and commercially, the shrine's foundation is inscribed with the name and New York address of the Harper firm. At the base of each column is a tall stack of weighty tomes, one of which is open to a title page reading "Harper's Monthly Magazine." The meaning of the illustration is clear: this magazine emerges from that cultural world both constituted and symbolized by books. By contrast, the covers of *Harper's Weekly* featured elaborate illustrations emphasizing the journal's connection to news and current events. The cover of the 4 March 1865 number, for example, is dominated by a full-page engraving of a scene from Sherman's march through South Carolina, which Union forces completed only a week earlier. While it did have some of the bookish features of the firm's monthly magazine, the two periodicals — one a weekly focusing on current events, the other a monthly that aspired to reach a more leisured, elite readership — nicely illustrate the differing ways and extents to which mid-nineteenth century publishers sought to connect magazines to book culture.

At the same time, book publishers sought to connect their work more closely to the activity of magazines — a lesson learned during the "paper wars" of the early 1840s, when mammoth weeklies found great success in publishing mostly British novels in serial form. While novels typically sold for $1, individual numbers of the *New World* (1840–45) and *Brother Jonathan* (1839–43) were priced at 2¢. "Extra" editions — in which especially popular titles appeared in toto — went for 10¢. The circulation of the weeklies soon topped ten and twenty thousand per week, causing Mathew Carey to complain that the market had become "glutted with periodical literature."[62] The weeklies' reign ended in 1845 when changes in the postal code prohibited them from mailing their wares at the rate reserved for newspapers. Their influence, however, was long lasting, as they showed book publishers how to reach larger, more diverse publics by providing the same material in different forms and at different prices. In 1842 Harper & Brothers had great success when it reissued all 157 volumes of its Family Library in cheap bindings at 25¢ per copy. Other publishers began issuing paperbound books as well, some of them complete, others in parts, with prices ranging from 25¢ to 50¢.[63]

The success of the mammoth weeklies also taught publishers that periodicals had the potential to reach a greater number of readers than any single book — that a magazine might "be floated as the flag of a book-house."[64] Thus began a period when large, general-interest publishers established their own magazines, viewing them not as independent concerns but as a means to support the firms' business in books. Through its magazine, a firm expected to attract and publish the work of young writers (who might later publish books through the firm), publish the work of established writers (who might also be published by the firm), and advertise and review its own new titles. House magazines also frequently excerpted or serialized works soon to appear in book form, on the assumption that doing so would increase demand for these texts. Each such magazine thus served as an important promotional tool, a means of communicating the values and prestige of the firm to readers throughout the country.

James R. Osgood & Co.'s publication and promotion of John De Forest's novel *Kate Beaumont* (1872) shows the extent to which a firm might use its magazine to support its book operations. The *Atlantic Monthly* (1857–), owned by the Osgood firm, published the novel in serial form between January and December of 1871. In March of the following year, the magazine published a favorable review of the novel, which had appeared in book form only months earlier. De Forest's novel, wrote the *Atlantic* reviewer, is "the first full and perfect picture of Southern society of the times before the war; certainly it is the most satisfactory."[65] The November issue printed an extended essay on De Forest's novels, treating *Kate Beaumont* as well as several other titles the firm had published over the past several years. *Kate Beaumont*, the article opined, was one of a handful of novels indicating "something fresh, strong, and advancing" in American literature.[66] Almost a decade later, when reviewing one of De Forest's subsequent novels — this one, significantly, published by D. Appleton & Co. — the *Atlantic* still showed an inordinate affection for the author's 1872 work: "there are a great many entertaining novels which are not nearly so good as *Kate Beaumont*, and this is one."[67]

Of course, these practices were not limited to fiction. Publishers regularly issued collections of essays and articles that had first appeared in their house magazines. Even at midcentury, the practice was so common that one observer noted that he would be hard-pressed to find a book *not* comprised of material that had originally been published in magazines or newspapers.[68] Nor were these practices limited to the elite monthly magazines. Frank Leslie serialized Mary Elizabeth Braddon's *Aurora Floyd* in his *Illustrated Newspaper*; in the same year, he published the novel in book form as part of Frank Leslie's Series of New Novels. Beadle & Co. and its successors (including Beadle and Adams) owned periodicals such as *Beadle's Monthly* (1866–67) and the *Star Journal* (1870–81) in which it published serialized fiction that it also released in book form. Of course, the firm also drew material for its dime novels from the magazine literature of the day. The first in the series, *Malaeska: The Indian Wife of the White Hunter* (1860), originally appeared in *Graham's* as a three-part serial in 1839. George Munro — "the manufacturer of twenty thousand, more or fewer, books, six days every week" — published a weekly titled the *Fireside Companion* (1867–1903). Later, he published and sold reprints of popular British magazines, such as the *Contemporary Review* (1866–), the *Nineteenth Century* (1877–1900), and the *Fortnightly Review* (1865–1934).[69]

Not surprisingly, both the proliferation and increasing importance of magazines had tremendous influence on the practices of American authors. Before 1840, periodicals could not guarantee authors a livelihood. This began to change in the early 1840s, however, with the emergence of two highly popular Philadelphia-based magazines: *Graham's* and *Godey's Lady's Book* (1830–98). By 1842 the circulation of each had topped thirty thousand, and their success allowed them both to pursue a business strategy heretofore untested among American periodicals: paying liberal rates for original submissions from the nation's best writers. *Graham's* attracted Henry Wadsworth Longfellow, James Russell Lowell, Edgar Allan Poe, and William Cullen Bryant with payments ranging from $2 to $7 per page; James Fenimore Cooper and Nathaniel Parker Willis earned even more. *Godey's* rates soon followed suit, as did those of *Sartain's Union Magazine* (1847–52). It is difficult to overestimate the importance of these changes. As Willis remembered, "The burst on author-land of *Graham's* and *Godey's* liberal prices was like a sunrise without a dawn."[70] Magazines boasted publicly about their rates of payment. "We have spent as high as fifteen hundred dollars on a single number for authorship alone," crowed *Graham's* in 1853. "This is more than twice the sum that has ever been paid by any other magazine in America." *Godey's* advertised itself with similar claims, noting that its owner had attracted the best American writers and artists "by the offer of a liberal compensation," spending "not less than two hundred thousand dollars" on contributions.[71]

Soon a small class of writers commanded high prices for their work (see Chapter 3). In the 1840s *Graham's* and *Godey's* paid Willis approximately $1,500 for his contributions, and the *Knickerbocker* (1833–65) promised Washington Irving an annual rate of $2,000.[72] Magazines competed to establish exclusive relationships with the most famous writers, recognizing that those writers' names were valuable commodities. In 1855 Robert Bonner, publisher and editor of the *New York Ledger* (1847–1903), established an exclusive contract with Sara Payson Willis (Fanny Fern), paying her $5,000 per year so that the *Ledger* could serve as the exclusive publisher of her essays. Of course, before the mid-1850s such arrangements were atypical—the "splendid exceptions," as one observer put it in 1847.[73] The smaller literary, religious, and professional magazines still did not pay at all, and the market for general-interest magazines supported only a handful of talented, established writers.[74] For the writer without a "name," things were even more difficult. "Of all the American periodicals," wrote William Gilmore Simms in 1845, "there is not one which pays all its contributors."[75] And those that did, wrote Nathaniel Parker Willis, "pay nobody whose 'name' would not enrich their table of contents."[76] For inexperienced writers, publication was generally assumed to be payment enough.

Nevertheless, as the century progressed, the paying opportunities for all writers, even the unknown ones, generally increased. Many of the new publisher-backed, general-interest monthly magazines developed large circulations among the growing middle class. These magazines paid for all submissions, though not equally, and had space enough to include works by unknown writers. The *Atlantic* had a base rate of $5 to $6 per page. *Harper's* and *Putnam's* paid about the same. These magazines did not simply expand the market for paying work; they also considerably altered how American writers understood the role that magazines might play in their careers. In the 1850s, John Burroughs, who would become the century's most popular nature writer, kept up with a number of American periodicals, including the *New Englander* (1843–92), the *United States Magazine and Democratic Review*, and the *North American Review* (1815–). Burroughs's true love, however, was the *Atlantic*. As he wrote later in life, that magazine served as "a sort of university" for him when he was young and did much "to stimulate and to shape my literary tastes and ambitions."[77] Indeed, the young Burroughs frequently imagined being published in the *Atlantic* and having his future books reviewed and advertised there as well.

In the late 1850s, when Burroughs began his career as a professional writer, he started out as many unknowns did, publishing in local newspapers and small quarterlies, such as Henry Clapp's *Saturday Press* (1858–66), which, as William Dean Howells noted, "never paid in anything but hopes of paying, vaguer even than promises."[78] But Burroughs wrote mainly toward the standards and conventions of the *Atlantic*, and in 1860 he finally had an essay accepted by James Russell Lowell, the magazine's editor. Professional success quickly followed. Over the next decade, Burroughs published multiple essays in the *Atlantic*, the *Knickerbocker*, the *Galaxy* (1866–78), *Putnam's*, *Appleton's Journal* (1869–81), and the *Nation* (1865–). His work earned not only critical praise but also considerable payment. In an 1878 journal entry, Burroughs marveled at his good fortune: "Could I have known 20 years ago all the good things that were in store for me, I should have been spoiled. My writing has brought more fame and money than I ever dared hope. For the past 15 years I have had a good income—the last five years as high as $3500 per annum, and have been almost entirely free to follow my own tastes."[79]

Burroughs's case is instructive in several ways. From the very beginning, he understood that magazines would be central to his career and its development. Indeed, his formative years were marked by an extended attempt to realize himself as a writer precisely within the standards dictated by the *Atlantic* and its peers. It is no surprise that his chosen métier — the nature essay — was a staple of these magazines. Burroughs regarded magazine publication, not book publication, as his central financial concern. In an 1876 letter, he explained that the *Galaxy* currently paid him the best rates and that "I shall drive my 'critter' to that market, since I have an eye on the paying part." Burroughs consistently earned far more selling individual essays to magazines than he did from the royalties on his books. In an 1868 letter, he reported that the *Atlantic* paid him $10 per published page; he earned a total of $250 for the essays he published in the magazine during 1869. Burroughs made only half that much in royalties from the first edition of *Wake-Robin*, his 1871 collection of essays.[80] To be sure, Burroughs was proud of his books. It meant a great deal that his own titles were under the same imprint as those of Ralph Waldo Emerson and Henry David Thoreau. But as a writer with an "eye on the paying part," Burroughs viewed book publication as a means of earning a bit more for essays he had already published in magazines.

Among writers of this period, Burroughs's success was not typical, but his increasing orientation toward magazines was. After 1860, magazines became the primary means professional writers used to establish their careers and earn the majority of their income. As a result, most writers consciously shaped their work — its style, subject matter, and format — according to the requirements of the magazine market.[81]

Creating and exploiting that market increasingly depended on advertising, which grew tremendously during this period. Many Americans, in fact, complained about its increasing presence in their lives. As one observer wrote in 1867, advertisements "invade every department of life, and no privacy or exclusiveness is a bar to them."[82] Some historians have argued that before 1890 the magazine was unimportant as a vehicle for advertising. In *Forty Years an Advertising Agent: 1865–1905* (1906), George P. Rowell wrote that he regularly advised clients that magazines were "not . . . at all worth the consideration of advertisers."[83] Citing Rowell several decades later, Frank Presbrey asserted that for advertisers in the mid-nineteenth century, not the magazine but "the newspaper was the great dominant medium."[84] The extensive advertising sections in magazines from the 1850s on, however, bring such definitive pronouncements into question. In the 1850s, two of the nation's most respected business journals, the *Merchants' Magazine and Commercial Review* (1839-70) and *DeBow's Review* (1846-80), averaged more than ten pages of advertising in each issue. During this same period, women's periodicals, religious weeklies, and agricultural journals also included substantial advertising sections.

To be sure, advertisers assumed that newspapers had the potential to reach larger audiences, particularly at the local and regional levels. But magazines had their own virtues as promotional tools. Perhaps most important, magazines were often devoted to some sort of vocational or avocational pursuit, and they therefore offered advertisers the opportunity to link reading tastes with purchasing habits. Purveyors of housewares, patent medicines, and sewing machines began advertising in women's periodicals. Notices for farm implements, cookware, and books appeared in farm journals. For certain advertisers, the publisher-backed monthly magazines that emerged at mid-century offered something especially appealing: the chance to reach the nation's emerging leisured class. As early as 1853, *Putnam's* promoted its "Advertiser" (an advertising section of up to sixteen pages inserted at the back of each issue), claiming that the magazine's circulation "is not only large almost beyond precedent, but is also of the *best kind — i.e.*, among intelligent readers and book buyers — it affords an unrivalled medium for Advertisements, especially of all matters concerned with books and the fine arts."[85] Several decades later, *Scribner's* made a similar claim. "It is now well understood," announced the editors, "that a first-class popular magazine furnishes to all men who seek a national market the very best medium for advertising that exists. It is both widely distributed to the prosperous and intelligent classes of society, and carefully read and preserved."[86]

Of course, not all businesses were interested in reaching "the prosperous and intelligent classes" of American society. Nevertheless, advertising sections in *Putnam's*, the *Atlantic*, or *Harper's* promoted a considerable variety of products: soap, sewing machines, pianos, linens, abdominal corsets, tooth powder. One also finds countless advertisements for printed materials. This should be no surprise, given that the nation's major publishers owned these magazines and operated them as promotional tools. Indeed, these magazines were often at their most inventive when promoting the books and periodicals owned by their parent institutions. Full pages in *Putnam's*, *Harper's*, and the *Atlantic* were dedicated to the promotion of certain publishers' wares — or even certain authors. "The Monthly Advertiser" in the May 1855 number of *Putnam's* included not only a full-page listing of the titles by Washington Irving currently published by G. P. Putnam & Co. but also eight full pages of tributes to Irving's genius.[87] In the late 1860s, the *Atlantic* concluded the editorial matter of each issue with "The Atlantic Advertiser and Miscellany," a substantial insert full of book chat and various promotional matter related to titles published by Ticknor and Fields (later Fields, Osgood & Co.).

It is difficult to know how readers responded, particularly given the advertisements' physical placement. In weeklies such as *Harper's Weekly* and the *Saturday Evening Post* (1821–), advertisements were limited to close-set columns or pages at the end of each issue. For subscribers to *Godey's*, the illustrated advertisements appearing in the magazine's back pages must have seemed positively understated when compared to the engravings and ornate colored plates sewn inside the front cover. In monthly magazines such as the *Atlantic*, advertisements were relegated to supplements, cover wrappers, and colored inserts, never sharing space with the content supplied by contributors. When individual issues were bound into a single volume, advertisements were typically removed as a part of the process, as they were considered not only outdated but also extraneous to the publication's enduring value. No doubt the editorial and literary content of the August 1855 issue of *Putnam's*—which included Herman Melville's "The Bell Tower" and Thoreau's "The Beach"—was tied to the business interests of Dix & Edwards, then the magazine's parent firm. Nevertheless, it seems the magazine was designed to hold these literary contributions wholly apart from the world of getting and spending.

Whether such placement served to deemphasize advertisements or to highlight them, it is clear that advertising became increasingly central to the operation of American magazines in the decades following 1850. After all, as Curtis pointed out, magazines required the "solid foundation" of capital. Popular religious weeklies such as the *Independent* (1848–1928) and the *Churchman* (1831–61) began to rely on revenue from advertising to sustain publication. By the mid-1870s, several advertising agencies began to specialize in placing advertisements in these journals' pages. The 1870s saw the emergence of inexpensive "mail-order monthlies," such as the *People's Literary Companion* (1869–1907) and the *Chicago Ledger* (1872–1936), several of which achieved circulations topping half a million. These periodicals, which were primarily vehicles for mail-order advertising, printed advertisements and miscellaneous editorial matter together on each page. Even the major monthly magazines—so often portrayed as ambivalent toward their commercial function—began to see advertising revenue as a reliable source of income, one perhaps more reliable than subscriptions.

These changes ultimately led to a watershed moment in the 1890s, when a range of magazine publishers began selling magazines at prices below their cost of production and made advertising their primary source of profit. At that point, magazine publishers radically reconceived their business model. Where once they sold magazines directly to readers, they now sold their readers' attention to advertisers. The circulation of monthlies such as *Munsey's Magazine*, *McClure's Magazine*, and the *Cosmopolitan* reached into the hundreds of thousands, and a new era in magazine publishing began.[88]

PART 3

The Cultural Work of National Magazines

Susan Belasco

· · ·

On 1 January 1840, Margaret Fuller wrote to encourage William Henry Channing to send her a contribution for the first issue of the *Dial* (1840–44), a new journal that she, Ralph Waldo Emerson, and other members of the Transcendental circle hoped would prove a powerful vehicle for intellectual, social, and literary thought. Channing, a Unitarian minister in Cincinnati and a magazine editor himself, was an enthusiastic supporter of the venture. Eager to have his article, Fuller reminded him that "you prophecied a new literature; shall it dawn on 1840."[89] The journal's finances were precarious, and all production costs had to be covered solely by subscription revenues. Authors were expected to contribute their labor, and neither Fuller nor Emerson received a salary for their duties as editors. The editors knew little about marketing their journal; Fuller and Emerson debated whether to order 1,500 or 2,000 copies of the first number, though at the time they had only thirty subscribers. Emerson was sure the magazine would sell and find a wide readership, but in fact it ceased publication after barely four years.[90] The hopes of Emerson and Fuller for a "new literature" nurtured in the pages of a magazine, as well as their lack of practical experience in running a periodical, were shared by many editors in the first half of the nineteenth century who knew little about how to attract subscribers, calculate expenses, develop advertisements, or judge the market demand for their periodicals. Furthermore, they had to persuade the American public that magazines, lacking the solid authority of the book and the flexible timeliness of the newspaper, were worth their price and the time required to read them.

At least part of what Fuller meant in 1840 by a "new literature" was the development of an American literature that would invigorate a literary scene still dominated by popular British writers and weak imitations of British periodicals. Magazines designed specifically for a national readership, such as the *Saturday Evening Post*, the *Knickerbocker*, and the *United States Magazine and Democratic Review*, went to considerable effort to publish American writers such as Washington Irving, Henry Wadsworth Longfellow, Lydia Huntley Sigourney, John Greenleaf Whittier, Nathaniel Hawthorne, Fanny Fern, and Caroline Kirkland. Despite these efforts, many other magazines, such as the *New York Mirror* (1823-57) and *Littell's Living Age* (1844-96), continued to reprint material chiefly from British periodicals. On the eve of the Civil War in 1860, Emerson's friend Moncure Conway tried again with a second version of the *Dial*, designed, as he said in the first number, to be a "legitimation of the spirit of the Age, which ASPIRES TO BE FREE," and published notices of books by Hawthorne, William Dean Howells, and even Walt Whitman.[91] Nonetheless, the efforts by new magazines to shape and reflect a national identity proved to be difficult. By 1880, however, editors, publishers, and contributors had overcome numerous obstacles to make magazines of many kinds a staple for an eager reading public. The founding of a third *Dial* in 1880 by Francis G. Browne in Chicago is a case in point. Published for the next thirty years, the literary journal had a steady readership for its book reviews, literary news, and lists of new books.

Increasingly throughout the nineteenth century, American magazines served many purposes and met many needs. Some magazines were calculated to appeal to large audiences, and some proved to be efficient promoters of national identity over regional differences. Other magazines appealed to narrower constituencies, setting themselves in opposition to mainstream politics and literature or creating solidarity and cohesiveness among widely dispersed segments of the population. As the divisions deepened between the North and the South, southerners sought to promote their views. Both the *Southern Literary Messenger* (1834-64) and *Russell's Magazine* (1857-60) were founded to showcase southern writers and opinions for what the editors hoped would eventually become a national audience. African Americans also sought a national audience. Edited by a free black, Thomas Hamilton, the short-lived *Anglo-African Magazine* (1859-60) was in many ways an effort to perform the cultural work of other national magazines by publishing the best work of mostly American writers. In the first issue, Hamilton proudly announced, "All the articles in the Magazine, not otherwise designated, will be the products of the pens of colored men and women."[92] As Hamilton explained, the central mission of the *Anglo-African Magazine* was to demonstrate the abilities of black men and women writers and to establish "an independent voice in the 'fourth estate.'"[93] Still other magazines sought to impart cultural lessons to people considered "other." The *Cherokee Messenger* (1844-46), the first periodical produced in Indian Territory, was published in English and Cherokee by the Baptist Mission Press and, strongly imbued with religious fervor, was intended to educate the Cherokee population while demonstrating Cherokees' embrace of the dominant white culture that had dispossessed them.[94] Finally, members of professional organizations and reform movements saw in magazines the opportunity to unite readers and provide an outlet for the exchange and distribution of ideas. In the period of prosperity between the mid-1840s and the mid-1850s, no interest or group seemed complete without its own magazine, whose various audiences are indicated in a few further examples: the *American Agriculturist* (1842–1964); the *Western Journal of Medicine and Surgery* (1840–55); *Scientific American* (1845–); the *Christian Inquirer* (1846–66); the *Home Journal* (1846–1901); and the *Child's Friend* (1843–58).

Regardless of whether a magazine was being designed for a national audience or a special interest group, a wide variety of formats could be used. Some magazines were scarcely distinguishable from newspapers, with text arranged in narrow, vertical columns; others looked more like books, bound in paper wrappers with articles printed one after another like chapters. In the early years, only a few were illustrated. However, magazines could never offer the timeliness of the increasing number of daily newspapers, nor did they have the cultural authority of books, especially for the middle and upper classes. Despite Emily Dickinson's enthusiasm for the three magazines to which her family subscribed — *Harper's New Monthly Magazine*, the *Atlantic Monthly*, and *Scribner's Monthly* — she wrote about the authority of books. For her, books were "Frigates" that had the power "To take us Lands away," as well as cherished companions: "Unto my Books — so good to turn — / Far ends of tired Days."[95] But many of the new monthly magazines shared characteristics with books that helped to communicate the same sense of permanent value. Semiannual volumes, continuously paged, were made available to subscribers, who were invited to return the individual issues to the publisher for binding in cloth or leather; subscribers could also buy bound volumes directly, without returning the individual copies. Similarly, the annuals and gift books that were popular during the antebellum period contained the materials of a magazine — articles, fiction, and poetry — bound in cloth or leather, like a book. Annuals and many periodicals, like books, were clearly meant to be preserved and treasured in the middle-class home library (see Chapter 9, Part 2).

If specialized magazines appealed to groups identified with a reform movement, profession, religious belief, or region, building a nationwide audience for a magazine demanded that its content be much less narrow and its format more attractive. As the editor of *Putnam's Monthly Magazine* wrote in 1853, "With all its present general features, it is intended that the Magazine shall have new and varied attractions for all classes of our wide circle of readers."[96] Other magazines began to feature more work of American authors and to contribute to the formation of a version of the "new literature" that Fuller called for, but one that was dedicated to an idealized vision of a unified America undivided by class, gender, and race. George R. Graham and Frank Leslie were important early influences on these magazines. In the 1840s and early 1850s, they founded magazines that appealed broadly to American audiences and made use of American materials and writers. Graham, who studied law, and Leslie, trained as an engraver in England, were innovative in the ways they paid authors and employed regular contributors. They also understood what many of their contemporaries did not: pictures sold. Subscribers frequently clipped illustrations, pasted them in albums, and even used them as decorations. In a letter written from California in 1851, Louise Amelia Knapp Smith Clappe described a rustic medical office that the doctor had "fondly decorated . . . with sundry pictures from Godey, Graham, and Sartain's Magazines, among which, fashion plates with imaginary monsters, sporting miraculous waists, impossible wrists and fabulous feet, largely predominated."[97] *Harper's New Monthly Magazine* used fifty woodcuts per issue in 1857; by 1880 that number had substantially increased.[98]

Graham and Leslie began their careers from very different directions. Graham's success was based on his close observation of other magazines and correction of what he viewed as their limitations and defects. To Graham, the sober format of the early magazines — unbroken pages of dense articles and lengthy reviews — was dull and uninviting. Each issue of *Graham's American Monthly Magazine* featured numerous illustrations and included book reviews, stories, poetry, and music. In a sustained effort to appeal to a national audience, Graham generally avoided controversial topics that might cause offense to any particular group.[99] In his "Editor's Table" commemorating the conclusion of the volume for 1844, he confidently observed, "In the coming year we propose to show our friends, a magazine thoroughly *American*, and of such merit as to put the blush upon all the English monthlies. There is no magazine, at home or abroad, that has been built upon the broad national basis that we chose for 'Graham's' in the outset of the enterprise; and hence none are so *widely* popular with the people."[100] This "thoroughly American" magazine designed for a united American people was propelled by the works of a large number of what the magazine called its "principal contributors," including Edgar Allan Poe (who also briefly served as editor), William Cullen Bryant, James Fenimore Cooper, Henry Wads-

---

FIGURE 7.1. "Literary Announcement for 1853," advertisement for magazines published by T. S. Arthur & Co. and L. A. Godey, Philadelphia, 1852 (broadside, 69 x 51 cm). "Clubbing terms" allowed groups of subscribers to receive periodicals such as *Arthur's Home Gazette* at reduced prices, and organizers of clubs with five or more subscribers received a "premium" — in this case, books published by T. S. Arthur & Co. American Antiquarian Society.

worth Longfellow, James Russell Lowell, Catharine Maria Sedgwick, Lydia Huntley Sigourney, William Gilmore Simms, Elizabeth Oakes Smith, Ann S. Stephens, Henry David Thoreau, and Nathaniel P. Willis.[101]

As popular as the literature in *Graham's* was, the magazine's use of illustrations generated strong interest on its own and influenced the appearance of other magazines designed for national audiences. While contemporary magazine editors printed from used plates, Graham employed an art staff to produce original woodcuts, steel and copper engravings, and mezzotints. Those illustrations were much more than mere embellishments. Taken together, the illustrations of idealized nature and peaceful domestic scenes promoted the sense of a harmonious America; they depicted a pastoral nation far removed from such divisive social issues as slavery, poverty, and immigration. Although some of these issues were addressed by special-interest magazines, especially those devoted to the abolition and temperance movements, magazines for general readers avoided these social problems, at least before the Civil War.

Like Graham, Frank Leslie also became an influential and successful publisher of an early national magazine. The head of the engraving department for the *Illustrated London News* before he immigrated to the United States in 1848, Leslie sought similar employment in his adopted country.[102] By 1852, he was working for Maturin Murray Ballou's *Gleason's Pictorial Drawing-Room Companion* (1851–59), which was modeled on the *Illustrated London News*. Like Graham, Ballou wanted to print only American writers, artists, and poets. Sylvanus Cobb, Lydia Huntley Sigourney, and Alice and Phoebe Cary were regular contributors; however, Ballou was not as interested in literature as Graham. Illustrations and light entertainment were integral to the success of Ballou's magazine, the tone of which was morally and socially conservative.[103] Leslie had bigger ideas. Having made some useful friends (such as P. T. Barnum, for whom he worked briefly) and having managed to save some money, in 1854 he established his own magazine, *Frank Leslie's Ladies' Gazette of Fashion* (1854–57). Thus began the first magazine empire in the United States. The following year, he founded a weekly, *Frank Leslie's Illustrated Newspaper*; over the next twenty-five years, his name would be associated with more than twenty periodicals. In the *Ladies' Gazette* and the many other magazines he would publish during his lifetime, Leslie showed few of Graham's scruples about reprinting British writers. But he well understood the importance of illustrations to the success of his periodicals and established the practice of incorporating oversized illustrations. In order to do so, he developed a technique that allowed him to separate a wood block into as many as thirty-two pieces, which then could be quickly prepared by a team of engravers and bolted together to produce large illustrations.[104]

While the careers of Graham and Leslie are illustrative of the entrepreneurial qualities that early magazine publishers had to possess in order to succeed, their magazines also chart the growth of editing as a specialized occupation. The publishers of antebellum magazines were often editors as well as owners, and the number of failed periodicals—both newspapers and magazines—during the first half of the nineteenth century attests to the difficulties they encountered. However, antebellum magazine editors were powerful within the realm of their own publications. Fanny Fern, among the most popular writers of mid-nineteenth-century America, graphically illustrated this power in *Ruth Hall* (1855), the first novel to describe the career of a woman periodical writer in America. Drawing on her own experiences, Fern described Ruth's trials in gaining access to editors and selling her articles. While Fern depicted some editors as autocratic and unprofessional, she also portrayed a new breed of editors and publishers who helped Ruth to live by her pen.[105] Fern's model for this new breed was her own longtime publisher, Robert Bonner of the *New York Ledger*, who practiced sound business principles, paid his contributors well, and developed advertising strategies that influenced later publishers.

Few had as long or as illustrative a career as Sarah Josepha Hale, chief editor for forty years, starting in 1837, of *Godey's Lady's Book. Godey's* became in the 1840s the premier national magazine for women, designed to capitalize on the ever-increasing number of loyal female readers of periodicals. The magazine published recipes, articles on fashion, music, and health, and works by many of the leading American writers of the day. First and foremost, however, the magazine was intended to be, as its publisher Louis A. Godey said, "The guiding star of female education—the beacon light of refined taste, pure morals and practical wisdom."[106] After Hale assumed the editorship under Godey's direction, she followed his lead. An able administrator and a hard worker, Hale strove to improve the quality of Godey's magazine by attracting well-known contributors and promising new writers, as well as by including articles on travel and history to supplement those on domestic matters. She also worked with several assistant editors who were also well-known authors, among them Sigourney and Eliza Leslie.[107]

In her monthly "Editor's Table," Hale wrote constantly of her strong belief in the moral superiority of women. Although she was careful to encourage women not to move outside the domestic sphere, Hale promoted the work of many women writers and editorialized about the importance for women of education, better health care, and property rights. But she did not stray far from a view of America that was essentially white, middle-class, and conservative. Committed to the ideal of a unified, harmonious America, Hale was reluctant to endorse abolition. In fact, slavery was never mentioned in the pages of *Godey's*, and Hale made no reference to the Civil War throughout the years of the conflict. Nonetheless, circulation declined during the war, and the years after the war were not prosperous ones for *Godey's*.

But the early success and staying power of the magazines edited by Graham, Leslie, and Hale had helped shape several new magazines in the 1850s — *Harper's New Monthly Magazine*, *Putnam's Monthly*, and the *Atlantic Monthly* — that in turn influenced magazine development after the Civil War. Despite differences in the orientation of these magazines, their editors and publishers adopted many of the same strategies as earlier editors to create a national audience. The early success of that effort, as well as the reach of those magazines, is illustrated in a letter written by Emerson during an extended lecture tour of the West in 1854. Describing the farmers in the free states and emphasizing their "new interest as colonists, & the historical importance of these days & of their work here," Emerson added, "But they are all violently preoccupied, and there is no thinking or reading in all this Siberia. Harper, Putnam, and the N.Y. Tribune, are the gentle boundaries of the wings of the Illinois & Wisconsin Muses."[108]

The publishers of the monthlies Emerson mentions managed these magazines along modern lines. *Harper's New Monthly Magazine*, edited by Henry J. Raymond and managed by Fletcher Harper (who would later establish *Harper's Weekly*), was a handsome magazine of 144 double-columned pages that sold for $3 per year or 25¢ per issue.[109] The magazine enlisted a number of regulars, such as George William Curtis, who contributed "The Editor's Easy Chair" for forty years, and Charles Parsons, who became the art editor in 1863 and soon employed many of America's best-known artists to provide illustrations.[110] The effective management of *Harper's Monthly* made the magazine "successful from the outset," as the publishers proudly proclaimed. The number of copies printed grew from 7,500 to 50,000 within the first six months. By 1865 the editors claimed to have an average circulation of 110,000.[111]

In part *Harper's* was designed to promote the firm's book business by offering serializations of, and extracts from, books it would eventually publish. In the initial issue of June 1850, the publishers explained that the general purpose of the new magazine was to present the "unbounded treasures of the Periodical Literature of the present day. Periodicals enlist and absorb much of the literary talent, the creative genius, the scholarly accomplishment of the present age. The best writers, in all departments and in every nation, devote themselves mainly to the Reviews, Magazines, or Newspapers of the day."[112] Thus, *Harper's* printed short fiction, articles about authors and topics of general interest, as well as columns on domestic political events—for example, the death of President Zachary Taylor and the debates over the Compromise of 1850—and international news briefs. But the magazine also served the ends of the publisher: it carried announcements for current and upcoming titles in Harper's Library of Select Novels, as well as other books that Harper & Brothers was publishing on travel and history, as well as schoolbooks. While the magazine reprinted many works by British authors, such as Charles Dickens, it also published American writers. Herman Melville, for instance, whose novels were published by the Harper firm, saw several of his short stories appear there during the 1850s. During the Civil War, the magazine published a few of his poems; Harper & Brothers published his book of poems, *Battle-Pieces and Aspects of the War*, in 1866.

Putnam's Monthly Magazine, also founded by an established book publisher, sought to promote and advertise American writers over British ones. From the beginning, G. P. Putnam & Co. wished to design a first-class literary magazine. Charles Frederick Briggs, Parke Goodwin, and George William Curtis, all experienced writers and editors, brought the idea for the magazine before George Palmer Putnam, the publisher of Washington Irving's works and of the best seller *The Wide, Wide World* (1850) by Susan Warner.[113] The confidence with which Putnam and the editors began this new venture is palpable in the "Introductory" to the first number: "The genius of the old world is affluent; we owe much to it, and we hope to owe more. But we have no less faith in the opulence of our own resources."[114] Despite its efforts to gain a broad audience for American writers, *Putnam's* could not sustain its readership. The firm was forced to sell the magazine to Dix & Edwards in 1855; it ceased publication in 1857, after circulation fell to 14,000 and the latter firm failed.[115]

Influenced more by George Graham's vision than Frank Leslie's, the *Atlantic Monthly* provided an enduring home for the "new literature" that Margaret Fuller envisioned in 1840.[116] Inspired by Francis H. Underwood, an antislavery activist and editor, as well as writers such as Emerson, Oliver Wendell Holmes, and James Russell Lowell, the *Atlantic* was founded with the cultural mission of guiding the age in literature, politics, science, and the arts. It was also firmly antislavery in political orientation. Lowell, the magazine's first editor, published established New England authors such as Nathaniel Hawthorne, Harriet Beecher Stowe, and Henry Wadsworth Longfellow. After Ticknor and Fields purchased the *Atlantic Monthly* from Phillips, Sampson

& Co. in 1859, the magazine sought to break out of the Northeast by including writers from other regions, including Rebecca Harding Davis, whose "Life in the Iron Mills" appeared in April 1861.

The first three editors — Lowell, James T. Fields, and William Dean Howells — steered the *Atlantic Monthly* from 1857 until 1881, and this stability demonstrated the increasing professionalism of editors. Lowell, who tended to be conservative and relatively conventional, deleted a line about the immortality of a pine tree from the first installment of Thoreau's "Chesuncook," published in June 1858, earning at least one furious note from Thoreau. During the Civil War, the *Atlantic* was generally pro-Union and pro-Lincoln, which limited its southern readership. Later the magazine promoted the goals of radical Republican Reconstruction, in part by the publication of articles by Frederick Douglass (December 1866 and January 1867). Fields, the editor during and after the war, printed Hawthorne's satirical and occasionally sharply critical "Chiefly about War Matters" in July 1862; but he had also published Julia Ward Howe's triumphant "Battle Hymn of the Republic" the preceding February.

During the Civil War, many magazine editors who aspired to a national readership found their audiences dwindling, especially in the South, where magazines published in the North were generally boycotted and circulation was generally hurt by high paper costs and distribution problems.[117] But in the aftermath of the war, magazine readership began to surge, especially since migration to the West created new markets and audiences. As its title confidently proclaimed, the *Nation* (1865–) was one of the new magazines designed to address current affairs for a national audience, especially the social and economic problems connected with Reconstruction, and to promote literature through its reviews. One of the first series of articles in the magazine was "The South as It Is." Written by John Richard Dennett, the purpose of the series was to provide a firsthand, realistic account of conditions in the South in the aftermath of the war. Founders of the magazine wanted to provide serious commentary on all aspects of American life by providing weekly news analysis, editorials, articles by foreign correspondents, and reviews of new books, art, and music.

Another magazine designed for a national readership after the war was *Scribner's Monthly*, which began publication in November 1870. The magazine immediately became popular because of the high quality of its illustrations, as well as the conservative religious and moral values of its first editor, Josiah Gilbert Holland, a popular poet and powerful literary figure of the 1870s. Holland, an editor with strong opinions about what American literature should be, refused to publish Whitman, observing in a letter to a friend that "He has offered me his stuff for publication, but it has seemed to me to be my duty to American literature to discountenance him entirely. He seems to me to be utterly a pest and an abomination."[118] Instead, Holland eagerly published William Cullen Bryant, Rebecca Harding Davis, Helen Hunt Jackson, Frances Hodgson Burnett, Bret Harte, Joel Chandler Harris, and Henry James. By 1880 the circulation of *Scribner's* under Holland's leadership had reached 100,000.[119]

In the midst of the development of new national magazines in the literary marketplace following the Civil War, the *Atlantic Monthly* underwent numerous changes. When William Dean Howells, the assistant editor of the magazine from 1866 to 1870, was made editor in 1871, he was charged with expanding the readership of the magazine. Howells wanted to promote realism in American literature and wished to cultivate a new generation of American writers. To that end, he solicited contributions from popular writers such as Mark Twain, whose "Old Times on the Mississippi" appeared between January and July 1875. Howells also serialized James's *The Portrait of a Lady* in fourteen installments, beginning in November 1880. While Howells greatly expanded the scope of articles and writers during the fifteen years of his involvement with the magazine, circulation fell from 50,000 to 12,000.[120] The *Atlantic Monthly* survived essentially by becoming what it remains today, an elite magazine read by a small but loyal audience. It thus found its niche in what had become a vastly expanded market for magazines.

By 1880 Frank Leslie was dead and George Graham was elderly and nearly blind, living on the support of George W. Childs and Charles J. Peterson, friends whom he had helped to achieve successful careers in publishing.[121] The legacy of Leslie and Graham was the national magazine, now firmly established as a feature of American life. These magazines were so well established, in fact, that commentators could wax nostalgic over their formative period of the 1840s and 1850s. In 1878 George William Curtis looked back to that era:

> It is a rueful thought that the old pea-green *Putnam* is now solemnly bound up and laid away in dusty and forgotten retirement with the *Portfolio* and the old *American Monthlies* and all the *emeriti*. The new readers have new writers to amuse them, and the tone and character of the magazine itself change. Yet upon those dead pages how many a thought and quip and fancy are still quick with life, and of an immortal freshness![122]

The magazine designed to reach a national audience, struggling in 1840 to define itself and promote the "new literature" Margaret Fuller envisioned, was by 1880 a distinctive part of American culture. With an impressive history, the magazine was poised to maintain its position for decades to come.

PART 4

Religious Periodicals and Their Textual Communities

Candy Gunther Brown

. . .

In 1861 the *Southern Baptist Messenger* (1851–62) published a letter in its correspondence column from P. West of Danville, New York. West had written after deriving "so much pleasure and satisfaction from reading the soul-cheering communications from the dear saints hitherto published in the *Messenger*." For this reader, the magazine offered the medium through which Christians could find "assurance that they were led through the same experiences of hopes and fears, temptations and triumphs." As an Old School Baptist, West felt personally responsible to the *Messenger*'s editor and to the periodical's community of readers. The "work of publishing pure Bible doctrine among those who truly love our Lord Jesus Christ" was a crucial task, and doing so sustained a "medium of correspondence between the members of Christ's body." This work was particularly important at a time when the "despised few" resisted the "opposing influence" of free-will doctrines within the larger Christian church.[123] West did not need or even want to learn anything new from the *Messenger*—but, rather, craved to hear convictions confirmed by repeated testimony from those who shared an understanding of the Christian life.

In corresponding with the *Messenger*, West interacted with geographically separated readers in a textual community that presented an alternative to local relationships. Texan Thomas Whiteley wrote to the *Messenger*, alluding to Malachi 3:16 and Hebrews 10:25, to describe "the assembling of yourselves" not in local church attendance but in the magazine's correspondence columns. Ellison Grisham of Florida similarly considered it "good for children of God to speak often one to another." Rather than turning to his pastor or fellow church members for spiritual counsel, he appealed to correspondents from the North, East, and South to explain "disputed points of Scripture." For Whiteley and Grisham, as for West, relationships within a textual community surpassed fellowship in a geographically specific place of worship.[124]

The *Southern Baptist Messenger* suggests the ritual power of communication networks sustained by nineteenth-century periodicals. By conveying the same texts at roughly the same time to scattered readers, religious periodicals reminded church members of their sectarian allegiances and prepared the community at large to "receive the truth when it is preached."[125] Readers cultivated a sense of interconnection through shared narrative frameworks, and periodicals confirmed a view of the world that many readers already assumed. Publishers and readers imagined a dramatic confrontation between purity and corruption. Even when the act of communicating did not change the outcome of this conflict, they felt satisfied by rehearsing a familiar explanation of how things were in the world.

Between 1840 and 1880, the relationship between textual communities and religious identities grew increasingly powerful. By one estimate, the 188 religious periodicals published between 1820 and 1852 accounted for 39 percent of the total number of periodicals published in that period; 120 of those religious periodicals represented a specific denomination, while the other 68 were "nondenominational Protestant." The 1880 census recorded 552 religious newspapers and periodicals, which spanned twenty-four different denominational categories, as well as 96 "unsectarian" journals (Table 7.3). The *Missouri Presbyterian Recorder* (1855-56?) considered print essential for communication among its members and with the world at large, unifying the denomination and guarding against rivals' misrepresentation. Other periodicals similarly sustained the collective identities of diverse religious groups: they facilitated the exchange of information, reminded adherents of core values, and responded to criticism from outsiders.[126] Religious minorities used print to resist assimilative pressures. As Jewish immigration increased in the 1840s and 1850s, publications rebutted Protestant criticism and facilitated communication among group members (see Chapter 6, Part 1). The *Israelite* (1854-74), established by Isaac Mayer Wise, attacked Protestant missionary propaganda. Catholic publishers offered alternatives to Protestant-issued Bibles, devotionals, and novels. Mary Ann Madden Sadlier was one of dozens of Irish Catholic women novelists who immigrated in the 1840s and used magazine stories to fortify readers against Protestant hegemony.[127]

New religious groups signaled their entrance into the American cultural milieu by issuing distinctive publications. William Miller began nursing ideas in 1818 that eventuated in the Seventh-Day Adventist Church. Miller did not attract a following until 1840, when Joshua Himes publicized his prophetic ideas through a periodical, *Signs of the Times* (1840-45, continued to 1846 as *Advent Herald, and Morning Watch*). After the Great Disappointment of 1844, when the world failed to end on schedule, James White resuscitated

TABLE 7.3. Number of religious periodicals by denomination, 1820–1852 and 1880

Denomination	1820–52	1880
Baptist	23	63
Christian	—	4
Congregational	3	14
Disciples/Campbellite	1	11
Dunkards	—	4
Episcopal	15	33
Evangelical	—	27
Friends	—	5
Jewish	3	16
Lutheran	3	22
Mennonite	—	9
Methodist	26	75
Moravian	—	2
Mormon	—	4
Presbyterian	18	42
Primitive Christian	—	2
Reformed/Dutch Reformed	1	11
Roman Catholic	11	70
Second Advent/Millennial	4	12
Spiritualist	—	7
Swedenborgian	—	3
Unitarian	1	4
United Brethren in Christ	1	7
Universalist	10	9
Nondenominational Protestant/Unsectarian	68	96
Total	188	552

Sources: For 1820–52 information, which enumerates "periodicals" published at some point in that period, Orville A. Roorbach, comp., *Bibliotheca Americana: Catalogue of American Publications* (New York: O. A. Roorbach, 1852), 644–52; for 1880 information, which enumerates "newspapers and periodicals," Francis A. Walker, *Compendium of the Tenth Census (June 1, 1880)* (Washington, D.C.: GPO, 1883), 1631.

the movement with two periodicals, *Present Truth* (1849) and the *Second Advent Review and Sabbath Herald* (1850– , now *Adventist Review*). Mary Baker Eddy heralded the founding of Christian Science with a market failure, *Science and Health, with Key to the Scriptures* (1875). However, the *Journal of Christian Science* (1883–) did more than Eddy's book to spread her ideas nationally and internationally. With the help of local Christian Scientist groups that distributed copies to neighbors and canvassed for subscribers, the journal gained a circulation of three thousand within four months, mark-

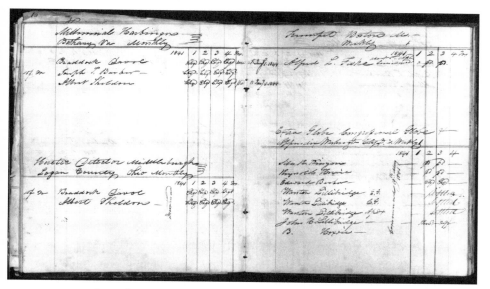

FIGURE 7.2. Post office subscription account book, 1837–55, listing religious periodicals published in Bethany, Va., and Logan County, Ohio, as well as magazines published in Washington, Boston, Providence, and New York. To assess charges, Oliver G. Palmer, the postmaster of Wyoming, R.I., maintained records of the periodicals that subscribers received through the post office (here, for 1841–44). American Antiquarian Society.

ing the beginning of a major movement.[128] Religious groups without organizational structures depended almost exclusively on the press for communication. Spiritualists, who did not establish churches or denominations, issued twenty to thirty periodicals at any one time between the late 1840s and the 1890s and as many as one hundred thousand books and pamphlets every year. Charles Taze Russell similarly relied upon publications to unify his new sect, which became the Jehovah's Witnesses. *Zion's Watch Tower and Herald of Christ's Presence* (1879–) garnered four million biweekly subscribers within eight years. Zion's Watch Tower Bible and Tract Society, incorporated in 1884, constituted the only official church structure established during Russell's lifetime.[129]

Evangelical Protestants, the most prolific of all religious groups, adopted the latest marketing strategies and printing technologies to achieve maximum influence. Evangelicals were quick to exploit more favorable postal rates after 1851 to increase the circulation of periodicals (Fig. 7.2).[130] Contrary to the assumption of many modern scholars that commercialization implicated Protestantism in secularization and cultural decline, evangelical Protestants configured commerce as a religious instrument, useful in competing against secular and religious alternatives.[131] As the Methodist *Christian Advocate and Journal* (1827–1938) phrased the issue in 1848, "People will have the gilding and tinsel; and if we intend to supply them, we must give them what they want."[132] Anxious to stay "up to the age," by 1860 the *Christian Advocate* included more articles classed as literary, scientific, commercial, and agricultural and had an expanding advertising department.[133] The Methodist Book Concern — since John Wesley's days "ready to adapt itself to modern methods" — had by its 1889 centennial expanded its lists from the doctrinal volumes, Sunday school books, and periodicals prevalent in the 1840s to include biography, travel, history, science, "harmless" fiction, and "entertaining and elevating" romances.[134]

In adapting to readers' changing preferences, religious publishers strengthened collective identity. As first-generation revival converts turned to the ongoing work of striving after holiness and socializing their children into church life, they used print to extend the reach of religion. To supplement the sporadic bursts of piety that revivals fostered, printed texts encompassed every life event from early childhood to the deathbed, in all moments and places of experience. The American Baptist Publication Society proclaimed in 1870 that its productions reached "the kitchen, the chamber, the closet, the shop, the railway car, the steamboat, — everywhere." Most important, publications reached homes. In newly emergent religious communities, the need for fellowship encouraged church members to envision one another as spiritual kin. As middle-class constituencies expanded within most denominations, families played a growing role in stimulating weekday devotion. Publications, presented by clergy and editors as operating within and cementing the family unit, coupled this narrowing inward with a broadening outward to intensify individuals' sense of membership in a textual community viewed as analogous to the church universal.[135]

The physical characteristics of publications reflected an increasingly middle-class, domestic model of religious community. Two advertisements appearing in the nondenominational *Mothers' Journal and Family Visitant* (1833–75), in 1841 and 1860, illustrate this cultural transition. The language of the earlier promotion demonstrated relatively scant concern for the paper's materiality: "every mother, who duly appreciates the responsibilities which rest upon her in training a soul for eternity, will gladly welcome this work to her fireside, if it be presented to her notice." Twenty years later, the same magazine advocated its purchase over other options not only because of its religious content but also because it exhibited a "much finer and higher style of steel plate, than are to be found in any other Dollar Magazine." This shift paralleled the simultaneous proliferation of refined literary objects in the secular market (see Chapter 9, Part 2). Indeed, religious publishers took full advantage of technological advances in wood engraving, lithography, and photography. Finely bound and elaborately illustrated religious gift books and annuals, such as *The Sacred Annual: A Gift for All Seasons, for 1851*, aimed to make "art subservient to the advancement of piety," by using "love of the beautiful" to direct minds to the "worship of the Holy." Likewise, the proliferation of illustrated "Lives of Christ" after the Civil War reflected Protestants' growing emphasis on facial features as an index of character. Illustrated publications attracted middle-class readers who assumed that visual attributes reinforced religious contents.[136]

Clerical editors helped reposition the religious community from local congregations to textual practices enacted at home. The Reverend Henry Keeling of the Virginia *Baptist Preacher* (1842–59) worried in 1844 that local congregations did not always enjoy a relationship of "intimate friendship and confidence" with their preachers. Addressing his "Beloved Patrons and Readers" thirteen years later, Keeling claimed to "feel towards you as a pastor does towards his people." He informed his congregation of readers that "by your subscription to the paper, you in a manner place yourselves in our parish — take a pew in our church — set before us on your seat, while we preach the gospel to you." Keeling made a pastoral visit by responding to correspondents who wrote to express "something of the personal, individual effects" of his ministry. Connecting textual and domestic models of community, Keeling preached "not from the pulpit, as you might sit away off some twenty or sixty feet — but at your fireside, in your own parlor face to face, as friend with friend or brother with brother." Imagining his congregation gathered around the domestic fireside, Keeling adopted conversational rhetoric that he thought more influential than preaching.[137]

Exalting Sabbath and home as "sacred enclosures of time and space," the American Tract Society's *Sabbath at Home* (1867–70) urged families to give careful attention to "the kind of topics of conversation, the kind of books read, the kind of visitors entertained." As more families spent Sabbath evenings at home, the magazine asked to be given a "place on the Sunday-evening table," linking the family circle with a larger community that observed the Sabbath together by reading the paper. One reader and contributor, Elizabeth Prentiss, articulated her sense of how the domestic and the textual connected. Prentiss read aloud or quoted memorized passages from *Sabbath at Home* and other religious texts to family seated around the domestic fireside. She marked texts and transcribed extracts from periodicals, books, hymns, and sermons to enclose in letters to friends, scrutinized paragraphs marked by others in periodicals sent to her, and purchased "lending" copies of especially useful books. By writing fiction grounded in painful domestic experiences, Prentiss saw herself as "preaching" a doctrine of holiness that enabled her readers—spread throughout the United States and Europe—to cope with necessary suffering. Prentiss could envision no other way to "reach so many minds and hearts" than by writing for such an expansive congregation.[138]

Because many nineteenth-century women had few opportunities to participate in communities wider than their immediate surroundings, religious periodicals played a special role in offering them a basis for collective identity. Caroline Hiscox, a Baptist minister's wife and editor of the nondenominational *Mothers' Journal and Family Visitant*, viewed her magazine in 1860 as a medium through which "many of our readers would be brought into close and friendly contact with each other as well as with us." Women participated in one another's religious growth as "thousands of mothers who read the *Journal*, could briefly narrate some circumstance in their own experience, or in their observation of the history of others, which would be of interest and profit to thousands of our readers." Representing her magazine as a "valuable household friend and companion," Hiscox associated textual and domestic communities: "Let us hear from many more, in different parts of the country. We wish to talk freely with them on these subjects, as we should if we could sit down in their homes with them for an hour, and converse without restraint." Adopting a conversational tone, Hiscox invited women to imagine themselves as personally connected to her and to correspondents around the country.[139]

The relative cheapness, speed, and range of distribution made periodicals particularly effective, because scattered readers received regular installments of communications almost simultaneously. Many religious and secular periodicals were rigidly organized into topical departments, so that readers did not need to peruse issues cover to cover as they might a book. Instead, they could find the same kinds of articles in the same place in every issue— such as local and national religious news, poetry, and articles for parents and youth. Departmentalization encouraged religious readers to interpret individual texts in the context of other articles and to view the complete set of departments as forming a curriculum essential to the well-informed Christian family. Although secular newspapers often juxtaposed articles connected primarily by calendrical coincidence, religious editors concerned themselves less with comprehensive coverage than with selection and placement of useful texts. Many articles published in religious papers were not news at all, but serialized excerpts from steady sellers and reprints from other religious and secular periodicals. Even the latest news, such as reports of recent revivals, made the most sense when linked with other reports of revivals and church growth. Together, such articles reinforced a larger narrative structure that explained Christians' relationship to the world.[140]

By organizing a wide range of genres by use, editors instructed readers to value the uses of texts above their formal qualities or authors' doctrinal or denominational intentions. Framing devices such as indexes, headings, and titles defined texts as useful in circumstances such as "Meditation" and "Family Worship." In 1855 the nondenominational *Beauty of Holiness* (1846–1901) reprinted excerpts from John Bunyan's *The Pilgrim's Progress*, David Brainerd's *Life*, Henry Ward Beecher's lectures, Robert Leighton's doctrines, Thomas Chalmers's sermons, and Charles Deems's hymns. Abstracting texts from their original contexts facilitated editorial reinterpretation. The *Western Christian*, established in Elgin, Illinois, in 1845 under the auspices of the North Western Baptist Anti-Slavery Convention, juxtaposed excerpts from Congregational revivalist Edward Payson and Unitarian William Ellery Channing, obscuring the former's predestinarianism and the latter's optimistic estimate of human nature by positioning both texts beneath the paper's masthead epigraph: "Go Ye into all the World and Preach the Gospel to Every Creature" (Mark 16:15). The *Western Christian* wielded Congregationalist and Unitarian texts to promote a Baptist interpretation of the evangelical mandate.[141]

Editors and readers continually reshaped the textual basis for community. Religious and secular editors regularly exchanged periodicals and reprinted selected items. Many of the same articles went the rounds of papers with multiple affiliations and regional emphases. The *Western Presbyterian*, a monthly published in Louisville in 1864, urged readers "living in different sections of the country" to share local news and texts pasted or summarized in their scrapbooks. The American Tract Society's *Sabbath at Home* asked readers to draw "their pencils around choice paragraphs," sharing them "with their friends" through the magazine. Serialization invited dialogue among authors, readers, and editors while authors were still composing. Harriet Beecher Stowe famously noted readers' responses while writing *Uncle Tom's Cabin*, published serially in the *National Era* in 1851–52. In a less-known incident, when Elizabeth Prentiss published *Pemaquid* (1877) serially for the *Christian at Work* (founded in 1866), she received conflicting advice about how to develop one character, Juliet. Prentiss's husband influenced her to "cut out" much about Juliet, because he "*loathes* so to read about bad people." After receiving "hundreds of letters daily" from readers, Prentiss's editor advised her to restore the omitted sections. In response to her textual community, Prentiss added another chapter. In many similar situations, editors, readers, and authors collectively constructed narratives.[142]

As religious publishing and reading practices expanded and diversified, they strengthened the collective identities of members of old and new religious groups. Like correspondents to the *Southern Baptist Messenger*, subsequent generations of readers and publishers have continued to imagine themselves in relation to their textual communities. In the face of wrenching cultural and political transitions, textual practices have offered some measure of stability — even if the textual communities themselves were always fluid. For the members of religious communication networks, textual rituals affirm that despite the onslaughts of religious and secular opponents, all is still well with the world.

Ideologies and Practices of Reading

Barbara Sicherman

. . .

"We are unquestionably a reading people," declared an Ohio educator in 1856.[1] Samuel Goodrich, author of an estimated 170 books for young people, was among the many who echoed that claim: "We . . . find a larger proportion of our people devoted to education, and reading, and meditation, and reflection than is to be met with in any other land."[2] Without endorsing such assertions of native superiority, foreign visitors also commented on the pervasiveness of reading in mid-nineteenth-century America.[3]

Just how many Americans read, as well as how much, what, and how they read, are questions that invite exploration. Unfortunately, despite some innovative recent scholarship, our knowledge of reading practices is limited, particularly for the period after the Civil War. In contrast to what we know about production and distribution, the consumption of books is almost wholly uncharted territory: we do not know whether more people read books or the same people read more books, let alone understand the meaning of reading in people's lives. Fuller understanding must await focused studies of readers' interactions with print. What can be said in the meantime?

First, and perhaps foremost, literacy was fast becoming a cultural imperative. By the second quarter of the nineteenth century, newspapers, school texts, children's books, and other instruments of an expanding communications network vigorously promoted literacy. Advocates of this emerging "ideology of literacy" depicted it as a potent technology that would foster morality, social cohesion, and economic advancement.[4] In contrast to England, where some viewed literacy as dangerous for the lower classes, few in the United States contended that it should be restricted — at least among those who were white. The logic of universal white male suffrage dictated at least a minimal level of popular literacy. The common-school movement, just taking hold at the beginning of the period, was dedicated to its achievement, while the spread of public libraries after 1850 made books more accessible. Despite heated debates about women's education throughout the century, there seems to have been no serious opposition to female literacy. Here an older tradition of Bible literacy linked to America's dissenting Protestant origins joined with the ideology of republican motherhood that required a certain level of female learning to produce virtuous male citizens. Only for enslaved African Americans was literacy considered inherently dangerous.

Although school attendance was voluntary and irregular, illiteracy declined sharply in the first half of the nineteenth century. According to the census of 1850, 22.6 percent of the total population and 10 percent of whites over the age of twenty could not read or write.[5] Illiteracy was considerably higher in the South (an estimated one out of seven people in North Carolina) and in other sparsely populated regions. By 1870 regional disparities diminished, and the literacy rates of the native- and foreign-born converged, with some variation among ethnic groups. A host of methodological and procedural problems make the census data about literacy impossible to use at face value (see Chapter 5, Part 2). But even if the estimate of 90 percent literacy among whites is exaggerated, Americans of European origin were highly literate by the standards of the day: the comparable estimate for England is 60 percent.[6] Numbers aside, what literacy meant depended on the social and cultural contexts in which it was acquired and used.

By 1850, about as many white women as men could read, an unusual circumstance at the time and one that largely accounts for the nation's high literacy rate. The rapid spread of female education after the Revolution, with a concomitant decline in fertility, helps explain the virtual disappearance of an earlier gender gap, at least in New England. Women were often the principal carriers of literacy in middle-class homes, teaching children or younger siblings to read and setting the cultural tone. At a time when domestic ideology was at its peak, literacy was a boon to many middle-class women — a source of intellectual growth, sociability, and pleasure. As "culture" in the sense of refinement became gendered female, women pursued intellectual interests outside the home, often in the informal and formal study clubs that proliferated after the Civil War. Free African American women, as well as men, established literary societies in the antebellum period, turning them to political account by working for abolition. Altogether, reading became so closely associated with women that they were often represented in words and images as the reading sex.

Literacy also brought economic opportunity to middle-class white women. The transformation of schoolteaching into a predominantly female vocation (59 percent of teachers were women in 1870) and women's astonishing success as authors after 1850 were pivotal in this context. Women not only constituted an important proportion of fiction writers; they also wrote poetry, advice books, and popular textbooks on history and science. The flourishing magazine market gave editors like Sarah Josepha Hale of *Godey's Lady's Book* influence and power, despite their own ambivalence about women's public roles. By 1880, with the establishment of women's colleges and the admission of women to formerly all-male institutions of higher learning, opportunities for professional employment were beginning to open, usually in segregated work environments. In cultural and economic terms, women's successful use of literacy depended on the rhetorically gendered division of labor and a segmented labor market.[7]

In contrast to the situation of white women, reading was forbidden to most enslaved African Americans. Despite this prohibition and the threat of punishment, an estimated 5 to 10 percent learned to read. Some acquired their knowledge from owners, preachers, or evangelical societies eager to promote Bible study. Others found ingenious ways to take advantage of intermittent opportunities.[8] Following Frederick Douglass, who depicted his progress to literacy as a step toward freedom and its attainment as an act of resistance, literacy became a trope for freedom in men's slave narratives; since literate slaves could read newspapers and signs and write their own passes, literacy was often literally an aid to freedom. Women writers of slave narratives and spiritual autobiographies were less likely to emphasize this equation.[9] Using literacy in the service of political goals, former slaves like Douglass and Harriet Jacobs partook of middle-class culture while indicting its racism. Similarly, African American newspaper editors not only advocated emancipation and full citizenship but strove to alter negative perceptions of blacks, and of workers more generally, by linking self-improvement with republicanism and natural rights.[10]

Perhaps no group believed as fervently in the ideology of literacy as African Americans (Fig. 8.1). In the aftermath of the Civil War, children and adults flocked to schools established by the Freedmen's Bureau, black and white missionary societies, and northern philanthropists. In *Up from Slavery* (1901), Booker T. Washington told the story of an entire race collectively learning to read and write. As a result of hard work under often dire circumstances, African American literacy increased to an estimated 30 percent in 1880 and 55 percent by 1900.[11] Despite their enthusiasm for education, the acquisition of literacy did not bring African American men and women significant opportunities for advancement, except as teachers in segregated southern schools.

As the number of readers increased, so did the quantity and variety of available reading material. Alongside the evangelical tracts and schoolbooks of an older era, new genres emerged, some offering pure (or, in the minds of critics, impure) entertainment. In addition to newspapers and both general and specialized periodicals, there were how-to manuals and advice books on subjects ranging from health, child rearing, and etiquette to public speak-

FIGURE 8.1. William Matthew Prior, *Mrs. Nancy Lawson* (1843). For portraitists and their subjects, a book denoted erudition, piety, or gentility, and depicting Nancy Lawson of Boston in a composition associated with white sitters may also have asserted African American accomplishment. © Shelburne Museum, Shelburne, Vt.

ing, managing a shop, and building a house. The most controversial genres, the penny press and the "cheap fiction" published serially in story papers and in dime novels, were considered cheap in content as well as in price. A middle-class women's market emerged with the popular "ladies' magazines" and domestic novels, the latter the best-sellers of the 1850s, and an important secular juvenile market (magazines as well as fiction) gained momentum in the 1860s.

This vast outpouring did not go unremarked. Clergymen, educators, and other cultural authorities voiced alarm at the dangerous conjunction of suspect new forms of print with mass consumption. The commercialization of what had once been a sacred activity and the loosening of reading from its earlier patriarchal and institutional moorings raised the specter of reading as an uncontrolled—and uncontrollable—activity. Rather than promoting education, meditation, and reflection, as Goodrich hoped, some feared that the "flood" of books would undermine morality, family values, and the social order.

What was at stake in these sometimes apocalyptic visions? Debates about reading were fueled by changes in American society, particularly with regard to the nature of work and leisure. Literacy was becoming a necessary skill for making one's way in the new white-collar sector that was emerging as the crucial dividing line between the middle and working classes. As middle-class childhood and youth lengthened, parental concern about reading and other forms of leisure grew. In a society so deeply imbued with religious and secular imperatives to work, it was reading's status as a leisure activity that excited the greatest suspicion. As in current debates about the impact of television, film, and popular music, the expansion of print culture raised the anxiety levels of those who posited an unmediated relationship between cultural consumption and its consequences.

Models of Reading

Virtually all contemporary commentators viewed reading as a potent technology. If they did not always concur on its goals and consequences, they agreed that when correctly practiced, reading had almost unlimited potential for good and, when improperly done, whether because of the matter or manner of reading, corresponding potential for harm. At least four approved models of reading coexisted in the mid-nineteenth century: the evangelical, the civic, the self-improving, and the cultural or cosmopolitan. These are ideal types, strategies advocated by those who hoped to instill their views in others. They are not the only possible models, nor are the distinctions among them absolute, but they represent important frameworks of meaning. Except for the civic model, they operated largely outside the institutions of formal education. The balance among them shifted, with the cultural model becoming more, and the evangelical less, important in the years after the Civil War. By then a fifth type of reading—for relaxation and perhaps even for pleasure— was gaining at least qualified approval.

By far the most powerful model of reading in the antebellum period was the evangelical: it was powerful both in institutional authority and in its conception of what reading could achieve. Not only was the Bible the most common reading fare, at least in New England, but as David Paul Nord has demonstrated, the religious press provided a major catalyst for an expanding national communications network, with the faithful constituting the first mass market for print.[12] This phenomenally successful and multifaceted publishing empire was in place by the mid-1830s (see Chapter 6, Part 1). In the evangelical model, the desired ends of reading were conversion and a life of Christian practice, outcomes that could occur only through reading in a deliberate and reflective manner. Operating on the assumption that reading could directly affect behavior, evangelicals believed that books themselves could hasten the conversion process. For the same reason, the corrupting power of the wrong reading prompted evangelical leaders to denounce what they called the "satanic press," which included "infidel" publications, romances, adventure stories, and most works of fiction.

In the end, evangelicals would "enter the lists with Satan." They used modern technologies, business practices, and distribution methods, packaging Christian texts in popular formats. Cheap tracts and even children's stories joined Bibles and "steady sellers" (many priced at 12½¢) in the evangelical repertoire.[13] The substitution of stories for textbooks in Sunday school libraries in the 1840s and 1850s signaled a shift to more utilitarian tactics. Foreign missionaries such as Adoniram Judson, the central figure in Baptist activities in Burma, relied on the expanding market and popular genres to gain converts.[14] And the American Anti-Slavery Society, adopting popular techniques from tract and Bible publishing, deluged southern states with over one million pieces of antislavery mail in its "pamphlet campaign" during 1835 alone. Revealing the possibilities of the new technology in the war for public opinion, the campaign brought complaints from northerners as well as southerners about the low cost of the pamphlets, the attempt to enlist women as activists, and the appeals to children through the distribution of hornbooks and primers: "A B stands for abolition."[15] Both domestic and foreign missionary societies were instrumental in teaching literacy to groups who were otherwise denied it, as the efforts of white and black missionaries in the South during Reconstruction demonstrate.

Coexisting with the evangelical ideal of reading was a civic model built around the development of common schools. No one did more to expound this vision than Horace Mann, secretary of the Massachusetts Board of Education from 1837 to 1848. Seeking to persuade citizens of a nation born out of tax revolt to support public education for all children of the commonwealth, he articulated the larger goals of education in twelve annual reports. More than a place to teach basic literacy, the common schools, according to Mann, would "create a more far-seeing intelligence, and a purer morality, than has ever yet existed among communities of men." By removing incentives to vice, and therefore to crime, intemperance, and even poverty, they seemed to him a panacea for all social ills. Education had a market value as well: Mann linked literacy to the economic advancement of individuals and of the common-wealth. Just as enhancing the "producer's producing power . . . [was] an end to be directly attained by increasing his intelligence," so, Mann assured the industrialists from whom he sought support, "the aim of industry is served, and the wealth of the country is augmented, in proportion to the diffusion of knowledge."[16]

Projecting a vision of a nation unified by a common politics and culture, Mann considered universal education the only sure foundation of republican institutions. Ostensibly secular, the civic model was in fact nonsectarian Prot-estant. With the influx of new immigrants, especially those from Ireland and Germany who challenged American religious and cultural unity, reformers like Mann counted on schools to produce disciplined citizens and promote a common national identity. They took it for granted that schools would pro-mote republicanism, Protestantism, and capitalism: to them, though not to the Irish immigrants who resisted the Protestant bias of the schools, these were universal values.[17]

Where Bibles, devotional tracts, and Sunday school literature constituted the evangelical genres, school texts were the means of promoting a broadly civic approach to literacy. The famous McGuffey series of graded readers — one for each elementary grade — first appeared between 1836 and 1857. Re-vised several times, the series constituted the basic classroom source in thirty-seven states and remained popular for forty years.[18] The largest category of books produced in the United States and the most profitable to pub-lishers (see Chapter 6, Part 2), textbooks self-consciously promoted moral and civic values. Designed to train character, selections in school readers were chosen less for their literary than their moral value: virtue was rewarded, vice punished, patriotic and nationalistic sentiments lauded. The Freedman's Readers (1865) for newly emancipated African Americans highlighted the virtues of home, religion, and work.[19]

The other models of reading are more difficult to characterize, in part because they were less dependent on institutions. Where the evangelical and civic approaches to literacy were highly organized, mainly on a top-down basis, a wide variety of informal endeavors of a "self-improving" na-ture flourished in the mid-nineteenth century. Reading for "useful knowl-edge," for general information, and for "self-culture" or character building all fit the self-improving rubric and might be pursued on one's own or with like-minded people. At times knowledge, information, and self-culture conjoined, at others they diverged, particularly late in the century, when knowledge became more specialized and increasingly the province of professionals, and culture became a body of works thought to embody a great tradition as well as a moral good.

"Diffusion of knowledge" was one of the great catchphrases of the antebellum era among both the more and the less educated, the former seeking to dispense it, the latter to attain it. Fostered by an ideology of self-improvement and by technological innovations that promoted the spread of print culture, opportunities for self-study proliferated for those lacking formal education. In addition to reading how-to books on anything from occupational skills to social graces, Americans could join debating or self-improvement societies, mechanics' or mercantile libraries, and attend lyceums or popular lectures.[20] The continuity between oral and print culture promoted the dissemination of knowledge.[21] On the one hand, it was the great age of the autodidact; on the other, much of the learning took place in social settings.

In the 1830s and 1840s, the diffusion of knowledge was broadly linked to the formation of character and to what some called "self-culture." Unitarian minister William Ellery Channing offered an influential formulation of the concept in an address to Boston workers in 1838. Channing assumed that workers were eager for improvement, but he cautioned them that self-culture was to be pursued for its own sake, in a "disinterested" manner, rather than for any anticipated material rewards. Defining "self-culture" as "the care which every man owes to himself, to the unfolding and perfecting of his nature," he included moral and social as well as intellectual culture. For Channing, reading was a matter of cultivating character, rather than accumulating information. Good books must "not be skimmed over for amusement, but read with fixed attention and a reverential love of truth." Although no substitute for experiencing nature, reading aided growth by providing access to superior minds, even for the most humble worker: "Let every man, if possible, gather some good books under his roof, and obtain access for himself and family to some social library. Almost any luxury should be sacrificed to this."[22]

A fourth framework for reading, the cultural or cosmopolitan, became more prominent after the Civil War, as Victorian values took hold among an expanding middle class. Inspired by a new intellectual elite that looked to Europe, the cosmopolitan approach evolved out of self-culture but could be detached from a broadly inclusive model of character building. This model added intellectual and, to a degree, aesthetic considerations to the traditional moral ones, as "culture" became the favored designation for study that led to refinement, rather than to character formation or the acquisition of knowledge.[23]

Interest in this sort of culture converged from many sources. An expanding urban middle class, with discretionary income and growing leisure, was eager to set itself apart from the less cultivated. Under the onslaughts of Darwinism and biblical criticism and the waning of Calvinist views of predestination, many Americans looked to culture for sources of values hitherto provided by religion. Books became symbols of the intangible cultural aspirations of the broad middle class. The moral value attached to books in general, rather than to the religious texts honored in Protestant tradition, was one of many signs that a reverence for culture was replacing an older religious sensibility. For a middle class moving away from a tightly bounded religion, Matthew Arnold's definition of culture as "a pursuit of our total perfection" held appeal.[24] All the more reason, in the eyes of arbiters of culture, to ensure that the right books were read rightly. To this end, a genre of advice literature about how and what to read emerged after 1870, while authorities debated the one hundred "best" books of all time. Seen in retrospect, such standardized lists helped transform the idea of culture from a process into a product, one that would later flourish commercially.

For many Americans, particularly those of higher social rank, the cultural model became disentangled from religion during the Gilded Age. Most still rejected a purely aesthetic standard in art that would later flower in modernism. But an increasingly elitist note crept into debates over culture. The *Nation* (1865–), depicting the United States as "a society of ignoramuses each of whom thinks he is a Solon," ridiculed the pretensions of those who had been influenced by the "common-schools, magazines, newspapers, and the rapid acquisition of wealth." The magazine's belief that true culture resulted from a process of "moral" as well as "mental" discipline that would "affect a man's whole character" was not unlike Channing's, but it set forth a class-linked model of culture that excluded most of the population.[25] It was a statement of hierarchy analogous to the efforts of urban elites and professionals late in the century to "sacralize culture" in ways that largely excluded working-class audiences from venues such as opera, theater, and museums.[26]

In practice, the distinctions among the four approved modes of reading were not absolute. A person might partake of several or even all of them in the course of a lifetime. Although religion remained a powerful force, by the end of the century many Americans had modified the strict rules that once guided them. The transformation of Henry Ward Beecher from a young hellfire preacher into an apostle of culture is emblematic. In his 1844 evangelical tract *Lectures to Young Men*, Beecher condemned fiction, along with theater, gambling, and other temptations of modern life. A trip to Europe where he had been overwhelmed by the beauties of culture and the move to a well-heeled Brooklyn congregation were among the experiences prompting him to reassess his wholesale rejection of modernity. His biographer goes so far as to claim that, by yoking romanticism with Christianity, Beecher's 1867 novel, *Norwood*, first published in a story paper, marked the end of New England Calvinism.[27]

Beecher's compromise between the evangelical and the cosmopolitan was exemplified by the Chautauqua movement, which brought culture to a white middle-class Protestant audience. Led by John H. Vincent, a Methodist minister who believed that religious and secular knowledge were not at odds, the movement began in 1874 as an outgrowth of a summer school for Sunday school teachers. Between 1878 and 1894, its home-study program, the Chautauqua Literary and Scientific Circle (CLSC), reached 225,000 individuals, approximately four-fifths of them women. There were more than ten thousand reading circles by 1900, most in small towns, many of them lacking public libraries. Self-improving as well as evangelical (in a modern mode) and cultural, the CLSC pioneered in adult education and university extension work, offering diplomas to those who completed its four-year cycle. In time, there were Jewish and Catholic Chautauquas and reading circles.[28]

By offering a prearranged curriculum, the CLSC institutionalized home study and centralized the kinds of programs that women's clubs across the nation had developed on their own after 1870. These clubs, many of which evolved from informal reading circles, provided women with opportunities for self-improvement that had previously been available principally to men. Combining collective learning and sociability, the clubs developed distinctive rituals of their own: they drafted constitutions, chose yearly topics, opened meetings with prayers or recitations of "memory gems," prepared and commented on papers, provided entertainment and food, and published yearbooks. Peaking in the 1890s when many joined the newly formed General Federation of Women's Clubs, the groups conducted campaigns to establish local public libraries and helped to launch the traveling library movement. Through their efforts, thousands of volumes by women writers were displayed in the library of the Woman's Building at the 1893 World's Columbian Exposition in Chicago.[29] At this landmark event, art and imagination were represented as female, science as male, visual depictions that symbolized contemporary understanding of the gendered division of labor that was even then being undermined by the growing consolidation of literary authority in academe.

Reading for Pleasure

A fifth framework of reading provided less a model than an antimodel for most of the century. Where the other modes had the imprimatur of weighty institutions and individuals, reading for amusement or pleasure found few outright champions, except perhaps for the publishers who reaped the profits. In a society that valued work so highly, the association of reading with leisure challenged traditional measures of worth: casual reading was nonproductive, a matter of easy consumption rather than sustained effort. At issue were what was read, who did the reading, and how. Closely linked to emerging categories of print that were not only suspect but aimed at a mass market, reading for pleasure, certainly reading *only* for pleasure, predictably alarmed cultural critics. So did the capacity of this material to enthrall readers, especially, moralists believed, those most in need of "protection": young people of both sexes and women of all ages.

By midcentury there was a wide variety of diverting reading from which to choose. Disparaged by all were the lurid "real" crime stories of the penny press and other sources of "dreadful pleasure," like the popular biographies of criminals, the notorious *National Police Gazette*, and the insider exposés of the "mysteries of the city" that afforded titillating opportunities for urban spectatorship (see Chapter 9, Part 3). Fiction was the characteristic vehicle of recreational reading (Fig. 8.2). It appeared in novels and magazines produced by mainstream publishers and in cheaper formats, such as story papers (newspaperlike magazines that featured serial stories) and paperback pamphlets, first published in the 1840s and later marketed as "dime novels." Introduced as a series by an enterprising publisher in 1860, "the dimes" sold an estimated four million copies by 1865, many to Civil War soldiers.[30] Some of this literature was frankly sensational. The novels of George Lippard, probably the most popular writer of the 1840s, featured seductions, rapes, orgies, and brutal murders by unrepentant killers. Though less graphic, the "sensation story," popular two decades later, remained suspect. Louisa May Alcott, herself the pseudonymous author of "blood and thunder" tales in the early 1860s, parodied the genre, with its "Indians, pirates[,] wolves, bears & distressed damsels in a grand tableau over a title like this 'The Maniac Bride' or 'The Bath of Blood. A thrilling tale of passion,' &c."[31]

The mass marketing of questionable new genres prompted anxious debate about the boundaries between good and bad books, useful and harmful reading. The particular grounds for inclusion and exclusion changed over the period. But efforts to draw boundaries continued, at least at the rhetorical

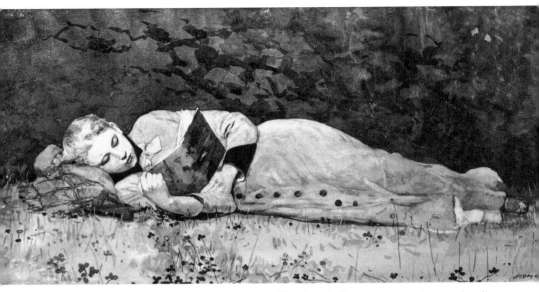

FIGURE 8.2. Winslow Homer's *The New Novel* (1877) offers an archetypal scene of reading, a young woman engrossed in a book and seemingly removed from daily cares. Museum of Fine Arts, Springfield, Mass.

level and sometimes practically as well. Congress went so far as to enact the restrictive Comstock Act in 1873, which banned the distribution of contraceptive information and other "obscene" literature through the mail.

Generalized opposition to fiction had so far abated that by 1870 Noah Porter, professor of moral philosophy at Yale College, could declare that "No intellectual enjoyment is so delightful" and that reading imaginative literature could impart "grace and finish to the character and life." Still, he warned, an exclusive diet of novels might turn the reader into "an intellectual voluptuary." By then, opposition centered on story papers and dime novels, the "cheap literature" condemned by Porter and others because it "stimulates and inflames the passions, ignores or misleads the conscience, and studiously presents views of life that are fundamentally false." Porter even suggested that it was "almost no worse that a procession of harlots should walk the streets of every city or village" than to have such books and newspapers distributed across the land.[32] Some feared that adventure stories of any kind would undermine the social order: "The uneventful life of school and shop, the working days and monotonous evenings, are set over against the dashing deeds and passionate joys of the putative heroes of the printed page, and appear all the more dull and profitless by the comparison."[33] From such fare, readers might infer that they "can be rich without toil and saving."[34] In addition to their obvious class bias, such views reveal the lingering suspicion of fantasy and a continued belief in an unmediated relationship between text and reader.

Gender and age as well as class considerations figured in these debates. There was ongoing concern that women's "addiction" to reading, particularly to "trashy" romances, would make them frivolous and unfit for useful womanhood.[35] By 1880, however, anxiety often focused on reading's dangers to boys. The appalling example of Jesse Pomeroy, a young murderer who attributed his crime to reading quantities of "blood and thunder" dime novels, seemed to confirm such fears.[36] The hyperbolic language of this discourse betrays deep-seated anxiety that middle-class youth would be contaminated by reading about behavior their elders associated with a degraded working class. Here the issue may have been less overt sexuality than the freewheeling depictions of smoking, drinking, and gambling, and the use of vulgar language ("Bowery slang")—habits the middle class wanted its sons to avoid and to which it considered them susceptible. The putative readers of cheap fiction and the working-class figures represented in it were alike to be avoided.

Despite such alarmist sentiments, more liberal voices maintained that any reading was better than none and, in a reversal of Gresham's law, that good books would drive out bad. In Horace Mann's view: "Let good books be read, and the taste for reading bad ones will slough off from the minds of the young, like gangrened flesh from a healing wound."[37] In high-culture circles, cheap fiction often received more literary than moral condemnation. Noting that the best of the story papers "reward virtue and punish vice," an 1879 article in the *Atlantic Monthly* declared them "not an unmixed evil. The legitimate charge against them is not that they are so bad, but only that they are not better." To his own query "Are they better than nothing?" the author answered a tentative yes: "The taste for reading, however perverted, is connected with something noble, with an interest in things outside of the small domain of self, with a praiseworthy curiosity about the great planet we inhabit. One is almost ready to say that, rather than not have it at all, it had better be nourished on no better food than story papers."[38]

The most consequential debates about books took place in connection with the public library movement (see Chapter 9, Part 1). Where some proponents argued against supplying novels, George Ticknor, a key figure in founding the Boston Public Library in 1853, insisted not only on including popular literature, at least the kind "tending to moral and intellectual improvement," but on circulating it—an even more daring proposition.[39] Disturbed by statistics that two-thirds or more of all books checked out of libraries were novels, librarians hoped to cultivate the "taste for reading" and then channel it in proper directions. From its founding in 1876, the American Library Association debated the principles of book selection, while local libraries excluded works considered "immoral" (many of them French novels), "sensational" (Mrs. E. D. E. N. Southworth and other domestic novelists), or "trashy and vicious" (*The Adventures of Huckleberry Finn* [1884]), as well as children's books by Horatio Alger ("sensational, impossible") and the Elsie Dinsmore stories ("tearfully sentimental and priggish"). It was a sign of the times that public libraries excluded not only dime novels but also Sunday school literature, the latter on the grounds of shallowness and falseness to life. In an age of burgeoning realism and declining piety, some guardians of culture considered "goody-goody" books as harmful as those that were "immoral." Literary tastes were changing. So were definitions of "trash."[40]

By the end of the period, large segments of the American public found satisfaction in leisure reading, much of it with no other apparent purpose than entertainment. As class divisions became more pronounced after the Civil War and opportunities to rise in rank fewer, critics began to valorize "escapist" or compensatory reading, a trend that would become more pronounced after 1890.[41] In this view, romances and the like were "valuable therapeutics . . . for the wearied brains and bodies of overworked shop-girls, clerks, house-keepers, bread-earners generally."[42] By then, the dangers of reading no doubt paled before other enticing new leisure opportunities. No longer was every act of reading considered so consequential that it might lead to the sacred or secular equivalent of salvation or damnation: sometimes reading might just be reading.

What kinds of satisfactions did leisure reading bring? In fact, we know little about responses to the more popular genres. Readers left few historical traces of those reading experiences, while scholars have typically paid greater attention to order and discipline than to pleasure. Like nineteenth-century critics, they have tended to associate pleasure reading with disparaged genres and to equate formulaic fiction with mere "escapism."

The consequences of reading are diverse and unpredictable. Leisure reading took many forms. At the casual end was the traveler, who might dip into a specially marketed "railroad literature" to stave off boredom (Fig. 8.3). For Daniel F. and Mary D. Child of Boston, reading was integral to daily life, its frequency and content influenced by mundane seasonal considerations (they read more in winter than in summer), rituals of family life (David read aloud while Mary did needlework), ephemeral events such as traveling shows and public readings, and by their antislavery and temperance convictions.[43] For some, most often those still young and in the process of self-definition, reading was as necessary as breathing, an occasion for emotional release and even

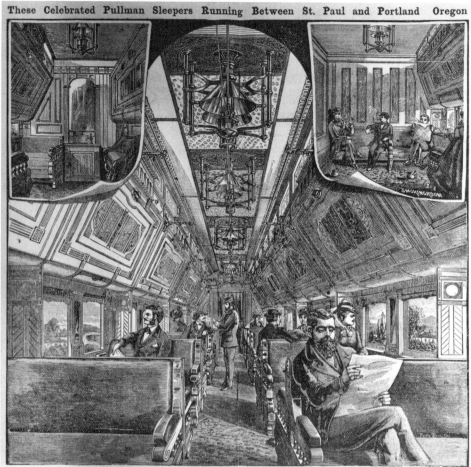

These Celebrated Pullman Sleepers Running Between St. Paul and Portland Oregon

Are the only Through Sleeping Cars run between the East and the Pacific Coast.

FIGURE 8.3. Advertisement for Pullman Sleepers showing passengers reading in railway cars, from *Short Line to the Pacific Coast, No. 20* (Chicago: Rand, McNally & Co., 1884). While publishers and booksellers marketed "railroad literature," the railroads advertised long-distance sleeping cars in which comfortable seats and ample illumination—both natural and artificial—enhanced the reading experience. American Antiquarian Society.

transformation. On returning from vacation, M. Carey Thomas headed for the local library, where she read for four days straight: "& the hours were seconds . . . It was like treading on air. It is the purest happiness—the one thing wh[ich] no man taketh from you."[44] Understanding such passionate encounters with books, as well as more ordinary kinds, requires a closer look at the contexts in which reading takes place.

Reading Practices

Authors and cultural authorities set goals for readers, but readers do not necessarily comply. To understand how men and women use print and the difference reading makes in their lives, we must turn from the pronouncements of critics to the behavior of historically situated readers. Instead of the models of authorial or textual determinacy that respectively dominated nineteenth-century cultural and late twentieth-century literary approaches to reading, historians are examining not only what people read but also how, why, and under what circumstances. Whether they view reading as a matter of fitting texts into a "pre-existing cultural frame" or as an activity that fosters "poaching" and "appropriation," practitioners of the new reading history no longer regard the reader as a kind of tabula rasa on which culture imprints itself.[45] Rather, readers are seen as active agents who interact in various ways with the texts they encounter. Meanings are constructed not only from what is read: the situations in which reading takes place, how it is practiced and with whom it is shared, its physical setting, the form and feel of a book—all are integral to the making of meanings.

Reading does not work the same way for everyone. What readers bring to their encounters with print is critical to the construction of meaning. As one of the most profound ways in which cultural values are transmitted, reading is social at its very core. What and how people read are influenced by the social location and conventions of particular communities of readers, whether they be families, formally constituted groups, informal local networks that can be documented with some precision, or broader reading or "interpretive communities." The latter include, in Janice Radway's view, "collections of people who, by virtue of a common social position and demographic character, unconsciously share certain assumptions about reading as well as preferences for reading material."[46] Of course, a reader often belongs to more than one reading community: a nineteenth-century farmer might read agricultural journals, antislavery publications, and political newspapers. Reading practices also change over a lifetime.

Using these insights, one can begin to assess the ways reading worked as a cultural system in nineteenth-century America. By examining reading practices in everyday life, it becomes possible to look for shared patterns of meaning as well as individual idiosyncrasy, the significance of reading across the life course, and the relationship between an activity that has often been represented as private to the rest of life. By examining readers in context, one moves not only beyond genre analysis (people typically read more than one) and generalizations about the American character based solely on American texts (given the popularity of British fiction), but also beyond the very notion of fixed categories and modes of reading. Access to print and skill in using it depended in part on currently popular analytic categories of class, gender, and race and on the intersections among them. But age, family culture, local networks, and individual aspiration also influenced what was read and how.[47] If options were limited for many, reading nevertheless opened up authentic possibilities for transformation.

Books and reading held a privileged place in the lives of nineteenth-century Americans of the comfortable classes. The Victorian culture of reading helped shape people's lives, though not in fixed or static ways. Cultural competence was a marker of class identity, for blacks as well as whites, distinguishing the middle from the lower classes and the genuinely cultured from the nouveaux riches: people might lose their money, but their culture was presumably a lifelong possession. The emergence of the middle-class domestic ideal—a family unit constituted around a male breadwinner, a housewife, and children freed from long hours of physical labor—enabled more people, in particular women and children, to devote time, energy, and resources to literary and aesthetic pursuits formerly reserved for the rich. As writer Mary Austin recalled of her youth in Carlinville, Illinois, in the late 1870s, "Everybody wanted culture in the same way that a few years earlier everybody wanted sewing machines . . . culture by this time . . . meant for one thing, more than another, the studious reading of books."[48]

The process of cultural transmission started early. With the waning of evangelicalism after the Civil War, literary activities often permeated middle-class family life, serving as entertainment as well as instruction. Families read aloud during long evenings at home. Children wrote poems for special occasions and performed prodigious feats by reciting "miles" of poetry from memory; some received monetary rewards for their efforts. They also engaged in parlor literary games, dramatized favorite stories, and produced home newspapers, an activity that peaked in the 1870s and 1880s.[49] The culture of reading was participatory and performative, stimulating writing as well as reading, especially among the daughters of the comfortable classes. Not only had diary keeping and letter writing become predominantly female arts, but girls often aspired to become authors, the most prestigious profession then open to their sex. Even before their teens, some sent off stories and poems, not only to *St. Nicholas* (1873–1943), a handsomely illustrated children's magazine, but also to prestigious periodicals such as *Harper's New Monthly Magazine*.

To suggest that reading was important in shaping middle-class identity is not to claim that it was inconsequential for workers or that there were fixed categories of "middle-class" and "working-class" reading or impermeable boundaries between them. We know little about the reading practices of the United States working class. But David Vincent's findings for England may apply at least in part: workers had less leisure time in which to read, less access to books at home, and less privacy for solitary reading than did members of the middle class, but their lives too — both on and off the job — were suffused with print.[50]

Given generally high literacy rates, the low cost of newspapers and paper-bound books, and the advent of reading rooms and libraries in urban areas, such class differences may have been less marked in the United States. In an 1890–91 survey of cotton textile workers' cost-of-living budgets, 77 percent reported some spending on newspapers and books, with significant regional and ethnic differences.[51] But expenditure is an inadequate indicator of workers' access to print, since books did not have to be owned to be enjoyed. Reading depended far less than other forms of cultural consumption on income; an observer in the 1840s estimated ten readers for every copy of a story paper.[52] Even in the middle class, few families owned enough books to satisfy avid readers; for them too, borrowing, whether from relatives, neighbors, employers, or libraries, was often the principal source of supply.

It is in this context that we must consider the claims of some cultural historians that specific genres appealed to different classes and that the "levels" of nineteenth-century cultural production corresponded with the class standing of their audience. Richard Brodhead, for example, suggests that "hierarchically arrayed literary 'levels' " developed in the postbellum era "as part of a larger action of social division" in which the middle class sought to separate itself from those beneath it.[53] Similarly, Michael Denning argues that young working-class men constituted the "bulk" of dime novel readers and that "the world of dime fiction was a separate world — in terms of production, reading public, and conventions" from the serial stories published in genteel magazines, as well as from "literary fiction."[54] What is the evidence for such claims?

Denning's analysis, in particular, has been challenged on several grounds: for exaggerating the working-class readership of dime novels and the importance of ideological formations in the ways workers read, for adducing insufficient historical evidence on workers' reading practices, and for assuming total separation between working-class and bourgeois cultural production.[55] A study of the Knights of Labor demonstrating that bourgeois ideology penetrated the working-class press undermines any assurance that ideological categories can be based solely on the venue of publication.[56] Denning's equation of cheap and commercial with sensational fiction is also overdrawn. During the 1870s, a flood of "cheap books" became available at ten and twenty cents. Often published in "cheap library" series, these works defy easy cultural labeling. Along with racier items, reprints of *Jane Eyre* (1846) and *Vanity Fair* (1848) can be found in the inventory of the well-known Seaside Library, which published more than 1,250 titles between 1877 and 1889. And more than 30 items each by Carlyle and Ruskin appeared on the 1887 list of Lovell's Library.[57] Given the many inexpensive editions of "standard" works, the convergence of writers of dime novels and domestic fiction, and the frequently sensational quality of the latter, caution is needed in equating levels of reading with either class or price.

If the verdict on readership is still out, anecdotal evidence suggests that there were broadly shared arenas of print culture. Men and women of the comfortable classes read, often apologetically, what they labeled "trash" — in practice, a flexible category, since one person's trash was often another's cherished work. Just as Shakespeare was broadly popular among theatergoers, so working-class audiences in the United States and England favored Dickens and other critically approved writers. The practice of serializing stories in newspapers, the most widely diffused form of print, encouraged such crossings. Lucy Larcom, a Lowell mill girl, read Dickens's *The Old Curiosity Shop* (1841) in a Philadelphia paper, while George Eliot, Homer, and Emerson turned up in ten- and twenty-cent editions in such unlikely places as "the backwoods of Arkansas and in the mining camps of Colorado."[58] We do not know how great the overlap in reading publics was, but it is likely that cultural stratification was not as marked in the Victorian era as it would later become.

Not only were the writings of many approved authors readily accessible but, as we have seen, the pursuit of knowledge was a widely dispersed ideal. Young women who worked in the Lowell mills were among those who, individually and collectively, took advantage of lectures, libraries, self-improvement circles, and other opportunities to engage in literary activities afforded by residence in the town. Inspired by their reading, some published stories and poetry in local magazines like the *Lowell Offering*. Lucy Larcom was one of those who went on to a literary career, while several became founders of public libraries in small New England towns.[59]

A journal kept by Edward Jenner Carpenter in 1844–45, while serving as an apprentice cabinetmaker in Greenfield, Massachusetts, suggests the difficulties of categorizing reading by class. Carpenter attended lyceum lectures and debates at the Literary Club with his peers; he also read an assortment of newspapers and books, many of the latter borrowed from friends or his employer. His reading included temperance newspapers, stories, and at least one novel, *Easy Nat; or, Boston Bars and Boston Boys* (1844), as well as Eugène Sue's recently published *The Mysteries of Paris* (1845), a work Carpenter was "considerably taken up with," but one often condemned as sensational and morally harmful. He also read historical adventures, romances, and other popular novels, a book about United States history, and a geography text. Viewed in the setting of his fellow apprentices, his literary activities seem to have been bound up with self-improvement, camaraderie, excitement, perhaps even self-discovery. Coming from a bookish but not well-off family, Carpenter later established a "periodical bookstore" and wholesale newspaper distribution business and served as town librarian of Brattleboro, Vermont, thereby parlaying his youthful interest in books into a career that guaranteed him a place in the middle class.[60]

Detailed personal accounts by non-elite individuals are rare. But during the antebellum period at least, when class lines still seemed fluid and artisans viewed themselves as occupying a middling social position between the elite and those below, workers participated in numerous literary activities, many of a self-improving nature. In a later period, the Knights of Labor and Jewish immigrant workers reinforced the self-improving tradition. Of course, both male and female workers were often drawn to less substantial fare—to the dismay of labor leaders.

Reading practices could also be mixed in interesting ways in elite communities, as in the case of Ella Clanton, daughter of a wealthy Georgia planter. Fourteen in 1848 when she began her journal, Clanton read thirty-nine novels in a three-month period; they were mainly popular stories of the day, seven by G. P. R. James, a British author of historical romances. She also read aloud from a seven-year-old copy of the *New World* (1839–45), one of the earliest story papers, pronouncing its fiction "beautiful" and "excellent." Clanton belonged to an informal network of male and female relatives and friends, mainly adults, with whom she exchanged books and magazines and discussed her reading. Later, as a mother who read more serious fare, she expressed concern about having read so much light fiction in her youth, but the adults in her life evidently did not disapprove of her selections at the time. In this local network, men and women, adults and young people, all read and discussed the same books, a circumstance that suggests less age and gender stratification in reading than is often supposed.[61]

As leisure opportunities grew, middle-class parents scrutinized their children's reading more closely. In addition to concerns about genre, they worried about the intensity with which adolescent girls devoured books. Disturbed by her daughter's interest in "trashy" serial stories, Lucy Stone tried to curtail Alice Stone Blackwell's access to the *New York Ledger* (1847–1903), a weekly story paper, even though by 1872 it published many respected writers. Fourteen-year-old Alice—whose diary is full of entries like "I felt that to wait till night for my *Ledger* meant insanity" — was outraged when her mother said she "never meant to let another [*Ledger*] come into the house. . . . To stop me off right in the midst of 'Mark Heber's Luck'! I straightway went off to bed mad, with tears in my eyes." Although Blackwell had only intermittent success in obtaining the *Ledger*, her negotiations suggest that middle-class children often had at least some access to reading that their parents considered inappropriate.[62]

Boys, in all likelihood, fared better: they were less subject to parental (mainly maternal) supervision and had more pocket money. Often identifying dime novels with the working class, their reading became a form of deliberate boundary crossing. Robert Morss Lovett, later a professor of English at the University of Chicago, said of his youthful passion for reading Beadle half-dime novels, "such reading was a major vice . . . and could only be indulged out-of-doors or in school behind a geography." He classified the boys' stories of Horatio Alger and "Oliver Optic" at a somewhat higher level, because they avoided "actual crime as material," but his mother said of them anyway, " 'They will give you a false view of life.' " This, Lovett observed, was "exactly what I wanted."[63]

The blurring of boundaries between genre and class applies as well to gender. It is often assumed that reading followed strict gender lines, particularly after 1860, with the separate marketing of books for boys and books for girls. In fact, there was greater crossover than has been acknowledged, a finding manifested in personal documents and in surveys of library borrowers that reveal considerable overlap between adolescent and adult male and female readers.[64] Of course, a book's borrower is not necessarily its reader or its only reader. Alice Stone Blackwell, for one, rarely read "girls' stories" between the ages of fourteen and sixteen, preferring tales of adventure. Her most passionate comments were reserved for works that were gender neutral or typically regarded as "boys' books," among them Charles Kingsley's *Westward Ho!* (1855). While women were the principal readers of domestic fiction, the significance of this reading in their lives has been exaggerated. Evidence from diaries, letters, and a few secondary studies reveals that women read many genres. Women of the comfortable classes read — and were encouraged to read — a wide range of books, including history, biography, and the classics (daughters as well as sons read Plutarch), a heady brew that might well undermine traditional gender messages. Men too sometimes crossed the gender divide, as Lovett did, despite the admission that "it was a shameful thing" to read the Dotty Dimple stories of "Sophie May."[65]

Growing up with contradictory messages, in which class and gender imperatives sometimes collided, some white middle- and upper-middle-class women found in the Victorian culture of reading a way of transcending traditional gender norms. One of them was M. Carey Thomas, from youth a passionate reader and seeker after culture. In her early teens, when reading's influence is probably greatest, she engaged in imaginative feminist readings of both Louisa May Alcott's *Little Women* (1868–69) and Thomas Carlyle's *On Heroes, Hero-Worship, and the Heroic in History* (1840): crossing gender as well as intellectual boundaries and appropriating both for her own purposes, she read herself as literary heroine and hero respectively. In her early twenties, these ambitions were reinforced by members of a feminist literary circle who read, wrote, dreamed, and schemed together; their later achievements included securing the admission of women to Johns Hopkins Medical School. Thomas never became the writer she aspired to be, but as president of Bryn Mawr College she fulfilled another enduring goal: educating women to their full intellectual potential. Their interpretive conventions and social reading practices helped women like Thomas first to imagine themselves as actors in the public sphere and then to carve out space for themselves there, as pioneers in education, the professions, and reform.[66]

Interactions with literature helped some readers cross racial and class as well as gender boundaries. In the face of severe discrimination, newly freed African Americans engaged in collective and individual literary ventures as a means of extending their educational and economic prospects. As a young teacher in Memphis in the 1880s, Ida B. Wells took elocution lessons, recited Lady Macbeth's soliloquies, joined the Chautauqua Literary and Scientific Circle, and participated in an African American lyceum that helped her launch a more satisfying career as a journalist.[67] For members of the working class, reading could provide a means of social ascent, as it did for Jack London, an ambitious outsider who tried to work his way into the middle class by a self-imposed course of reading.[68]

For those more comfortably situated, reading was sometimes a form of imaginative "slumming." For women especially, growing up in a society bent on "protecting" them, reading about members of other classes offered a taste of the forbidden — their earliest association with people they would not normally encounter, except perhaps as servants or Sunday school pupils. Jane Addams even claimed that because novels countenanced a "wide reading of human life," they enabled middle-class people like herself to "find in ourselves a new affinity for all men" and perhaps even a commitment to "remedying . . . social ills."[69] Despite her sometimes acute awareness that literature might become a substitute for action, for Addams herself the imaginative experience opened up by reading helped pave the way for a life of social action.

Print may never have been more powerful than in the years between 1840 and 1880. Its new abundance and variety, as well as the easy transit between oral and print cultures, contributed to the dominance of the medium. By the end of the period, the valorization of self-culture was diminishing as literature became the province of professional critics. The importance of reading as a leisure activity declined after 1890, for the middle as well as the working classes. Despite a sharp rise in the number of magazines that entered people's homes, new forms of entertainment, especially movies and radio, would soon hold wider appeal, coming to rival, and for many to surpass, the importance of reading as a means of sociability and self-definition.

What can we learn from the study of reading in past times? Beyond uncovering the behavioral patterns of particular individuals and groups, the history of reading can shed light on reading's impact on cultural formations and on intellectual and emotional life. But not in uncomplicated ways. Some scholars have claimed that by the nineteenth century reading was both more private and less intense an activity than it once had been. The stories of reading subjects suggest otherwise. Not only were literary activities deeply embedded in family and social life, but people read to one another, exchanged books as tokens of love or friendship, talked endlessly about them, and used stories and characters as referents for their lives. Reading could be an intense experience — emotionally, intellectually, spiritually. Fiction may have elicited such responses most often, but so could religious texts and even geology treatises, judging by Mary Austin's mystical encounter with Hugh Miller's *The Old Red Sandstone* (1851), during which, she claimed, "the earth itself became transparent, molten, glowing."[70] Such passionate responses may have characterized only a small proportion of readers' encounters with print, but as more people could read and had more opportunity to do so, it may well be that such responses became more, rather than less, common. To recognize the variability of reading is to perceive that tastes and practices were multiple and complex, changing over time and the course of a life. Like nineteenth-century critics whose ideal reading was to apprehend the thoughts of the author at the time of writing, twentieth-century scholars too often treated reading as an independent variable, rather than as a practice embedded in social life.

Historians have variously argued that print helped to create a common national outlook that transcended regional and, presumably, class differences in nineteenth-century America or that, by classifying readers along lines of age, gender, ethnicity, and class, it served as an instrument of fragmentation. Presumably it did both. Print's capacity to draw readers into imagined communities was not a one-way proposition. If there were moments of substantial unity, such as continental expansion, these were never absolute. Print media represented a variety of special interests — including those based on section, sect, occupation, avocation, generation, gender, race, and age. But even in cases like the ethnic press, assimilationist as well as separatist messages appeared. With such diverse offerings, the task of integration fell to readers. How men and women, individually or collectively, made sense of what they read is a subject that remains largely unexplored. That is the very considerable task of the next generation of historians of reading.

CHAPTER 9

Sites of Reading

Reading is a material act, in part as a result of the diverse physical settings in which people read. Three such sites are the library, the home, and the city: communal space, domestic space, and public space. In the mid-nineteenth century, institutions across the United States, ranging from colleges to churches to mercantile associations, established libraries. Shared ownership of, and access to, reading matter helped such communities to define themselves and their missions. By 1880 these institutions began to include the towns and cities that supported public libraries. Domestic reading took place in different rooms within the home, at different times of day, and in different social circumstances: private but also public, silent but also aloud. The setting itself helped determine whether reading functioned to reinforce various types of family bonding or to help establish personal privacy. Within a home, a plenitude of domestic objects—both decorative and useful, and for the most part industrially produced—was generated by the literary arena, from handkerchiefs and candlesticks to authors' busts and portraits. City streets were similarly crammed with objects to be "read," ranging from banknotes to newspapers to broadsides. Urban reading occurred not only in such public buildings as libraries, post offices, and banks but also, perhaps especially, on and around the streets themselves. Surprisingly perhaps, there too reading could be a private act as well a public one, but one that was ever more necessary for survival in an increasingly urban world.

PART 1

Libraries

Kenneth E. Carpenter

. . .

On 26 August 1871 the *Portsmouth (N.H.) Journal* reprinted an article by the novelist Sylvanus Cobb Jr. from the *New York Ledger* entitled "True Story of Swiftville Library." This "same old story . . . told over and over again" was set in a farming community on Maine's Androscoggin River. Four men—Daniel, who was eighty-five years of age, another man of seventy, and Daniel's son and son-in-law—were husking corn one late autumn day and talking as they worked. The younger men wished that their children had more advantages: "Our school, of only three months in the year, don't seem to be quite enough," said the son-in-law. Daniel's son replied, "That's so. And yet it wouldn't make so much matter if we only had good books and papers for them to read; but we can't afford that, you know." If such could be provided, "not only would they thus find means for storing their minds with useful knowledge, but they would find more comfort and pleasure at home." Another of the men interjected: "How much better it would be for the children to have interesting and profitable reading than to be killing time in hunting up non-sensical and profitless games." That set Daniel calculating in his head: if he had never drunk "spirit" (though he never had overdone it), he could have built a library. He thereupon decided never to drink again and to put the savings toward a library. The others agreed to do likewise, and together they persuaded others—a total of forty-two townspeople—to do the same. If each citizen contributed but 30¢ per week, the total would come to $655 per year. The group formed a society, chose officers, and made each contributor an equal shareholder. Daniel provided a suitable room in his house, but "at length" the community erected a library building that also contained an "audience hall" for public meetings. Daniel Swift died at the age of ninety-six; but shortly before his death, they carried him up to the library building. When the young people knew he was there, "they came in, gathered around him, and blessed him; and he raised his streaming eyes to Heaven, and repeated aloud the words of Simeon of old: 'Lord, now lettest thy servant depart in peace; for mine eyes have seen thy salvation!' "[1]

Although this story is fictional, its main points—the evangelical character of library founding, the desire to provide advantages for children through books, and its civic model of voluntarism (including, in this case, self-taxation) and formal organization—would have been recognized by 1880 in communities throughout the United States. In the early decades of the nineteenth century, American educators, church leaders, government officials, reformers, and scholars argued that social benefits would surely follow from improved access to books, among them the creation of an educated citizenry for a strong democracy; the moral and religious education of a large and rapidly growing population; a heightened sense of the country's heroic past; and the enhancement of the new nation's standing in the world. Ordinary Americans sought pleasure, instruction, and social advancement in the latest books from an expanding publishing industry. Between 1840 and 1880, these motives and

SITES OF READING

expectations joined with a growing economy, a rapidly developing educational system, and a highly religious population to support the quickening expansion of libraries in various forms, financed by various means. Some developments in this period may seem unfamiliar to us, such as the proliferation of school-district, Sunday school, and social libraries, but in their day they provided readers with access to a wide range of books. More familiar institutions, such as free public and academic research libraries, put down roots in these decades, even though their flowering came later.

Many nineteenth-century Americans would have been familiar with one or more of the multiple kinds of libraries that were common in the North and West and in southern cities. Some of these institutions were primarily depots — often just a wooden bookshelf in the corner of a church, schoolroom, or private home — from which books could be borrowed, taken away, read, and returned. Others dedicated extensive space to amass collections that could only be read on site. Still others, founded out of a desire to encourage personal improvement, provided newspapers and periodicals in comfortable reading rooms. Still others offered reading materials to diverse and targeted audiences, such as prisoners, patients in hospitals, sailors, and factory workers. Although many of these institutions were essentially private, such as the collections of associations of lawyers and doctors or those of learned societies, a large number were "public" in the mid-nineteenth-century sense: a small payment bought anyone access to commercial circulating libraries, and working- and middle-class readers could join social libraries for inexpensive membership fees.

Graph 9.1 demonstrates not only that the overall number of libraries steadily grew but also that many hundreds of libraries already existed by the 1840s. The vast majority of these institutions were established by voluntary associations, which were generally small and impermanent. Given these qualities, it is certainly the case that many libraries have left little by which to document their existence. Some libraries existed only in a formal sense, such as the township libraries established by the states of Michigan and Indiana (in the graph, they account for the 1855 spike in Middle West numbers), which were often not maintained by the townships or were established in name only.

Township libraries were part of an ongoing quest for a sustainable means of giving Americans access to books they did not individually own. In the early decades of the century, library advocates maintained a long-established argument that voluntary or philanthropic means were the best ways to provide such access, but in the decades after 1840, many state governments provided financial support to foster school-district and township libraries. In 1839 Horace Mann, secretary of the Massachusetts Board of Education, made

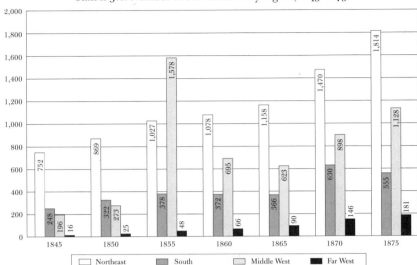

GRAPH 9.1. Number of U.S. libraries by region, 1845–1875

Source: Haynes McMullen, *American Libraries before 1876* (Westport, Conn.: Greenwood, 2000), 48, table 3.3.

Note: McMullen's extensive data cards have been converted into a searchable database, available through the Davies Project at Princeton University (http://www.princeton.edu/~davpro). This database should be used with caution, however: as McMullen notes, it is impossible to count nineteenth-century American libraries definitively.

libraries the main focus of a state report. For Mann, schools were the preliminary means of forming a "powerful and exemplary people," and libraries were the subsequent method: "with no books to read, the power of reading will be useless." [2] Mann wanted to diffuse information, to be sure, but more crucially he wanted good reading to heighten the wisdom of the citizenry. To him, a straightforward solution was the creation of school-district libraries, small collections that children and adults alike could use and that the state could fund—and control. These libraries could be stocked with the right books, not the cheap literature hawked by book peddlers. Under Mann's guidance and in imitation of the Harper's Family Library, the Massachusetts Board of Education commissioned solid fare from notable writers, such as Francis Lieber and Alonzo Potter, and arranged for the Boston firm of Marsh, Capen, Lyon, & Webb to publish these works as a "library," shipped complete with its own bookcase. Indicative of the importance of the effort, Edward Everett, then governor of the commonwealth, chaired the Board of Education, and Jared Sparks, a historian and sometime president of Harvard College, was one of its key members. [3]

SITES OF READING

In promoting school-district libraries, Mann was following the lead of New York. In 1835 the state legislature had passed a law enabling school districts to create publicly accessible libraries through taxation. A windfall from the sale of western lands in 1838 permitted the state to make a large investment, and by 1841 most of the state's eleven thousand school districts had libraries.[4] Where Mann emphasized mental improvement, advocates for school-district libraries in New York focused on moral betterment.[5] Of course, intellectual and moral improvement were never far apart, for morality was as much an escape from vice as a positive acquisition, and the idleness that led to vice had its antidote in reading good books. Improvement of any kind depended on the collected books being read, but in many cases these small libraries do not seem to have been heavily used.[6] The reading public's hunger for books ran more to novels and romances than to "improving" works.

The association of publicly accessible collections of books with educational institutions was not exclusive to the school-district library. Some school and college libraries allowed their collections to be used by certain members of the public. In the 1840s and 1850s, the Harvard College Library was known as the "Public Library at Cambridge." The City School Library in Lowell, Massachusetts, was open to all citizens of the town. In 1870 the Institute for Colored Youth in Philadelphia loaned out some three thousand books.[7] What distinguished the school-district library was its support through taxation and public money, a characteristic that relates it to contemporaneous New England experiments in the public funding of libraries and allows us to see it as a predecessor of the free public library that would begin to take root in the 1850s.[8]

State support brought with it restrictions on the contents and scope of collections. Works that were explicitly partisan, sectarian, or hostile to the Christian religion were deemed inappropriate, as was most fiction.[9] Other funding sources allowed different collecting policies. Church and Sunday school libraries, for instance, collected just the kinds of sectarian publications that school-district libraries eschewed. Church libraries for adult, typically clerical, use were often essentially learned libraries, while others contained current evangelical literature.[10] The Sunday school libraries served children, supplying multitudes of young people with a large number of printed works, especially those of tract societies, many of which were denominational.[11]

Sunday school libraries were widespread in the United States. The 1850 census reported almost two thousand of them; by 1870 that number had grown to almost thirty-four thousand. Notably, these libraries existed for both white Americans and African Americans. Bethel's Sabbath School in Baltimore, an African American library, owned a collection of more than a thousand books.[12] But although the number of Sunday school libraries had increased dramatically by midcentury, and although these libraries collectively held a large percentage of the circulating library books in the United States, the individual libraries tended to be small. According to the census, the average size of such a collection was 273 books in 1850, 334 in 1860, and 249 in 1870.[13]

The church and Sunday school libraries served evangelical purposes, but even more avowedly so did the libraries aiming to reach the unchurched, especially unchurched young men away from home in cities. That was the goal of the Young Men's Christian Association movement, which began in Britain, was imported first in the United States to Boston in 1851, and then spread rapidly, especially after the Civil War.[14] From the start and through the 1870s and 1880s, a library was an important draw for YMCAs, as it was for other local organizations that aimed to reach the young. Libraries or reading rooms with newspapers and periodicals were standard (reading rooms and libraries were not necessarily one and the same).[15]

These libraries sought to control reading by limiting the kinds of books they provided. Readers who wanted a wider selection of books were apt to find it elsewhere. In cities, they often resorted to social libraries — apprentices', mechanics', or mercantile libraries — which collected membership dues. These institutions, recognizing that to attract members they needed to offer popular literature, had less restrictive collection policies, and competition from commercial circulating libraries encouraged them to admit women. Many social libraries did not survive their first generation or amass large collections.[16]

Of the many kinds of social libraries, mercantile libraries on average seem to have survived longer than the others. When founded in 1820, the New York Mercantile Library held several hundred books and had two hundred members. By 1875 it held more than 160,000 volumes, making it the fourth largest library in the United States; it also had more than eight thousand members. Given the size of its collection, the New York Mercantile Library was clearly exceptional, and in its organization and purpose it was exemplary. Operated and owned by its members, the library and its collection were funded through dues readily affordable to mercantile clerks — at the time of the Civil War, between $2 and $5 annually. The library originally focused on collecting standard works for moral improvement, but as members demanded more fiction, the library wisely broadened its collections. By 1870 fiction accounted for 70 percent of the library's purchases.[17] The New York Mercantile Library Association, made up of budding businessmen, managed its library "as a nonprofit, commercial enterprise."[18] It is not surprising, then, that it opened its doors to those outside the profession it was meant to serve. Notably, by 1870 women were among the library's most devoted users. The Mercantile Library offered many attractions beyond its circulation of books and its reading room. It sponsored lectures, offered classes, and mounted exhibits and displays.[19] Most important for the young men who made up its target audience, it provided a transitional space between "the home they had left and the one they would presumably make."[20]

Social libraries were considered public because they were open to anyone who could pay for a membership. By the middle of the century, "public" began to assume a new meaning as it became associated with tax-supported municipal libraries. In 1851, Edward Everett, the former governor and recently resigned president of Harvard, and George Ticknor, author and first Smith chair of French and Spanish at Harvard, strongly articulated their visions for a free public library. Everett believed "that a Public Library, well supplied with books in the various departments of art and science, and open at all times for consultation and study to the citizens at large, is absolutely needed to make our admirable system of Public Education complete."[21] He wanted a library dedicated to study and scholarship, what would later be called a research library. So did Ticknor, who had cherished this desire ever since his student days at Göttingen. His friend Joseph Green Cogswell was the librarian of just such an institution, the newly established Astor Library in New York City. But Ticknor also wanted a library that would circulate multiple copies of the "pleasant literature of the day" in order to instill an "appetite for healthy general reading." "This appetite, once formed, . . . will, in the majority of cases, demand better and better books; and can, I believe, by a little judicious help, rather than by any direct control or restraint, be carried much higher than is generally thought possible."[22] The Massachusetts legislature had in 1848 enacted a law allowing for the establishment of a municipal library supported by taxation — the first of its kind in the nation's history — and in 1854 Everett's and Ticknor's visions became a reality when the Boston Public Library opened its doors. That the new institution was intended to serve both ways of using books was represented spatially by the divided form of the library building: books circulated through the lower hall, while scholarly materials that did not circulate were found in the upper hall.

The Boston Public Library did not have to struggle to build the research collection. Gifts of money and materials flowed in, but like other free public libraries, it found that the citizenry did not readily ascend the reading ladder. Library annual reports indicate that circulation declined when public libraries sought to force the reading of "higher" literature by cutting back on fiction. In effect, publicly financed institutions were caught in the same

FIGURE 9.1. "Saturday Night," illustration from "New York Mercantile Library," *Scribner's Monthly* 1 (February 1871), depicting the crush of Saturday night visitors to the library, both male and female, individually and in small groups. American Antiquarian Society.

dilemma as social libraries. However much those in charge—members in membership libraries, trustees in public libraries—might wish to foster reading as a means of self-improvement, reading purely for pleasure was what a large proportion of the population wanted.

The shifting meaning of "public" moved hand in hand with an expanding patronage. When new public libraries opened their doors, for instance, women took advantage of the access afforded them that the social libraries had sometimes denied them. An account of the New Bedford Public Library in 1857 reported, "A striking and delightful feature of our operations is the large number of females who visit the rooms both as takers of our books, and readers of our periodicals. Nearly one-half of the names upon our books are those of females." In Exeter, New Hampshire, the "eagerness" for books even had the drawback of preventing "many females from mingling in the crowd." In fact, "at times the librarian had to have a police officer present to enforce order."²³ (See Fig. 9.1.)

The number of free public libraries grew slowly throughout the second half of the century. By 1880 only eighteen other states had followed Massachusetts's lead and allowed municipalities to fund libraries through taxation. Many free public libraries in this period depended not on public money but on substantial gifts and bequests, often for buildings or endowed funds.[24] An 1894 study reported that 566 free public libraries in the nation had collections of one thousand or more volumes. Of that total, 70 percent were supported by taxation. A disproportionate number of the free public libraries were located in Massachusetts (212), but twenty states had at least 5.[25] The causes of the slow spread of public libraries have not been adequately examined. Certainly opposition to levying taxes for a library was often an important reason. Probably just as important was the lack in many communities of a positive effort on behalf of establishing a public library.[26] Behind this lack of advocacy must lie a number of reasons, one of which was very likely the long history of library closures in rural communities and small towns: many libraries were founded only to become moribund and die after members had read the initial collection. It was also difficult, especially in small towns, to make the capital expenditure for a library building. The standard way for a community to deal with this difficulty was to wait for or seek out a gift.

The impetus for free public library development would increase substantially only in the last decade of the century. By then a growing number of states had passed enabling legislation to permit taxation for libraries. Andrew Carnegie drew attention to the importance of libraries in the December 1889 issue of the *North American Review*, where he argued that libraries were the best single field for philanthropy because placing books within the reach of aspiring citizens effectively fostered the genuine progress of the people.[27] In 1890 the Free Public Library Commission of Massachusetts was founded, and similar organizations soon followed in other states. These commissions, whose membership often included women, were sometimes founded at the urging of women's clubs, and the growing empowerment of American women may have been closely related to the new era of the free public library.

Just as the dramatic growth in the number of public libraries and their concomitant cultural influence would come in the 1890s and after the turn of the century, so too would the transformation of academic or learned libraries into research libraries with large endowments, growing and coherent collections, sophisticated cataloging, and impressive reading rooms take place in the decades far beyond 1880. Although a few individuals had a vision of research libraries early in the century, more advocates of such libraries began to appear around midcentury, at a time when steps were also being taken to create learned libraries. In 1850 the Boston book collector George Livermore argued, counter to the patriotic sense of many Americans, that libraries in the United States were inadequate for scholarly research. He admitted that the nation was rich in the number of its libraries and that those libraries as a whole contained an impressive number of books. They were mostly the *same* books, however, and Livermore called on the nation and its libraries to increase and diversify their holdings. Libraries, he believed, "should contain all those works which are too costly, too voluminous, or of *too little value* in the common estimation, to be found elsewhere, down even to the smallest tracts." Scholars needed access to broad, detailed, and sometimes unpredictable forms of knowledge, because even an "old almanac or a forgotten pamphlet" might enable a scholar "to verify or correct some important point which would otherwise have remained in dispute."[28] Livermore was not alone in making this argument, but its logic had not yet become commonplace in discussions of libraries.

In criticizing the state of American libraries as a whole, Livermore was writing not out of despair but out of a consciousness of new possibilities. The nationalist strain in his argument revealed a certain anxiety about the relationship of the United States to Europe. Americans "must have," he wrote, "a large national library, to which we can point men of other countries as the substantial evidence of interest in the promotion of literature and science." In this nationalistic rhetoric there was an expression of national pride, but also a recognition that the United States lagged behind Europe. Livermore understood that Americans wanted to see themselves as Europeans' equals and to be perceived as such. Libraries were a means to that end, not merely in literary culture and esoteric research. Library collections were also seen as vehicles for fostering an economically advanced, industrial civilization, with an infrastructure and institutions comparable to those of Europe.

Because Livermore's ideal was a great national library on the model of the British Museum and the much larger Bibliothèque Nationale, it is not surprising that he urged that the recently created Smithsonian Institution be made into such a library. Five years earlier, Rufus Choate, the primary Senate proponent of using James Smithson's bequest to fund a national library, asked on the Senate floor, "Why should a German or an Englishman sit down to a repast of five hundred thousand books, and an American scholar, who loves truth as well as he, be put on something less than half allowance?"[29] The establishing act, signed by President Polk on 10 August 1846, called for considerable sums to be devoted to a library "composed of valuable works pertaining to all departments of human knowledge."[30] A library was consequently part of the program that the secretary of the Smithsonian Institution, physicist Joseph Henry, presented to the regents in 1847, and the Smithsonian began to form a "complete collection of the transactions and proceedings of all the learned societies in the world."[31]

The first librarian of the Smithsonian, Charles Coffin Jewett, unable to gather all that a scholar might need, called for the Smithsonian to collect "catalogues of all the different libraries in the United States," plus "catalogues of memoirs, and of books in foreign libraries, and other materials . . . for rendering the institution a centre of bibliographical knowledge, whence the student may be directed to any work which he may require." Jewett's plan was becoming practicable because libraries of all sorts nationwide were beginning to publish their own catalogs. Institutions that issued these works ranged from the Public School Library of New Orleans (1848), to mercantile libraries in Philadelphia (1850) and San Francisco (1854), to the Young Ladies' Lyceum at Wesleyan Female College in Cincinnati (1859).[32] Such catalogs were not new, but in the 1840s and 1850s, they increasingly classified books by genre. By 1850 Jewett was also working on an audacious proposal for a national union catalog to be produced by creating stereotyped citations for the individual books held by American libraries.[33] Although Jewett publicized his plan in *On the Construction of Catalogues and Libraries* (1853), it was never put into practice. That Smithsonian publication, however, contained an extensive set of rules that became "the basic guide to cataloging practice" in the United States and remained so until the mid-1870s.[34]

A consciousness of American deficiencies also inspired individuals with foreign ties—through birth, study, or travel—to found libraries. In 1848 John Jacob Astor's bequest of $400,000 allowed for the founding in New York of the Astor Library. Its first librarian, Joseph Green Cogswell, had studied at Göttingen, where experience with the greatest learned library of the day forever changed him and his compatriots who studied there—among them, Edward Everett and George Ticknor. The Astor Library was momentously important. Here for the first time was a library of learning established to serve the public. It was not controlled by shareholders, university overseers, or Congress, but instead by specially chosen trustees whose power derived from an act of the New York state legislature. Its funding did not depend on the willingness of shareholders to tax themselves or on the appropriations of a governmental body. Instead, much of Astor's bequest was turned into what was by far the largest endowment for an American library at that time. Given this strong financial foundation, Cogswell became the first librarian who could plan for the long term. He realized that the Astor Library could be "formed upon system," as he put it in his report for 1853.[35] That meant developing policies about the overall shape of the library and determining precisely what should be acquired and how to go about doing so.[36] Cogswell sought gifts from governments and institutions here and abroad and from representatives of other countries stationed in the United States: edited historical documents, laws, court cases, legislative proceedings, reports of government departments on agriculture, education, finance, population, prisons, railroads, and, more notably, publications of the British Patent Office (which were heavily used by researchers interested in the latest technological developments). Contemporaries recognized such advantages and the cumulative, positive result likely to flow from them; that, of course, further helped the Astor. Scholars drew up lists of desiderata, foreign governments and learned societies sent publications, and Americans made significant gifts. It looked as if the Astor would become the greatest American library.

In the annual report of 1851, which seems to have served as a manifesto, Cogswell explained his priorities. He wrote that he selected with "due regard to the claims of every department of learning," but that "as it is in the most costly that the wants are greatest, large sums have necessarily been applied to works of that description, including those on civil engineering, public improvements, architecture, and the arts generally, and the voluminous accounts of the voyages and researches for scientific, geological and archaeological discoveries."[37] In the 1853 report, he was even more explicit about wanting books of a practical nature: "It will be a leading object of the library to provide a complete 'Bibliothèque Industrielle,' or collection of books for the special benefit of practical industry. A convenient and commodious room will be prepared for it on the first floor of the building, in which every accommodation will be afforded to those who wish to consult it."[38] That report also noted that William B. Astor had placed at Cogswell's disposal £2,500 for such books.[39] Despite such gifts and its initial promise, the Astor Library was ultimately unable to acquire the necessary resources to equal the greatest European libraries.

College and university libraries did not collect as widely as the Astor, but the institutions' presidents expressed the same nationalism. Columbia's Nathaniel Fish Moore, in an address to alumni in 1848, reviewed the great libraries of the past and of Europe at the present time in order to "show how greatly wanting our country is as yet in this respect."[40] Harvard's James Walker echoed these comments but went further in relating the library to scholarship: "What the College needs, as a place of earnest study directed by teachers aiming to be on a level with the highest problems of the day, is a large fund, the income of which shall be sufficient to obtain every important work in every branch of learning and inquiry, wherever published, and as soon as published. To expect high and various scholarship, as scholarship is now understood, without providing such means and facilities, is to expect an impossibility."[41] For Walker, the definition of scholarship was itself changing. That consciousness ultimately lay behind the gradual transformation of academic libraries in the latter part of the nineteenth century.

The relationship between academic libraries, new methods of instruction, and an increased emphasis on research was reciprocal (see Chapter 10, Part 1). Like changes in higher education generally during this period, these elements came into being gradually. In 1831 Brown University, under the leadership of Francis Wayland, set out to raise $25,000 for library materials and organized a Joint Library Committee, consisting of members of the Brown Corporation and the faculty. When funds became available in 1840, Wayland created a new joint committee to oversee expenditures. Such an infrastructure was crucial but rare, however, and it could not guarantee steady library development any more than could a building. The libraries of the University of Virginia, where the library was in the central campus structure, South Carolina College, which in 1840 erected the first separate library building in an American college or university, and Harvard, which built the second in 1841, did not thereby get a long-term boost. Library development required more, even, than occasional large sums for purchases.

In 1842 Harvard raised nearly $17,000 to fill gaps in its collection, but once that fund was expended, little money remained for purchases, and the library grew primarily through gifts of books and other material. Funds for ongoing acquisitions of currently published material, plus an infrastructure for selection and ordering, were required. That happened at Harvard in 1859, when William Gray made the first of his promised annual gifts of $5,000 and Harvard's president established a library committee. It allocated expenditures among various disciplines, solicited lists of books for purchase, and established procedures for purchasing (for example, identifying agents to supply books). Once the new books began to arrive in significant numbers, a decision was made not to supplement the old printed catalog or bring out a new one but rather to use some of the gift to produce a public card catalog. After the Gray gifts were spent, the library returned to its usual state of poverty. That changed only after Charles William Eliot became president in 1869 and began to emphasize endowed funds, which increased tremendously during the 1870s and 1880s, as did purchases, the processing of materials, and their use. In 1869–70, 197 purchases and 1,323 gifts were recorded; by 1877–78, those numbers had jumped to 5,566 purchases and 2,796 gifts. Soon after his arrival in 1877, Harvard's new librarian, Justin Winsor, inaugurated policies and practices that increased use of the library, including allowing greater access to books and producing a guide to the catalog. Harvard's situation became better than most, thanks to its endowed funds and to Winsor's pioneering work in systematizing library operations and rationalizing policies.

For academic libraries, like research universities, the period after the Civil War consisted of a "series of scattered, discrete events [that] provided precedents and stimuli for subsequent developments." [42] For instance, Yale in 1870–71 acquired the library of the political scientist Robert von Mohl; in 1871 a Detroit businessman purchased the library of a German economist for the University of Michigan; and in 1873 a San Francisco businessman paid for the library of Francis Lieber for the University of California. Systematic development was not possible, however, for academic libraries were dependent on the larger institutions to which they belonged for financial support, for the determination of the scope of collections, and for the use that gave them importance. As science advanced, libraries spent significant amounts of their funds on scientific periodicals. Humanistic scholarship emphasized the history and literature of classical antiquity, the major countries of western Europe, and the United States. The libraries echoed such valuations. American scholarship on eastern and southern Europe, on the Middle East, Asia, Latin America, and, of course, Africa did not exist; neither, then, did the library resources, except for some holdings in the Astor Library and scattered, often uncataloged materials elsewhere. The social sciences were only beginning to be an area of scholarship, and so relevant holdings were almost nonexistent.

American librarians first assembled for a national conference in 1853. In that year, Charles B. Norton published a call for such a meeting in *Norton's Literary Gazette*.[43] More than eighty librarians and others interested in libraries responded and gathered in New York for what appears to have been a successful conference. Charles Coffin Jewett, elected president of the meeting, delivered several talks on the state of libraries and librarianship, in particular emphasizing his plan for a national union catalog. But although the attendees unanimously resolved to form "a permanent Librarians' Association," no organization developed and no meetings followed. One of the reasons was that Jewett, the most prominent librarian in the United States, lost his position as assistant secretary and librarian at the Smithsonian in 1854 because of an internal struggle over the direction of the institution.[44]

In 1876, twenty-three years after that first conference, librarians gathered again in Philadelphia. While the attractions of the Centennial Exhibition may have encouraged attendance, the conferees were nonetheless very serious about improving the practices of librarianship. Of the 103 registrants, about two-thirds were librarians, the remaining number being made up mostly of library trustees, bibliographers, and educators (one in the last category, Henry Barnard, had also attended the 1853 conference).[45] Ninety registrants were men; thirteen were women. A variety of libraries were represented: thirteen academic, twenty-four free public, and forty-three of other kinds, including private and subscription libraries. Before the conference came to a close, a resolution for a library association was introduced. The fledgling American Library Association had 41 members by the end of 1876, 110 by 1877, and 197 by 1878. While the ALA and its efforts grew slowly over the next several decades, the association steadily increased in authority.[46] Its annual conferences and publications stimulated the missionary spirit that has since characterized American librarianship. American librarians fought for legislation to further the establishment of new libraries, and they sought "the best reading for the largest number at the least expense."[47] Over time, the ALA and its activities, including its promotion of efficient library practices, helped to create a climate that stimulated other actors, notably Andrew Carnegie, to take the steps that would make public libraries commonplace in the twentieth century.

Modern librarians have often considered 1876 "to mark the beginning of the modern era in American librarianship."[48] That year witnessed not only the founding of the ALA but also the publication by the U.S. Bureau of Education of its survey titled *Public Libraries in the United States of America* and the launching of the *American Library Journal*, the nation's first periodical devoted to libraries and librarianship.[49] But the *Journal* ran at a deficit for a decade, and to talk of the professionalization of library management before 1880 is misleading: most volunteer or employed librarians were not trained in librarianship; most libraries did not embrace standardized practices; and the majority of American libraries grappled with quite different issues than better-known institutions such as the Astor and Boston Public libraries. Significant disagreement persisted about the benefits of standardization; Justin Winsor, the first president of the ALA, spoke in his 1879 presidential address about "the dangers of cooperation as well as its virtues."[50] The ALA would remain small for many years, and its best-attended conferences were the ones at summer playgrounds: 186 were present at Thousand Islands (1887), and 242 in the White Mountains (1890).[51]

If the library community took many years to reach the organizational levels of the twentieth century, it is fair to say that there was a growing discussion of "best practices" in the latter part of the nineteenth century, and these discussions contained the seeds of later organizational developments. Most of the participants in such exchanges, however, came from the largest libraries, and many of them moved from one institution to another, spreading their particular visions of librarianship and libraries in the process. The influential William Frederick Poole, for instance, served as librarian at the Boston Mercantile Library, the Boston Athenæum, the Cincinnati Public Library, the Chicago Public Library, and the Newberry Library. Workers whom he trained then carried his vision far afield. Librarians wrote to each other with questions and observations about cataloging, collecting, and other important matters, and some published articles about such topics. Many of the larger libraries published bulletins or annual reports that included current practices in library management.[52]

Before 1880, then, many promising beginnings had not developed as it seemed they would. After Justin Winsor left for Harvard in 1877, the Boston Public Library foundered for nearly two decades.[53] The Smithsonian Institution did not become a national library, and the Library of Congress between 1840 and 1880 had almost no funds for purchases. The Library of Congress grew faster than any other library, thanks to its acquisition of two major collections of Americana and, after 1870, of books received as copyright deposits, but the development of its international collections essentially took place in the twentieth century. Nevertheless, libraries seem never to have discarded materials when they declined. Even when they changed direction—as the New York State Library did in 1878, when it consciously decided no longer to be a general research library—libraries retained the materials already acquired.[54] The period ended on the cusp of a fundamental restructuring. University libraries were about to become the dominant sites for developing extensive collections, with the exception of a very few major public institutions and some major rare book collections of wealthy individuals. In the arena of libraries for general reading, Andrew Carnegie was about to transform the library scene, literally and symbolically, through his gifts of funds for library buildings. But it is important to remember, in light of earlier attempts to provide for libraries, that Carnegie's philanthropy always required a commitment from the community that it would finance operations. Philanthropy alone was not enough, as it rarely had been. One of the key lessons of the period was that all libraries, whether academic libraries like Harvard's or subscription libraries like the fictional Swiftville Library discussed at the opening of this essay, would require ongoing support in order to survive.

Homes, Books, and Reading

Louise Stevenson

. . .

In the centennial year 1876, a student learning penmanship might copy and re-copy this sentence: "The present is emphatically an age of books; everybody reads more or less daily." In the same year, a book catalog quoted Henry Ward Beecher, the well-known preacher, lecturer, and author, as saying that every man should surround his children with books. He saw them as no luxury but rather among "the necessaries of life." [55]

Indeed, books in homes connected individuals to their families and friends, to people across the society, and to the marketplace. Books existed both as objects from the marketplace and as texts for readers, simultaneously express-ing the central cultural role of literature and helping to maintain it. Books also found representation in the decorative arts, either purchased or homemade. The more that middle-class readers bought elegantly bound books, as well as representations based on them in Staffordshire figurines, white porcelain Parian-ware busts, and other mementos, the more those readers' domestic world intersected with the marketplace.

The nineteenth-century publishing world made available an abundance of books at a range of prices. Cultural arbiters claimed to have witnessed an explosion in book publishing. Book ownership seemed to have reached such an extent that an 1876 cultural commentator was moved to decry the "craze" of purchasing books and to yearn for the olden days of early New England when, he thought, the few books a minister might own could find a place on his desk shelves. [56] Mid-nineteenth-century readers could choose from inexpensive editions, usually called a "people's," or "household," edi-tion, of standard authors costing 75¢ or $1.00, or more costly sets in half or full calf, with gilt edges, such as the thirty-four volumes of James Fenimore Cooper's works for $75.00. Washington Irving's *Life of George Washington* (1860) was available in cloth for $2.00, in sheepskin for $2.50, half calfskin covers for $3.25, and full calfskin covers for $4.00. A smaller, cloth-covered edition for about $1.00 was printed in reduced type and had no portraits or map. A Bible, the book households most frequently owned, cost as little as 75¢ or as much as $75.00, if it had leather bindings, engravings, maps, and other reference aids.

Gift books, bought as Christmas or New Year's presents or as birthday gifts from the late 1820s through the 1850s, offered a selection of fiction, biography, poetry, or inspirational works. They cost as little as $1.25 for children's books and $1.50 for adults' books. The steel engravings and decorative bindings of gift books accounted for as much as 60 percent of their price. More expensive volumes had illuminated title pages, about a dozen steel engravings, and elaborate leather bindings. For example, D. Appleton & Co. offered *Beauties of the Court of Queen Victoria* (1849) with fourteen portraits "engraved by the best artists," richly bound in cloth with full gilt on the edges, and an ornamented spine. Advertising copy described both *The American Landscape Annual* and *The Diadem*, subtitled *A Souvenir for the Drawing-Room and Parlor; and Gift Book for all Seasons*, as quarto-sized, "splendidly illustrated with steel engravings," and priced at $4.00 when bound in morocco. Gift books pleased both the eye and the mind of their givers and recipients. People gave books to express the sentiments that they felt for another, whether as friend, relative, or lover. The words in gift books were meant to give expression to these feelings much as the worth of the object was intended to convey the magnitude and sincerity of their feelings. Displayed in recipients' homes, gift books served to remind viewers and readers that someone close by felt the sentiments expressed in their pages.[57]

Urban dwellers generally owned more books than did those who lived in rural places or on the frontier. However, an analysis of estate inventories from two counties on the antebellum Ohio frontier shows that numerous people, above and below the median wealth level, owned books. Model budgets of the 1850s suggest that a working family's income of $600 allowed less than $10 a year for reading matter and other amusements, making luxuries of books costing even 75¢. Still, paperbacks of British novels cost as little as 5¢, and story papers, which serialized novels, cost 5¢ or 6¢. Readers stretched their budgets through various strategies. Committed readers could buy 25¢ paperbacks, borrow from libraries and friends, and plan their purchases to complement those of a friend or family member with whom they frequently exchanged books. Journals and diaries of families in western states tell how they looked forward to packages of magazines and newspapers sent by relatives and friends. Neither these strategies nor the impact of personal taste on what people read are reflected in model budgets, tax records, and estate inventories, which tell but a partial story of book ownership. Some less well-to-do families owned more books than did their economic betters. Schoolteachers, college professors, writers, lawyers, ministers, and other modestly paid professionals sometimes owned more books than their level of wealth might suggest.[58]

The proliferation of book ownership paralleled the emergence of book decor within the home. Many well-to-do families had separate rooms devoted to books and reading, as did the du Ponts of Delaware, who prospered as gunpowder manufacturers, and the Hamiltons of Fort Wayne, Indiana. In 1851, Alexander Jackson Downing designed a "cottage for a country-clergyman," with a parlor, dining room, kitchen, bedroom, and library on the first floor. House plans from the 1850s and 1860s show that lower-middle-class families bought houses with libraries. The small, two-story brick house in Galena, Illinois, where Ulysses S. Grant, a less-than-prosperous member of the middle class, spent his years before the Civil War, had a study or library on the first floor. After the Civil War brought about considerable increase in prices, architect Samuel Sloan designed a house in 1867 for a mechanic's or clerk's family that cost $1,500 and had no library included in its three-room first floor, and a residence for $3,100 with a first-floor library.[59]

Whatever their income level, people displayed objects that suggested their participation in the world of books. Even though working-class families might possess few or no books, representations of books, their characters, and their authors might enter their homes. People with less disposable income for pleasure purchases might take home inexpensive handkerchiefs with literary motifs, won as prizes at fairs or church bazaars, or peddlers might sell them pottery decorated with book representations or the illustrations from popular books. Since so few of these handkerchiefs now exist, most of them, especially the most popular, probably were used until they wore out. Wealthier people also decorated their homes according to certain literary inspirations. For example, a set of gilded candlesticks manufactured in Philadelphia in 1848 and 1849 had likenesses of the major characters from James Fenimore Cooper's *The Last of the Mohicans: A Narrative of 1757* (1826) standing on white marble bases. Between handkerchiefs and gilded girandoles, the marketplace had almost limitless possibilities, at various prices, for bringing home references to books.[60]

At prices affordable to the middle class, decorative objects for children and adults featured authors and characters from books. The decorative motifs on imported British pottery drew heavily from British literature, demonstrating the transatlantic nature of the period's literary culture. On children's pottery, including cups, saucers, and small plates, appeared figures from nursery rhymes (Jack-be-Nimble) and folk tales (Cinderella), suggesting the mixing of the spoken and printed word, as well as from the *Arabian Nights* and *Robinson Crusoe*. Images of reading were also popular decorative motifs. Transfer printing on china often showed a young child teaching an animal to read, a mother reading to her two little children, or a boy and girl sharing a book. Adults might buy Parian-ware sculpture busts in various sizes of famous literary figures, including Shakespeare, Goethe, Petrarch, Homer, Milton, and even Washington Irving. The novels of Charles Dickens and Sir Walter Scott provided much inspiration. Little Nell from *The Old Curiosity Shop* had her portrait in Parian ware. Mr. Pickwick's image appeared on mugs, and his form was modeled into a bottle shape. Consumers might decorate their homes with Staffordshire figurines of heroes and heroines of the Waverley novels, Scott himself, and his favorite greyhound. Or they might choose images of Romeo and Juliet, Robert Burns, Don Quixote, Iago and Othello, Robert and Elizabeth Barrett Browning, the robber Dick Turpin popularized by William Harrison Ainsworth's *Rookwood* (1834), and many other authors and fictional characters.[61] Visual images of authors and characters of novels and poetry also were collected for display on walls, shelves, and parlor tables. Many daguerreotype collections of portraits of European and American celebrities included authors. For viewing in stereoscopes or projection through magic lanterns, consumers might choose images from American book culture, including illustrations of Benjamin Franklin's Poor Richard, Cooper's novels, *Pilgrim's Progress*, or Robert Burns's "The Cotter's Saturday Night."[62] Shakespeare found his way into every material form imaginable, from a card game, to a library furniture suite with his portrait in relief, to elegant folio editions of his plays.[63]

Houses themselves, fictional or real, also linked readers to books. After visiting famous literary sites, tourists brought home mementos: a glass tumbler marking John Greenleaf Whittier's birthplace; souvenir spoons of Nathaniel Hawthorne's, Henry Wadsworth Longfellow's, and Whittier's birthplaces or houses. Even if they could not visit faraway tourist attractions, readers could view stereoscope images of Shakespeare's birthplace and Washington Irving at his home, "Sunnyside." People such as African American abolitionist Charlotte Forten spent evenings with friends poring over *Homes of American Authors* (1853) and other illustrated books. They wrote famous authors for their photographs or cartes de visite, placed them in albums, and then displayed these albums in their parlors.[64] The names of houses — as well as of pets and children — sometimes had their source in nineteenth-century books. Well-to-do readers named houses "Le Bocage" after the best-selling *St. Elmo* (1866), "Rochester" after the character in *Jane Eyre* (1847), or "Belmont" after Portia's country seat in *The Merchant of Venice*.[65]

Harriet Beecher Stowe's *Uncle Tom's Cabin* (1852) provided the richest American source for literary material culture at every price range from its publication date until well past 1880 (Fig. 9.2). It quickly became a popular play, performed in many versions on both sides of the Atlantic and, by one account,

322　　　　SITES OF READING

FIGURE 9.2. Literary artifacts associated with *Uncle Tom's Cabin*, 1852–c. 1880. Translated into many languages, adapted for the theater, and sufficiently well known to be used in advertising, its stories and characters were depicted in prints suitable for framing, musical compositions, and card games. American Antiquarian Society.

at the court of the King of Siam. Illustrations were printed on inexpensive mugs and plates and even on handkerchiefs. Little Eva and Uncle Tom were paired in Staffordshire figures and on more expensive French porcelain vases. An image of Little Eva teaching Uncle Tom to read appeared on preprinted canvas for needleworkers to complete in their leisure time.[66]

The richness of this marketplace teaches two lessons. First, the decorative arts magnified and fed off the popularity of literary culture. In an age of fertilization between media, artists promoted books. The sculptor John Rogers capitalized on the popularity of well-known works, such as Henry Wadsworth Longfellow's *The Courtship of Miles Standish* and Washington Irving's "The Legend of Sleepy Hollow," and painter Eastman Johnson composed a portrait of John Greenleaf Whittier's "Barefoot Boy," which reached a larger audience as a low-cost chromolithograph (see Fig. 1.2).[67] Second, the extensive world of literary material culture complicates mid-nineteenth-century authors' condemnations of materialism and the marketplace. In Emerson's *Nature* (1836), the everyday man who will transcend material things is promised kingdoms vaster than those of Caesar. In *Uncle Tom's Cabin*, Stowe reveals how the rule of materialism in human affairs distorts all human relationships between friends, parents and children, husbands and wives. While Emerson, Stowe, and other authors guided their readers to values independent of commerce, their words gained power from the material reinforcements that the international marketplace provided.

Although households at all income levels had access to literary material culture, sharing a world of things does not necessarily mean living in identical worlds of meaning. As the preceding list illustrates, the quantity and variety of book-related commodities was almost overwhelming, and future investigations will likely reveal yet more ways in which literature and its related products entered the marketplace. Still, consumers did not experience this marketplace all at once. No one store, even a bookstore, carried all these objects. Consumers encountered them piecemeal in a variety of shops and trade catalogs. At commercial sites, books and book objects competed with other goods. Even though literary imagery was prevalent in many media, images relating to American political and military history, natural scenery, and commercial and philanthropic institutions dominated. Moreover, readers were active participants in the marketplace. When books entered the home, individuals' personal and social worlds of meaning absorbed them, and that meaning could be as various as the number of readers.

The sites of reading within middle-class homes suggest the relationship of books and sociability. Where people read depended largely on the availability of light and heat or cool shade. By 1830 widespread domestic use of the wood stove permitted both public and private rooms to have economical sources of heat. On sunny days, people might read while sitting on window seats or with chairs backed up to a window. Well beyond Thomas Edison's improved electric light bulb of 1879, families' nighttime reading remained centered in the parlor or downstairs family room. Families read by one or two candles or a kerosene lamp that around 1840 became a standard feature on parlor tables.

Fueled by expensive whale oil, Argand or astral lamps projected up to ten candlepower, far more light than most households enjoyed. In 1877 a woman wrote her mother that she was buying an oil lamp so that we "can do more than play checkers after dark."[68] Poorer families sometimes could not even afford the least expensive tallow candle. Dependence on one or two parlor lamps, candles, or the fireplace meant that nighttime reading was by necessity a social experience. However, even in daylight, when far more settings permitted reading, mid-nineteenth-century letters and diaries reveal that reading was as frequently a social experience as it was a private one.

When people read in daily life had much to do with their age and sex. Children too young to attend school either played with or looked at books when their older family members had time to help them. School-age children generally read after school, in the evenings with their family, or on Sunday afternoons. One woman recalled that as a young mill worker she and her brother would read before going to work, and factory rules suggest that workers often tried to read while tending their machines; probably most men and women read after work.[69] Single women returned to their apartments and either read alone or joined the family with whom they boarded. In a household, usually the wife and young women who had completed their formal education were responsible for housework. Early in the day, duties such as dusting, mopping, and swabbing were not conducive to reading. When families schooled their children at home, the mother and her older daughters might hear younger children's lessons in the morning. After cleaning up the midday meal, which fathers who worked within walking distance often shared, women settled in the parlor while someone read and others did needlework. Even women who had servants said that they read "by patches and snatches . . . during the laborious duties of housekeeping."[70] Some families managed to combine reading and work at other times. As a young farm boy driving a team of horses, Hamlin Garland was so inspired by Milton's *Paradise Lost* that he harangued his team until he lost control of it.[71] Women might read to one another during food preparation and cooking. In the evenings, men joined the family circle, sometimes reading aloud while women darned, mended, and made clothes. There would usually be one oral reader, one or more silent men or women readers, and perhaps other women involved in activities such as sketching, writing, or needlework. Even while doing needlework for pleasure, people could keep books at the center of things. Among the small items that women could sew as gifts were bookmarks and book weights.[72]

Sometimes books simply provided opportunities for fun. Young people amused themselves by producing home magazines or newspapers in the style and form of popular literature. During the Civil War, some Virginia children

FIGURE 9.3. *The Game of Authors* (Salem, Mass.: G. M. Whipple and A. A. Smith, 1861). Introduced in 1861, the card game appeared by the 1870s in diverse editions featuring a variety of British and American writers, classic and modern. American Antiquarian Society.

spoofed *Godey's Lady's Book*.[73] Sophie du Pont wrote a parody of Mary Mitford's *Our Village* (1824–32) called "Our Parlor" in the author's stilted, overblown, and minutely detailed language.[74] When visiting or receiving visitors, friends read together; books, their themes, characters, and authors were frequent subjects of conversation. Friends entertained one another by looking through albums of cartes de visite, often containing photographic portraits of celebrity authors, or collections of steel engravings, including images from books. On evenings sometimes called "literaries," families read together or took turns reading extracts from favorite books. They gave these presentations a visual dimension by staging tableaux of favorite scenes. At antebellum masques, the Hartford, Connecticut, elite dressed as fictional characters. At home, people entertained themselves with various card games, including one called *Authors* that became popular in the late 1860s and featured the portrait of a different author and the titles of his or her more famous works on each card (Fig. 9.3). In 1867 a Nevada mother reported that her children played *Authors* with "zest," and introduced guests at their house to the game. Other card games turned on familiar quotations from popular authors or names of popular fictional characters.[75]

Family portraits and stereographs reveal religious reading as a significant practice in domestic religious life. Jews read the Bible to observe holy days, such as Tishah B'Av.[76] For Protestants, Bible study was supposed to be a daily occurrence. Visual images often show a family group seated about a parlor table on which lies a Bible, sometimes alone and sometimes with other objects, including carte de visite albums, gift books, and stereoscopes. Such portraits suggest that the family followed the practice recommended by many authors of advice books on home management, decoration, or reading, even though few written sources mention such public devotions. With the Bible at the center of its life, a family might think, as one diary writer did, that home ought to be "a little heaven on earth."[77] Advice-book writers told readers to set aside a time for daily worship in the early morning and the evening, and on Sunday to save an hour for Bible reading before or after church services. The father was supposed to conduct the worship and reading services as the chief representative of God in the home.[78]

Bibles, especially the weightier and more decorated versions available in the marketplace, were often displayed in middle-class homes. A Bible might have gilt edges, an elaborately tooled or embossed leather cover, and a heavy clasp. Nineteenth-century publishers added supplemental material to help domestic readers better understand scriptures. Home Bibles often contained a concordance, chronological charts, tables of biblical weights and measures, maps of the Holy Land, and guides to proper names. Some Bibles added formal pages as repositories of births, deaths, marriages, and photographs and even more supplementary material such as the Lord's Prayer, information on the geology of the Holy Land, and elaborate illustrations. Families pressed flowers from weddings and funerals and locks of hair from deceased loved ones between pages. As the daughter of a pioneer to Colorado in the 1880s remembered, "We had a big family Bible . . . it must have been made to sell, certainly not made to read; it was too heavy unless one laid it on the floor."[79]

For many mid-nineteenth-century Americans, reading was both an edifying pastime and one crucial to social bonding. It entertained families and friends while supplying a common vocabulary and world of allusion and imagery. To reflect upon issues of the self and society, readers copied meaningful passages into quotation and commonplace books, recorded their thinking in journals and diaries, and wrote of their reading in letters to friends. Even though readers consumed tremendous numbers of books and magazines, many of them took time to capture and explore the import of authors' words for their own lives. Some felt that the settings, plots, characters, and vocabulary of books extended their ability to express emotions and describe thoughts. In readers' correspondence, commentary upon books had a conventional space along with mention of family doings and the weather. By borrowing phrases and lines, readers borrowed an author's authority, made their own ideas sound less ordinary, and reminded others of common experiences. Describing what reading mattered to distant friends helped correspondents share knowledge of one another's thoughts. As one reader said, "it is delightful to read the same books as our friends and be able to compare our thoughts with theirs."[80] In the 1860s and 1870s, one young mother regularly wrote her mother a four-page letter, usually devoting one page to a discussion of reading. The daughter told where she procured books, what she had been reading, and what she planned to read; she sometimes commented on the content. In 1870 she recommended Louisa May Alcott's *Little Women* (1868–69) and *An Old-Fashioned Girl* (1870). Though she called them "children's books," she deemed them the "best ones I ever read."[81] Another daughter lamented after her mother's death that the two usually spoke of frivolous subjects, except for their "conversations upon books and characters."[82]

Lines from books, applied to events outside the home, could make them familiar to readers within the home. A Civil War officer wrote his family in Delaware that they would know what he meant about life in camp if they imagined inserting "two lines of Ovid" into his letter.[83] To clarify what she meant, a daughter in an Iowa farm family that read Dickens described a visitor as standing "with an old hood tipt on her head [and] an old coat of Mr. Smiths over her slim skirts reminding me of Davy Coperfields Aunt Betsy."[84] Another reader, who wanted to tell her correspondent the extent of her distress, quoted from Sir Walter Scott's poetry: "what are hearts made of . . . flesh or stone?"[85]

Between a man and a woman, books sometimes played a role in negotiating the terms of the relationship and then in cementing it, literally helping to lay the foundations of a new home. Upon first meeting a young man, a young woman might estimate his character from his account of his reading. While courting, a couple often sat together reading, determining by their likes and dislikes their attraction for each other and finding ways to discuss their own thoughts and feelings in the religious and amorous sentiment of poetry and prose. They could reveal their selves by indirection and maintain standards of modesty, which banned explicit revelations.[86] In a mature relationship, a married couple often found joy and comfort in reading together. A Nevada diarist wrote that her husband read to her while she nursed a child. She cried, he laughed at her, and then "We both blubbered over the story and laughed at each other for so doing."[87] Sophie du Pont recalled after her husband's death that listening in the evening to him read and then conversing with him about it had been "the greatest of pleasures."[88] Men usually assumed the prerogative of recommendation and prescription. One man told his sister to avoid Mason Locke Weems's *The Life of Gen. Francis Marion* (1809) because it was "such nonsense, such vulgarity [that it was] not fit for a woman to read."[89] A suitor recommended to a Philadelphia woman that he did not "want her to read Mrs. Hemans because he thinks it will make a person too sensitive."[90]

Less frequently, women took the initiative. From the time her younger brother Henry went to school in Philadelphia until his first year at the United States Military Academy, Sophie du Pont wrote him about family household doings and her reading. Her "dear Harry" was not the reader she was, and she worried that he preferred novels. She advised reform, for his "liveliness and vivacity" had led him "to neglect cultivating a taste for reading books of an instructive nature." "Young people are always more fond of what excites the feelings and speaks to the fancy, than what requires the coolness of reason and reflection to enjoy. The perusal of so many works of the imagination produced its usual affect [*sic*], I mean, giving a distaste for all other kinds of reading." She wanted him to undertake more reading to improve himself, including works of history, government, and biography.[91]

Far more often than young men, young women seem to have used books to think about their future lives and how they wished to be known. Considering women authors, one female diarist concluded, "It is a remarkable fact that those women who have made themselves eminent by the display of the intellectual powers in their writings have almost universally been single — for example Miss More, Edgeworth, Hamilton, Taylor, Adams. I should not have said this was remarkable for it is almost incompatible to attend properly to the domestic duties of a family and to literary pursuits."[92] A young teacher, unsure of her vocational direction and the foundations of her religious belief, having just finished a biography of the founder of Mount Holyoke Female Seminary, Mary Lyon, felt herself incapable "of ever reaching her [Lyon's] standard, but if I might approach it, I should be glad."[93] Several women found that an old favorite, *Patronage* (1813) by Maria Edgeworth, provided a source for emulation. Sophie du Pont found "the characters of all the Percy family, are just what men and women should be; not the sentimental sighing among heroes and heroines of novels, but noble men, and truly fine women."[94] Reading also supplied a crucial means for exploring the meaning of religion within a familial framework. Former mill worker Harriet Robinson interpreted the Trinity so that it included a mother figure. Robinson's biographer concludes that she "remade the Trinity into the image of her own happy family."[95] As her own death approached, an older reader found in books, including a biography of Sir Walter Scott, answers that helped her sidestep the austere messages of Presbyterianism and reconsider her final extraterrestrial destination as a place for reunion with friends and family.[96]

By the 1880s, some cultural leaders had begun to denigrate the relationship between the home and literary culture. In William Dean Howells's *The Rise of Silas Lapham* (1885), John Rogers's decorative sculptures of Civil War scenes and fictional characters merit derision. Late nineteenth-century advisers on house decoration warned against decorating parlors or living rooms with ornamental books, "premium chromos," and "hideous plaster busts of popular men."[97] Gift books lost popularity and received belittling commentary. An 1885 biographer of Nathaniel Parker Willis, who had risen to prominence as a gift book editor and contributor, sneered at the genre and its illusions.

> It was a needlework world, a world in which there was always moon light on the lake and twilight in the vale; where drooped the willow and bloomed the eglantine, and jessamine embowered the cot of the village maid; where the lark warbled in the heavens and the nightingale chanted in the grove 'neath the mouldering ivy-mantled tower; where vesper chimes and the echoes of the bugle-ugle-ugle horn were borne upon the zephyr across the yellow corn; where Isabella sang to the harp (with her hair down) and the tinkling guitar of the serenader under her balcony made response; a world in which there were fairy isles, enchanted grottoes, peris, gondolas, and gazelles.[98]

As literary critics began to champion realism, they turned hostile to works that they termed less than masculine. Successful midcentury authors such as Willis and Stowe had written for undifferentiated middle-class readers; but now taste was changing. New writers and critics, including Howells and Henry James, gained prominence and wrote for discriminating readers seeking polished and refined cultural productions. Early twentieth-century critics accused Willis, Stowe, and their contemporaries of having avoided the pressing questions of the day and the sexual reality implicit in human relationships. Still other critics felt that social cachet had displaced moral growth as the objective of self-culture.[99] The material culture and organizational history of middle-class life, however, show that many of its members' tastes changed more slowly than those of literary critics.

Simultaneously, technology eroded the domestic life that had supported nineteenth-century literary culture. New inventions of the last quarter of the nineteenth century meant that reading and other domestic leisure activities now interacted in new ways, modifying how and where the middle class enjoyed books. Reading could become a more private experience in the age of electric light. Competition from entertainment such as vaudeville, film, and the phonograph would encourage the decline of reading as a social pastime. The links between the marketplace, consumers, and domestic life re-formed to make a new culture that we call modern.[100]

PART 3

City Streets and the Urban World of Print

David M. Henkin

·   ·   ·

In the historical imagination, the nineteenth-century American city appears as a place of cacophonous commotion, even as the reader sits in silent solitude, engrossed in the private pleasures of a novel. Much of the literature on the history of the book from the early modern era onward emphasizes the increasing privatization of the act of reading and illuminates its domestic setting. The public spaces of the bustling city would thus appear an unlikely locale to chart the power and impact of the written word in its modern incarnation.

But while printing had always exhibited an urban bias, during the middle of the nineteenth century, large American cities came to play an even greater and more hegemonic role in the expanding network of literate communication. In the 1850s, New York alone (which accounted for only 2 percent of the U.S. population) claimed 18 percent of the nation's newspaper circulation, handled 22 percent of its mail, and produced more than 36 percent of its publishing revenue. Together, the twelve largest cities boasted newspapers with a circulation amounting to about 60 percent of the national total, despite housing only 7.5 percent of the American population.[101] Although the development and extension of postal service, telegraphic transmission, newspapers, magazines, and novels promised to close the gaps between urban and nonurban life, this was not in fact what happened during the four decades surrounding the Civil War. Reading in urban America became both distinctive and paradigmatic. Big cities dominated the national print culture while nurturing new uses of the written and printed word.

America's growing metropolitan centers, which by the Civil War included such western places as Cincinnati, New Orleans, San Francisco, and Chicago, did not simply boast more presses and wider distribution networks.

Cities also hosted institutions of literary exchange and intellectual ferment in which ideas germinated and books circulated. The middle third of the nineteenth century saw the decline of an older type of intellectual sociability centered in the salon, the coffee house, the literary society, and the merchants' exchange in favor of new modes of impersonal interaction and circulation, modeled upon, but competing with, emerging establishments of commercial leisure. Urban reading institutions were increasingly oriented toward unidentified potential consumers. Though many of the new reading rooms and circulating libraries that emerged in big cities during the antebellum era originated as bulwarks against anonymity and promiscuity, the most successful and enduring of them grew in competitive collaboration with the penny papers, dime novels, theatrical performances, and oyster houses that epitomized the new urban environment.

City people produced and consumed books in distinctive patterns during the nineteenth century, but the impact of writing and print on city life went well beyond books themselves. Throughout urban America, living in a city involved frequent encounters with writing and continual reliance on printed artifacts. Even those forms of reading that seem unrelated to the exigencies of urban life had a disproportionate and peculiar impact in cities. City people were particularly dependent on paper money, for example, not only because of the urban location and identity of most of the institutions that issued currency during the state-banking era, but also because the promiscuous intermingling of bills and people from diverse points of origin increased both the variety of banknotes in circulation and the likelihood that a banknote would be the only thing to pass between two anonymous individuals. The introduction of uniform national currency in 1863 blunted the threat of such encounters by discouraging counterfeiting and obviating the need to assess the solvency of the corporations whose notes were in circulation. Banknotes thus required far less reading after the Civil War than before. Nonetheless, paper transactions remained characteristically urban by obscuring the forms of personal identity that anchored financial dealings in small towns and rural communities.

Similarly, the exchange of letters was far more common and conspicuous in cities, which received more frequent postal service and generated proportionally greater volumes of mail. In 1852, to take one measure, 28 percent of all letters mailed in the United States were posted in one of six cities (the five largest and San Francisco). New Yorkers in 1856 sent thirty letters per capita, more than six times the national average. Country mail, like country newspapers, conformed to slower rhythms and produced little in the way of outdoor frenzy and public assembly. In a semifictional 1839 account of life in

Michigan, Caroline Kirkland contrasted the much-anticipated pleasures of the small-town weekly mail with the urban experience of "those who get their letters and papers at all sorts of unexpected and irregular times . . . a dropping in at all hours, seasonable and unseasonable." Urban post offices were vehicles of unpredictable, promiscuous contact and sites of intense public sociability.[102] Here too the Civil War era marked an important transition, as a Republican Congress instituted free home delivery of letters in large cities and severed some of the links between private correspondence and public self-presentation. Even after home delivery became available, however, city post offices retained some of their distinctive character as spaces of anonymous circulation. In his 1869 guide to the sensations of New York, Junius Browne reported that the city's post offices were "the favorites of intriguers of both sexes, and are frequently made rendezvous for interdicted communication and illicit pleasures."[103]

If banknotes and mail were disproportionately urban in their origin and impact, other types of reading material were more peculiar to the experience of the metropolis. Certainly the urban institution that had the greatest impact on new reading practices was the metropolitan press (see Chapter 7, Part 1). By midcentury, cities had become both the site and the focus of a new form of daily journalism. Inexpensive daily papers appeared in New York, Philadelphia, Boston, and Baltimore during the mid-1830s, quickly becoming the best-selling journals in their respective cities and spawning a rash of followers, many of which folded during the depression of 1837. Those penny papers that survived grew substantially during the next decade and influenced both the content and conduct of their more traditional six-penny rivals. By the 1840s, cheap dailies such as the *New York Herald* and the *New York Tribune*, despite obvious differences in politics and style, had become recognized exemplars of a new urban journal, devoted to stories about the city in which they were published.[104] Changes in postal rates beginning in 1845 stripped the newspaper of its traditional privilege to circulate cheaply throughout the country at the expense of letter writers. By the middle of the century, the big-city press had undergone a crucial and surprising shift: instead of bridging geographical distances and eroding geographical differences, urban newspapers became more local.[105]

In America's large cities, newspapers began addressing specifically urban audiences and representing distinctively urban experiences. In this respect, the persistent and striking proliferation of small-town newspapers during the nineteenth century is potentially misleading. Urban newspapers bore little resemblance to their contemporary rural counterparts, which were typically weekly publications put out in small editions by printers whose principal business lay in other activities. Unlike these country papers and unlike most newspapers in smaller cities, which retained an integral relationship to partisan politics through the end of the antebellum era, metropolitan dailies of the midcentury devoted considerable attention to the timely reporting of local events and used a steady and varied supply of local advertising to become less centered on promoting a partisan agenda.[106] The cheap urban daily was a unique institution that transformed its readers' perceptions of community and institutionalized the *day* as a significant unit of news in their lives.

For the majority of Americans who lived outside the world of the big city, the revolutionary explosion of cheap daily newspapers during and after the 1830s had a different, much less direct impact. Articles from major urban dailies were frequently reprinted in the provincial press, while Sunday editions of daily papers circulated in significant numbers beyond the metropolis. Weeklies such as the *New York Ledger*, *Frank Leslie's Illustrated Newspaper*, and *Harper's Weekly* brought various urban scenes and sensibilities before a staggeringly large, mixed readership of city and country readers in the decades following 1850. Finally, individual copies of daily papers might enjoy an afterlife far from their point of origin. But in none of these cases did the particular urban experience of the new daily paper extend beyond the city limits.

For city residents, the newspaper appeared as part of the world of the street. Hawked by roving bands of newsboys, arrayed conspicuously in news racks, clutched by omnibus passengers, or posted to walls, the new dailies left the confines of the coffee house and jostled for attention amid a crowded cityscape. In the experience of many New Yorkers, Philadelphians, Chicagoans, and San Franciscans, news — however distant — broke first in broad view on public thoroughfares. Though authorized by a national print establishment armed with the latest cylinder presses and special access to telegraph wires, this news was mediated by the strident shouts of vendors or the outdoor commotion surrounding the release of an "extra." Walt Whitman learned of the outbreak of the Civil War, for example, walking along New York's Broadway on his way home from the opera: hearing "the loud cries of the newsboys," he proceeded to buy an extra edition of one of the local dailies. Then, instead of retreating to domestic privacy for a silent encounter with the printed page, Whitman joined a growing crowd of "thirty or forty," as they "listen'd silently and attentively . . . under the lamps at midnight" to reports of the firing on Fort Sumter. Such scenes of collective reading occurred frequently over the course of the war, institutionalizing the emerging public space of the newspaper as bulletin board. Herman Melville's 1862 poem "Donelson" is organized as a series of news bulletins posted on successive days before an anxious urban crowd. In between recording the conventional, pithy announcements northern city-dwellers came to know well during the war years ("GLORIOUS VICTORY TO THE FLEET!"; "WE SILENCED EVERY GUN"), Melville imagines longer verse reports that form the bulk of his poem. The social setting of "Donelson" was by no means imaginary. In 1865 New York lawyer George Templeton Strong spotted an announcement going up, letter by letter, outside the offices of the *Commercial Advertiser*. When fully assembled, the text of the bulletin advised him that Petersburg and Richmond had fallen and that the war had come to a close.[107]

By the time of the Civil War, the metropolitan daily and the city street were profoundly linked as arenas of public interaction. Both publishers and readers understood this relationship, which was captured most neatly in the rise during the early 1860s of a certain type of personal advertisement still familiar to modern city-dwellers. Sometimes these advertisements connected acquaintances who were otherwise unable to locate each other or who needed to exercise particular discretion. Other notices sought to re-create the circumstances of an initially anonymous public encounter between strangers. An item would announce, "If the young lady who, on Monday afternoon, at about four o'clock, took a Sixth Avenue small car at the corner of Varick and Water Streets, and left it at the corner of Waverly Place, and wore a black and white check dress, trimmed in front and below with black silk, edged with crimson, fur cape and muff and black bonnet with green velvet behind, desires to become acquainted with one who admires her very much," and the writer would provide a postal address.[108] Other personal advertisements referred explicitly to glances and acknowledgments exchanged in these encounters, optimistically invoking a private conspiracy but displaying it in full view. Like the streets on which they appeared, news sheets were spaces in which anonymous strangers could gain easy access to information, make quick public impressions, expose themselves to the gaze of others, and expect to meet one another again.

The metropolitan daily press anchored a set of outdoor reading practices that were intensely, and in several respects, promiscuous. Newsboys, in addition to hawking daily papers, would also distribute brothel advertisements and peddle obscene literature. One of these boys, Edward Scofield, was arrested in 1842 and again in 1847 for his participation in this trade. Ann Street in Lower Manhattan emerged as the main street of what one historian has called a "zone of printed erotica."[109] By the end of the period, distinctive texts and reading habits pioneered in and around New York's sporting press of the 1840s had spread throughout the bachelor cultures of America's largest cities. Richard K. Fox's revival of the *National Police Gazette* in the 1870s provided the centerpiece of this culture and became a constant presence in the spaces in which bachelors congregated for the next several decades.[110]

More broadly, the circulation of newspapers in public space belonged not simply to a promiscuous culture of male reading habits but to the larger category of ephemeral signage that became central to the midcentury experience of big cities. Like the broadside, the handbill, the trade card, the parade banner, and countless other written artifacts of everyday urban existence, big-city newspapers were addressed anonymously to residents and visitors as they passed through public space. Taken together, all of these texts formed an increasingly compelling and indispensable tool in the negotiation of city life. Traditional, face-to-face modes of advertising products, organizing collective action, and communicating with neighbors, which had served the needs of more compact and manageable cities in the early national era, gave way to a collage of words addressed in public space to an impersonal readership. Signs helped publicize and promote riots, rallies, parades, and celebrations and served as pivotal communication devices within the context of crowd activity. Inflammatory posters precipitated New York's Astor Place Riot (1849) and stirred Boston's response to the fugitive slave trial of Anthony Burns (1854). Meanwhile in San Francisco during the reign of the Committee of Vigilance (1856) and in Chicago in the aftermath of the Great Fire (1871), bills broadcast authoritarian visions of law and order. On less tumultuous occasions, placards and banners promoted the competing issues and candidates of rival political causes, introducing pithy aphorisms into popular political parlance. Ephemeral texts were equally important to the leisure culture of urban America, publicizing the attractions at Barnum's Museum, the concerts on Jenny Lind's national tour in 1850, or the performances of popular minstrel troupes. These light, flimsy, and mobile signs littered the streets, blending politics, religion, and entertainment in a shared language of urban publicity.

Alongside the ephemeral texts that evoked the transitory and chaotic features of America's unwieldy cityscapes emerged a class of sturdier, less flashy signs that covered buildings, blocked sidewalks, and dominated cityscapes. The sheer volume of this monumental signage was portrayed rather dramatically in 1857 when Chicago police captain John Wentworth decided to enforce a previously inert statute barring the obstruction of sidewalks by signs. Over the course of a single night, "Wentworth's Sign-Raid" netted a prodigious quantity of illegal urban landmarks and left them in a pile on State Street (Fig. 9.4).[111] All of this signage did not merely impede movement; it reinforced the sense that midcentury urban spaces were increasingly designed to be read.

THE "PILE" OF PRISONERS GUILTY OF OBSTRUCTING ON THE SIDEWALKS, ARRESTED IN THE STREETS OF CHICAGO, ON THE NIGHT OF JUNE 18. PHOTOGRAPHED BY C. H. LILLIBRIDGE, CHICAGO.

FIGURE 9.4. Depiction of John Wentworth's Chicago sign raid in 1857, from *Frank Leslie's Illustrated Newspaper*, 11 July 1857. The newspaper in which this engraving appeared made sly reference to itself and its Chicago agent in the left foreground of the image. American Antiquarian Society.

For newcomers entering the city for the first time, a legible cityscape offered an avenue of impersonal access to an unfamiliar environment. In what remains the classic description of a young man at the urban threshold in colonial America, Benjamin Franklin describes wandering pathetically through the streets of Philadelphia in the early eighteenth century, without acquaintances, a walking embodiment of urban ignorance and outsider status. Not knowing "where to look for Lodging," he fell asleep in a Quaker meeting house and set out the next day, examining the faces of strangers in search of a point of entry. Meeting a "young Quaker Man whose Countenance I lik'd," he approached and asked where strangers might find a place to stay: "We were then near the Sign of the Three Mariners. Here, says he, is one Place that entertains Strangers, but it is not a reputable House; if thee wilt walk with me,

I'll show thee a better." Franklin's guide vindicated the physiognomic diagnosis by personally escorting him through the city, offering insider knowledge as a necessary supplement to the inadequate iconic sign of the three mariners.[112] By contrast, a century later Horace Greeley arrived alone in New York, equally bereft of personal ties and resources, spotted a *written* "lodging sign," and thereby secured his first residence in urban America.[113] Such signs institutionalized the presence of the urban stranger and allowed residents and visitors with even limited facility with the Roman alphabet to make their way around without knowing or speaking to anyone. Signs proliferated not only in the dense older cities on the Atlantic coast but also along the urban frontier, where boosters and builders developed an acute self-consciousness about how their fledgling communities might appear to prospective settlers and investors. In Gold Rush San Francisco, to take the most documented example, local printers produced—and new arrivals posted—tens of thousands of illustrated letter-sheets and envelopes, many of which exhibit what one scholar characterizes as "a particular fascination . . . with signs on buildings" in the instant city.[114]

In this sense, urban texts during the middle of the century were the products of a network of sign painters, job printers, engravers, lithographers, daguerreotypists, municipal leaders, and commercial entrepreneurs, all of whom helped envision city streets from the perspective of the urban stranger. Marcus Ormsbee's 1865 photograph of Lower Hudson Street in New York neatly captures a slice of the artisanal world in which the everyday texts of urban America were manufactured (Fig. 9.5). Flanking a building shared by a druggist and a carpenter, Leonard Ring's sign-painting establishment and Croker's printing shop are classic exhibits in the new verbal cityscape. The human figures in the foreground are arrayed and subsumed under signs posted by tradesmen who clearly understood the photogenic appeal of the written word. Throughout this period, producers of urban signs and print ephemera typically collaborated or cohabited with those who specialized in the visual representation of the growing city. Often the two enterprises were combined under the same roof. New York's lithography firm of Sarony, Major & Knapp, which produced many popular city views during the 1850s and 1860s, also specialized in trade cards, posters, maps, and "labels of every description." In Philadelphia, leading antebellum lithographers such as Augustus Koellner and Peter Duval offered job services for making circulars, handbills, banknotes, and visiting cards alongside their more famous and enduring landscapes and urban portraits. Much like their entrepreneurial counterparts in the newspaper business, a new generation of job printers— drawing upon innovative techniques of visual representation and mechanical

FIGURE 9.5. Marcus Ormsbee's 1865 photograph of Lower Hudson Street, New York. Collection of the New-York Historical Society.

reproduction—produced the material culture of the city as well as its public image.[115]

The full array of tradesmen who printed and posted ephemeral texts for an urban public is hard to reconstruct, especially since many of these texts did not identify their makers, and defies easy categorization. But it is clear that numerous firms from all corners of the urban printing industry were engaged in the production and sale of signs, banners, and bills. In Cincinnati in 1840, for example, when that city's population barely exceeded forty thousand, an advertising directory in a popular guidebook listed eleven distinct businesses that explicitly catered to the demand for urban signage, eight of them involving print. Two of these were newspaper offices, one of which offered "Cards, Blanks, Pamphlets, Handbills, and every variety of Book and Job Printing," while the other promised to do "any kind of Printing at short notice, as Books, Pamphlets, Cards, Handbills, Steam-boat Bills, &c. &c." A third, the engraver and printer J. Brewster, sought the special attention of

"Druggists and others in want of beautiful Showbills and Labels," done in "his XYLOGRAPHIC style." The others included a paper warehouse, two type foundries, a book and job printer, and the stationer and bookseller E. Morgan & Co., whose five "Power Presses" could be used for "Circulars, Cards, Bills of lading, notes and Check books, printed at the shortest notice," when they were not busy churning out biographies of Tecumseh or directories such as the very volume in which these advertisements appeared.[116]

Such business patterns were typical; ephemeral urban texts formed an important sideline for printers, engravers, booksellers, and suppliers of varying degrees of prominence. Frank W. Brenckle, who achieved some stature in Chicago as a "society stationer and printer" and as publisher of the *Saturday Evening Post* in that city, began his career around 1871 as a boy who had expertise in printing handbills and visiting cards.[117] City directories from San Francisco in the late 1870s list printers under such categories as "Show Card Writers" and producers of "Advertising Signs." For the most part, sign painting belonged to a separate occupational category and was identified both in city directories and in its own advertising with house painting and ornamental painting. The Cincinnati painters O. Lovell & Son advertised their standing in "the Sign and House Painting business," and a New Orleans directory from just after the Civil War listed twenty-one businesses under that category. The line between sign printers and sign painters was not always firm. Shubael Childs, who was trained as a wood engraver in Boston, moved to the new city of Chicago in 1837 only to find little work in that trade. Expanding his repertoire to include sign painting, wood carving, and some printing, he remained in business until his death in 1870.[118]

Perhaps the most fascinating line of work that developed around the new habits of urban reading was that of the bill poster, an occupational status advertised in Chicago in 1855 and in San Francisco two decades later. George G. Foster, in his popular 1850 sketches, *New York by Gas-Light*, represented the bill poster as an intrepid connoisseur who, much like the author, prowled nearly deserted streets of the city late at night "with his hieroglyphic paper bed-blankets over one arm and his paste-bucket hanging upon the other."[119] From the perspective of the bill poster, the passions and pursuits of city people appeared in all of their variety and conflict. A lithographic cartoon from 1862, which was an advertisement for a bill-posting company, made the same point more humorously, depicting the awkward juxtapositions and collisions of urban life as the *Bill-Poster's Dream* (Fig 9.6).[120]

What this profusion of texts on city streets meant to readers is a big and unwieldy question, because there were so many readers. Signs, bills, banners, and newspapers were the most widely read texts in nineteenth-century urban

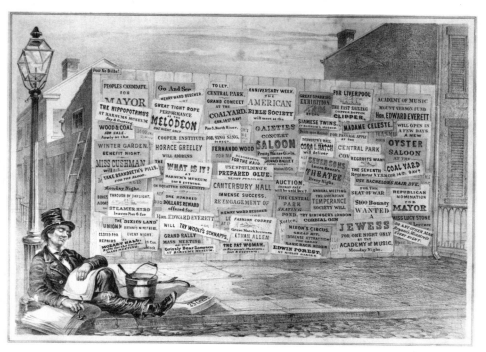

FIGURE 9.6. B. Derby's *The Bill-Poster's Dream: Cross Readings, to Be Read Downwards* (lithograph, 35 x 49 cm; New York: Ross & Tousey, 1862) depicts a riot of printed bills covering a fence, beneath the notice "Post No Bills!" American Antiquarian Society.

America. Every observer who noted the existence of a publicly posted word was also testifying to, and implicitly commenting upon, a reading experience, though much of this testimony lacks the self-consciousness recorded by readers of longer, more bounded texts.

Visitors to large cities in the United States were the most likely to reflect publicly upon urban signage. English travel writer Isabella Lucy Bird was struck in the 1850s that "large squares of calico, with names in scarlet or black upon them, hang across the streets, to denote the whereabouts of some popular candidate or 'puffing' storekeeper." A decade later, French visitor Ernest Duvergier de Hauranne noticed the same trend in New York toward "emphatic advertisement" and the same juxtaposition of commercial and civic concerns. "Everything is done in this way," he noted after spotting a recruitment sign for Civil War volunteers, "even serious things, even the purchase of human blood!" Others found more comfort in the spectacle of so many publicly posted words. British journalist Edward Dicey observed during the war that "all the shop-notices . . . are in English," which he cited in support of the proposition that "there is far less of a foreign look about New York than I had expected."[121]

Images of American cities after the Civil War suggest, not surprisingly, a greater number of signs in other languages, but English continued to dominate the legible cityscapes of the United States throughout the century. For many foreign arrivals, including Russian Jewish immigrant Abraham Bisno at the age of fifteen in 1881, city signs proved instrumental in mastering a new alphabet and an unfamiliar tongue.[122] Even English signs, however, could convey foreignness or heterogeneity. In his novelistic depiction of Cincinnati, German immigrant Emil Klauprecht mobilized city signage to represent the juxtaposition of social difference in the streets of the metropolis:

> The numerous signs and notices on the buildings are totally attuned to the prevailing confusion of tongues. Here old Mother *Germania* greets us from the midst of a faded sign of Hambach castle with the patriotic inscription: 'Lager Beer and Swiss Cheese'; over there is *Ireland* with a harp surrounded by a wreath of shamrocks. Here is *France* embodied in the person of the great emperor offering 'Boarding' to French laborers and travelers, while his neighbor, perfidious Albion at the 'Robert Peel,' serves 'Tom and Jerry' and pickled pigs' feet with a Pickwickian bow. Here, where a languid romantic tune with zither accompaniment sounds from a shop selling cigars and liquor, we stroll over to *Spain* at the 'Alhambra Exchange'; . . . a hop further lies *Hungary*, or the 'Kossuth House,' displaying an earnest bearded young man, a former Hungarian patriot.[123]

More settled urbanites were also wont to fill their diaries, letters, and published recollections with anecdotes about telling or striking signs that appeared in public space. Others registered their awareness of public texts in more brash and creative ways. Teenaged Martha Clements saw in the proliferation of playbills and handbills an opportunity to amuse or scandalize passersby. Cutting and pasting the printed words appearing in these bills, Clements rearranged them to form obscene messages, which she then pasted on her fence — much to the dismay of a neighbor who had her prosecuted for indecency in 1830.[124] The susceptibility of public signs to scandalous modification and reappropriation loomed larger as signs became a more ubiquitous feature of the American cityscape. A comic anecdote published during the Civil War era told of an urban sign painter who got only as far in one job as the words "dealer in all sorts of ladies" — and then fell and sprained his ankle. Until the next day, the story went, "citizens made themselves busy . . . in surmises, scurrilous innuendoes, and injurious quizzings; which could hardly be overcome when the finishing lettering '*and Gentlemen's ready-made Clothing,*' was at last added." [125] By the last third of the century, more urbanites had come to appreciate the fact that words published before an urban readership (much like other kinds of published words) acquired lives of their own that could subvert the controlling intentions of their original authors.

Of course, not all readers and writers wielded the same authority within this growing medium. Access to printing presses or even to the services of a job printer required money, and the right to project monumental epigraphs over the cityscape was granted selectively by a complex real estate market. Some of the power of urban texts, especially signboards, lay in the claims those texts made on behalf of their named proprietors. In a new model of sign use introduced in New York's Central Park during the 1860s, the authority of the sign over its readers became more explicit. While Frederick Law Olmsted gave direct instructions to remove commercial notices and ban inscriptions from the park grounds, an array of posted advisories guided visitors through the area and regulated their conduct. Signs proclaiming that "driving on central park at a greater rate [of] speed than 7 miles per hour is prohibited," or that "pedestrians are not permitted to walk along the drive," were among the earliest systematic uses of impersonal, permanent, and stationary signboards to govern public behavior in an American city.[126] While urban texts served the purposes of a bewildering array of authors, including small-time tradesmen, union organizers, antidraft rioters, and mischievous teenagers, some users staked a greater claim to the attention of readers than others.

Among readers, the distribution of access was also uneven. Though the overwhelming majority of adults, both immigrant and native born, in large northern cities were literate, not all read with equal facility or sophistication. Lengthy newspaper stories presented in dense columns of minuscule type often required a higher degree of literacy than the ability to sign one's name. Signs, handbills, and trade cards were much easier to read but were sometimes incomplete or deceptive. Jokes about newcomers to the city misreading public signs formed a staple of popular discourse about the city. The best known of these anecdotes, Barnum's claim to have duped visitors to the American Museum whose curiosity led them "to the egress," emphasized the hidden demands of ostensibly simple signs. Urban texts weeded out gullible readers, sometimes with more serious implications. Failure to discern the legitimacy of a banknote passed in a commercial transaction could prove more costly. The bank teller or clerk who could distinguish spurious notes from legitimate currency at a glance embodied a form of urban connoisseurship that figured more generally in the practices and culture of city reading. Urban texts were not private codes; they addressed readers inclusively and indifferently. Nonetheless, some readers claimed particular privileges as interpreters.

Widespread perception that city living required special reading skills helped sustain popular interest, both urban and rural, in texts that treated cities as mysteries to be elaborated and decoded in print. Under this general rubric, a host of publications sought to make some sense of the city, including some ostensibly straightforward reference works. Official city guides and directories, the first of which appeared in 1785 in Philadelphia, listed local businesses and offered practical information, often under the imprimatur of the municipal government. By 1840 city directories had become standard texts, typically seeking to represent a city's major public buildings and institutions as evidence of civic order and anchors of prospective economic growth. Many of these guidebooks featured pictures, enlisting the skills of leading lithographers and photographers to offer readers a sense of the frenetic metropolis as a manageable, legible entity. David T. Valentine's *Manual of the Corporation of the City of New York* (issued regularly during the 1840s, 1850s, and 1860s), the most famous of the official city guides, employed lithographs by the firm of Sarony, Major & Knapp to create an authoritative iconography of Lower Manhattan. In George Robinson Fardon's 1856 album of "beautiful views and public buildings" of San Francisco, published by forces sympathetic to that city's vigilance committee, photographic images of order and stability stood alone, unaccompanied by the information that characterized the more official texts. In both cases, the message was the same.[127]

Other midcentury guides to the metropolis dramatized rather than contained the chaos of urban life, promising to expose the hidden dangers and pleasures of the city to a readership that could remain at a safe distance. Instead of relying on the authority of the municipal corporation, the camera, or some imagined bird's-eye view of the city, this alternative model of guidebook (which drew on French precedents dating back to the beginning of the eighteenth century) invoked the privileged access of the urban connoisseur.[128] Foster's *New York by Gas-Light*, which originally appeared in the pages of the *Tribune*, stands as an early example of this extremely popular genre of sensationalist journalism. In rhetoric and imagery, these urban guides shared much with an emerging genre of melodramatic fiction: the city-mysteries novels modeled on Eugène Sue's *Les Mystères de Paris* (1842). From the mid-1840s on, many of the most successful works of nineteenth-century American fiction fit more or less comfortably within this category. The popular *Mysteries and Miseries of New York* (1848) by Ned Buntline (Edward Zane Carroll Judson), like its counterparts appearing first in serial installments in the popular press, was reprinted in a book format that quickly sold close to one hundred thousand copies. A slew of titles followed in its wake, turning every American city into the object of literary unmasking. Some of these novels, such as Henry Boernstein's *The Mysteries of St. Louis* (1851) and Emil Klauprecht's *Cincinnati; or, The Mysteries of the West* (1854–55), were published originally in German by immigrant authors. Other works that did not explicitly invoke Sue in their titles nonetheless belong to this genre, such as George Lippard's *The Quaker City* (1845), which sold sixty thousand copies in its first year and an average of thirty thousand more in each of the next five years—becoming the best-selling novel written by an American before *Uncle Tom's Cabin*.[129]

Despite the obvious differences between journalistic surveys of places and people in the contemporary city and lurid fictional tales of crime and tragedy, the boundaries between the two genres were porous enough that scholarly discussions of urban sensationalism often conflate them. Texts such as *Sunshine and Shadow in New York* (1868), *Lights and Shades in San Francisco* (1876), and *Boston Inside Out!* (1880), to name but a few representative titles, were not novels at all, but rather guidebooks. James McCabe's *Lights and Shadows of New York Life* (1872) interspersed sensational descriptions of vice with architectural illustrations, biographies of leading journalists and tycoons, and explanations of the workings of city government.

In the 1880s, these genres of city writing began to be displaced by more earnest forms of muckraking journalism and realist fiction. In other respects, it was the 1870s that signaled a new chapter in the relationship between cities and writing in the United States. Letter delivery had reduced some of the publicity involved in reading one's mail. State-authorized banknote issues had been taxed out of existence, and the task of sorting out the legitimacy of paper money had moved from ordinary consumers to the Secret Service. Chromolithography marked an important shift in the nature of trade cards and posters, emphasizing color and image rather than text. Significantly taller buildings and elevated railroad lines, especially in New York and Chicago, dwarfed the monumental signboards that had in many places dominated the cityscape. The 1870s also saw the rise of new paradigms of daily news, including the *New York Daily Graphic*, the *Chicago Daily News*, and Joseph Pulitzer's *Post-Dispatch* in St. Louis. Urban dailies thereafter would emphasize illustration, visual appeal, and an image of cities as more cohesive, less chaotic spaces.[130] One thing did not change, however: urban living continued to depend on distinctive practices of reading that remain as central to the identity of the city as noise, smell, and physical contact.

CHAPTER 10

Cultures of Print

Nineteenth-century Americans possessed multiple affinities and affiliations, which helped shape their individual and collective identities. These associational dimensions of identity — such as family, nationality, vocation, religion, and region — were often profoundly shaped by "cultures of print": specific sorts of reading practices, particular patterns and institutions of publication. Learned culture had connections to colleges and universities as well as historical, scientific, and kindred societies, many of them (notably the Smithsonian Institution) founded around midcentury. Among affinitive cultures of print, the ranks of learnedness were perhaps the most consciously exclusive: individuals could not simply choose to join. In this period, learned culture was in transition. The earlier professions of law, medicine, and the ministry were joined by academic versions of erudition, but the establishment of professional cultures with their own argots and associations lay largely in the future.

Other Americans developed print cultures based upon ethnicity. German American cultures of print may have been the most visible, because they were anchored by German-language publishers, separate schools in such cities as St. Louis, and other institutions. African Americans, particularly free blacks in the urban North, established vibrant reading communities, although their newspapers and occasional printing firms were more economically tenuous. Hispanic Americans produced varied cultures of print in western cities such as San Antonio, Santa Fe, Los Angeles, and San Francisco, as well as in eastern cities such as New York and Philadelphia (for a more extensive treatment of Hispanic American cultures of print, see volume 4 of *A History of the Book in America*). All of these groups shared certain tensions of living outside the Anglo-American, Protestant mainstream in an era of intense racism and xenophobia. In their reading, writing, and publishing, they attempted to mediate between cementing ethnic identity and associating themselves with mainstream values that included literacy itself.

It is more difficult to speak of regional cultures of print, for within any "region" there were diverse people and communities. However, in the years surrounding the Civil War and the transcontinental consolidation of the United

States, areas outside the Northeast were increasingly defined as distinct—by northeasterners and by their own inhabitants. Southern cultures of print, especially, revealed both the differences and the connections between "regional" and "national" identity. White southerners had varying degrees of literacy and connections to education and book culture, depending upon their location as well as their economic status. They might procure reading material locally, but that fare was local (newspapers), regional (expressly southern magazines and, to a lesser extent, books), and national (books and magazines published in America's metropolitan centers). Black southerners, most of them enslaved and barred from formal education before the Civil War, avidly sought to join the literate nation afterward. Their culture of print may have been the furthest from the learned cultures that took higher education for granted. But it quickly came to include schools and colleges, the institutions that would help blur the boundaries between race and erudition.

PART 1

Erudition and Learned Culture

David D. Hall

. . .

Ralph Waldo Emerson famously declared in "The American Scholar" (1837) that "books are for the scholar's idle time." This assertion of intellectual independence from the authority of the printed past was belied by Emerson's own reading and, as the history of learned culture between 1840 and 1880 reveals, belied as well by the ever-strengthening connections between the practice of scholarship and distinctive forms of print. These forty years saw remarkable changes in how those books deemed necessary or valuable were collected, described, and put to use. After 1840, Europe took on a fresh importance as the source of new disciplines and new models for how scholarship should be organized and as the training ground for scholars in the making. Not that Americans shed the moral and civic dimensions of learnedness that Emerson also articulated in 1837. For more than a few, the well-being of the nation or, as some would begin to say by midcentury, of "culture," depended on the authority of the learned to differentiate the sham, the temporary, or the merely utilitarian from forms of knowledge regarded as pure, enduring, or true. While clerical or gentlemanly ideals of learnedness lived on in such rhetoric, they were increasingly overlaid with an awareness of scholarship as requiring more substantial forms of patronage, institutions that encouraged collaborative work, and distinctive forms of print.[1]

In that context, six trends stand out: first, the founding of specialized periodicals, each coinciding with the emergence or clarification of academic fields; second, the accumulating of older books, many of them in languages other than English, on a scale hitherto impossible, a process closely linked with the strengthening of enumerative bibliography and a new attention to textual scholarship; third, the creation of additional sites of learned cultural production, such as the seminary, the research university with its graduate programs, the professional society, and the government bureau; fourth, heightened expectations about securing claims to priority of discovery, which in turn put new pressure on editors and publishers; fifth, a shift in intellectual relations with Europe, from merely keeping up or preparing translations, the focus of the 1840s and 1850s, to the possibility of Americans becoming productive scholars on the European model; and sixth, during the 1870s and as a cumulative consequence of the other trends, a clear tilt of the precarious balance between democratic inclusiveness and specialized exclusiveness in favor of the latter — a shift the consequences of which included the substantial exclusion of women from the ranks of learned culture. These six trends transcend the disciplinary boundaries that will help organize the following pages.

Scientific geology is a good place to begin. In the 1830s, a combination of interests — local learned societies, state governments wanting to enhance economic development, self-taught naturalists, some of whom also sensed the possibilities for economic gain — promoted geological surveys in state after state. Thus was launched the career of James Hall. Out of the New York state survey, where Hall cut his teeth as a surveyor, emerged the Association of American Geologists (1840), which held annual meetings in various cities. After absorbing another society, the newly founded American Society of Naturalists, in 1847 the AAG transformed itself into an institution that has endured to this day, the American Association for the Advancement of Science (AAAS). That same year, Hall published the first of the thirteen volumes of *Palaeontology of New York*, illustrated with lithographs based on drawings done by his wife. In New York, as in many other states, public support for such work was sometimes lacking, and Hall ended up financing much of the publication himself.[2]

A turning point for the nascent community of geologists had come in 1841 when, at the invitation of the Lowell Institute, the British geologist Charles Lyell arrived in Boston to give a course of lectures. During his travels around the country and again on a second trip in 1845, Lyell met almost everyone engaged in local surveys, all of whom were delighted to give him specimens that enhanced his own collections. In return, Lyell advised them on aligning local terminologies for geological strata with those he and others had developed for Britain.[3] In 1846 a young Swiss geologist, Louis Agassiz, arrived in Boston, also at the behest of the Lowell Institute. He joined the Harvard College faculty the next year. Connected as few locals were with the wider world of scientific periodicals, learned societies, and the practices of exchange arising out of them, Agassiz and Lyell embodied what the American geologists lacked but were eager to acquire. In the short run, however, Hall's interactions with Lyell and Agassiz underscored his own isolation, as he pointedly remarked in the preface to the first volume of the *Palaeontology*: "situated [in Albany] where I can have no recourse to scientific friends except by letters, with a scanty library of works on Palaeontology and no authentic collections for the comparison of species already described, I have been forced to depend upon my own resources in every department."[4]

The Yale geologist James Dwight Dana made his mark initially as an author of textbooks at a moment in the history of science when textbooks played a distinctive role in systematizing the state of knowledge. The aptly titled *System of Mineralogy*, issued in 1837 by a New Haven publisher, was taken over by Wiley & Putnam of New York in 1844. *A Manual of Geology* (1863) was published by T. Bliss & Co. of Philadelphia and copublished by Trübner & Co. of London, one sign among many of the international recognition Dana was acquiring. The four years (1838–42) he spent with the government-sponsored Wilkes expedition to the Pacific necessitated thirteen more years to complete his share of the expedition's reports, each limited to a hundred printed copies because political rivalries stinted governmental appropriations. Nor could Yale afford a professorial appointment until an admiring colleague, Edward Salisbury, endowed a chair for Dana. As Benjamin Silliman's son-in-law, Dana became associated with the *American Journal of Science* (1818–) and as its editor assured that it remained family property. Apart from textbooks and expedition reports, the most important venues for Dana's research and reflections were this periodical and, early on, the transactions of local learned societies.[5]

His was the common condition of American natural scientists. Scientific research required organization, substantial patronage, and publications with elaborate illustrations and tables of data that were expensive to produce. Periodicals were important as a means of keeping up with research elsewhere, but they were also acquiring a new significance in relation to timeliness of publication and claims of priority of discovery. To meet these needs, in 1839 the American Philosophical Society began to issue a new quarterly, the *Proceedings*, to compensate for the much slower pace of its *Transactions*.[6]

Other assistance came from the federal government.[7] The substantial bequest of the British chemist James Smithson, received in the United States in 1838, led to the creation of the Smithsonian Institution "for the increase and diffusion of knowledge." In 1846 the regents of the Smithsonian funds appointed the experimental physicist Joseph Henry, then a member of the Princeton faculty, to the new post of secretary. Henry, who saw clearly the need for an organization able to make timely grants to specialists and to publish their research in a dependable periodical, founded in 1848 the *Smithsonian Contributions to Knowledge* (1848–1916). As a scientist in his own right, Henry had experienced the frustration of being unexpectedly anticipated by others in the field and of having to circulate his own publications privately. Now, in addition to founding the *Smithsonian Contributions* and other periodicals, he sought to ensure that the Smithsonian received, by exchange, copies of the publications of learned societies throughout the Western world.[8]

Henry and others of like thinking fashioned an influential, albeit informal, social and political network that extended from Washington, D.C., to Cambridge, Massachusetts, and encompassed not only the Smithsonian but also the other federal agencies that supported research — the Naval Observatory, the Bureau of the Census, the Coast Survey, the Bureau of Ethnology. The annual meetings of the AAAS were invariably accompanied by informal fetes hosted by the well-to-do, affairs that could lead to federal money. Astronomer Maria Mitchell reported in 1855 that Alexander Bache, head of the Coast Survey and Mitchell's fellow member of the AAAS, made these social occasions "the opportunities for working sundry little wheels, pulleys, and levers; the result of all which is that he gets his enormous appropriations of $400,000 out of Congress, every winter, for the maintenance of the United States Coast Survey." Another AAAS member reported in 1868 that "by far the greatest good is done outside the walls of the section rooms."[9]

In the aftermath of the Civil War, Congress continued to finance a series of geographical surveys of the trans-Mississippian West. To cite but one example, the survey of the fortieth parallel, authorized in 1867, was planned and led by the young geologist Clarence King, with John Wesley Powell as his chief assistant. The resulting report (7 vols., 1870–80) — each of its volumes written by a different participant, replete with scientific tables, photographs, and engravings, and financed by the government — became a striking example of the requirements of such scientific publication.[10]

The opportunities, but also the limits, of the new scientific associations are revealed in the career of the upstate New York lawyer Lewis Henry Morgan, who became fascinated with the nearby Iroquois. The papers Morgan wrote about them were brought together in an important, though locally printed, book, *The League of the Iroquois* (1851). Five years later, Morgan attended the annual meeting of the AAAS, which offered support for his research. In 1865, after almost another full decade of ongoing investigations, he finally submitted a lengthy manuscript on comparative kinship systems to the *Smithsonian Contributions to Knowledge*. Much to Morgan's disappointment, the manuscript languished for five more years in the hands of editor Joseph Henry, delayed by the process of review and because it was the largest and most expensive book the Smithsonian had yet undertaken to publish. Ironically, it was to avoid such delays that Joseph Henry had instituted the *Smithsonian Contributions* two decades earlier, but the acclaim that *Systems of Consanguinity and Affinity of the Human Family* (1870) eventually received led to Morgan's election to the National Academy of Sciences and to the creation of a new subsection on anthropology, which he chaired, within the AAAS.[11]

To aspiring men of letters, the situation of the humanities and social sciences in 1840 seemed rather more precarious than that of the natural sciences. When Joseph Green Cogswell reflected on the condition of learned culture in New York City in 1840, he was pessimistic. A former educator who had been one of the earliest Americans to go abroad after the War of 1812 to study in Germany, Cogswell declared that the city had no university worthy of the name and no library comparable in size and quality to the great libraries of Europe.[12] Like the local and national learned societies, none of them truly national in scope despite their titles, colleges and seminaries commanded little in the way of resources — few paid positions, and these mostly involving rote instruction within a fixed curriculum; no scholarship funds to support postgraduate training; and meager holdings of scholarly books.

It is not surprising, then, that provincialism abounded. George Fitzhugh, who never attended college and only once traveled north of the Mason-Dixon line, lived quietly on a Virginia plantation as a self-described "desultory" reader, chiefly of British quarterly reviews, until the political crisis of 1848 in Europe aroused him to publish pamphlets, followed in 1854 and 1857 by two book-length critiques of "free society" and wage labor, each published locally in Richmond. The Protestant writers of New England who came to be known as "Transcendentalists" were only marginally better off. The influence on them of the British quarterly reviews, together with their efforts to obtain and translate the literature of German romanticism — a broader enterprise that involved Margaret Fuller and several other women — bespoke a dependence on European high culture and the fragility of any literary or religious avant-garde.[13] German idealism had another major outlet in Henry Brokmeyer, a disciple of Hegel who immigrated to St. Louis in the 1850s, where he found a few kindred spirits with whom he could share his translation of Hegel's *Logic*. Although the manuscript remained unpublished for want of money to subsidize such a massive book, the "St. Louis Hegelians" were able to launch the first purely philosophical quarterly in the Anglo-American world, the *Journal of Speculative Philosophy* (1867-93), in which the mathematician and philosopher Charles Saunders Peirce would begin to publish his philosophical work.[14]

The provincial nature of these developments must not be allowed to obscure the changes that were taking place in the structure and practice of scholarship in the humanities and the social sciences. Cogswell's postgraduate experience in Europe pointed toward one change that had several consequences: a veritable explosion in the number of Americans who, after 1840 and especially after 1865, went to Germany to receive advanced training.[15] One fledgling institutional setting affected especially by this development was the seminary. Here and in colleges sponsored by the Protestant denominations, the task of the learned was to sustain the authority of Christianity and, more specifically, the authority of scripture.[16] This task gained a new importance among those Protestants who came into contact with biblical scholarship as practiced in early nineteenth-century Germany.[17] The University of Tübingen had rapidly become famous as the capital of the "higher criticism" that treated the Old and New Testaments as historical documents, to be approached through the methods of history and philology in order to understand how scripture developed over time. Keeping up on this side of the Atlantic with German scholarship was no small challenge. At Presbyterian-affiliated Princeton Seminary, Charles Hodge, who was elected professor of Oriental and biblical literature in 1822 without knowing German at the time, created another journal dedicated to providing translations of and reports on European, chiefly German, scholarship, which he edited until 1871: originally titled the *Biblical Repertory* (1825), the name underwent several changes, but after 1837 was commonly known as the *Princeton Review*. Like its Andover Seminary-based rival, the *Bibliotheca Sacra* (1844-), it was transformed into a magazine concerned more generally with theology and the condition of the church.[18]

This commerce in books and information was almost entirely in one direction, from Germany to America, although Andover Seminary professor Edward Robinson's important *Biblical Researches in Palestine* was published in 1841 in London, Boston, and (translated into German) Halle.[19] But if books flowed west, people mainly traveled in the opposite direction, for by the 1840s it was becoming more common, and by 1870 almost a requirement, for scholars of the Bible and philology to engage in postgraduate study at a German university. The purpose in going was not to earn a degree. Rather, postgraduate education entailed listening to lectures, with many, if not most, of the Americans moving from university to university. One person who did travel west was the Swiss-born, German-educated Philip Schaff. Appointed a *privatdocent* in Berlin in 1843, that fall he accepted a professorship of church history and biblical literature at a German Reformed seminary in Mercersburg, Pennsylvania. There he introduced German concepts of development and historicism into what must have struck him as a quite different philosophical climate.[20] Moving to New York in 1863, Schaff used his remarkable administrative skills to develop two interdenominational organizations before being appointed a professor of church history at Union Theological Seminary in 1870. That same year, he was invited to organize American participation in a British-initiated project to revise the King James translation of the Bible. In 1880, one year before the revised New Testament was published to great acclaim, Schaff and a handful of others founded the Society of Biblical Literature and Exegesis.[21]

The full measure of German scholarship lay in its consequences for what would eventually come to be known as the humanities. At the center of this story were philology and history. William Dwight Whitney went to Yale in 1849 to study with Edward Elbridge Salisbury, who had graduated from Yale in 1836, went to Germany using family money to study Sanskrit and Arabic, and was appointed in 1841, without salary, to the Yale faculty as the nation's first professor of Arabic and Sanskrit. Drawing again on his personal resources, a year later he founded the American Oriental Society and became the editor of its journal. Whitney was the first person to seek advanced training with Salisbury, who in 1850 dispatched him to Berlin and Tübingen. When Whitney returned in 1853, Salisbury arranged a faculty appointment at Yale and personally paid his salary. Though Whitney remained extremely active in the Oriental Society, editing its journal for some twenty-five years and contributing half of its contents during this period, he also acted to enhance the authority of his own discipline, founding in 1869 the American Philological Association, which grew out of a discussion group in New Haven; in turn, the association began to issue transactions.[22]

The small community of philologists and their allies in classics and modern languages prepared many editions of texts and grammars in Hebrew, Greek, and the modern languages for an expanding classroom market. Whitney's work in this vein was overshadowed, however, by his extensive work with Sanskrit literature and grammar.[23] Others turned their attention to Old English, a subject taught and studied before the Civil War by a few southerners and after the war by a cluster of northerners, chief among them Francis Andrew March, whose contributions included a handbook titled *Method of Philological Study of the English Language* (1865) and *A Comparative Grammar of the Anglo-Saxon Language* (1870).[24] Basil Gildersleeve, a Virginian who studied in Germany, where he earned a doctorate in 1855, became the first person appointed to a chair at newly founded Johns Hopkins (1876). With the university's assistance, he created the *American Journal of Philology* (1880–), which featured regular reports summarizing the contents of European philological journals (the rationale being that most were not available in American libraries). Another goal was to publish promptly the latest scholarship by Americans and, if possible, by Europeans. In a choice of words that reflected the anxieties of authority among the humanists, Gildersleeve also wanted his journal to provide "specialist" reviews.[25]

Another fruit of the new discipline, and a sign of the transition to collaborative forms of scholarship, were the dictionaries prepared under the auspices of philologists. The fifth edition of Noah Webster's *American Dictionary of the English Language* (1868) was edited by Noah Porter of Yale, with Whitney and his Latinist colleague James Hadley among his assistants. (Porter had persuaded the dictionary's longtime publisher, Charles Merriam of Springfield, that the rise of philology had made Webster's own etymologies "notorious.")[26] A more substantial achievement of the American philologists was *An Encyclopedic Lexicon of the English Language* (6 vols., 1889–91), published by the Century Company and edited by Whitney. The emergence of philology as a discipline gave the humanities a new gravitas in colleges and universities. But the more far-reaching changes lay in how scholarship and the figure of the scholar were understood and how the study of texts was transformed. The eighteenth-century German classicist Friedrich August Wolf had argued for a rigorously historical or developmental understanding of texts and language.[27] Americans who studied in Germany were hampered in practicing critical scholarship in this vein until the movement after 1860 to introduce postgraduate instruction in colleges and universities. Henry Adams, who joined the Harvard faculty as a professor of history in 1871, trained his first doctoral students in a new kind of course, a "seminar" employing the "historical method." The outcome was a collaborative book that Adams personally financed, *Essays in Anglo-Saxon Law* (1876), containing the doctoral dissertations of three of his students, a longer essay by Adams himself, a five-page, closely printed list of "authorities," and a seventy-five-page appendix of Anglo-Saxon law suits translated from the Latin or Anglo-Saxon originals.[28]

Adams thanked two persons for assistance in translating from the Anglo-Saxon, Francis Andrew March and his older Harvard colleague Francis James Child. Child, who received an honorary doctorate in philology from Göttingen in 1854, spent much of his career preparing grammars and editions of texts, most notably a five-volume edition of the poems of Edmund Spenser (1855) with a historical and philological apparatus. But his heart was in a project that became driven by an ambition for completeness: an edition of English and Scottish popular ballads, based on manuscript and printed sources and involving the widest possible search for sources and parallels in other European languages, especially Old German and Old Norse. Working from manuscripts he studied during summers in Europe, Child enlisted copyists, collectors, and archivists in Britain, Scandinavia, and continental Europe to locate and provide him every possible version of the texts he needed, all of which he incorporated into the five-volume *English and Scottish Popular Ballads* (1882–98).[29]

At the outset of his career, Child could not have relied on the Harvard College Library, or any other institutional or public collection, for the books he needed. American scholars in the 1840s were required, perforce, to form their own private collections, as did George Ticknor in Boston, who assembled a 13,000-volume library, "the choicest collection of Spanish books out of Spain," in the course of writing a history of Spanish literature.[30] This situation began to change once the men who had gone to Germany began to campaign for better resources at home (see Chapter 9, Part 1). Ticknor himself played a key role in creating the Boston Public Library (chartered 1848), which benefited from an acquisitions fund of $50,000 donated by Joshua Bates that the trustees and librarian used to purchase books in Europe. To this nucleus were joined important donations or deposits: much of Ticknor's library, the 11,000 volumes owned by the radical minister and biblical scholar Theodore Parker, the collection of manuscripts and early New England imprints assembled in the mid-eighteenth century by Thomas Prince, and Thomas Barton's collection of editions of Shakespeare.[31] Justin Winsor, who became the librarian in 1868, undertook to inventory the Shakespeare quartos and folios owned in America and then followed with a bibliography of the Barton collection. By the time Winsor left to become head of Harvard's library in 1877, the Boston Public Library collection had almost tripled, in less than a decade, to 320,000 volumes. At Harvard, Winsor revolutionized access and cataloging practices by insisting that the library function as a "laboratory" to aid scholars and would-be scholars, a category that for him included the undergraduates.[32] In New York, a fruitful partnership evolved between librarian Joseph Green Cogswell and John Jacob Astor and, after the latter's death, his sons.

By 1853 the Astor Library, which Cogswell opened to scholars and eventually the general public, contained almost 80,000 volumes, a quarter of them classified as "history."[33]

Another New Yorker of great wealth, the bachelor and devout Presbyterian James Lenox, was also buying books during these years with the aid of two London rare-book dealers, the American-born Henry Stevens and the German-born Bernard Quaritch. Fascinated with the history of the Bible in English, Lenox sought every possible edition, in 1847 purchasing the first Gutenberg Bible to be owned in America. Like many other American collectors at midcentury, including his great rival, John Carter Brown of Providence, Lenox also valued Americana relating to the early discovery and exploration of the Americas.[34] Lenox was reluctant to share his extraordinary collections, however, as was another of this generation's great collectors, George Brinley of Hartford, Connecticut. Brinley came to own an amazing number of imprints relating to America, and especially early New England, though he too could not resist buying a Gutenberg Bible. Fortunately, when his library was dispersed at auction after his death in 1875, most of the choice items were purchased by institutions such as Yale and the American Antiquarian Society, thanks to a generous credit provided to them by the Brinley estate.[35]

The transformation in the scale and nature of private book collecting had immediate consequences for bibliographical practice in America. As collecting proceeded, dealers and buyers needed more precise information about old books in order to ascertain how rare or desirable a given copy was, a tendency fed by the collectors' preferences for specific authors and subjects and for ever-higher quality in the books they acquired. Thus emerged the earliest American efforts at systematic enumerative bibliography as a means of ordering the archive of print, and thus were assembled collections that in turn nurtured new kinds of scholarship. John Carter Brown relied on the bookseller and publisher John Russell Bartlett for some of his purchases and eventually employed him to catalog the collection. For the second edition of that catalog, printed in parts after 1875, Bartlett made significant improvements in his bibliographical descriptions.[36]

Meanwhile, Edmund Bailey O'Callaghan, a Catholic scholar and archivist of New York state, prepared a bibliography of the "Jesuit Relations," and the French-born Henry Harrisse, stimulated by his encounter with Samuel Barlow, a New York collector of Americana, studied the imprints relating to Christopher Columbus based on Barlow's holdings. Harrisse's *Notes on Columbus* (1866) was accompanied that same year by an effort, published as *Bibliotheca Americana Vetustissima* (1866), "to list every book which referred to America" printed before 1551. Henry Stevens was similarly ambitious. In 1848 he urged the Smithsonian to publish a work he promised to prepare, "Bibliographia Americana" to the year 1700, to encompass "all books relating to America . . . and all books printed in America," though the closest Stevens came to completing the project were proof sheets or printed catalogs based mainly on books that passed through his London shop.[37] A greater accomplishment was that of the New York book dealer and auctioneer Joseph Sabin, who decided in 1856 to attempt a comprehensive listing of books relating to America. The first part of his *Bibliotheca Americana: A Dictionary of Books Relating to America, from Its Discovery to the Present Time* was published in January 1867; by 1881, the year he died, Sabin had overseen the preparation of 80 parts, though the work, 172 parts in all, would not be completed until 1936. Less specifically bibliographical was a project of Hubert Howe Bancroft, a former midwesterner and ex-gold-rusher turned merchant and publisher in San Francisco. Bancroft, who became fascinated with the early history of the West and used his wealth to collect manuscripts and imprints relating to the Native Americans and the Spanish, employed contract writers and multitudes of copyists to assemble the five-volume *Native Races of the Pacific States of North America* (1874–75).

The passage from book collecting to bibliography was paralleled by the flowering of book collecting in areas that supported new kinds of scholarship, an example being work on Shakespeare. A New York journalist and man of letters, Richard Grant White, had previously become fascinated with the way the texts of Shakespeare's plays had been transmitted and had used his command of the texts to disprove, in essays published in *Putnam's Monthly* in 1853, an English scholar's claim to have discovered annotations in a 1632 folio that were contemporary with the playwright. Thereafter White edited a new edition of the plays, finding "all the necessary books," including copies of the First Folio, in the hands of a private collector and the Astor Library.[38] In Philadelphia, Henry Howard Furness, a lawyer, the son of a learned clergyman, and a great admirer of Shakespeare, organized with others the first Shakespeare Society in America in 1852, a social setting for talking about the plays and sharing books that the members owned. For Furness, the apparatus was everything. After his wife inherited a fortune in 1871, he devoted himself to preparing a variorum edition of each play, together with extensive citations to the interpretive or historical literature. The first five volumes, containing the texts of four plays, of *A New Variorum Shakespeare* were published by 1880, though the full series of twenty-seven volumes would not be completed until 1955. It remains, with Child's *Ballads*, the best example of how the "historical method" was beginning to transform textual study.[39]

Such transformations came at a price. To the young University of Michigan historian Charles Kendall Adams, the flourishing of historical study meant that newcomers and specialists alike were confronted with an "almost overwhelming abundance of materials." Responding to this situation, Adams prepared *A Manual of Historical Literature* (1882) for the purpose of separating the "best" authorities from others and indicating the "best order and method" of using books.[40] This genre of manuals or guides was needed in every field, not only history, as were guides to the burgeoning periodical literature, such as William F. Poole's *Index to Periodical Literature*, first published in 1853. These examples of dealing with periodicals offer but a taste of how knowledge was being assessed, stored, and retrieved at a time of great expansion in the quantity of scholarship published, principally in periodicals.

As part of the process by which learned culture was intellectually and institutionally reorganized between 1840 and 1880, it became more deeply male. The AAAS, for example, had admitted Nantucket resident Maria Mitchell to membership in 1849, in the wake of her prize-winning discovery of the first "telescopic comet" two years earlier. Mitchell, the most important female American scientist of the nineteenth century, was also elected to membership in both the American Academy of Arts and Sciences and the American Philosophical Society; in 1865 she became professor of astronomy at Vassar College. By 1872 there were forty-six women in the AAAS — about 7 percent of its total membership. But in 1873 the AAAS voted to institute a new elite membership category, termed "fellows," that would be open only to those members who were "professionally engaged in science, or have by their labors aided in advancing science." Such fellows would have to be elected by a process far more demanding than that required for ordinary membership. This new category — similar to strategies employed by many other American learned societies during the 1870s — responded to the need of many members of such organizations to assert their hard-won professional credentials (doctoral degrees, college professorships, government positions) and to distinguish themselves from amateurs and generalists. From the very beginning there had been opposition within the ranks of learned societies to admitting amateurs in the name of democratic inclusiveness, but only in the early 1870s did that opposition prevail. The professionalism it was attempting to institutionalize was largely gendered male (Figs. 10.1 and 10.2). Only two women became "fellows" of the AAAS between 1873 and 1880. Sometimes the association between professionalism and gender took on an openly aggressive edge. During the 1880 meeting of the AAAS, the American Chemical Society held a stag dinner at which members declaimed in verse and song the many troubles caused by women. The proceedings of this dinner were taken down in short-

FIGURE 10.1. Tompkins Matteson, *Dedication of the Dudley Observatory*, 1857. The ceremony on 28 August 1856, in Schenectady, N.Y., which took place during the AAAS meeting in Albany, was attended mostly by men, but a few women appear in the visual record of the occasion. Albany Institute of History and Art.

hand, printed privately, and distributed to the society's members under the title *The Misogynist Dinner of the American Chemical Society*.[41]

To be sure, none of these changes was by any means complete. As late as 1880, for example, the line between the specialist and the generalist, between professional and amateur, remained indistinct. During these decades, too, censorship on moral, religious, and political grounds remained an ever-present possibility, something southerners before the Civil War experienced firsthand, as did the men who studied biblical scholarship in Germany and young social scientists such as William Graham Sumner of Yale. For that matter, older clerical and gentlemanly ideals of learnedness endured and even continued to be dominant, albeit in somewhat modified form, as gender largely came to replace class as a determinant for acceptance into the club of the learned. Nevertheless, as some had begun to realize by 1880, the new tendencies were leading to an understanding of scholarship that increasingly

FIGURE 10.2. The Priestley Centennial of 1874, commemorating the anniversary of the discovery of oxygen, included a few women chemists, but they did not appear in the event's official photograph. Reproduced with the permission of the Special Collections Library, The Pennsylvania State University Libraries.

lay in tension with the Emersonian vision of the "scholar" as moral agent and prophet of culture.[42]

African American Cultures of Print

Jeannine Marie DeLombard

. . .

> Mrs Bacon. Mrs N. G. Bacon Miss ester armstrong & sister Ms
> Matthews Miss Cooper = Miss Jackson Miss Oliver presented to
> the said lodge a melodeon = Likewise Mrs A. Webber made &
> presented a handsome Grecian cover = for to cover the melodeon–
> also Mrs Freeman presented a handsome Stool A piece of poetry
> composed by A Webber especially for the Ladies = was sung; ac-
> companied by the composer . . . on the melodeon.
>
> 2 June 1859, Thermometer Book of Amos Webber[43]

The seventy-eight-year life of Amos Webber—janitor, Odd Fellow, Mason, and Civil War veteran—follows many of the currents that shaped free African

Americans' reading and publishing practices in nineteenth-century America. Born in rural Pennsylvania in 1826, Webber spent most of his life in the urban centers of Philadelphia and Worcester. Following his better-known predecessor, Henry Highland Garnet, Webber learned biblical lessons, along with the fundamentals of literacy, in a school founded by the Bethlehem Colored Methodist Church. But unlike the celebrated black orator and preacher, Webber spent his life engaged in unskilled labor as a servant, handyman, and messenger. The steadiness of this work, however, enabled Webber to buy a house in each city, allowed his wife Lizzie to work at home, and made them both solid members of the North's free black middle class. Webber and his wife were active in African American orders of the Odd Fellows, the Masons, and their female auxiliaries, for which Amos occasionally composed and presented speeches and poetry. Indeed, despite her illiteracy, Lizzie Webber, like Anna Murray Douglass (wife of the famous antislavery author and orator Frederick Douglass), participated in such indirect "reading" through her associational work. More literate than his wife, Amos Webber recorded and commented on these and other public activities in the "Thermometer Record and Diary" he wrote from 1854 to the end of his life in 1904. (In keeping with nineteenth-century Americans' fascination with tracking meteorological and scientific data, Webber carefully documented weather conditions twice daily over these fifty years.) The "Daily Pages" of his nine-volume journal chronicle a wide range of events, from the comings and goings of his coworkers to natural disasters, strikes, and elections. Incorporating clippings, transcriptions and other material from *Scientific American*, *Frank Leslie's Illustrated Newspaper*, and newspapers from Detroit and New York as well as his hometown of Worcester, Webber's "Thermometer Book" offers a rare record of one African American man's reading as well as his social and political commentary on that reading.[44]

Like other members of black organizations in the North, Webber engaged in a literacy that was both private *and* communal in nature; furthermore, like some club members, he entered print as both subject and author. His leadership role in local black organizations was frequently noted in the press, but he also wrote for the papers, publishing a letter to the editor in the *Worcester Evening Gazette* and contributing to the era's burgeoning black press as a reporter and columnist for the *Boston Advocate* in 1885 and 1886. Actively involved in local and regional black associational life, Webber made contact with African American communities stretching from Canada to Florida. Underground Railroad responsibilities may have been the impetus for Webber's 1859 trip to Canada, and if so, he probably encountered Ontario's significant community of expatriate African Americans. As a member of Company D in the

Fifth Massachusetts (Colored) Cavalry during the Civil War, Webber participated in capturing Richmond; he was still stationed in Virginia when, a mere seventeen days later, the American Missionary Association established freedpeople's schools in that city, which soon had a daily attendance of 1,500 students.[45] In 1881–82 his five-month sojourn to Palatka, Florida, where he was feted with a banquet by the local Masons, was duly noted in Florida's *Putnam County Journal*, a notice reprinted in the *Worcester Evening Gazette*.[46]

Of course, Amos Webber would not achieve the fame nor garner the scholarly attention of his fellow newspaperman and memoirist Frederick Douglass. Often described as the nineteenth century's representative African American, Douglass emphasized the ways literacy and publication transformed his own life. Beginning in childhood with his proscribed literacy and defiant self-education, followed by his organization of a Sabbath school for fellow slaves, membership in the East Baltimore Mental Improvement Society, and escape attempts using counterfeit written passes, Douglass's story culminated in his writing a string of popular personal narratives, as well as groundbreaking short fiction, and editing a series of respected newspapers. Unquestionably, Douglass's life and career reflect the centrality of reading, writing, and publishing to an African American political activism that engaged the slavery crisis as well as the nationwide struggle against racism, civic exclusion, and economic exploitation. But we should not allow Douglass's monumental shadow to obscure other stories.[47]

In addition to the slave narrative, belles lettres, and the abolitionist press, the mid-nineteenth century saw African Americans participating in other kinds of manuscript and print production, ranging from pamphleteering to diary keeping and the circulation of friendship albums. Likewise, the private, often secret, education of slaves was complemented by the development of African American literary societies, the struggle for black and integrated schools in the antebellum North, and the mass movement for freedpeople's education in the postwar South. In this sense, Amos Webber is an equally representative African American, for he shared in many of the defining characteristics of nineteenth-century black reading and writing: his church-based education, his associational activities, his political activism, his occasional print publication, his involvement in both the black and the mainstream press, and, crucially, his membership in an internally diverse African American reading community spanning the illiterate, the semiliterate, and the literate, as well as slave and free, northerners and southerners.

Like Douglass and other representatives of local, regional, and national African American communities, Webber occasionally seems to have endorsed uplift ideology: a belief that the elevation of poor and working-class African Americans was the responsibility of the black elite, who could ultimately achieve equality and defeat racism through education, upward mobility, and exemplary behavior. It bears noting that the very preliminary research on early African American reading, authorship, and publishing in the North has depended largely on the public and private records of those in the black elite and middle class. The same institutional and informal racism that restricted access to education and literacy throughout nineteenth-century America made African American reading and writing highly circumscribed forms of cultural expression in what was still very much an oral culture, both North and South. But even as comparatively privileged black Americans depicted participation in print culture as the gateway to political, economic, religious, and social inclusion in mainstream America, they were creating cultural forms, practices, and networks of their own.

In the antebellum years, when party politics and the legal profession effectively excluded African Americans, print offered an important venue in which to agitate for social and political change as well as to demonstrate to a white-supremacist dominant culture the equality of blacks as fellow human beings. Crucial to the transformation from the spoken to the printed word was the pamphlet, which often contained speeches or convention proceedings. In contrast to both the abolitionist-sponsored slave narrative and the struggling black press, the pamphlet offered black authors a unique degree of editorial autonomy because it was comparatively cheap to produce and disseminate. The exemplar of black pamphleteering remains David Walker, whose radical *Appeal, in Four Articles; Together with a Preamble, to the Coloured Citizens of the World* (1829) incorporated elements of African American oral culture (patterns of speech and preaching) and invited performance for the benefit of the illiterate.[48] Famously, Walker sought to reach this diverse audience by providing copies of the *Appeal* to a covert and still quite mysterious distribution network of fugitive slaves, itinerant preachers, seamen, and others who circulated through African American communities in the North and the South.[49]

Like the "Coloured Citizens of the World" to whom Walker directed his pamphlet, members of free African American communities were united rather than divided by their wide range of reading practices.[50] Combining moral uplift with education and politics and blending oral and print traditions, such organizations as Boston's Afric-American Female Intelligence Society, New York's Phoenix Society and Phoenixonian Literary Society, and Philadelphia's Colored Reading Society, Library Company of Colored Persons, and Female Literary Association had their origins in the mutual aid societies that mushroomed across the Northeast in the late eighteenth and early nineteenth centuries. Originally founded to ensure funds for burials and other economic exigencies, in the late 1820s and early 1830s these working-class organizations developed literary offshoots that sponsored a wide range of activities. In the increasingly segregated culture of Jacksonian America, local schools for African American students were either nonexistent, under-funded, or subject to racist attacks, and black readers could be denied access to public venues such as libraries and reading rooms. Literary societies carved a space for black readers, both novice and expert, to educate themselves and one another. Guiding their members' reading and creating opportunities for critical analysis of published works ranging from Greek and Roman classics to current African American newspapers, such organizations also encouraged the production, dissemination, and critique of original compositions.[51]

Typically organized along gender lines, African American literary soci-eties offered both sexes valuable lessons in political organization, even as they refuted long-standing racist assumptions of blacks' ignorance, laziness, im-morality, and even bestiality. With their constitutions, elections, and bylaws, these organizations were modeled on political communities. They offered protected spaces in which members could develop and refine oratorical, rhe-torical, and literary skills requisite to civic inclusion. For African American women caught between the urgent need for political activism and the intense pressure to conform to the prevailing bourgeois ideology of separate spheres, literary societies presented a socially acceptable forum in which to pursue educational opportunities, cultivate literary and political skills, and even on rare occasions address a public audience through the medium of print. Not surprisingly, both the early African American female orator and essayist Maria Stewart and the prolific black poet Sarah Forten were active in their local lit-erary societies.[52] The importance and influence of such societies extended to expatriate African American communities as far-flung as Liberia and Canada. In an 1861 speech delivered in Monrovia, the Episcopal minister, scholar, and educator Alexander Crummell called for "some influential persons" to "at-tempt to gather, in clubs or a society, the aspiring matrons and young women, in our communities, for reading, composition, and conversation upon im-proving topics."[53] Seven years earlier, journalist and teacher Mary Ann Shadd Cary had already organized such a group, the Windsor Ladies Club, the first women's literary society in Ontario, if not in all of Canada.[54]

The sociability, diversity, and activism that characterized African Ameri-can reading appear vividly in the journals of young Charlotte Forten (later Grimké). Granddaughter of eminent black Philadelphia businessman, aboli-tionist, and pamphleteer James Forten and niece of activist poet and lecturer Sarah Forten, Charlotte keenly felt a responsibility "to labor earnestly and faithfully to acquire knowledge, to break down the barriers of prejudice and oppression."[55] Moving at age sixteen to Salem, Massachusetts, in late 1853 to pursue an education in the local public schools (which, unlike those in Philadelphia, were racially integrated), Forten soon began keeping a diary. Begun in part to document "the interesting books that I read," Forten's journal provides a detailed record of not only the young woman's reading but also that of her friends and family.[56] Notwithstanding an acquaintance's complaint that "we never talked or read anything but Anti-Slavery" and her own lament, after having spent a pleasurable evening with "intelligent, well-educated people with good literary tastes," that "among *us* they are too rare," Forten's diary tracks the extraordinary number and range of publications exchanged by members of her circle in a seemingly never-ending round of visits and letters.[57] In addition to keeping up with the most recent antislavery newspapers, Forten and the households to which she was attached regularly read the *Spectator*, the *Atlantic Monthly*, and the African Methodist Episcopal Church's *Christian Recorder* (1852–1960). Possessed of limited funds herself, Forten nevertheless consumed print in a wide range of formats, from the most recent serial installment of Charles Dickens's *Little Dorrit* (1855) to an "English copy of Longfellow's poems," the elegant format of which enhanced "the fascination of the poetry."[58] An avid reader and writer of poetry and prose, Forten pursued an impressively broad course of reading that included classics such as Plutarch's *Lives* and different translations of the *Iliad*, as well as contemporary works like Thomas Babington Macaulay's *History of England* (1849–57) and David Livingstone's *Missionary Travels and Researches in South Africa* (1857). At the heart of Forten's reading community was the African American historian, journalist, and printer William Cooper Nell, whose direct access to both American and European publication-exchange networks ensured that every visit or letter brought "his usual budget of scraps for me to read."[59] Furthermore, Forten's friends and family showed each other selected passages from personal journals, shared letters, and exchanged drafts of unpublished poetry and fiction. In addition to her more formal participation in literary societies, reading clubs, lyceums, and school exercises, Forten read aloud and was read to at sewing circles, in sick rooms, and on seaside outings. For Forten and her circle, reading extended into other activities, such as performing tableaux, attending literary lectures, reciting poetry, acting in parlor theatricals, touring private libraries, and translating beloved works.[60] In a world where literary celebrities were becoming an important part of consumer culture, Forten and her friends sighed over engravings of "Scott and His Friends at Abbotsford" and "gazed admiringly" at the illustrations in *Homes of American Authors*.[61]

Despite her commitment to uplift ideology and to her own self-improvement through reading and writing, Forten could be quite frank about her dissatisfaction with some aspects of African American literate culture. Once, having spent part of a January day writing in a friend's "exquisite album," she commented in her own private diary, "Writing in albums is my special aversion."[62] Owned by her friend Sarah Remond, the album probably resembled the black morocco-bound volume filled with calligraphy and watercolors kept by Amy Matilda Cassey, founding member of Philadelphia's mixed-gender Gilbert Lyceum, the Philadelphia Female Anti-Slavery Society, and the national Moral Reform Association. African American women's friendship albums helped establish and maintain the elite, East Coast network of male and female friendship in which Forten and her family circulated. One can only speculate as to the reasons behind Forten's aversion: inscribed by both men and women and filled with sentimental effusions as well as occasional political commentary, these genteel volumes forged a distinctive identity among free African Americans even as they reinforced bourgeois ideals of femininity and confirmed one's inclusion in — or exclusion from — the North's black elite.[63]

Perhaps Forten simply felt her time could be better spent. Her disciplined reading regimen notwithstanding, Forten repeatedly deplored her own "want of energy, perseverance, and application," regretting at the age of twenty that "I have read an immense quantity, and it has all amounted to nothing, because I have been too indolent and foolish to take the trouble of *reflecting.*"[64] Forten's anxiety about her reading practices speaks to the larger cultural imperatives that shaped African American participation in print culture. Although she frequently expressed great pleasure in her reading, Forten, like many of her contemporaries, notably middle-class, northern African Americans, assumed that consuming fiction was a frivolous diversion from the civic and intellectual purposes of reading.[65] Nowhere, perhaps, was this attitude toward reading so clearly and persistently articulated as in the burgeoning black press, notably *Freedom's Journal* (1827–29) and the *Colored American* (1837–41).

Like Amos Webber, the young Forten both consumed and contributed to the periodical press, black-owned and otherwise, publishing her writing in the *Liberator* (1831–65), the *National Anti-Slavery Standard* (1840–72), the *Christian Recorder*, and the *Atlantic Monthly*.[66] But as activist T. Morris Chester would insist in an 1862 address commemorating the twenty-ninth anniversary of the Philadelphia Library Company of Colored Persons, African Americans had a special responsibility to support black newspapers. Asserting that "every family should subscribe for one if it is only to acquire the habit of supporting one of your own enterprises," he reminded his audience that political and literary considerations were just as important as economic ones, for African American newspapers "express your sentiments on all the great questions under discussion" and thus, by "subscribing for one, you not only encourage a sentinel guarding your liberties, but manifest a laudable desire to contribute to the success of your own literature."[67]

Nineteenth-century black newspapers were in dire need of such support: most were short-lived before the Civil War. Simultaneously advocating a political agenda, serving as a forum for African American writers, and conveying information was a difficult balance, made more challenging by the need to attract subscribers, donors, and advertisers.[68] The very few black newspapers that sustained extended print runs, such as Frederick Douglass's *North Star* (1847–51), *Frederick Douglass' Paper* (1851–59), *Douglass' Monthly* (1858–63), and his *New National Era* (1870–74), or Mary Ann Shadd Cary's *Provincial Freeman* (1853–59), depended heavily upon the celebrity of their editors, extensive fundraising campaigns, or infusions of cash from (often white) philanthropists.[69] The longest-running black newspaper, the *Christian Recorder*, survived on subsidies from its sponsor, the African Methodist Episcopal Church. (The current emphasis on journalistic objectivity should not obscure the importance of the *Christian Recorder* and the African American Protestant press more generally as an important black literary forum.)[70] For the most part, however, limited advertising and faltering subscription lists simply could not support an independent black newspaper over sustained periods. As Syracuse editor and activist Samuel Ringgold Ward diagnosed the problem in a wry postmortem of his own failed paper: "The *Impartial Citizen* breathed its last, after a lingering illness of the spine, and obstructions, impurities and irregularities of the circulation."[71]

Unlike diary keeping and pamphleteering, newspaper publishing was an intensely collaborative enterprise at all levels, including that of reception. Arguing that half of the nation's free people of color "might peruse, and the whole be benefitted," editors Samuel Cornish and John Russworm directed *Freedom's Journal* in the late 1820s to both literate and illiterate members of the black public. The ironically apprehensive comments of an anonymous white observer suggest that they were justified in doing so:

> a few years since, being in a slave state, I chanced one morning, very early, to look through the curtains of my chamber window, which opened upon a back yard. I saw a mulatto with a newspaper in his hand, surrounded by a score of coloured men, who were listening, open mouthed, to a very inflammatory article the yellow man was reading. Sometimes the reader dwelt emphatically on particular passages, and

I could see his auditors stamp and clench their hands. I afterwards learned that the paper was published in New-York, and addressed to the blacks. It is but reasonable to suppose that such scenes are of common occurrence in the slave states, and it does not require the wisdom of Solomon to discern their tendency.[72]

Such collective reading practices fostered a shared—and politicized—racial identity: the *Boston Daily Evening Transcript* had anxiously noted "a marked difference in the deportment of our colored population" after the publication of Walker's *Appeal*, affirming that "*we know* that the larger portion of them have read it, or *heard* it read."[73] But as the southern scene described above illustrates, such group reading also prompted discussion and debate. Politically and culturally generative as such dialogue undoubtedly was, it could prove disastrous to black periodicals that, unlike pamphlets, depended upon a sustained, committed, and, above all, unified readership.

The embattled history of the nineteenth-century black press reflects the tensions within the free black population in and beyond the North, as well as in the larger interracial reform community. Newspapers amplified and conducted the era's central debates within and across these constituencies, often at their peril. Noting that "From the press and the pulpit we have suffered much by being incorrectly represented," Cornish and Russworm had famously insisted in their inaugural issue that the time had come "to plead our own cause" in the pages of the nation's first black newspaper.[74] But what exactly should the black press advocate? Conflicts over tactics would shape the black press in the 1840s and 1850s. Frederick Douglass's gradual break with William Lloyd Garrison's abolitionism was prompted in part by his determination to edit his own newspaper, the *North Star*, an inevitable rival to the white abolitionist's influential but perpetually struggling *Liberator*.[75] Douglass's editorial partnership with activist and future novelist Martin Delany dissolved amid their growing discord over Delany's emigrationist agenda.[76] And tensions mounted between Douglass and Henry Highland Garnet when Douglass resisted Garnet's efforts to launch a national black press organization.[77] Farther north, Mary Ann Shadd Cary, at first an enthusiastic supporter of *Voice of the Fugitive* (1851–53), former slave Henry Bibb's newspaper for Canada West's expatriate African American community, was prompted to begin her own *Provincial Freeman* after an increasingly rancorous debate with Henry and Mary Bibb over the question of white philanthropy.[78] The black press revealed the spirited controversy that marked the diversity of African American communities within and beyond the United States.

With the rare exception of wartime papers such as the *Cincinnati Colored Citizen* (1863–69) and the bilingual *New Orleans L'Union* (1862–64), the coming of the Civil War posed yet another impediment to the black press. By 1890, however, nearly six hundred black publications had been founded throughout the reunited nation. Along with increasing racial segregation and thus concentration of African American populations, this explosion of black print activity was fueled by the effects of Reconstruction: more education, higher earnings, the sponsorship of social and religious organizations, and an audience of African American voters.[79] Post-Reconstruction African American periodicals reflected the breadth of their origins. No longer united by the crisis of slavery and a corresponding reform orientation, the black press added a fascination with sensationalism and "high society" to more traditional editorial commitments to moral uplift and political organization.[80]

During and after the Civil War, too, came unprecedented efforts to introduce systematized education to African Americans throughout the South. The first such efforts occurred very early in the war, when the American Missionary Association (AMA, founded in 1846 with the merger of several antislavery societies, and predominantly Congregationalist by 1860) opened a school for so-called contrabands in Fortress Monroe, Virginia, in September 1861. An interracial cadre of female and male teachers taught former slaves in Fortress Monroe, Port Royal, and eventually throughout the South, frequently under extremely difficult conditions: insufficient food, shelter, and clothing for students and teachers alike; the often involuntary wartime transience of scholars; and hostility and outright violence from white southerners and Union troops.[81] Students in freedpeople's schools ranged from those "too young even for the alphabet" to the elderly. Morning, afternoon, night, and Sabbath classes were held to accommodate the number and diversity of those who sought education.[82] Along with contrabands and emancipated slaves, the student body included black southerners who had enlisted as Union soldiers. The political symbolism of literacy for African American soldiers was particularly vivid: as one chaplain observed of Louisiana's Corp d'Afrique, "a majority of the men seemed to regard their books an indispensable portion of their equipment, and the cartridge-box and spelling book are attached to the same belt."[83] Complementing and competing with the AMA was the American Freedman's Union Commission, a coalition of northern secular societies and western religious organizations that embraced the nonsectarian, nonevangelical values of Garrisonian abolitionism.[84]

Along with these predominantly white organizations, free black southerners like teacher Mary Peake, literate former slaves like nurse Susie King Taylor, returning former fugitives like author Harriet Ann Jacobs, and free black northerners like Charlotte Forten played a crucial role in educating the freedpeople. So did such national and local African American organizations as the African Civilization Society, the African Methodist Episcopal Church, the Consolidated American Baptist Missionary Convention, and the Freedmen's Mutual Improvement Society.[85] African American teachers and organizations remained in the minority, however.

The Freedmen's Bureau, created in March 1865, did not have an explicit educational mandate but coordinated northern societies' efforts and laid foundations for public education.[86] Such organizations ostensibly aimed to "create a comprehensive system of black education that would enable the mass of freed people to read newspapers and labor contracts and write letters; provide them with rudimentary lessons in moral behavior and insure a steady, reliable supply of teachers of their own race in the years to come."[87] This broad pedagogical agenda accommodated conflicting ideological approaches. Some proponents of freedpeople's education seemed dedicated to producing a liberated, enlightened African American citizenry that would achieve economic mobility and uphold its civic responsibilities, thereby demonstrating its equality to whites and effectively challenging racism. Other aid societies emphasized the limits, not the rights, of citizenship, stressing obedience, not challenge to the political and social order.[88]

Many schools used standard primers familiar to beginning scholars throughout the nation, such as McGuffey's readers, Webster's spellers, Clark's grammars, and Greenleaf's arithmetic, all of which tacitly endorsed the same middle-class northern values and behaviors espoused by most of the teachers, regardless of race and institutional affiliation.[89] But other primers were created especially for freedpeople. The earliest, *The Picture Lesson Book* (1862), received approbation from the *Chicago Tribune*:

> On the title page, a neat vignette presents a colored child and a white teacher. Turning the leaf, and before an open cabin door we see seated a white teacher and his black pupil. . . . This book is the initial volume of a reform that turns a new page in history. It is the first book ever printed for the elevation and education of the black race, — the American slave. . . .
> In its general aspects, it is just such a stepping-stone to knowledge as you would throw down before the feet of your pet child, — neat and bold in typography, ornate with wood cuts, elegant in embossed muslin.[90]

The Congregationalist American Tract Society developed a "Freedman's Library" of primers, spellers, and readers, as well as a monthly paper and volumes of didactic prose. The *Freedman's Third Reader* (1865) and the *Freedman* (1864–69), its four-page monthly newspaper intended for both classroom and household use, reinforced themes of piety, domesticity, temperance, thrift, industry, discipline, and order, combining these textual messages with engravings that featured exemplary bourgeois white children and racially caricatured black characters. Although Lewis Tappan initiated the *Freedman* to counteract the influence of the *Anglo-African* (1859–65), another newspaper—the *Freedman's Torchlight* (1866), a four-page monthly published by the black-run African Civilization Society—proved a more direct competitor, offering reading, grammar, and history lessons in a black evangelical framework designed to inculcate racial pride. White abolitionist author and editor Lydia Maria Child offered yet another alternative with her *Freedmen's Book* (1865), which sought to affirm black intellect and activism through short biographies of famous black figures, such as writers Ignatius Sancho and Phillis Wheatley, scientist Benjamin Banneker, and leaders Toussaint L'Ouverture, Madison Washington, and Frederick Douglass.[91]

The difficulty of accurately gauging student perception of such texts is evident from white teacher Lucy Chase's intensely racist description of one pupil's response to an image in the *Lincoln Primer* depicting freedpeople as they celebrated emancipation: "One day a very black, thick-lipped, broadnosed, savage looking boy of mine . . . made the discovery of the picture and made merry, from his wooly crown to his shambling shoes, 'So glad they're free, dun gone and put it in a book!' "[92] More telling perhaps are the recorded attempts of individual black communities to exert control over their own and their children's education for the sake of racial pride and autonomy. Along with anecdotal evidence of the widespread preference for southern black teachers, these efforts are evident in the work of the Savannah Education Association (which ran autonomous black-supported schools with entirely African American faculty), the successful demand of freedpeople in Hagerstown, Maryland, to choose their own teacher, and the founding of an unaffiliated black school in Albemarle County, Virginia.[93]

Far easier to gauge is the postwar rise of African American higher education, particularly in the South, where Howard University (1867) and AMA-chartered colleges such as Atlanta University (1865), Fisk University (1866), and Hampton Institute (1868) quickly followed in the wake of Freedmen's Bureau–supported common, secondary, and normal schools. Joining such earlier northern institutions as Pennsylvania's Lincoln University (1854) and Ohio's Wilberforce University (1856), these institutions of higher learning initially focused largely on teacher training (in order to keep up with the demand for literacy education). They soon became central to the development of a black professional class and an African American intellectual establishment in the late nineteenth and early twentieth centuries.[94]

FIGURE 10.3. Winslow Homer, *Sunday Morning in Virginia*, 1877. In contrast to his better-known painting *The New Novel* (Fig. 8.2), painted the same year, this one placed reading in an explicit social and political context — the education of former slaves at the very end of Reconstruction — that served purposes other than the evocation of idle fantasies. Cincinnati Art Museum.

If, as Frederick Douglass famously proclaimed, the control of literacy was the source of "the white man's power to enslave the black man," then the "pathway from slavery to freedom" for African American men and women alike would appear to lie in the written word.[95] Accordingly, throughout the nineteenth century, a wide range of African Americans determinedly trod that path, from Amos Webber's recording scientific and political observations in his "Thermometer Book" and Charlotte Forten's documenting her rigorous reading regimen to freedpeople of all ages acquiring elementary literacy in fraught circumstances (Fig. 10.3). Toward century's end, African Americans would continue to assess and increasingly begin to debate the political, social, and economic value of literacy and print culture. The heated dispute between W. E. B. DuBois and Booker T. Washington over the relative merits of a liberal education as opposed to a technical one reflected a broader post-Reconstruction shift in emphasis, as African Americans turned their energies

CULTURES OF PRINT

from acquiring and promoting literacy to weighing the aims and methods of black education. But African Americans' relationship, both individual and collective, to reading and the printed word would endure as a pressing issue throughout the period that has become known as the nadir of black history — especially after the segregationist Supreme Court decisions in *Plessy v. Ferguson* (1896) and *Cumming v. Richmond County Board of Education* (1899). From the print campaign against lynching conducted by journalist and pamphleteer Ida B. Wells to the controversial attempts to preserve and convey oral black folk culture by "dialect" poets Frances Ellen Watkins Harper and Paul Laurence Dunbar, reading and publishing would remain crucial to African American political as well as cultural survival.

PART 3

Literacies, Readers, and Cultures of Print in the South

Amy M. Thomas

. . .

The South is a large chunk of a continent,
with a great accumulation of subregions that
elsewhere would serve for countries.
Michael O'Brien[96]

Upper South, Deep South, border states. Seacoast, piedmont, mountains. Plantation elite, slaves, yeomen farmers, free African Americans, rural and urban poor. The South's diverse geography is matched only by the diversity of its inhabitants. The region's geographies indelibly shaped its economics and politics and, in turn, southerners' abilities to become literate, gain access to reading materials, and use them in their daily lives. From 1840 to 1880, southerners experienced dramatic changes in the nature and meaning of literacy, reading, and print culture, as slavery, the Civil War, and Reconstruction influenced their lives. Acknowledging the diverse literacies, print cultures, and readers of the many "Souths" offers a rich history of the region and a national book history defined not in opposition to, but inclusive of, the diverse regions comprising it. Too often "the South" has played the role of the embarrassing second cousin below the Mason-Dixon line — illiterate and unwilling to support a native publishing industry. The story is much more complicated, and its details have implications for the North as well.

Literacy had multiple meanings for antebellum southerners. Enslaved African Americans saw literacy as a tool for communal advancement, resistance, and self-determination. Slaves in every southern state sought to become literate, despite meager learning conditions and restrictive laws. Federal Writers' Project interviews of ex-slaves, conducted in the 1930s, document the lengthy and laborious process enslaved people underwent to gain literacy. Rarely were slaves taught by a trained teacher or in a classroom; instead, most were self-taught, often using Webster's "blue-back" speller as their guide. Lack of access to materials made learning to write much more difficult than learning to read. The motive for overcoming these obstacles named most frequently by former slaves was the desire to read the Bible.[97]

Southern slaveholders understood the power of literacy for slaves and believed that controlling it was crucial to perpetuating the institution of slavery. At the same time, many slaveholders held the same Christian beliefs that inspired slaves to learn to read, and the imprint of these beliefs is seen in the history and nature of antiliteracy laws. Slaveholding southerners carefully distinguished between types of literacy for slaves: they saw writing as a dangerous tool that enabled slaves to escape by forging passes, but reading as an essential skill (and right) for practicing Christians. Until 1829, southern antiliteracy laws focused on prohibiting the teaching of writing and teaching slaves in groups. In response to David Walker's *Appeal, in Four Articles; Together with a Preamble, to the Coloured Citizens of the World* (1829), an antislavery text written by a free African American, Georgia passed the first law prohibiting the teaching of reading to individual slaves. Louisiana, North Carolina, and Alabama passed similar laws in 1830, as did South Carolina in 1831, after the Nat Turner Rebellion. The Alabama, Georgia, and South Carolina laws extended to free African Americans as well. Fear of texts like Walker's also prompted the passage of laws preventing the writing, printing, and distribution of antislavery materials in Georgia, Alabama, Florida, Louisiana, Mississippi, North Carolina, Tennessee, and Virginia. South Carolina had passed a law prohibiting the importation and circulation of antislavery literature in 1820.[98] Despite the passage of ever-stricter laws governing literacy, some Christian slaveholders resisted their implementation. In 1845, for instance, members of a Presbyterian congregation in Chester, South Carolina, owned 213 slaves, 23 of whom were church members, and almost all of them could read. In addition to religious beliefs, region (up-country versus low-country) and political perspectives (unionists versus nullifiers) also shaped South Carolinians' views of their state's antiliteracy laws.[99]

Regional variations also influenced the education of free African Americans in the South, particularly in their efforts to establish schools. Washington, D.C., was the southern city with the most schools for free African Americans—at least seventy-two. Nashville, Savannah, and Charleston also had many such schools, as did Mobile, thanks to guarantees made to Creoles under the Louisiana Purchase. In contrast, Richmond strictly enforced its antiliteracy laws, and free African Americans were forced to learn in secret. Although antiliteracy laws often applied to free African Americans, many were taught to read and write as conditions of apprenticeships. In North Carolina, for instance, the terms of indenture for free African Americans in the 1850s included provisions for teaching reading and writing skills.[100]

Similar regional differences shaped the education of antebellum southern whites. The common-school movement faced the same obstacles in the South as in the North: opposition to taxes and state control. In the South, the movement progressed unevenly and at a slower pace than in the North. In the coastal slave states, large slaveholders were concentrated in the east, and state constitutions ensured heavy representation from these areas. With an established history of providing education for their own children, planters had little interest in paying taxes to extend education to common whites. Residents of the piedmont and western regions of the coastal slave states typically were small farmers who held few or no slaves and who were interested in the creation of a common-school system. Residents of western Virginia fought throughout the antebellum period for common schools, but an eastern-dominated state legislature effectively undermined their efforts. In contrast, North Carolina developed the strongest common-school system in the South. Dominated by the piedmont region, North Carolina had lower rates of slaveholding than Virginia and South Carolina and an established tradition of antislavery sentiment, rooted in populous evangelical Baptist and Methodist churches.[101]

Local and statewide factors affected people's access to literacy and education in particular places. The Edgefield district in South Carolina is illustrative. In 1860, only a quarter of the children whose parents were landless attended school, compared to two-thirds of the children from the wealthiest families. In the poorest households, 20 percent of the dwellers were illiterate; in the wealthiest families, the number was 2 percent. But the causes of this disparity belie the stereotype that southerners opposed education. Located in the southwestern part of the state, Edgefield residents' views of education often differed from those of the state's coastal residents, who dominated the legislature. Edgefield's yeomen and middling classes petitioned the state legislature for a common-school system in 1811, and in response a "Bill to Establish Free Schools throughout the State" was passed. Seventy-five of Edge-field's wealthiest slaveholders immediately attempted to have the Free School Act repealed. When their efforts failed, they wielded political influence to undermine the effort to create a free school system. County school commissioners used public school funds to establish academies that would admit only wealthy families' tutored children. In 1847 Edgefield commissioners restricted free schooling to the children of parents who were indigent or unable to work or whose property was worth less than $500. These severe restrictions stigmatized public schools, and many eligible children did not attend. Most yeoman, artisan, and middling parents with children were neither poor enough to qualify for free schooling nor wealthy enough to send their children to field schools or academies.[102]

The same planter-elite views of education that thwarted common schooling for poor whites and restricted literacy for African Americans provided elite white women with access to the most advanced education available to women in the nation. The first college in the nation established to provide women with higher education equivalent to men's was Georgia Female College, founded in Macon in 1839. Women's colleges offered training in mathematics and the sciences, with the study of ancient languages lagging slightly behind. Ironically, elite southern women could enjoy a rigorous higher education because the planter class was confident that it would never be used, as it was in the North, to advance women professionally. Instead, education for elite southern women became a sign of their gentility.[103]

Reading also was a marker of gentility for women of the planter aristocracy. Reading and writing were crucial to plantation mistresses' developing identities. They read widely, from southern productions such as Augusta Jane Evans's *Beulah* (1859) and the *Southern Literary Messenger* (1834–64) to *Harper's New Monthly Magazine*, Dickens's *The Life and Adventures of Nicholas Nickleby*, and Madame Germaine de Staël's *Corinne*. Reading performed the conservative function of initiating women into traditional roles, while also enabling them to challenge those roles. In particular, reading fiction enabled slaveholding women to enter into "imaginative worlds" where they could explore and affirm aspects of their identities denied by their communities.[104] Their reading experiences parallel those of the white, middle-class Victorian women studied by Barbara Sicherman.[105] The uses of reading were the same—identity formation—but the norms for women's identities and gender roles differed. Region, though seemingly invisible, was one of the factors that shaped the reading experiences of white, middle-class northern women as well.

The reading experiences of individuals who belonged to the same social group could be dramatically different. Ann Hardeman joined her brother and sister-in-law's plantation household outside Jackson, Mississippi, in 1849 to care for the six children orphaned by her sister. An unmarried woman without property or income, Hardeman depended financially upon her relatives and had to be resourceful about gaining access to reading materials. For example, when a colporteur stopped at the Hardeman home in 1851, she "purchased (or my bro[the]r did for me) 2 vols of the 'Women of Israel' & 'Mammas Birthday.' "[106] She read the Sunday school library books the children borrowed, yet her choices were more than expedient: in 1852 and again in 1861, she copied a list of virtues (such as good temper and industry) from a book she identified only as "S.S. book called the 'Premium,' " suggesting that her reading and journal writing helped her create a sense of order in her often challenging life.[107] A devout Methodist, Hardeman found Grace Aguilar's *The Women of Israel* (1851) both instructive and entertaining. Her religious beliefs may explain the paucity of fictional works she read: only one entry in her seventeen-year journal mentioned a novel. Hardeman's experience also demonstrates the often idiosyncratic nature of reading. By 1860 the children were old enough that her daily responsibilities changed substantially, and her family began giving her a monthly cash allowance, but her reading did not change. She seems to have been an occasional reader by nature as much as by circumstance.[108]

David Golightly Harris's circumstances also led him to be an occasional reader, though his life differed considerably from Ann Hardeman's. A small farmer in the South Carolina piedmont, Harris represents both the middle group of white southerners (between the planter aristocracy and nonslaveholding yeomen farmers) and the majority of slaveholders, those who owned fewer than twenty slaves. Because his daily life was consumed with managing ever-expanding farm holdings, Harris's opportunities for reading were rare. Space and quiet were difficult to come by as well in the three-room house he shared with his wife and seven children: "I some times try to read, but the children are so noisy and troublesome that I lay aside my book and seek repose in bed." When he was able to read, Harris preferred nonfiction, such as Elisha Kent Kane's *The United States Grinnell Expedition in Search of Sir John Franklin: A Personal Narrative* (1854). He purchased his books on his monthly trips to nearby Spartanburg village: "To day I bought the life of T P Barnum. I anticipate grate pleasure in reading the history of the man of humbugery. To night I have finished reading the Explorations of Fremont in Rocky Mountains. I find it quite dull as a naritive b[ut] intere[s]ting as a history of an wild and unknowned section of the country." Harris sought both instruction and pleasure in Phineas T. Barnum's and John C. Frémont's works, an understandable expectation for a farmer with a limited cash income.[109]

Though he also lived in a small house with many household members, Thomas Wharton's urban location afforded him opportunities for reading that David Harris could only dream of. An architect for the New Orleans Custom House, Wharton's professional and personal interests led him to immerse himself in the city's culture of reading. He was an active member of the New Orleans Lyceum Library, which served the city's public school students and adult subscribers. In 1858 Wharton organized a lyceum lecture series as a library fundraiser on such topics as "the claims of the English language." He attended other lectures by visitors to the city, such as Ellen Key Blunt: "Her 'Evangeline' was good, but her best were 'Poe's Raven' and her father's 'Star Spangled Banner.' " He frequented the numerous booksellers in town, purchasing books for himself and his family members: with his supervisor, Major P. G. T. Beauregard, Wharton "Went off for half an hour to 'Steele's' & 'White's' and out [of] the stores of elegant volumes for the New Year selected each a 'gem.' " The Wharton household also attended art exhibits based on literary works, including the panorama of the *Grand Illuminated Historic Voyage of Dr. Kane's Exploration* at the Armory Hall and a tableau of *Pilgrim's Progress*, which his son found "deeply interesting," as they had read the book together. Wharton's experience suggests that differences between rural and urban life may have shaped readers' experiences at least as strongly as regional differences between North and South.[110]

Wharton's experience also demonstrates the dynamic nature of regional identity for readers. "Identities" is more to the point, for there were many layers to Wharton's regional identifications. Born in Hull, England, he had immigrated with his family to the United States in 1830 when he was sixteen. He moved to New Orleans in 1845 and resided there until his death in 1862. His active involvement in New Orleans' civic life, such as his tenure on the school board, and his support for secession and the Confederacy suggest that he deeply identified with his adopted home.[111] He was simultaneously English, American, southern, Louisianan, and New Orleanian. Like Ann Hardeman and David Harris, Wharton wrote self-consciously about southern identity only during the Civil War period. In this they were like most antebellum southerners who understood "region" primarily as the particular place in which they lived—New Orleans, Spartanburg, and Jackson—rather than "the South."[112]

The power of the local is reflected in their reading choices, particularly in the importance of newspapers and magazines to all three readers: Wharton was an avid reader of the *Daily Picayune*; Harris subscribed to the *Farmer and Planter*, a monthly magazine published in Columbia, South Carolina; and Hardeman read the weekly Nashville Methodist newspaper, the *Advocate*. Low subscription prices and eclectic, locally focused content made newspapers and magazines popular for southerners as well as northerners. Wharton's, Hardeman's, and Harris's newspaper and periodical choices reflect the breadth and diversity of reading material available in the local southern press.

At the same time, these readers selected reading materials that reflected national or American concerns. Many of the books they chose were published in the North, such as Harris's choice of Frémont's *Narrative of the Exploring Expedition to the Rocky Mountains in the Year 1842* (New York, 1846) or Hardeman's *The Two Friends* (Philadelphia, 1827), an American Sunday-School Union publication. None of these readers commented on where their books were published, suggesting that their identities as southerners and Americans comfortably coexisted. These separate yet related identities were embodied in other publications issued by both southern and northern presses. For example, Wharton, a recent convert, read Thomas F. Curtis's *The Progress of Baptist Principles in the Last Hundred Years* in 1858, and he may have chosen the first edition, published in Boston in 1855, or an 1857 Charleston, South Carolina, edition.[113] In December 1854, Wharton wrote his most animated journal entry about reading, recounting his "great interest" in the newly issued report on the New Orleans yellow fever epidemic of 1853. Published by the job printing office of the *Picayune*, the report was issued in a revised version by a Philadelphia firm in 1855 and a New York firm in 1857. There is no question why Wharton would be so interested in this publication, nor why it would quickly have national appeal.

The publishing history of antebellum southern authors also exemplifies readers' dual regional and American identities. For example, in 1834 Augustus Longstreet began publishing his humorous sketches about Georgia country and city life in his Augusta newspaper, the *States Rights Sentinel*. The *Sentinel* press issued the sketches in book form as *Georgia Scenes* in 1835, and their popularity attracted Harper & Brothers in New York, which published an edition in 1840 and was issuing a new edition of *Georgia Scenes* as late as 1897. In contrast, Caroline Gilman, Caroline Lee Hentz, Maria McIntosh, Mary Virginia Terhune, and Augusta Jane Evans became best-selling American authors by choosing northern publishers, with their larger market, extensive distribution systems, and higher royalties. They achieved their fame by transforming the northern domestic novel into a vehicle to promote and defend southern culture.[114] The best-known southern male authors—John Pendleton Kennedy, William Gilmore Simms, and Edgar Allan Poe—made similar choices. Poe and Simms, however, also contributed to southern publishing through journals: the *Southern Literary Messenger* and the *Southern and Western Magazine and Review* (1845), respectively. Such reviews were prestigious and promoted a distinctively southern literary culture. Indeed, periodicals published much of the South's intellectual work long before the late 1850s, when proslavery rhetoric was at its highest.[115]

The Richmond publishing and bookselling firm of J. W. Randolph demonstrates that a northern-based, national publishing industry did not obviate southerners' desires to produce and consume their own books. The more than three thousand titles listed in the firm's 1850 catalog of books for sale suggest that Richmond residents had access to a wealth of printed material, northern and southern publications alike. As a publisher in the state capital, J. W. Randolph focused on legal works, a key to the firm's longevity (1845–97). But it also sought to meet the broader needs of Richmond and regional readers by publishing works in the fields of agriculture and history, such as Edmund Ruffin's *Premium Essay on Agricultural Education* (1853) and reprints of Robert Beverley's *History of Virginia* (1855) and Thomas Jefferson's *Notes on the State of Virginia* (1853). Randolph also made room in its list for original southern literary works, including *Southern and South-Western Sketches* by a "Gentleman of Richmond" (1852), J. W. Page's *Uncle Robin in His Cabin in Virginia and Tom without One in Boston* (1853), and James Bartley's *Lays of Ancient Virginia and Other Poems* (1855).[116] The S. H. Goetzel firm of Mobile, Alabama, made the unusual choice for any antebellum publisher, South or North, to specialize in literature. The firm established itself in 1857 with the publication of Octavia Walton LeVert's *Souvenirs of Travel* and two books by Alexander Beaufort Meek, *Romantic Passages in Southwestern History; Including Orations, Sketches, and Essays* and *Songs and Poems of the South*, which went through at least four editions that year.[117]

Uncle Robin was one of three titles about slavery published by J. W. Randolph in the antebellum period out of fifty-eight titles issued by the firm, a proportion that supports the argument that antebellum southerners were not obsessed with slavery.[118] Though these works were a minor part of Randolph's list, they demonstrate how proslavery writings increased in tandem with the growth of the antislavery movement. Two of the three were published in the volatile 1850s. Page, who never published another work, felt compelled to respond to Stowe's *Uncle Tom's Cabin*, and Thornton Stringfellow's *Scriptural and Statistical Views in Favor of Slavery* (1856) further bespoke the powerful role of evangelical Christian beliefs for both proslavery and antislavery advocates. Thomas R. Dew's *An Essay on Slavery* (1849) was originally published as *Review of the Debate in the Virginia Legislature of 1831 and 1832*

(1832) by T. W. White of Richmond. Prompted by the Nat Turner Rebellion, the legislature's debate was marked by the long-standing political divisions within the state. Dew sided with eastern planter interests and devoted his essay to criticizing proposals for the gradual abolition of slavery advanced by representatives from western counties. His essay was reprinted in 1852 in *The Pro-Slavery Argument*, published in Charleston by Walker & Richards. Increasing sectional friction also marked the history of religious publishers in the South. The founding of separate southern publishing concerns, following divisions in the national denominations (see Chapter 6, Part 1), demonstrated southern efforts to establish a regional literature at the height of the power of national publishers — in this case, such religious publishers as the American Tract Society. It foreshadowed what happened to the southern world of print with the outbreak of the Civil War.[119]

Print culture was crucial to the creation of the Confederacy. New publishers came into being, and established firms transformed their production to meet the needs of the Confederate government and its people.[120] J. W. Randolph's legal line changed from a Virginian to a Confederate orientation. Many of the firm's new titles addressed practical topics for fighting a war, such as skirmishing drills and cooking for troops. Randolph published works for general readers as well, including songs and literary works, such as *God Will Defend the Right* by a Lady of Richmond (1861), William Shakespeare Hays's *The Drummer Boy of Shiloh* (1863), and Margaret Junkin Preston's *Beechenbrook: A Rhyme of the War* (1865). S. H. Goetzel's publications from 1863 show a continued appeal to diverse interests: *The Confederate States Almanac*, William Joseph Hardee's *Rifle and Infantry Tactics*, Sallie Rochester Ford's *Raids and Romance of Morgan and His Men*, as well as British authors George Eliot's *Silas Marner* and Charles Dickens's *Great Expectations*, among other works. The Confederate best-seller *Macaria; or, Altars of Sacrifice* (1864), by Augusta Jane Evans, was published by West & Johnston in Richmond (as well as by J. Bradburn in New York). *Macaria* held particular power for women readers, many of whom described it in their letters and diaries. Indeed, elite women read intensely for instruction and pleasure during the war, finding in books a sense of order and control that the war had undermined. White women increasingly claimed a public, political identity in their private writings and their published novels, songs, and poems.[121]

Newspapers and broadsides were particularly important publication formats for Confederate readers. The publication history of Mary Devereux Clarke's poem "The Battle of Manassas" (1861) is illustrative. Clarke wrote the piece as she traveled to an encampment where she would serve as a nurse. Her sense of immediacy was matched by that of an officer, who took her poem

FIGURE 10.4.
This page from *Norton's Literary Gazette* 2 (June 1852), a New York trade periodical, prints advertisements from regional booksellers, stationers, printers, and publishers located in such southern cities as New Orleans, Mobile, and Columbus, Georgia. American Antiquarian Society.

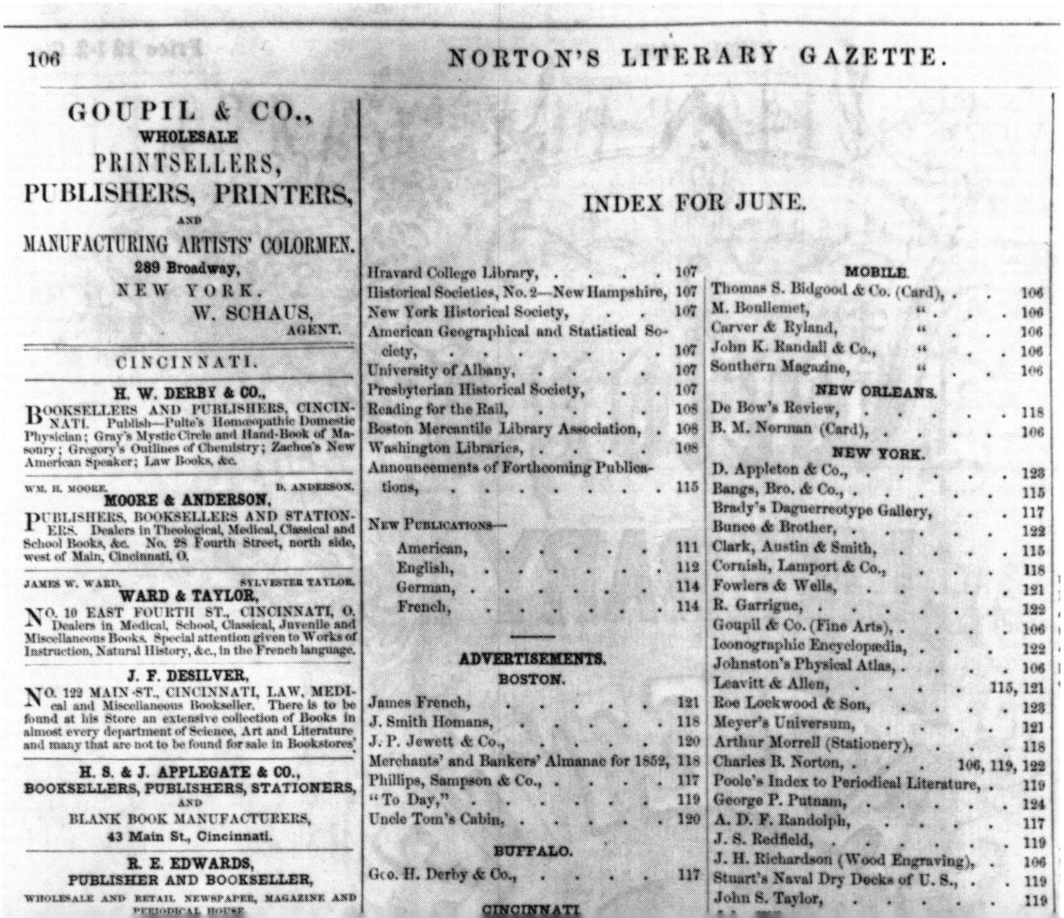

106 NORTON'S LITERARY GAZETTE.

GOUPIL & CO.,
WHOLESALE
PRINTSELLERS,
PUBLISHERS, PRINTERS,
AND
MANUFACTURING ARTISTS' COLORMEN.
289 Broadway,
NEW YORK.
W. SCHAUS,
AGENT.

CINCINNATI.

H. W. DERBY & CO.,
BOOKSELLERS AND PUBLISHERS, CINCINNATI. Publish—Pulte's Homœopathic Domestic Physician; Gray's Mystic Circle and Hand-Book of Masonry; Gregory's Outlines of Chemistry; Zachos's New American Speaker; Law Books, &c.

WM. H. MOORE, D. ANDERSON.
MOORE & ANDERSON,
PUBLISHERS, BOOKSELLERS AND STATIONERS. Dealers in Theological, Medical, Classical and School Books, &c. No. 28 Fourth Street, north side, west of Main, Cincinnati, O.

JAMES W. WARD, SYLVESTER TAYLOR.
WARD & TAYLOR,
NO. 10 EAST FOURTH ST., CINCINNATI, O. Dealers in Medical, School, Classical, Juvenile and Miscellaneous Books. Special attention given to Works of Instruction, Natural History, &c., in the French language.

J. F. DESILVER,
NO. 122 MAIN ST., CINCINNATI, LAW, MEDICal and Miscellaneous Bookseller. There is to be found at his Store an extensive collection of Books in almost every department of Science, Art and Literature and many that are not to be found for sale in Bookstores.

H. S. & J. APPLEGATE & CO.,
BOOKSELLERS, PUBLISHERS, STATIONERS,
AND
BLANK BOOK MANUFACTURERS,
43 Main St., Cincinnati.

R. E. EDWARDS,
PUBLISHER AND BOOKSELLER,
WHOLESALE AND RETAIL NEWSPAPER, MAGAZINE AND PERIODICAL HOUSE

INDEX FOR JUNE.

Hravard College Library,	107
Historical Societies, No. 2—New Hampshire,	107
New York Historical Society,	107
American Geographical and Statistical Society,	107
University of Albany,	107
Presbyterian Historical Society,	107
Reading for the Rail,	108
Boston Mercantile Library Association,	108
Washington Libraries,	108
Announcements of Forthcoming Publications,	115
New Publications—	
American,	111
English,	112
German,	114
French,	114

ADVERTISEMENTS.

BOSTON.

James French,	121
J. Smith Homans,	118
J. P. Jewett & Co.,	120
Merchants' and Bankers' Almanac for 1852,	118
Phillips, Sampson & Co.,	117
"To Day,"	119
Uncle Tom's Cabin,	120

BUFFALO.

Geo. H. Derby & Co.,	117

CINCINNATI

MOBILE.

Thomas S. Bidgood & Co. (Card),	106
M. Boullemet, "	106
Carver & Ryland, "	106
John K. Randall & Co., "	106
Southern Magazine, "	106

NEW ORLEANS.

De Bow's Review,	118
B. M. Norman (Card),	106

NEW YORK.

D. Appleton & Co.,	123
Bangs, Bro. & Co.,	115
Brady's Daguerreotype Gallery,	117
Bunce & Brother,	122
Clark, Austin & Smith,	115
Cornish, Lamport & Co.,	118
Fowlers & Wells,	121
R. Garrigue,	122
Goupil & Co. (Fine Arts),	106
Iconographic Encyclopædia,	122
Johnston's Physical Atlas,	106
Leavitt & Allen,	115, 121
Roe Lockwood & Son,	123
Meyer's Universum,	121
Arthur Morrell (Stationery),	118
Charles B. Norton,	106, 119, 122
Poole's Index to Periodical Literature,	119
George P. Putnam,	124
A. D. F. Randolph,	117
J. S. Redfield,	119
J. H. Richardson (Wood Engraving),	106
Stuart's Naval Dry Docks of U. S.,	119
John S. Taylor,	119

TERMS.

HALF COLUMN, each insertion,	. . .	$5 00
Do do six months,	. . .	25 00
ONE COLUMN, each insertion,	. . .	10 00
Do do six months,	. . .	50 00
TWO COLUMNS, each insertion,	. . .	18 00
Do do six months,	. . .	100 00
ONE PAGE, each insertion,	. . .	30 00
Do do six months,	. . .	150 00

AGENTS.

BOSTON,	A. K. Loring, with Phillips, Sampson & Co.
Do	Petridge & Co.
CAMBRIDGE,	John Bartlett.
NEW HAVEN,	S. Babcock.
PHILADELPHIA,	H. C. Baird.
BALTIMORE,	Jas. S. Waters.
CHARLESTON,	W. C. Richards.
ALBANY,	Joel Munsell.
BUFFALO,	G. H. Derby & Co.
CHICAGO,	A. H. Burley & Co.
CINCINNATI,	H. W. Derby & Co.
Do	R. E. Edwards.
LOUISVILLE,	Morton & Griswold.
Do	C. Hogan & Co.
NASHVILLE,	W. T. Berry.
ST. LOUIS,	John Halsall.
NEW ORLEANS,	B. M. Norman.

SAMPSON LOW, 169 Fleet Street, London,
Agent for England and the Continent.

and read it to his troops. He asked to publish it in the *Richmond Enquirer*; a North Carolina editor issued it in broadside form. Clarke wrote, "I have had applications for it from all parts of the Confederate states, and shall get the Edt. of the N.O. Picayune to issue it in New Orleans in the same style."[122] Thomas Wharton may have read Clarke's poem in the *Picayune*; his references to reading during the war are limited to newspapers. The same was true for David Harris, who hungrily read newspapers before he served in the army and when he was home on leave. Ann Hardeman made no references to reading, perhaps reflecting the disruption of her household, which relocated to Haynesville, Alabama, during the war.

The diverse reading materials published in the Civil War South were produced in extraordinary conditions. The experience of textbook publisher Sterling, Campbell & Albright is representative. Founded in February 1862 in Greensboro, North Carolina, the firm published the "Our Own" reader series, marketed in Virginia and South Carolina as well as North Carolina. The firm employed a hand press until it purchased a used, damaged Adams power press. In 1863 the bindery used by the firm was damaged in a fire, destroying seven to eight thousand dollars' worth of textbooks in sheets. A paper shortage in Greensboro forced the firm to search for supplies throughout southern cities. Unable to purchase stereotype plates in the South (the one southern manufacturer, located in Nashville, had been seized in February 1862), the firm purchased plates from an Edinburgh manufacturer in early 1864. The firm's textbook production for the Confederacy came to an end in May 1865, when United States military orders closed the press and banned the sale of its schoolbooks. Reopened in August, the firm began publishing textbooks again, edited by Federal authorities to remove passages redolent of proslavery sentiments and southern nationalism.[123]

The Confederacy took early steps to protect authorship and freedom of speech. In 1862 Secretary of War George Randolph expressed the hope that "this revolution may be successfully closed without the suppression of one single newspaper in the Confederate States, and that the experience may be able to challenge comparison with our enemy." Although many southern newspapers harshly criticized the Davis administration, none was ever suppressed.[124] In 1861 the Provisional Congress of the Confederacy transferred U.S. copyrights to the antebellum works of Confederate authors and granted new works copyright protection for twenty-eight years. The latter resolution also contained a groundbreaking provision to extend Confederate copyright protection to works by foreign authors. However, although southern publishers attempted to negotiate contracts with foreign authors, none succeeded because no country recognized Confederate independence.

Nevertheless, individual publishers attempted to honor the spirit of the Confederacy's international copyright as well as the familiar practice of trade courtesy: when S. H. Goetzel failed in his efforts to negotiate a contract with Edward Bulwer-Lytton for *A Strange Story* (1862), he sent the author $1,000, ten cents for each of the ten thousand copies of the novel published by his firm in 1863.[125]

The revolution of the Confederate printing and publishing industries was paralleled by a revolution in the education of southern African Americans. Efforts to educate freed slaves began early in the war, well before the Freedmen's Bureau was established in 1865. The first general report of the bureau's inspector of schools documented at least five hundred "native schools," established and maintained by ex-slaves, and Sabbath schools in every southern state, "all of them giving elementary instruction, and reaching thousands who cannot attend the week-day teaching." Formed in 1865 by the leaders of the African American community in Savannah, the Georgia Educational Association sought to supervise and offer financial assistance for schools throughout the state. By 1866 the agency was responsible for more than two-thirds of Georgia's schools for African Americans.[126] The act creating the Freedmen's Bureau made no provision for education; lacking the economic resources to establish schools, the bureau instead coordinated the efforts of southern African Americans and northern benevolent societies. By 1869 the bureau was overseeing the education of more than 150,000 students who attended approximately three thousand schools. Regional patterns from the antebellum period continued to shape school development. For example, the northern benevolent societies concentrated their efforts in Virginia and North Carolina and in areas liberated early in the war, such as Louisiana and parts of South Carolina. Postbellum school development progressed more quickly in cities than in rural areas. In Alabama, more than half the counties lacked schools; eventually, with Freedmen's Bureau assistance, schools were developed in neglected areas such as Selma and Tuscaloosa.[127]

After the war, African Americans worked to make universal schooling part of southern state constitutions. When Congress failed to pass a civil rights bill outlawing segregated schools, Reconstruction-era state conventions became the site for grappling with this controversial issue. Only Louisiana and South Carolina banned legal segregation. Other state constitutions remained silent on the issue, and the states later passed restrictive laws after readmission to the Union.[128] Political legacies from the antebellum period shaped the debates and outcomes in each state. For example, unpropertied Virginia whites, who had gained the right to vote only in 1851, were apprehensive about extending civic rights to African Americans. Elite white convention representatives, concerned that free schooling would erase distinctions between lower-class whites and African Americans, used the issue of segregation to divide Republicans of the two races. When the General Assembly outlawed integrated schools in 1870, African American Virginians concentrated on securing control and adequate funding of their schools. White southerners, particularly those denied access to public schooling in the antebellum period, supported the development of public schools once segregation calmed their fears of race mixing. But that was not the whole story. In Spotsylvania, African Americans and unpropertied whites joined in 1872 to vote for public schools.[129] By 1872 in Texas, 1,500 schools educated more than half of the state's children. By 1875, approximately half of Mississippi's, Florida's, and South Carolina's children, black and white, were enrolled in school.[130] In the late 1880s, however, Jim Crow laws began to reverse these gains.

The growing body of southern readers embraced reading materials of all types. Newspaper and periodical publication increased dramatically during the 1870s. In Mississippi, for example, the 14 newspapers in print at the end of the war grew to 111 in 1870, with a circulation of 71,868.[131] Newspapers published by and for African Americans were founded in all states, including the *Arkansas Weekly Mansion* (Little Rock), the *Africo-American Presbyterian* in Charlotte, North Carolina, the *Georgetown Planet* in Georgetown, South Carolina, the *Southern Sentinel* in Talladega, Alabama, the *People's Advocate* in Alexandria, Virginia, and the *Black Republican* in New Orleans. Many postwar literary magazines relied on the eclectic contents essential to antebellum weekly newspapers' appeal, such as *Scott's Monthly Magazine* (founded in Atlanta, 1865), *The Land We Love* (Charlotte, North Carolina, 1866), and the *Richmond Eclectic* (1866).

The end of the war saw southern publishers and authors return to prewar patterns of publication. Some publishers, such as Mobile's S. H. Goetzel, did not survive the war. After a few lean years, the J. W. Randolph firm of Richmond returned to its prewar list, with legal works at the center, complemented by almanacs and agricultural and business-related titles. The firm, which became J. W. Randolph & English in 1868, continued to publish original literary works as well, such as *Riego; or, The Spanish Martyr: A Tragedy in Five Acts* (1872), by John Robertson, a Lynchburg, Virginia, judge. Augusta Jane Evans, author of *Macaria*, though a fervid supporter of the "lost cause," returned to northern publishers, and her *St. Elmo* (1867), published by Carleton of New York, became one of the most popular novels of the nineteenth century. Like Augustus Longstreet in the antebellum period, Joel Chandler Harris first began publishing his Uncle Remus tales in the *Atlanta Constitution* in the late 1870s; their popularity led them to be published in *Scribner's*

Monthly and then issued in book form by D. Appleton & Co. of New York and Houghton, Mifflin & Co. of Boston.

David Harris's and Ann Hardeman's postwar reading choices suggest that the Civil War did not leave a permanent divide along the Mason-Dixon line for readers. Soon after the war ended, Hardeman and Harris read books published in the North. On 3 June 1866, Hardeman's sister read aloud *The Household Bouverie; or, The Elixir of Gold: A Romance by a Southern Lady* (1860), published in New York.[132] (Catherine Ann Ware Warfield, the "southern lady," like Evans, returned to her northern publisher after the war.) Harris devoted his Sunday reading on 8 September 1867 to a Beadle & Co. dime novel, James Lorenzo Bowen's *The Missing Bride: A Story of Life in the West* (1867): "A book of but little importance, but it served to beguile the tedious day." This was the first time that either reader mentioned reading a novel, a change that may have been rooted in the growing popularity and acceptance of fiction nationally. For Hardeman, it may have been that her religious strictures against fiction lessened a bit as she aged; she was sixty-three when her sister read her *The Household Bouverie*, and she died two years later, in 1868. As before the war, neither Hardeman nor Harris felt compelled to note the place of publication of their reading material.

Harris did note the place of publication of his postwar newspapers. In February 1868, he wrote, "Some time ago I subscribed to three newspapers: the *Weekly Age*, Philadelphia, the *Day Book*, N.Y., & *The Metropolitan Record*, N.Y. To day I have read them & find it pleasant to read the writing of a good Democrat."[133] The subscription choices of this Civil War veteran demonstrate how complex regional and political affiliations could be in this time period. The full title of the *Day Book* was the *New York Weekly Day-Book Caucasian*; when "Caucasian" was dropped from the masthead in the early 1870s, the newspaper added the inscription "Devoted to white supremacy, state equality, and federal union." It appears that Harris looked to the North for a Democratic newspaper because the Spartanburg newspaper that survived the war, the *Carolina Spartan*, moderated its sectional politics. The *Spartan*'s prewar motto, "Devoted to Southern Rights, Politics, Agriculture, and Miscellany," was changed to "Devoted to Education, Agricultural, Manufacturing, and Mechanical Arts" in the postwar period. Harris's newspaper subscriptions also illustrate the impact on an individual reader of the dramatic growth in newspaper and periodical publishing in the 1870s (Fig. 10.5). A year after Harris began reading northern newspapers, a second newspaper was founded in Spartanburg, but its editor was a Republican. A few years before Harris's death in 1875, three additional newspapers were founded, and Harris may have found support for his political views in the local press.[134]

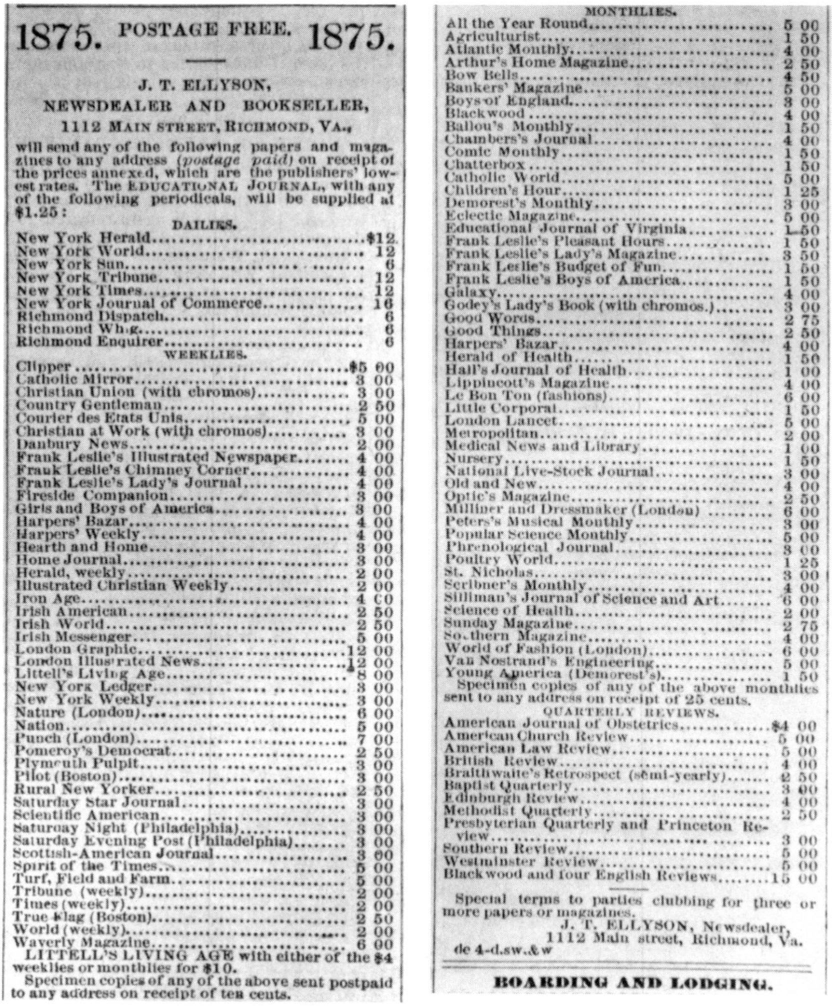

1875. POSTAGE FREE. 1875.

J. T. ELLYSON,
NEWSDEALER AND BOOKSELLER,
1112 MAIN STREET, RICHMOND, VA.,

will send any of the following papers and magazines to any address (*postage paid*) on receipt of the prices annexed, which are the publishers' lowest rates. The EDUCATIONAL JOURNAL, with any of the following periodicals, will be supplied at $1.25:

DAILIES.

New York Herald	$12
New York World	12
New York Sun	6
New York Tribune	12
New York Times	12
New York Journal of Commerce	16
Richmond Dispatch	6
Richmond Whig	6
Richmond Enquirer	6

WEEKLIES.

Clipper	$5 00
Catholic Mirror	3 00
Christian Union (with chromos)	3 00
Country Gentleman	2 50
Courier des Etats Unis	5 00
Christian at Work (with chromos)	3 00
Danbury News	2 00
Frank Leslie's Illustrated Newspaper	4 00
Frank Leslie's Chimney Corner	4 00
Frank Leslie's Lady's Journal	4 00
Fireside Companion	3 00
Girls and Boys of America	3 00
Harpers' Bazar	4 00
Harpers' Weekly	4 00
Hearth and Home	3 00
Home Journal	3 00
Herald, weekly	2 00
Illustrated Christian Weekly	2 00
Iron Age	4 00
Irish American	2 50
Irish World	2 50
Irish Messenger	5 00
London Graphic	12 00
London Illustrated News	12 00
Littell's Living Age	8 00
New York Ledger	3 00
New York Weekly	3 00
Nature (London)	6 00
Nation	5 00
Punch (London)	7 00
Pomeroy's Democrat	2 50
Plymouth Pulpit	3 00
Pilot (Boston)	3 00
Rural New Yorker	2 50
Saturday Star Journal	3 00
Scientific American	3 00
Saturday Night (Philadelphia)	3 00
Saturday Evening Post (Philadelphia)	3 00
Scottish-American Journal	3 00
Spirit of the Times	5 00
Turf, Field and Farm	5 00
Tribune (weekly)	2 00
Times (weekly)	2 00
True Flag (Boston)	2 50
World (weekly)	2 00
Waverly Magazine	6 00

LITTELL'S LIVING AGE with either of the $4 weeklies or monthlies for $10.

Specimen copies of any of the above sent postpaid to any address on receipt of ten cents.

MONTHLIES.

All the Year Round	5 00
Agriculturist	1 50
Atlantic Monthly	4 00
Arthur's Home Magazine	2 50
Bow Bells	4 50
Bankers' Magazine	5 00
Boys of England	3 00
Blackwood	4 00
Ballou's Monthly	1 50
Chambers's Journal	4 00
Comic Monthly	1 50
Chatterbox	1 50
Catholic World	5 00
Children's Hour	1 25
Demorest's Monthly	3 00
Eclectic Magazine	5 00
Educational Journal of Virginia	1 50
Frank Leslie's Pleasant Hours	1 50
Frank Leslie's Lady's Magazine	3 50
Frank Leslie's Budget of Fun	1 50
Frank Leslie's Boys of America	1 50
Galaxy	4 00
Godey's Lady's Book (with chromos.)	3 00
Good Words	2 75
Good Things	2 50
Harpers' Bazar	4 00
Herald of Health	1 50
Hall's Journal of Health	1 00
Lippincott's Magazine	4 00
Le Bon Ton (fashions)	6 00
Little Corporal	1 50
London Lancet	5 00
Metropolitan	2 00
Medical News and Library	1 00
Nursery	1 50
National Live-Stock Journal	3 00
Old and New	4 00
Optic's Magazine	2 50
Milliner and Dressmaker (London)	6 00
Peters's Musical Monthly	3 00
Popular Science Monthly	5 00
Phrenological Journal	3 00
Poultry World	1 25
St. Nicholas	3 00
Scribner's Monthly	4 00
Silliman's Journal of Science and Art	6 00
Science of Health	2 00
Sunday Magazine	2 75
Southern Magazine	4 00
World of Fashion (London)	6 00
Van Nostrand's Engineering	5 00
Young America (Demorest's)	1 50

Specimen copies of any of the above monthlies sent to any address on receipt of 25 cents.

QUARTERLY REVIEWS.

American Journal of Obstetrics	$4 00
American Church Review	5 00
American Law Review	5 00
British Review	4 00
Braithwaite's Retrospect (semi-yearly)	2 50
Baptist Quarterly	3 00
Edinburgh Review	4 00
Methodist Quarterly	2 50
Presbyterian Quarterly and Princeton Review	3 00
Southern Review	5 00
Westminster Review	5 00
Blackwood and four English Reviews	15 00

Special terms to parties clubbing for three or more papers or magazines.

J. T. ELLYSON, Newsdealer,
1112 Main street, Richmond, Va.
de 4-d.sw.&w

BOARDING AND LODGING.

FIGURE 10.5. Advertisement in the *Richmond Daily Dispatch*, 22 January 1875, by Richmond newsdealer and bookseller J. T. Ellyson, listing more than one hundred periodicals, few of which were published in the South. American Antiquarian Society.

Readers' regional and national identities became even more complex as they sought to understand the meanings of the Civil War. The postwar period witnessed an explosion of biographies of Confederate commanders, published by both southern and northern presses, often simultaneously. For example, James D. McCabe Jr.'s *Life and Campaigns of General Robert E. Lee* (1866), the first biography of Lee, was published by the National Publishing Company, a Philadelphia-based subscription firm with offices in Atlanta, St.

Louis, Cincinnati, and Davenport, Iowa.[135] J. W. Randolph & English's *The Life and Campaigns of Major-General J. E. B. Stuart* (1885) also carried the imprint of Boston's Houghton, Mifflin & Co. In the 1880s, the Richmond publishing firm increased its offerings of fiction, most of which depicted the Civil War era, such as Mary Jane Haw's *The Beechwood Tragedy: A Tale of the Chickahominy* (1889), an expanded version of a short story she published during the Civil War. After more than fifty years of publishing and bookselling, Randolph closed its doors in 1897.

A number of southern authors rose to national prominence in the late 1870s and early 1880s, as readers, southern and northern, hungered for depictions of life during and before the Civil War. Two stories published by George Washington Cable and Thomas Nelson Page in *Scribner's Monthly* (renamed *Century Illustrated Magazine* in November 1881) reflected the diverse perspectives on the present and past that southerners held in the post-Reconstruction period. Page's "Marse Chan" (1884) offered a nostalgic look back, including an idealized view of slavery in Ol' Virginia, infamously articulated by Sam, the slave who has served Marse Chan since his birth: "Dem wuz good ole times, marster—de bes' Sam ever see!"[136] Yet even as Page told a seemingly simple story with, as many critics argue, a racist agenda, he offered readers a complicated view of the Civil War. Marse Chan, like his father, was a Whig who opposed secession and the war, enlisting only after Virginia declared for secession. By making Sam the story's central narrator, Page, wittingly or not, humanized his African American character in ways not seen before in southern literature. Readers then and now are led to see the world through Sam's eyes and have been often more struck by the depths of his humanity than that of his noble "Marse Chan."

George Washington Cable also set his post-Reconstruction literary works in the past, and in "Madame Delphine" (1881) he delivered a searing critique of both time periods. When Madame Delphine denounces the Black Code preventing her daughter Olive, an octoroon, from marrying a white man, crying, "They do not want to keep us separated; no, no! But they *do* want to keep us despised!"; and when her counselor and friend, Father Jerome, implores his parishioners, "God help you, monsieur, and you, madame, . . . to beat upon the breast with me and cry, 'I, too, Lord—I, too, stood by and consented,'"[137] many readers would have seen in Cable's depiction of 1820s New Orleans a mirror image of the present, as the Compromise of 1877 enabled every southern state to enact Jim Crow laws. Cable was so concerned about this trend that he turned to writing essays on the topic, all of which were published in the *Century*. His essay "The Freedman's Case in Equity" (January 1885) was answered by Henry W. Grady's "The New South" (April 1885), to which Cable responded with "The Silent South" (August 1885). The *Century* published a number of letters to the editor as well, each articulating a slightly different view of the issue.

Rather than choosing one position, the editors of the *Century* published works by authors whose diverse perspectives mirrored those of their readers, northern as well as southern. As a May 1885 editorial stated, "The country, the section, or the man that is not an infidel to truth, will never fear honest freedom of debate." Much work remains to be done before history of the book scholarship reflects the specificity and diversity of the views of the South presented in the *Century*. The literature written by post-Reconstruction southern authors provides a model for future work in its focus on particular places —eastern Virginia for Page and New Orleans for Cable—rather than attempting to speak for a monolithic South. Our knowledge of print culture in the South, from the antebellum period through Reconstruction, needs to be deepened by case studies of readers, publishers, and publications. Only by documenting the many Souths of the nineteenth century will we have a history of the book of this region commensurate with the richness of its peoples.

CHAPTER 11

Alternative Communication Practices
and the Industrial Book

As book manufacturing became industrialized and the language of profes-sionalism pervaded publishing and authorship alike, important alternative communication practices continued, notably oratory, handwriting, and ama-teur production of printed matter. One might expect that investigations of those practices would reveal eddies of "tradition" unaffected by the dynamic mainstream, arenas bypassed by the industrial book or allowing withdrawal from its gathering power. That may sometimes have been the case, but the story is not so simple. The oratory associated with reform movements was fixed, even on outlying Nantucket, in an increasingly potent culture of print. The precision and repeatability of print changed the way handwriting was taught and used, even as handwriting also came to be associated with indi-vidual character. Amateur writers could not have functioned without access to low-priced new products of industrial technology, and those writers often aspired to authorial careers. Indeed, the very notion of amateurism could develop only in relation to the figure of the professional. Abandoning as-pirations for magazine or book publication after a negative response from Thomas Wentworth Higginson, Emily Dickinson preserved her poetry in let-ters to friends and in carefully crafted, handwritten "fascicles"—venerable forms of publication long associated with private circulation, now imagined also against the emergent world of professional authorship. Even alternative practices of communication were far from immune to the industrial forces that so powerfully shaped the history of the book in America between 1840 and 1880.

PART 1

Speech, Print, and Reform on Nantucket

Lloyd Pratt

·   ·   ·

On the evening of 11 August 1841, Frederick Douglass took the stage at the Atheneum Library on the island of Nantucket, Massachusetts. History marks this as the moment when Douglass "rose and found his voice" while telling his life story to the abolitionists and curiosity-seekers gathered at the first Nantucket Anti-Slavery Convention.[1] Douglass spoke at the urging of a Nantucketer, a white native of the island who had heard Douglass address a meeting of free blacks on the mainland in New Bedford, Massachusetts. Although Douglass had often spoken before groups of black people, the Nantucket speech was his first before a predominantly white audience.

We can assume that Douglass's remarks that evening anticipated his contribution to the American literary canon, *Narrative of the Life of Frederick Douglass, an American Slave, Written by Himself* (1845). His fortunate audience, in other words, most likely heard the debut of one of the most significant personal narratives ever written by an American. Douglass's listeners that night also witnessed the beginning of his career as an institutionally affiliated reformer and the first signs of his future role as an influential speaker, writer, editor, and newspaperman. Douglass's previous public remarks, such as those delivered to his fellow slaves beneath the trees on his master's plantation, as well as those given in New Bedford, had been directed to small, often informal audiences. His speech at the Nantucket Atheneum marked a turning point: it led the prominent abolitionist William Lloyd Garrison to recruit Douglass for the movement's national lecture circuit, launching Douglass's long and auspicious public career.

If the story of Douglass's finding his voice is a familiar one, the story of the institutional setting of his debut is considerably less so. Douglass had chosen a telling venue for his move into the public spotlight. Nantucket's Atheneum was more than a passive backdrop; by the time of Douglass's appearance, it linked Nantucket's social reformers to kindred spirits across the nation. Both the printed and the spoken words of an increasingly well-established national reform network found early shelter under the Atheneum's roof.[2] As Douglass's successful debut might suggest, the role of the Atheneum as a node of reform culture illuminates a larger story of how the mutually reinforcing relationship between the spoken and written word fueled the expansion of American reform communities.

Incorporated in 1834, after the merger of two private library associations, the Atheneum announced in 1835 that it would begin to function as a subscription library, thereby significantly widening its audience and increasing access to print. Shortly thereafter, the Atheneum's shareholders decided to organize a series of lectures modeled on the lyceums that had sprung up across the nation since 1826. The next forty years were the golden age of Nantucket's Atheneum. It hosted speeches by leading American reform intellectuals, and its library came to house the books, periodicals, and ephemera written by and about them. When Douglass took the stage that evening, his audience was destined to be much wider than the crowd gathered before him. The Atheneum was importing, purveying to locals, and exporting those staple resources of nineteenth-century American reformers, from abolitionists to temperance activists and beyond: printed and spoken words. Its ties to a vast network of reformers, which were realized in its collection of reform publications and through the presence of reform speakers, ensured that Douglass's claims were intelligible to local reformers and, at the same time, quickly available to the national reform community. Without the framework provided by the Atheneum, Douglass's words might very well have died on its stage.

In a way, Nantucket was an unlikely site for such an auspicious event. To be sure, the island was hardly obscure or distant from the centers of American culture. As early as 1782, J. Hector St. John de Crèvecœur even made the case that it was *the* representative American community.[3] At the time of Douglass's visit six decades later, Nantucket was a thriving place of some ten thousand residents, rendered prosperous by virtue of the market for whale oil. The voyage across Nantucket Sound was far less onerous than several days of journeying through America's interior.

Even so, Nantucketers were regularly cut off from the mainland, especially during the winter. Early in the nineteenth century, for instance, when Nantucket's harbor had been frozen over for several weeks, cutting off all communication from off-island, one islander described how he had belatedly learned that the War of 1812 was over: "Thomas Fisher arrived from [Martha's] Vineyard this evening in a Boat & Landed at Smith's point. He came for the sole purpose of bringing the welcome intelligence. He brought Boston papers which contained [this] information." Two winters later, the same man complained again: "The harbour being closed up with Ice displays a very dreary aspect to us who are confined to an Island; Strong walls, bolts & bars are quite unnecessary to confine us to this little spot; the natural fortifications which now surround us are stronger than all the art that the ingenuity of man can invent."[4]

Nor did the situation much improve over the decades that followed. In February 1844, Nantucketers learned that because of the ice in the harbor, one local newspaper could not be printed for more than a week "for want of Paper."[5] In December 1853, the *Nantucket Inquirer* reported that a lecture at the Atheneum had been canceled — twice — "on account of the failure of the steamer."[6] As late as 1875, the *Inquirer and Mirror* published a notice headed "The Weather and the Mails," detailing the misadventures of the ship *Island Home* in its efforts to reach Nantucket: "On Sunday, the Island Home again reconnoitered our position but found the ice too heavy, and to our intense mortification, turned back." Among the ship's cargo were the usual newspapers carrying word from the mainland.[7]

In other words, Nantucket was in some ways as cut off from Boston or even New Bedford as if it had been situated deep in the American hinterland, a place somewhere along the periphery of the emerging — and dispersing — national culture. For that very reason, it is striking just how deeply enmeshed Nantucket was in the nation's cultural currents, especially those linked to social reform. By the year of Douglass's lecture, the island had given rise to at least three general booksellers; two specialty bookshops carrying antislavery materials; a private circulating library advertising several hundred publications for rent; the Commercial News and Whig Reading Room (a periodical reading room advertising access to hundreds of national and international newspapers); two local newspapers; two printers; a private school library open to alumni, students, and members of the school's founding family; at least two church libraries consisting of one hundred or more volumes; and the Atheneum itself, whose library held more than thirty-two hundred volumes.[8] These figures do not take into account the personal libraries on the island or individual subscriptions for periodicals such as Garrison's *Liberator* and the *National Anti-Slavery Standard*, not to mention the abbreviated libraries secreted onboard Nantucket's sailing vessels. Quantitatively, at least, Nantucket was an early home to the industrial book.

The Atheneum was at the center of this activity. It provided the major link between Nantucket's own reformers and the larger national, and international, movements to which they belonged. Those connections were firmly in place by the time Frederick Douglass lectured at the Atheneum. The 1841 printed *Catalogue of the Library of the Nantucket Atheneum* shows how. If Douglass chose to descend from the stage and make his way to the library, he would have found bookshelves 96 through 101 lined with the roster of American literature that we often associate with this period, including, for a start,

ALTERNATIVE COMMUNICATION PRACTICES

James Fenimore Cooper's novels, Washington Irving's *The Crayon Miscellany* (1835) and *The Sketch Book of Geoffrey Crayon* (1819-20), and Hawthorne's *Twice-Told Tales* (1837). Intermingled with those American texts he would also have found the novels of Walter Scott, eight volumes of Charles Dickens, and Samuel Richardson's *Pamela* (1740). If Douglass decided to seek out sympathetic fellow travelers in his incipient role as reformer, he would quickly realize he was not limited to the people attending the convention. Shelves 84 through 91 would have introduced him to William Ellery Channing's *Slavery* (1835) and *Emancipation* (1840), Lydia Maria Child's *An Appeal in Favor of That Class of Americans Called Africans* (1833), a translation of Erasmus's *The Complaint of Peace, to Which Is Added, Antipolemus; or, The Plea of Religion, Reason, and Humanity, against War* (1813), Horace Mann's *Lecture on Education* (1840), the first volume of the *Permanent Temperance Documents of the American Temperance Society* (1835), the monthly *The Reformer: A Religious Work* (1820-31), and Ralph Waldo Emerson's *Nature* (1836). Finally, if he had the time and inclination, Douglass could discover the publications held by several major American libraries, for the Nantucket Atheneum held the published catalogs of the Boston Athenæum (1827), the Mercantile Library Association of New York (1837), and the Library of Congress (1839).[9]

Nantucket's Atheneum would have been only a starting point for extending Douglass's sense that he belonged to a larger reform community connected by a commerce in speech and print. He might have known even before he stepped ashore to contact Captain E. J. Pompey, who had been repeatedly advertised in the *Colored American* (1837-42) as that newspaper's sales agent on Nantucket.[10] In Pompey's absence, Douglass could choose to direct his steps to the door of George Bradburn, who only a few months before had written an essay republished in the *Colored American* protesting the treatment of black passengers on American railways.[11] And if Douglass wanted timely information about the national antislavery community, he had several options. The 23 June 1841 number of the *Nantucket Inquirer* would have informed him of the mission of the new *National Anti-Slavery Standard*, which Lydia Maria Child had just moved to New York to edit.[12] If Douglass wished to purchase a copy of the most recent number of the *Standard*, he had only to walk a few blocks across town to Obed Barney's general store. As the *Inquirer* reported on 13 January 1841, in a notice titled "Light for the People,"

An Anti-Slavery Library has been established in the room over Obed Barney's store, recently occupied by J. Cowan. It comprises as extensive a collection of the standard Anti-slavery productions of British and American authors, as can be found in any Anti-Slavery depository in the country. The leading A. S. periodicals can also be examined in the room. — The public generally, are invited to take advantage of this means of obtaining correct information, FREE OF EXPENSE, respecting the present condition of 3,000,000s of American citizens, and the most effectual means for bettering their condition.[13]

The work of Barney's Anti-Slavery Library was supported later that same month by an Anti-Slavery Fair, among whose offerings were at least two other antislavery publications, Maria Weston Chapman's annual *The Liberty Bell* for 1841 and "the Slave Boy, by Mrs. Opie."[14] When Douglass visited Nantucket seven months later, he might have been introduced to another community of reformers with whom the island's antislavery reformers almost certainly shared members: advocates of temperance. Not two weeks after his visit, various local temperance associations, "united against the grand enemy of human peace and health, of social order, morality and happiness," erected in the public square near the Atheneum "a triumphal pavilion, of classic design, adorned with characteristic insignia, surrounded with appropriate [temperance] mottos, and surmounted by the banner of the Union."[15]

Like similar institutions around the nation, the Nantucket Atheneum was part of a complex network that constituted reformers as a political force *and* as a buying audience. The books and periodicals generated by the abolitionist, temperance, peace, feminist, education, labor, and other reform movements, together with the adjunct libraries, lyceums, and speaker bureaus, nurtured those movements, expanding their reach and providing a tangible product around which their core supporters could congregate. And reformers such as Douglass supported themselves and their movements through their work as paid writers, speakers, and publishers: Douglass spoke again in Nantucket in both 1842 and 1843. Meanwhile, commercial publishing houses fueled their expanding businesses by exploiting this growing market. Beginning in the 1840s, reform-minded people became what publishers would now call a niche market — one that seemed to be continually expanding. Acting out of their own ideological commitments, but also recognizing and addressing that expanding market, publishers such as Burgess, Stringer & Co., Greeley & McElrath, Redding & Co., and Fowler & Wells entered the field of reform publishing, while continuing to maintain a diversified list of publications not strictly reformist in nature.

In August 1846, the Atheneum building and its collections were destroyed in a blaze that consumed much of Nantucket's village center. But while the "Great Fire" was a major event in the history of the island, it proved to have relatively little impact on Nantucket's involvement in social reform. A new Atheneum library was quickly reconstituted from cash donations and contributions of books and ephemera from the mainland. Among the latter were several hundred pamphlets, a collection rediscovered during a renovation of the Atheneum undertaken in the 1990s. The invited outside speakers, as well as the island's native reformers, would still have found themselves at home with the pamphlets dealing with abolitionism, peace, and prison reform that were awaiting their perusal in the Atheneum's new collection.

In fact, the web of reform lecturers and their printed matter grew even thicker in the 1850s. Frederick Douglass returned for a third visit to the Atheneum stage in 1850. If on this occasion he had also chosen to wander about, he would most likely have been able to find his own *Narrative* on the island. Had the Atheneum itself, by some egregious oversight, failed to purchase the book (and catalogs suggest it might have), Douglass could have walked a few blocks across town to one of the island's two antislavery bookstores. Douglass was followed to the stage of the Atheneum in the 1850s by reformers known as much from title pages or mastheads of newspapers as from their public speaking: these included education reformer Horace Mann, transcendentalist Ralph Waldo Emerson, labor and peace activist Elihu Burritt, civil disobedient and essayist Henry David Thoreau, abolitionist clergyman Theodore Parker, publisher and one-time Fourierite Horace Greeley, feminist preacher (and Nantucket native) Lucretia Coffin Mott, antislavery activist and future Union Army officer Thomas Wentworth Higginson, and comprehensive reformer and orator Wendell Phillips.[16]

Like Douglass, most of these women and men would have been able to find and purchase on Nantucket works that they had written, edited, or published. If the Atheneum failed to supply them with those materials, they could visit the Commercial News Room, a subscription newsroom that advertised "some Seventy or Eighty of the best journals of the country, as well as papers from foreign countries."[17] Or they could ask around among the locals, a number of whom subscribed to off-island reform newspapers, as subscription receipts from the period indicate. At the very least, they could turn to the island's own *Inquirer* or *Weekly Mirror* (which in 1865 merged to become the *Inquirer and Mirror*) for news of reforms on the mainland and for information about where to buy reform materials.[18] The link between the commercial enterprises of publishing, printing, and professional authorship and the moral enterprise of reform was an intimate one on Nantucket, as it was across the nation. When a reform speaker boarded the packet leaving Nantucket for New Bedford or Boston, printed matter remained behind to embody the re-

Speech, Print, and Reform   397

form community and link its far-flung members, as well as to connect those reformers to a commercial network. Douglass, Emerson, and Greeley might have been occasional visitors, but their words were permanent residents.

The situation changed in the 1860s. With the notable exception of the temperance movement, the influence and purchasing power of reformers declined after the Civil War, on Nantucket as elsewhere in the nation. The whaling industry had shifted away from Nantucket decades earlier, and it collapsed during the 1850s, largely because of the increasing use of kerosene. Thanks also to the gold rush of the 1840s, the island experienced a rapid exodus that reduced its population by half, to little more than four thousand, in less than a decade. To compound that blow, the island suffered further during the Civil War. Unlike some other New England towns, whose factories manufactured supplies for the Union forces, Nantucket had little to offer in the way of industrial production. In the 1870s, however, an industry first introduced to the island in the 1820s began to flourish in earnest: tourism. Large, new hotels were built on Nantucket, and the sea air began to supply a steadier income than the sea itself. A growing emphasis on entertaining diversions may have helped shift the island's cultural life away from its earlier interest in reform culture.

Even as early as the 1840s, reformers had competed with a rapidly expanding roster of popular entertainments. The reform lecturers who continued to appear at the Atheneum began to have competition from the spectacle of panoramas, light musical concerts, and tightrope acts. The lectures themselves were affected also by the parallel transformation of the lyceum movement. While the lyceum had initially emphasized the scientific and practical education of industrial workers through an ongoing course of lectures, it later came to favor single talks intended more as literary and intellectual diversions. Reformers found themselves placed within this latter category. Early on, lecturers were booked through personal transactions with their hosts, but after the 1850s the whole affair became increasingly professionalized, with speaker bureaus assuming the responsibility of booking lecturers and arranging fee structures. Reformers were not immune to the lure of simpler logistics and a guaranteed fee—and many ended up as one of several "acts" managed by a speaker's bureau. By the 1870s, such omnibus arrangements were commonplace, so that erudite reformers shared the same bill with lustier entertainments. Former connections between lecturing and publishing were thus loosened.

So were the connections between print and reform. In 1875 the Nantucket Atheneum hosted a lecture by Rev. Mrs. Phebe (Coffin) Hanaford. Hanaford, a Nantucketer, had left the island to become the first ordained female minister in New England, in the Universalist Church. A temperance reformer in her youth, she came to author the antislavery novel *Lucretia, the Quakeress* (1853) and an 1865 biography of Abraham Lincoln; after the Civil War, Hanaford devoted the last fifty years of her life to the passionate advocacy of women's rights, helping to organize the American Woman Suffrage Association in 1869. In 1875, the *Inquirer and Mirror* reported, Hanaford spoke hopefully "in favor of the Press, as an engine of reform"—as an ally fighting on behalf of industrial workers and "for political equality for women; for the opening of the doors of all our Colleges; for the raising of those twin pillars of reform in our world—enlightened motherhood, enfranchised." Her Atheneum lecture was titled "The Possibilities and Opportunities of Humanity in Our Times."[19]

But Hanaford's hopes were misplaced. By 1875, prospects for the working class and the equality of women were not good, and the sorry end of Reconstruction lay only two years ahead. Nor, finally, was it any longer reasonable to regard the press as "an engine of reform." The mainstream press had for the most part come to accept and justify the status quo. The reform press itself was beating a retreat from its earlier association with the social vanguard and was in the process of becoming either marginalized or even, by virtue of the recently passed Comstock Act, criminalized. None of Phebe Hanaford's feminist lectures was ever printed: the only one of her many books that dealt with women—her magnum opus, *Women of the Century* (1877, later titled *Daughters of America*)—was published by a Boston firm, B. B. Russell, which specialized in biographies of antebellum abolitionists, American presidents, and other prominent political figures of the Gilded Age, along with a smattering of nostalgic books about old-time New England, but which avoided tackling more current reforms.

Ten years after Hanaford's appearance, in 1885, Frederick Douglass returned to the stage of the Nantucket Atheneum for a fourth, and final, visit. By this time, Nantucket had become best known as a repository of quaint, old-fashioned New England customs and characters, luring tourists with the aura of isolation its residents had once lamented. Douglass was now about sixty-seven years old, and the third version of his autobiography had appeared three years earlier. A full forty-four years had passed since his initial appearance at the Atheneum, his very first speech delivered to a predominantly white audience, the momentous evening on which he "rose and found his voice." A packed house greeted the "distinguished gentleman" on this occasion. "By particular request," Douglass "prefaced his address with a brief reminiscence of his early life, his escape from slavery, and his subsequent career." Turning to his main subject, he "dwelt at length upon the career of John Brown."

The *Inquirer and Mirror* described his lecture this way: "While much that was historical in the address was familiar to most of the audience, many of the reminiscences with which it was interspersed were new and greatly enhanced its interest."[20] Reform culture's adept triangulation of print, speech, and commerce had made the names "John Brown" and "Frederick Douglass" centerpieces of the American vernacular. Yet, on Nantucket at least, the moment of reform that Douglass represented was over — its outlines both "familiar" and "historical," its few remaining unknown details registering only as "reminiscence."

PART 2

Handwriting in an Age of Industrial Print

Tamara Plakins Thornton

· · ·

The penmanship class of the Gilded Age typically began with the command to "Open books." Only later did the teacher order her class to "Open inkstands," "Take pens," and "Write."[21] The books in question were copybooks, mass-produced and marketed by large publishing houses, ubiquitous in the schoolroom, and available, in the words of one contemporary penman, at every "cross-roads grocery."[22] Their dominance in postbellum handwriting instruction made possible the fulfillment of goals dear to the hearts of Victorian Americans: the mastering of the body by the will and the consequent formation of character; and the enforcement of conformity and obedience in the interests of a broader societal discipline. As part of what were increasingly designated "national" or "American" systems of penmanship,[23] printed copybooks served yet another objective. Penmanship authorities imagined the formation of a national character in classrooms across America, one intimately linked to the rise of America as a business civilization. In the aftermath of the Civil War, print realized the cultural and social possibilities of script. But those possibilities did not end with the agenda of pedagogues. Away from the classroom, Victorians closed their copybooks and opened their autograph albums. There no teacher supervised the writing process, and no copy text dictated the product of the pen. There Victorians signed their names as individuals.

Well before the Civil War, penmanship pedagogy was recognized as teaching pupils far more than just how to write. Antebellum Americans understood

that when children learned how to form their letters, they were forming characters in both senses of the word. "A neat handwriting," read one typical copy
phrase, "is a letter of recommendation," attesting to the writer's ability to meet
both a mercantile employer's practical demands as well as such qualifications
as honesty and reliability.[24] Children learned too that character was a standardized product, just like the model alphabets and copy phrases imitated
over and over down the length of the page.[25]

In the real world of the antebellum classroom, it was difficult to enforce
uniformity and discipline. In the common schools, it was an often ill-trained
teacher's responsibility to "set the copy" at the top of pupils' copybooks,
and so penmanship models varied with the teacher. Nor could anything like
standardization or discipline be enforced. In a one-room schoolhouse, the
students were of every age and skill level. Teachers, busy with setting copies
and repairing quill pens, could not supervise activity.[26] And students, as a
perusal of antebellum exercise books reveals, sometimes took the opportunity
to depart from the lesson of the day.[27]

By the 1860s, however, the mass production and national distribution of
copybooks made the enforcement of uniformity and discipline in the handwriting lesson a practical possibility. Other factors were at work, of course
—from the use of steel pens to the ever more common age-graded classroom—but perhaps the key innovation was the use of stereotyped engraving,
steel-plate engraving, and, most commonly, lithography to reproduce handwriting on the printed page.[28] Across the top of each copybook page ran the
copy text, the model to be imitated on the machine-ruled lines below. With
the work of setting copy taken over by the instructional materials themselves,
teachers were freed up to supervise the penmanship drill. Manuals stipulated
the minutest details of correct finger, hand, arm, and body positions and the
sets of commands and counts to which students were to write "in concert,"
executing the same letter stroke at exactly the same time.[29] The teacher's careful monitoring of the drill prevented straying from both the physical regimen and the printed models of script. Without such "direction or criticism,"
warned the superintendent of the St. Louis schools, the pupil "acquires a
sort of individuality of hand-writing, that proves difficult to change."[30] Each
penmanship lesson, then, became a lesson in character formation, conformity
to standardized models, and social discipline (Figs. 11.1 and 11.2).

It was not technological innovation by itself that transformed penmanship
education, however, but the exploitation of that technology by rival penmen
and publishers targeting particular markets.[31] Take, for example, the dominant system of the Gilded Age, Spencerian penmanship. Born in 1800, Platt
Rogers Spencer established himself as an Ohio writing master by the age of

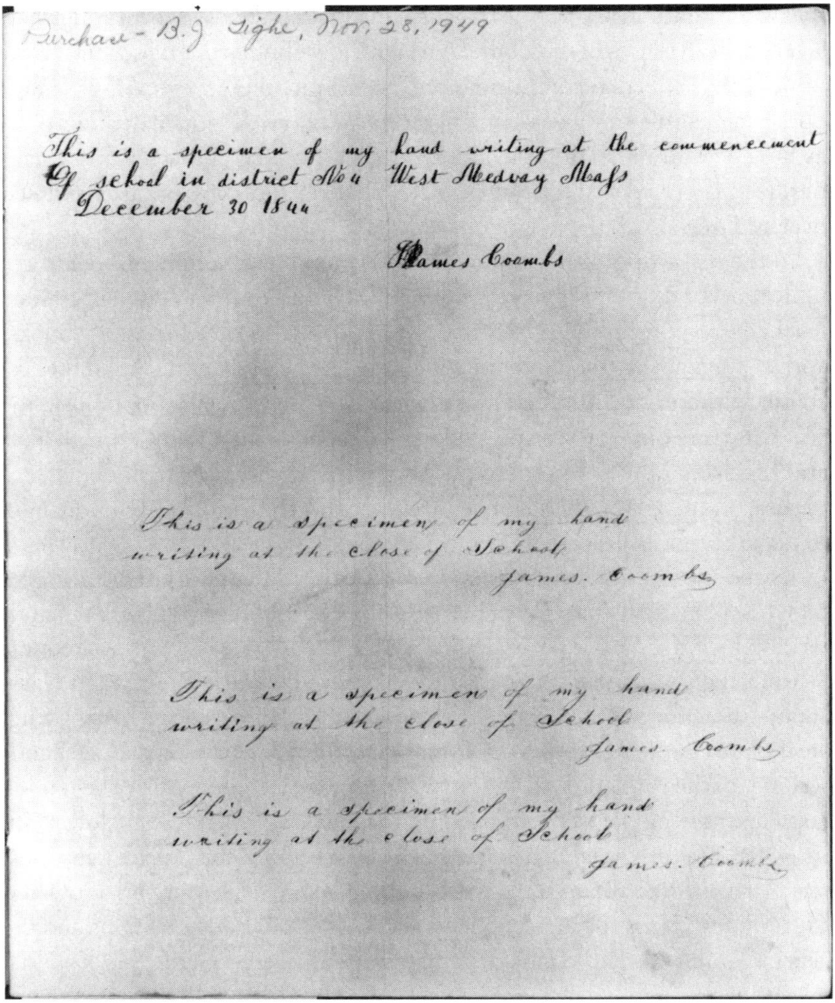

Purchase - B. J. Tighe, Nov. 28, 1949

This is a specimen of my hand writing at the commencement
Of school in district No 4 West Medway Mass
December 30 1844

James Coombs

This is a specimen of my hand
writing at the close of School
James. Coombs

This is a specimen of my hand
writing at the close of School
James. Coombs

This is a specimen of my hand
writing at the close of School
James. Coombs

FIGURE 11.1. Student James Coombs in 1844 recorded a school term's progress in penmanship in a copybook bought from Thomas Groom & Co., Boston manufacturers of "Account, Writing, and Blank Books." American Antiquarian Society.

fifteen, but his career as a penmanship impresario really only began in 1848, when he published a set of engraved copy-slips in Geneva, Ohio. By the 1860s, the copy-slips were superseded by a graded series of copybooks, keyed to use in the common schools and supplemented with instructional manuals and charts, brought out by a publisher of educational materials based in New York. When Spencer died in 1864, the "Spencerian authors," at one point numbering thirty-eight of his relatives and associates, continued the expan-

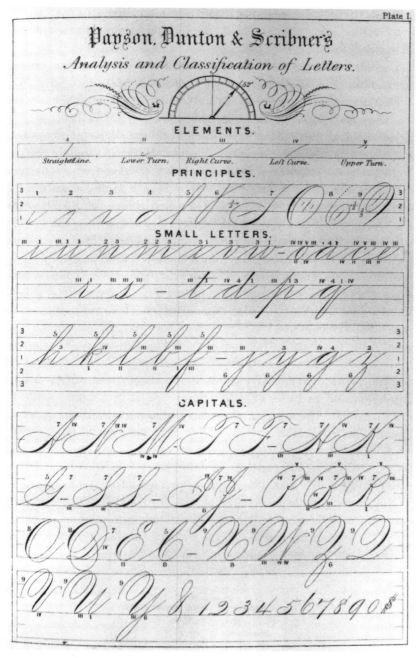

FIGURE 11.2. Plate 1, "Analysis and Classification of Letters," *The Payson, Dunton, & Scribner Manual of Penmanship* (New York and Chicago: Potter, Ainsworth, & Co., 1873). American Antiquarian Society.

sion of this penmanship empire. Eventually, school systems in forty-two states along with an ever-growing chain of Spencerian mercantile colleges adopted the system.[32]

The Spencerians had their rivals, but all contributed to a single national penmanship establishment consisting of professional penmen, mercantile colleges, national publishing houses, and centralized school systems. Private business colleges, first appearing in the 1840s and reaching their heyday in the decades after the Civil War, acted as the institutional base for professional penmen.[33] The expanding chains of colleges provided a lucrative market for instructional materials, of course, but because the big money lay in the public schools, it was the imprimatur granted by the mercantile colleges that had the higher value. The adoption of a set of materials for an entire school district only lent further prestige to the system, as attested to by the testimonials of school officials printed in the back of some copybooks.[34] Because the largest markets were in the burgeoning urban school systems, copybooks were published in graduated series to match the organization of these schools in age-graded classes. Instruction manuals and classroom charts, the latter for teachers lacking the skill to demonstrate letters on the blackboard, accompanied the copybooks, as did pens, pen wipers, ink, even storage cases for penmanship materials.[35]

Penmanship systems bore the names of professional penmen and carried the prestige of the penmen's mercantile college connections, but the national distribution and marketing of these systems went well beyond the scope of a lone entrepreneur. Hence we see the creation of authorial syndicates; the main rivals of "the Spencerian authors," for example, were the "P., D., & S. Authors."[36] And the days of self-publishing in Geneva, Ohio, were over as well. Some copybooks were issued by multiple publishers in multiple cities. Others were published by national houses that specialized in schoolbooks, or by such mainstream publishers as D. Appleton & Co. and J. B. Lippincott & Co. Indeed, in establishing the claim of a system to be truly national, the prestige of the publisher may have been as important as that of the penman. In an advertisement for one penmanship manual, for example, special note was taken that the manual appeared "under the auspices of the largest and perhaps the most discriminating publishing house in America, D. Appleton & Co., New York."[37] Author, publisher, and market thus worked in concert to exploit the potential of new technology and to consolidate a national system of penmanship.

Because a good deal of money was at stake, competition among systems of penmanship instruction was keen. The rivalry between Spencer and Payson, Dunton, & Scribner deteriorated into a pamphlet war, with charges and countercharges of plagiarism. Nor were they alone in making those kinds of allegations.[38] It might seem that penmanship instruction would have been as various as the rival systems, but because no system deviated substantially from the Spencerian model, a truly national system did in fact exist. Indeed, one can almost measure the extent of acceptable variation. Spencer advocated a 52-degree slope of the writing line, as did Payson, Dunton, & Scribner and G. A. Gaskell, among others. But S. A. Potter boldly called for 51, and Porter & Coates, 53.[39] The vision of "a uniform lithographed system of penmanship" had been achieved.[40]

The creation of a national system of penmanship involved more than the consolidation of a penmanship establishment that marketed a standardized script to a nationwide market. When the Spencerian authors decorated their copybooks with images of the United States Capitol and the bald eagle, they were participating in the process of defining a national community.[41] In the aftermath of the Civil War, the "national" was synonymous with the North, apparent from the list of northeastern and midwestern cities from which copybooks were issued.[42] *Sterling's Southern Series of Writing Books* (1867), published in Macon, Georgia, and written by the author of such Confederate-era textbooks as *Our Own Primer* (1862), struck the only discordant note in this postbellum process of defining the nation.[43] Even more critically, as a natural extension of the role handwriting instruction had long played in the process of character formation, the postbellum penmanship establishment took on the task of forming a national character, a task made possible by the national distribution of a distinctively and self-consciously American script. Our "commercial college men," wrote one Gilded Age penman, used European penmanship models as the basis for "perfecting a superior national style." They "are now seeking to modify the forms that have become Americanized and render them still more American; to impart such a style as will occupy less space, have more freedom in its execution, and answer more fully in other respects the purposes of business in this day of despatch."[44] If national identity was to be synonymous with the North, the national character needed to be synonymous with northern business civilization, a laissez-faire world in which efficiency and speed held sway.

In the lithographed letters of copybooks, handwriting in the Gilded Age denoted conformity to standardized models of character and to the demands of a corporate economy. But other products of the press—autograph facsimile albums, graphology manuals, and autograph albums—sustained an alternative understanding of handwriting as an expression of individuality. The clearest evidence that Victorian Americans were capable of more than one way of thinking about handwriting was a belief that, as one writer summarized it in 1855, "not only is it a wise provision of Providence that the hand-writing of every man should be different from that of every other, but a man's penmanship is an unfailing index of his character."[45] In midcentury, hand-writing analysis was new, and it lacked intellectual respectability.[46] Far more developed and bearing no stigma of the occult was a related practice, auto-graph collecting. Many Americans were first introduced to the notion that autographs of the famous were artifacts of personality when in 1836 Edgar Allan Poe published a series of magazine articles on "autography." They in-cluded printed facsimiles of famous signatures, apparently the first to be published in America, accompanied by brief character sketches. Within a few years, Americans could purchase whole albums of autograph facsimiles, mass-marketed in cheap editions. For those who wanted to buy autographs, mail-order catalogs advertised signatures for sale, and by the 1880s, auto-graph dealers published specialty journals that included news and commen-tary as well as lists of items for sale.[47]

Autograph collectors did not claim that every person's handwriting was unique and an index of character. Instead, they believed that, as most people conform themselves to common models of character, their handwriting does the same. But a few rare individuals, men (and only very occasionally women) of genius, had risen above what one Gilded Age autograph collector de-scribed as "the common herd,"[48] and their triumphant individuality might therefore be savored in their idiosyncratic scripts. There was no contradiction between perceiving handwriting as a form of both studied self-presentation and unconscious self-revelation. It was understood that handwriting meant one thing for the Victorian masses, quite another for a small number of un-usual individuals. Indeed, it was precisely because most people felt that it was their duty and fate to conform that they were drawn to those driven by other imperatives. By the 1870s and 1880s, however, there were signs that this dichotomy was breaking down. One was the transformation of handwrit-ing analysis, which had focused on the scripts of famous men and women, into the universally applicable "science" of graphology.[49] Another was the changing nature of autograph collecting.

To be sure, postbellum Americans continued to collect the signatures of the famous, but they were seeking out the signatures of the not-so-famous as well, collecting them in a new species of bound matter, the autograph album.[50] Before the Civil War, something akin to autograph albums had existed. They were sized and shaped like small books, rightly suggesting that their contents consisted of vertical texts, not horizontal signatures, and these albums had been titled just that: "Flora's Album," "The Young Lady's Album," or just plain "Album"—but never "Autographs." The true autograph album dates from about 1860 and was commonplace by the 1870s, thus sharing the same pattern of popularity as the copybook. Even today most people have a mental picture of these Victorian albums: They are small, wider than they are high, and on their leather covers, tooled and gilded into ornate designs and pictures, is the title "Autographs." Inside, cousins and school chums dated the pages, penned a sentimental or humorous ditty, and most important, signed their names. No copy text at the top of the page, no lines running down the paper, demanded conformity. Here was a place to express and to savor individuality.

In mass-producing copybooks and autograph albums alike, Gilded Age publishers marketed both a mechanism of uniformity and the possibility of individuality. If handwriting worked to create authorized versions of the Victorian self, it also held out the enticing possibility that alternate versions were possible, each as unique as the man or woman who put pen to paper. Open the book to find a copy text and a ruled page, and there is no choice but to copy the standardized model and obey the rules. But open the book to find a blank page, and there is no script to follow.

PART 3

Amateur Authorship

Ann Fabian

. . .

About halfway through *Moby-Dick*, Ishmael describes a beggar on the London docks. A one-legged man holds up a picture of three whales and three boats "representing the tragic scene in which he lost his leg." Not everyone believes this beggar's story, but, says Ishmael, "the time of his justification has now come." It is not that his story is necessarily true, but rather that "his three whales are as good whales as were ever published in Wapping, at any rate."[51] In one sense, this begging artist is a figure of the amateur—a man whose works of art would never be printed in the modest commercial establishments located on the streets of Wapping, the neighborhood behind the docks. But he is also a professional—a man trying to find a market for his pictures and make a living by selling his art.

Historians of the book have been trained to see the history of authorship in the United States in the nineteenth century as a slow emergence of an organized profession out of a chaos of amateurism. "The terms of professional writing are these," William Charvat wrote, "that it provides a living for the author, like any other job; that it is a main and prolonged, rather than an intermittent or sporadic, resource for the writer; that it is produced with the hope of extended sale in the open market, like any article of commerce; and that it is written with reference to buyers' tastes and reading habits."[52] Those bent on a profession of letters, he might have added, defined themselves against those they labeled "amateurs." Our idea of the amateur writer derives in part from the condescension of would-be professionals.

The amateur and the professional came into being together. We pretend that there are clear distinctions between the professional and the amateur, but most literary careers must have contained elements of both. What did it mean to be an amateur? Was it to be a part-time author, a one-time author, or a poor, incompetent, aspiring, or unpaid author? Was it to be young and unschooled? Or was it to be outside the mainstream of the emerging literary establishment — to be a woman, an African American, a former slave, a Native American? Was it to tell stories based on experience rather than insight, inspiration, education, or genius? To make things even more confusing, some aspiring professional writers exploited vestiges of the eighteenth-century ideal of the gentleman writer, pretending to protect a pure (and amateur) literary tradition from the inroads of hacks who pandered to the market and made money off the popular taste for sensation and sentiment.

It was not hard for Charvat to find contemporary evidence to support his case that the very possibility of a professional literary career, and therefore the demise of the amateur, was an event of national significance. Writing in support of international copyright in 1844, William Gilmore Simms described James Fenimore Cooper's career in terms that would have made perfect sense to Charvat. Cooper's success had had an important "effect . . . upon the native intellect, in stimulating its movements, giving courage to its exertions, and converting it from a concern of amateurship and *dilettantism* into an employment and a profession." Simms deemed Cooper's effect "absolutely wonderful!" adding that "the Literature of a people depends wholly upon the fact that it is made a profession. Nothing has ever come from amateur performances in letters or the arts."[53]

It is hardly surprising that most of those who published on the subject looked down on amateurs from the heights of the profession. Writing in the *United States Magazine and Democratic Review* in the summer of 1845, an author calling himself "Mimin" described "the various divisions and subdivisions into which the trade of authorship is divided." "[W]e recognize two classes," he wrote, "authors by profession, and amateur writers: those who regard study and composition as the business of their lives, and those who

ALTERNATIVE COMMUNICATION PRACTICES

look upon them merely as incidental occupations." Amateurs, Mimin argued, distorted the market, selling their works on the cheap, undermining the worth of good literature, and stalling the development of a national culture. Amateurs kept themselves outside the guild of authorship, refusing to learn from each other and to listen to the critics who served an important role in Mimin's portrait of the profession. "An amateur in almost every walk is regarded as much inferior to the working member of the craft," he concluded.[54]

By the mid-1840s, those calling themselves amateurs were neither above nor outside the market. As it became possible to live by the pen, commentators cast the figure of the unpaid "gentleman amateur" as a throwback to an outmoded, aristocratic, and un-American literary tradition. That a world of "gentlemanly amateurs" had ever existed was perhaps more fantasy than reality, but it served a useful rhetorical purpose for those determined to make the case for the literary profession. In the literary marketplace, magazine editors took advantage of the aspirations of amateurs who were happy just to appear in print, and magazine proprietors paid little for many of the poems and essays that filled their pages. In fact, according to Mimin, amateur writers and editors perpetuated a pious fraud, defending themselves as guardians of culture not debased by commerce, while profiting at every turn from culture's commercialization.

As magazine publishing expanded in the 1840s and 1850s, editors were tempted to pick up cheap materials both from foreign periodicals and from native amateurs. Little surprise, then, that some editors had kind words for their amateur contributors. Editors of the *Southern Literary Messenger*, for example, boasted on the back page that its "CONTRIBUTORS are numerous, embracing Professional and Amateur Writers of the First Distinction."[55] In a column assessing the literary production of the last season, the editors of the Cincinnati-based *Ladies' Repository* praised the "literary ability displayed" in several works of history and biography, "written all of them by amateur authors." The books suggested "that there is still a vast amount of undeveloped history in every part of the country, inviting the appreciative labors of our writers, while the fields of biography are alike extensive and rich in the most interesting forms of historical matter. Into these it is hoped our non-professional writers will freely enter."[56]

Inside many Whig and Democratic magazines, aspiring professionals warned against both the dangers of reprinting English materials and the temptation to publish amateur authors. Stolen English materials polluted American minds with foreign ideas and put a damper on the development of native genius. Amateurs who wrote at their leisure misappropriated the income true authors needed to live. From the professional's perspective, amateur writers did more harm than good. They were foolish to entertain literary aspirations, and editors were wrong to encourage them:

> There never was a greater mistake than the belief, in which so many otherwise sensible men and women indulge, that they could write well for magazines and for the papers if they would but try. It is an error, a delusion, and one which works a great deal of mischief among people of literary tastes but of small literary training. There is not a periodical of any note, either in this country or any other, that would not soon be ruined by the exclusive contributions of a corps of amateur writers.[57]

These professionals focused their animosity on the amateur writers who competed with them for space on the pages of periodicals. But what happens if we try to imagine the era of the industrial book from the amateur's point of view? How did the enormous expansion of print and the development of professional careers shape the experience of amateur writers? And how do we identify the amateur author at midcentury?

William Gilmore Simms pictured the amateur as a "gentleman in nightgown and slippers." But he also noted that amateurs presented their tales as told "by one who apologized . . . for this wandering into forbidden grounds — possibly alleging a vacant mind, or an erring mood, for the solitary trespass; and promising if forgiven for this, never, in like manner, to offend again."[58] Perhaps it is by their apologies that we can identify amateur authors. Apologies actually served amateur writers in a number of ways. Many women writers negotiated the demands of the marketplace by pretending to shun literary ambition and backing into literary careers as a desperate means to meet traditional domestic duties. A veneer of amateurism thus permitted female professionalism.

The rhetoric of apology served amateur writers and professionals who wished for whatever reason to pose as amateurs. It was so common a feature of amateur literary production that unschooled and unpublished writers adopted it as a necessary opening gambit. Consider, for example, the "Preface" a writer calling herself Hannah Crafts attached to her unpublished novel, "The Bondwoman's Narrative": "In presenting this record of plain unvarnished facts to the generous public I feel a certain degree of diffidence and self-distrust. I ask myself for the hundredth time How will such a literary venture, coming from a sphere so humble be received?"[59] Crafts uses the few lines of her preface to accomplish several things. She apologizes for coming before the public, but at the same time, she enlists her public's generosity, praising her readers' virtues before they have even begun her tale. She also calls attention to her own humble social position and pledges, as do most midcentury amateurs, to confine herself to the facts, to those things about which she can claim a special, experiential knowledge. That she assembled her unvarnished facts in the service of a novel did not seem to trouble her. She based her confidence on the special knowledge she had gained as a writer who had been a slave.

When William Gilmore Simms assessed the state of American authorship in 1844, he singled out the War of 1812 as an essential event in the development of the profession of letters. It was no accident, he said, that Cooper's career followed "closely upon the footsteps of war!"[60] The war cut off the supply of British books, and just as the embargo on British goods had encouraged domestic manufacture, so the embargo on British ideas encouraged American authors. According to Simms, patriotism spurred a market for American writings and finally permitted American writers to live by their pens.

The Civil War played a similar role in the history of amateur authorship, creating a demand for the unvarnished accounts of soldiers' wartime experiences. Books and stories by Union soldiers who were captured and confined in Confederate prisons offer particularly instructive examples of postwar amateur authorship. Prisoner writers still apologized, testifying that they appeared in print only at the urgent "solicitation of friends." "Without any aspirations whatever to literary notoriety, I have endeavored to give a plain, unvarnished narrative of facts and incidents of prison life, as they occurred, under my observation, during twenty-two months in various rebel prisons," one typical account of a former prisoner began.[61]

"I had no thoughts of publishing a book until several weeks after my escape," another confessed. "I kept a diary, or journal, from the time of my capture. After reading portions of it to some of my friends, they persuaded me to amplify and put it in a readable form."[62] To reassure his readers that his amplifications had not gone beyond the bounds of his experience, this writer, like many of his fellow amateurs, made sure to offer a provenance for his literary production: "The rough manuscript was, for the most part, written during my imprisonment at Columbia, sitting on the ground, and writing on my knee. Captain Kelly, 1st Kentucky Cavalry, brought a part of that manuscript through the lines by concealing it in the crown of an old regulation hat. I escaped with the remainder concealed in the lining of my jacket." He also gave his manuscript an aura of authenticity by describing the nearly heroic measures behind the simplest acts of composition. "I had no pencil of my own," he noted in the middle of an account of a night spent in a swamp. But his companion "had a short piece which he kindly lent me. Having no knife, I was obliged to sharpen it by picking the wood away from the lead with my finger nails."[63]

Such descriptions give a visceral immediacy to amateur accounts. And immediacy, not literary polish or philosophical insight, was the chief selling point of amateur tales. As good amateurs, these writers pledged to confine themselves to things they had seen, heard, or felt, leaving the work of describing the war's larger meanings to professional writers and commentators. Working within the bounds of a carefully constructed modesty, former prisoners took their accounts of experience into the postwar literary marketplace.

A few prisoners' stories appeared with the imprint of such New York houses as Harper & Brothers, but more were the work of hometown presses and newspaper printing offices — outfits such as the Methodist Book Concern of Cincinnati, the Railroad City Publishing House of Indianapolis, or the Daily Wisconsin Printing House in Milwaukee. Narratives by former prisoners appeared in congressional reports and popular magazines; they appeared as straightforward commercial publications with commissioned illustrations, as bound journalism, as subscription volumes, and as self-published books and cheap pamphlets that former soldiers hawked themselves on street corners and in railroad stations.[64]

While most former prisoners explicitly distanced themselves from professional authors and promised to retail their experiences in print only once, one group in the postwar United States gave a different meaning to "amateur." Young members of the National Amateur Press Association celebrated their inexperience and embraced amateurism as a necessary stage on the route to a professional career. For them, the label "amateur" meshed easily with the wider social trend toward professionalism. The Amateur Press Association held its first meeting in September 1869 "at the residence of Mr. Charles Scribner, the publisher. No. 12 East 38th Street, New York."[65] The young and aspiring publishers Scribner welcomed into his home were part of a popular pastime of hobby printing (Fig. 11.3) that had grown enormously after Benjamin O. Woods began to market his inexpensive Novelty Press in 1867.

Hundreds of youths started their own papers and small publications in the 1870s and 1880s (Fig. 11.4). Some of these were surely just engaging in child's play, but the roles they took on as editors, writers, and printers were modeled on the actual culture of print professionalism. Like their grown-up mentors, they exchanged pieces among themselves, looked for good adventure stories to publish, held meetings, elected officers, passed resolutions, staged competitions, and granted prizes. "There is, undoubtedly, no occupation which would be of more profit to a boy (or girl) than editing an amateur paper," one enthusiast wrote in 1872. "Actual business, instruction and amusement are combined. Although it may be said to divert the mind from the ordinary

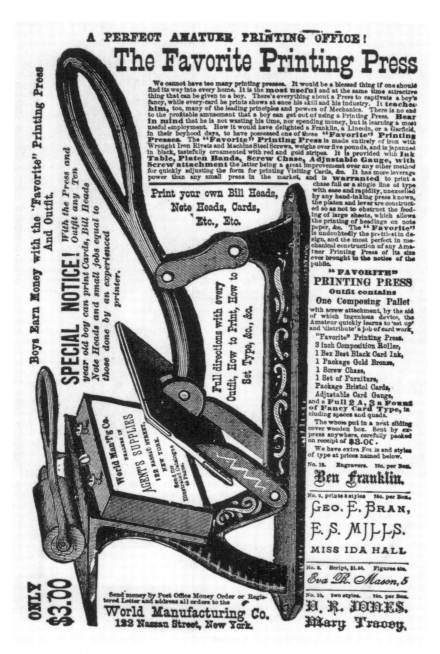

FIGURE 11.3. Advertisement for "The Favorite Printing Press," from Harold E. Sterne, *A Catalogue of Nineteenth Century Printing Presses*, 2nd ed. (New Castle, Del.: Oak Knoll, 2001). Produced by the World Manufacturing Co. of New York, c. 1883, it was sold with ink, roller, and three fonts of type (samples at lower right) for only three dollars.

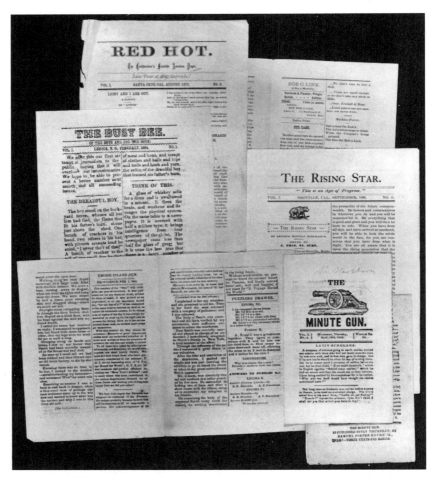

FIGURE 11.4. Six amateur newspapers, ranging in date from 1846 to 1886 and in place of publication from Worcester, Mass., to Lenoir, N.C., to Santa Cruz, Calif. Most such papers were monthlies and were usually printed on a single folded sheet. American Antiquarian Society.

school duties, yet it is thought that what is gained through journalistic experience amply makes up for what is lost at school."[66]

What teachers had to say about this assertion we do not know, but as we might expect from youths on their way to careers in publishing, the amateurs left ample records of their doings. That record, like the culture of the United States in the 1870s, is hardly unblemished. The boys who first met at Scribner's house in 1869 were the publishers of papers that still bore the mark of the war. They called their papers *The Loyal Union*, *The Yankee Peddler*,

The Patriot, and *The Young American.* They published stories about brave youths in battle. But when they met in Washington, D.C., ten years later, some young amateurs behaved like the rest of the country and moved their organization into the segregated world of Jim Crow. Delegates at a sparsely attended session elected a young African American, Herbert A. Clarke, as third vice president. On Clarke's election, the North Carolina chapter seceded, and the young publishers set up their own "Southern association of white amateurs," complete with an " 'Amateur Anti-Negro Admission Association,' better known as the 'A.A.A.A.' "[67]

These youthful white segregationists probably kept the word "amateur" in their sorry organization for alliterative reasons, but its presence suggests how important the label amateur was to their enterprise. Amateur defined who they were. The word's meanings had settled somewhat since the early years of the century. These boys were not amateurs because they were outside the market; members of the Amateur Press Association sold their publications. They were not amateurs because they were lovers of literature or refined gentlemen. They were amateurs because they aspired to become professionals. Those who sought to remake the model of American literary careers by substituting the professional as a norm for the amateur had succeeded. To be an amateur in this literary world was to be on its margins; these boys were on the margins not because they lacked talent or ambition but only because they were young.

When William Dean Howells described the "Man of Letters as a Man of Business" in a column in *Scribner's Magazine* in 1893, he called up an older vision of the amateur as the artist outside the market. "People feel that there is something profane, something impious, in taking money for a picture, or a poem, or a statue," he wrote. "Most of all, the artist himself feels this."[68] As Howells saw it, the artist feels it morally — as sin or shame. Since the war, he thought, business had taken over the arts. At the beginning of the century, artists lived by their art only part-time. In their incomplete professionalism, they were more easily able to tap the amateur's graces. It might have distressed a man like Simms, but in Howells's terms writers were better off when they were less successful as men of business. The literary world Howells surveyed had been made to suit not the professionals, exactly, but the hacks. In the age of the industrial book, hope for the future of art lay in that part of every artist that might still be called the amateur.

Coda

Scott E. Casper

. . .

The Centennial Exhibition closed on 10 November 1876, but not before leaving its own residue in print: guidebooks, maps, a history of the fair compiled from reports in *Frank Leslie's Illustrated Newspaper*. Marietta Holley's humorous novel *Josiah Allen's Wife as a P.A. and P.I.: Samantha at the Centennial* appeared the next year from the American Publishing Company, a leading Hartford subscription publisher. The exhibition had played host to the American Library Association as well as the American Book Trade Association. And it had provoked a copyright lawsuit, *Centennial Catalogue Co. v. Porter*, in which the publisher of the fair's official catalog sought unsuccessfully to bar another publisher from producing a similar work, even before the official work existed. Stories of the Centennial Exhibition made their way to communities across the nation, in local newspapers and in visitors' letters home as well as in the magazines that circulated nationwide by 1876.

On 11 November, *Publishers' Weekly* proclaimed the exhibition "a splendid success, greatly to the credit of the nation in general and of Philadelphia in particular." Perhaps the book trade could "do better another time" at displaying its wares, and perhaps most of the exhibiting publishers had not recouped their costs. Nevertheless, "The book trade of the country may congratulate itself on having taken in this great national representation a highly creditable part." The Centennial Exhibition was over, but its organizers planned a continuing exhibit in its Main Building. Seeing an opportunity, the ABTA queried its members about maintaining the book trade's presence in the new undertaking.[1] By the next May, the "International Exhibition of 1877"—a fragment of the previous year's—was on display. The ABTA abandoned its two-story iron pavilion, which sat empty except for the ABTA's monogram and an ice-cooler, in favor of expanded space on the main floor. Firms that had crowded onto the pavilion's second story now made "an extremely pretty and striking display, on account of their oddity and diversity," and the "handsome showcases of E. Steiger, Porter & Coates, Harding, Holman, American Sunday-School Union, Presbyterian Board," and J. B. Lippincott & Co. now appeared "to their full advantage."[2] But most of these were Philadelphia firms. The nationwide representation of the Centennial Exhibition evaporated along with the throngs of visitors, and the "permanent exhibition" proved short-lived. So did the ABTA.

The truly permanent exhibition of America's book trades was the books themselves, the industrial products that found their way into bookshops, homes, and libraries throughout the United States. By 1880 the value of products of the printing trades and related industries topped $189 million, a far cry from the $29 million of just thirty years earlier; these industries employed more than 112,000 workers, more than five times the number in 1850. Despite two nationwide depressions and the bankruptcies of numerous individual firms, the national book trade system thrived as well: in the financial arrangements of discounted sales to dedicated retailers; in the credit networks that linked publishers, jobbers, and booksellers; and in the pages of *Publishers' Weekly*, if not in a formal organization such as the ABTA. Courtesy of the trade survived challenges from the so-called pirates of the 1870s and 1880s, although passage of international copyright legislation in 1891 would considerably limit its application. Many of the pioneering publishers were gone: George Palmer Putnam died in 1872; Fletcher, the last of the Harper brothers, in 1877; James T. Fields, in 1881.

Their successors continued to define the "American book," but never without complications. On 17 December 1877, the *Atlantic Monthly* hosted a dinner to mark the seventieth birthday of John Greenleaf Whittier. More than fifty prominent literary men convened at Boston's Brunswick Hotel; women were admitted after dinner. At the head table sat Whittier, Henry Wadsworth Longfellow (who also turned seventy that year), Ralph Waldo Emerson (seventy-four), Oliver Wendell Holmes (whose seventieth-birthday breakfast the *Atlantic* would host two years later), William Dean Howells (at forty a generation younger), and the publisher Henry Oscar Houghton (fifty-four). Houghton's firm, Hurd & Houghton, published the *Atlantic*; the next year it would merge with James R. Osgood & Co., successor to Ticknor and Fields. Two years later, after Houghton forced Osgood out, it would become Houghton, Mifflin & Co. Houghton introduced the evening's entertainment with a tribute to the twenty-year-old *Atlantic* and its many contributors and then introduced Whittier to "rapturous applause."[3] Longfellow, Emerson, Howells, and Holmes offered their own praises and read from Whittier's poetry. It was the perfect celebration of a particular notion of American literature: centered in Boston and indeed in a single magazine, dominated by the antebellum generation of authors now in the twilight of their lives. Emerson read "Ichabod," written twenty-seven years earlier to denounce Daniel Webster's support of the Compromise of 1850. But Whittier's once-incendiary abolitionism had receded from memory in an era when white Americans nationwide were trying to repress the memory of slavery, the Civil War, and emancipation. Now more popular as the author of *Snow-Bound* (1866), a quiet "Winter Idyl," Whittier was so national a figure that he had been invited to write a poem for the opening ceremony of the Centennial Exhibition.

Whittier's birthday banquet has been best remembered for Mark Twain's unusual speech, testimony to the transcontinental reach of "American literature." Twain spun a tale of his days in Nevada's mining country, thirteen years earlier. As he told it, he had "knocked at a miner's lonely cabin in the foothills of the Sierras just at nightfall." Upon hearing Twain's name, the miner told him that three other "littery" men had preceded him: Longfellow, "built like a prize-fighter"; Emerson, "a seedy little bit of a chap"; and Holmes, "fat as a balloon" with "double chins all the way down to his stomach."[4] The "littery" men had kept the miner up all night as they played cards and traded fractured aphorisms from American poetry. Twain told his exhausted host that these unwanted guests had been impostors, and the story came to an end. This burlesque amused Longfellow and Holmes, apparently confused Emerson, and caused Twain lasting remorse for presumably insulting his literary elders. It also testified to the emergence of literary celebrity in America by the 1870s: incongruously, drunken gamblers in a cabin in the Sierra Mountains could bandy about the names of eminent eastern authors as well as snippets of American verse, even if they mismatched quotations and authors. Emerson, Longfellow, and Holmes were national literature for a continental nation, connected by the transcontinental railroad in 1869 and by distribution systems that publishers had established since before the Civil War.

That same continental connectedness made Twain's depiction of "littery" rubes partial at best, anachronistic at worst. By 1877, print culture suffused the Pacific slope. San Francisco was a publishing hub, not merely of newspapers and job printing but also of literary magazines such as the *Overland Monthly* (1868–1935) and of the publisher A. L. Bancroft & Co. Literary culture there and in such boom towns as Virginia City, Nevada, approximated eastern gentility: middle-class citizens read the *Atlantic Monthly*, played *Authors*, and enjoyed literary evenings. Canvassers peddled subscription books deep in mining country. The literary nation, in other words, consisted not just of cultural markers — names like "Emerson" and "Longfellow" — but also of the connecting technologies of transportation and distribution that moved the printed word eastward as well as westward.

Indeed, one of America's best-sellers of 1879 came from San Francisco: Henry George's *Progress and Poverty*. George's indictment of the widening breach between industrial capitalists and laborers is well known to historians of American industry and economy; less well known are the origins of *Progress and Poverty* in George's own career as a working printer. When Henry George was born in 1839, his father was a Philadelphia publisher and seller of Protestant Episcopal Church books and Sunday school books. The livelihood from this business enabled young Henry to attend school until he was fourteen, at which time his father abandoned publishing because "the general book houses had encroached so much on denominational business."[5] Henry held several clerical jobs and then went to sea in 1856. Upon his return the next year, his father found him a position with the printers King & Baird. There he learned to set type until he was fired after a quarrel with the foreman nine months later. Unemployed, George learned of a strike at the *Philadelphia Argus*. In six days — the only scab labor he ever did — he made $9.50. But the depression of 1857 made work scarce, and prospects in Oregon urged him to cross the continent. He found work as a compositor in San Francisco, making a minor's pay of $12 per week when journeymen were making $30. George joined the Eureka Typographical Union upon his twenty-first birthday and entered the journeymen's ranks. For the next decade, he alternated between regular positions and "subbing," twice forming partnerships to buy and run newspapers. He also began to express a political consciousness in print. In 1865 he wrote a letter to the editor of San Francisco's *Journal of the Trades and Workingmen*, praising the paper's voice "for the working classes . . . at a time when most of our public prints pander to wealth and power and would crush the poor man beneath the wheel of the capitalist's carriage."[6] The same year, when San Franciscans demolished the presses of four Democratic newspapers in response to Abraham Lincoln's assassination, George wrote a letter to the editor of the *Alta California* lamenting the president's murder.

Years later, George's son wrote that Henry George first considered the problem of industrial depressions when a veteran printer in King & Baird's shop observed the disparity of wages in old and new countries. Equally likely, George's critique of capitalism and monopoly took shape during his California printing career, which included frequent periods of privation. His first newspaper partnership, in the *San Francisco Evening Journal* in 1861, thrived initially because "There was no wire connection with the East." Once the transcontinental telegraph was completed that October, "the papers that were in the press association monopoly had so much advantage" that papers such as the *Evening Journal* could not compete.[7] Seven years later, the publisher of the *San Francisco Herald* hired George to travel to New York and attempt to win the *Herald* access to the Associated Press news service. When the AP refused, George and a partner established a bureau in Philadelphia to send eastern news to San Francisco via telegraph. Other papers complained to Western Union, which promptly changed its rates to undercut the bureau. The telegraphic monopoly became one of George's first political causes. In 1871 he self-published and printed *Our Land and Land Policy, National and State*, a pamphlet whose ideas would become the germ of *Progress and Poverty*. He also joined the new *San Francisco Evening Post*—the city's first penny newspaper, at a time when one-cent pieces had to be imported from the east for newsboys to make change—as editor, using its pages to crusade against the increasingly powerful railroad interests.[8]

George wrote *Progress and Poverty* between September 1877 and March 1879 and sent the manuscript to D. Appleton & Co. in New York. Appleton was the American publisher of the British political economist Herbert Spencer's *Social Statics*, as well as of an "International Scientific Series" into which *Progress and Poverty* might fit. But the firm rejected George's book: "It has the merit of being written with great clearness and force, but it is very aggressive. There is very little to encourage the publication of any such work at this time and we feel we must decline it." George's brother and two friends visited William H. Appleton in New York, who restated the conviction that the book "would not pay."[9] When Harper & Brothers and Charles Scribner's Sons also rejected *Progress and Poverty*, George began the process of publishing it himself in San Francisco. He had just begun a weekly newspaper, the *State*, at a printing office owned by a former partner. He closed the paper and turned to his book, setting the first sticks of type himself. He revised chapters as the printers continued the composition. His old partner displayed faith in George's book by volunteering to underwrite the stereotyping. Another friend suggested subscription publication, and George produced an "informal 'Author's Edition' of five hundred copies," along with a prospectus.[10] He sent unbound copies of that edition to publishers on both sides of the Atlantic. And then, reversing its earlier decision, D. Appleton & Co. offered to publish it if George supplied the plates, which he did. The book appeared in a two-dollar edition (with royalty to George of 15 percent), and reviews began to notice *Progress and Poverty*. It sold in England, Europe, and Australia as well as the United States; there was also an edition in German. By October 1880, George estimated that the circulation had reached 75,000 or 100,000 copies. *Truth*, a New York penny paper aimed at working-class readers, serialized it, and D. Appleton & Co. produced a one-dollar edition. The John W. Lovell Co., known as a publisher of cheap, paperbound "libraries" and as a "pirate" that disregarded the courtesy of the trade, also published *Progress and Poverty*: in a twenty-cent edition that brought George few royalties but many more readers.[11]

Among the readers of that edition was twenty-one-year-old Hamlin Garland, then chafing at his family's farming existence in South Dakota.[12] George's ideas found fertile soil in the Midwest and Great Plains in these years of incipient populist revolt. But it was Garland's own background as a consumer of printed words that ultimately enabled him to weave George's ideology into a new vision of American literature. Garland's memory of his earliest reading included *Beauty and the Beast*, *Aladdin and His Wonderful Lamp*, and *Mother Goose*, but also *The Female Spy*, "a Tale of the Rebellion."[13] In a rural school outside Osage, Iowa, McGuffey's readers exposed him to a cornucopia of Anglo-American literature. Shakespeare's characters "all became a part of our thinking and helped us to measure the large figures of our own literature, for Whittier, Bryant and Longfellow also had place in these volumes," and "extracts from *The Deer Slayer* and *The Pilot* gave us a notion that in Cooper we had a novelist of weight and importance, one to put beside Scott and Dickens." Out of school, Garland enjoyed the *New York Weekly*, a story paper, and "Beadle's Dime Novels"; years later, he thought it "impossible for any print to be as magical to any boy these days as those weeklies were to me in 1871." He also relished Edward Eggleston's *The Hoosier Schoolmaster* (1871), a serialized "chronicle of everyday life" and "a perfectly successful attempt to interest western readers in a story of the middle border."[14] Old books such as Jane Porter's *The Scottish Chiefs* and new story papers, classic British literature and American tales, almanacs and biographies and cheap fiction: all enthralled young Garland.

Middle-class tastes and habits also inflected Garland's reading, especially after his family moved into town. Urban America, whether New York or San Francisco, was certainly growing rapidly by 1880, but more Americans still lived in rural areas and the towns that served as their county seats and market hubs. Osage, the seat of Mitchell County, was such a town, with a population of 1,846 in 1885.[15] An emergent class structure included prosperous learned professionals and business owners; a middle class of clerks and teachers and small-business owners; skilled craft workers; and unskilled workers and agricultural laborers.

The institutions of print there emanated from and catered to the professional and middling classes. Schools included Cedar Valley Seminary, which was a Baptist institution founded in 1862, and a public school that had eight grades by 1885. Fourteen leisured women and men founded the Shakespearean Class in 1881. After the men withdrew, the remaining women renamed it the Shakespearean Club—a literary society akin to the women's reading groups appearing nationwide in the 1890s. Two local newspapers served Osage's citizens; Chicago papers were also readily available. General stores sold books, as did a bookshop and stationery store operated by the son of the *Mitchell County Press*'s editor. The Osage Library Association, a subscription library established in 1871, became the tax-supported Sage Public Library five years later, the same year the American Library Association was founded. Residents could also borrow books from church libraries and the reading rooms of local associations or order books by mail from catalogs such as Montgomery Ward's. Subscription book agents frequented Osage, as they did towns across rural America. Some publishers tried to enlist agents within the town, calculating that neighbor-to-neighbor sales might succeed better than impersonal door-to-door canvassing. In Osage, as elsewhere in the United States, discourses about beneficial and pernicious reading surrounded ordinary citizens who read across the boundaries of genre and respectability. The *Osage News* reprinted a Kansas City newspaper article in 1884 decrying "dime novels, flashy story papers and illustrated papers that make crime attractive."[16] But citizens like Hamlin Garland read more promiscuously than Comstock-era moralists might have wished.

Garland's conception of the literary developed at Cedar Valley Seminary. At sixteen he joined a Sunday school class where he mingled with students from the seminary, prompting him to attend that autumn. His family returned to the farm the next year, but Garland continued to attend the winter terms until 1881, boarding in town during the week and going home every Friday. In the seminary, which for Garland "symbolized freedom from the hay fork and the hoe," he endured elocution drills and learned the cachet of softened hands, store-bought clothes, and nice shoes.[17] From the "pitifully small" school library, he borrowed Scott, Dickens, Thackeray, and especially Hawthorne and abandoned his juvenile fare: "never again did I fall to the low level of *Jack Harkaway*," formerly one of his favorite Beadle dime novels. "I now possessed a literary touchstone with which I tested the quality of other books and other minds."[18] But Garland was forging more than a middle-class literary sensibility. With his father, he felt the religious faith of his upbringing dim as he read the lectures of the agnostic Robert Ingersoll, printed in Chicago newspapers and later collected into *Some Mistakes of Moses* (1879). Home from the seminary on weekends, attending a lyceum at the rural schoolhouse, he encountered the poetry of Californian Joaquin Miller, "at once American and western."[19] After his family left Iowa for the South Dakota plains in 1881, Garland read the book that was sweeping the West: *Progress and Poverty*. George's indictment of individual land ownership fueled Garland's discontent with "pioneering the plain."[20] He left for Boston, further schooling, and a different life.

Six years later, twenty-seven-year-old Hamlin Garland returned to Iowa to visit the places of his youth. For him, the country surrounding Osage now possessed an "atmosphere" he could deploy for literary purposes. "This was my country — my people," and he wondered why nobody had told their stories the way New Englanders' had seen print for decades. Influenced by literary realism and Henry George's political economy, Garland "perceived life without its glamour": the backbreaking labor that farm families performed day after day, "the essential tragedy and hopelessness of most human life under the conditions into which our society was swiftly hardening."[21] This was not the middle-class ideal of self-made men and feminine domesticity, the midcentury ideal now crumbling under the weight of social, political, and cultural divisions between owners and workers, city and country. Instead, it was the hallmark of Garland's short stories, beginning with "A Prairie Heroine," which he thought "entirely too grim to find a place in the pages of the *Century* or *Harper's*." He sent the story to the *Arena*, a "frankly radical" new Boston monthly, whose editor, Benjamin Orange Flower, accepted it immediately and sent Garland $100, apologizing that he could not "match the prices of magazines like the *Century*." The *Century* itself soon accepted Garland's "A Spring Romance" with a check for $500 and a letter of praise from Richard Watson Gilder. That letter mattered the most to an author whose literary standards derived from the East, even if his political ideology rang with western populism: "I regarded Gilder as second only to Howells in all that had to do with the judgment of fiction."[22] The *Arena*'s editor proposed collecting Garland's stories into a book, which became *Main-Travelled Roads* (1891), an American book for a new context. Harper & Brothers soon acquired the rights to republish it. For the next twenty years, Garland, the "son of the middle border" who made a career in Boston, published his fictional and autobiographical narratives with America's most venerable firm.

By the 1880s, the industrial book dominated American publishing, a field defined largely by trade publishers that had built a system of distribution, finance, and communication. In the last twenty years of the century, composition — the skilled trade in which Henry George had begun his working life — became the last significant element of the printing process to be mechanized. The introduction of the linotype and monotype machines would begin a decisive change in the workplace, as typesetters at their cases were replaced by operators at their keyboards. Alternatives to the national trade publishing system always existed in the pages of local newspapers, the products of local printers, and the work of publishers outside the trade such as the John W. Lovell Co. But those alternatives were increasingly embedded in national systems: weekly small-town newspapers purchasing syndicated material; subscription publishers competing with the trade for such works as Ulysses S.

Grant's *Personal Memoirs* (1885–86); reform movements establishing printing concerns to disseminate their ideas across the United States, as religious publishing societies had done since the 1820s. The "American book," too, had developed several clear definitions by 1880. In one sense, it meant the increasingly canonized world of the Whittier dinner, a conception of American literature ratified in the 1880s and 1890s in book series such as Houghton, Mifflin & Co.'s American Men of Letters and in an emergent academic discipline. In another sense, it embraced the California and frontier tales of the dime novels that Hamlin Garland devoured before he rejected them for loftier fare. Tamer versions of such tales, as well as stories from all over the United States, also became the stuff of Harper & Brothers' books and the *Atlantic Monthly*'s local-color fiction. If middle-class notions of education and refinement could lead a young man like Garland to "literature," Americans' diverse reading always transgressed the boundaries of the "literary." Garland's and George's own writings reveal the ways middle-class ideals failed to describe or ameliorate many Americans' realities. The national trade publishing system had created the means for conceptualizing the "American book." But the larger world of print continuously called that conception into question, particularly as American culture itself became more fragmented in the decades after 1880.

NOTES

Abbreviations

AAS	American Antiquarian Society, Worcester, Mass.
ALGPC	*American Literary Gazette and Publishers' Circular*
AM	*Atlantic Monthly*
APCLG	*American Publishers' Circular and Literary Gazette*
GPO	Government Printing Office
HL	Houghton Library, Harvard University, Cambridge, Mass.
HML	Hagley Museum and Library, Wilmington, Del.
Procs. AAS	*Proceedings of the American Antiquarian Society*
PW	*Publishers' Weekly*
USMDR	*United States Magazine and Democratic Review*
WMGL	Winterthur Museum, Gardens, and Library, Winterthur, Del.

Introduction

1. "Report of the Convention," *PW* 10 (22 July 1876): 167. The description of the American Book Trade Association's conference in this and succeeding paragraphs is derived from this issue of *PW*; subsequent citations are to quoted material.

2. Ibid., 168–69.

3. Ibid., 175–76, 184, 186; *PW* 9 (27 May 1876): 702–3.

4. "The Excursion," *PW* 10 (22 July 1876): 193.

5. "Report of the Convention," 181.

6. "Enrolment List of the Convention," *PW* 10 (22 July 1876): 194–96.

7. William Dean Howells, "A Sennight of the Centennial," *AM* 38 (July 1876): 99.

8. Francis A. Walker, ed., *United States Centennial Commission, International Exhibition, 1876: Reports and Awards*, vol. 8 (Washington, D.C.: GPO, 1880), 604–6.

9. Ibid., 541–43.

10. "Machinery Hall," *PW* 10 (1 July 1876): 38.

11. Walker, *United States Centennial Commission*, 573–77.

12. The complete list of awards in this category is in ibid., 579–618.

13. "Machinery Hall," 37.

14. Walker, *United States Centennial Commission*, 588. For Cervi's ancestry, see Manuscript Schedules, Brooklyn (19th Ward), Kings County, N.Y., 144, in Ninth Census of the United States, 1870, where the Italian immigrant lived in a boardinghouse with two New York–born bookbinders, two book finishers (one born in Ireland), a printer, and a compositor. Beckett appeared in the Manuscript Schedules, Cambridge, Middlesex County, Mass., 55, in Tenth Census of the United States, 1880.

15. "The Centennial Exhibition: How Shall Prizes Be Awarded?" *PW* 9 (29 January 1876): 117; "The Awards at Philadelphia," *PW* 9 (27 May 1876): 702; "The Award Question Again," *PW* 10 (8 July 1876): 130–31; "The Award Question," *PW* 10 (12 August 1876): 326.

16. Michael Winship, *American Literary Publishing in the Mid-Nineteenth Century: The Business of Ticknor and Fields* (Cambridge: Cambridge University Press, 1995), 12–13.

17. Ibid., 157–58.

18. "Individual Book Exhibits," *PW* 10 (1 July 1876): 16–27; quotations at 16, 22–23, 26.

19. "The A.B.T.A. at the Centennial," *PW* 9 (15 January 1876): 60–61.

20. "The Opening of the Exhibition," *PW* 9 (13 May 1876): 609.

21. "Centennial Notes," *PW* 9 (8 April 1876): 473.

22. Alfred D. Chandler Jr., *The Visible Hand: The Managerial Revolution in American Business* (Cambridge, Mass.: Belknap Press of Harvard University Press, 1977), 123–44, 209–15; Jeremy Atack and Peter Passell, *A New Economic View of American History from Colonial Times to 1940*, 2nd ed. (New York: W. W. Norton, 1994), 481.

23. S. N. D. North, *The History and Present Condition of the Newspaper and Periodical Press of the United States, with a Catalogue of the Publications of the Census Year* (Washington, D.C.: GPO, 1884), 73.

24. "Centennial Notes," *PW* 9 (26 February 1876): 253; George P. Rowell & Co., comp., *Centennial Newspaper Exhibition, 1876* (New York: George P. Rowell & Co., 1876), iv.

25. George P. Rowell & Co., *Centennial Newspaper Exhibition*, vi, 292, 301. On patent insides, see Charles Johanningsmeier, *Fiction and the American Literary Marketplace: The Role of Newspaper Syndicates, 1860–1900* (Cambridge: Cambridge University Press, 1997), 37. Rowell's exhibition catalog described the stock material as being on the outside, not the inside, of the sheets.

26. "Individual Book Exhibits," 24.

27. Ibid., 16.

28. Richard H. Brodhead, *Cultures of Letters: Scenes of Reading and Writing in Nineteenth-Century America* (Chicago: University of Chicago Press, 1993), 120, 133.

29. "Individual Book Exhibits," 18. On the dictionary controversy, see Kenneth Cmiel, *Democratic Eloquence: The Fight over Popular Speech in Nineteenth-Century America* (New York: Morrow, 1990), 82–90.

30. Rose Marie Cutting, "America Discovers Its Literary Past: Early American Literature in Nineteenth-Century Anthologies," *Early American Literature* 9 (1975): 226–51; Ezra Greenspan, *George Palmer Putnam: Representative American Publisher* (University Park: Pennsylvania State University Press, 2000), 216–17, 383, 386–88.

31. [Sydney Smith], review of Adam Seybert, *Statistical Annals of the United States of America*, in *Edinburgh Review* 33 (January 1820): 79.

32. James D. McCabe, *The Illustrated History of the Centennial Exhibition* (Philadelphia: National Pub. Co., 1876), 644; Walker, *United States Centennial Commission*, 328.

33. Walker, *United States Centennial Commission*, 68.

34. Ibid., 203–4.

35. J. D. B. DeBow, *Statistical View of the United States . . . Being a Compendium of the Seventh Census* (Washington, D.C.: Beverley Tucker, Senate Printer, 1854), 142, 150–51; U.S. Bureau of the Census, *Historical Statistics of the United States: Colonial Times to 1957* (Washington, D.C.: GPO, 1960), 207–8, 211, 213.

36. Anne M. Boylan, *Sunday School: The Formation of an American Institution, 1790–1880* (New Haven: Yale University Press, 1988), 31–33.

37. Walker, *United States Centennial Commission*, 212–13.

38. DeBow, *Statistical View of the United States*, 126; Bureau of the Census, *Statistics of the Population of the United States at the Tenth Census (June 1, 1880)* (Washington, D.C.: GPO, 1883), 744–51.

39. See esp. Stuart M. Blumin, *The Emergence of the Middle Class: Social Experience in the American City, 1760–1900* (Cambridge: Cambridge University Press, 1989), the introduction of which distinguishes middle-class "awareness" from Marxist class consciousness, drawing upon the work of Anthony Giddens. On the ambivalence of a "provincial middle class" toward urban middle-class culture, see Catherine E. Kelly, *In the New England Fashion: Reshaping Women's Lives in the Nineteenth Century* (Ithaca, N.Y.: Cornell University Press, 1999). Brian Roberts offers a similar argument about middle-class California migrants' relation to print culture about the Gold Rush in *American Alchemy: The California Gold Rush and Middle-Class Culture* (Chapel Hill: University of North Carolina Press, 2000). For the development of middle-class economic patterns and cultural styles west of New England, see John Mack Faragher, *Sugar Creek: Life on the Illinois Prairie* (New Haven: Yale University Press, 1986), esp. 173–215; and Susan Lee Johnson, *Roaring Camp: The Social World of the California Gold Rush* (New York: W. W. Norton, 2000).

40. On the links and distinctions between emerging definitions of professionalism and the middle class, see Burton J. Bledstein, *The Culture of Professionalism: The Middle Class and the Development of Higher Education in America* (New York: W. W. Norton, 1976), and "Introduction: Storytellers to the Middle Class," in *The Middling Sorts: Explorations in the History of the American Middle Class*, ed. Burton J. Bledstein and Robert D. Johnston (New York: Routledge, 2001), 1–25.

41. DeBow, *Statistical View of the United States*, 126; Joseph C. G. Kennedy, *Population of the United States in 1860; Compiled from the Original Returns of the Eighth Census* (Washington, D.C.: GPO, 1864), 656–57; Francis A. Walker, *Ninth Census, Volume III: The Statistics of the Wealth and Industry of the United States* (Washington, D.C.: GPO, 1872), 832; Bureau of the Census, *Statistics of the Population (Tenth Census)*, 744.

42. Lee Soltow and Edward Stevens, *The Rise of Literacy and the Common School in the United States: A Socioeconomic Analysis to 1870* (Chicago: University of Chicago Press, 1981), 58–88.

43. [Catharine E. Beecher], *The Duty of American Women to Their Country* (New York: Harper & Brothers, 1845), 112–31.

44. Walker, *United States Centennial Commission*, 88–90.

45. Ibid., 96–97.

46. Jon Reyhner and Jeanne Eder, *American Indian Education: A History* (Norman: University of Oklahoma Press, 2004), 72–73.

47. William G. McLoughlin, *After the Trail of Tears: The Cherokees' Struggle for Sovereignty, 1839–1880* (Chapel Hill: University of North Carolina Press, 1993), 86–96.

48. George P. Rowell & Co., *Centennial Newspaper Exhibition*, 168; Reyhner and Eder, *American Indian Education*, 78–79; John M. Coward, "Explaining the Little Bighorn: Race and Progress in the Native Press," *Journalism Quarterly* 71 (1994): 540–49.

49. David J. Whittaker, "The Web of Print: Toward a History of the Book in Early Mormon Culture," *Journal of Mormon History* 23 (1997): 1–41; Douglas D. Alder, Paula J. Goodfellow, and Ronald G. Watt, "Creating a New Alphabet for Zion: The Origin of the Deseret Alphabet," *Utah Historical Quarterly* 52 (1984): 275–86.

50. "The New Century," *Woman's Journal* 7 (13 May 1876): 156.

51. Robert W. Rydell, *All the World's a Fair: Visions of Empire at American International Expositions, 1876–1916* (Chicago: University of Chicago Press, 1984), 33–35.

52. *New York Herald*, 11 May 1876; *Centennial Exposition Guide* (Philadelphia: G. Lawrence, [1876?]), quoted in Rydell, *All the World's a Fair*, 28–29; McCabe, *Illustrated History*, 493.

53. Clement Eaton, *Freedom of Thought in the Old South* (Durham, N.C.: Duke University Press, 1940), 127–43, 162–95; David Grimsted, *American Mobbing, 1828–1861: Toward Civil War* (New York: Oxford University Press, 1998), 115.

54. The concept of "imagined communities" defined by print derives from Benedict Anderson, *Imagined Communities: Reflections on the Origin and Spread of Nationalism* (London: Verso, 1983). Specific applications of Anderson's argument to the Union and Confederacy include Drew Gilpin Faust, *The Creation of Confederate Nationalism: Ideology and Identity in the Civil War South* (Baton Rouge: Louisiana State University Press, 1988); and Alice Fahs, *The Imagined Civil War: Popular Literature of the North and South, 1861–1865* (Chapel Hill: University of North Carolina Press, 2001).

55. *Manufactures of the United States in 1860; Compiled from the Original Returns of the Eighth Census* (Washington, D.C.: GPO, 1865), 715–18; Joseph C. G. Kennedy, *Preliminary Report of the Eighth Census* (Washington, D.C.: GPO, 1862), 131; Fahs, *Imagined Civil War*, 21, 38.

56. DeBow, *Statistical View of the United States*, 142; Bureau of the Census, *Statistics of the Population (Tenth Census)*, 916–18, and *Report of the Manufactures of the United States at the Tenth Census (June 1, 1880)* (Washington, D.C.: GPO, 1883), 66–67.

CHAPTER 1
Manufacturing and Book Production

1. *Report of the Commissioner of Patents, for the Year 1850; Part 1: Arts and Manufactures*, 31st Cong., 2nd sess., House Executive Document 32 (Washington, D.C.: GPO, 1851; serial set 600), 398.

2. George A. Kubler, *A New History of Stereotyping* (New York: J. J. Little & Ives, 1941); Michael Winship, "Printing from Plates in the Nineteenth Century United States," *Printing History* 5, no. 2 (1983): 15–26.

3. Michael Schudson, *Discovering the News: A Social History of American Newspapers* (New York: Basic Books, 1978).

4. William Dean Howells, "The Country Printer," *Scribner's Magazine* 13 (May 1893): 539–58, esp. 545–46; Jacob Abbott, *The Harper Establishment; or, How the Story Books Are Made* (New York: Harper & Brothers, 1855), esp. 20–23, 42–44, 119–23.

5. See recapitulation at the end of Riverside Press, Press Earnings, 1867–71, HL; and 1868 inventory laid into envelope at front of Charles Hamilton, Printer Work and Expense Book, 1875–1905, AAS.

6. Theodore Low De Vinne, *The Practice of Typography: A Treatise on . . . Plain Printing Types* (New York: Century, 1900), 20-27.

7. Ibid., 18-19.

8. Maurice Annenberg, *Type Foundries of America and Their Catalogs*, 2nd ed., with additions by Stephen O. Saxe (New Castle, Del.: Oak Knoll, 1994).

9. See Thomas MacKellar, *The American Printer: A Manual of Typography*, 15th ed. (Philadelphia: MacKellar, Smiths, & Jordan, 1885), 27; and Theodore Low De Vinne, *The Printers' Price List: A Manual* (New York: Francis Hart & Co., 1871), 429.

10. Richard L. Hopkins, *Origin of the American Point System for Printer's Type Measurement* (Terra Alta, W.Va.: Hill & Dale, 1976), 29, 39-40.

11. Rob Roy Kelly, *American Wood Type: 1828-1900* (New York: Van Nostrand Reinholt, 1969).

12. Michael Winship, "'The Greatest Book of Its Kind': The Publishing History of *Uncle Tom's Cabin*," *Procs. AAS* 109 (1999): 323-25.

13. *New American Cyclopaedia: A Popular Dictionary of General Knowledge*, ed. George Ripley and Charles A. Dana, vol. 13 [Parr-Redwitz] (New York: D. Appleton & Co., 1861), 589; "Measuring Type or Matter," in J. Luther Ringwalt, *American Encyclopædia of Printing* (Philadelphia: Menamin & Ringwalt, 1871), 303-4.

14. John F. Trow, *Specimen Book of the Letterpress, Stereotype, Electrotype, and Wood-Cut Printing Establishment of John F. Trow* (New York: John F. Trow, 1856).

15. Ringwalt, *American Encyclopædia of Printing*, 24-25, 478-82; W. W. Pasko, ed., *American Dictionary of Printing and Bookmaking* (New York: H. Lockwood & Co., 1894), 75, 548, 561-64; Walker Rumble, *The Swifts: Printers in the Age of Typesetting Races* (Charlottesville: University Press of Virginia, 2003), [44]-83, 143-44. More generally, see John S. Thompson, *History of Composing Machines* (Chicago: Inland Printer, 1904); and Richard E. Huss, *The Development of Printers' Mechanical Typesetting Methods, 1822-1925* (Charlottesville: University Press of Virginia, 1972).

16. Judith A. McGaw, *Most Wonderful Machine: Mechanization and Social Change in Berkshire Paper Making, 1801-1885* (Princeton: Princeton University Press, 1987), 96-116.

17. John Bidwell, "The Brandywine Paper Mill and the Anglo-American Book Trade, 1787-1837" (Ph.D. thesis, Oxford University, 1992), 177-78, 247, 297; Dard Hunter, *Papermaking: The History and Technique of an Ancient Craft*, 2nd ed. (New York: Knopf, 1947), 351-68, 544-46; Lyman Horace Weeks, *A History of Paper-Manufacturing in the United States, 1690-1916* (New York: Lockwood Trade Journal, 1916), 302.

18. James M. Willcox, "Paper Making in the United States," in *Report of the Commissioner of Patents, for the Year 1850*, 404; W. J. Barrow Research Laboratory, *Strength and Other Characteristics of Book Papers, 1800-1899*, Permanence/Durability of the Book, no. 5 (Richmond, Va.: W. J. Barrow Research Laboratory, 1967), 15-16, 23.

19. Hunter, *Papermaking*, [374]-99, 555-75; Edwin Sutermeister, *The Story of Papermaking* (Boston: S. D. Warren, 1954), [49]-111; Barrow, *Strength and Other Characteristics*, table 3.

20. Hunter, *Papermaking*, [400]-408; Willcox, "Paper Making," 406.

21. Barrow, *Strength and Other Characteristics*, 16-17, table 3.

22. Many such orders survive in the Tileston and Hollingsworth Papers (1765-1963), AAS.

23. De Vinne, *Printers' Price List*, 18, 21–22; Warren S. Tryon and William Charvat, eds., *The Cost Books of Ticknor and Fields and Their Predecessors, 1832–1858* (New York: Bibliographical Society of America, 1949).

24. The wholesale paper trade is documented in the correspondence files of the Tileston and Hollingsworth Papers. D. Monachesi and Albert B. Yohn, eds., *The Stationer's Hand-Book: A Practical Business Guide* (New York: Office of Publishers' Weekly, 1876), illustrates the variety of the stationery business.

25. Frank H. Norton, ed., *Frank Leslie's Historical Register of the United States Centennial Exposition, 1876* (New York: Frank Leslie's Publishing House, 1877), 70, 268–69, 272–73, 293–95; James D. McCabe, *The Illustrated History of the Centennial Exhibition* (Philadelphia: National Pub. Co., 1876), 494–98, 712, 714–16; *Old "No. 1": The Story of Isaiah Thomas and His Printing Press* (Worcester, Mass.: AAS, 1989), unpaged.

26. Stephen O. Saxe, *American Iron Hand Presses* (New Castle, Del.: Oak Knoll, 1992), vii–xi, 3–13, 43–47; Rollo G. Silver, *The American Printer, 1787–1825* (Charlottesville: University Press of Virginia, 1967), 47–53; Pasko, *American Dictionary of Printing and Bookmaking*, 577.

27. Ringwalt, *American Encyclopædia of Printing*, 21.

28. Frank E. Comparato, *Chronicles of Genius and Folly: R. Hoe & Company and the Printing Press as a Service to Democracy* (Culver City, Calif.: Labyrinthos, 1979), 3–23, 359–64; James Moran, *Printing Presses: History and Development from the Fifteenth Century to Modern Times* (Berkeley: University of California Press, 1973), [113]–16; Pasko, *American Dictionary of Printing*, 9.

29. Moran, *Printing Presses*, [101]–9; Comparato, *Chronicles of Genius and Folly*, 5–9, 37–43.

30. Moran, *Printing Presses*, [173]–96; Comparato, *Chronicles of Genius and Folly*, 261–70, 289, 317–26; Ringwalt, *American Encyclopædia of Printing*, 86–88.

31. Moran, *Printing Presses*, [143]–55; Ralph Green, *History of the Platen Jobber* (Chicago: Printing Office of Philip Reed, 1953).

32. Ringwalt, *American Encyclopædia of Printing*, 119–20, 172, 190, 217–19, 441, 447; Pasko, *American Dictionary of Printing*, 156, 196–97, 245, 461–63, 490–91, 526.

33. See note 5 above.

34. George Bruce, *A Priced List of Printing Types and Materials* (New York: G. Bruce, 1856), 5.

35. R. Hoe & Co. catalog (New York: R. Hoe & Co., 1867), 11. For the 1871 prices of a full range of presses, see De Vinne, *Printers' Price List*, 434–39.

36. Comparato, *Chronicles of Genius and Folly*, 537.

37. De Vinne, *Printers' Price List*, 76. De Vinne surely based these figures on Francis Hart & Co., where he was a junior partner.

38. Abbott, *Harper Establishment*, 20–23, 42–44, 119–21.

39. De Vinne, *Printers' Price List*, 69–70.

40. Michael Winship, *American Literary Publishing in the Mid-Nineteenth Century: The Business of Ticknor and Fields* (Cambridge: Cambridge University Press, 1995), 123.

41. Sue Allen, *American Book Covers, 1830–1900* (Washington, D.C.: Library of Congress, 1998); William Tomlinson and Richard Masters, *Bookcloth, 1823–1980* (Stockport, U.K.: Dorothy Tomlinson, 1996), 76.

42. Joseph W. Rogers, "The Rise of American Edition Binding," in *Bookbinding in America: Three Essays*, ed. Hellmut Lehmann-Haupt (New York: R. R. Bowker, 1941; repr., 1968), [145]-58; Frank E. Comparato, *Books for the Millions: A History of the Men Whose Methods and Machines Packaged the Printed Word* (Harrisburg, Pa.: Stackpole, 1971), 155-204; Harold E. Sterne, *Catalogue of Nineteenth Century Bindery Equipment* (Cincinnati: Ye Olde Printery, 1978).

43. *Literary World* 10 (22 May 1852): 367.

44. For evidence of this practice, see Ticknor and Fields, Sheet Stock Books, 1860-70, HL.

45. G. Thomas Tanselle, "Book-Jackets, Blurbs, and Bibliographers," *The Library*, 5th ser., 26 (1971): 91-134; Oinonen Book Auctions, *The Ken Leach Collection of Nineteenth Century American Books in Original Dust Jackets and Boxes*, Sale no. 71 (Northampton, Mass., 1984).

46. Winship, *American Literary Publishing*, 128; De Vinne, *Printers' Price List*, 361, 367; Ticknor and Fields (and successors), Cost Book Fair H, May 1875-December 1877, 176, HL.

47. Bamber Gascoigne, *How to Identify Prints: A Complete Guide to Manual and Mechanical Processes from Woodcut to Ink-Jet* (New York: Thames & Hudson, 1986), sec. 20c.

48. James Parton, "Popularizing Art," *AM* 23 (March 1869): 351. More generally, see Peter C. Marzio, *The Democratic Art: Pictures for a 19th-Century America* (Boston: Godine, 1979).

49. Lucien Goldschmidt and Weston J. Naef, *The Truthful Lens: A Survey of the Photographically Illustrated Book, 1844-1914* (New York: Grolier Club, 1980), 145, 206.

50. "Inventories, Valuations, etc., 1860-1875," in Houghton Mifflin Co., Correspondence and Records, 1832-1944, HL; Bruce, *Priced List*, 5.

CHAPTER 2
Labor and Labor Organization

1. Minutes of Typographical Union No. 2, Philadelphia, 1852-87, 17 June 1876. The current location of the original manuscripts is unknown. The photocopies used here are in the possession of David Montgomery.

2. Ibid.

3. See Eric Hobsbawm, "The Labour Aristocracy in Nineteenth-Century Britain," in *Labouring Men: Studies in the History of Labour* (1964; repr., Garden City, N.Y.: Anchor Books, 1967), 321-70.

4. W. J. Rorabaugh, *The Craft Apprentice: From Franklin to the Machine Age in America* (New York: Oxford University Press, 1986), 154. For a more general discussion of the declension model, see Bruce Laurie, *Artisans into Workers: Labor in Nineteenth-Century America* (New York: Hill & Wang, 1989), 15-46.

5. Bruce Laurie, Theodore Hershberg, and George Alter, "Immigrants and Industry: The Philadelphia Experience, 1850-1880," *Journal of Social History* 9 (1975): 229, table 9.

6. Daniel Walkowitz, *Worker City, Company Town: Iron and Cotton-Worker Protest in Troy and Cohoes, New York, 1855-1884* (Urbana: University of Illinois Press, 1978), 101-21.

7. Laurie, Hershberg, and Alter, "Immigrants and Industry," 229.

8. Illinois Bureau of Labor Statistics, *Third Biennial Report* (Springfield, Ill.: H. W. Rokker, 1884), 346–49, 380–81.

9. Massachusetts Bureau of Statistics of Labor, "The Condition of Workingmen's Families," *Sixth Annual Report* (Boston: Wright & Potter, 1875), 191–450.

10. Illinois Bureau of Labor Statistics, *Third Biennial Report*, 381.

11. Moore quoted in George A. Stevens, *New York Typographical Union No. 6: Study of a Modern Trade Union and Its Predecessors* (Albany: J. B. Lyon, 1913), 166, 168, 177–89.

12. In 1850 Pennsylvania ranked second to New York in the value of its publishing output, with a total of $1.7 million as against $6.1 million. See Ronald J. Zboray and Mary Saracino Zboray, "The Boston Book Trades, 1789–1850: A Statistical and Geographical Analysis," in *Entrepreneurs: The Boston Business Community, 1750–1850*, ed. Conrad Wright and Katheryn P. Viens (Boston: Massachusetts Historical Society, 1997), 213.

13. See ibid., esp. 221–23.

14. Quoted in Rorabaugh, *Craft Apprentice*, 151.

15. Ibid., 152.

16. *Boston Evening Traveler*, 9 April 1853.

17. Ethelbert Stewart, "Early Organizations of Printers," *Bulletin of the Bureau of Labor* 61 (Washington, D.C.: GPO, 1905): 905–8 and app. A, no. 12, 987–1000.

18. Charlotte E. Morgan, *The Origin and History of the New York Employing Printers' Association: The Evolution of a Trade Association* (New York: Columbia University Press, 1930), 50–51.

19. *Philadelphia Public Ledger*, 30 July 1849.

20. Quoted in Stevens, *New York Typographical Union No. 6*, 222.

21. Quoted in Morgan, *Origin and History*, 68–69.

22. For a different interpretation of employer collusion, see William S. Pretzer, "The Quest for Autonomy and Discipline: Labor and Technology in the Book Trades," *Procs. AAS* 96 (1986): 95–96.

23. Morgan, *Origin and History*, 13.

24. Quoted in Stevens, *New York Typographical Union No. 6*, 255.

25. Morgan, *Origin and History*, 33.

26. *Massachusetts Spy* (Worcester), 14 April 1854.

27. See Irene Tichenor, "Master Printers Organize: The Typothetæ of the City of New York, 1865–1906," in *Small Business in American Life*, ed. Stuart Bruchey (New York: Columbia University Press, 1980), 169–91.

28. Ibid., 175.

29. Ibid., 177–78.

30. See Lloyd Ulman, *The Rise of the National Trade Union: The Development and Significance of Its Structure, Governing Institutions, and Economic Policies* (Cambridge, Mass.: Harvard University Press, 1955).

31. Stewart, "Early Organizations of Printers," 911–22.

32. Executive Council, International Typographical Union, *A Study of the International Typographical Union, 1852–1963* (Colorado Springs: ITU, 1964), 2:17, 39.

33. See Arthur R. Porter Jr., *Job Property Rights: A Study of the Job Controls of the International Typographical Union* (New York: King's Crown Press, 1954).

34. Minutes of Typographical Union, 27 June, 10 October 1863.

35. Seymour Martin Lipset, Martin A. Trow, and James S. Coleman, *Union Democracy: The Internal Politics of the International Typographical Union* (Garden City, N.Y.: Doubleday, 1956), 33.

36. Zboray and Zboray, "Boston Book Trades," 253–59.

37. *The Charter and By-Laws of the Philadelphia Typographical Society, with the Members' Names* (Philadelphia, 1843). See also *Philadelphia Public Ledger*, 11 August 1849.

38. Sean Wilentz, *Chants Democratic: New York City and the Rise of the American Working Class, 1788–1850* (New York: Oxford University Press, 1984), 406, table 15.

39. See Laurie, Hershberg, and Alter, "Immigrants and Industry," 232–38.

40. *The Pennsylvanian* (Philadelphia), 11 August 1835. For an original interpretation of the "maleness" of printing, see Ava Baron, "An 'Other' Side of Gender Antagonism at Work: Men, Boys, and the Remasculinization of Printers' Work," in *Work Engendered: Toward a New History of American Labor*, ed. Ava Baron (Ithaca, N.Y.: Cornell University Press, 1991), 47–69.

41. This brief treatment necessarily compresses a more complicated story: women's exclusion from printing was no more linear than the decline of the craft. Instead, there were moments of breakthrough, which in turn evoked opposition. See, for instance, Stewart, "Early Organizations of Printers," 884; Executive Council, *Study of the International Typographical Union*, 1:234–36; and Stevens, *New York Typographical Union No. 6*, 421–29.

42. See *The Printer* (New York), April 1863 and August 1864. See also *Typographical Journal* 26 (1905): 494–95.

43. United States Senate, Committee on Education and Labor, *Report of the Committee of the Senate upon the Relations between Labor and Capital, and Testimony Taken by the Committee*, 48th Cong., 2nd sess. (Washington, D.C.: GPO, 1885), 1:41, 43. See also Walker Rumble, *The Swifts: Printers in the Age of Typesetting Races* (Charlottesville: University Press of Virginia, 2003).

44. Stevens, *New York Typographical Union No. 6*, 114–40, 143–46. See also Stewart, "Early Organizations of Printers," 954–56.

45. Stewart, "Early Organizations of Printers," 867–68; Stevens, *New York Typographical Union No. 6*, 143–46.

46. On tramping in general, see Eric Hobsbawm, "The Tramping Artisan," in *Labouring Men*, 41–74.

47. Stewart, "Early Organizations of Printers," 867; Stevens, *New York Typographical Union No. 6*, 150.

48. Stevens, *New York Typographical Union No. 6*, 441–42.

49. Stewart, "Early Organizations of Printers," 911–17.

50. *Constitution and By-Laws of the Philadelphia Typographical Union, No. 2* (Philadelphia: Co-Operative Print, 1870), 14.

51. Minutes of Typographical Union, 15 May 1866, 16 October 1869; Elizabeth Faulkner Baker, "The Printing Foreman — Union Man: A Historical Sketch," *Industrial and Labor Relations Review* 4 (January 1951): 223–35.

52. Executive Council, *Study of the International Typographical Union*, 1:296.

53. See Stevens, *New York Typographical Union No. 6*, 197; and David Montgomery, "Workers' Control of Machine Production in the Nineteenth Century," in *Workers' Con-*

trol in America, ed. David Montgomery (New York: Cambridge University Press, 1979), 15–18.

54. *Philadelphia Public Ledger*, 7 November 1838.

55. Morgan, *Origin and History*, 58–60.

56. See Minutes of the Typographical Union No. 2 Business Committee, 1850–61. The current location of the original manuscripts is unknown. The photocopies used here are in the possession of David Montgomery.

57. See, for example, ibid., 2 September 1850, 11 December 1858; and Minutes of Typographical Union, 11 December 1858.

58. See, for example, Minutes of Typographical Union, 10 March 1860.

59. Ibid., 14 April 1860.

60. Ibid., 18 October 1859.

61. Ibid. See also ibid., 16 June 1866, 19 August, 21 November 1868, and 19 August 1882.

62. Ibid., 12 April, 18 December 1875, 17 June, 16 September 1876.

63. Ibid., 20 April, 18 May 1878.

64. James L. Homer, *An Address Delivered before the Massachusetts Charitable Mechanic Association, on the Celebration of Their Tenth Triennial Festival* (Boston: Homer, Palmer and Joseph Adams, 1836).

65. *Boston Courier*, 13 April 1850; Joseph T. Buckingham, *Personal Memoirs and Recollections of Editorial Life* (Boston: Ticknor, Reed, and Fields, 1852), 1:81–82.

66. See Gary J. Kornblith, "Becoming Joseph T. Buckingham: The Struggle for Artisanal Independence in Early Nineteenth-Century Boston," in *American Artisans: Crafting Social Identity*, ed. Howard Rock et al. (Baltimore: Johns Hopkins University Press, 1995), 124–26.

67. *Boston Courier*, 2 June 1832.

68. Quoted in Kornblith, "Becoming Joseph T. Buckingham," 131.

69. Quoted in Stewart, "Early Organizations of Printers," 982.

70. See, for example, *Constitution and By-Laws of the Philadelphia Typographical Union No. 2*, 23–24; and Stewart, "Early Organizations of Printers," 987–1000.

71. Morgan, *Origin and History*, 53–57.

72. See, for example, the *Philadelphia Public Ledger*, 22 July and 21 August 1850.

73. Stevens, *New York Typographical Union No. 6*, 454–55. See also Minutes of Typographical Union, 17 March, 21 April 1866, 21 December 1867, 19 September 1868, 16 January 1869, and 26 February 1870.

74. Baron, "Gender Antagonism at Work," 54, 59–67.

75. Baker, "Printing Foreman," 224–25.

76. Quoted in ibid., 226. See also George E. Barnett, "The Printers: A Study in American Trade Unionism," *American Economic Association Quarterly* 10 (October 1909): 228.

77. Executive Council, *Study of the International Typographical Union*, 1:84–87, 2:296–313; Baker, "Printing Foreman," 226–28.

78. Porter, *Job Property Rights*, 9–35; Lipset et al., *Union Democracy*, 17–32.

79. Minutes of Typographical Union, 2 and 16 December 1871, 20 January 1872.

80. J. Thomas Scharf and Thompson Westcott, *History of Philadelphia, 1609–1884* (Philadelphia: L. H. Everts & Co., 1884), 3:2026–30.

81. Minutes of Typographical Union, 13 August 1864, 20 October 1866, 15 May 1880.

82. Ibid., 16 December 1871, 19 September 1874, 21 February 1880.

83. Ibid., 21 July 1879, 7 October 1882.

84. Ibid., 21 October 1880.

85. Ibid., 20 July 1878.

86. Ibid., 21 February 1880.

87. Ibid., 7 October 1882.

88. Ibid., 19 August, 7 October 1882.

89. Ibid., 1 October, 17 December 1881.

90. Harry W. Laidler, *Boycotts and the Labor Struggle: Economic and Legal Aspects* (New York: Russell & Russell, 1913), esp. 31–68; Michael Gordon, "The Labor Boycott in New York City, 1880–1886," *Labor History* 16 (1975): 187–227.

91. Minutes of Typographical Union, 30 January, 1 February 1884; David Nasaw, *Children of the City at Work and at Play* (New York: Anchor Press, 1985), 62–87.

92. Kenneth Fones-Wolf, *Trade Union Gospel: Christianity and Labor in Industrial Philadelphia, 1865–1915* (Philadelphia: Temple University Press, 1989), esp. 38–94. See also Minutes of Typographical Union, 21 June and 19 July 1884.

93. Minutes of Typographical Union, 17 October, 21 November 1885.

94. Ibid., 21 November 1885, 16 January, 20 March 1886.

95. Ibid., 20 April 1886.

96. Quoted in Baker, "Printing Foreman," 234. For information on Francis, see Charles Francis, *Printing for Profit* (Indianapolis: Bobbs-Merrill, 1917).

CHAPTER 3

Authors and Literary Authorship

1. Nathaniel Hawthorne to Elizabeth C. Hawthorne, 13 March 1821, in *Letters, 1813–1843*, ed. Thomas Woodson et al., vol. 15 of *The Centenary Edition of the Works of Nathaniel Hawthorne* (Columbus: Ohio State University Press, 1984), 139.

2. Ralph Waldo Emerson, "The Poet," in *Essays: Second Series* (Boston: James Munroe & Co., 1844), 41.

3. Richard H. Brodhead, *Cultures of Letters: Scenes of Reading and Writing in Nineteenth-Century America* (Chicago: University of Chicago Press, 1993), 115.

4. Michael Winship, *American Literary Publishing in the Mid-Nineteenth Century: The Business of Ticknor and Fields* (Cambridge: Cambridge University Press, 1995), 13–15, 133–34.

5. Ibid., 135; *The House of Putnam, 1837–1872: A Documentary Volume*, ed. Ezra Greenspan, vol. 254 of *Dictionary of Literary Biography* (Detroit: Gale, 2002), 162.

6. Raymond L. Kilgour, *Messrs. Roberts Brothers Publishers* (Ann Arbor: University of Michigan Press, 1952), 110–11.

7. Donald Sheehan, *This Was Publishing: A Chronicle of the Book Trade in the Gilded Age* (Bloomington: Indiana University Press, 1952), 80–82.

8. Winship, *American Literary Publishing*, 133.

9. Ibid., 44.

10. Eugene Exman, *The Brothers Harper: A Unique Publishing Partnership and Its Impact upon the Cultural Life of America from 1817 to 1853* (New York: Harper & Row, 1965), 286.

11. Ellen C. Pratofiorito, "Selling the Vision: Marketability and Audience in Antebellum American Literature" (Ph.D. diss., Rutgers University, 1998), 63, 82–83.

12. "The Pay of Authors," *Congregationalist and Boston Recorder*, 10 October 1867, 184; James C. Austin, *Fields of the Atlantic Monthly: Letters to an Editor, 1861–1870* (San Marino, Calif.: Huntington Library and Art Gallery, 1953), 85.

13. Samuel Longfellow, *The Life of Henry Wadsworth Longfellow* (Boston: Ticknor & Co., 1886), 2:35. The *Bibliography of American Literature*, comp. Jacob Blanck et al. (New Haven: Yale University Press, 1963), 4:469–76, lists twenty-eight publications by Ingraham in 1845, all of which appeared in printed white paper wrappers.

14. Michael Anesko, *Friction with the Market: Henry James and the Profession of Authorship* (New York: Oxford University Press, 1986), 31–33 and app. B ("Henry James's Literary Income").

15. Warren S. Tryon, *Parnassus Corner: A Life of James T. Fields, Publisher to the Victorians* (Boston: Houghton Mifflin, 1963), 334–49; Susan Coultrap-McQuin, *Doing Literary Business: American Women Writers in the Nineteenth Century* (Chapel Hill: University of North Carolina Press, 1990), 123.

16. Contracts between Maria S. Cummins and Ticknor and Fields, 20 March 1860, and between Maria S. Cummins and J. E. Tilton & Co., 22 March 1864 and 30 April 1864, Cummins Family Papers, folder 2, Phillips Library, Peabody Essex Museum, Salem, Mass.; *J. E. Tilton & Co.'s Publications* (Boston, 1865): 22; *J. E. Tilton & Co.'s Publications* (Boston, 1866): 32; "An Important English Copyright Case," *ALGPC* 6 (15 January 1866): 174–76.

17. Maria Cummins to Maria Franklin Kittredge Cummins, 9 April, 13 April 1860, Maria Cummins Collection (7076), The Clifton Waller Barrett Library of American Literature, The Albert H. Small Special Collections Library, University of Virginia Library, repr. in Heidi L. M. Jacobs, "Maria Susanna Cummins's London Letters: April 1860," *Legacy* 19 (2003): 246, 249.

18. Michael Winship, "'The Greatest Book of Its Kind': A Publishing History of *Uncle Tom's Cabin*," *Procs. AAS* 109 (1999): 309–32.

19. Ezra Greenspan, *George Palmer Putnam: Representative American Publisher* (University Park: Pennsylvania State University Press, 2000), 254–56.

20. Gail Hamilton [Mary Abigail Dodge], *A Battle of the Books* (Cambridge: Hurd & Houghton, 1870), 285.

21. Herman Melville, *Moby-Dick; or, The Whale*, ed. Harrison Hayford, Hershel Parker, and G. Thomas Tanselle, vol. 6 of *The Writings of Herman Melville* (Evanston and Chicago: Northwestern University Press and the Newberry Library, 1988), 683–89.

22. Herman Melville to Catherine Gansevoort Lansing, 25 July 1876, in *Correspondence*, ed. Harrison Hayford et al., vol. 14 of *The Writings of Herman Melville* (Evanston and Chicago: Northwestern University Press and the Newberry Library, 1993), 437.

23. Eric Gardner, "'This Attempt of Their Sister': Harriet Wilson's *Our Nig* from Printer to Readers," *New England Quarterly* 66 (1993): 226–46.

24. *Anglo-African Magazine* 1 (December 1859): 400.

25. *American Magazine Journalists, 1741–1850*, ed. Sam G. Riley, vol. 73 of *Dictionary of Literary Biography* (Detroit: Gale, 1988), 270–71.

26. Sarah Robbins, "Gendering Gilded Age Periodical Professionalism: Reading Harriet Beecher Stowe's *Hearth and Home* Prescriptions for Women's Writing," in *"The Only Efficient Instrument": American Women Writers and the Periodical, 1837–1916*, ed. Aleta Feinsod Cane and Susan Alves (Iowa City: University of Iowa Press, 2001), 49.

27. Nathaniel Hawthorne to Elizabeth Peabody, 13 August 1857, in *Letters, 1857–1864*, ed. Thomas Woodson et al., vol. 18 of *The Centenary Edition of the Works of Nathaniel Hawthorne* (Columbus: Ohio State University Press, 1987), 89–90.

28. *The Journals and Miscellaneous Notebooks of Ralph Waldo Emerson*, ed. William H. Gilman et al. (Cambridge: Belknap Press of Harvard University Press, 1965), 5:120.

29. Michael Winship, "Hawthorne and the 'Scribbling Women': Publishing *The Scarlet Letter* in the Nineteenth-Century United States," *Studies in American Fiction* 29 (2001): 4.

30. Sheila Post-Lauria, *Correspondent Colorings: Melville in the Marketplace* (Amherst: University of Massachusetts Press, 1996), 151.

31. "Novels and Novel-Reading," *Hours at Home: A Popular Monthly of Instruction and Recreation* 10 (February 1870): 358.

32. Rebecca Harding Davis, "Women in Literature," *Independent*, 7 May 1891, 1.

33. "Authors and Writers," *United States Literary Gazette* 1 (March 1825): 346–47.

34. "The Dinner to Mr. Dickens," *New York Tribune*, 21 February 1842, 4.

35. "National Literature, and the International Copy-right Treaty," *United States Review* 2 [*USMDR* 33] (August 1853): 99; Meredith L. McGill, *American Literature and the Culture of Reprinting, 1834–1853* (Philadelphia: University of Pennsylvania Press, 2003), 275. The *United States Review* had formerly been known, from its 1837 inception, as the *United States Magazine and Democratic Review* and would be renamed the *United States Democratic Review*, 1856–59.

36. Kristie Hamilton, *America's Sketchbook: The Cultural Life of a Nineteenth-Century Genre* (Athens: Ohio University Press, 1998), 8.

37. Nathaniel Hawthorne to William D. Ticknor, 19 January 1855, in *Letters, 1853–1856*, ed. Thomas Woodson et al., vol. 17 of *The Centenary Edition of the Works of Nathaniel Hawthorne* (Columbus: Ohio State University Press, 1987), 304.

38. Nathaniel Hawthorne, *The Scarlet Letter*, ed. William Charvat et al., vol. 1 of *The Centenary Edition of the Works of Nathaniel Hawthorne* (Columbus: Ohio State University Press, 1962), 37, 45.

39. H. Trusta [Elizabeth Stuart Phelps], *The Last Leaf from Sunny Side, with a Memorial of the Author, by Austin Phelps* (Boston: Phillips, Sampson, & Co., 1853), 86.

40. [Henry James], "The Schönberg-Cotta Family," *Nation* 1 (1865): 345.

41. Catharine M. Sedgwick, "Cacoethes Scribendi," *Atlantic Souvenir* (1830): 17–38.

42. Louisa May Alcott to Miss Churchill, 25 December [1878?], Berg Collection, New York Public Library, repr. in Louisa May Alcott, *Little Women*, ed. Anne Hiebert Alton (Orchard Park, N.Y.: Broadview, 2001), 511.

43. Elizabeth Stoddard, "From Our Lady Correspondent," *San Francisco Daily Alta California*, 22 October 1854, 2; repr. in Elizabeth Stoddard, *The Morgesons and Other Writings, Published and Unpublished*, ed. Lawrence Buell and Sandra A. Zagarell (Philadelphia: University of Pennsylvania Press, 1984), 314.

44. Harriet Beecher Stowe, "How May I Know That I Can Make a Writer?" *Hearth and Home*, 30 January 1869, 88, and "How Shall I Learn to Write?" *Hearth and Home*, 16 January 1869, 49.

45. *The Journals of Charlotte Forten Grimké*, ed. Brenda Stevenson (New York: Oxford University Press, 1988), 92, 156, 475.

46. Review of *The Garies and Their Friends*, by Frank J. Webb, *Frederick Douglass' Paper*, 4 December 1857, quoted in Carla L. Peterson, *"Doers of the Word": African-American Women Speakers and Writers in the North (1830–1880)* (New York: Oxford University Press, 1995), 173-74.

47. Nancy Glazener, *Reading for Realism: The History of a U.S. Literary Institution, 1850–1910* (Durham, N.C.: Duke University Press, 1997).

48. Ella K. Blake to Susan Warner, 9 February 1879, Constitution Island Association Warner Collection, Special Collections, U.S. Military Academy, West Point, N.Y., quoted in Susan S. Williams, "Widening the World: Susan Warner, Her Readers, and the Assumption of Authorship," *American Quarterly* 42 (1990): 573; Paul D. Swanwick to Maria Cummins, 28 July 1854, Cummins Family Papers, folder 2, Phillips Library, Peabody Essex Museum, Salem, Mass., quoted in Susan S. Williams, "'Promoting an Extensive Sale': The Production and Reception of *The Lamplighter*," *New England Quarterly* 69 (1996): 193.

49. Review of *Little Women*, by Louisa May Alcott, *Portland (Maine) Advertiser* ([1870?]), Alcott-Pratt Collection, HL, quoted in Janet S. Zehr, "The Response of Nineteenth-Century Audiences to Louisa May Alcott's Fiction," *American Transcendental Quarterly*, n.s., 1 (1987): 324.

50. Journal entry from August 1872, in *Louisa May Alcott: An Intimate Anthology* (New York: New York Public Library and Doubleday, 1997), 173-74.

51. Michael J. Deas, *The Portraits and Daguerreotypes of Edgar Allan Poe* (Charlottesville: University Press of Virginia, 1989), 15-18.

52. Ludwig [Rufus W. Griswold], "Death of Edgar Allan Poe," *New-York Daily Tribune*, 9 October 1849, 2.

53. George Selwyn, "Walt Whitman in Camden," in *Authors at Home: Personal and Biographical Sketches of Well-Known American Writers*, ed. J. L. Gilder and J. B. Gilder (New York: Cassell, 1889), 338-39.

54. David S. Reynolds, *Walt Whitman's America: A Cultural Biography* (New York: Knopf, 1995), 387, 516, 563-70.

55. Nathaniel Hawthorne, *The English Notebooks, 1853–1856*, ed. Thomas Woodson and Bill Ellis, vol. 21 of *The Centenary Edition of the Works of Nathaniel Hawthorne* (Columbus: Ohio State University Press, 1997), 113; Rita Gollin, *Portraits of Nathaniel Hawthorne: An Iconography* (DeKalb: Northern Illinois University Press, 1983), viii-xvi, 34-37.

56. Herman Melville to Evert A. Duyckinck, February 12, 1851, in *Correspondence*, 180.

57. John S. Hart, *The Female Prose Writers of America* (Philadelphia: E. H. Butler & Co., 1852), vii-viii.

58. Mrs. A. J. Graves, *Woman in America* (New York: Harper & Brothers, 1847), 190.

59. Phelps Ward was the daughter of Austin and Elizabeth Stuart Phelps, cited in note 39 above; the daughter assumed her mother's name after the mother's death in 1852.

60. R. H. Stoddard et al., *Poets' Homes: Pen and Pencil Sketches of American Poets and Their Homes* (Boston: D. Lothrop, 1879), 2:98.

61. "Four Luminaries of American Letters," *Frank Leslie's Illustrated Newspaper*, 14 August 1880; Ednah Dow Cheney, *Louisa May Alcott: The Children's Friend* (Boston: L. Prang, 1888).

62. *Louisa May Alcott: Her Life, Letters and Journals*, ed. Ednah D. Cheney (Boston: Roberts Brothers, 1889), iv.

63. Louisa May Alcott to Thomas Niles, [1885], in ibid., 364.

64. Thomas Wentworth Higginson, "Letter to a Young Contributor," *AM* 9 (April 1862): 401–11.

65. Gilder and Gilder, *Authors at Home*, i.

CHAPTER 4

The National Book Trade System

1. Lea & Blanchard correspondence, 1850 II, items #50709 and #51569, and Lea & Blanchard ledger, 1849–53, 63, 656, in Lea & Febiger Archives, Collection #2278, The Historical Society of Pennsylvania; Lea & Blanchard ledger, 1854–60, 305, Library Company of Philadelphia. Unpublished material from The Historical Society of Pennsylvania is quoted by permission. Omitted from Taft's total are several further small orders of less than $10, which presumably represent special orders for customers rather than purchases for stock.

2. Lea & Blanchard correspondence, 1850 I, items #48591, #50045, and #50143, and 1850 II, item #50688.

3. Adolf Growoll, *Book-Trade Bibliography in the United States in the XIXth Century* (New York: Dibdin Club, 1898), xxxiii–xxxv, lxxvi.

4. See, for example, advertisements for the "Literary Bulletin" in *PW* 1 (18 January 1872): 26, and the "Monthly Book Circular" in *PW* 2 (5 September 1872): 240, as well as those by Henry L. Hinton & Co. for "The Library Table" in *American Bookseller* 1 (1 April 1876): 259, and by the American News Company for "Our Book Circular" in *American Bookseller* 2 (1 July 1876): 45.

5. U.S. Bureau of the Census, *Historical Statistics of the United States: Colonial Times to 1957* (Washington, D.C.: GPO, 1960), 8, 14, 427.

6. George Rogers Taylor, *The Transportation Revolution, 1815–1860* (New York: Holt, Rinehart & Winston, 1951), 139–40; Michael Winship, *American Literary Publishing in the Mid-Nineteenth Century: The Business of Ticknor and Fields* (Cambridge: Cambridge University Press, 1995), 151–52.

7. Edwin T. Freedley, *Philadelphia and Its Manufacturers: A Hand-Book Exhibiting the Development, Variety, and Statistics of the Manufacturing Industry of Philadelphia in 1857* (Philadelphia: Edward Young, 1858), 157.

8. Winship, *American Literary Publishing*, 151 and app. A, 193–203.

9. Madeleine B. Stern, "Dissemination of Popular Books in the Midwest and Far West during the Nineteenth Century," in *Getting the Books Out: Papers of the Chicago Conference on the Book in 19th-Century America*, ed. Michael Hackenberg (Washington, D.C.: Center for the Book, Library of Congress, 1987), 87–91.

10. "The Baker & Taylor Company," *American Stationer* 39 (9 April 1896): 655-56.

11. Ibid., 656.

12. Jack Cassius Morris, "The Publishing Activities of S. C. Griggs and Company, 1848-1896; Jansen, McClurg and Company, 1872-1886; and A. C. McClurg and Company, 1886-1900; with Lists of Publications" (master's thesis, University of Illinois, 1941).

13. See, for example, *American Bookseller* 2 (1 July 1876): 40.

14. Winship, *American Literary Publishing*, 152-53.

15. The *American Bookseller* ceased to list itself as the "Official Organ of the American Book Trade Association" with its 15 October 1877 issue.

16. Michael Winship, "Getting the Books Out: Trade Sales, Parcel Sales, and Book Fairs in the Nineteenth-Century United States," in *Getting the Books Out*, 4-25.

17. Quoted in *The Booksellers' League: A History of Its Formation and Ten Years of Its Work*, ed. Adolf Growoll (New York: Booksellers' League, 1905), 34-35.

18. The best source on the nature of the nineteenth-century retail bookshop is Adolf Growoll, *The Profession of Bookselling: A Handbook of Practical Hints for the Apprentice and the Bookseller*, 3 vols. (New York: Office of Publishers' Weekly, 1893-1913).

19. St. Louis Mercantile Library, Accession Books, nos. 1, 3, 5-6 (shelfmark A16), and copy of Smith's *Life at the South* (Buffalo: Geo. H. Derby & Co., 1852), in the collections of Washington University Library, St. Louis (shelfmark PS 2878.S5.5 L5 1852).

20. George Palmer Putnam, "Rough Notes of Thirty Years in the Trade," *APCLG* 1, octavo series (15 July 1863): 244.

21. Ibid.

22. Ibid.; "Publishers' Notice," *Booksellers' Advertiser, and Monthly Register of New Publications, American and Foreign* 2 (1 March 1836): 1; Ezra Greenspan, *George Palmer Putnam: Representative American Publisher* (University Park: Pennsylvania State University Press, 2000), 47, 49.

23. "The American Publishers' Circular," *APCLG* 1 (1 September 1855): 1.

24. "George Palmer Putnam," *Publishers' and Stationers' Weekly Trade Circular* 2 (26 December 1872): 697-98.

25. James D. Norris, *R. G. Dun & Co., 1841-1900: The Development of Credit-Reporting in the Nineteenth Century*, Contributions in Economics and Economic History, no. 20 (Westport, Conn.: Greenwood, 1978), 49-54.

26. D. Appleton & Co. and Wiley & Putnam, "A Card," *Literary World* 1 (6 February 1847): 17; "The Newspapers of the Trade," *Norton's Literary Almanac for 1852* (New York: Charles B. Norton, 1852), 42; Greenspan, *George Palmer Putnam*, 114-15.

27. "Reasons for the Change of Plan in 'The Home Book Circular,' and Explanation of the Intended System," *Appleton's Literary Bulletin* 1 (June 1843): 1.

28. D. Appleton & Co. and Wiley & Putnam, "A Card," 17.

29. Greenspan, *George Palmer Putnam*, 207-8.

30. Perry Miller, *The Raven and the Whale* (New York: Harcourt, Brace & Co., 1956), 238.

31. C[harles] F[enno] Hoffman, "The Literary World," *Literary World* 2 (7 August 1847): 1.

32. "Newspapers of the Trade," 42.

33. Miller, *Raven and the Whale*, 183, 238; Greenspan, *George Palmer Putnam*, 207;

Growoll, *Book-Trade Bibliography*, xxviii, xliii. The annual had various titles: *Norton's Literary Almanac for 1852; Norton's Literary Register and Bookbuyers' Almanac for 1853; Norton's Literary and Educational Register for 1854;* and *Norton's Literary Register; or, Annual Book List, for 1856* (announced for 1855 but not published until the following year).

34. "American Publishers' Circular," 1; Growoll, *Book-Trade Bibliography*, xli.

35. "Mr. Charles B. Norton," *APCLG* 2 (2 February 1856): 61.

36. "Booksellers' Credits," *APCLG* 3 (5 December 1857): 741.

37. "Booksellers' Credits: Six Months or Four," *APCLG* 4 (9 January 1858): 13–14.

38. "Supplement to the Publishers' Weekly: The American Book Trade Convention," *PW* 6 (8 August 1874): 4.

39. Advertisement for *PW*, in *Publishers' Trade List Annual* (New York: Office of the Publishers' Weekly, 1873), front pastedown endpaper.

40. "Annual Summaries; Important to Publishers," *PW* 3 (2 January 1873): 3.

41. "Uniformity in Booksellers' Catalogues," *APCLG* 2 (2 February 1856): 61.

42. O. A. Roorbach, comp., *Bibliotheca Americana: Catalogue of American Publications; Including Reprints and Original Works, from 1820 to 1848, Inclusive* (New York: Orville A. Roorbach, 1849), iii.

43. "The Trade Directory," *PW* 16 (12 July 1879): 28.

44. Jay W. Beswick, *The Work of Frederick Leypoldt: Bibliographer and Publisher* (New York: R. R. Bowker, 1942), 34.

45. "Trade Directory," 28–29.

46. C. N. Caspar, *Caspar's Directory of the American Book, News and Stationery Trade* (Milwaukee: C. N. Caspar's Book Emporium; New York: Office of Publishers' Weekly, 1889), v. Four years earlier, Caspar had published a *Directory of the Antiquarian Booksellers and Dealers in Second-Hand Books of the United States* (Milwaukee: C. N. Caspar, 1885), to which he added a brief supplement in 1887.

47. Beswick, *Frederick Leypoldt*, 29–30.

48. Ibid., 24–25.

49. Ibid., 45–47, 97.

50. Ibid., 50.

51. L. Thorvel Solberg, "The 'Booksellers' Bible,' " *PW* 5 (17 January 1874): 50.

52. "National Organization of the Book Trade," *PW* 1 (28 March 1872): 268.

53. "The First Step," *PW* 4 (11 October 1873): 376; "The Book Trade Convention," *PW* 5 (21 February 1874): 178–79.

54. K. Funk & Co., "Foreign Authors and 'The Standard Series,' " *PW* 17 (15 May 1880): 499.

55. Quoted in Henry Walcott Boynton, *Annals of American Bookselling, 1638–1850* (New York: John Wiley & Sons, 1932), 186.

56. David Kaser, *Messrs. Carey & Lea of Philadelphia: A Study in the History of the Booktrade* (Philadelphia: University of Pennsylvania Press, 1957), 150.

57. Ticknor and Fields, Letter Book, foreign, 1866–77, 69, HL.

58. Ellen B. Ballou, *The Building of the House: Houghton Mifflin's Formative Years* (Boston: Houghton Mifflin, 1970), 279.

59. Rosalind Remer, *Printers and Men of Capital: Philadelphia Book Publishers in the New Republic* (Philadelphia: University of Pennsylvania Press, 1996), 55–65.

60. M. Pollard, *Dublin's Trade in Books, 1550–1800* (Oxford: Clarendon Press, 1989), 74, 143–45, 170.

61. Kaser, *Messrs. Carey & Lea*, 95–110; John Tebbel, *A History of Book Publishing in the United States*, vol. 1 (New York: R. R. Bowker, 1972), 223; James J. Barnes, *Authors, Publishers and Politicians: The Quest for an Anglo-American Copyright Agreement, 1815–1854* (Columbus: Ohio State University Press, 1974), 49–53.

62. Eugene Exman, *The Brothers Harper: A Unique Publishing Partnership and Its Impact upon the Cultural Life of America from 1817 to 1853* (New York: Harper & Row, 1965), 22–24, 48–58; Kaser, *Messrs. Carey & Lea*, 149–53.

63. Barnes, *Authors, Publishers and Politicians*, 5–29.

64. Exman, *Brothers Harper*, 52; *Archives of Harper & Brothers, 1817–1914*, microfilm (Cambridge: Chadwyck-Healey, 1980), reels 22–24.

65. Ticknor and Fields, Letter Book, foreign, 1855–59, 14, HL.

66. Ibid, 16.

67. Ibid.

68. Warren S. Tryon, *Parnassus Corner: A Life of James T. Fields, Publisher to the Victorians* (Boston: Houghton Mifflin, 1963), 302–3.

69. "The Dickens Controversy," *Atlantic Advertiser and Miscellany*, 1, bound with *AM* 20 (August 1867).

70. Ticknor and Fields, Letter Book, foreign, 1866–77, 175, 223–25.

71. See the extant documents for *Sheldon et al. v. Houghton*, 21 F. Cas. 1239 (Circuit Court, Southern District, State of New York, December 1865) (No. 12,748); Ballou, *Building of the House*, 70–79. Judge Shipman's decision is reported in "An Interesting Case to Publishers," *ALGPC* 7 (1 January 1866): 150–52.

72. "Interesting Case to Publishers," 150.

73. Regarding a perceived weakening in trade courtesy, see Ballou, *Building of the House*, 78–79; and Tebbel, *History of Book Publishing*, 1:414.

74. "'The Evening Post's' Libel Suit," *PW* 43 (25 February 1893): 359–61.

75. Donald Sheehan, *This Was Publishing: A Chronicle of the Book Trade in the Gilded Age* (Bloomington: Indiana University Press, 1952), 69.

76. "Publishers' First Announcements," *PW* 3 (2 January 1873): 5.

77. John W. Lovell, "The Canadian Incursion," *PW* 15 (19 April 1879): 470–71.

78. K. Funk & Co., "Foreign Authors and 'The Standard Series,'" 499.

79. Quoted in Charles Madison, *Book Publishing in America* (New York: McGraw-Hill, 1966), 52–53.

80. "The 'Standard Series' Controversy," *PW* 17 (15 May 1880): 495.

81. J. R. S., "Short Discounts," *PW* 17 (31 January 1880): 88.

82. "To Booksellers throughout the United States," *Publisher's Trade List Annual* (New York: Office of Publishers' Weekly, 1880), n.p.; "Catalogue of Books Published by John Wurtele Lovell," *Publisher's Trade List Annual* (New York: Office of Publishers' Weekly, 1880), n.p.

83. "'Standard Series' Controversy," 495.

84. See *The House of Holt, 1866–1946: A Documentary Volume*, ed. Ellen D. Gilbert, vol. 284 of *Dictionary of Literary Biography* (Detroit: Gale, Thomson/Gale, 2003), 33–44.

85. For a longer version of this essay that also includes book import and export figures recorded in the British parliamentary papers, see Michael Winship, "The Transatlantic Book Trade and Anglo-American Literary Culture in the Nineteenth Century," in *Reciprocal Influences: Literary Production, Distribution, and Consumption in America,* ed. Steven Fink and Susan S. Williams (Columbus: Ohio State University Press, 1999), 98–122. The original essay is adapted here with the permission of the Ohio State University Press.

86. The British government did, however, exercise some control over the internal book trade through its "taxes on knowledge," and the record of government receipts from the duty on paper—not repealed until 1861—provides useful statistics for British book production in the first half of the nineteenth century. For a statistical study of the British book trade that draws on these and other sources, see Simon Eliot, *Some Patterns and Trends in British Publishing, 1800–1919* (London: Bibliographical Society, 1994).

87. *Statutes at Large of the United States of America, 1789–1873,* 5 (1846): 557–58, 9 (1851): 47–48, 11 (1859): 192, 12 (1863): 187, 551, 13 (1866): 213. See also *Tariff Proceedings, 1839–57,* 62nd Cong., 1st sess., Senate Document 72, 3 vols. (Washington, D.C.: GPO, 1911; serial set 6086–88); and Donald Marquand Dozer, "The Tariff on Books," *Mississippi Valley Historical Review* 36, no. 1 (June 1949): 73–75.

88. Great Britain, *Parliamentary Papers,* 1850 (85), 52:341, and 1852 (1466), 52:34–35.

89. Ticknor and Fields, Letter Book, foreign, 1855–59, 115–16, HL.

90. Ibid., 340, 347–48; Ticknor and Fields, Foreign Order Book, 1858–61, 8–11, and Purchase Book, 1857–58, 369, 387, HL.

91. *The Cost Books of Ticknor and Fields and Their Predecessors, 1832–1858,* ed. Warren S. Tryon and William Charvat (New York: Bibliographical Society of America, 1949), 52–53.

92. Ticknor and Fields, Letter Book, foreign, 1855–59, 452.

93. Ibid., 357; Ticknor and Fields, Foreign Order Book, 1858–61, 33, and Purchase Book, 1857–58, 511.

CHAPTER 5
The Role of Government

1. For alternative accounts of copyright in this period, see Alice D. Schreyer, "Copyright and Books in Nineteenth-Century America," in *Getting the Books Out: Papers of the Chicago Conference on the Book in 19th-Century America,* ed. Michael Hackenberg (Washington, D.C.: Center for the Book, Library of Congress, 1987), 121–36; and Peter Jaszi, "Toward a Theory of Copyright: The Metamorphoses of Authorship," *Duke Law Journal* 41 (1991): 455–502.

2. For a survey of American copyright law from 1790 to 1840, see my "Copyright in the Early Republic," in *An Extensive Republic: Print, Culture, and Society in the New Nation,* ed. Robert A. Gross and Mary Kelley, vol. 2 of *A History of the Book in America* (Chapel Hill: University of North Carolina Press, forthcoming).

3. For a detailed discussion of the antebellum campaign for international copyright, see James J. Barnes, *Authors, Publishers and Politicians: The Quest for an Anglo-American*

Copyright Agreement, 1815–1854 (Columbus: Ohio State University Press, 1974). Much of my discussion of the debate over international copyright is adapted from my *American Literature and the Culture of Reprinting, 1834–1853* (Philadelphia: University of Pennsylvania Press, 2003).

4. See *Petition of Thomas Moore, and Other Authors of Great Britain, Praying Congress to Grant to Them the Exclusive Benefit of Their Writings within the United States*, 24th Cong., 2nd sess., Senate Document 134 (Washington, D.C., 1837; serial set 298).

5. For lists of American authors who supported international copyright, see Kenneth Cameron, "The Quest for International Copyright in the Thirtieth Congress," *ESQ: A Journal of the American Renaissance* 51 (1968): 108–36; William Cullen Bryant et al., *An Address to the People of the United States in Behalf of the American Copyright Club* (New York: American Copyright Club, 1843); and R. R. Bowker, *Copyright: Its Law and Its Literature* (New York: Office of Publishers' Weekly, 1886).

6. For representative tradesmen's petitions against the proposed law, see *Memorial of the Columbia Typographical Society*, 25th Cong., 2nd sess., Senate Document 190 (Washington, D.C., 1838; serial set 316); *Memorial of the New York Typographical Society*, 25th Cong., 2nd sess., Senate Document 296 (Washington, D.C., 1838; serial set 317); *Memorial of a Number of Persons Concerned in Printing and Publishing*, 27th Cong., 2nd sess., Senate Document 323 (Washington, D.C., 1843; serial set 399). Both pro- and anti-international copyright petitions are indexed in Thorvald Solberg, *Copyright in Congress, 1789–1904* (Washington, D.C.: GPO, 1905).

7. On the politics of the antebellum struggle over international copyright, see "The International Copyright Question," *USMDR* 12 (February 1843): 113–22; and Evert Duyckinck, "Literary Prospects of 1845," *American Review* 1 (February 1845): 146–51. For Young America's support of international copyright, see Perry Miller, *The Raven and the Whale* (New York: Harcourt, Brace & Co., 1956), 94–103.

8. John Jay's 1848 petition synthesized the most persuasive points made by international copyright advocates: *Memorials of John Jay and of William C. Bryant and Others, in Favor of an International Copyright Law*, 30th Cong., 1st sess., House Miscellaneous Document 76 (Washington, D.C., 1848; serial set 523).

9. For attacks on international copyright that highlighted its inconsistency with Whig principles, see "Literary Property," *USMDR* 2 (June 1838): 289–311; and Philip H. Nicklin, *Remarks on Literary Property* (Philadelphia: P. H. Nicklin and T. Johnson, 1838).

10. See, for example, the 1838 *Memorial of the New York Typographical Society*.

11. British copyright law was extended to Ireland under the Copyright Act of 1801. For the immigration of Irish printers to the United States, see Richard Cargill Cole, *Irish Booksellers and English Writers, 1740–1800* (Atlantic Highlands, N.J.: Humanities Press International, 1986), 40–61, 148–190. For the vexed relationship of the Irish and British book trades at the end of the eighteenth century, see M. Pollard, *Dublin's Trade in Books, 1550–1800* (New York: Oxford University Press, 1989).

12. Carey's pamphlet was circulated to members of the Senate as the treaty was being discussed (Barnes, *Authors, Publishers and Politicians*, 256). Carey republished *Letters* in 1868 in response to a revived campaign for international copyright. In a new preface, he shifted his attack from the London press to large eastern publishers' control over western reading and ridiculed copyright advocates' eagerness to require payments to foreign au-

thors while neglecting pensions for the widows of Civil War dead. See *Letters on International Copyright* (Philadelphia: A. Hart, 1853; repr., New York: Hurd & Houghton, 1868).

13. For Putnam's career-long advocacy of international copyright, see Ezra Greenspan, *George Palmer Putnam: Representative American Publisher* (University Park: Pennsylvania State University Press, 2000); on *Putnam's Monthly*, see 289–95. For *Harper's New Monthly Magazine*, see Edward E. Chielens, ed. *American Literary Magazines: The Eighteenth and Nineteenth Centuries* (Westport, Conn.: Greenwood, 1986), 168.

14. Eugene Exman, *The Brothers Harper: A Unique Publishing Partnership and Its Impact upon the Cultural Life of America from 1817 to 1853* (New York: Harper & Row, 1965), 358.

15. Richard Fawkes, *Dion Boucicault: A Biography* (New York: Quartet Books, 1979), 91.

16. *Congressional Globe*, 46th Cong., 2nd sess., 14 April 1870, 2683.

17. Thorvald Solberg, *Copyright Enactments of the United States, 1783–1906*, 2nd ed. (Washington, D.C.: GPO, 1906), 36–41.

18. Copyright cases involving plays and musical performances constitute the largest subset of cases organized by type of text, with at least twenty-eight such cases heard between 1840 and 1880. Court reports and legal texts are the next largest group, with fourteen cases heard in this period.

19. Eaton S. Drone, *A Treatise on the Law of Property in Intellectual Productions in Great Britain and the United States* (Boston: Little, Brown, & Co., 1879), v.

20. *Gray v. Russell*, in *Decisions of the United States Courts Involving Copyright and Literary Property, 1789–1909*, Copyright Office Bulletins 13–16, comp. and ed. Wilma S. Davis and Mark A. Lillis (Washington, D.C.: Copyright Office, Library of Congress, 1980), 14:1120, 1124.

21. British and American abridgment cases are peppered with these phrases. For example, in ibid., see the American cases *Folsom v. Marsh* (1841; 13:991–1003), *Emerson v. Davies* (1845; 13:850–68), and *Story v. Holcombe* (1847; 15:2473–81), and the references within these cases to British precedents *Sayre v. Moore* (1785), *Roworth v. Wilkes* (1807), and *Bramwell v. Halcomb* (1836).

22. *Story v. Holcombe*, in ibid., 15:2475.

23. *Gray v. Russell*, in ibid., 14:1124.

24. *Folsom v. Marsh*, in ibid., 13:995.

25. Ibid., 13:1000, 1002.

26. *Stowe v. Thomas*, in ibid., 15:2484–86.

27. *White-Smith Music Publishing Company v. Apollo Company*, in ibid., 15:2978.

28. Drone, *Treatise*, 198–99. Drone summarizes the trend of the nineteenth-century courts thus: "to be entitled to protection, the author has simply to show something material and valuable produced by himself and not copied from the protected matter of another" (199). Although Drone defends retaining an author's rights to abridgment as well as to translation and dramatization, as had been conferred by the 1870 copyright revision, his emphasis on "protected matter" indicates that this strengthening of copyright protection assumes a robust public domain from which authors can draw to create new works.

29. *Boucicault v. Fox* (1862), in Davis and Lillis, *Decisions*, 13:401. For an analysis of the attempt to distinguish written law from both literature and literary criticism, see Susan

Stewart, *Crimes of Writing: Problems in the Containment of Representation* (New York: Oxford University Press, 1991), 15–30.

30. *Martinetti v. Maguire*, in Davis and Lillis, *Decisions*, 14:1726.

31. *Bartlett v. Crittenden*, in ibid., 13:164.

32. *Kiernan v. Manhattan Quotation Telegraph Co.*, in ibid., 14:1498.

33. *Boucicault v. Fox*, in ibid., 13:397.

34. *Baker v. Selden*, in ibid., 13:82.

35. Ibid., 13:84–85.

36. George Haven Putnam, *International Copyright Considered in Some of Its Relations to Ethics and Political Economy* (New York: G. P. Putnam's Sons, 1879), typically argued that the reciprocal treaties entered into by the "Continental powers" (13) had left the United States behind the times.

37. See "Extract from *The Report of the British Commission*," repr. in George Haven Putnam, comp., *The Question of Copyright*, 2nd ed. (New York: G. P. Putnam's Sons, 1896), 269–73.

38. For the history of international copyright in the postbellum period, see Bowker, *Copyright*, [28]–32; Putnam, *Question of Copyright*, 40–63; and Aubert J. Clark, *The Movement for International Copyright in Nineteenth Century America* (Washington, D.C.: Catholic University of America Press, 1960), 84–181.

39. *Bleistein v. Donaldson Lithographing*, in Davis and Lillis, *Decisions*, 13:269–79.

40. Act of 4 March 1909, in Solberg, *Copyright Enactments*, 66.

41. Ernest W. Winkler, *Check List of Texas Imprints, 1846–1860* (Austin: Texas State Historical Association, 1949); Ernest W. Winkler and Llerena B. Friend, *Check List of Texas Imprints, 1861–1876* (Austin: Texas State Historical Association, 1963). For similar variety, see Cecil K. Byrd, *A Bibliography of Illinois Imprints, 1814–58* (Chicago: University of Chicago Press, 1966); and *A Check List of Nevada Imprints, 1859–1890* (Chicago: Historical Records Survey, 1939).

42. Hendrik Edelman, "The Government and the Immigrant Press: Notes on Some Nineteenth Century New Jersey Government Publications in the German Language," *Journal of the Rutgers University Library* 43 (1981): 25–31.

43. On the 1840 census, see Patricia Cline Cohen, *A Calculating People: The Spread of Numeracy in Early America* (Chicago: University of Chicago Press, 1982), 175–204.

44. Lee Soltow and Edward Stevens, *The Rise of Literacy and the Common School in the United States: A Socioeconomic Analysis to 1870* (Chicago: University of Chicago Press, 1981), 5.

45. Francis A. Walker, *The Statistics of the Population of the United States . . . from the Original Returns of the Ninth Census* (Washington, D.C.: GPO, 1872), 1:xxx.

46. Francis A. Walker, *Compendium of the Tenth Census (June 1, 1880)*, pt. 2 (Washington, D.C.: GPO, 1883), 1637, 1655.

47. Carl F. Kaestle, *Pillars of the Republic: Common Schools and American Society, 1780–1860* (New York: Hill & Wang, 1983), 75–103.

48. Theodore D. Woolsey et al., *The First Century of the Republic: A Review of American Progress* (New York: Harper & Brothers, 1876), 287–89.

49. George Tucker, *Progress of the United States in Population and Wealth, as Exhibited by the Decennial Census* (New York: Hunt's Merchants' Magazine, 1856), 146.

50. Hinton Rowan Helper, *Compendium of the Impending Crisis of the South* (New York: A. B. Burdick, 1860), 92.

51. Thomas Prentice Kettell et al., *First Century of National Existence: The United States as They Were and Are* (Hartford: L. Stebbins, 1875), 402.

52. George F. Hoar, *National Education: Speech of Hon. George H. Hoar, of Massachusetts, in the House of Representatives, February 7, 1871* (Washington, D.C.: Congressional Globe Office, 1871), 1–2.

53. Catharine Beecher, *Educational Reminiscences and Suggestions* (New York: J. B. Ford & Co., 1874), 239–40.

54. Samuel C. Busey, *Immigration: Its Evils and Consequences* (New York: De Witt and Davenport, [1856]), 127–30.

55. Walker, *Compendium of the Tenth Census,* 1637.

56. Quoted in Thomas B. Stockwell, ed., *A History of Public Education in Rhode Island, from 1636 to 1876* (Providence: Providence Press, 1876), 89–90.

57. Ibid., 90.

58. See, for example, John G. Sproat, *"The Best Men": Liberal Reformers in the Gilded Age* (London: Oxford University Press, 1968), 32; and A. T. Lane, "American Labour and European Immigrants in the Late Nineteenth Century," *Journal of American Studies* 11 (1977): 241–60.

59. Richard Burket Kielbowicz, *News in the Mail: The Press, Post Office, and Public Information, 1700–1860s* (New York: Greenwood, 1989), 31–81.

60. Richard R. John, "Private Enterprise, Public Good? Communications Deregulation as a National Political Issue, 1839–1851," in *Beyond the Founders: New Approaches to the Political History of the Early American Republic,* ed. Jeffrey L. Pasley, Andrew W. Robertson, and David Waldstreicher (Chapel Hill: University of North Carolina Press, 2004), 328–54.

61. Kielbowicz, *News in the Mail,* 109–14, 124–25, 129–30.

62. Amy M. Thomas, "Who Makes the Text? The Production and Use of Literature in Nineteenth-Century America" (Ph.D. diss., Duke University, 1992), chap. 1.

63. Congressman Abraham W. Venable of North Carolina, speaking on a bill for the reduction of postage on letters, periodicals, and pamphlets, in the *Congressional Globe,* 31st Cong., 2nd sess., 18 December 1850, 74.

64. Kielbowicz, *News in the Mail,* 86–87.

65. Molly McGarry, "Spectral Spiritualities: Nineteenth-Century Spiritualism, Moral Panics, and the Making of U.S. Obscenity Law," *Journal of Women's History* 12 (Summer 2000): 8–29; quotation at 20.

66. *An Act for the Suppression of Trade in, and Circulation of, Obscene Literature and Articles of Immoral Use, Statutes at Large of the United States of America, 1789–1873* 17 (1873): 598–600.

67. McGarry, "Spectral Spiritualities," 19.

68. See Richard Burket Kielbowicz, *Origins of the Second-Class Mail Category and the Business of Policymaking, 1863–1879,* Journalism Monographs, no. 96 (Columbia, S.C.: Association for Education in Journalism and Mass Communication, 1986).

69. Ibid., 14–20.

70. Kielbowicz, *News in the Mail,* 127–29; Barnes, *Authors, Publishers, and Politicians,*

6-24; Isabelle Lehuu, *Carnival on the Page: Popular Print Media in Antebellum America* (Chapel Hill: University of North Carolina Press, 2000), 59-75.

71. Kielbowicz, *News in the Mail*, 98-100; Jen A. Huntley-Smith, "Publishing the 'Sealed Book': James Mason Hutchings and the Landscapes of California Print Culture, 1853-1886" (Ph.D. diss., University of Nevada, Reno, 2000), 66-75.

72. Michael Winship, *American Literary Publishing in the Mid-Nineteenth Century: The Business of Ticknor and Fields* (Cambridge: Cambridge University Press, 1995), 148-52.

73. *Joint Resolution in Relation to the Public Printing,* June 23, 1860, *Statutes at Large of the United States of America, 1789-1873* 12 (1863): 117-20.

74. R. W. Kerr, *History of the Government Printing Office* (Lancaster, Pa.: Inquirer Printing and Pub. Co., 1881; repr., New York: B. Franklin, 1970), 66-68.

75. Ibid., 42.

76. Ibid., 8-10.

77. Ibid., 79, 83; *100 GPO Years, 1861-1961: A History of United States Public Printing* (Washington, D.C.: GPO, 1961), 46-54.

78. Ridley E. Kessler Jr., "A Brief History of the Federal Depository Library Program: A Personal Perspective," *Journal of Government Information* 23 (1996): 369-71.

79. Benjamin Perley Poore, *A Descriptive Catalogue of the Government Publications of the United States, September 5, 1774-March 4, 1881* (Washington, D.C.: GPO, 1885).

80. Ron Tyler, "Illustrated Government Publications Related to the American West, 1843-1863," in *Surveying the Record: North American Scientific Exploration to 1930*, ed. Edward C. Carter II (Philadelphia: American Philosophical Society, 1999), 147-72.

81. Kerr, *History*, 12, 45-47; *100 GPO Years*, 53-54.

82. Robert D. Armstrong, "'The Matter of Printing': Public Printing in the Western Territories of the United States," *Journal of Government Information* 21 (1994): 37-47, and "'The Only Alternative Course': Incidents in Nevada Printing History," *Papers of the Bibliographical Society of America* 95 (2001): 97-115.

CHAPTER 6

Alternative Publishing Systems

1. Horace Bushnell, "The Kingdom of Heaven as a Grain of Mustard Seed," *New Englander and Yale Review* 2 (1844): 606.

2. David P. Nord, *Faith in Reading: Religious Publishing and the Birth of Mass Media in America* (New York: Oxford University Press, 2004), 71-86, 152; Eugene Exman, *The Brothers Harper: A Unique Publishing Partnership and Its Impact upon the Cultural Life of America from 1817 to 1853* (New York: Harper & Row, 1965), 17.

3. Candy Gunther Brown, *The Word in the World: Evangelical Writing, Publishing, and Reading in America, 1789-1880* (Chapel Hill: University of North Carolina Press, 2004), 51.

4. Nord, *Faith in Reading*, 152; James Penn Pilkington, *The Methodist Publishing House: A History*, vol. 1, *Beginnings to 1870* (Nashville: Abingdon, 1968), 192, 294-398.

5. Paul C. Gutjahr, *An American Bible: A History of the Good Book in the United States, 1777-1880* (Stanford, Calif.: Stanford University Press, 1999), 106-9.

6. Quoted in John Andrew Hostetler, *God Uses Ink: The Heritage and Mission of the Mennonite Publishing House after Fifty Years* (Scottdale, Pa.: Herald Press, 1958), 48.

7. Joseph C. G. Kennedy, *Preliminary Report on the Eighth Census, 1860* (Washington, D.C.: GPO, 1862), 211, table 37; Francis A. Walker, *A Compendium of the Ninth Census* (Washington, D.C.: GPO, 1872), 509, table 37.

8. John C. Nerone, "The Press and Popular Culture in the Early Republic: Cincinnati, 1793-1843" (Ph.D. diss., University of Notre Dame, 1982), 197-98.

9. "The Methodist Book Concern Report," *PW* 17 (15 May 1880): 498.

10. Hostetler, *God Uses Ink*, 36-39; Ernst W. Olson, *Augustana Book Concern: Publishers to the Augustana Synod since 1889* (Rock Island, Ill.: Augustana Book Concern, 1934), 6-9.

11. An excellent discussion of these schisms and their influence on religious publishing can be found in Nord, *Faith in Reading*, 152-58.

12. Willard M. Rice, *History of the Presbyterian Board of Publication and Sabbath-School Work* (Philadelphia: Presbyterian Board of Publication and Sabbath-School Work, 1889); *Presbyterian Board of Publication, Its Present Operations and Plans* (Philadelphia: Presbyterian Board of Publication, 1848).

13. P. E. Burroughs, *Fifty Fruitful Years, 1891-1941: The Story of the Sunday School Board of the Southern Baptist Convention* (Nashville: Broadman Press, 1941), 18.

14. Karl Eric Valois, "'To Revolutionize the World': The American Tract Society and the Regeneration of the Republic, 1825-1877" (Ph.D. diss., University of Connecticut, 1994), 368; *Fifty-Second Annual Report of the American Tract Society* (New York: American Tract Society, 1877), 16, 108; Gutjahr, *American Bible*, 33, 188.

15. David Paul Nord, "Free Grace, Free Books, Free Riders: The Economics of Religious Publishing in Early Nineteenth-Century America," *Procs. AAS* 106 (1996): 241-72.

16. Examples of selling stock to support religious publishing enterprises are documented in Pilkington, *Methodist Publishing House*, 1:374; and Hostetler, *God Uses Ink*, 51.

17. *An Appeal to the Christian Public, on the Evil and Impolicy of the Church Engaging in Merchandise, and Setting Forth the Wrong Done to Book Sellers* (Philadelphia: King & Baird, 1849), 4-6; *An Expose of the Rise and Proceedings of the American Bible Society, during the Thirteen Years of Its Existence, by a Member* (New York, 1830), 15; "Religious Publishing Societies," *APCLG* 3 (28 March 1857): 193.

18. Burroughs, *Fifty Fruitful Years*, 28.

19. For a detailed overview of the distribution strategies of the ATS, see Valois, "To Revolutionize the World," 152-209.

20. Nathan O. Hatch, *The Democratization of American Christianity* (New Haven: Yale University Press, 1989), 142.

21. Stephen Elmer Slocum Jr., "The American Tract Society, 1825-1975: An Evangelical Effort to Influence the Religious and Moral Life of the United States" (Ph.D. diss., New York University, 1975), 85-92.

22. American Tract Society, *Twenty-Fifth Annual Report* (New York: American Tract Society, 1851), 74.

23. Peter Wosh, *Spreading the Word: The Bible Business in Nineteenth-Century America* (Ithaca, N.Y.: Cornell University Press, 1994), 175-99.

24. Daniel Gurden Stevens, *The First Hundred Years of the American Baptist Publica-*

tion Society (Philadelphia: American Baptist Publication Society, 1925), 27, 31; American Baptist Publication Society, *Thirty-Second Annual Report* (Philadelphia: American Baptist Publication Society, 1856), 35.

25. Congregational Board of Publication, *Twenty-Sixth Annual Report* (Boston: Congregational Board of Publication, 1855), 8.

26. Brown, *Word in the World*, 66–67.

27. "The Methodist Book Concern Report," 498, quoting the report of Phillips & Hunt, "book agents, to the Quadrennial General M. E. Conference at Cincinnati."

28. Roger Finke and Rodney Stark, *The Church of America, 1776–1990* (New Brunswick, N.J.: Rutgers University Press, 1992), 113.

29. John Tebbel, *A History of Book Publishing in the United States* (New York: R. R. Bowker, 1975), 2:247.

30. Robert C. Healey, *A Catholic Book Chronicle: The Story of P. J. Kenedy & Sons, 1826–1951* (New York: P. J. Kenedy & Sons, 1951), 34.

31. Ibid., 25.

32. Tebbel, *History of Book Publishing*, 2:248.

33. Ibid., 1:530; Charles A. Madison, *Jewish Publishing in America: The Impact of Jewish Writing on American Culture* (New York: Sanhedrin, 1976), 74–77.

34. Madison, *Jewish Publishing in America*, 25–42.

35. Brown, *Word in the World*, 66.

36. Allan Fisher, *Fleming H. Revell Company: The First 125 Years, 1870–1995* (Grand Rapids, Mich.: Fleming H. Revell, 1995), 7–11; Jan Blodgett, *Protestant Evangelical Literary Culture and Contemporary Society* (Westport, Conn.: Greenwood, 1997), 25.

37. Esek Cowen, *A Treatise on the Civil Jurisdiction of a Justice of the Peace, in the State of New-York* (Albany: Wm. Gould & Co.; New York: Gould & Banks, 1821); Benjamin Vaughan Abbott, *Clerks' and Conveyancers' Assistant: A Collection of Forms of Conveyancing, Contracts, and Legal Proceedings* (New York: Baker, Voorhis & Co., 1868); *ALGPC* 14 (1 April 1870): 310.

38. Charles Warren, *A History of the American Bar* (Boston: Little, Brown, 1911), 540–54; "American Law Books, 1860–1900," in Betty W. Taylor and Robert J. Munro, eds., *American Law Publishing, 1860–1900: Historical Readings* (Dobbs Ferry, N.Y.: Glanville, 1984), 2:341–47; "A Symposium of Law Publishers," *American Law Review* 23 (1889): 396ff., repr. in ibid., 2:383–406.

39. Francesco Cordasco, *Medical Publishing in 19th Century America: Lea of Philadelphia; William Wood & Company of New York City; and F. E. Boericke of Philadelphia* (Fairview, N.J.: Junius Vaughn, 1990), esp. 3–9, 17–27. For the *Medical News and Library* as "lighter medical literature" than the *American Journal of the Medical Sciences*, see "Prospectus," *Medical News and Library* 1 (1843): 2, quoted in ibid., 24.

40. See, for example, numerous advertisements in *American Phrenological Journal* 22 (July 1855): 22–23. For publication lists and the agent system, see *Life Illustrated* (New York: Fowlers & Wells, 1855), and *Illustrated Annual of Phrenology* (New York: Fowler & Wells, 1866), Broadsides Collection, AAS. For circulation and printing figures, see "The Past and Future of the Journal," *American Phrenological Journal* 4 (October 1842): 318–19; and "A Miscalculation," *American Phrenological Journal* 17 (April 1853): 95.

41. Clarence Danhof, *Change in Agriculture: The Northern United States, 1820–1870*

(Cambridge, Mass.: Harvard University Press, 1969), 55–56; Hellmut Lehmann-Haupt et al., *The Book in America: A History of the Making and Selling of Books in the United States*, 2nd ed. (New York: R. R. Bowker, 1951), 235; William E. Ogilvie, *Pioneer Agricultural Journalists* (New York: Beekman, 1974), 29–37.

42. Cynthia H. Peters, "Rand, McNally and Company in the Nineteenth Century: Reaching for a National Market," in *Chicago Mapmakers: Essays on the Rise of the City's Map Trade*, ed. Michael P. Conzen (Chicago: Chicago Historical Society for the Chicago Map Society, 1984), 64–72.

43. Michael P. Conzen, "Maps for the Masses: Alfred T. Andreas and the Midwestern County Atlas Map Trade," in *Chicago Mapmakers*, 47–63; Scott E. Casper, *Constructing American Lives: Biography and Culture in Nineteenth-Century America* (Chapel Hill: University of North Carolina Press, 1999), 291–99.

44. *New York Musical Review and Choral Advocate* 6 (4 January 1855): 7; *New York Times*, 5 January 1855, 8, quoted in Dena J. Epstein, introduction to Board of Music Trade of the United States of America, *Complete Catalogue of Sheet Music and Musical Works, 1870* (repr., New York: Da Capo, 1973), vii.

45. "War among the Music Dealers," *Dwight's Journal of Music* 6 (13 January 1855): 118. An excellent synopsis of the price war appears in James H. Stone, "The Merchant and the Muse: Commercial Influences on American Popular Music before the Civil War," *Business History Review* 30 (1956): 8–12.

46. These statistics are compiled from Harry Dichter and Elliott Shapiro, "Dictionary of Early American Music Publishers," in *Early American Sheet Music: Its Lure and Its Lore, 1768–1889* (New York: R. R. Bowker, 1941), 165–248.

47. Ernst C. Krohn, *Music Publishing in the Middle Western States before the Civil War*, Detroit Studies in Music Bibliography, no. 23 (Detroit: Information Coordinators, 1972).

48. Dichter and Shapiro, *Early American Sheet Music*, 91.

49. Krohn, *Music Publishing*, 10–14, 35, 40.

50. Stone, "Merchant and the Muse," 7; *Catalogue of Music, Published by Firth, Hall & Pond, Publishers and Importers of Music* (New York: Firth, Hall & Pond, 1846).

51. *New-York Musical Review and Gazette* 6 (16 June 1855): 197, quoted in Epstein, introduction, viii. It is unclear exactly how many publishers initially joined the Board of Music Trade. Stone gives the number as fifteen, including two of the original price-cutters, and claims that membership doubled by the end of 1855; Epstein lists twenty-seven initial signatories to the board's articles of association, including New York's Horace Waters — who Stone claims joined the board only in 1858. Stone, "Merchant and the Muse," 8–9; Epstein, introduction, viii.

52. Stone, "Merchant and the Muse," 7, 11; "The Board of Music Trade," *Dwight's Journal of Music* 13 (15 May 1858): 55.

53. *Complete Catalogue of Sheet Music and Musical Work Published by the Board of Music Trade of the United States of America, 1870* (New York: Board of Music Trade, 1871).

54. See Nicholas E. Tawa, *High-Minded and Low-Down: Music in the Lives of Americans, 1800–1861* (Boston: Northeastern University Press, 2000).

55. *Dwight's Journal of Music* 7 (22 September 1855): 198.

56. *Dwight's Journal of Music* 9 (3 May 1856): 37, (7 June 1856): 88; 10 (28 February 1857): 175; 12 (27 February 1858): 379.

57. Richard Crawford, *America's Musical Life: A History* (New York: W. W. Norton, 2001), 131–35, 140–51; Carol A. Pemberton, "Lowell Mason," in *American National Biography*, ed. John A. Garraty and Mark C. Carnes (New York: Oxford University Press, 1999), 14:656–57.

58. Crawford, *America's Musical Life*, 129–31, 164–68.

59. Statistics compiled from Dichter and Shapiro, "Dictionary." Because this study likely underrepresented small and short-lived firms, persistence rates may have been slightly lower, but the contrast with the antebellum period is striking.

60. "Ditson & Co.'s New Music Store," *Dwight's Journal of Music* 11 (22 August 1857): 166–67; repr. in *APCLG* 3 (29 August 1857): 546–47. This republication, as well as an item on the Board of Music Trade's annual convention (*APCLG* 3 [20 June 1857]: 388), suggests the trade publishers' recognition of their counterparts in music publishing. Russell & Richardson, also of Boston, opened its own ornate store, complete with fireproof safe, six months before Ditson's. See advertisement in *Dwight's Journal of Music* 10 (7 March 1857): 183.

61. William Arms Fisher, *One Hundred and Fifty Years of Music Publishing in the United States: An Historical Sketch with Special Reference to the Pioneer Publisher, Oliver Ditson Company, Inc., 1783–1933* (Boston: Oliver Ditson, 1933), 74–75.

62. Epstein, introduction, xi–xv.

63. For figures for school population and funding, see Lawrence A. Cremin, *American Education: The National Experience* (New York: Harper & Row, 1980), 182–85. Book expenditures appear in Eugene Exman, *The House of Harper: One Hundred and Fifty Years of Publishing* (New York: Harper & Row, 1967), 166–67.

64. On the fitful emergence of public school systems, see Cremin, *American Education*, 148–85; and Henry G. Good and James D. Teller, *A History of American Education*, 3rd ed. (New York: Macmillan, 1973), 127–58.

65. *Common School System of Connecticut* (pamphlet, 1830), quoted in "History of Common Schools in Connecticut," *American Journal of Education* 5 (June 1858): 144.

66. J. C. Barnes, paper read at the Publishers' Board of Trade, in "The Abuses in the School-Book Business," *American Educational Monthly* 6 (June 1870): 217.

67. G. & C. Merriam, "The Springfield Series" (1842), Broadsides Collection, AAS.

68. David Vincent, *Literacy and Popular Culture: England, 1750–1914* (Cambridge: Cambridge University Press, 1989), 73–92.

69. Henry J. Perkinson, "American Textbooks and Educational Change," in *Early American Textbooks, 1775–1900* (Washington, D.C.: U.S. Department of Education, 1985), xii–xiii.

70. Walter Sutton, *The Western Book Trade: Cincinnati as a Nineteenth-Century Publishing and Book-Trade Center* (Columbus: Ohio State University Press for the Ohio Historical Society, 1961), 179–83.

71. Exman, *House of Harper*, 167.

72. William H. McGuffey, *McGuffey's New Sixth Eclectic Reader* (Cincinnati: Sargent, Wilson & Hinkle, c. 1857), front and end matter.

73. "Valuable School Books, Published by Thomas, Cowperthwait & Co., Philadelphia, and for Sale by Booksellers Generally throughout the United States" (1848), Broadsides Collection, AAS.

74. Sutton, *Western Book Trade*, 180–82.

75. Advertisement, *APCLG* 5 (2 April 1859): 163.

76. Keith Whitescarver, "School Books, Publishers, and Southern Nationalists: Refashioning the Curriculum in North Carolina's Schools, 1850–1861," *North Carolina Historical Review* 79 (2002): 28–49; Karen C. Carroll, "Sterling, Campbell, and Albright: Textbook Publishers, 1861–1865," *North Carolina Historical Review* 63 (April 1986): 169–98; O. L. Davis Jr., "The Educational Association of the C.S.A.," *Civil War History* 10 (1964): 67–79, and "E. H. Cushing: Textbooks in Confederate Texas," *Library Chronicle of the University of Texas* 8 (1966): 46–50.

77. "Southern Books for Southern Children" (c. 1872), Broadsides Collection, AAS.

78. "School-Book Agencies," *American Educational Monthly* 2 (February 1865): 38–41; "Text Books," *American Educational Monthly* 2 (May 1865): 136–38; "Shall the Truth Be Told about School-Books?" *American Educational Monthly* 5 (January 1868): 30–32.

79. "Uniformity of Text-Books," *American Educational Monthly* 4 (April 1867): 154–55.

80. *Massachusetts Teacher*, c. July 1870, quoted in "School-Book Agents," *American Educational Monthly* 6 (August 1870): 348–49.

81. Barnes paper, in "Abuses in the School-Book Business," 217–22.

82. "The Reformation," *American Educational Monthly* 6 (June 1870): 236; Donald Sheehan, *This Was Publishing: A Chronicle of the Book Trade in the Gilded Age* (Bloomington: Indiana University Press, 1952), 207.

83. *PW* published minutes of the board's quarterly meetings as late as July 1873 and described a special meeting of the board in October 1874. *PW* 3 (July 1873): 27; "The Reform in the Board," *PW* 6 (31 October 1874): 482.

84. *ALGPC* 15 (1 February 1870): 158.

85. "Publishers' Board of Trade," *ALGPC* 17 (1 May 1871): 3; *PW* 11 (17 March 1877): 293; "American School-Books," *PW* 12 (14 July 1877): 53; Sheehan, *This Was Publishing*, 208–9. For an example of board-sanctioned arbitration, see *Weekly Trade Circular* 1 (11 April 1872): 325.

86. Sheehan, *This Was Publishing*, 47–48, 209–10; Ellen B. Ballou, *The Building of the House: Houghton Mifflin's Formative Years* (Boston: Houghton Mifflin, 1970), 330–32.

87. Irving G. Hendricks, "The Early History of California State-Printed Textbooks," *Historical Society of Southern California Quarterly* 46 (1964): 223–38. Other states considered or adopted legislation requiring long-term contracts with schoolbook publishers. See, for example, "The Text-Book Question," *PW* 14 (20 April 1878): 407; "State School-Book Legislation," *PW* 15 (15 February 1879): 198; and "State-Made School-Books," *PW* 15 (29 March 1879): 395.

88. Exman, *House of Harper*, 170; Ballou, *Building of the House*, 337.

89. See Donald Farren, "Subscription: A Study of the Eighteenth-Century American Book Trade" (D.L.S. thesis, Columbia University, 1982), as well as the numerous references to subscription publishing in Hugh Amory and David D. Hall, eds., *The Colonial Book in the Atlantic World*, vol. 1 of *A History of the Book in America* (Cambridge: Cambridge University Press, 2000), esp. 80–81, 206 (fig. 6.1), 286 (fig. 8.2).

90. Michael Hackenberg, "The Subscription Publishing Network in Nineteenth-Century America," in *Getting the Books Out: Papers of the Chicago Conference on the Book in*

19th-Century America, ed. Michael Hackenberg (Washington, D.C.: Center for the Book, Library of Congress, 1987), 45–75.

91. "The Subscription Book Trade," *Weekly Trade Circular* 2 (25 July 1872): 94.

92. Hackenberg, "Subscription Publishing Network," 54, 63.

93. Keith Arbour, *Canvassing Books, Sample Books, and Subscription Publishers' Ephemera, 1833–1951, in the Collection of Michael Zinman* (Ardsley, N.Y.: Haydn Foundation for the Cultural Arts, 1996), xii–xv, xx–xxiv; a useful bibliography of canvassers' memoirs and other firsthand descriptions of their experience appears on xii n. 3. Mrs. J. W. Likins's description of selling *Roughing It* appears in *Six Years Experience as a Book Agent: Including My Trip from New York to San Francisco via Nicaragua* (San Francisco: Women's Printing Union, 1874), 104–11. Amy M. Thomas, "'There Is Nothing So Effective as a Personal Canvass': Revaluing Nineteenth-Century American Subscription Books," *Book History* 1 (1998): 140–55, analyzes the experience of an officer's widow peddling a Civil War book for Harper & Brothers. For a solid overview of the trade, including the marketing of Ulysses S. Grant's *Memoirs*, see Walter A. Friedman, *Birth of a Salesman: The Transformation of Selling in America* (Cambridge, Mass.: Harvard University Press, 2004), 34–55.

94. Elisha Bliss, "Subscription Books," *New York Tribune*, 28 October 1874, 8. On the value of having agents sell one book at a time, see Sheehan, *This Was Publishing*, 192–93.

95. "Subscription Publishers and Underselling," *ALGPC* 15 (15 July 1870): 164–65.

96. "Subscription Book Trade," 93–94.

97. S. R. Crocker, "Subscription Books," *Literary World* 5 (August 1874): 40.

98. "Subscription Publishers and Underselling," 165.

99. Sheehan, *This Was Publishing*, 190–95; Thomas, "'There Is Nothing So Effective,'" 150–52.

CHAPTER 7

Periodicals and Serial Publication

1. Joseph C. G. Kennedy, *Preliminary Report on the Eighth Census, 1860* (Washington, D.C.: GPO, 1862), 174, table 15. The table reports the values for book, job, and newspaper printing, but "newspaper" in the census reports is often used to refer to periodicals generally, which seems to be the case here.

2. Francis A. Walker, *A Compendium of the Ninth Census* (Washington, D.C.: GPO, 1872), 508.

3. Ibid., 510.

4. Ibid., 511–12.

5. For the segregation of newspaper from other periodical statistics, see the various tables in the appendix to Alfred McClung Lee, *The Daily Newspaper in America: The Evolution of a Social Instrument* (New York: Macmillan, 1937), 705–53. For estimates of magazine production, see the extensive notes in Frank Luther Mott, *A History of American Magazines*, vol. 1 (New York: D. Appleton & Co., 1930), 342 n. 6; ibid., vol. 2 (Cambridge, Mass.: Harvard University Press, 1938), 4 n. 2; and ibid., vol. 3 (Cambridge, Mass.: Harvard University Press, 1938), 5 n. 2.

6. Walker, *Compendium of the Ninth Census*, 508–9. The newspaper directories of George P. Rowell & Co. and N. W. Ayer & Son for 1880 both record a somewhat lower

number of newspapers overall than does the census for that year. Lee suggests that the differences may have resulted from different practices for counting newspapers; see *Daily Newspaper in America*, 707, 721–22.

7. J. D. B. DeBow, *Statistical View of the United States . . . Being a Compendium of the Seventh Census* (Washington, D.C.: Beverley Tucker, Senate Printer, 1854), 154.

8. Francis A. Walker, *Compendium of the Tenth Census (June 1, 1880)* (Washington, D.C.: GPO, 1883), 1630, table 133.

9. Walker, *Compendium of the Ninth Census*, 508, table 37.

10. On syndication, see Charles A. Johanningsmeier, *Fiction and the American Literary Marketplace: The Role of Newspaper Syndicates in America, 1860–1900* (Cambridge: Cambridge University Press, 1997), 34–63.

11. Elizabeth L. Eisenstein, "From the Printed Word to the Moving Image: Technology and the Rest of Culture," *Social Research* 64 (1997): 1049.

12. See, for instance, Charles Dudley Warner, *The American Newspaper: An Essay Read before the Social Science Association at Saratoga Springs, Sept. 6, 1881* (Boston: J. R. Osgood & Co., 1881).

13. Kevin G. Barnhurst and John Nerone, *The Form of News: A History* (New York: Guilford, 2001), chap. 1.

14. The distinction between transmission and ritual models of communication is made in James W. Carey, *Communication as Culture: Essays on Media and Society* (London: Allen & Unwin, 1988), 14–23. See also Charles Clark, *The Public Prints: The Newspaper in Anglo-American Culture, 1665–1740* (New York: Oxford University Press, 1993), 4–5.

15. On the electoral tactics of the second party system of Whigs and Democrats, see Robert Gray Gunderson, *The Log Cabin Campaign* (Lexington: University Press of Kentucky, 1957); Robert V. Remini, *The Election of Andrew Jackson* (Philadelphia: Lippincott, 1963); and John G. Gasaway, "Tippecanoe and the Party Press Too: Mass Communication, Politics, Culture, and the Fabled Presidential Election of 1840" (Ph.D. diss., University of Illinois at Urbana-Champaign, 1999). On the party-press system and its infrastructure, see Richard Kielbowicz, *News in the Mail: The Press, Post Office, and Public Information, 1700–1860s* (Westport, Conn.: Greenwood, 1989); Richard R. John, *Spreading the News: The American Postal System from Franklin to Morse* (Cambridge, Mass.: Harvard University Press, 1995); Jeffrey L. Pasley, *"The Tyranny of Printers": Newspaper Politics in the Early American Republic* (Charlottesville: University Press of Virginia, 2001); Barnhurst and Nerone, *Form of News*, chaps. 3–5; and John L. Brooke, "To Be 'Read by the Whole People': Press, Party, and Public Sphere in the United States, 1789–1840," *Procs. AAS* 110 (2002): 41–118.

16. *Niles' Weekly Register* 43 (15 September 1832): 39.

17. "The Organized Press, and the Case of Gales & Seaton," *Niles' Weekly Register* 45 (4 January 1834): 306–9.

18. For other uses of "manufacturing public opinion," see the following, all *New York Times*: "The Proposed Tilden Mass Meeting," 21 January 1877, 2; "New Jersey Democracy," 14 September 1874, 5; and untitled editorial article, 20 February 1874, 4.

19. Glenn C. Altschuler and Stuart M. Blumin, "Limits of Political Engagement in Antebellum America: A New Look at the Golden Age of Participatory Democracy," *Journal of American History* 84 (1997): 855–85.

20. John L. Thomas, *"The Liberator," William Lloyd Garrison: A Biography* (Boston: Little, Brown, 1963), 131; Augusta Rohrbach, " 'Truth Stronger and Stranger than Fiction': Reexamining William Lloyd Garrison's *Liberator*," *American Literature* 73 (2001): 729–30.

21. See Douglas Andrew Gamble, "Moral Suasion in the West: Garrisonian Abolitionism, 1831–1861" (Ph.D. diss., Ohio State University, 1973).

22. See the entries for these cities in Karl J. R. Arndt and May E. Olson, *German American Newspapers and Periodicals, 1732–1955: History and Bibliography* (Heidelberg: Quelle & Meyer, 1961). On German publishing more generally, see Robert E. Cazden, *A Social History of the German Book Trade in America to the Civil War* (Columbia, S.C.: Camden House, 1984); see also Ken Fones-Wolf and Elliott Shore, "The German Press and Working-Class Politics in Gilded-Age Philadelphia," in *The German-American Radical Press: The Shaping of a Left Political Culture, 1850–1940*, ed. Elliott Shore et al. (Urbana: University of Illinois Press, 1992), 63–77.

23. For the importance of manliness among printers, see Ava Baron, "Questions of Gender: Deskilling and Demasculinization in the U.S. Printing Industry, 1830–1915," *Gender and History* (Great Britain) 1 (1989): 178–99.

24. On southern criticism of the American Anti-Slavery Society publication operation, see Leonard Richards, *"Gentlemen of Property and Standing": Anti-Abolition Mobs in Jacksonian America* (New York: Oxford University Press, 1970), 71–73, 150, 162.

25. Frank Luther Mott, *American Journalism: A History of Newspapers in the United States through 260 Years, 1690 to 1950* (New York: Macmillan, 1950), 316.

26. Lee, *Daily Newspaper in America*, 262–63.

27. David J. Russo, "The Origins of Local News in the U.S. Country Press, 1840s–1870s," *Journalism Monographs* 65 (1980): 1–43.

28. Lee, *Daily Newspaper in America*, 263.

29. "The Magnetic Telegraph — Some of Its Results," *Littell's Living Age* 6 (26 July 1845): 194.

30. Daniel J. Czitrom, *Media and the American Mind: From Morse to McLuhan* (Chapel Hill: University of North Carolina Press, 1982), 3–29; Menahem Blondheim, *News over the Wires: The Telegraph and the Flow of Public Information in America, 1844–1897* (Cambridge, Mass.: Harvard University Press, 1994), and "The Click: Telegraphic Technology, Journalism, and the Transformation of the New York Associated Press," *American Journalism* 17 (Fall 2000): 27–52. See also Richard Schwarzlose, *The Nation's Newsbrokers*, 2 vols. (Evanston: Northwestern University Press, 1988).

31. The 4 March 1880 issue of the *Daily Graphic* included examples of fourteen different methods of graphic reproduction on two facing pages. There is no necessary reason to think that the halftone example jumped out at the 1880 readership; not for another twenty years would halftones become the most common form of illustration.

32. The numerous examples in Michael L. Carlebach's *The Origins of Photojournalism in America* (Washington, D.C.: Smithsonian Institution, 1992) are instructive. See, for instance, a photograph (a cabinet card, or large carte de visite) of Winnebago Indians receiving annuity payments in Wisconsin, c. 1871, and the wood engraving of the same scene (140–41). In the woodcut, the line between whites and Native Americans is accentuated; the Native Americans are presented with orientalized features and romanticized dress and

posture. In the original photo, the Native Americans are wearing Euro-American clothes, but the woodcut shows them in colorful native attire and invents a warrior on horseback and a statuesque, bare-breasted woman.

33. Barnhurst and Nerone, *Form of News*, chap. 6.

34. See David Kaser, *Books and Libraries in Camp and Battle: The Civil War Experience* (Westport, Conn.: Greenwood, 1984).

35. Menahem Blondheim, " 'Public Sentiment Is Everything': The Union's Public Communications Strategy and the Bogus Proclamation of 1864," *Journal of American History* 89 (2002): 869–99.

36. Louis M. Starr, *Bohemian Brigade: Civil War Newsmen in Action* (New York: Knopf, 1954); J. Cutler Andrews, *The North Reports the Civil War* (Pittsburgh: University of Pittsburgh Press, 1955), and *The South Reports the Civil War* (Princeton: Princeton University Press, 1970). On Sherman's interactions, see John F. Marszalek, *Sherman's Other War: The General and the Civil War Press* (Memphis: Memphis State University Press, 1981).

37. Mark E. Neely, *The Fate of Liberty: Abraham Lincoln and Civil Liberties* (New York: Oxford University Press, 1991). Jeffery A. Smith views Lincoln's record in a harsher light in *War and Press Freedom: The Problem of Prerogative Power* (New York: Oxford University Press, 1999), chap. 5.

38. Robert S. Harper, *Lincoln and the Press* (New York: McGraw Hill, 1951); John Nerone, *Violence against the Press: Policing the Public Sphere in U.S. History* (New York: Oxford University Press, 1994), chap. 5.

39. Adrian Cook, *Armies of the Streets: The New York City Draft Riots of 1863* (Lexington: University Press of Kentucky, 1974), 87–90.

40. George P. Rowell & Co., *American Newspaper Directory, Edition for 1876* (New York: George P. Rowell & Co., 1876), iii–iv.

41. David Bailey, *Eastward Ho! Leaves from the Diary of a Centennial Pilgrim* (Highland County, Ohio: David Bailey, 1877), 60.

42. *Frank Leslie's Illustrated Historical Register of the Centennial Exposition* (New York: Frank Leslie's Pub. House, 1876), 274.

43. George P. Rowell & Co., comp., *Centennial Newspaper Exhibition, 1876* (New York: George P. Rowell & Co., 1876), xii.

44. Walter Lippmann, "Two Revolutions in the American Press," *Yale Review* 20 (1931): 433–41; Robert Ezra Park, "The Natural History of the Newspaper," *American Journal of Sociology* 29 (1955): 80–98; Mott, *American Journalism*, chap. 12; Michael Schudson, *Discovering the News: A Social History of American Newspapers* (New York: Basic Books, 1978), chap. 2.

45. Gerald J. Baldasty, *The Commercialization of News in the Nineteenth Century* (Madison: University of Wisconsin Press, 1992), 3–4.

46. Gerald J. Baldasty, *E. W. Scripps and the Business of Newspapers* (Urbana: University of Illinois Press, 1999), 1–8, 19–32; Richard L. Kaplan, "The Economics and Politics of Nineteenth-Century Newspapers: Market Segmentation and Partisanship in the Detroit Press, 1865–1900," *American Journalism* 10 (Winter/Spring 1993): 84–101.

47. Mark Wahlgren Summers, *The Press Gang: Newspapers and Politics, 1865–1878* (Chapel Hill: University of North Carolina Press, 1994), 303.

48. For some prominent examples, see Nerone, *Violence against the Press*, chap. 6.

49. Barnhurst and Nerone, *Form of News*, 99–104.

50. Blondheim, "Click," 27–52.

51. For example, in 1863 the *New York Times* complained that the *Philadelphia Sunday Mercury* reprinted telegraphic dispatches that had first appeared in the *Times*; see "News from Washington: Stealing News," *New York Times*, 18 February 1863, 1. See the similar complaint in 1874 about the *New York Herald* and *New York Tribune*: untitled editorial, *New York Times*, 7 April 1874, 4.

52. James W. Carey, "Technology and Ideology: The Case of the Telegraph," in *Communication as Culture*, 201–30.

53. David T. Z. Mindich, *Just the Facts: How Objectivity Came to Define American Journalism* (New York: New York University Press, 1998), chap. 3.

54. Kaplan, "Economics and Politics," 84–101. In *Politics and the American Press: The Rise of Objectivity, 1865–1920* (New York: Cambridge University Press, 2002), chap. 5, Kaplan argues that partisanship remained the rule until the election of 1896, which threw party allegiances into turmoil.

55. George William Curtis, "Editor's Easy Chair," *Harper's New Monthly Magazine* 26 (January 1863): 279.

56. Ibid.

57. Ibid., 277.

58. See, for example, "Publisher's Successes," *Putnam's Monthly* 11 (January 1868): 122.

59. "Literary Speculations by One Who Has Had Enough of Them," *United States Review* 1 [*USMDR* 32] (June 1853): 535.

60. Mott, *History of American Magazines*, 2:4.

61. Jacob Blanck identifies such publications as "twilight books" in the preface to *Bibliography of American Literature* (New Haven: Yale University Press, 1955), 1:xxi.

62. Earl L. Bradsher, *Mathew Carey* (New York: Columbia University Press, 1912), 93; Carey quoted in Mott, *History of American Magazines*, 1:361.

63. Eugene Exman, *The Brothers Harper: A Unique Publishing Partnership and Its Impact upon the Cultural Life of America from 1817 to 1853* (New York: Harper & Row, 1965), 158–67.

64. J. G. Holland, "*Scribner's Monthly*: Historical," *Scribner's Monthly* 22 (June 1881): 302.

65. "Recent Literature," *AM* 29 (March 1872): 364.

66. "Mr. De Forest's Novels," *AM* 32 (November 1873): 611.

67. "Books of the Month," *AM* 48 (December 1881): 860.

68. "Books and Their Influences," *USMDR* 37 (July 1856): 556–69.

69. "George Munro," *Biographer* 1 (1883): 19–21.

70. Mott, *History of American Magazines*, 1:506; Ellery Sedgwick, "Magazines and the Profession of Authorship in the United States, 1840–1900," *Papers of the Bibliographical Society of America* 94 (2000): 404; Henry A. Beers, *Nathaniel Parker Willis* (Boston: Houghton, Mifflin & Co., 1885), 240.

71. *Graham's American Monthly Magazine* 43 (November 1853): 554; *Godey's Lady's Book* 40 (February 1850): 88.

72. Mott, *History of American Magazines*, 1:510–11.

73. "Pay of Authors," *Littell's Living Age* 13 (8 May 1847): 257.

74. Sedgwick, "Magazines and the Profession of Authorship," 404.

75. William Gilmore Simms, "Walks among the Publishers," *Southern and Western Magazine* 2 (November 1845): 356.

76. N. P. Willis, "The Pay for Periodical Writing," *Evening Mirror* (12 October 1844): 2.

77. John Burroughs, Autobiographical Fragments, 15 March 1906, 48, John Burroughs Papers, Berg Collection, New York Public Library.

78. William Dean Howells, "First Impressions of Literary New York," *Harper's New Monthly Magazine* 91 (June 1895): 63.

79. John Burroughs, Journal, 26 May 1878, John Burroughs Papers, Department of Archives and Special Collections, Vassar College.

80. John Burroughs to Myron Benton, 1 December 1868, 28 February 1871, Burroughs Papers, New York Public Library.

81. Sedgwick, "Magazines and the Profession of Authorship," 402.

82. George Wakeman, "Advertising," *Galaxy* 3 (15 January 1867): 202.

83. George P. Rowell, *Forty Years an Advertising Agent, 1865–1905* (1906; repr. New York: Franklin Pub. Co., 1926), 179.

84. Frank Presbrey, *The History and Development of American Advertising* (New York: Doubleday, 1929), 302.

85. "Putnam's Monthly Advertiser," *Putnam's Monthly* 2 (July 1853): [1].

86. "To The Public," *Scribner's Monthly Advertiser*, 1, in *Scribner's Monthly* 1 (November 1870).

87. "Putnam's Monthly Advertiser," *Putnam's Monthly* 5 (May 1855): i–ix.

88. Ellen Gruber Garvey, *The Adman in the Parlor: Magazines and the Gendering of Consumer Culture, 1880s to 1910s* (New York: Oxford University Press, 1996), 9.

89. Margaret Fuller to William Henry Channing, 1 January 1840, in *Letters of Margaret Fuller*, ed. Robert Hudspeth (Ithaca, N.Y.: Cornell University Press, 1983), 2:111.

90. Joel Myerson, *The New England Transcendentalists and the Dial* (Cranbury, N.J.: Associated University Presses, 1980), 47–49.

91. "A Word to Our Readers," *Dial* 1 (January 1860): 11.

92. [Thomas Hamilton], "Apology," *Anglo-African Magazine* 1 (January 1859): 4.

93. Ibid., 1.

94. James E. Murphy and Sharon M. Murphy, *Let My People Know: American Indian Journalism, 1828–1978* (Norman: University of Oklahoma Press, 1981), 20.

95. [There is no Frigate like a Book] and [Unto my Books—So good to turn—], in *The Complete Poems of Emily Dickinson*, ed. Thomas H. Johnson (Boston: Little, Brown, 1955), 553, 296; Jack L. Capps, *Emily Dickinson's Reading, 1836–1886* (Cambridge, Mass.: Harvard University Press, 1966), 128–43. See also Nancy Glazener, *Reading for Realism: The History of a U.S. Literary Institution, 1850–1910* (Durham, N.C.: Duke University Press, 1997), 93–94.

96. "New Volume—1854," *Putnam's Monthly Magazine* 2 (December 1853): back cover.

97. Louise Amelia Knapp Smith Clappe, "Letter Third: A Trip into the Mines" (20 September 1851), in *The Shirley Letters from the California Mines, 1851–52*, ed. Carl I. Wheat (New York: Knopf, 1922), 31.

98. For example, in the June 1880 number of *Harper's New Monthly Magazine*, there are eighty-five illustrations, including those that accompany "The Editor's Drawer."

99. Mott, *History of American Magazines*, 1:547.

100. "Editor's Table," *Graham's American Monthly Magazine* 25 (December 1844): 296.

101. See the volume title pages of *Graham's American Monthly Magazine* for 1845 and 1850.

102. Biographical details of Frank Leslie may be found in Budd Leslie Gambee Jr., *Frank Leslie and His Illustrated Newspaper, 1855–1860* (Ann Arbor: University of Michigan, Department of Library Science, 1964), 1–30.

103. Mott, *History of American Magazines*, 1:409–12.

104. Ibid., 2:452–65.

105. Fanny Fern, *Ruth Hall* (New York: Mason Brothers, 1855), 231.

106. "Editor's Table," *Godey's Lady's Book* 19 (December 1839): 284.

107. Mott, *History of American Magazines*, 1:580, 584.

108. Ralph Waldo Emerson to Henry James Sr., 8 February 1854, in *The Letters of Ralph Waldo Emerson*, ed. Eleanor M. Tilton, vol. 8 (New York: Columbia University Press, 1991), 393.

109. For an overview, see Mott, *History of American Magazines*, 1:383–405; Exman, *Brothers Harper*, 303–22; and Eugene Exman, *The House of Harper: One Hundred and Fifty Years of Publishing* (New York: Harper & Row, 1967), 69–79.

110. Exman, *House of Harper*, 71–72, 102–20.

111. Alfred Hudson Guernsey, "Making the Magazine," *Harper's New Monthly Magazine* 32 (December 1865): 2; Edward E. Chielens, ed., *American Literary Magazines: The Eighteenth and Nineteenth Centuries* (New York: Greenwood, 1986), 166.

112. "A Word at the Start," *Harper's New Monthly Magazine* 1 (June 1850): 1.

113. For an overview, see Mott, *History of American Magazines*, 1:419–31; and Ezra Greenspan, *George Palmer Putnam: Representative American Publisher* (University Park: Pennsylvania State University Press, 2000), 285–321.

114. "Introductory," *Putnam's Monthly* 1 (January 1853): 1.

115. Greenspan, *George Palmer Putnam*, 314–16, 373.

116. For an overview, see Mott, *History of American Magazines*, 1:493–515; and Ellery Sedgwick, *The Atlantic Monthly, 1857–1909: Yankee Humanism at High Tide and Ebb* (Amherst: University of Massachusetts Press, 1994).

117. Mott, *History of American Magazines*, 2:6–9.

118. J[osiah] G[ilbert] Holland to Edmund C. Stedman, 22 March 1879, Edmund C. Stedman Collection, Columbia University, quoted in Robert Scholnick, "Whitman and the Magazines: Some Documentary Evidence," *American Literature* 44 (1972): 228.

119. Mott, *History of American Magazines*, 3:467.

120. Sedgwick, *Atlantic Monthly*, 158.

121. J. Albert Robbins, "George Graham, Philadelphia Publisher," *Pennsylvania Magazine of History and Biography* 75 (1951): 292.

122. "Editor's Easy Chair," *Harper's New Monthly Magazine* 56 (January 1878): 302.

123. *Southern Baptist Messenger* 11 (1 May 1861): 18.

124. *Southern Baptist Messenger* 7 (1 February 1857): 19.

125. *Annual Report of the American Baptist Publication Society* 42 (1866): 36.

126. Orville A. Roorbach, comp., *Bibliotheca Americana: Catalogue of American Publications* (New York: O. A. Roorbach, 1852), 644–52; Mott, *History of American Magazines*, 1:341–70; *Missouri Presbyterian Recorder* 1 (January 1855): back.

127. Charles A. Madison, *Jewish Publishing in America: The Impact of Jewish Writing on American Culture* (New York: Sanhedrin, 1976), 6–14; Mary Stephana Cavanaugh, *Catholic Book Publishing History in the United States, 1785–1850* (Rochester, N.Y.: University of Rochester, 1954), 122; Colleen McDannell, "Catholic Women Fiction Writers, 1840–1920," *Women's Studies* 19 (1991): 395–405.

128. David Morgan, *Protestants and Pictures: Religion, Visual Culture, and the Age of American Mass Production* (New York: Oxford University Press, 1999), 163; Paul K. Conkin, *American Originals: Homemade Varieties of Christianity* (Chapel Hill: University of North Carolina Press, 1997), 118–35, 167–73, 237–53; Georgine Milmine, *The Life of Mary Baker G. Eddy and the History of Christian Science* (New York: Doubleday, Page & Co., 1909; repr. [by Willa Cather and Georgine Milmine], Lincoln: University of Nebraska Press, 1993), 176, 312–13 (page citations are to the reprint edition); Gillian Gill, *Mary Baker Eddy* (Reading, Mass.: Perseus, 1998), 325–30.

129. Ann Braude, *Radical Spirits: Spiritualism and Women's Rights in Nineteenth-Century America* (Boston: Beacon, 1989), 26; Conkin, *American Originals*, 147.

130. John Tebbel, *A History of Book Publishing in the United States*, vol. 1 (New York: R. R. Bowker, 1972), 214–40.

131. For one of many secularization narratives, see R. Laurence Moore, *Selling God: American Religion in the Marketplace of Culture* (New York: Oxford University Press, 1994), 10.

132. *Christian Advocate and Journal* 23 (1 October 1848): 161, quoted in James Penn Pilkington, *The Methodist Publishing House: A History*, vol. 1, *Beginnings to 1870* (Nashville: Abingdon, 1968), 366, 459–60.

133. *Christian Advocate* 35 (5 January 1860): 2; 39 (7 January 1864): 8.

134. *Centennial of the Methodist Book Concern* (New York: Hunt & Eaton, 1890), 75.

135. *Annual Report of the American Baptist Publication Society* 46 (1870): 21; Christine Leigh Heyrman, *Southern Cross: The Beginnings of the Bible Belt* (New York: Knopf, 1997), 159–60; Colleen McDannell, *The Christian Home in Victorian America, 1840–1900* (Bloomington: Indiana University Press, 1986), xi.

136. *Mothers' Monthly Journal* 6 (September 1841): cover; "Editor's Miscellany," *Mothers' Journal and Family Visitant* 25 (January 1860): 38; H. Hastings Weld, *Sacred Annual* (Philadelphia: T. E. Collins Jr., 1851), 3–4; Richard L. Bushman, *The Refinement of America: Persons, Houses, Cities* (New York: Knopf, 1992), 322; Morgan, *Protestants and Pictures*, 10.

137. *Baptist Preacher* 3 (June 1844): 104; 16 (January 1857): 23.

138. *Sabbath at Home: An Illustrated Religious Magazine for the Family* 1 (January 1867): 1–2, 60; George L. Prentiss, *The Life and Letters of Elizabeth Prentiss* (New York: A. D. F. Randolph & Co., 1882), 255–81, 391.

139. *Mother's Journal and Family Visitant* 25 (January 1860): 33–37.

140. Wesley Norton, *Religious Newspapers in the Old Northwest to 1861: A History, Bibliography, and Record of Opinion* (Athens: Ohio University Press, 1977), 4; David Paul Nord, *Communities of Journalism: A History of American Newspapers and Their Readers* (Urbana: University of Illinois Press, 2001), 253-54; David D. Hall, *Worlds of Wonder, Days of Judgment: Popular Religious Belief in Early New England* (New York: Knopf, 1989), 49.

141. *Beauty of Holiness* 7 (January 1855): 1, (February 1855): 35-64, (March 1855): 79; *Western Christian* 1 (28 June 1845): 1-3.

142. *Western Christian* 2 (24 September 1846): 2; *Western Presbyterian* 1 (15 January 1864): 39-40; *Sabbath at Home* 1 (March 1867): 189; Susan Belasco Smith, "Serialization and the Nature of *Uncle Tom's Cabin*," in *Periodical Literature in Nineteenth-Century America*, ed. Kenneth M. Price and Susan Belasco Smith (Charlottesville: University Press of Virginia, 1995), 71; Prentiss, *Life and Letters*, 483-84.

CHAPTER 8
Ideologies and Practices of Reading

1. *Ohio Journal of Education* 5 (1856): 97, quoted in Lee Soltow and Edward Stevens, *The Rise of Literacy and the Common School in the United States: A Socioeconomic Analysis to 1870* (Chicago: University of Chicago Press, 1981), 74.

2. Samuel Griswold Goodrich, *Recollections of a Lifetime; or Men and Things I Have Seen* (New York: Miller, Orton & Mulligan, 1856), 2:391.

3. Sections of this essay draw on Barbara Sicherman, "Reading and Middle-Class Identity in Victorian America: Cultural Consumption, Conspicuous and Otherwise," in *Reading Acts: U.S. Readers' Interactions with Literature, 1800-1950*, ed. Barbara Ryan and Amy M. Thomas (Knoxville: University of Tennessee Press, 2002), 137-60.

4. Soltow and Stevens, *Rise of Literacy*, 58-88.

5. John K. Folger and Charles B. Nam, *Education of the American Population* (Washington, D.C.: GPO, 1967), 113. The census enumeration of illiteracy counted whites and "free colored persons." Estimates of illiteracy in the total population were generally extrapolated from the assumption, now recognized as mistaken, that all enslaved people were illiterate.

6. Ronald J. Zboray, *A Fictive People: Antebellum Economic Development and the American Reading Public* (New York: Oxford University Press, 1993), 83-84, 196-201, 233; Carl F. Kaestle et al., *Literacy in the United States: Readers and Reading since 1880* (New Haven: Yale University Press, 1991), 18-25.

7. Nina Baym, *Woman's Fiction: A Guide to Novels by and about Women in America, 1820-1870* (Ithaca, N.Y.: Cornell University Press, 1978), and *American Women Writers and the Work of History, 1790-1860* (New Brunswick, N.J.: Rutgers University Press, 1995); Mary Kelley, *Private Woman, Public Stage: Literary Domesticity in Nineteenth-Century America* (New York: Oxford University Press, 1984); Susan Coultrap-McQuin, *Doing Literary Business: American Women Writers in the Nineteenth Century* (Chapel Hill: University of North Carolina Press, 1990); Mary P. Ryan, *The Empire of the Mother: American Writing about Domesticity, 1830 to 1860* (New York: Institute for Research in History and Haworth Press, 1982); Patricia Okker, *Our Sister Editors: Sarah J. Hale*

and the Tradition of Nineteenth-Century American Women Editors (Athens: University of Georgia Press, 1995).

8. Janet Duitsman Cornelius, *"When I Can Read My Title Clear": Literacy, Slavery, and Religion in the Antebellum South* (Columbia: University of South Carolina Press, 1991).

9. See Harriet A. Jacobs, *Incidents in the Life of a Slave Girl, Written by Herself*, ed. Jean Fagan Yellin (Cambridge, Mass.: Harvard University Press, 1987), 40; and Katherine Clay Bassard, "Gender and Genre: Black Women's Autobiography and the Ideology of Literacy," *African American Review* 26 (1992): 119–29.

10. See the essays in *The Black Press: New Literary and Historical Essays*, ed. Todd Vogel (New Brunswick, N.J.: Rutgers University Press, 2001), esp. Vogel's "The New Face of Black Labor," 37–54.

11. *Twelfth Census of the United States, Taken in the Year 1900: Population, Part II* (Washington, D.C.: U.S. Census Office, 1902), cv. The 45 percent illiteracy figure for 1900 includes those who could read but not write.

12. William J. Gilmore, *Reading Becomes a Necessity of Life: Material and Cultural Life in Rural New England, 1780–1835* (Knoxville: University of Tennessee Press, 1989), 257; David Paul Nord, *Faith in Reading: Religious Publishing and the Birth of Mass Media in America* (New York: Oxford University Press, 2004). See also Leonard I. Sweet, "Communication and Change in American Religious History: A Historiographical Probe," in *Communication and Change in American Religious History*, ed. Leonard I. Sweet (Grand Rapids, Mich.: Eerdmans, 1993), 1–49.

13. Nord, *Faith in Reading*, 131.

14. Joan Jacobs Brumberg, *Mission for Life: The Story of the Family of Adoniram Judson* (New York: Free Press, 1980), 45, 65–66, 70, 139.

15. Leonard L. Richards, *"Gentlemen of Property and Standing": Anti-Abolition Mobs in Jacksonian America* (New York: Oxford University Press, 1970), 52, 58.

16. Horace Mann, "Report for 1848," in *Life and Works of Horace Mann* (Boston: Lee & Shepard, 1891), 4:260, 277; Mann quoted in Merle Curti, *The Social Ideas of American Educators: With New Chapter on the Last Twenty-Five Years* (1935; repr., Paterson, N.J.: Littlefield, Adams, 1965), 113.

17. Carl F. Kaestle, *Pillars of the Republic: Common Schools and American Society, 1780–1860* (New York: Hill & Wang, 1983), 75–103, 161–81.

18. Nila Banton Smith, *American Reading Instruction* (Newark, Del.: International Reading Association, 1986), 103–9; Richard L. Venezky, "A History of the American Reading Textbook," *Elementary School Journal* 87 (1987): 250–52.

19. For an instructive comparison of the McGuffey's and Freedman's readers, see Louise L. Stevenson, *The Victorian Homefront: American Thought and Culture, 1860–1880* (New York: Twayne, 1991), 71–100.

20. A useful starting point is Joseph F. Kett, *The Pursuit of Knowledge under Difficulties: From Self-Improvement to Adult Education in America, 1750–1990* (Stanford, Calif.: Stanford University Press, 1994), esp. 38–141. See also Richard D. Brown, *Knowledge Is Power: The Diffusion of Information in Early America, 1700–1865* (New York: Oxford University Press, 1989), esp. 160–96, 218–44; and Carl Bode, *The American Lyceum: Town Meeting of the Mind* (New York: Oxford University Press, 1956).

21. Donald M. Scott, "The Popular Lecture and the Creation of a Public in Mid-Nineteenth-Century America," *Journal of American History* 66 (1980): 781–809, "Print and the Public Lecture System, 1840–60," in *Printing and Society in Early America*, ed. William L. Joyce et al. (Worcester, Mass.: AAS, 1983), 278–99, and "Knowledge and the Marketplace," in *The Mythmaking Frame of Mind: Social Imagination and American Culture*, ed. James Gilbert et al. (Belmont, Calif.: Wadsworth, 1993), 91–112. See also Kenneth Cmiel, *Democratic Eloquence: The Fight over Popular Speech in Nineteenth-Century America* (New York: Morrow, 1990); and Elizabeth McHenry and Shirley Brice Heath, "The Literate and the Literary: African Americans as Writers and Readers — 1830–1940," *Written Communication* 11 (1994): 419–44.

22. William E. Channing, "Address on Self-Culture," in *The Works of William E. Channing, D.D.*, 20th ed. (Boston: American Unitarian Association, 1871), 1:354, 378, 379.

23. On U.S. Victorian culture, see David D. Hall, "The Victorian Connection," and Daniel Walker Howe, "Victorian Culture in America," in *Victorian America*, ed. Daniel Walker Howe (Philadelphia: University of Pennsylvania Press, 1976); and Stevenson, *Victorian Homefront*.

24. Matthew Arnold, *Culture and Anarchy: An Essay in Political and Social Criticism* (London: Smith, Elder, 1869), viii.

25. "Chromo-Civilization," *Nation* 19 (24 September 1874): 202.

26. Lawrence W. Levine, *Highbrow/Lowbrow: The Emergence of Cultural Hierarchy in America* (Cambridge, Mass.: Harvard University Press, 1988).

27. William G. McLoughlin, *The Meaning of Henry Ward Beecher: An Essay on the Shifting Values of Mid-Victorian America, 1840–1870* (New York: Knopf, 1970), 20–25, 55–58, 63–64, 119–33.

28. Andrew C. Rieser, *The Chautauqua Moment: Protestants, Progressives, and the Culture of Modern Liberalism* (New York: Columbia University Press, 2003); Theodore Morrison, *Chautauqua: A Center for Education, Religion, and the Arts in America* (Chicago: University of Chicago Press, 1974), 53–70; Kett, *Pursuit of Knowledge*, 160–65, 171–75, 182–89; Thomas F. O'Connor, "American Catholic Reading Circles, 1886-1909," *Libraries and Culture* 26 (1991): 334–47.

29. Jeanne M. Weimann, *The Fair Women* (Chicago: Academy Chicago, 1981), 353–92.

30. On cheap books, see Frank L. Schick, *The Paperbound Book in America: The History of Paperbacks and Their European Background* (New York: R. R. Bowker, 1958), 48–66; and Michael Denning, *Mechanic Accents: Dime Novels and Working-Class Culture in America* (London: Verso, 1987). On Civil War reading, see David Kaser, *Books and Libraries in Camp and Battle: The Civil War Experience* (Westport, Conn.: Greenwood, 1984).

31. Louisa May Alcott to Alfred Whitman, 22 June 1862, in *The Selected Letters of Louisa May Alcott*, ed. Joel Myerson and Daniel Shealy (Boston: Little, Brown, 1987), 79.

32. Noah Porter, *Books and Reading; or, What Books Shall I Read and How Shall I Read Them?* (1871; repr., New York: Charles Scribner's Sons, 1883), 9, 98–99, 231–32. The discourse on reading is analyzed by Isabelle Lehuu, *Carnival on the Page: Popular Print Media in Antebellum America* (Chapel Hill: University of North Carolina Press, 2000), chap. 6; and Stevenson, *Victorian Homefront*, chap. 2.

33. M. F. Sweetser, "What the People Read," in *Hints for Home Reading: A Series of Papers on Books and Their Use*, ed. Lyman Abbott (New York: G. P. Putnam's Sons, 1880), 12–13.

34. Porter, *Books and Reading*, 98.

35. Ibid., 7–8.

36. W. H. Bishop, "Story-Paper Literature," *AM* 44 (September 1879): 384; Joseph Cook, "How to Make Dull Boys Read," in Abbott, *Hints for Home Reading*, 70–77.

37. Horace Mann, "Report for 1839," in *Life and Works*, 3:45.

38. Bishop, "Story-Paper Literature," 393. See also "Beadle's Dime Books," *North American Review* 99 (July 1864): 303–9.

39. George Ticknor to Edward Everett, 14 July 1851, in *Life, Letters, and Journals of George Ticknor*, ed. George S. Hillard (Boston: James R. Osgood & Co., 1876), 2:301–2.

40. Esther Jane Carrier, *Fiction in Public Libraries, 1876–1900* (New York: Scarecrow, 1965), 188–89, 267–362; Dee Garrison, *Apostles of Culture: The Public Librarian and American Society, 1876–1920* (New York: Free Press, 1979), chap. 4.

41. Nancy Glazener, *Reading for Realism: The History of a U.S. Literary Institution, 1850–1910* (Durham, N.C.: Duke University Press, 1997), 105, 147–88.

42. Lindsay Swift, "The Public Library in Its Relation to Literature," *Library Journal* 25 (July 1900): 327, quoted in Carrier, *Fiction in Public Libraries*, 116.

43. Ronald J. Zboray and Mary Saracino Zboray, "Reading and Everyday Life in Antebellum Boston: The Diary of Daniel F. and Mary D. Child," *Libraries and Culture* 32 (1997): 285–323.

44. "Journal," August 23 [1878], *The Papers of M. Carey Thomas in the Bryn Mawr College Archives*, ed. Lucy Fisher West (Woodbridge, Conn., 1982), microfilm edition, reel 2. See also Barbara Sicherman, "Reading and Ambition: M. Carey Thomas and Female Heroism," *American Quarterly* 45 (1993): 90–91.

45. Influential statements of these views include Robert Darnton, *The Forbidden Best-Sellers of Pre-Revolutionary France* (New York: W. W. Norton, 1994), 186; and Roger Chartier, "Texts, Printing, Readings," in *The New Cultural History*, ed. Lynn Hunt (Berkeley: University of California Press, 1989), 154–75.

46. Janice Radway, "Interpretive Communities and Variable Literacies: The Functions of Romance Reading," *Daedalus* 113 (Summer 1984): 54.

47. For a reading network of farmers "forged through kinship, exchange, and neighborliness," see Sally McMurry, "Who Read the Agricultural Journals? Evidence from Chenango County, New York, 1839–1865," *Agricultural History* 63 (Fall 1989): 3.

48. Mary Austin, *Earth Horizon: Autobiography* (Boston: Houghton Mifflin, 1932), 100.

49. Paula Petrik, "The Youngest Fourth Estate: The Novelty Toy Printing Press and Adolescence, 1870–1886," in *Small Worlds: Children and Adolescents in America, 1850–1950*, ed. Elliott West and Paula Petrik (Lawrence: University Press of Kansas, 1992), 125–42.

50. David Vincent, *Literacy and Popular Culture: England, 1750–1914* (Cambridge: Cambridge University Press, 1989).

51. David Paul Nord, "Working-Class Readers: Family, Community, and Reading in Late Nineteenth-Century America," *Communication Research* 13 (April 1986): 156–81.

52. Ronald J. Zboray, "Technology and the Character of Community Life in Antebellum America: The Role of Story Papers," in Sweet, *Communication and Change*, 204.

53. Richard H. Brodhead, *Cultures of Letters: Scenes of Reading and Writing in Nineteenth-Century America* (Chicago: University of Chicago Press, 1993), 103.

54. Denning, *Mechanic Accents*, 4.

55. See, for example, Jochen Schulte-Sasse, "Can the Disempowered Read Mass-Produced Narratives in Their Own Voice?" *Cultural Critique* 10 (Fall 1988): 171–99.

56. Robert E. Weir, *Beyond Labor's Veil: The Culture of the Knights of Labor* (University Park: Pennsylvania State University Press, 1996), esp. 145–94.

57. Raymond Howard Shove, *Cheap Book Production in the United States, 1870 to 1891* (Urbana: University of Illinois Library, 1937), 56–64, 74–82. See also *Publishers for Mass Entertainment in Nineteenth Century America*, ed. Madeleine B. Stern (Boston: G. K. Hall, 1980).

58. Quoted in Shove, *Cheap Book Production*, 39.

59. Harriet H. Robinson, *Loom and Spindle; or, Life among the Early Mill Girls* (New York: T. Y. Crowell & Co., 1898), esp. chaps. 3, 6; Lucy Larcom, *A New England Girlhood: Outlined from Memory* (Boston: Houghton, Mifflin & Co., 1889); Elfrieda B. McCauley, "The New England Mill Girls: Feminine Influence in the Development of Public Libraries in New England" (D.L.S. diss., Columbia University, 1971).

60. Christopher Clark, ed., "The Diary of an Apprentice Cabinetmaker: Edward Jenner Carpenter's 'Journal,' 1844–45," *Procs. AAS* 98 (1988): 303–94; quotation at 327.

61. Amy M. Thomas, "Who Makes the Text? The Production and Use of Literature in Antebellum America" (Ph.D. diss., Duke University, 1992), 8–98.

62. *Growing Up in Boston's Gilded Age: The Journal of Alice Stone Blackwell, 1872–1874*, ed. Marlene Deahl Merrill (New Haven: Yale University Press, 1990), 67, 105.

63. Robert Morss Lovett, "A Boy's Reading Fifty Years Ago," *New Republic* 48 (10 November 1926): 334–36. On Alger's readers, see Carol Nackenoff, *The Fictional Republic: Horatio Alger and American Political Discourse* (New York: Oxford University Press, 1984), 181–205.

64. Christine Pawley, *Reading on the Middle Border: The Culture of Print in Late-Nineteenth-Century Osage, Iowa* (Amherst: University of Massachusetts Press, 2001), esp. 61–116; Zboray, *Fictive People*, 156–79. On crossover reading, see also Ronald J. Zboray and Mary Saracino Zboray, "Political News and Female Readership in Antebellum Boston and Its Region," *Journalism History* 22 (Spring 1996): 2–14; and Thomas C. Leonard, "News at the Hearth: A Drama of Reading in Nineteenth-Century America," *Procs. AAS* 102 (1993): 379–401.

65. Lovett, "Boy's Reading," 335. Even when reading the same books, men and women did not necessarily read them the same way; see Barbara Sicherman, "Sense and Sensibility: A Case Study of Women's Reading in Late-Victorian America," in *Reading in America: Literature and Social History*, ed. Cathy N. Davidson (Baltimore: Johns Hopkins University Press, 1989), 210–12; and Susan K. Harris, *The Courtship of Olivia Langdon and Mark Twain* (Cambridge: Cambridge University Press, 1996), 106–34.

66. Sicherman, "Reading and Ambition," 73–103; Helen Lefkowitz Horowitz, "'Nous Autres': Reading, Passion, and the Creation of M. Carey Thomas," *Journal of American History* 79 (1992): 68–95.

67. *The Memphis Diary of Ida B. Wells*, ed. Miriam DeCosta-Willis (Boston: Beacon, 1995); *Crusade for Justice: The Autobiography of Ida B. Wells*, ed. Alfreda M. Duster (Chicago: University of Chicago Press, 1970).

68. Joan D. Hedrick, *Solitary Comrade: Jack London and His Work* (Chapel Hill: University of North Carolina Press, 1982), 32–36.

69. Jane Addams, *Democracy and Social Ethics* (New York: Macmillan, 1902), 8–9.

70. Austin, *Earth Horizon*, 103–4.

CHAPTER 9
Sites of Reading

1. Sylvanus Cobb Jr., "True Story of Swiftville Library," *Portsmouth Journal*, 26 August 1871, 1.

2. *Common School Journal* 2 (15 April 1840): 120.

3. *School Advertiser* (August 1839), bound in, as issued, with Marsh, Capen, Lyon, & Webb, *The School Library: Published under the Sanction and by Authority of the Board of Education of the State of Massachusetts* (Boston, 1839).

4. See Sidney Ditzion, "The District-School Library, 1835–55," *Library Quarterly* 10 (1940): 545–77; William P. Page, *School District Libraries* (printed letter; Brooklyn, 8 February 1841), 3.

5. Page, *School District Libraries*, 2.

6. Ditzion, "District-School Library," 575–76.

7. See *Catalogue of the City School Library, Lowell, Mass., Established May 20, 1844* (Lowell, 1845); Roger Lane, *William Dorsey's Philadelphia and Ours: On the Past and Future of the Black City in America* (New York: Oxford University Press, 1991), 139.

8. For contemporaneous developments, see Robert Ellis Lee, *Continuing Education for Adults through the American Public Library, 1833–1964* (Chicago: American Library Association, 1966), 3.

9. Ditzion, "District-School Library," 568–72.

10. *Catalogue and By-laws of the Sears Library of St. Paul's Church Boston; also, the Catalogue of the Sunday School Library of St. Paul's Church* (Boston: John Cotton, 1827) recorded even sixteenth-century books, and a catalog of books sought by the West Parish Association (*Constitution of the West Parish Association, Together with Reports of Committees on the Sunday Schools, and the Library* [Boston: Wm. Bellamy, 1825], [19]–24) showed the desire to create a learned library, presumably particularly for the use of clergy.

11. F. Allen Briggs, "The Sunday School Library in the Nineteenth Century," *Library Quarterly* 31 (1961): 174–77; Anne M. Boylan, *Sunday School: The Formation of an American Institution, 1790–1880* (New Haven: Yale University Press, 1988), 48–52.

12. Christopher Phillips, *Freedom's Port: The African American Community of Baltimore, 1790–1860* (Urbana: University of Illinois Press, 1997), 166.

13. Francis A. Walker, *A Compendium of the Ninth Census* (Washington, D.C.: GPO, 1872), 505, table 35; Briggs, "Sunday School Library," 176–77.

14. Although the YMCAs were then primarily in the large cities attracting immigrants from the countryside, they were also formed in towns whose young men needed to be prepared "to go out from us [to be] clothed in the Christian panoply, and having on the

breastplate of righteousness"; see *Journal of Proceedings of the First Annual Convention of Young Men's Christian Associations of the United States and British Provinces* (Washington, D.C.: Central Committee of the Y.M.C.A., 1854), 45.

15. C. Howard Hopkins, *History of the Y.M.C.A. in North America* (New York: Association Press, 1951), 195. YMCAs also distributed tracts; see, for example, *Quarterly of the Young Men's Christian Associations of America* 2 (May 1868): 98–99.

16. Thomas Augst, *The Clerk's Tale: Young Men and Moral Life in Nineteenth-Century America* (Chicago: University of Chicago Press, 2003), 175.

17. Ibid., 167–73.

18. Ibid., 165.

19. Ibid., 166, 173.

20. Ibid., 175.

21. Edward Everett to the mayor of Boston, 7 June 1851, in Horace G. Wadlin, *The Public Library of the City of Boston: A History* (Boston: The Trustees, 1911), 23–26.

22. Ticknor to Edward Everett, 14 July 1851, in *The Life and Letters of George Ticknor* (Boston: James R. Osgood & Co., 1876), 2:300–302. The same sentiments are expressed in *Report of the Trustees of the Public Library of the City of Boston, July 1852*, City Document no. 37 (Boston: J. H. Eastburn, 1852), 17–19; repr. in Jesse Shera, *Foundations of the Public Library: The Origins of the Public Library Movement in New England, 1629–1855* (Chicago: University of Chicago Press, 1949), app. 5, 283–85.

23. William J. Rhees, *Manual of Public Libraries, Institutions, and Societies, in the United States, and British Provinces of North America* (Philadelphia: J. B. Lippincott & Co., 1859), 154, 208.

24. William I. Fletcher, *Public Libraries in America* (Boston: Roberts Brothers, 1894), 143–46.

25. Ibid., 152–54.

26. For an illuminating, detailed study of the transformation of a small-town social library into a free public institution, see Christine Pawley, *Reading on the Middle Border: The Culture of Print in Late-Nineteenth-Century Osage, Iowa* (Amherst: University of Massachusetts Press, 2001), esp. 61–69.

27. Andrew Carnegie, "The Best Fields for Philanthropy," *North American Review* 149 (December 1889): 689–98. See also George S. Bobinski, *Carnegie Libraries: Their History and Impact on American Public Library Development* (Chicago: American Library Association, 1969).

28. [George Livermore], "Public Libraries," *North American Review* 71 (July 1850): 189.

29. Rufus Choate, "Speech on the Bill for the Establishment of the Smithsonian Institution, Delivered in the Senate of the United States, January 8, 1845," in *The Works of Rufus Choate*, ed. Samuel Gilman Brown (Boston: Little, Brown & Co., 1862), 2:264.

30. Quoted in Cyrus Adler, "The Smithsonian Library," in *The Smithsonian Institution, 1846–1896: The History of Its First Half Century*, ed. George Brown Goode (Washington, D.C., 1897), 270.

31. Ibid., 272. See also the separately paginated appendixes, "Publications of Learned Societies and Periodicals in the Library of the Smithsonian Institution," in *Smithsonian Contributions to Knowledge* 7 (1855) and 8 (1856).

32. Quoted in Adler, "Smithsonian Library," 272. These catalogs and hundreds of kindred works comprise the Public Library Catalogues Collection, AAS. For a bibliography of American library catalogs, see Robert Singerman, *American Library Book Catalogues, 1801–1875: A National Bibliography* (Urbana-Champaign: Graduate School of Library and Information Science, University of Illinois, 1996). For a study of catalogs, including their arrangement, see Jim Ranz, *The Printed Book Catalogue in American Libraries, 1723–1900* (Chicago: American Library Association, 1964).

33. Samuel Foster Haven of AAS learned of the plan, wrote to Jewett, and received a reply dated 24 January 1850; see Joseph A. Borome, *Charles Coffin Jewett* (Chicago: American Library Association, 1951), 46–49. Michael H. Harris suggests that Jewett was contemplating the plan as early as 1847; see *The Age of Jewett: Charles Coffin Jewett and American Librarianship, 1841–1868*, ed. Michael H. Harris (Littleton, Colo.: Libraries Unlimited, 1975), 30.

34. Charles Coffin Jewett, *On the Construction of Catalogues of Libraries, and of a General Catalogue* (Washington, D.C.: Smithsonian Institution, 1853); Harris, *Age of Jewett*, 30, 131.

35. *Annual Report of the Trustees of the Astor Library, for the Year 1853* (Albany, N.Y., 1854), 27; also quoted in Harry Miller Lydenberg, "The Astor Library, 1848–1895," in *History of the New York Public Library: Astor, Lenox and Tilden Foundations* (New York: New York Public Library, 1923), 32.

36. See Joseph Green Cogswell to George Ticknor, 27 May 1840 and 23 October 1848, in *Life of Joseph Green Cogswell as Sketched in His Letters*, ed. Anna Eliot Ticknor (Cambridge, Mass.: Riverside Press, 1874), 225, 242.

37. *Annual Report of the Trustees of the Astor Library, for the Year 1851* (Albany, N.Y., 1852), 5.

38. *Annual Report of the Trustees of the Astor Library, for the Year 1853*, 13–14.

39. Ibid., 29–30.

40. Nathaniel Fish Moore, *Address to the Alumni of Columbia College, Delivered in the College Chapel, March 16, 1848* (New York, 1848).

41. *Twenty-eighth Annual Report of the President of Harvard College to the Overseers . . . for the Academical Year 1852–53* (Cambridge, Mass.: Metcalf & Co., 1854), 9.

42. Roger L. Geiger, *To Advance Knowledge: The Growth of American Research Universities, 1900–1940* (New York: Oxford University Press, 1986), 1.

43. Harris, *Age of Jewett*, 33.

44. George Burwell Utley, *The Librarians' Conference of 1853: A Chapter in American Library History* (Chicago: American Library Association, 1951).

45. "The Convention of Librarians," *PW* 10 (7 October 1876): 600.

46. Edward G. Holley, *Raking the Historic Coals: The A.L.A Scrapbook of 1876* (N.p.: Beta Phi Mu, 1967), 17–19.

47. Wayne A. Wiegand, *Irrepressible Reformer: A Biography of Melvil Dewey* (Chicago: American Library Association, 1996), 61, notes that Dewey conceived the ALA motto in 1879.

48. Haynes McMullen, *American Libraries before 1876* (Westport, Conn.: Greenwood, 2000), 3.

49. Holley, *Raking the Historic Coals*, 3–4.

50. Ibid., 9–14.

51. Conference attendance numbers, locations, and ALA presidents up through 1917 are given in Wayne Wiegand, *The Politics of an Emerging Profession: The American Library Association, 1876–1917* (New York: Greenwood, 1986), app. 3, 245–50.

52. William Landrum Williamson, *William Frederick Poole and the Modern Library Movement* (New York: Columbia University Press, 1963).

53. Walter Muir Whitehill, *Boston Public Library: A Centennial History* (Cambridge, Mass.: Harvard University Press, 1956), 109.

54. Kenneth E. Carpenter, "New York State Library," in *International Dictionary of Library Histories*, ed. David H. Stam (Chicago: Fitzroy Dearborn, 2001), 2:621–23.

55. George N. Comer, *Penmanship Made Easy* (Boston: G. C. Rand and Avery, 1864), [4]; *Descriptive Catalogue of Books, Bibles and Photograph Albums* (Philadelphia: Quaker City Pub. House, 1880).

56. Charles Wyllys Elliott, *The Book of American Interiors* (Boston: J. R. Osgood & Co., 1876), 62–63.

57. Quotations from *G. G. Evans' Great Gift Book Sale* (Philadelphia: G. G. Evans, 1858), 47. On gift books, see Frederick W. Faxon, *Literary Annuals and Gift Books: A Bibliography with a Descriptive Introduction* (Boston: Boston Book Co., 1912); Ralph Thompson, *American Literary Annuals and Gift Books, 1825–1865* (New York: H. W. Wilson, 1936); and Isabelle Lehuu, *Carnival on the Page: Popular Print Media in Antebellum America* (Chapel Hill: University of North Carolina Press, 2000), 76–101.

58. For figures on the Ohio frontier, see Lee Soltow and Edward Stevens, *The Rise of Literacy and the Common School in the United States: A Socioeconomic Analysis to 1870* (Chicago: University of Chicago Press, 1981), 79. For 1850s budgets, see Edgar W. Martin, *The Standard of Living in 1860* (Chicago: University of Chicago Press, 1942), 394–95. For reading in the Midwest and West, see John Kent Folmar, ed., *"This State of Wonders": The Letters of an Iowa Frontier Family, 1858–1861* (Iowa City: University of Iowa Press, 1986); Richard D. Lillard, "A Literate Woman in the Mines: The Diary of Rachel Haskell," *Mississippi Valley Historical Review* 31 (1944): 81–98; and Pawley, *Reading on the Middle Border*.

59. *Horticulturalist* 6 (July 1851): 313–16 and frontispiece; Samuel Sloan, *Sloan's Homestead Architecture, Containing Forty Designs for Villas, Cottages, and Farm Houses, with Essays on Style, Construction, Landscape Gardening, Furniture*, 2nd ed. (Philadelphia: J. B. Lippincott & Co., 1867), 142–44, 148–50.

60. See Judith Reiter Weissman and Wendy Lavitt, *Labors of Love: America's Textiles and Needlework, 1650–1930* (New York: Knopf, 1987), 204–5. The candelabra were manufactured by Cornelius & Co., Philadelphia, 1848–51; accession no. 91.61, WMGL.

61. Robinson and Leadbeater, *Catalog of Figures* (N.p., c. 1885); Noel Riley, *Gifts for Good Children: The History of Children's China* (Somerset, U.K.: Richard Dennis, 1991), esp. pt. 1 (1790–1890); P. A. Halfpenny, *English Earthenware Figures, 1740–1840* (Woodbridge, Suffolk, U.K.: Antique Collectors' Club, 1991); Griselda Lewis, *A Collector's History of English Pottery*, 4th ed. (Woodbridge, Suffolk, U.K.: Antique Collectors' Club, 1987); Jeffrey B. Snyder, *Historical Staffordshire: American Patriots and Views* (Atglen, Pa.: Schiffer, 1995); P. D. Gordon Pugh, *Staffordshire Portrait Figures* (London: Barrie & Jenkins, 1970).

62. For example, see T. H. McAllister, *Catalogue of Stereopticons, Dissolving-View Apparatus, Magic Lanterns* (New York: T. H. McAllister, 1867); C. T. Milligan, *Illustrated Catalogue of Stereopanopticons* (Philadelphia: C. T. Milligan, 1881); and J. Jay Gould, *Catalog of Chromos, Engravings, Album Gems . . . Embossed Pictures, Flower Seeds, Novelties, &c.* (Boston: J. Jay Gould, 1875).

63. J. W. Hamburger, Catalog (New York: J. W. Hamburger, c. 1870); Burns & Trainique, Cabinet Makers and Upholsterers, "The Shakespeare Stand" (broadside; New York: Burns & Trainique, c. 1850–59), WMGL.

64. *The Journals of Charlotte Forten Grimké*, ed. Brenda Stevenson (New York: Oxford University Press, 1988), 71–72; Bessie M. Lindsey, *American Historical Glass* (Rutland, Vt.: C. E. Tuttle, 1967), 410; George B. James Jr., *Souvenir Spoons: Containing Descriptions and Illustrations of the Principal Designs Produced in the United States* (Boston: A. W. Fuller, 1891); G. W. Tomlinson, *Card Photographs: Distinguished Personages, Works of Art, etc.* (Boston: G. W. Tomlinson, 1864).

65. Jacqueline Ann Hinsley, "The Reading Tastes of Educated Women of a Manufacturing Family in America, 1810–1835" (master's thesis, University of Delaware, 1976), 57–58.

66. Riley, *Gifts for Good Children*, 106–7; Lewis, *Collector's History of English Pottery*, 211; Pugh, *Staffordshire*, 4; Robinson and Leadbeater, Catalog of Parian ware (Stoke-on-Trent, Staffordshire, U.K., c. 1885), WMGL; Weissman and Lavitt, *Labors of Love*, 205; Margaret Vincent, *The Ladies' Work Table* (Allentown, Pa.: Allentown Art Museum, 1988), 31; Margaret Landon, *Anna and the King of Siam* (New York: Harper Collins, 1944), 348.

67. John Rogers, *Groups of Statuary* (New York: John Rogers, 1877).

68. Gabrielle Shubrick Crofton to Julia Shubrick, n.d., Crofton-Shubrick Letters, HML.

69. Claudia L. Bushman, *"A Good Poor Man's Wife": Being a Chronicle of Harriet Hanson Robinson and Her Family in Nineteenth-Century New England* (Hanover, N.H.: University Press of New England, 1981), 39.

70. Sophie du Pont to Clementina Smith, 26 June 1832, HML.

71. Hamlin Garland, *A Son of the Middle Border* (New York: Macmillan, 1917), 187.

72. See the following manuscript materials in the Joseph Downs Collection of Manuscripts and Ephemera, WMGL: Frances Burgess, Diaries, 1864–65; Martha Fletcher, Journal, 1863–65; Miss J. E. Markley, Memorandum Book, 1850–52; Lucinda Foote, "A Common Place Book Containing Variety: Written in Haste without Premeditation, 1832–35, 1846, 1876"; George Jaques, Diary and Memoranda, 1840–46, 1852–56; Journal of Josephine Clara Lakin, written while attending State Normal School, 1860–62; Hannah Rogers [Mason], "Diary; or, An Account of the Events of Everyday, 1825–36"; Mary Elizabeth Steen, Diary, 1847–61; James Edward Wright, Diaries, 1851–66. In addition, see *A Treasury of Needlework Projects from Godey's Lady's Book*, comp. Arlene Zeger Wiczyk (New York: Arco, 1972), 90.

73. Evelyn D. Ward, *The Children of Bladensfield during the Civil War* (New York: Viking, 1978), 95.

74. Sophie du Pont, "Our Parlour," 1837, ms., Sophie du Pont Papers, HML; Sophie du Pont to Henry du Pont, 9 March 1830, HML.

75. Lillard, "Literate Woman in the Mines," 91, 93, 95. For the game *Authors* and other

card games, see advertisements in trade catalogs; for example, Moss & Co., in *Toy Books, Games, &c.* (New York: McLoughlin Bros., 1872).

76. Dianne Ashton, *Rebecca Gratz: Women and Judaism in Antebellum America* (Detroit: Wayne State University Press, 1997), 109.

77. James C. Mohr, ed., *The Cormany Diaries: A Northern Family in the Civil War* (Pittsburgh: University of Pittsburgh Press, 1982), 73.

78. For advice books, see, for instance, Julia McNair Wright, *The Complete Home: An Encyclopedia of Domestic Life and Affairs* (Philadelphia: J. C. McCurdy & Co., 1879), 197-98; and Colleen McDannell, *The Christian Home in Victorian America, 1840–1900* (Bloomington: Indiana University Press, 1986), 77-85.

79. Colleen McDannell, *Material Christianity: Religion and Popular Culture in America* (New Haven: Yale University Press, 1995), 67, 89.

80. Sophie du Pont to Clementina Smith, 27 May 1834, HML.

81. Gabrielle Josephine Shubrick Crofton to Julia Sophie du Pont Shubrick, 26 August 1870, Crofton-Shubrick Letters, HML.

82. Josephine Clara Lakin, Journal, 19 May 1862, WMGL.

83. Daniel Woodall to his sister, 2 April 1862, Daniel Woodall Papers, Historical Society of Delaware, Wilmington.

84. Quoted in Folmar, *"This State of Wonders,"* 68.

85. Sophie du Pont to Henry du Pont, 30 July 1846, HML.

86. Josephine Clara Lakin, Journal, 13 December 1863, WMGL; James Hadley, *Diary (1843–1852) of James Hadley, Tutor and Professor of Greek in Yale College, 1845–1872*, ed. Laura Hadley Moseley (New Haven: Yale University Press, 1951), 100, 140, 200, 236, 238.

87. Lillard, "Literate Woman in the Mines," 98.

88. Sophie du Pont to "My dear friend," 28 March 1865, HML.

89. Hinsley, "Reading Tastes of Educated Women," 49 n. 101.

90. Mary Elizabeth Steen, Diary, 26 August 1853, WMGL.

91. Sophie du Pont to Henry du Pont, 16 October 1831, HML.

92. Hannah Rogers [Mason], Diary, 5 August 1827, WMGL.

93. Josephine Clara Lakin, Journal, 3 December 1862, 18 March 1863, WMGL.

94. Sophie du Pont to Henry du Pont, 25 August 1830, HML.

95. Bushman, *"Good Poor Man's Wife,"* 98-99.

96. Alison M. Scott, "'These Notions I Imbibed from Writers': The Reading Life of Mary Ann Wodrow Archbald, 1762-1841" (Ph.D. diss., Boston University, 1995), 186-92.

97. Ella Rodman Church, *How to Furnish a Home* (New York: D. Appleton & Co., 1881), 7.

98. Henry A. Beers, *Nathaniel Parker Willis* (Boston: Houghton, Mifflin & Co., 1885), 78-79.

99. For discussion of these issues, see Joan D. Hedrick, *Harriet Beecher Stowe: A Life* (New York: Oxford University Press, 1994), chaps. 23-24; and Richard H. Brodhead, *Cultures of Letters: Scenes of Reading and Writing in Nineteenth-Century America* (Chicago: University of Chicago Press, 1993), chaps. 3-4.

100. On the changed character of reading, see Robert S. Lynd and Helen Merrell Lynd, *Middletown: A Study in Modern American Culture* (New York: Harcourt, Brace, 1929), 230-42.

101. Allan Pred, *Urban Growth and City-Systems in the United States, 1840–1860* (Cambridge, Mass.: Harvard University Press, 1980), 222–26.

102. Ibid., 224–25; Caroline Kirkland, *A New Home, Who'll Follow? Or Glimpses of Western Life* (New York: C. S. Francis, 1839; repr., ed. with an intro. by Sandra A. Zagarell, New Brunswick, N.J.: Rutgers University Press, 1990), 177 (page citation is to the reprint edition); Richard R. John, *Spreading the News: The American Postal System from Franklin to Morse* (Cambridge, Mass.: Harvard University Press, 1995), 161–67.

103. Junius Henri Browne, *The Great Metropolis: A Mirror of New York* (Hartford: American Pub. Co., 1869), 423.

104. Michael Schudson, *Discovering the News: A Social History of American Newspapers* (New York: Basic Books, 1978), 12–60. For a more skeptical view of the momentousness of the change, see John C. Nerone, "The Mythology of the Penny Press," *Critical Studies in Mass Communication* 4 (1987): 376–404.

105. Despite countervailing technological and economic impulses toward centralization, the local character of the daily newspaper only intensified during the second half of the century, spreading to smaller cities as well. Thomas C. Leonard, *The Power of the Press: The Birth of American Political Reporting* (New York: Oxford University Press, 1986), 166–67.

106. Andie Tucher, *Froth and Scum: Truth, Beauty, Goodness, and the Ax Murder in America's First Mass Medium* (Chapel Hill: University of North Carolina Press, 1994), 87–89.

107. Walt Whitman quoted in Edward Robb Ellis, *The Epic of New York City* (New York: Coward-McCann, 1966), 262; Herman Melville, *Battle-Pieces and Aspects of the War* (New York: Harper & Brothers, 1866), 33–52; Allan Nevins and Milton Halsey Thomas, eds., *The Diary of George Templeton Strong* (New York: Macmillan, 1952), 3:574 (3 April 1865). For another account of public reading at the newspaper bulletin board, see *New York Herald*, 4 July 1862.

108. *New York Times*, 21 December 1861. For more on this genre of advertising, see David Henkin, *City Reading: Written Words and Public Spaces in Antebellum New York* (New York: Columbia University Press, 1998), 125–26, 176–77.

109. Helen Lefkowitz Horowitz, *Rereading Sex: Battles over Sexual Knowledge and Suppression in Nineteenth-Century America* (New York: Knopf, 2002), 245.

110. Howard P. Chudacoff, *The Age of the Bachelor: Creating an American Subculture* (Princeton, N.J.: Princeton University Press, 1999), 185–216.

111. A. T. Andreas, *History of Chicago from the Earliest Period to the Present Time* (Chicago: A. T. Andreas, 1884–86), 2:83.

112. Benjamin Franklin, *Writings* (New York: Library of America, 1987), 1329–30.

113. Horace Greeley, *Recollections of a Busy Life* (New York: J. B. Ford, 1869), 10.

114. See Peter Hales, *Silver Cities: The Photography of American Urbanization, 1839–1915* (Philadelphia: Temple University Press, 1984), 11–65; and Joseph Armstrong Baird Jr., *California's Pictorial Letter Sheets, 1849–1869* (San Francisco: David Magee, 1967), 18.

115. Robert Jay, *The Trade Card in Nineteenth-Century America* (Columbia: University of Missouri Press, 1987), 20–27; Nicholas B. Wainwright, *Philadelphia in the Romantic Age of Lithography* (Philadelphia: Historical Society of Pennsylvania, 1958), 30–90.

116. Charles Cist, *Cincinnati in 1841: Its Early Annals and Future Prospects* (Cincinnati: Charles Cist, 1841).

117. Andreas, *History of Chicago*, 3:690.

118. *McKenney's Pacific Coast Directory* (San Francisco: L. M. McKenney, 1876–78); Cist, *Cincinnati in 1841*; *Business Directory of the Principal Southern Cities* (New York: Dunkley & Woodman, 1866–67); Andreas, *History of Chicago*, 2:488.

119. *Chicago Directory for 1855* (Chicago: Chicago Printing Co., 1855); *Pacific Coast Business Directory* (San Francisco: Henry G. Langley, 1867); George G. Foster, *New York by Gas-Light and Other Urban Sketches*, ed. Stuart Blumin (Berkeley: University of California Press, 1990), 75.

120. Henkin, *City Reading*, 71.

121. Lucy Isabella Bird, *The Englishwoman in America* (London: J. Murray, 1856; repr., Madison: University of Wisconsin Press, 1966), 386–87; Ernest Duvergier de Hauranne, *A Frenchman in Lincoln's America: Huit Mois en Amerique; Lettres et Notes de Voyage, 1864–1865* (Paris: Lacroix, Verboeckhoven, 1866; repr., ed. and trans. Ralph H. Bowen, Chicago: Lakeside Press, 1974), 1:22 (page citations for Bird and Duvergier are to the reprint editions); Edward Dicey, *Six Months in the Federal States* (London: Macmillan, 1863), 1:12–13. There were, of course, some well-known exceptions to the pattern of English-only signage in nineteenth-century American cities. See, for example, Benjamin Lloyd's sensational chapter on "Sign-board Literature" on the streets of San Francisco's Chinatown, in B. E. Lloyd, *Lights and Shades in San Francisco* (San Francisco: A. L. Bancroft & Co., 1876), 241–43.

122. Abraham Bisno's recollection that he "learned English from signs" is quoted in Michael Denning, *Mechanic Accents: Dime Novels and Working-Class Culture in America* (London: Verso, 1987), 36.

123. Emil Klauprecht, *Cincinnati; or, The Mysteries of the West* (1854–55; repr., trans. Steven Rowan, ed. Don Heinrich Tolzmann, New York: Peter Lang, 1996), 8.

124. Henkin, *City Reading*, 78–79.

125. Ibid., 59.

126. Ibid., 65–67.

127. John Kouwenhoven, *The Columbia Historical Portrait of New York: An Essay in Graphic History* (New York: Harper & Row, 1972), 149; Jay, *Trade Card in Nineteenth-Century America*, 21; George Robinson Fardon, *San Francisco Album: Photographs of the Most Beautiful Views and Public Buildings* (San Francisco: Chronicle Books, 1999), 22–23.

128. On the Parisian antecedents, see Priscilla Parkhurst Ferguson, *Paris as Revolution: Writing the Nineteenth-Century City* (Berkeley: University of California Press, 1994), esp. 47–54.

129. On the links between Stowe's novel and the city-mysteries texts, see Werner Sollors, *Beyond Ethnicity: Consent and Descent in American Culture* (New York: Oxford University Press, 1986), 141–48.

130. David Paul Nord, *Communities of Journalism: A History of American Newspapers and Their Readers* (Urbana: University of Illinois Press, 2001), 126–28; Leonard, *Power of the Press*, 131.

CHAPTER 10

Cultures of Print

1. Jack Morrell and Arnold Thackray, *Gentlemen of Science: Early Years of the British Association for the Advancement of Science* (Oxford: Clarendon Press, 1981), provides a careful account of tensions that reappeared in America.

2. John M. Clarke, *James Hall of Albany, Geologist and Palaeontologist, 1811–1898* (Albany, N.Y., 1923), 48–62, 130–77, 180; Lillian B. Miller et al., *The Lazzaroni: Science and Scientists in Mid-Nineteenth-Century America* (Washington, D.C.: Smithsonian Institution, 1972), 72. For other examples of private funding, see ibid., 53, 205.

3. Leonard G. Wilson, *Lyell in America: Transatlantic Geology, 1841–1853* (Baltimore: Johns Hopkins University Press, 1998), chaps. 1–3, 5; Martin J. S. Rudwick, *The Great Devonian Controversy: The Shaping of Scientific Knowledge among Gentlemanly Specialists* (Chicago: University of Chicago Press, 1985). See ibid., 368, for how one partisan utilized James Hall's work.

4. Quoted in Clarke, *James Hall*, 163–64.

5. Daniel Coit Gilman, *The Life of James Dwight Dana, Scientific Explorer, Mineralogist, Geologist, Zoologist, Professor in Yale University* (New York: Harper & Brothers, 1899).

6. Derek J. De Sola Price, *Little Science, Big Science . . . and Beyond* (New York: Columbia University Press, 1986), chap. 3; Simon Newcomb, "Abstract Science in America, 1765–1876," *North American Review* 122 (January 1876): 110.

7. The uncertainties of national and state support as well as other forms of patronage are described in Robert V. Bruce, *The Launching of Modern American Science, 1846–1876* (New York: Knopf, 1987), chaps. 10, 12, 17.

8. Albert E. Moyer, *Joseph Henry: The Rise of an American Scientist* (Washington, D.C.: Smithsonian Institution, 1997), chap. 6.

9. Phebe Mitchell Kendall, comp., *Maria Mitchell: Life, Letters, and Journals* (Boston: Lee and Shepard, 1896), 23; Sally Gregory Kohlstedt et al., *The Establishment of Science in America: 150 Years of the American Association for the Advancement of Science* (New Brunswick, N.J.: Rutgers University Press, 1999), 17.

10. Clarence King et al., *Report of the Geological Exploration of the Fortieth Parallel*, 7 vols., Professional Papers of the Engineer's Department, U.S. Army, no. 18 (Washington, D.C.: GPO, 1870–80).

11. Thomas R. Trautmann, *Lewis Henry Morgan and the Invention of Kinship* (Berkeley: University of California Press, 1987), chaps. 7, 10; Carl Resek, *Lewis Henry Morgan: American Scholar* (Chicago: University of Chicago Press, 1960), 97–99.

12. Thomas Bender, *New York Intellect: A History of Intellectual Life in New York City from 1750 to the Beginnings of Our Own Time* (New York: Knopf, 1987), 109. Frank Luther Mott, *A History of American Magazines*, vol. 1 (New York: D. Appleton & Co., 1930), 669–71, includes a brief sketch of the magazine Joseph Green Cogswell owned and edited at this time, *New York Review*.

13. This activity of translation may be followed in Bayard Quincy Morgan, *A Critical Bibliography of German Literature in English Translation, 1481–1927*, 2nd ed. (New York: Scarecrow, 1965).

14. Henry A. Pochmann, *German Culture in America: Philosophical and Literary Influences, 1600–1900* (Madison: University of Wisconsin Press, 1957), 257–94; Frank Luther Mott, *A History of American Magazines*, vol. 3 (Cambridge, Mass.: Harvard University Press, 1938), 385–87. A content analysis of the journal is in Pochmann, *German Culture in America*, 278–80.

15. Carl Diehl, *Americans and German Scholarship, 1770–1870* (New Haven: Yale University Press, 1978), 52–61. According to Diehl's careful survey (correcting overestimations of the numbers involved), up to about 1870, Göttingen and Berlin attracted the lion's share of American students, with Heidelberg and Halle among the also-rans. Relatively few went to study the natural sciences; the number who registered in theology, significant at the beginning, fell to less than 10 percent of current students by the 1860s.

16. My account omits learnedness within Catholicism, e.g., the translation of the Latin Vulgate prepared by Patrick Kenrick and the doctorates earned by Americans at seminaries in Rome and France. See Gerald P. Fogarty, *American Catholic Biblical Scholarship: A History from the Early Republic to Vatican II* (San Francisco: Harper & Row, 1989).

17. Of the ninety-three doctoral degrees granted in America between 1861 and 1900, half were in Hebrew studies. Robert A. McCaughey, *International Studies and Academic Enterprise: A Chapter in the Enclosure of American Learning* (New York: Columbia University Press, 1984), 36.

18. Marion Ann Taylor, *The Old Testament in the Old Princeton School (1812–1929)* (San Francisco: Mellen Research University Press, 1992), 51–54, 73.

19. Jerry Wayne Brown, *The Rise of Biblical Criticism in America, 1800–1870: The New England Scholars* (Middletown, Conn.: Wesleyan University Press, 1969), 119.

20. James Hastings Nichols, *Romanticism in American Theology: Nevin and Schaff at Mercersburg* (Chicago: University of Chicago Press, 1961); David W. Lotz, "Philip Schaff and the Idea of Church History," in *A Century of Church History: The Legacy of Philip Schaff*, ed. Henry W. Bowden (Carbondale: Southern Illinois University Press, 1988), 1–35.

21. [Philip Schaff], *Anglo-American Bible Revision: Its Necessity and Purpose* (New York: American Sunday-School Union, 1879).

22. Diehl, *Americans and German Scholarship*, 119; Louise Stevenson, *Scholarly Means to Evangelical Ends: The New Haven Scholars and the Transformation of Higher Learning in America, 1830–1890* (Baltimore: Johns Hopkins University Press, 1986), 24.

23. Diehl, *Americans and German Scholarship*, chap. 6; McCaughey, *International Studies and Academic Enterprise*, 43–44.

24. Their contributions are briefly noted in *The Cambridge History of American Literature*, ed. William P. Trent et al. (New York: Macmillan, 1933), 3:478–80.

25. Ward W. Briggs Jr. and Herbert W. Benario, eds., *Basil Lanneau Gildersleeve: An American Classicist* (Baltimore: Johns Hopkins University Press, 1986), 43. Gildersleeve's experiences in Germany and at Johns Hopkins are chronicled in *The Letters of Basil Lanneau Gildersleeve*, ed. Ward W. Briggs Jr. (Baltimore: Johns Hopkins University Press, 1987).

26. Noah Porter to Charles Merriam, June 1857, quoted in Stevenson, *Scholarly Means to Evangelical Ends*, 25.

27. Diehl, *Americans and German Scholarship*, chap. 2.

28. [Henry Adams], *The Education of Henry Adams: An Autobiography* (Boston: Houghton Mifflin, 1918), 301–3; *The Letters of Henry Adams*, ed. J. C. Levenson et al. (Cambridge, Mass.: Harvard University Press, 1982), 2:270–71; Ernest Samuels, *The Young Henry Adams* (Cambridge, Mass.: Harvard University Press, 1948), 254, 290.

29. G. L. Kittredge, "Francis James Child," preface to *The English and Scottish Popular Ballads*, ed. Francis James Child (Boston, 1882–98), 1:xxii–xxxi. See Jo McMurtry, *English Language, English Literature: The Creation of an Academic Discipline* (Hamden, Conn.: Archon Books, 1985), chap. 3, and esp. 106–7, on the immense scale of his correspondence and the uses he made of the British periodical *Notes and Queries*; Steven Swann Jones, "Francis James Child," in *American Literary Critics and Scholars, 1850–1880*, ed. John W. Rathbun and Monica M. Grecu, vol. 64 of *Dictionary of Literary Biography* (Detroit: Gale, 1988), 23–28.

30. Luther Farnham, *A Glance at Private Libraries* (Boston: Crocker & Brewster, 1855), 1, 2, 31, 35.

31. Laura V. Marti, "Thomas Barton," in *American Book Collectors and Bibliographers: Second Series*, ed. Joseph Rosenblum, vol. 187 of *Dictionary of Literary Biography* (Detroit: Gale, 1997), 9.

32. Wayne Cutler and Michael H. Harris, eds., *Justin Winsor, Scholar-Librarian* (Littleton, Colo.: Libraries Unlimited, 1980), 137.

33. *Annual Report of the Trustees of the Astor Library, for the Year 1853* (Albany, N.Y., 1854), 11–20.

34. Victor Hugh Paltsits, "The Bibliographical Transactions of James Lenox with Bernard Quaritch," *Papers of the Bibliographical Society of America* 40 (1946): 181–204; Wyman W. Parker, *Henry Stevens of Vermont: American Rare Book Dealer in London, 1845–1886* (Amsterdam: N. Israel, 1963), chaps. 3, 6, 11, 17; Harry M. Lydenberg, *History of the New York Public Library* (New York: New York Public Library, 1923), chap. 2.

35. Brinley's career is briefly sketched in Randolph G. Adams, *Three Americanists: Henry Harisse, Bibliographer; George Brinley, Book Collector; Thomas Jefferson, Librarian* (Philadelphia: University of Pennsylvania Press, 1939). See also *Catalogue of the American Library of the Late Mr. George Brinley*, 5 vols. (Hartford, Conn., 1878–93).

36. John Duncan Haskell Jr., "John Russell Bartlett (1805–1886): Bookman" (Ph.D. diss., George Washington University, 1977), is an indispensable source of information. A proper history of the shifting standards for enumerative bibliography would be transatlantic, taking note especially of Anthony Panizzi's efforts with the catalog of the British Museum.

37. Parker, *Henry Stevens*, esp. 177–80; Haskell, "Bartlett," 169–70.

38. Richard Grant White, *Shakespeare's Scholar: Being Historical and Critical Studies of His Text, Characters, and Commentators* (New York: D. Appleton & Co., 1854), xii, xv; Alfred Van Renssalaer Westfall, *American Shakespearean Criticism, 1607–1865* (New York: H. W. Wilson, 1939), 158.

39. James M. Gibson, "Horace Howard Furness: Book Collector and Library Builder," in *Shakespeare Study Today*, ed. Georgianna Ziegler (New York: AMS, 1986), 169–91; Henry L. Savage, "The Shakespeare Society of Philadelphia," *Shakespeare Quarterly* 3

(1952): 341–52; David Laird, "Horace Howard Furness," in Rathbun and Grecu, *American Literary Critics and Scholars*, 66–70.

40. Charles Kendall Adams, *A Manual of Historical Literature, Comprising Brief Descriptions of the Most Important Histories in English, French and German* (1882; rev. ed., New York: Harper & Brothers, 1889), iii–iv.

41. Margaret Rossiter, *Women Scientists in America: Struggles and Strategies to 1940* (Baltimore: Johns Hopkins University Press, 1982), 73–79, 275.

42. These tensions are mapped in Laurence R. Veysey, *The Emergence of the American University* (Chicago: University of Chicago Press, 1965); and Bruce Kuklick, *The Rise of American Philosophy: Cambridge, Massachusetts, 1860–1930* (New Haven: Yale University Press, 1977).

43. Nick Salvatore, *We All Got History: The Memory Books of Amos Webber* (New York: Times–Random House, 1996), 66. Webber refers to the Carthagenian Lodge, founded in 1848, one of Philadelphia's two black orders of Odd Fellows.

44. All information on Amos Webber is drawn from ibid., esp. 11, 41, 66, 238, 276–77. On Anna Murray Douglass's participation in the East Baltimore Mental Improvement Society, see Elizabeth McHenry, *Forgotten Readers: Recovering the Lost History of African American Literary Societies* (Durham, N.C.: Duke University Press, 2002), 13.

45. Joe M. Richardson, *Christian Reconstruction: The American Missionary Association and Southern Blacks, 1861–1890* (Athens: University of Georgia Press, 1986), 33.

46. Salvatore, *We All Got History*, 261, 372 n. 64.

47. McHenry, *Forgotten Readers*, 1–3.

48. David Walker, *Appeal, in Four Articles; Together with a Preamble, to the Coloured Citizens of the World, but in Particular, and Very Expressly to Those of the United States of America* (Boston, 1829).

49. Richard Newman, Patrick Rael, and Phillip Lapsansky, eds., *Pamphlets of Protest: An Anthology of Early African American Protest Literature, 1790–1860* (New York: Routledge, 2001), 3–14; Richard Newman, *The Transformation of American Abolitionism: Fighting Slavery in the Early Republic* (Chapel Hill: University of North Carolina Press, 2002), 86–106; Peter P. Hinks, *To Awaken My Afflicted Brethren: David Walker and the Problem of Antebellum Slave Resistance* (University Park: Pennsylvania State University Press, 2000), 116–72.

50. Free blacks in the United States numbered 386,303 in 1840, 44 percent of them in the North. Twenty years later, free blacks numbered 488,070, 46 percent in the North. Joseph C. G. Kennedy, *Population of the United States in 1860* (Washington, D.C.: GPO, 1864), 598–604.

51. McHenry, *Forgotten Readers*, 50–57. See also Julie Winch, "'You Have Talents — Only Cultivate Them': Philadelphia's Black Female Literary Societies and the Abolitionist Crusade," in *The Abolitionist Sisterhood: Women's Political Culture in Antebellum America*, ed. Jean Fagan Yellin and John C. Van Horne (Ithaca, N.Y.: Cornell University Press, 1994), 101–18.

52. McHenry, *Forgotten Readers*, 56, 63–64, 68–78.

53. Alexander Crummell, "The English Language in Liberia," in Newman et al., *Pamphlets of Protest*, 299.

54. Heather Murray, *Come Bright Improvement! The Literary Societies of Nineteenth-Century Ontario* (Toronto: University of Toronto Press, 2002), 71.

55. *The Journals of Charlotte Forten Grimké*, ed. Brenda Stevenson (New York: Oxford University Press, 1988), 140 (12 September 1856).

56. Ibid., 58 (May 1854).

57. Ibid., 73 (17 June 1856), 236 (6 July 1857).

58. Ibid., 121 (8 January 1855), 204 (21 March 1857), 212 (18 April 1857).

59. Ibid., 258 (27 September 1857).

60. Ibid., 170 (3 December 1856), 187 (31 January 1857), 295 (22 March 1858), 335 (31 August 1858).

61. Ibid., 72 (16 June 1854), 286 (14 February 1858).

62. Ibid., 277 (10 January 1858).

63. Erica R. Armstrong, "A Mental and Moral Feast: Reading, Writing, and Sentimentality in Black Philadelphia," *Journal of Women's History* 16, no. 1 (2004): 78–102.

64. Stevenson, *Journals of Charlotte Forten Grimké*, 316 (15 June 1858).

65. McHenry, *Forgotten Readers*, 105.

66. Brenda Stevenson, introduction, *Journals of Charlotte Forten Grimké*, 23, 36, 48.

67. T. Morris Chester, "Negro Self-Respect and Pride of Race," in Newman et al., *Pamphlets of Protest*, 309.

68. Jane Rhodes, "Race, Money, Politics, and the Antebellum Black Press," *Journalism History* 20, nos. 3–4 (1994): 1–12.

69. The best account of Douglass's editorial experiences remains Benjamin Quarles, *Frederick Douglass* (New York: Da Capo, 1997), 80–98. On the *Provincial Freeman* and its early competitor, *Voice of the Fugitive*, see Jane Rhodes, *Mary Ann Shadd Cary: The Black Press and Protest in the Nineteenth Century* (Bloomington: Indiana University Press, 1998), 51–134.

70. McHenry, *Forgotten Readers*, 137.

71. *Voice of the Fugitive*, 5 November 1851, quoted in Rhodes, *Mary Ann Shadd Cary*, 72.

72. *The Liberator*, 14 May 1831, quoted in Hinks, *To Awaken My Afflicted Brethren*, 154–55.

73. *Boston Daily Evening Transcript*, 28 September 1830, quoted in Hinks, *To Awaken My Afflicted Brethren*, 151.

74. "To Our Patrons," *Freedom's Journal*, 16 March 1827.

75. On the Garrison-Douglass break, see Waldo E. Martin Jr., *The Mind of Frederick Douglass* (Chapel Hill: University of North Carolina Press, 1984), 18–55.

76. For an alternative understanding of the Douglass-Delany collaboration and subsequent split, see Robert S. Levine, *Martin Delany, Frederick Douglass, and the Politics of Representative Identity* (Chapel Hill: University of North Carolina Press, 1997), 18–57.

77. Frankie Hutton, *The Early Black Press in America, 1827–1860* (Westport, Conn.: Greenwood, 1993), 10–15.

78. Rhodes, *Mary Ann Shadd Cary*, 25–99.

79. Roland E. Wolseley, *The Black Press, U.S.A.*, 2nd ed. (Ames: Iowa State University Press, 1990), 37–38.

80. Rhodes, *Mary Ann Shadd Cary*, 202–5. See also Wolseley, *Black Press*, 38–42.

81. Richardson, *Christian Reconstruction*, 27–30.

82. Stevenson, *Journals of Charlotte Forten Grimké*, 394 (5 November 1862).

83. Quoted in Richardson, *Christian Reconstruction*, 25.

84. Ibid., 71–74; Ronald E. Butchart, *Northern Schools, Southern Blacks, and Reconstruction: Freedmen's Education, 1862–1875* (Westport, Conn.: Greenwood, 1980), 77–95.

85. Butchart, *Northern Schools, Southern Blacks*, 174. For a detailed account of African Americans' participation in the AMA, see Clara Merritt DeBoer, *His Truth Is Marching On: African-Americans Who Taught the Freedmen for the American Missionary Association, 1861–1877* (New York: Garland, 1995). Individuals' accounts of teaching in freedpeople's schools include Susie King Taylor, *A Black Woman's Civil War Memoirs: Reminiscences of My Life in Camp with the 33rd U.S. Colored Troops, Late 1st South Carolina Volunteers*, ed. Patricia W. Romero and Willie Lee Rose (New York: Marcus Weiner, 1988); Stevenson, *Journals of Charlotte Forten Grimké*, 374–511; and Harriet A. Jacobs, *Incidents in the Life of a Slave Girl, Written by Herself*, ed. Jean Fagan Yellin (Cambridge, Mass.: Harvard University Press, 2000), 247, 271–73.

86. Eric Foner, *A Short History of Reconstruction* (New York: Harper & Row, 1990), 65. See also Richardson, *Christian Reconstruction*, 75–84.

87. Jacqueline Jones, *Soldiers of Light and Love: Northern Teachers and Georgia Blacks, 1865–1873* (Chapel Hill: University of North Carolina Press, 1980), 26.

88. Butchart, *Northern Schools, Southern Blacks*, 20, 23.

89. Ibid., 136; Robert C. Morris, *Reading, 'Riting, and Reconstruction: The Education of Freedmen in the South, 1861–70* (Chicago: University of Chicago Press, 1981), 174. See also Stevenson, *Journals of Charlotte Forten Grimké*, 391–511.

90. *Chicago Tribune*, quoted in American Tract Society, *Forty-eighth Annual Report* (Boston: American Tract Society, 1862), 35, quoted in Morris, *Reading, 'Riting, and Reconstruction*, 190.

91. L[ydia] Maria Child, *The Freedmen's Book* (Boston: Ticknor and Fields, 1865); Butchart, *Northern Schools, Southern Blacks*, 136–46, 151–55; Morris, *Reading, 'Riting, and Reconstruction*, 207–9 and figs. 6–9. The American Tract Society series also included biographies of these figures. For an instructive comparative analysis of the primers' contrasting portrayals of Toussaint L'Ouverture, see Butchart, *Northern Schools, Southern Blacks*, 137–38, 152–53. For further discussion of *The Freedman's Book*, see Morris, *Reading, 'Riting, and Reconstruction*, 202–7; and Carolyn L. Karcher, *The First Woman in the Republic: A Cultural Bibliography of Lydia Maria Child* (Durham, N.C.: Duke University Press, 1994), 487–504.

92. Quoted in Morris, *Reading, 'Riting, and Reconstruction*, 209.

93. Butchart, *Northern Schools, Southern Blacks*, 171–76.

94. See Richardson, *Christian Reconstruction*, esp. chap. 8.

95. Frederick Douglass, *Narrative of the Life of Frederick Douglass, An American Slave; Written by Himself* (Boston: Anti-Slavery Office, 1845), 33.

96. Michael O'Brien, "Finding the Outfield: Subregionalism and the American South," *Historical Journal* 38 (1995): 1047.

97. Janet Duitsman Cornelius, *"When I Can Read My Title Clear": Literacy, Slavery, and Religion in the Antebellum South* (Columbia: University of South Carolina Press, 1991), 3, 61, 73.

98. E. Jennifer Monaghan, "Reading for the Enslaved, Writing for the Free: Reflections on Liberty and Literacy," *Procs. AAS* 108 (1998): 316-18, 331-38.

99. Cornelius, *"When I Can Read My Title Clear,"* 37-58.

100. Ibid., 78-80; John Hope Franklin, *The Free Negro in North Carolina* (Chapel Hill: University of North Carolina Press, 1943), 129-30.

101. Carl F. Kaestle, *Pillars of the Republic: Common Schools and American Society, 1780-1860* (New York: Hill & Wang, 1983), 203-9; Jane Dailey, *Before Jim Crow: The Politics of Race in Postemancipation Virginia* (Chapel Hill: University of North Carolina Press, 2000), 15.

102. Orville Vernon Burton, *In My Father's House Are Many Mansions: Family and Community in Edgefield, South Carolina* (Chapel Hill: University of North Carolina Press, 1985), 80-90.

103. Christie Anne Farnham, *The Education of the Southern Belle: Higher Education and Student Socialization in the Antebellum South* (New York: New York University Press, 1994), 11, 24-28.

104. Elizabeth Fox-Genovese, *Within the Plantation Household: Black and White Women of the Old South* (Chapel Hill: University of North Carolina Press, 1988), 259-63, 268.

105. Barbara Sicherman, "Sense and Sensibility: A Case Study of Women's Reading in Late-Victorian America," in *Reading in America: Literature and Social History*, ed. Cathy N. Davidson (Baltimore: Johns Hopkins University Press, 1989), 201-25, and "Reading and Ambition: M. Carey Thomas and Female Heroism," *American Quarterly* 45 (1993): 73-103.

106. Ann Hardeman, Journal, 9 May 1851, in *An Evening When Alone: Four Journals of Single Women in the South, 1827-67*, ed. Michael O'Brien (Charlottesville: University Press of Virginia, 1993), 232.

107. Ibid., 243-244 (15 August 1852), 372 (21 September 1861).

108. Ibid., 294 (13 February 1860).

109. *Piedmont Farmer: The Journals of David Golightly Harris, 1855-1870*, ed. Philip N. Racine (Knoxville: University of Tennessee Press, 1990), 41, 94-96 (entries for 11 January 1859, 28 December 1858, 14 January 1857); Racine, introduction, in ibid., 1-2.

110. *Queen of the South—New Orleans, 1853-1862: The Journal of Thomas K. Wharton*, ed. Samuel Wilson Jr., Patricia Brady, and Lynn D. Adams (New Orleans: Historic New Orleans Collection; New York: New York Public Library, 1999), 137, 178, 187-90, 218 (entries for 9 September, 10 December 1858, 12 January 1859, 31 December 1858, 31 March 1857, 3 February 1860).

111. Ibid., 261 (20 November 1861).

112. Michael O'Brien, "On Observing the Quicksand," *American Historical Review* 104 (1999): 1204.

113. Wilson et al., *Queen of the South*, 160 (8 May 1858).

114. Elizabeth Moss, *Domestic Novelists in the Old South: Defenders of Southern Culture* (Baton Rouge: Louisiana State University Press, 1992), 2, 7, 18.

115. Michael O'Brien, "On the Mind of the Old South and Its Accessibility," in *Rethinking the South: Essays in Intellectual History* (Baltimore: Johns Hopkins University Press, 1988), 21-22, 34.

116. J. W. Randolph, *Catalogue of Books, Stationery, Music and Musical Instruments, and Fancy Goods* (Richmond, Va.: J. W. Randolph, 1850).

117. Robert Bell, "S. H. Goetzel, Publisher; Mobile, Alabama, 1857–1865," *Book Club of California Quarterly Newsletter 34* (Spring 1969): 29.

118. O'Brien, "On the Mind of the Old South," 33–35.

119. James Penn Pilkington, *The Methodist Publishing House: A History*, vol. 1, *Beginnings to 1870* (Nashville: Abingdon, 1968), 294–314; John W. Kuykendall, *Southern Enterprize: The Work of the National Evangelical Societies in the Antebellum South* (Westport, Conn.: Greenwood, 1982), 122–58.

120. T. Michael Parrish and Robert M. Willingham Jr., *Confederate Imprints: A Bibliography of Southern Publications from Secession to Surrender: Expanding and Revising the Earlier Works of Marjorie Crandall and Richard Harwell* (Austin, Tex.: Jenkins, 1984), 9, 12.

121. Drew Gilpin Faust, *Mothers of Invention: Women of the Slaveholding South in the American Civil War* (Chapel Hill: University of North Carolina Press, 1996), 153–75.

122. Quoted in ibid., 167.

123. Karen C. Carroll, "Sterling, Campbell, and Albright: Textbook Publishers, 1861–1865," *North Carolina Historical Review* 63 (1986): 170–93.

124. E. Merton Coulter, *The Confederate States of America, 1861–1865*, vol. 7 of *A History of the South* (Baton Rouge: Louisiana State University Press, 1950), 499–503.

125. Coulter, *Confederate States of America*, 508; Bell, "S. H. Goetzel, Publisher," 30–31. For the text of the copyright provisions, see Resolution 15, 7 March 1861, and Chapter 65, 21 May 1861, in *The Statutes at Large of the Provisional Government of the Confederate States of America*, ed. James M. Matthews (Richmond: R. M. Smith, 1864), 93, 157–61.

126. James D. Anderson, *The Education of Blacks in the South, 1860–1935* (Chapel Hill: University of North Carolina Press, 1988), 6–7, 12–13. Anderson's reference is to John W. Alvord, *Inspector's Report of Schools and Finance*, U.S. Bureau of Refugees, Freedmen, and Abandoned Lands (Washington, D.C.: GPO, 1866), 9–10.

127. Renee F. Cooper, "Reconstruction and Education: Voice from the South, 1865–1871," *Prologue: The Journal of the National Archives* 27 (1995): 127–28; Eric Foner, *Reconstruction: America's Unfinished Revolution, 1863–1877* (New York: Harper & Row, 1988), 97, 144, 366; Peter Kolchin, *First Freedom: The Responses of Alabama's Blacks to Emancipation and Reconstruction* (Westport, Conn.: Greenwood, 1972), 80–82.

128. David Tyack and Robert Lowe, "The Constitutional Moment: Reconstruction and Black Education in the South," *American Journal of Education* 94 (1986): 243–46.

129. Dailey, *Before Jim Crow*, 15, 24–25, 70.

130. Foner, *Reconstruction*, 366–68.

131. E. Merton Coulter, *The South during Reconstruction, 1865–1877*, vol. 8 of *A History of the South* (Baton Rouge: Louisiana State University Press, 1947), 285; William C. Harris, *Day of the Carpetbagger: Republican Reconstruction in Mississippi* (Baton Rouge: Louisiana State University Press, 1979), 596.

132. O'Brien, *Evening When Alone*, 379 (3 June 1866).

133. Racine, *Piedmont Farmer*, 458–59 (23 February 1868).

134. John Hammond Moore, *South Carolina Newspapers* (Columbia: University of South Carolina Press, 1988), 224–29.

135. "Agents Wanted for the Most Popular and Best Selling Subscription Books Published . . . : National Publishing Company . . . : 'Life and Campaigns of Genr'l. R. E. Lee' " (Georgia[?], 1866), broadside, Special Collections, Perkins Library, Duke University.

136. Thomas Nelson Page, "Marse Chan," *Century* 27 (April 1884): 935. A serial installment of Cable's novel *Dr. Sevier* appeared in the same issue.

137. George W. Cable, "Madame Delphine," *Scribner's Monthly* 22 (July 1881): 436; ibid., (May 1881): 28.

CHAPTER 11
Alternative Communication Practices and the Industrial Book

1. Robert B. Stepto, *From behind the Veil: A Study of Afro-American Narrative* (Urbana: University of Illinois Press, 1979), 3–31.

2. For the institutional history of Nantucket's Atheneum, see Susan Beegel, "The Nantucket Atheneum Spreads Its Wings Again," in *The Nantucket Atheneum: A Commemorative Review*, ed. Hobson Woodward (Nantucket, Mass.: Nantucket Journal, 1996), 10–17. Information on the history of Nantucket is drawn from Lisa Norling, *Captain Ahab Had a Wife: New England Women and the Whalefishery, 1720–1870* (Chapel Hill: University of North Carolina Press, 2000); and Nathaniel Philbrick, *Away off Shore: Nantucket Island and Its People, 1602–1890* (Nantucket, Mass.: Mill Hill, 1994).

3. J. Hector St. John de Crèvecœur, *Letters from an American Farmer* (1782; repr., ed. Susan Manning, Oxford: Oxford University Press, 1997), 83–150.

4. Obed Macy Journal, 16 February 1815, 31 January 1817, Macy Family Papers (1729–1959), Nantucket Historical Association, Nantucket, Mass.

5. Ibid., 3 February 1844.

6. "Atheneum Lectures," *Nantucket Inquirer*, 5 December 1853.

7. "The Weather and the Mails," *Nantucket Inquirer and Mirror*, 6 February 1875.

8. Information in this paragraph is drawn from the following articles in the *Nantucket Inquirer*: "New Books," 3 February 1841; "Hunt's Merchants' Magazine and Commercial Review," 7 August 1841; [untitled], 25 December 1841; "New Books," 4 January 1840; "William A. Jenks" and "To Borrowers," 2 April 1840; "Circulating Library," 5 July 1837; "Anti-Slavery," "Commercial News and Whig Reading Room," and "Coffin School Library," 1 January 1840; "Anti-Slavery Fair" and "Whig Reading Room," 23 January 1841; and "Coffin School Library," 18 September 1841.

9. *Catalogue of the Nantucket Atheneum, with the By-Laws of the Institution* (Boston: Freeman and Bolles, 1841).

10. *Colored American*, 15 July 1837, 7 November 1840, 30 January 1841.

11. "From the Liberator. Railroad Corporations," *Colored American*, 1 May 1841.

12. *Nantucket Inquirer*, 23 June 1841.

13. "Light for the People," *Nantucket Inquirer*, 13 January 1841.

14. *Nantucket Inquirer*, 23 January 1841.

15. Ibid., 25 August 1841.

16. Ibid., 13 January, 12 November 1855, 17 November 1856, 17 January, 9 February, 21 March 1857; *Nantucket Weekly Mirror*, 4 April 1857; Hobson Woodward, "The Atheneum Is Pleased to Present . . . ," in Woodward, *Nantucket Atheneum*, 38–46.

17. *Nantucket Weekly Mirror*, 10 February 1855.

18. "Anti-Slavery Standard," *Nantucket Inquirer*, 23 June 1841.

19. *Nantucket Inquirer and Mirror*, 14 August 1875.

20. Ibid., 27 August 1885.

21. *Guide to Williams & Packard's System of Penmanship for Teachers and Adepts* (New York: Slote, Woodman & Co., 1869), 4.

22. N. Hinman, "Then and Now," *Western Penman* 4 (February 1873): 34–35.

23. Examples include Levi Rightmyer, *Rightmyer's American System of Penmanship, in Thirteen Numbers* (New York: Benziger Brothers, 1866); J. W. Payson et al., *Payson, Dunton, & Scribner's National System of Penmanship, in Twelve Numbers* (Boston: Crosby & Ainsworth, 1866); *American Standard System of Penmanship* (New York: Woolworth & Co., 1879); and *Barnes' National System of Penmanship* (New York: A. S. Barnes & Co., 1886).

24. James French, *Gentlemen's Writing Book* (Boston: James French, 1845).

25. On Victorian penmanship pedagogy, see Tamara Plakins Thornton, *Handwriting in America: A Cultural History* (New Haven: Yale University Press, 1996), chap. 2.

26. For a contemporary description, see William A. Alcott, *On Teaching Penmanship* (Boston: Lilly, Wait, Colman, & Holden, 1833).

27. See, for example, the copybooks of Reuben Comins and Lincoln Varney, Penmanship Collection, and Alice Arnold Holmes, "Cyphering Book," Folio vol. "H," Manuscript Department, AAS.

28. For explicit references to these technologies, see S. A. Potter, *Penmanship Explained* (Philadelphia: Cowperthwait & Co., 1868), 12, 114–15; "P., D., & S. Authors," in *Payson, Dunton, & Scribner Manual of Penmanship* (New York and Chicago: Potter, Ainsworth, and Co., 1873), 1, 115; and *Barnes' National System*, back cover.

29. See, for example, "Spencerian Authors," in *Theory of Spencerian Penmanship* (New York: Ivison, Blakeman, Taylor & Co., 1874), 5–13; *Payson, Dunton, & Scribner Manual*, 17–36; and *Guide to Williams & Packard's System*, 1–5.

30. *Twenty-seventh Annual Report of the Board of President and Directors of the St. Louis Public Schools* (St. Louis: Slawson & Co., 1882), 201.

31. For the penmen's perspective on these changes, see Hinman, "Then and Now"; and "The Unparalleled Progress of Writing during the Past Twenty-Five Years," *Penman's Art Journal* 2 (October 1878): 4–5.

32. Thornton, *Handwriting in America*, 47–49. "Copy-slips" were rectangular strips of paper with handwritten or engraved penmanship exemplars to be imitated by the pupil.

33. The links between penmen and the business colleges are especially clear in such journals as the *Penman's Art Journal*.

34. See, for example, P. R. Spencer et al., *Spencerian System of Practical Penmanship, in 12 Numbers*, no. 5 (New York: Ivison, Phinney, Blakeman & Co., 1864).

35. *Guide to Williams & Packard's System*, 4; *Payson, Dunton, & Scribner Manual*, 11, 17–18, 115; Potter, *Penmanship Explained*, 36, 103, 107–8.

36. See "Spencerian Authors"; and "P., D., & S. Authors."

37. H. W. Ellsworth, *Ellsworth's Systematically Arranged Copybooks, Complete in Eight Numbers*, no. 3 (New York: H. W. Ellsworth and D. Appleton & Co., 1861). Among the other publishers listed on the front cover was J. B. Lippincott & Co., Philadelphia.

38. *Payson, Dunton & Scribner's Refutation of the Absurd Claims of the Spencerial System to Originality* (Boston: Payson, Dunton & Scribner, 1869); Robert C. Spencer, *P. R. Spencer Defended by His Sons: Spencerian Penmanship Proven to Be Original with Him* (New York: Ivison, Blakeman, Taylor, & Co., 1870); Potter, *Penmanship Explained*, 109–13.

39. "Spencerian Authors," 18; "P., D., & S. Authors," 45; G. A. Gaskell, *Gaskell's Compendium of Forms, Educational, Legal and Commercial* (Chicago: William M. Farrar, 1882), 72; Potter, *Penmanship Explained*, 61; *A Practical System of Penmanship* (Philadelphia: Porter & Coates, 1884), inside cover.

40. Potter, *Penmanship Explained*, 12.

41. P. R. Spencer et al., *Spencerian System*.

42. *Ellsworth's Systematically Arranged Copybooks*, for example, listed publishers in New York, Boston, Philadelphia, Buffalo, Chicago, Cincinnati, and St. Louis.

43. Richard Sterling, *Sterling's Southern Series of Writing Books* (Macon, Ga.: J. W. Burke & Co., 1867).

44. Gaskell, *Gaskell's Compendium of Forms*, 58.

45. "Autographs," *National Magazine* 7 (October 1855): 358.

46. On handwriting analysis, see Thornton, *Handwriting in America*, 73–86.

47. Edgar Allan Poe, "Autography," *Southern Literary Messenger* 2 (February 1836): 205–12, (August 1836): 601–4. On autograph collecting, see Thornton, *Handwriting in America*, 86–88.

48. "A Chapter on Autographs," *American Antiquarian* 1 (August 1870): 3.

49. On graphology, see Thornton, *Handwriting in America*, 92–105.

50. My discussion is based on an examination of seventy-seven albums in the collections of AAS.

51. Herman Melville, *Moby-Dick; or, The Whale* (New York: Harper & Brothers, 1851), 357–58.

52. William Charvat, *The Profession of Authorship in America, 1800–1870: The Papers of William Charvat*, ed. Matthew J. Bruccoli (Columbus: Ohio State University Press, 1968), [3].

53. William Gilmore Simms, "International Copyright Law," *Southern Literary Messenger* 10 (1844): 13.

54. Mimin, "Amateur Authors and Small Critics," *USMDR* 17 (July–August 1845): 62, 63.

55. *Southern Literary Messenger* 10 (1844): 768.

56. "New York Literary Correspondence," *Ladies' Repository: A Monthly Periodical Devoted to Literature, Arts and Religion* 19 (1859): 634.

57. An American Writer, "A Letter to the Proprietors of Harpers' Magazine," *American Whig Review* 16 (July 1852): 14.

58. Simms, "International Copyright Law," 14.

59. Hannah Crafts, *The Bondwoman's Narrative*, ed. Henry Louis Gates (New York: Warner Books, 2002), [3].

60. Simms, "International Copyright Law," 12.

61. C. Roach, *The Prisoner of War and How Treated* (Indianapolis: Railroad City Pub. House, 1865), 4. On Civil War writing, see Alice Fahs, *The Imagined Civil War: Popular Literature of the North and South, 1861–1865* (Chapel Hill: University of North Carolina Press, 2001).

62. Willard W. Glazier, *The Capture, the Prison Pen, and the Escape: Giving a Complete History of Prison Life in the South* (New York: United States Pub. Co., 1868), vii.

63. Ibid., vii–viii, 251.

64. See, for example, A. O. Abbott, *Prison Life in the South: At Richmond, Macon, Savannah, Charleston, Columbia, Charlotte, Raleigh, Goldsborough, and Andersonville, during the Years 1864 and 1865* (New York: Harper & Brothers, 1865); B. F. Booth, *Dark Days of the Rebellion; or, Life in Southern Military Prisons* (Indianola, Iowa: Booth Pub. Co., 1897); Henry M. Davidson, *Fourteen Months in Southern Prisons* (Milwaukee: Daily Wisconsin Printing House, 1865); J. Madison Drake, *Fast and Loose in Dixie: An Unprejudiced Narrative of Personal Experience as a Prisoner of War at Libby, Macon, Savannah, and Charleston* (New York: Authors' Pub. Co., 1880); T. H. Mann, "A Yankee in Andersonville," *Century* 40 (July 1890): 447–61; and Chas. L. Cummings, *The Great War Relic* (Harrisburg, Pa.: George E. Reed, 1887).

65. *The Amateurs' Guide for 1872: A Complete Book of Reference, Relative to the Amateur Editors, Authors, Printers and Publishers of America* (Chicago: Amateur Pub. Co., 1871), 7; Truman J. Spencer, *The History of Amateur Journalism* (New York: Fossils, 1957).

66. *Amateurs' Guide for 1872*, 16.

67. John T. Nixon, *History of the National Amateur Press Association* (Crowley, La.: John T. Nixon, 1900), 55.

68. William Dean Howells, "The Man of Letters as a Man of Business," *Scribner's Magazine* 14 (October 1893): 429.

Coda

1. "The Close of the Exhibition," *PW* 10 (11 November 1876): 774; "The Permanent National Exhibition," *PW* 10 (11 November 1876): 775–76.

2. "The Permanent Exhibition," *PW* 11 (12 May 1877): 523–24.

3. Arthur Gilman, "Atlantic Dinners and Diners," *AM* 100 (November 1907): 652; Gilman's description of the Whittier birthday dinner is at 651–53. Other descriptions of the event, notably Mark Twain's speech, include Albert Bigelow Paine, *Mark Twain: A Biography* (New York: Harper & Brothers, 1912), 2:603–10; William Dean Howells, *My Mark Twain: Reminiscences and Criticisms*, ed. Marilyn Austin Baldwin (1910; repr., Baton Rouge: Louisiana State University Press, 1967), 50–54; Henry Nash Smith, "'That Hideous Mistake of Poor Clemens's,'" *Harvard Library Bulletin* 9 (Spring 1955): 145–80; and Richard S. Lowry, *"Littery Man": Mark Twain and Modern Authorship* (New York: Oxford University Press, 1996), 24–43.

4. Mark Twain, "Whittier's Birthday," in *Plymouth Rock and the Pilgrims and Other Salutary Platform Opinions*, ed. Charles Neider (New York: Harper & Row, 1984), 50–54.

5. Henry George Jr., *The Life of Henry George: First and Second Periods* (1900), vol. 9 of *Complete Works of Henry George* (Garden City, N.Y.: Doubleday, Page & Co., 1911), 5.

The discussion of George's early life in this paragraph is derived from ibid., 8–11, 42–46, 95, 99–120, 144–53, 160–62. See also Charles Albro Barker, *Henry George* (New York: Oxford University Press, 1955).

6. George, *Life of Henry George*, 159.

7. Ibid., 109, 120.

8. Ibid., 180–86, 227, 236–49.

9. Henry George Jr., *The Life of Henry George: Third Period* (1900), vol. 10 of *Complete Works of Henry George* (Garden City, N.Y.: Doubleday, Page & Co., 1911), 315–16. The initial printing, publishing, and reception of *Progress and Poverty* is described in ibid., 315–34.

10. Ibid., 321.

11. Ibid., 355–56, 397, 404–5.

12. Hamlin Garland, *A Son of the Middle Border* (New York: Macmillan, 1917), 313.

13. Ibid., 68, 89.

14. Ibid., 112–14.

15. The description of Osage is derived from Christine Pawley, *Reading on the Middle Border: The Culture of Print in Late-Nineteenth-Century Osage, Iowa* (Amherst: University of Massachusetts Press, 2001), 9–56.

16. *Osage (Iowa) News*, 26 June 1884, quoted in ibid., 37.

17. Garland, *Son of the Middle Border*, 197–201.

18. Ibid., 219.

19. Ibid., 223. Garland's reading of Ingersoll is in ibid., 192.

20. Ibid., 312.

21. Ibid., 355, 366.

22. Ibid., 410–12.

General Works

The best earlier general histories of the American book and of American publishing are Hellmut Lehmann-Haupt et al., *The Book in America: A History of the Making and Selling of Books in the United States*, 2nd ed. (New York: R. R. Bowker, 1951); and John Tebbel, *A History of Book Publishing in the United States*, 4 vols. (New York: R. R. Bowker, 1971–81). Both contain a useful overview of the period from 1840 to 1880, but for the postbellum period Donald Sheehan, *This Was Publishing: A Chronicle of the Book Trade in the Gilded Age* (Bloomington: Indiana University Press, 1952), is indispensable. Histories and biographies of the major publishing firms and publishers, while more focused, are also rich sources of information. Chief among these are Eugene Exman's two studies, *The Brothers Harper: A Unique Publishing Partnership and Its Impact upon the Cultural Life of America from 1817 to 1853* (New York: Harper & Row, 1965), and *The House of Harper: One Hundred and Fifty Years of Publishing* (New York: Harper & Row, 1967); Warren S. Tryon, *Parnassus Corner: The Life of James T. Fields, Publisher to the Victorians* (Boston: Houghton Mifflin, 1963), and Michael Winship, *American Literary Publishing in the Mid-Nineteenth Century: The Business of Ticknor and Fields* (Cambridge: Cambridge University Press, 1995), which describe the preeminent literary publishing firm of the period; Ellen B. Ballou, *The Building of the House: Houghton Mifflin's Formative Years* (Boston: Houghton Mifflin, 1970), which chronicles the successor firm to Ticknor and Fields; and Ezra Greenspan, *George Palmer Putnam: Representative American Publisher* (University Park: Pennsylvania State University Press, 2000). Nineteenth- and early twentieth-century house histories and memoirs are also valuable, especially Samuel G. Goodrich, *Recollections of a Lifetime; or Men and Things I Have Seen*, 2 vols. (New York and Auburn, N.Y.: Miller, Orton & Mulligan, 1856); James C. Derby, *Fifty Years among Authors, Books and Publishers* (New York: G. W. Carleton & Co., 1884); George Haven Putnam, *Memoir of George Palmer Putnam, Together with a Record of the Publishing House Founded by Him*, 2 vols. (New York: G. P. Putnam's Sons, 1903; repr., 1 vol., 1912); and J. Henry Harper, *The House of Harper: A Century of Publishing in Franklin Square* (New York: Harper & Brothers, 1912). Though now several decades old, G. Thomas Tanselle, *Guide to the Study of United States Imprints*, 2 vols. (Cambridge, Mass.: Harvard University Press, 1971), indexes the books and articles that document the American book trade. A few volumes in the *Dictionary of Literary Biography* (*DLB*) series contain useful information about American publishers; see especially *American Literary Publishing Houses, 1638–1899*, ed. Peter Dzwonkoski, vol. 49 of *DLB* (Detroit: Gale, 1986); *The House of Scribner, 1846–1904*, ed. John Delaney, vol. 13 of *DLB Documentary Series* (Detroit: Gale, 1995); and *The House of Putnam, 1837–1872: A Documentary Volume*, ed. Ezra Greenspan, vol. 254 of *DLB* (Detroit: Gale, 2002).

The record of American publication can be found in the serial lists of new publications regularly published in trade periodicals from the period, recorded in Adolf Growoll, *Book-Trade Bibliography in the United States in the XIXth Century* (New York: Dibdin Club, 1898; repr., New York: Brick Row Book Shop, 1939), and discussed more fully below in the bibliographical notes for Chapter 4. The most important of these trade periodicals were *Publishers' Weekly* and its predecessors, including *Norton's Literary Gazette*, the *American Publishers' Circular and Literary Gazette*, and the *American Literary Gazette and Publishers' Circular*. Also indispensable are the series of compilations of American books in print, inaugurated in 1849 by Orville A. Roorbach and listed in both Growoll and Tanselle: *Bibliotheca Americana: Catalogue of American Publications . . . 1820–1848* (New York: O. A. Roorbach, 1849; repr. with supplement, New York: G. P. Putnam, 1850), updated in 1852 in a new edition that was supplemented by separate volumes published in 1855, 1858, and 1861. Roorbach's catalog was continued by James Kelly, *The American Catalogue of Books . . . Jan., 1861, to Jan. [1871]*, 2 vols. (New York: J. Wiley & Son, 1866, 1871), which in turn was superseded by the series of volumes titled *The American Catalogue of Books* that were published from 1870 to 1872 in New York by the *Trade Circular and Literary Bulletin* (later the *Publishers' and Stationers' Weekly Trade Circular*) and from 1880 until 1910 by *Publishers' Weekly*.

A number of important archival and manuscript collections document the book trade between 1840 and 1880. The richest of these is undoubtedly the Ticknor and Fields business records and correspondence, which are part of the Houghton Mifflin archives in the Houghton Library at Harvard University; a small but important portion of that archive was published as Warren S. Tryon and William Charvat, eds., *The Cost Books of Ticknor and Fields and Their Predecessors, 1832–1858* (New York: Bibliographical Society of America, 1949). Other important survivals include the major portion of the archives of Harper & Brothers held by the Columbia University Library (available on microfilm as the *Archives of Harper & Brothers, 1817–1914* [Cambridge: Chadwyck-Healey, 1980], but see the review of the microfilm by Michael Winship in *Papers of the Bibliographical Society of America* 79 [1985]: 462–68); the archives of Little, Brown & Co., which are also held by the Houghton Library and include the business records of Roberts Brothers; and the archives of Charles Scribner & Co. in the collections of the Princeton University Library. American copyright records, also valuable, are largely held at the Library of Congress and fully described in G. Thomas Tanselle, "Copyright Records and the Bibliographer," *Studies in Bibliography* 22 (1969): 77–124. Further information about the book trades is contained in the United States decennial census records of manufacturing: *Abstract of the Statistics of Manufactures, according to the Returns of the Seventh Census* (Washington, D.C.: Bureau of the Census, 1858); *Manufactures of the United States in 1860; Compiled from the Original Returns of the Eighth Census* (Washington, D.C.: GPO, 1865); *Ninth Census, Volume III: The Statistics of the Wealth and Industry of the United States* (Washington, D.C.: GPO, 1872); and *Report on the Manufactures of the United States at the Tenth Census (June 1, 1880)* (Washington, D.C.: GPO, 1883).

A wide variety of sources documents the activities of nineteenth-century authors and readers. George Haven Putnam, *Authors and Publishers: A Manual of Suggestions for Beginners in Literature* (New York: G. P. Putnam's Sons, 1883), is an early authors' manual that includes "a description of publishing methods and arrangements, directions for the preparation of mss. for the press, explanations of the details of book-manufacturing . . . with general hints for authors." The editorial material in the many critical editions of American authors that have been published under the auspices of the Modern Language Association's Center for the Editions of American Authors (later the Center for Scholarly Editions) contains much information about the process of seeing a manuscript through the press, and modern editions of the collected letters of American authors are also a valuable resource. Also of use is the information included in relevant author bibliographies, especially those in *Bibliography of American Literature*, comp. Jacob Blanck et al., 9 vols. (New Haven: Yale University Press, 1955–91), and published as part of the Pittsburgh Series in Bibliography. Noah Porter, *Books and Reading; or, What Books Shall I Read and How Shall I Read Them?* (New York: C. Scribner & Co., 1871; and many later editions), is likely only the best known of many nineteenth-century readers' guides. The work of William Charvat, especially *Literary Publishing in America* (Philadelphia: University of Pennsylvania Press, 1959), has been fundamental for much recent work in the history of American authorship and reading. Cathy N. Davidson, ed., *Reading in America: Literature and Social History* (Baltimore: Johns Hopkins University Press, 1989), is an influential collection of scholarly work on American reading practices, while the essays in James L. Machor, ed., *Readers in History: Nineteenth-Century American Literature and the Contexts of Response* (Baltimore: Johns Hopkins University Press, 1993), deploy a variety of literary-critical approaches to considering reader response. The articles in Michele Moylan and Lane Stiles, eds., *Reading Books: Essays on the Material Text and Literature in America* (Amherst: University of Massachusetts Press, 1996), explore how the material text is connected to issues of authorship, publishing, and reader response.

Since the mid-1990s, an increasing number of useful resources have appeared in electronic form, and many are now available over the Internet. With a very few exceptions, these are not cited here due to the historical instability of URLs, the restricted access to some resources that are available only by license through controlled portals, and the uncertain authority of others. While any future history of the book in America will undoubtedly depend on such resources, they have not yet achieved the stability of the printed resources that are noted here.

CHAPTER 1

Manufacturing and Book Production

The best general discussion of book manufacturing and production during the industrial era is Philip Gaskell, "Book Production: The Machine-Press Period, 1800–1950," in *A New Introduction to Bibliography* (Oxford: Oxford University Press, 1972), [189]–310, although this overview does not focus specifically on the United States. Nineteenth-century sources that document American practice are J. Luther Ringwalt, *American Encyclopædia of Printing* (Philadelphia: Menamin & Ringwalt, 1871); and W. W. Pasko, ed., *American Dictionary of Printing and Bookmaking* (New York: H. Lockwood & Co., 1894). Theodore Low De Vinne, *The Printers' Price List: A Manual* (New York: Francis Hart & Co., 1871), provides a record of manufacturing costs. Richard-Gabriel Rummonds, *Nineteenth-Century Printing Practices and the Iron Handpress*, 2 vols. (New Castle, Del.: Oak Knoll, 2004), reprints extracts from the many printers' manuals that describe the working of the nineteenth-century printing office. Book production in one of the most up-to-date plants of the antebellum period is described in Jacob Abbott, *The Harper Establishment; or, How the Story Books Are Made* (New York: Harper & Brothers, 1855).

Theodore Low De Vinne's four volumes in *The Practice of Typography* series (1900–1904) document nineteenth-century practices of composition and typefounding; of particular value is his *Treatise on . . . Plain Printing Type* (New York: Century Co., 1900). De Vinne's volumes are supplemented by information in Thomas MacKellar, *The American Printer: A Manual of Typography* (Philadelphia: L. Johnson & Co., 1866, and later editions); and Lucien Alphonse Legros and John Cameron Grant, *Typographical Printing Surfaces: The Technology and Mechanism of Their Production* (London: Longmans, Green & Co., 1916). A comprehensive record of American type foundries can be found in Maurice Annenberg, *Type Foundries of America and Their Catalogs*, 2nd ed., with additions by Stephen O. Saxe (New Castle, Del.: Oak Knoll, 1994). A general account of stereotyping and electrotyping is Michael Winship, "Printing from Plates in the Nineteenth Century United States," *Printing History* 5, no. 2 (1983): 15–26, though George A. Kubler's various studies, especially *A New History of Stereotyping* (New York: J. J. Little & Ives, 1941), also provide much information about the history of different processes used for making plates. The development of mechanical typesetting is best documented in Richard E. Huss, *The Development of Printers' Mechanical Typesetting Methods, 1822–1925* (Charlottesville: University Press of Virginia, 1972).

Dard Hunter, *Papermaking: The History and Technique of an Ancient Craft*, 2nd ed. (New York: Knopf, 1947), is the best general account of papermaking and includes a great deal of information relevant to the United States. Chronicles of nineteenth-century American papermaking include Joel Munsell, *A Chronology of Paper and Paper-Making* (Albany: J. Munsell, 1856, and later editions); and Lyman Horace Weeks, *A History of Paper-Manufacturing in the United States, 1690–1916* (New York: Lockwood Trade Journal Co., 1916). W. J. Barrow Research Laboratory, *Strength and Other Characteristics of Book Papers, 1800–1899*, Permanence/Durability of the Book, no. 5 (Richmond, Va.: W. J. Barrow Research Laboratory, 1967), gives the results from scientific tests of the paper used in 500 books printed from 1800 to 1899, over 90 percent of which were published in the United States. Judith A. McGaw, *Most Wonderful Machine: Mechanization and Social Change in Berkshire Paper Making, 1801–1885* (Princeton: Princeton University Press, 1987), is a sophisticated, scholarly examination of both papermaking and industrialization.

The development of power-driven printing machines is described at length in James Moran, *Printing Presses: History and Development from the Fifteenth Century to Modern Times* (Berkeley: University of California Press, 1973). Frank E. Comparato, *Chronicles of Genius and Folly: R. Hoe & Company and the Printing Press as a Service to Democracy* (Culver City, Calif.: Labyrinthos, 1979), gives a fascinating account of the history of the largest American industrial manufacturer of printing presses. Harold E. Sterne, *A Catalogue of Nineteenth Century Printing Presses*, 2nd ed. (New Castle, Del.: Oak Knoll, 2001), reproduces numerous illustrations of presses, both hand- and power-driven, from original trade catalogs, while Stephen O. Saxe, *American Iron Hand Presses* (New Castle, Del.: Oak Knoll, 1992), describes and illustrates the iron hand presses manufactured and used in the United States.

The classic study of nineteenth-century American publishers' bindings is Joseph W.

Rogers, "The Rise of American Edition Binding," in *Bookbinding in America: Three Essays*, ed. Hellmut Lehmann-Haupt (New York: R. R. Bowker, 1941; repr. with additional note, 1967), [135]–185b; but it should be supplemented, especially on design, by Sue Allen, *American Book Covers, 1830–1900* (Washington, D.C.: Library of Congress, 1998) and *Gold on Cloth: American Book Covers, 1830–1910* (New Haven: Endpapers Press, forthcoming). William Tomlinson and Richard Masters, *Bookcloth, 1823–1980* (Stockport, U.K.: Dorothy Tomlinson, 1996), is exhaustive and, though largely based on the records of the English Winterbottom firm, includes information relevant to the United States. Frank E. Comparato, *Books for the Millions: A History of the Men Whose Methods and Machines Packaged the Printed Word* (Harrisburg, Pa.: Stackpole, 1971), explores the development and impact of binding machinery during the industrial era; Harold E. Sterne, *Catalogue of Nineteenth Century Bindery Equipment* (Cincinnati: Ye Olde Printery, 1978), reproduces illustrations of many of the tools and machines that were used in the nineteenth-century American bindery.

An indispensable guide to understanding illustration processes is Bamber Gascoigne, *How to Identify Prints: A Complete Guide to Manual and Mechanical Processes from Woodcut to Ink-Jet* (New York: Thames & Hudson, 1986). Sinclair Hamilton, *Early American Book Illustrators and Wood Engravers, 1670–1870: A Catalogue of a Collection of American Books, Illustrated for the Most Part with Woodcuts and Wood Engravings, in the Princeton Library*, 2 vols. (Princeton: Princeton University Press, 1968), documents what was the most widely used method of book illustration. Donald McNeely Stauffer, *American Engravers upon Copper and Steel*, 2 vols. (New York: Grolier Club, 1907; with supplemental volume by Mantle Fielding [Philadelphia, 1917], and artist's index by Thomas Hovey Gage [Worcester, Mass.: American Antiquarian Society, 1921]), does the same for the intaglio process. A less useful list for color-plate books is Whitman Bennett, *A Practical Guide to American Color Plate Books* (New York: Bennett Book Studios, 1949; repr. with corrections, Ardsley, N.Y.: Haydn Foundation, 1980); and it should be supplemented by an extensively illustrated exhibition catalog of these works: William S. Reese, *Stamped with a National Character: Nineteenth Century American Color Plate Books* (New York: Grolier Club, 1999). An excellent and comprehensive study of chromolithography in the United States is Peter C. Marzio, *The Democratic Art: Pictures for a 19th-Century America* (Boston: Godine, 1979), while Lucien Goldschmidt and Weston J. Naef, *The Truthful Lens: A Survey of the Photographically Illustrated Book, 1844–1914* (New York: Grolier Club, 1980), an important exhibition catalog, explores the use of photography for book illustration.

CHAPTER 2
Labor and Labor Organization

There is no modern, detailed history of printers or their unions in the industrial era from the 1840s into the 1880s. A number of institutional histories written at the turn of the twentieth century, however, can be read with great profit. These include Ethelbert Stewart, *A Documentary History of the Early Organizations of Printers* (Indianapolis: International Typographical Union, 1907); George A. Stevens, *New York Typographical Union No. 6: Study of a Modern Trade Union and Its Predecessors* (Albany: J. B. Lyon, 1913); and George E. Barnett, *The Printers: A Study in American Trade Unionism* (Cambridge,

Mass.: American Economic Association, 1909). Seymour Martin Lipset, Martin A. Trow, and James S. Coleman, *Union Democracy: The Internal Politics of the International Typographical Union* (New York: Doubleday, 1956), carries the story of printer unionism into the modern era, focusing on its two-party political system. Printers and technology are covered most thoroughly in W. J. Rorabaugh, *The Craft Apprentice: From Franklin to the Machine Age in America* (New York: Oxford University Press, 1986), which focuses on the deskilling of the journeyman printer, as do any number of histories of cities in which printers figured prominently, the most heralded being Sean Wilentz, *Chants Democratic: New York City and the Rise of the American Working Class, 1788–1850* (New York: Oxford University Press, 1984). An additional treatment of printers, printing, and technology is Elizabeth Faulkner Baker, *Printers and Technology: A History of the International Printing Pressmen and Assistants' Union* (New York: Columbia University Press, 1957). Fredson Bowers, "Old Wine in New Bottles: Problems of Machine Printing," in *Editing Nineteenth-Century Texts*, ed. John M. Robson (Toronto: University of Toronto Press, 1967), makes a contribution. Though much scholarship stresses the economic side of the story and, within that context, the deskilling of the printer, the model of craft declension for many workers, including journeymen printers, has been overdrawn. For seminal work in this spirit, see Benson Soffer, "A Theory of Trade Union Development: The Role of the 'Autonomous' Workman," *Labor History* 1 (1960): 141–63; and David Montgomery, "Workers' Control of Machine Production in the Nineteenth Century," *Labor History* 17 (1976): 485–509. The "maleness" implied in Montgomery's work is explored more fully in Ava Baron, "An 'Other' Side of Gender Antagonism at Work: Men, Boys, and the Remasculinization of Printers' Work," in *Work Engendered: Toward a New History of American Labor*, ed. Ava Baron (Ithaca, N.Y.: Cornell University Press, 1991), 47–69. The most revealing sources on printers are first-person accounts, of which there are many due to the literacy of printers and their respect for the written word. A good number are listed in Rorabaugh, *Craft Apprentice*; one should also consult government reports for testimony of printers, such as U.S. Senate, Committee on Education and Labor, *Report of the Committee of the Senate upon the Relations between Labor and Capital, and Testimony Taken by the Committee*, 5 vols. (Washington, D.C.: GPO, 1885).

CHAPTER 3
Authors and Literary Authorship

The study of American authorship has over the past fifty years undergone three primary stages: first, a concern with its economic, publishing, and material history; second, a concern with authorship as a mode of (high) cultural subversion that was supported by, but sometimes conflicted with, commercial aspects of the literary marketplace; and third and most recent, a concern with authorship as a facet of larger cultural formations that de-center the notion of originality and literary proprietorship. The classic starting point is William Charvat's essays, collected in *The Profession of Authorship in America, 1800–1870: The Papers of William Charvat*, ed. Matthew J. Bruccoli (Columbus: Ohio State University Press, 1968). Michael Davitt Bell provides an important extension of Charvat's work in "Beginnings of Professionalism," in *The Cambridge History of American Literature*, ed. Sacvan Bercovitch, 8 vols. (Cambridge: Cambridge University Press, 1994–

2005), 2:11–73, reprinted in Bell, *Culture, Genre, and Literary Vocation: Selected Essays on American Literature* (Chicago: University of Chicago Press, 2001), 67–133. Burton Bledstein, *The Culture of Professionalism: The Middle Class and the Development of Higher Education in America* (New York: W. W. Norton, 1976), provides a historical overview of professionalism in general. The particular issues faced by women writers are explored in Mary Kelley, *Private Woman, Public Stage: Literary Domesticity in Nineteenth-Century America* (Oxford: Oxford University Press, 1984); Susan Coultrap-McQuin, *Doing Literary Business: American Women Writers in the Nineteenth Century* (Chapel Hill: University of North Carolina Press, 1990); Frances Smith Foster, *Written by Herself: Literary Production by African American Women, 1746–1892* (Bloomington: Indiana University Press, 1993); Carla L. Peterson, *"Doers of the Word": African-American Women Speakers and Writers in the North (1830–1880)* (New York: Oxford University Press, 1995); and Joyce W. Warren, *Women, Money, and the Law: Nineteenth-Century Fiction, Gender, and the Courts* (Iowa City: University of Iowa Press, 2005).

The second stage, which focuses on market culture from an authorial perspective, particularly on the formation of high, or "classic," American literature and the various ways in which authors resisted, critiqued, or participated in a burgeoning mass market economy, includes Ann Douglas, *The Feminization of American Culture* (New York: Knopf, 1977); Nina Baym, "Melville's Quarrel with Fiction," *PMLA* 94 (1979): 903–23; Michael T. Gilmore, *American Romanticism and the Marketplace* (Chicago: University of Chicago Press, 1985); Jane Tompkins, *Sensational Designs: The Cultural Work of American Fiction, 1790–1860* (Oxford: Oxford University Press, 1985); Richard H. Brodhead, *The School of Hawthorne* (New York: Oxford University Press, 1986); Lawrence Buell, *New England Literary Culture from Revolution through Renaissance* (Cambridge: Cambridge University Press, 1986); R. Jackson Wilson, *Figures of Speech: American Writers and the Literary Marketplace from Benjamin Franklin to Emily Dickinson* (New York: Knopf, 1989); Nicholas K. Bromell, *Literature and Labor in Antebellum America* (Chicago: University of Chicago Press, 1993); Richard F. Teichgraeber, *Sublime Thoughts/Penny Wisdom: Situating Emerson and Thoreau in the American Market* (Baltimore: Johns Hopkins University Press, 1995); Cindy Weinstein, *The Literature of Labor and the Labors of Literature* (New York: Cambridge University Press, 1995); Michael Newbury, *Figuring Authorship in Antebellum America* (Stanford, Calif.: Stanford University Press, 1997); and Terence Whalen, *Edgar Allan Poe and the Masses: The Political Economy of Literature in Antebellum America* (Princeton: Princeton University Press, 1999). Key studies of individual authors that combine a material history with a concern with market issues include Michael Anesko, *Friction with the Market: Henry James and the Profession of Authorship* (New York: Oxford University Press, 1986); and Richard S. Lowry, *"Littery Man": Mark Twain and Modern Authorship* (New York: Oxford University Press, 1996).

The most recent wave of criticism, which reconceives and in some cases decenters authorship by locating it in broader cultural concerns, includes Richard H. Brodhead, *Cultures of Letters: Scenes of Reading and Writing in Nineteenth-Century America* (Chicago: University of Chicago Press, 1993); Nancy Glazener, *Reading for Realism: The History of a U.S. Literary Institution, 1850–1910* (Durham, N.C.: Duke University Press, 1997); Steven Fink and Susan S. Williams, eds., *Reciprocal Influences: Literary Production, Distribution, and Consumption in America* (Columbus: Ohio State University Press, 1999);

John L. Idol Jr. and Melissa Ponder, eds., *Hawthorne and Women: Engendering and Expanding the Hawthorne Tradition* (Amherst: University of Massachusetts Press, 1999); Kirsten Silva Gruesz, *Ambassadors of Culture: The Transamerican Origins of Latino Writing* (Princeton: Princeton University Press, 2002); Jennifer Cognard-Black, *Narrative in the Professional Age: Transatlantic Readings of Harriet Beecher Stowe, George Eliot, and Elizabeth Stuart Phelps* (New York: Routledge, 2004); Anne Boyd, *Writing for Immortality: Women and the Emergence of High Literary Culture in America* (Baltimore: Johns Hopkins University Press, 2004); Sarah Wadsworth, *In the Company of Books: Literature and Its "Classes" in Nineteenth-Century America* (Amherst: University of Massachusetts Press, 2006); and Bruce Michelson, *Printer's Devil: Mark Twain and the American Publishing Revolution* (Berkeley: University of California Press, 2006). In tandem with this work, a number of excellent revisionist biographies have also appeared. Joan D. Hedrick, *Harriet Beecher Stowe: A Life* (New York: Oxford University Press, 1994), and Brenda Wineapple, *Hawthorne: A Life* (New York: Random House, 2003), are particularly concerned with gender issues, while Lawrence Buell, *Emerson* (Cambridge, Mass.: Harvard University Press, 2003), resituates a classic American author in a transatlantic context.

The iconology of authors and its relation to literary celebrity has been an ongoing concern throughout these various stages. Particularly helpful studies of individual authors include Morris Star, "A Checklist of Portraits of Herman Melville," *Bulletin of the New York Library* 71 (1967): 468–73; Rita Gollin, *Portraits of Nathaniel Hawthorne: An Iconography* (DeKalb: Northern Illinois University Press, 1983); Ed Folsom, "'This Heart's Geography Map': The Photographs of Walt Whitman," *Walt Whitman Quarterly Review* 4 (1986–87): 1–72; and Michael J. Deas, *The Portraits and Daguerreotypes of Edgar Allan Poe* (Charlottesville: University Press of Virginia, 1989). Thomas N. Baker explores the history of "sentimental celebrity" in *Sentiment and Celebrity: Nathaniel Parker Willis and the Trials of Literary Fame* (New York: Oxford University Press, 1999), while Barbara Hochman, *Getting at the Author: Reimagining Books and Reading in the Age of American Realism* (Amherst: University of Massachusetts Press, 2001), locates issues of celebrity within broader shifts in the relation between reader and author.

CHAPTER 4

The National Book Trade System

For a general understanding of the economic history of the nineteenth-century United States, George Rogers Taylor, *The Transportation Revolution, 1815–1860* (New York: Holt, Rinehart & Winston, 1951), and Alfred D. Chandler Jr., *The Visible Hand: The Managerial Revolution in American Business* (Cambridge, Mass.: Belknap Press, 1977), are fundamental. Important specific studies of distribution and the book trades can be found in the various essays printed in Michael Hackenberg, ed., *Getting the Books Out: Papers of the Chicago Conference on the Book in 19th-Century America* (Washington, D.C.: Center for the Book, Library of Congress, 1987).

For information on book distribution and trade communication, *Publishers' Weekly*, the *American Bookseller*, and the numerous earlier trade periodicals are indispensable as contemporary sources. Adolf Growoll was also responsible for two further useful works in addition to his *Book-Trade Bibliography* (cited above in General Works), though both were published several decades after 1880: *The Profession of Bookselling: A Handbook of Practical Hints for the Apprentice and the Bookseller*, 3 vols. (New York: Office of the Publishers' Weekly, 1893-1913), and a volume he edited, *The Booksellers' League: A History of Its Formation and Ten Years of Its Work* (New York: Booksellers' League, 1905). Jay W. Beswick, *The Work of Frederick Leypoldt: Bibliographer and Publisher* (New York: R. R. Bowker, 1942), details the evolution of *Publishers' Weekly*.

The courtesy of the trade merits frequent mention in accounts of nineteenth-century American publishing but is treated extensively in few. The best overview is in Sheehan, *This Was Publishing* (cited above in General Works). Three house histories provide examples of courtesy practices and, as a group, trace the development of courtesy through much of the century: David Kaser, *Messrs. Carey & Lea of Philadelphia: A Study in the History of the Booktrade* (Philadelphia: University of Pennsylvania Press, 1957), sets courtesy practices within the American trade in foreign reprints in the 1820s and 1830s; Exman, *The Brothers Harper* (also cited in General Works), recounts the growth of a major publisher that decisively shaped courtesy practices; and Ballou, *The Building of the House* (also cited in General Works), follows the story into the 1860s and 1870s. The annual Commerce and Navigation reports collected statistics on imports and exports of the United States, including the international trade in books, and are printed as part of the U.S. Serial Set.

CHAPTER 5

The Role of Government

No legal history adequately covers mid-nineteenth-century American copyright law, although Benjamin Kaplan, *An Unhurried View of Copyright* (New York: Columbia University Press, 1967), succinctly traces the main lines of American legal thinking from its roots in British copyright law through the mid-twentieth century. The texts of federal copyright decisions can be found in Wilma S. Davis and Mark A. Lillis, comps. and eds., *Decisions of the United States Courts Involving Copyright and Literary Property, 1789-1909, with an Analytical Index*, Copyright Office Bulletin nos. 13-16 (Washington, D.C.: Copyright Office, Library of Congress, 1980). The index includes a subject index, lists of works and artists involved or mentioned in the copyright cases, and a list of congressional acts related to copyright, but not a chronological index to the cases. The legislation can be found in *Copyright Enactments: Laws Passed in the United States since 1783 Relating to Copyright* (Washington, D.C.: Copyright Office, Library of Congress, 1973). Thorvald Solberg, *Copyright in Congress, 1789-1904* (Washington, D.C.: GPO, 1905), includes a chronological record of congressional proceedings relating to copyright. Two nineteenth-century collections of the discussions of issues regarding copyright are R. R. Bowker, *Copyright: Its Law and Its Literature* (New York: Office of Publishers' Weekly, 1886), which includes an extensive "Bibliography of Literary Property" by Thorvald Solberg that lists both books and articles, and George Haven Putnam, comp., *The Question of Copyright* (New York: G. P. Putnam's Sons, 1891). James J. Barnes, *Authors, Publishers and Politicians: The Quest for an Anglo-American Copyright Agreement, 1815-1854* (Columbus: Ohio State University Press, 1974), has the most thorough account of the antebellum struggle for international copyright, while Aubert J. Clark, *The Movement for International Copyright in Nineteenth Century America* (Washington, D.C.: Catholic University of America Press, 1960), provides an overview of the entire century. The British side of the question is described in Simon Nowell-Smith, *International Copyright Law and the Publisher in the Reign of Queen Victoria* (Oxford: Clarendon Press, 1968). Meredith L. McGill, *American Literature and the Culture of Reprinting, 1834–1853* (Philadelphia: University of Pennsylvania Press, 2003), details what was at stake for those who resisted passage of an international copyright law during the antebellum period. Melissa J. Homestead, *American Women Authors and Literary Property, 1822–1869* (Cambridge: Cambridge University Press, 2005), examines copyright in the context of nineteenth-century women's legal status.

A vein of recent scholarship emphasizes the significance of governmental policy and administration, often overlooked by social and cultural historians, in everyday life. For a variety of such work, see Peter B. Evans, Dietrich Rueschemeyer, and Theda Skocpol, eds., *Bringing the State Back In* (Cambridge: Cambridge University Press, 1985). A signal application of this approach is Richard R. John, *Spreading the News: The American Postal System from Franklin to Morse* (Cambridge, Mass.: Harvard University Press, 1995), which with Richard B. Kielbowicz, *News in the Mail: The Press, Post Office, and Public Information, 1700–1860s* (New York: Greenwood, 1989), provides the essential overview of the nineteenth-century postal system. David M. Henkin, *The Postal Age: The Emergence of Mass Communications in Nineteenth-Century America* (Chicago: University of Chicago Press, 2006), places the postal system within a cultural framework. For a broader view that also encompasses copyright, journalism, and communications technologies, see Paul Starr, *The Creation of the Media: Political Origins of Mass Communications* (New York: Basic Books, 2004); Oz Frankel, *States of Inquiry: Social Investigations and Print Culture in Nineteenth-Century Britain and the United States* (Baltimore: Johns Hopkins University Press, 2006), examines how the federal government employed print to study Indian cultures, explore the West, and investigate the post–Civil War South. On the processes and evolution of the census, see Margo J. Anderson, *The American Census: A Social History* (New Haven: Yale University Press, 1988), as well as the decennial reports of the Census Office, notably Francis A. Walker, *The Statistics of the Population of the United States . . . from the Original Returns of the Ninth Census* (Washington, D.C.: GPO, 1872), and *Compendium of the Tenth Census (June 1, 1880)* (Washington, D.C.: GPO, 1883). Governmental printing has received considerable attention. Culver H. Smith, *The Press, Politics, and Patronage: The American Government's Use of Newspapers, 1789–1875* (Athens: University of Georgia Press, 1977), is the most comprehensive treatment of the different systems; also useful are Stephen W. Stathis, "The Evolution of Government Printing and Publishing in America," *Government Publications Review* 7A (1980): 377–90; and Frank Hennessy, "Printing and Pirates: The Genesis of the U.S. Government Printing Office," *Government Publications Review* 14 (1987): 103–11. Important insider histories are R. W. Kerr, *History of the Government Printing Office (at Washington, D.C.); With a Brief Record of the Public Printing for a Century* (Lancaster, Pa.: Inquirer Printing and Publishing Co., 1881; repr., New York: B. Franklin, 1970); and *100 GPO Years, 1861–1961: A History of United States Public Printing* (Washington, D.C.: GPO, 1961). Finally, in 1885 the GPO produced Benjamin Perley Poore, *A Descriptive Catalogue of the Government Publications of the United States, September 5, 1774–March 4, 1881* (Washington, D.C.: GPO, 1885), a won-

BIBLIOGRAPHICAL ESSAY

derful barometer of the increasing volume and variety of federal publications, especially after 1840.

CHAPTER 6
Alternative Publishing Systems

The best overarching treatments of religious publishing in this period include David Paul Nord, *Faith in Reading: Religious Publishing and the Birth of Mass Media in America* (New York: Oxford University Press, 2004); Paul C. Gutjahr, *An American Bible: A History of the Good Book in the United States, 1777–1880* (Stanford, Calif.: Stanford University Press, 1999); John P. Dessauer, Paul D. Doebler, and Hendrik Edelman, *Christian Book Publishing and Distribution in the United States and Canada* (Tempe, Ariz.: Christian Booksellers Association, 1987); and Candy Gunther Brown, *The Word in the World: Evangelical Writing, Publishing, and Reading in America, 1789–1880* (Chapel Hill: University of North Carolina Press, 2004).

More specific treatments of various publishing enterprises are also rewarding. Stephen Elmer Slocum Jr., a former president of the American Tract Society, wrote "The American Tract Society, 1825–1975: An Evangelical Effort to Influence the Religious and Moral Life of the United States" (Ph.D. diss., New York University, 1975). David Morgan, *Protestants and Pictures: Religion, Visual Culture, and the Age of American Mass Production* (New York: Oxford University Press, 1999), has a great deal of useful information on the ATS, as well as illustrations in religious publishing; Peter Wosh, *Spreading the Word: The Bible Business in Nineteenth-Century America* (Ithaca, N.Y.: Cornell University Press, 1994), treats the development of the American Bible Society. Many denominations have chronicled their publishing enterprises; the best of these histories include James Penn Pilkington, *The Methodist Publishing House: A History*, vol. 1, *Beginnings to 1870* (Nashville: Abingdon, 1968); and Lemuel Call Barnes et al., *Pioneers of Light: The First Century of the American Baptist Publication Society, 1824–1924* (Philadelphia: American Baptist Publication Society, 1924).

Virtually every "variation on the trade" invites deeper scholarly attention than it has received. For a useful overview of "Important Special Publishers," see Lehmann-Haupt et al., *The Book in America*, 232–41 (cited above in General Works); Walter Sutton, *The Western Book Trade: Cincinnati as a Nineteenth-Century Publishing and Book-Trade Center* (Columbus: Ohio State University Press for the Ohio Historical Society, 1961), describes how Cincinnati thrived in specific arenas — notably schoolbooks and subscription publishing — long after the city faded as a national publishing hub. Richard W. Clement, *Books on the Frontier* (Washington, D.C.: Library of Congress, 2003), deals with early book trade ventures from Kentucky to California, as well as readers' experiences in the West. On publishing for the major professions, see the reprinted articles in Betty W. Taylor and Robert J. Munro, *American Law Publishing, 1860–1900*, 4 vols. (Dobbs Ferry, N.Y.: Glanville, 1984); Erwin C. Surrency, *A History of American Law Publishing* (New York: Oceana, 1990); and Francesco Cordasco, *Medical Publishing in 19th Century America: Lea of Philadelphia; William Wood & Company of New York City; and F. E. Boericke of Philadelphia* (Fairview, N.J.: Junius Vaughn, 1990).

Dena J. Epstein's introduction to the 1973 reprint of the Board of Music Trade's *Complete Catalogue of Sheet Music and Musical Works, 1870* (New York: Da Capo, 1973) is the invaluable history of the board. Harry Dichter and Elliott Shapiro, *Early American Sheet Music: Its Lure and Its Lore, 1768–1889* (New York: R. R. Bowker, 1941), includes a list of American music publishers, compiled from "advertisements in newspapers, trade journals, city directories, sheet music copies, and collectors' own treasured lists." This list includes several famous musicians and trade firms that may have published only one song, and it undercounts short-lived firms that left few traces in surviving sheet music or city directories. Subsequent studies identify additional firms, particularly away from the Atlantic seaboard; see Ernst C. Krohn, *Music Publishing in the Middle Western States before the Civil War*, Detroit Studies in Music Bibliography, no. 23 (Detroit: Information Coordinators, 1972); and Dena J. Epstein, *Music Publishing in Chicago before 1871: The Firm of Root & Cady, 1858–1871*, Detroit Studies in Music Bibliography, no. 14 (Detroit: Information Coordinators, 1969).

Although William Holmes McGuffey is a fixture in histories of education, schoolbook publishing has received little scholarly attention; the best discussion remains Sheehan's in *This Was Publishing* (cited above in General Works). House histories exist for several firms, such as Ernest Carroll Moore, *Fifty Years of American Education: A Sketch of the Progress of Education in the United States from 1867 to 1917* (Boston: Ginn, 1917). On subscription publishing, Keith Arbour's introduction to *Canvassing Books, Sample Books, and Subscription Publishers' Ephemera, 1833–1951, in the Collection of Michael Zinman* (Ardsley, N.Y.: Haydn Foundation for the Cultural Arts, 1996), places these sales artifacts into the context of the industry. Michael Hackenberg, "The Subscription Publishing Network in Nineteenth-Century America," in *Getting the Books Out* (cited above in the bibliographical notes for Chapter 4), 45–75, offers a superb introduction to the business of subscription publishing in each region of the United States and pays noteworthy attention to the often-neglected period before the Civil War.

CHAPTER 7

Periodicals and Serial Publication

For basic records of newspapers and holdings, researchers can rely on census records, compiled by S. N. D. North in *The History and Present Condition of the Newspaper and Periodical Press of the United States, with a Catalogue of the Publications of the Census Year* (Washington, D.C.: GPO, 1884). By the 1860s advertising agencies had begun to produce directories of newspapers, which included circulation figures, political affiliations, and other descriptive data useful for advertisers. The most useful are the annual directories produced by George P. Rowell & Co.: *Rowell's American Newspaper Directory* (New York: Printers' Ink Publishing Co., 1869–1908). Information from *Rowell's* is compiled in the many useful tables and charts in Alfred McClung Lee, *The Daily Newspaper in America: The Evolution of a Social Instrument* (New York: Macmillan, 1937). Advertising directories tended to neglect publications that were either short-lived or not congenial to advertising for political or other reasons. The United States Newspaper Program's *National Union List* (4th ed., Dublin, Ohio: OCLC, 1993) of newspaper holdings by year of publication, although more complete, has not yet been analyzed to yield a statistical picture that would supersede North's or Lee's.

The relationship between commercialization and the public sphere frames much of the scholarship on newspapers in this period. A previous generation of historians of journalism, notably Edwin Emery and Henry Ladd Smith (*The Press and America* [New York: Prentice-Hall, 1954]) and Frank Luther Mott (*American Journalism: A History of Newspapers in the United States through 250 Years, 1690–1940* [New York: Macmillan, 1941]), argued that the marketplace freed newspapers from captivity to political parties. This position was elaborated and revised by Michael Schudson, *Discovering the News: A Social History of American Newspapers* (New York: Basic Books, 1978), which understood the rise of a "democratic market society" in the mid-nineteenth century as the crucial moment in the construction of a culture of news, as opposed to partisan newspapering. Scholars sympathetic to partisan newspapering have tended to view commercialized newspapers as corroding a popular system of mass politics. Studies of the relationship between political newspapers and the postal service depict an open-ended system that reflected republican values, while studies of early telegraphic news by Daniel Czitrom (*Media and the American Mind: From Morse to McLuhan* [Chapel Hill: University of North Carolina Press, 1982]) and Menahem Blondheim (*News over the Wires: The Telegraph and the Flow of Public Information in America, 1844–1897* [Cambridge, Mass.: Harvard University Press, 1994]) show technological and commercial bottlenecks creating a centralized and hierarchical news system. Gerald Baldasty proposes that this history means that commercialization caused a decline in political culture, in *The Commercialization of News in the Nineteenth Century* (Madison: University of Wisconsin Press, 1992). Subsequent scholarship using the notion of the public sphere questions what seems to be nostalgia for the party period. Michael Schudson, *The Good Citizen: A History of American Civic Life* (Cambridge, Mass.: Harvard University Press, 1999), and Glenn Altschuler and Stuart Blumin, *Rude Republic: Americans and Their Politics in the Nineteenth Century* (Princeton: Princeton University Press, 2000), both move beyond Emery and Mott in recognizing the persistence of partisan journalism but argue that it was neither very popular nor engaging. In *Politics and the American Press: The Rise of Objectivity, 1865–1920* (New York: Cambridge University Press, 2002), Richard Kaplan argues on the basis of Detroit's history that partisan journalism persisted until at least the last decade of the century. The many changes in news forms and technologies in the period are discussed in Kevin G. Barnhurst and John Nerone, *The Form of News: A History* (New York: Guilford, 2001). The rise of illustrated news is best discussed in Joshua Brown, *Beyond the Lines: Pictorial Reporting, Everyday Life, and the Crisis of Gilded Age America* (Berkeley: University of California Press, 2002).

Frank Luther Mott's magisterial *A History of American Magazines*, 5 vols. (vol. 1, New York: D. Appleton & Co., 1930; vols. 2–5, Cambridge, Mass.: Harvard University Press, 1938–68), remains the most comprehensive source for information on American magazines in the nineteenth century. Other notable histories include James Playsted Wood, *Magazines in the United States*, 3rd ed. (New York: Ronald Press, 1971); and John W. Tebbel and Mary Ellen Zuckerman, *The American Magazine, 1741–1990* (New York: Hawthorn Books, 1969). Kenneth M. Price and Susan Belasco Smith, eds., *Periodical Literature in Nineteenth-Century America* (Charlottesville: University Press of Virginia, 1995), includes important essays on a variety of subjects; for a similar collection on precursors to the nineteenth-century magazine, see Sharon Harris and Mark Kamrath, *Periodical Literature in Eighteenth-Century America* (Knoxville: University of Tennessee Press, 2005). Studies focusing on a single nineteenth-century magazine, editor, or publisher offer crucial insight into magazines' business practices and their increasing integration within American print culture. In addition to house histories cited above, see for example Albert Johannsen, *The House of Beadle and Adams and Its Dime and Nickel Novels: The Story of a Vanished Literature* (Norman: University of Oklahoma Press, 1950); Arthur John, *The Best Years of the Century: Richard Watson Gilder, Scribner's Monthly, and the Century Magazine, 1870–1909* (Urbana: University of Illinois Press, 1981); and Ellery Sedgwick, *The Atlantic Monthly, 1857–1909: Yankee Humanism at High Tide and Ebb* (Amherst: University of Massachusetts Press, 1994). Similarly, works that focus on single nineteenth-century authors (such as biographies, autobiographies and memoirs, and critical studies) often show the profound influence that magazines had upon the development of American authorship: notably, William Dean Howells, *Literary Friends and Acquaintance* (New York: Harper & Brothers, 1900). For an overview of the developments in advertising in American periodicals during this period, see James D. Norris, *Advertising and the Transformation of American Society, 1865–1920* (New York: Greenwood, 1990); and James Playsted Wood, *The Story of Advertising* (New York: Ronald Press, 1958). An enlightening study of book publishers' use of magazines for advertising is Susan Geary, "The Domestic Novel as a Commercial Commodity: Making a Best Seller in the 1850s," *Papers of the Bibliographical Society of America* 70 (1976): 365–93.

A number of scholars have developed theories for explaining the relationship between religious print and collective identities. For the ritual uses of communication networks, see James W. Carey, *Communication as Culture: Essays on Media and Society* (London: Allen & Unwin, 1988); and David Paul Nord, *Communities of Journalism: A History of American Newspapers and Their Readers* (Urbana: University of Illinois Press, 2001). For an insightful interpretation of how religion shapes imagined identities, see Paul Ricoeur, *Figuring the Sacred: Religion, Narrative, and Imagination*, trans. David Pellauer and ed. Mark I. Wallace (Minneapolis: Fortress, 1995). On the overwhelming cultural influence of nineteenth-century religious periodicals, see for instance Carol Sue Humphrey, "Religious Newspapers and Antebellum Reform," in *Media and Religion in American History*, ed. William David Sloan (Northport, Ala.: Vision, 2000), 104–18. An extraordinarily useful reference is Gaylord P. Albaugh, *History and Annotated Bibliography of American Religious Periodicals and Newspapers Established from 1740 through 1830* (Worcester, Mass.: American Antiquarian Society, 1994).

CHAPTER 8

Ideologies and Practices of Reading

There are several useful reviews of U.S. scholarship on reading: David D. Hall, "Readers and Reading in America: Historical and Critical Perspectives," *Proceedings of the American Antiquarian Society* 103 (1994): 337–57; Janice Radway, "Beyond Mary Bailey and Old Maid Librarians: Reimagining Readers and Rethinking Reading," *Journal of Education for Library and Information Science* 35 (1994): 1–21; and Carl F. Kaestle, "The History of

Readers," in Carl F. Kaestle et al., eds., *Literacy in the United States: Readers and Reading since 1880* (New Haven: Yale University Press, 1991), 33–72. On the complex subject of literacy, see Lee Soltow and Edward Stevens, *The Rise of Literacy and the Common School in the United States: A Socioeconomic Analysis to 1870* (Chicago: University of Chicago Press, 1981); Carl F. Kaestle, "Studying the History of Literacy," in Kaestle et al., *Literacy in the United States*, 3–32; John K. Folger and Charles B. Nam, *Education of the American Population* (Washington, D.C.: GPO, 1967); and Harvey J. Graff, *The Literacy Myth: Literacy and Social Structure in the Nineteenth-Century City* (New York: Academic Press, 1979).

On models and sites of reading having to do with religion, see Nord, *Faith in Reading*; Brown, *The Word in the World* (cited above in the bibliographical notes for Chapter 6); and Anne M. Boylan, *Sunday School: The Formation of an American Institution, 1790–1880* (New Haven: Yale University Press, 1988), chap. 2. On the civic model, see Carl F. Kaestle, *Pillars of the Republic: Common Schools and American Society, 1780–1860* (New York: Hill & Wang, 1983). On self-improving activities, see Joseph F. Kett, *The Pursuit of Knowledge under Difficulties: From Self-Improvement to Adult Education in America, 1750–1990* (Stanford, Calif.: Stanford University Press, 1994), esp. 38–141; and Richard D. Brown, *Knowledge Is Power: The Diffusion of Information in Early America, 1700–1865* (New York: Oxford University Press, 1989). On culture, see Louise L. Stevenson, *The Victorian Homefront: American Thought and Culture, 1860–1880* (New York: Twayne, 1991); Ronald J. Zboray, *A Fictive People: Antebellum Economic Development and the American Reading Public* (New York: Oxford University Press, 1993); and Joan Shelley Rubin, *The Making of Middlebrow Culture* (Chapel Hill: University of North Carolina Press, 1992), chap. 1. Nina Baym, *Novels, Readers, and Reviewers: Responses to Fiction in Antebellum America* (Ithaca, N.Y.: Cornell University Press, 1984), describes a specific class of readers—book reviewers in periodicals—and their prescriptive role for readers.

Ideologies of African American literacy are analyzed in Dana Nelson Salvino, "The Word in Black and White: Ideologies of Race and Literacy in Antebellum America," in *Reading in America: Literature and Social History*, ed. Cathy N. Davidson (Baltimore: Johns Hopkins University Press, 1989), 140–56; and Viola J. Harris, "African-American Conceptions of Literacy: A Historical Perspective," *Theory into Practice* 31 (1992): 276–86. For analysis of literary societies, see Elizabeth McHenry, *Forgotten Readers: Recovering the Lost History of African American Literary Societies* (Durham, N.C.: Duke University Press, 2002); and Julie Winch, "'You Have Talents—Only Cultivate Them': Philadelphia's Black Female Literary Societies and the Abolitionist Crusade," in *The Abolitionist Sisterhood: Women's Political Culture in Antebellum America*, ed. Jean Fagan Yellin and John C. Van Horne (Ithaca, N.Y.: Cornell University Press, 1994), 101–18. For studies of literacy and education among southern African Americans, enslaved and free, see the bibliographical notes for Chapter 10 below.

On women's reading practices, see Mary Kelley, *Learning to Stand and Speak: Women, Education, and Public Life in America's Republic* (Chapel Hill: University of North Carolina Press, 2006), and "Reading Women/Women Reading: The Making of Learned Women in Antebellum America," *Journal of American History* 83 (1996): 401–24; and Drew Gilpin Faust, *Mothers of Invention: Women of the Slaveholding South in the American Civil War* (Chapel Hill: University of North Carolina Press, 1996), chap. 7; for the postbellum era, Barbara Sicherman, "Sense and Sensibility: A Case Study of Women's Reading in Late-Victorian America," in Davidson, *Reading in America*, 201–25, and "Reading *Little Women*: The Many Lives of a Text," in *U.S. History as Women's History: New Feminist Essays*, ed. Linda K. Kerber et al. (Chapel Hill: University of North Carolina Press, 1995), 245–66, 414–24. On women's study clubs, see Theodora Penny Martin, *The Sound of Our Own Voices: Women's Study Clubs, 1860–1910* (Boston: Beacon, 1987); Anne Ruggles Gere, *Intimate Practices: Literacy and Cultural Work in U.S. Women's Clubs, 1880–1920* (Urbana: University of Illinois Press, 1997); Karen J. Blair, *The Clubwoman as Feminist: True Womanhood Redefined, 1868–1914* (New York: Holmes & Meier, 1980), 57–71; Anne Ruggles Gere and Sarah R. Robbins, "Gendered Literacy in Black and White: Turn-of-the-Century African-American and European-American Club Women's Printed Texts," *Signs* 21 (1996): 643–78; Elizabeth Long, *Book Clubs: Women and the Uses of Reading in Everyday Life* (Chicago: University of Chicago Press, 2003), 31–58; and Anne Firor Scott, "Women and Libraries," *Journal of Library History* 21 (1986): 400–405. Men's reading has been less studied, but see Thomas Augst, *The Clerk's Tale: Young Men and Moral Life in Nineteenth-Century America* (Chicago: University of Chicago Press, 2003); and Michael Denning, *Mechanic Accents: Dime Novels and Working-Class Culture in America* (London: Verso, 1987).

On reading practices in local communities, see William J. Gilmore, *Reading Becomes a Necessity of Life: Material and Cultural Life in Rural New England, 1780–1835* (Knoxville: University of Tennessee Press, 1989); Ronald J. Zboray and Mary Saracino Zboray, *Everyday Ideas: Socioliterary Experience among Antebellum New Englanders* (Knoxville: University of Tennessee Press, 2006), "Reading and Everyday Life in Antebellum Boston: The Diary of Daniel F. and Mary D. Child," *Libraries and Culture* 32 (1997): 285–323, and "'Have You Read. . . ?': Real Readers and Their Responses in Antebellum Boston and Its Region," *Nineteenth-Century Literature* 52 (1997): 139–70; and Christine Pawley, *Reading on the Middle Border: The Culture of Print in Late-Nineteenth-Century Osage, Iowa* (Amherst: University of Massachusetts Press, 2001).

CHAPTER 9
Sites of Reading

The only attempts to survey large pieces of the institutional history of American libraries are now somewhat dated: Jesse Shera, *Foundations of the Public Library: The Origins of the Public Library Movement in New England, 1629–1855* (Chicago: University of Chicago Press, 1949); Sidney Ditzion, *Arsenals of a Democratic Culture: A Social History of the American Public Library Movement in New England and the Middle States from 1850 to 1900* (Chicago: American Library Association, 1947); and Arthur T. Hamlin, *The University Library in the United States: Its Origins and Development* (Philadelphia: University of Pennsylvania Press, 1981). Apart from the Library of Congress and New York Public Library, almost no major histories of libraries have been published, and those that have been are limited in their examination to a single institution. Some excellent book-length work on aspects of American library history during this period has been done, notably Wayne Wiegand, *The Politics of an Emerging Profession: The American Library Association, 1876–1917* (New York: Greenwood, 1986), and *Irrepressible Reformer: A Biography of*

Melvil Dewey (Chicago: American Library Association, 1996). Several essays in Thomas Augst and Wayne A. Wiegand, eds., *Libraries as Agencies of Culture* (Madison: University of Wisconsin Press, 2003), situate nineteenth-century libraries in contexts other than institutional development. The journal *Libraries & Culture*, now *Libraries & the Cultural Record*, has been an important publishing outlet for scholarship on libraries. For a comprehensive guide to the scholarly literature, see Donald G. Davis Jr. and John Mark Tucker, *American Library History* (Santa Barbara, Calif.: ABC-CLIO, 1989). On the primary literature, one can consult *Libraries in American Periodicals before 1876*, comp. Larry J. Barr, Haynes McMullen, and Steven G. Leach, ed. Haynes McMullen (Jefferson, N.C.: McFarland, 1983); and Robert Singerman, *American Library Book Catalogues, 1801–1875: A National Bibliography* (Urbana-Champaign: Graduate School of Library and Information Science, University of Illinois, 1996). Much work remains to be done to make the widely scattered source materials on library history more widely accessible.

Domestic literary culture has two major subtopics: the material culture of books and reading and the technology necessary to reading. Because these subjects are new, most of the relevant secondary work has yet to move beyond description. On the material culture, see Ronald J. Zboray and Mary Saracino Zboray, "Books, Reading and the World of Goods in Antebellum New England," *American Quarterly* 48 (1996): 587–622; Isabelle Lehuu, *Carnival on the Page: Popular Print Media in Antebellum America* (Chapel Hill: University of North Carolina Press, 2000); and Stevenson, *The Victorian Homefront* (cited above in the bibliographical notes for Chapter 8), the first two chapters of which are founded on a comprehensive survey of commercial offerings. Colleen McDannell addresses the more specialized subject of religion and material culture in *Material Christianity: Religion and Popular Culture in America* (New Haven: Yale University Press, 1995). Virtually all the books on readers and domestic reading describe the experiences of Christian, primarily Protestant, readers. For an introduction to the domestic reading of Jews, see Dianne Ashton, *Rebecca Gratz: Women and Judaism in Antebellum America* (Detroit: Wayne State University Press, 1997).

To discover what books readers might have purchased and in what formats manufacturers offered them, nineteenth-century commercial media present research opportunities. Advertisements and publishing news found in publishers' trade journals and manufacturers' trade catalogs—as well as ephemera such as trade cards and contemporary visual images—display how publishers presented books to the public, including their prices, varied formats, and bindings. These sources suggest how publishers perceived their market and what books they estimated might be popular with particular segments of the reading public. The American Antiquarian Society (Worcester, Mass.), the Hagley Museum and Library (Wilmington, Del.), and the Winterthur Museum, Gardens, and Library (Winterthur, Del.) house rich repositories of these sources. Scholars may also discover this world of material culture in numerous specialized books on various decorative arts, including pottery, glass, and metalware, although these works do not display the full range of marketplace choices. The technology of lighting and heat receives attention in Jane C. Nylander, *Our Own Snug Fireside: Images of the New England Home, 1800–1860* (New York: Knopf, 1993); and Jack Larkin, *The Reshaping of Everyday Life* (New York: Harper & Row, 1988).

Cultural histories of the nineteenth-century American city have emphasized two central features of the relationship between reading and urban life. On the role of the metropolitan press in mediating and representing relationships within an unwieldy environment, see Gunther Barth, *City People: The Rise of Modern City Culture in Nineteenth-Century America* (New York: Oxford University Press, 1980); and Andie Tucher, *Froth and Scum: Truth, Beauty, Goodness, and the Ax Murder in America's First Mass Medium* (Chapel Hill: University of North Carolina Press, 1994). On the proliferation of texts purporting to decode the mystery of the city, see Stuart M. Blumin, "George G. Foster and the Emerging Metropolis," introduction to *New York by Gas-Light and Other Urban Sketches*, by George G. Foster (Berkeley: University of California Press, 1990); and John F. Kasson, *Rudeness and Civility: Manners in Nineteenth-Century America* (New York: Hill & Wang, 1990), 70–111. Paul Joseph Erickson, "Welcome to Sodom: The Cultural Work of City-Mysteries Fiction in Antebellum America" (Ph.D. diss., University of Texas at Austin, 2005), offers the most comprehensive research to date into the city-mystery phenomenon.

More commonly, cities have been fruitfully examined as centers of intellectual life, home to various institutions that encouraged new forms of intellectual sociability. Thomas Bender, *New York Intellect: A History of Intellectual Life in New York City, from 1750 to the Beginnings of Our Own Time* (New York: Knopf, 1987) is probably the best-known work in this field. Literary historians have also been interested in the relationship between print culture and urban culture in this period. David S. Reynolds, *Beneath the American Renaissance: The Subversive Imagination in the Age of Emerson and Melville* (Cambridge, Mass.: Harvard University Press, 1988), takes seriously the material connections and thematic continuities between the popular urban publications and the now-canonical literary works of the 1840s and 1850s; while Dana Brand, *The Spectator and the City in Nineteenth-Century American Literature* (Cambridge: Cambridge University Press, 1991), explores the way cities themselves were represented in a range of literary texts, including city-mystery novels.

CHAPTER 10

Cultures of Print

An older survey remains the best point of entry to the history of learned culture: Herbert W. Schneider, *A History of American Philosophy* (New York: Columbia University Press, 1946). The essays in Alexandra Oleson and Sanborn C. Brown, eds., *The Pursuit of Knowledge in the Early American Republic: American Scientific and Learned Societies from Colonial Times to the Civil War* (Baltimore: Johns Hopkins University Press, 1976), and its sequel, Alexandra Oleson and John Voss, eds., *The Organization of Knowledge in Modern America, 1860–1920* (Baltimore: Johns Hopkins University Press, 1979), are invaluable.

Much of the best work on learned culture concerns sites or institutions, coteries or "connections," practices, and vehicles of culture. Colleges and universities (in the form that the latter began to take in the 1860s and 1870s) figure largely in this body of work. Still useful is an older survey, especially the chapters on post–Civil War developments: Richard Hofstadter and Walter P. Metzger, *The Development of Academic Freedom in the United States*, 2 vols. (New York: Columbia University Press, 1955). The early chapters of Bruce Kuklick, *The Rise of American Philosophy: Cambridge, Massachusetts, 1860–1930* (New

Haven: Yale University Press, 1977), discuss the transition from moral philosophy to other modes of work. Studies of important sites of cultural production include Bender, *New York Intellect* (cited above in the bibliographical notes for Chapter 9), and Louise L. Stevenson, *Scholarly Means to Evangelical Ends: The New Haven Scholars and the Transformation of Higher Learning in America, 1830–1890* (Baltimore: Johns Hopkins University Press, 1986). Studies of coteries or connections include Charles Capper and Conrad Edick Wright, eds., *Transient and Permanent: The Transcendentalist Movement and Its Contexts* (Boston: Massachusetts Historical Society, 1999); and Drew Gilpin Faust, *A Sacred Circle: The Dilemma of the Intellectual in the Old South, 1840–1860* (Baltimore: Johns Hopkins University Press, 1977). E. Brooks Holifield, *The Gentlemen Theologians: American Theology in Southern Culture, 1795–1860* (Durham, N.C.: Duke University Press, 1978), a close examination of urban Presbyterian ministers, is an excellent (and rare) combination of social and intellectual history. David D. Hall, "The Victorian Connection," in *Victorian America*, ed. Daniel Walker Howe (Philadelphia: University of Pennsylvania Press, 1976), 81–94, describes a transatlantic group of intellectuals allied with Bender's metropolitan gentry in creating periodicals such as the *Nation*. Book collecting can primarily be approached through histories of particular collectors; the classic study and starting point is Carl L. Cannon, *American Book Collectors and Collecting from Colonial Times to the Present* (New York: H. W. Wilson, 1941).

Thomas L. Haskell, *The Emergence of Professional Social Science: The American Social Science Association and the Nineteenth-Century Crisis of Authority* (Urbana: University of Illinois Press, 1977), and Mary O. Furner, *Advocacy and Objectivity: A Crisis in the Professionalization of American Social Science, 1865–1905* (Lexington: University Press of Kentucky, 1975), deal with the nascent social sciences. The outstanding study of American science for this period is Robert V. Bruce, *The Launching of Modern American Science, 1846–1876* (New York: Knopf, 1987). Also of importance are A. Hunter Dupree, *Science in the Federal Government: A History of Policies and Activities* (Baltimore: Johns Hopkins University Press, 1957); Sally Gregory Kohlstedt, *The Formation of the American Scientific Community: The American Association for the Advancement of Science, 1848–60* (Urbana: University of Illinois Press, 1976); Margaret W. Rossiter, *The Emergence of Agricultural Science: Justus Liebig and the Americans, 1840–1880* (New Haven: Yale University Press, 1975), and *Women Scientists in America: Struggles and Strategies to 1940* (Baltimore: Johns Hopkins University Press, 1982); and William H. Goetzmann, *Army Exploration in the American West, 1803–1863* (New Haven: Yale University Press, 1959).

The recent emphasis in American cultural studies on participation and exclusion, or (nationalistic) democratic versus (cosmopolitan) elite versions of culture, has obscured the structures and practices of learned culture and the exchanges and parallels with Europe that were of importance for Americans in the mid-nineteenth century. The international connections may be approached through Henry A. Pochmann, *German Culture in America: Philosophical and Literary Influences, 1600–1900* (Madison: University of Wisconsin Press, 1957), which is strongest on the Transcendentalists; and Carl Diehl, *Americans and German Scholarship, 1770–1870* (New Haven: Yale University Press, 1978). For comparative perspectives, see Noel Annan, "The Intellectual Aristocracy," in *Studies in Social History: A Tribute to G. M. Trevelyan*, ed. J. H. Plumb (London: Longmans, Green, 1955),

241–87; Christopher Kent, "Higher Journalism and the Mid-Victorian Clerisy," *Victorian Studies* 13 (1969): 181–98; and John J. Gross, *The Rise and Fall of the Man of Letters: Aspects of English Literary Life since 1800* (London: Weidenfeld & Nicolson, 1969).

Work on early African American book history has just begun; see McHenry, *Forgotten Readers* (cited above in the bibliographical notes for Chapter 8); Richard Newman, Patrick Rael, and Phillip Lapsansky, eds., *Pamphlets of Protest: An Anthology of Early African American Protest Literature, 1790–1860* (New York: Routledge, 2001); and Frances Smith Foster, "A Narrative of the Interesting Origins and (Somewhat) Surprising Developments of African-American Print Culture," *American Literary History* 17 (2005): 714–40. As Rael has noted, the scholarship on general African American periodical publishing is of limited usefulness; but see the essays by Todd Vogel ("The New Face of Black Labor" [37–54]) and Robert Fanuzzi ("Frederick Douglass's 'Colored Newspaper': Identity Politics in Black and White" [55–70]) in *The Black Press: New Literary and Historical Essays*, ed. Todd Vogel (New Brunswick, N.J.: Rutgers University Press, 2001). For a comprehensive biography of one African American editor, see Jane Rhodes, *Mary Ann Shadd Cary: The Black Press and Protest in the Nineteenth Century* (Bloomington: Indiana University Press, 1998). The role of the American Missionary Association—which is still active as the missionary component of the United Church of Christ—in the education of the freedpeople remains controversial: laudatory accounts include Joe M. Richardson, *Christian Reconstruction: The American Missionary Association and Southern Blacks, 1861–1890* (Athens: University of Georgia Press, 1986); and Clara Merritt DeBoer, *His Truth Is Marching On: African-Americans Who Taught the Freedmen for the American Missionary Association, 1861–1877* (New York: Garland, 1995); more critical studies include Robert C. Morris, *Reading, 'Riting, and Reconstruction: The Education of Freedmen in the South, 1861–70* (Chicago: University of Chicago Press, 1981); Ronald E. Butchart, *Northern Schools, Southern Blacks, and Reconstruction: Freedmen's Education, 1862–1875* (Westport, Conn.: Greenwood, 1980); and Jacqueline Jones, *Soldiers of Light and Love: Northern Teachers and Georgia Blacks, 1865–1873* (Chapel Hill: University of North Carolina Press, 1980). For concise yet thorough overviews that situate nineteenth-century black literacy, education, and print culture in the broader context of American and African American history and culture, see the relevant entries in William L. Andrews, Frances Smith Foster, and Trudier Harris, eds., *The Oxford Companion to African American Literature* (New York: Oxford University Press, 1997).

On stereotypes about the South and their implications for the history of the book, see Michael O'Brien, "On the Mind of the Old South and Its Accessibility," in *Rethinking the South: Essays in Intellectual History* (Baltimore: Johns Hopkins University Press, 1988), 19–37; and Susan-Mary Grant and Peter J. Parish, eds., *Legacy of Disunion: The Enduring Significance of the American Civil War* (Baton Rouge: Louisiana State University Press, 2003). On the variety of literacies in the South, see Janet Duitsman Cornelius, *"When I Can Read My Title Clear": Literacy, Slavery, and Religion in the Antebellum South* (Columbia: University of South Carolina Press, 1991); Heather Andrea Williams, *Self-Taught: African American Education in Slavery and Freedom* (Chapel Hill: University of North Carolina Press, 2005); E. Jennifer Monaghan, "Reading for the Enslaved, Writing for the Free: Reflections on Liberty and Literacy," *Proceedings of the American Antiquarian Society* 108 (1998): 309–41; Keith Whitescarver, "Political Economy, Schooling, and Literacy in the South: A Comparison of Plantation and Yeomen Communities in North Carolina, 1840–1880" (Ph.D. diss., Harvard University, 1995); and Bruce Fort, "The Politics and Culture of Literacy in Georgia, 1800–1920" (Ph.D. diss., University of Virginia, 1999). On education, see David Freedman, "African American Schooling in the South Prior to 1861," *Journal of Negro History* 84 (1999): 1–47; Christie Anne Farnham, *The Education of the Southern Belle: Higher Education and Student Socialization in the Antebellum South* (New York: New York University Press, 1994); James D. Anderson, *The Education of Blacks in the South, 1860–1935* (Chapel Hill: University of North Carolina Press, 1988); and Daniel J. Whitener, "Public Education in North Carolina during Reconstruction, 1865–1876," in *Essays in Southern History*, ed. Fletcher M. Green (Chapel Hill: University of North Carolina Press, 1949), 67–90.

On southern literature, see Elizabeth Moss, *Domestic Novelists in the Old South: Defenders of Southern Culture* (Baton Rouge: Louisiana State University Press, 1992); Louis D. Rubin Jr. et al., eds., *The History of Southern Literature* (Baton Rouge: Louisiana State University Press, 1985); and Jay B. Hubbell, *The South in American Literature, 1607–1900* (Durham, N.C.: Duke University Press, 1954). *Documenting the American South* (http://docsouth.unc.edu), a digital publishing project sponsored by the University Library of the University of North Carolina at Chapel Hill, provides Internet access to books, diaries, posters, artifacts, letters, oral history interviews, and songs. For model studies of southern printers and publishers, see Cathleen Ann Baker, "The Press That Cotton Built: Printing in Mobile, Alabama, 1850–1865" (Ph.D. diss., University of Alabama, 2004); Florence M. Jumonville, *Bibliography of New Orleans Imprints, 1764–1864* (New Orleans: Historical New Orleans Collection, 1989); and Karen C. Carroll, "Sterling, Campbell, and Albright: Textbook Publishers, 1861–1865," *North Carolina Historical Review* 63 (1986): 169–98. The essential study of Civil War print genres is Alice Fahs, *The Imagined Civil War: Popular Literature of the North and South, 1861–1865* (Chapel Hill: University of North Carolina Press, 2001). Often-overlooked studies of Confederate print culture include T. Michael Parrish and Robert M. Willingham Jr., *Confederate Imprints: A Bibliography of Southern Publications from Secession to Surrender: Expanding and Revising the Earlier Works of Marjorie Crandall and Richard Harwell* (Austin, Tex.: Jenkins, 1984); W. Harrison Daniel, "Bible Publication and Procurement in the Confederacy," *Journal of Southern History* 24 (1958): 191–201; and Bell Irvin Wiley, "Camp Newspapers of the Confederacy," *North Carolina Historical Review* 20 (1943): 327–35.

CHAPTER 11

Alternative Communication Practices and the Industrial Book

Carl Bode, *The American Lyceum: Town Meeting of the Mind* (New York: Oxford University Press, 1956; repr., Carbondale: Southern Illinois University Press, 1968), remains the standard resource on the lyceum movement, athenaeum culture, and their relationship to reform. See also John E. Tapia, "Adult Education in Nineteenth-Century America," *Circuit Chautauqua: From Rural Education to Popular Entertainment in Early Twentieth-Century America* (Jefferson, N.C.: McFarland, 1997), 11–26. For oratory and performance during this period, see Gregory Clark and S. Michael Halloran, eds., *Oratorical Culture in Nineteenth-Century America: Transformations in the Theory and Practice of Rheto-*

ric (Carbondale: Southern Illinois University Press, 1993); Kenneth Cmiel, *Democratic Eloquence: The Fight over Popular Speech in Nineteenth-Century America* (New York: Morrow, 1990); and James Perrin Warren, *Culture of Eloquence: Oratory and Reform in Antebellum America* (University Park: Pennsylvania State University Press, 1999).

Other than Tamara Plakins Thornton, *Handwriting in America: A Cultural History* (New Haven: Yale University Press, 1996), secondary sources on Victorian handwriting, especially of an analytical nature, are sparse. On penmanship pedagogy, see Barbara Joan Finkelstein, "Governing the Young: Teacher Behavior in American Primary Schools, 1820–1880; A Documentary History" (Ed.D. diss., Columbia University, 1970); Janet Weiss, "Educating for Clerical Work: A History of Commercial Education in the United States since 1850" (Ed.D. diss., Harvard Graduate School of Education, 1978); and William E. Henning, *An Elegant Hand: The Golden Age of American Penmanship and Calligraphy*, ed. Paul Melzer (New Castle, Del.: Oak Knoll, 2002). On autograph albums, see W. K. McBeil, "The Autograph Album Custom: A Tradition and Its Scholarly Treatment," *Keystone Folklore Quarterly* 13 (Spring 1968): 29–40; Robert P. Stevenson, "The Autograph Album: A Victorian Girl's Best Friend," *Pennsylvania Folklife* 34 (1984): 34–43; and Katharine Morrison McClinton, *Antiques of American Childhood* (New York: Clarkson N. Potter, 1970), 124–34. For thought-provoking analyses of the cultural functions and meanings carried by the medium of handwriting, see Jonathan Goldberg, *Writing Matter: From the Hands of the English Renaissance* (Stanford, Calif.: Stanford University Press, 1990); and David S. Shields, *Civil Tongues and Polite Letters in British America* (Chapel Hill: University of North Carolina Press, 1997).

Readers interested in the history of amateur authorship should begin with Charvat, *The Profession of Authorship in America* (cited above in the bibliographical notes for Chapter 3); Richard Layman and Joel Myerson, eds., *The Professions of Authorship: Essays in Honor of Matthew J. Bruccoli* (Columbia: University of South Carolina Press, 1996); and Ronald Weber, *Hired Pens: Professional Writers in America's Golden Age of Printing* (Athens: Ohio University Press, 1997). Work on the professional careers of individual authors helps illuminate the evolution of the concept of the amateur. See, for example, Mary Ann Wimsatt, "The Professional Author in the South: William Gilmore Simms and Antebellum Literary Publishing," in Layman and Myerson, *Professions of Authorship*, 121–34; and Steven Fink, *Prophet in the Marketplace: Thoreau's Development as a Professional Writer* (Princeton: Princeton University Press, 1992). On one-time authors far from the mainstream of literary publishing, see Ann Fabian, *The Unvarnished Truth: Personal Narratives in Nineteenth-Century America* (Berkeley: University of California Press, 2000). On soldiers and prisoners who wrote of Civil War experiences, see William Best Hesseltine, *Civil War Prisons: A Study in War Psychology* (Columbus: Ohio State University Press, 1930); and Allan Nevins, James I. Robertson Jr., and Bell I. Wiley, *Civil War Books: A Critical Bibliography* (Baton Rouge: Louisiana State University Press, 1967). On hobby printers, see Paula Petrik, "The Youngest Fourth Estate: The Novelty Toy Printing Press and Adolescence, 1870–1886," in *Small Worlds: Children and Adolescents in America, 1850–1950*, ed. Paula Petrik and Elliot West (Lawrence: University Press of Kansas, 1992), 125–42.

INDEX

Note: Page numbers in italics refer to figures, tables, or graphs.

Apprentices, printing, 74, 84
Arena, The (periodical), 423
Arkansas Weekly Mansion (periodical), 386
Arnold, Matthew, 287
Art exhibits based on literary works, 378
Arthur, Timothy S., 32–33, *262–63*
"Art of Fiction, The" (James), 104
Associated Press, 25, 241, 246–47, 419
Association of American Geologists, 348
Association of Editors and Printers of Western Mass., 75–76
Association of Music Teachers, 208
Astor, John Jacob, 312, 355
Astor, William B., 314
Astor Library, 309, 312–14, 356
Atlanta Constitution (newspaper), 245, 386
Atlanta University, 371
Atlantic Monthly: and advertising, 256–57; author compensation, 93, 252, 254; Burroughs and, 255; and Centennial Exhibition, 6, 27; on cheap fiction, 291; cultural mission of, 266–69; Dickinson and, 260; Forten and, 366; Whittier's birthday party, 417
Audubon, at Centennial Exhibition, 27
Aurora Floyd (Braddon), 252
Aurora Leigh (Barrett Browning), 144
Austin, Mary, 295, 301
Authors: African American, 104; amateur, 409–11; biographical sketches of, 113; commodification of, by readers, 105–6; compensation of, 91–94, 253–54; female, 90, 102–3, 288, 329, 410–11; foreign, 139–40, 178; images of, 106–9, 112–13, 322; and literary market, 91–99, 116, 237–38; and magazines, 254–55; male, 90; nineteenth-century American, 90, 100, 102; professional, 99, 407–8, 410–11; and publicity, 109–10; published by Ticknor and Fields, 157; reform, 33; relationships with publishers, 94; rights of, and American copyright law, 158; southern, 379, 389–

90; Spencerian, 402; writers vs., 100. *See also individual author names*
Authors (game), 326, *326*, 418
Authors at Home (Gilder and Gilder), 107–8, 116
Authorship, 90–91, 97–99, 101–2, 105, 115, 407–9
Autobiography (Gough), 32
Autograph albums and collecting, 406–7

B. B. Russell, 399
Bache, Alexander, 350
Bailey, Gamaliel, 235
Baker, Daniel, 117–18
Baker, Peter C., 76
Baker & Taylor Co., 122
Baker, Pratt & Co., 122
Baker, Voorhis & Co., 204
Baker v. Selden, 176–77
Ballou, Maturin M., 264
Bancroft, A. L., 418
Bancroft, Hubert H., 220, 357
Bangs & Co., 126
Bangs, Merwin & Co., 24
Baptist Mission Press, 260
Baptist Preacher (periodical), 275
Baptists, 3, 195, 197, 199, 260, 274, 370
Barber, B. B., 122
"Barefoot Boy" (Whittier), 66, *67*, 324
Baring Brothers, 154
Barlow, Samuel, 356
Barlow, William W., 123
Barnard, Henry, 214, 317
Barnes, A. S., *19*, 117, 214, 218–19
Barnes, J. C., 213, 218
Barney, Obed, 395–96
Barnum, P. T., 241, 343
Bartlett, John R., 356
Bartlett, W. H., 68
Bartlett v. Crittenden, 175
Bartley, James, 380
Barton, Thomas, 355
Bates, Joshua, 355
"Battle Hymn of the Republic" (Howe), 93, 268

American Lead Pencil Co., 7; American Library Association at, 316–17; Brewer & Tileston, 28; Campbell Press Building, 53; education exhibits, 30–31, 34, 36–37; foreign publishers, 29; journeymen printers and, 10; legacy of, 416–17; Machinery Hall, 6; Main Building, 17–18; national image, 37–39; Newspaper Pavilion, 25, 244–45; printing press display, 53; prizes, furor over, 11–12; stationery exhibits, 6–7; Thaddeus Davids & Co., *8*

Central Labor Union, 87–88

Central Park signs, 343

Century Co., 354

Century Illustrated Magazine, 389–90

Cervi, Romeo, 10, 425 (n. 14)

Chace, Jonathan, 178

Chace Act, 16, 178

Challen, Howard, 136

Chambers, Cyrus, Jr., 61

Channing, William H., 258, 286

Chapel heads, 79–80

Chapman, Maria W., 396

Chapman & Hall, 142–43, 156–57

Character, penmanship and, 400–401, 405

Charles Scribner's Sons, 420

Charvat, William, 99, 407–8

Chase, Lucy, 371

Chattanooga Times (newspaper), 245

Chautauqua Literary and Scientific Circle, 288

Cheney, Ednah D., 115

Cherokee Advocate (newspaper), 35

Cherokee Messenger (periodical), 259–60

Cherokee public school system, 35

Chester, T. Morris, 366

"Chesuncook" (Thoreau), 268

Chicago, Ill., 4, 205, 336

Chicago Daily News, 245, 345

Chicago sign raid, 336, *337*

Chicago Tribune (newspaper), 370

"Chiefly about War Matters" (Hawthorne), 268

Child, Daniel F., 292

Child, Francis J., 30, 355

Child, Lydia Maria, 104, 371, 395

Child, Mary D., 292

Child labor, 9–10

"Children's Hour, The" (Longfellow), 93

Childs, George W., 135, 269, 357

Childs, Shubael, 340

Choate, Rufus, 312

Christian Advocate and Journal, 274

Christian at Work (periodical), 277

Christian Recorder (periodical), 365–67

Christian Science, 272

Chromolithography, 66, *67*, 110, *111*, 345

Churches. *See specific denominations*

Church libraries, 307–8

Church of Jesus Christ of Latter-day Saints, 36

Cincinnati (Klauprecht), 345

Cincinnati Colored Citizen (newspaper), 369

Cincinnati Philanthropist (newspaper), 235

City directories, 340, 344

City mysteries (genre), 289, 344–45

City School Library, Lowell, Mass., 307

Civic model of reading, 283–85

Civil rights, Reconstruction-era, 385–86

Civil War: amateur authorship and, 411–12; *Atlantic Monthly* and, 268; dispatches from, and inverted pyramid style, 247; and nationalizing trends, 38; newspapers and, 242–44, 248, 335; and periodicals, 225, 250; and schoolbooks, 217, 384

Clanton, Ella, 298

Clapp, Henry, 254

Clarel (Melville), 95

Clarke, Herbert A., 415

Clarke, Mary D., 381, 384

Clay, Henry, 164

Clayton v. Stone, 174–75

Clements, Martha, 342

Clerks, Industrial Revolution and, 32

Clymer, George, 54

Cobb, Lyman, 214

Cobb, Sylvanus, Jr., 264, 303–4

Cogswell, Joseph G., 309, 312–14, 351–52, 355–56

Cole, Thomas, 28

"Collected by a Valetudinarian" (Stoddard, E.), 116

Collected editions, 29, 144

Collective bargaining, 80

Collective reading practices, 367–68

Collender v. Griffith, 175

Colored American (periodical), 366, 395

Colportage, 199

Columbian press, 54

Commerce and Navigation reports, 148

Commercial News and Whig Reading Room, Nantucket, 394, 397

Commercial travelers, 127

Common-law copyright, 167, 175

Common press, 53–54

Common schools, 375–76. *See also* Schools

Communication networks, 119, 271

Company D, Fifth Massachusetts (Colored) Cavalry, 361–62

Competition: among American publishers, 17; mammoth weeklies and, 142; Post Office and, 182; reprinters as, 76, 145–47; in schoolbook trade, 212–13, 216–17

Competitive bidding, 74

Compilations, copyright of, 169–70

Complete Catalogue of Sheet Music and Musical Works (Board of Music Trade), 208, 212

Complete List of Booksellers, Stationers, and News Dealers (Dingman), 136

Composing and distributing machines, 47–48

Compositors, 47, 72–73, 78, 190–91

Compromise of 1850, 417

Comstock, Anthony, 185

Comstock Act, 185, 290, 399

Confederate States of America, 5, 38, 217, 243, 347, 381–85, 389. *See also* South, the

Congregational hymn singing, 209–10

Congregationalists, 199, 370

Congressional Record, 191

Conkling, Roscoe, 37

Consolidated American Baptist Missionary Convention, 370

Contemporary Review (periodical), 253

Continental (periodical), 249

Contract system, for public printing, 188

Cook, David C., 201

Coombs, James, *402*

Cooper, James Fenimore, 99, 253, 261, 319, 321, 395, 408, 411, 421

Copybooks, 401, *402*, 403, *403*, 405

Copyright cases, 167–69, *170–72*

Copyright deposits, 318

Copyright infringement, 212

Copyright laws: authors and, 158; changes to, and business practices, 166–67; Confederate States of America and, 384–85; enforcement of, 167; expanding reach of, 165, 169–72, 178; fair use guidelines, 172–73; Great Britain and, 94, 141, 156; limits on, 174–75; and performance rights, 159; printing plates and, 46; United States and, 17, 160–63; in works for hire, 176. *See also* International copyright laws

Cornish, Samuel, 367–68

Corp d'Afrique, 369

Corporatism: and labor relations, 83, 88–89

Correspondents, 247

Cosmopolitan model of reading, 286–87

Courtesy of the trade: Chace Act and, 16; challenges to, 93; collected editions and, 29; the Confederacy and, 385; as de facto copyright protection, 159; John W. Lovell Co. and, 420; in music publishing, 203, 205, 208; and national book trade system, 24; practice of, 142–

Literary exchange, institutions of, 332
Literary figures, images of, 106–9, 112–13, 322
Literary market, 91–99, 116; authors and, 237–38
Literary property, 144. *See also* Copyright laws
Literary societies, 280, 362, 364
Literary tradition, American, 30
Literary World (periodical), 62, 133–34
Literature: abolitionist, 37–38, 96, 104; American, 5, 26–30, 258, 417; and boundary crossings, 300; in library of Nantucket Atheneum, 394–95
Lithography, 65–66, 68, 338
Lithotints, 66
Littell's Living Age (periodical), 259
Little, Brown and Co., 191, 204
Little Women (Alcott), 90, 113, 300
Livermore, George, 311–12
Lockwood, George R., 18
Log Cabin (newspaper), 233
Logic (Hegel), 352
London, Jack, 300
Longfellow, Henry Wadsworth: 59, 155, 322, 365; "The Children's Hour," 93; "The Courtship of Miles Standish," 324; *Evangeline*, 92; and periodicals, 92, 166, 253, 259, 261–64, 267; *The Song of Hiawatha*, 27; and Whittier's birthday party, 417–18
Longstreet, Augustus, 379
Lothrop, D., *129*
Louisa May Alcott (Cheney), 115
Louisiana's Corp d'Afrique, 369
Louis Prang & Co., 66
Lovell, John W., 146–47, 420, 423
Lovell, O., 340
Lovell's Library, 297
Lovett, Robert M., 299
Low, Sampson, 121, 151
Lowell, James Russell, 253–54, 264, 267, 268
Lowell Institute, 348–49
Lowell Offering (periodical), 297

Lower Hudson Street, New York, 338, *339*
Loyal Union, The (newspaper), 414
Lucretia, the Quakeress (Hanaford), 399
Lutherans, 196–97
Lyell, Charles, 348–49
Lyon, Mary, 329

Macaria (Evans), 381
Machinery Hall, Centennial Exhibition, 6, 53, 245
"Madame Delphine" (Cable), 389
Magazines: and amateur writers, 409; the business of, 248–58; after Civil War, 266; connection of, to books, 250–52; cultural work of, 258–70; imported, 155; and national identity, 259; postal rates for, 185–87; production of, 249–50; specialized vs. nationwide, 260–61. *See also* Periodicals; *specific magazine titles*
Mahon, Charles, 54
Main-Travelled Roads (Garland), 423
Malaeska: The Indian Wife (dime novel), 27, 252
Mammoth weeklies, 142, 187, 251
Mann, Horace, 214, 284–85, 291, 305–7, 395, 397
Manual of Geology, A (Dana), 349
Manual of Historical Literature, A (Adams), 358
Manual of the Corporation of the City of New York (Valentine), 344
March, Francis A., 354–55
Market, literary, 91–99, 116, 237–38
"Marse Chan" (Page), 389
Marsh, Capen, Lyon & Webb, 306
Martinetti v. Maguire, 174
Marx, Karl, 238
Mason, Lowell, 209
Massachusetts, 306, 309, 311
Massachusetts Charitable Mechanic Association (MCMA), 82
Massachusetts Teacher (periodical), 217–18

Material culture, literary, 321–24, *323*
Mathews, Cornelius, 100–101
Matrices, electrotype, 43
Matteson, Tompkins, *359*
McCabe, James D., Jr., 345, 388
McClellan, H. B., 389
McElrath, Thomas, 238
McGuffey, William H., 214, 219
McGuffey's readers, 3, 216, 285, 370, 421
McIntosh, Maria, 379
McNally, Andrew, 205
Medical News and Library (periodical),
   117
Medical publishing, 204–5
Meek, Alexander B., 380
Melville, Herman: *Battle-Pieces and
   Aspects of the War*, 267; "The Bell
   Tower," 257; *Clarel*, 95; "Donelson,"
   334–35; early work as an author, 90;
   Moby-Dick, 95, 407; and periodicals,
   166; *Pierre*, 92; and publicity, 109, 116
Mennonites, 196
Mercantile colleges, 404
Mercantile libraries, 308
*Merchants' Magazine and Commercial
   Review*, 255
Merriam, Charles, 354
Merriam, G. & C., 28, 213–14, *215*
Methodist Book Concern, 195–97, 199,
   274, 412
Methodist Church, 195, 197, 199, 201
Methodist Episcopal Church, 197
Metropolitan Record, The (newspaper),
   387
Middle class, 4–5, 32–33, 286–87, 330,
   424, 427 (n. 39)
Military information, control of, 243
Miller, Hugh, 301
Miller, Joaquin, 422
Miller, William, 271
Millerites, 236
"Mimin," on authorship, 408–9
Minhag America (prayer books), 200
*Misogynist Dinner of the American Chemi-
   cal Society, The* (proceedings), 359

"Miss Grief" (Woolson), 116
Missing Bride, The (Bowen), 387
Missionary societies, 35, 284
Missouri Presbyterian Recorder (periodi-
   cal), 271
Mitchel, William H., 47–48
Mitchell, J. B., 1, 3
Mitchell, Maria, 350, 358
Mitchell, S. Augustus, 216
Mitford, Mary, 156, 326
Moby-Dick (Melville), 95, 407
Modern Mephistopheles, A (Alcott), 115
Mohl, Robert von, 316
Monopolies, 240–41
Moods (Alcott), 90
Moody, Dwight L., 201
Moore, Ely, 72–73, 75–76, 82
Moore, Nathaniel F., 314
Mordecai, Alfred, 191
Morgan, Charlotte, 75
Morgan, E., 340
Morgan, Lewis H., 351
Mormon publications, 36
Moses Dodd, 92
Mothers' Journal and Family Visitant
   (periodical), 274, 276
Mott, Frank L., 250
Mott, Lucretia Coffin, 397
Movable type process, 42
Mrs. Nancy Lawson (Prior), 282
Munro, George P., 146–47, 250, 252
Murphy, W. F., 6
Murray, Lindley, 213
Music publishing: consolidation of, 210;
   and copyright, 206–8; and courtesy of
   the trade, 203, 205; discounted sales,
   208; distribution networks, 207; firms,
   222–23; reprint business, 212; sacred,
   209–10; volatility in, 206–7
Mutual aid societies, 363–64, 370
Mystères de Paris, Les (Sue), 297, 344
Mysteries and Miseries of New York (Bunt-
   line), 344–45
Mysteries of Paris, The (Sue), 297, 344
Mysteries of St. Louis (Boernstein), 345

New York Book Publishers' Association, 15, 17, 125–26
New York by Gas-Light (Foster), 340, 344
New York Commercial Advertiser (newspaper), 146
New York Daily Graphic (newspaper), 345
New York draft riots, 244
New Yorker Staats-Zeitung (newspaper), 51
New York Evening Post (newspaper), 145
New York Herald (newspaper), 6, 108–9, 239, 333
New York Illustrated News (newspaper), 241
New York Ledger (newspaper), 298–99, 334
New York Mercantile Library, 308–9, *310*
New York Mirror (periodical), 259
New York Musical Review and Choral Advocate (periodical), 209
New York Printers' Association, 75
New York Publishers' Association, 24, 131, 134
New York State Library, 318
New York Sun (newspaper), 184
New York Times (newspaper), 6, 206, 245
New York Tribune (newspaper), 184, 238, 333
New York Typographical Association, 79
New York Typothetæ, 76, 83
New York Weekly Day Book Caucasian (newspaper), 387, 421
New York World (newspaper), 48
Nichols, H. H., 188–89
Niles, Hezekiah, 233–34
Nineteenth Century (periodical), 253
No Name series, 115
Noncopyrighted music, 206–8
Nord, David Paul, 284
North, S. N. D., 25
North American (newspaper), 88
North American Review (periodical), 254, 311
North Carolina, 375
North Star (newspaper), 236, 367–68

Norton, Charles B., 121, 134–35, 316
Norton's Literary Advertiser (periodical), 134
Norton's Literary Gazette (periodical), 17, 134, 316, *382–83*, 441 (n. 33)
Norwood (Beecher), 288
Novelty Press, 412

O. Lovell & Son., 340
O'Callaghan, Edmund B., 356
Ochs, Adolph, 245
Octoroon, The (Boucicault), *168*, 176
Oldach & Mergenthaler, 10
Old Curiosity Shop, The (Dickens), 297
Old English, 354
Old Red Sandstone, The (Miller), 301
"Old Times on the Mississippi" (Twain), 269
Oliver Ditson & Co., 209–10, *211*, 212, 219, 223
Olmsted, Frederick Law, 343
On Heroes, Hero-Worship, and the Heroic in History (Carlyle), 300
On the Construction of Catalogues and Libraries (Jewett), 312
Oratory, 392
Ormsbee, Marcus, 338, *339*
Osage Library Association, 422
Osage News (newspaper), 422
Osgood, James R., 3, 26–27, 30, 62, 252, 417
"Our Lady Contributors" (engraving), 111
Our Land and Land Policy, National and State (George), 420
Our Nig (Wilson), 96
"Our Own" reader series, 384
Our Village (Mitford), 326
Overland Monthly, 418

P. Blakiston's Son, 204
P. J. Kenedy & Sons, 200
P. S. Duval, 66
Packet lines, 153–54
Page, J. W., 380
Page, Thomas N., 389

Planographic process, 65–66
Platen jobbers, 56–57
Plays and Poems (Boker), 167
Plessy v. Ferguson, 373
Poe, Edgar Allan: and "autography," 406;
　Eureka, 92; and periodicals, 253, 261,
　379–80; portrait of, for readers, 106–
　7; and publicity for new authors, 116;
　royalty contract, 91–92
Poems (Browning), 142–43
Poems (Ingelow), 147
Poems (Tennyson), 141, 156
Poems on Various Subjects (Wheatley), 112
Poetry, compensation for, 93
Poets' Homes (Stoddard), 113
Polk, James K., 312
Pomeroy, Jesse, 291
Poole, William F., 318, 358
Population growth, U.S., 120
Porter, Noah, 290, 354
Porter & Coates, 3, 28, 405, 416
Portrait of a Lady, The (James), 93, 269
Portsmouth Journal, 303
Post, Emily, 104
Posters, 336
Post Office: censorship, 185; and GPO,
　191; local publishers and, 187; as meet-
　ing place, 333; postage rates, 182–83,
　183, 185, 333; and print distribution,
　128–29, 179, 233, 251; and professional-
　ism, 192; and shipment of books, 120;
　subscription account book, *273*
Potter, Alonzo, 306
Potter, S. A., 405
Poulson's American Daily Advertiser, 50
Powell, John W., 192, 350
Pratt, Woodford & Co., 117
Prentiss, Elizabeth, 275–77
Presbrey, Frank, 255
Presbyterians, 196–99, 201, 416
Present Truth (periodical), 272
Press (newspaper), 85, 87–88
Presses: African American, 368–69;
　American, localization of, 25; commer-
　cial, 246; hometown, 412; party, 232–

34, 237–42, 245, 248; penny, 237–40,
245, 289, 333; reform, 32–33, 235–36,
246, 395–96, 398–99. *See also* Printing
presses; *individual publisher names*
Preston, Margaret J., 381
Price-fixing, 76
Priestley Centennial (1874), *360*
Primary Geography (Mitchell), 216
Prince, Thomas, 355
Princeton Review (periodical), 352
Princeton Seminary, 352
Printers: apprentices, 74, 84; book, 9–10,
　340; job, 9–10, 338–40; journeymen,
　9–10, 70–72, 77–78, 84; tramp, 71, 79
Printing, book, and stationery trades: in
　1850, *10–11*; in 1860, *12–13*, 38; in 1870,
　14–15; in 1880, *16–17*; child labor in,
　9–10; health of workers, 79; value of
　products, 417; women and, 9, 48, 59,
　61–62, 78, 433 (n. 41)
Printing establishments: federal, autho-
　rized, 191–92; labor force, 9–10, 73–74,
　74, 190, 417; newspapers, 339, 412;
　southern, 38
Printing plates, 41, 45–47, 239
Printing presses: ancillary inventions, 57;
　cylinder, 42, 55, 57; hand, 42, 54–55;
　jobbing-platen, 56–57; large, 59; Light-
　ning, 56, 238; mass production of, 6;
　production rates, 58, *58*; rotary, 1, 41,
　53, 56–57; steam-powered, 42, 66; web,
　245; wooden, 53–54
Printing processes, 5, 7–9, 41, 46–47, 51,
　64–65, 92
Print unionism, 83–84
Prior, William M., 282
Private libraries, 305
Proceedings (periodical), 350
Professionalism: of authors, 99, 407–
　8, 410–11; evolution of, 33; in federal
　civilian bureaucracies, 192; in learned
　societies, 358–59; literary, 102–3; in
　penmanship, 404
Profession of Authorship in America, The
　(Charvat), 99

Tilghman, Benjamin C. and Richard, 51
Times (London), 55
Token, The (periodical), 96
Trade associations, 24, 83–84, 88
Trade bibliography, 135–38
Trade Circular and Literary Bulletin (periodical), 135
Trade communication, 131, 138, 141
Trade courtesy. *See* Courtesy of the trade
Trade periodicals, 131–37, 151
Trade publishers, 13, 91, 203
Trade sales, semiannual, 15–16, 24, 125–26, *126*, 126–27, 138
Tramp printers, 71, 79
Transactions (periodical), 350
Transatlantic trade, 30, 148, 150–57
Transcendentalists, 97, 351–52
Transcontinental telegraph, 419–20
Translations, and copyright law, 26, 173
Traubel, Horace, 115
Traveling library movement, 288
Traveling sales agents, 127, 216, 218
Treadwell, Daniel, 55–57
Treatise on the Law of Property in Intellectual Productions, A (Drone), 169
Troup, Augusta Lewis, 48
Trow, John F., 47–48, 76
Trübner, Nicolas, 121, 151–53, 156
Trübner & Co., 156, 349
"True Story of Swiftville Library" (Cobb), 303–4
Truman & Smith, 214, 216
Trusta, H. (Elizabeth Stuart Phelps), 102–3
Trusts, formation of, 24
Truth (newspaper), 420
Tucker, George, 180–81
Twain, Mark, 27, 206, 220–21, 230, 269, 418
Twice-Told Tales (Hawthorne), 109
Two Friends (American Sunday-School Union), 379
Tyler, Moses Coit, 29
Type, 43–46
Typecasting machinery, 42, 44

Type Founders' Association of the United States, 44
Type foundries, 43–45, *44*, 340
Type-revolving presses, 56
Typesetting, mechanical, 47–48

Uncle Remus tales (Harris), 386
Uncle Robin in His Cabin (Page), 380
Uncle Tom's Cabin (Stowe): as American literature, 28; author's compensation for, 94; demand for and production of, 62; literary artifacts associated with, 322–23, *323*; Page's response to, 380; plates for, 47; popularity in England, 30; publication of, 16, 95–96, 322–24; serialization of, 235, 277; unauthorized translation of, 173
Underselling, 76, 128, 138, 222
Underwood, Francis H., 267
Uniform national currency, 332
Uniform Trade-List Circular (periodical), 136
Unions and unionism, 72–73, 76–85, 87–88. *See also specific union publications; specific unions*
United Brethren Publishing House, 1
United States Literary Gazette (periodical), 100
United States Magazine and Democratic Review, 100–101, 250, 254, 259, 408, 437 (n. 35)
University libraries, 314–16, 318
University of California library, 316
University of Deseret (University of Utah), 36
University of Michigan library, 316
University of Tübingen, 352
University of Virginia library, 315
University Publishing Co., 217
Up from Slavery (Washington), 281
Upham, Charles, 172–73

Vail, Stephen, 50
Valentine, David T., 344
Van Antwerp, Bragg & Co., 219

Wise, Isaac Mayer, 200, 271

With Walt Whitman in Camden
(Traubel), 115

Wm. Bradwood, 6

Wm. Hall & Son, 206–7

Wolf, Friedrich A., 354

Woman's Building, World's Columbian
Exposition (1893), 288

Woman's Pavilion, Centennial Exhibition,
36

Women: African American, 112, *112*, 364;
authors, 90, 94, 102–3, 109–10, 288,
329, 410–11; chemists, and Priestley
Centennial, *360*; and education, 246,
376; and learned culture, 348, 358–
59; library access, 308–9; and literacy,
280–81, 299; in printing trades, 9,
48, 59, 61–62, 74, 78, 190, 433 (n. 41);
southern, 376, 381; suffrage movement,
246; white, *111*, 376; and Whittier's
birthday party, 417. *See also* Gender
roles

Women of Israel, The (Aguilar), 377

Women of the Century (Hanaford), 399

Women's Typographical Union No. 1, 48

Woodhull, Victoria, 185

Wood, William., 18, 204

Woods, Benjamin O., 412

Wood type, 45

Wood v. Abbott, 175

Woolson, Constance Fenimore, 116

Worcester, Joseph Emerson, 28

Worcester, Samuel, 216, 219

Worcester Evening Gazette, 361

Working card system (union cards), 79

Working conditions, 69, 78–79

Writings of George Washington (Sparks),
172

Yale University, 316, 349, 353, 356

Yankee Peddler, The (newspaper), 414

Young, Brigham, 36

Young America group, 100

Young American, The (newspaper), 415

Young Men's Christian Association
(YMCA), 308, 467–68 (n. 14)

*Zion's Watch Tower and Herald of Christ's
Presence* (periodical), 273